Reading Latin

TEXT AND VOCABULARY

Second edition

Reading Latin, first published in 1986, is a bestselling Latin course designed to help mature beginners read classical Latin fluently and intelligently, primarily in the context of classical culture, but with some medieval Latin too. It does this in three ways: it encourages the reading of continuous texts from the start without compromising grammatical rigour; it offers generous help with translation at every stage; and it integrates the learning of classical Latin with an appreciation of the influence of the Latin language upon English and European culture from antiquity to the present.

The *Text and Vocabulary*, richly illustrated, consists at the start of carefully graded adaptations from original classical Latin texts. The adaptations are gradually phased out until unadulterated prose and verse can be read. The accompanying *Grammar and Exercises* volume supplies all the grammatical help needed to do this, together with a range of reinforcing exercises for each section, including English into Latin for those who want it. It also contains a full and detailed reference grammar at the back. For each section, a selection of Latin epigrams, mottoes, quotations, everyday Latin, word-derivations, examples of medieval Latin and discussions of the influence of Latin upon English illustrate the language's impact on Western culture.

Reading Latin is principally designed for college/university and adult beginners, but also for those in the final years of school. It is also ideal for those people who may have learned Latin many years ago, and wish to renew their acquaintance with the language. The optional *Independent Study Guide* provides a great deal of help to the student learning without a teacher.

The second edition has been fully revised and updated, with revisions to the early chapters including a new one on stories from early Roman history, and extensively redesigned to make it easier and clearer to navigate. The vocabulary has been moved into the same volume as the text and placed alongside it, so that the *Text and Vocabulary* could function as a self-standing beginner's reader independent of the whole course if desired. Moreover, a visual distinction has been made between those texts which are essential to follow the course and those which could be omitted and simply read in translation if time is very limited.

PETER JONES was Senior Lecturer in Classics at the University of Newcastle upon Tyne until his retirement. He has written many books for the student of Latin and Greek, most recently *Reading Ovid* (Cambridge, 2007), *Reading Virgil* (Cambridge, 2011) and (with Keith Sidwell) the *Reading Latin* textbook series.

KEITH SIDWELL is Emeritus Professor of Latin and Greek, University College Cork and Adjunct Professor in the Department of Classics and Religion at the University of Calgary. He has written on Greek drama, later Greek literature and Neo-Latin writing: his books include *Lucian: Chattering Courtesans and Other Sardonic Sketches* (2004) and *Aristophanes the Democrat* (Cambridge, 2009). As well as co-authoring the *Reading Latin* series with Peter Jones, he is the author of *Reading Medieval Latin* (Cambridge, 1995).

Reading Latin
Text and Vocabulary

Second edition

Peter Jones
and Keith Sidwell

 CAMBRIDGE
UNIVERSITY PRESS

CAMBRIDGE
UNIVERSITY PRESS

University Printing House, Cambridge CB2 8BS, United Kingdom

Cambridge University Press is part of the University of Cambridge.

It furthers the University's mission by disseminating knowledge in the pursuit of education, learning and research at the highest international levels of excellence.

www.cambridge.org
Information on this title: www.cambridge.org/9781107618701

First edition © Cambridge University Press 1986
This second edition © Peter Jones and Keith Sidwell 2016

First edition published 1986
Second edition published 2016

Printed in the United Kingdom by TJ International Ltd. Padstow Cornwall

A catalogue record for this publication is available from the British Library

ISBN 978-1-107-61870-1 Paperback

Contents

Illustrations

Maps

Figures

Preliminary remarks

The course: time to be taken and principles of construction

Reading Latin (*Text and Vocabulary* and *Grammar and Exercises*) is aimed at mature beginners in the sixth form (11th–12th grade), universities and adult education who want to learn classical or medieval Latin. Trials were carried out between 1981 and 1984 at a number of schools, summer schools, universities (at home and in the United States, Canada, New Zealand and Denmark) and adult education centres, and the final version of the first edition was given to the Press in September 1984.

This second edition has benefited from twenty-five years' experience with the first edition. In that time it has become clear that there was too much Plautus, and the transition from the Plautus to the Ciceronian prose of Section 4 was too abrupt. As a consequence, we have cut Plautus' *Bacchides* (old Section 2), whose plot was also found to be excessively complicated, and moved *Amphitruo*, appropriately re-written and slightly extended, back from old Section 3 to replace it; and created a brand new Section 3, concentrating on the early history of Rome. Here we tell the stories of Aeneas, Romulus and Remus, the rape of Lucretia and Hannibal, all of which played a vital part in constructing the Romans' sense of their own identity.

We have also introduced the 'momentum' principle into the *Text*, i.e. some portions of a passage appear with their translation appended, but with their full vocabulary still in the vocabulary list. This will enable the reading of the *Text* to be speeded up without depriving the teacher of the chance to home in on any lexical or grammatical features judged to need attention. However, the teacher needs to be warned that the test exercises may cover material found in the momentum sections.

We also decided to move the Running and Learning vocabularies, previously placed in the accompanying *Grammar, Vocabulary and Exercise* volume, onto the facing pages of the *Text*. Each double-page spread now contains Latin text and the vocabulary needed to translate it; and the total Latin–English vocabulary to be learned now appears at the back of the *Text* volume as well as of the *Grammar* volume. As a result, the two volumes are now called *Reading Latin: Text and Vocabulary* and *Reading Latin: Grammar and Exercises*.

Our experience strongly suggests that it takes longer to develop a reading ability in Latin than it does in Greek. Consequently, in schools and adult education, where time is restricted, *Reading Latin* should be treated as a two-year course.

In universities, on a timetable of three to four hours a week, the first year's target should be the end of Section 4, by which time most of the major grammar will have been covered, though better classes may be able to get well into Section 5.

The principles on which we constructed the course are broadly those of *Reading Greek*, with three important exceptions. First, it became clear early on that Latin needs more exercise work than Greek does, and that English into Latin restricted to the level of the phrase or single verb has an important part to play (there are also English into Latin sentences and simple prose work for those who want them). Secondly, we became convinced that if students are ever to read Latin with any confidence they must be encouraged from the very beginning to understand it, word by word and phrase by phrase, in the same order as it was written. A large number of exercises are devoted to this end. In particular, we encourage students to analyse out loud their understanding of a sentence as they translate it and to indicate what they anticipate next. Thirdly, the role of the Latin language in the development of English in particular and Western civilisation and romance languages in general is ineradicable. If we ignored that tradition, and concentrated narrowly on classical Latin, we felt that we would be depriving students of an understanding of Latin's true importance for the Western world. Consequently, while the course teaches classical Latin, the sections of *Dēliciae Latīnae* take the students into the worlds of pre-classical, post-classical, Vulgate and medieval Latin and explore Latin's influence upon English vocabulary today. All the reading material which was attached in the first edition to these *Dēliciae Latīnae* sections in the *Grammar, Vocabulary and Exercises* volume has been moved in the second edition to the end of the *Text and Vocabulary* volume, pp. 283–328. But the word-building and derivation exercises remain under the *Dēliciae Latīnae* from Sections 1B to 4E.

Methodology

Users of *Reading Greek* will be familiar with the methodology that we propose. There are two working volumes: *Text and Vocabulary* (*TV*) and *Grammar and Exercises* (*GE*), and a support-book for those working mostly on their own (Peter Jones and Keith Sidwell, *An Independent Study Guide to Reading Latin* [second edition, Cambridge 2017]).

Note: teachers are advised to mark in their texts the new syntax and accidence that is being introduced in each section.

Step one: with the help of the running vocabularies in the *Text*, or with the teacher prompting, read and translate the appropriate section of the Latin *Text*. In the course of the translation, the teacher should draw out and formalise on the board *only the grammar that is set to be learned for that section* (this can, of course, be done before the *Text* is tackled, if the teacher so desires, but our experience suggests it is far better to let the students try to see for themselves, under the teacher's guidance, how the new grammar works).

Step two: when that is done, students should learn thoroughly the *Learning vocabulary* for the section. Words set to be learned will not be glossed in running vocabularies again, unless they occur in the *Text* with a different meaning. On p. 329 there is a total vocabulary of all words set to be learned with their full range of meanings given in this course, and a note of where they should have been learned (teachers should use this information when devising their own tests).

Step three: the grammar of the section should be reviewed and learned thoroughly from the *GE* volume, and a selection of the exercises tackled. It is extremely important to note that the exercises should be regarded as a *pool out of which the teachers/students should choose what to do, and whether in or out of class*. Teachers will note that we now regularly offer Either/Or options. Some of the simpler exercises we have already split into necessary and optional sections, but this principle should be applied to all of them. Most of these should be done and graded *out of class* (this saves much time), but the *Reading exercises* should all be done orally and the students encouraged to analyse out loud their understanding of the passage as they read it. This technique should, in time, be passed on to the reading of the *Text*. It will help you to learn if you read out the Latin of the *Text* and exercises as much as possible.

We are aware that some teachers of the first edition of the course have created online interactive exercises which have proved a success with their students, and we hope that these might eventually be made more widely available through Cambridge University Press once suitably updated. Any further developments in this respect will be announced through the webpage of the *Grammar and Exercises* volume.

Step four: use as much *Dēliciae Latīnae* (or extra reading: see note after *step five* below) as time allows or personal taste dictates.

Step five: on to the next section of the *Text*, and repeat.

Dēliciae Latīnae

Note that in the second edition, we have moved all extra reading material (real Latin – and sometimes unreal Latin – except the word-building and derivation exercises) from the *Grammar* volume to the end of this *Text*. This material includes *Dēliciae Latīnae* from sections 1B to 4C, passages of *Rēs Gestae Dīuī Augustī* and other writers in sections 4D–G, and passages of Virgil's *Aeneid* and other writers in section 5A–G. This now appears as 'Additional reading for sections 1B to 5G', pp. 283–328 of the *Text*.

Students who want to have more practice with real Latin can now flip directly to these passages, which are equipped with vocabulary and notes at the level of the sections to which they are linked. Once more, it must be stressed that these readings are not an integral part of the course, though, naturally, using them will help develop and strengthen the student's reading abilities.

After *Reading Latin*

There are many classical Latin readers designed for the post-beginners' stage. Three that are tied specifically to *Reading Latin* (and *Wheelock's Latin*) are Peter Jones, *Reading Ovid: Stories from the* Metamorphoses (Cambridge, 2007), Peter Jones, *Reading Virgil*: Aeneid *I and II* (Cambridge, 2011) and Noreen Humble and Carmel McCallum-Barry, *Myths of Rome: An Intermediate Latin Reader* (Cambridge, forthcoming). All have introductions, same-page running and learning vocabularies, grammatical help (cross-referred to *Reading Latin*, *Wheelock* and *The Oxford Latin Grammar*), commentary and discussion.

A note for medieval Latinists

Since classical Latin is the foundation on which medieval developed, and to which medieval writers consistently looked back, it is essential to start Latin studies with classical Latin. The *Dēliciae Latīnae* section offers plenty of contact with later Latin, especially the Vulgate (probably the most important Latin text ever written). You should aim to get into, and preferably complete, Section 5 of *Reading Latin*, before moving on to Keith Sidwell, *Reading Medieval Latin* (Cambridge, 1995). This consists of selections of Latin, in historical sequence in four sections, from the first to the twelfth century AD, with commentary on the cultural changes of the times. The texts are accompanied by extensive linguistic notes and, at the back, a working reference grammar of medieval Latin, and a vocabulary (or spellings) of words not found in standard classical Latin dictionaries.

Acknowledgements

We give our warmest thanks to all our testing institutions, both at home and overseas. In particular, we should like to thank I. M. Le M. DuQuesnay (then of the University of Birmingham, now of Newnham College, Cambridge) and Professor J. A. Barsby (University of Otago at Dunedin, New Zealand), who both gave up wholly disproportionate amounts of their time to the early drafts of the course; Janet Cann† and Professor David West† (University of Newcastle upon Tyne), who suffered with the course from its very beginnings, and can have learned nothing through their suffering, though they both taught us very much; J. G. Randall (University of Lancaster), whose *Parua Sagācī* taught us much about the technique of reading Latin as it comes and who put at our disposal his index of Latin sentences; Professor E. J. Kenney (Peterhouse, Cambridge), who took the tortured Latin of the trial text and put it skilfully out of its suffering; Dr J. G. F. Powell (University of Newcastle upon Tyne, now Professor of Latin at Royal Holloway, London), who ran an expert eye at the last minute over the whole course and saved us from much error of fact and judgement and whose notes on Latin word-order are the basis for section **W** of the Reference Grammar; Dr R. L. Thomson (University of Leeds) for contributing the essays on the Latin language in the Appendix; Sir Desmond Lee† for the comedy and prose translations; Professor West† for the Lucretius and Virgil translations; J. J. Paterson (University of Newcastle upon Tyne) for work on the historical introductions to Sections 4 and 5; Professor E. Phinney† (University of Massachusetts) for scrutinising the whole text for solecisms; our patient indefatigable typist Ms (now Dr) Janet Watson (University of Newcastle upon Tyne); Professor B. A. Sparkes (University of Southampton), who brought to the illustrations the same scholarship and imagination which so graced the pages of the *Reading Greek* series.

Finally, we gratefully acknowledge a loan of £750 from the Finance Committee of the J.A.C.T. Greek Project and a grant of £3,000 from the Nuffield 'Small Grants' Foundation which enabled the three-year testing programme to begin.

The generous support of these institutions and the selfless commitment of the individuals mentioned above have been indispensable ingredients in the production of this course. Responsibility for all error is to be laid firmly at our door.

Second edition

We owe especial thanks to Professor David Langslow (University of Manchester) for thoroughly revising the grammatical Glossary and the whole Reference

Grammar, adding an important new linguistic and comparative philological element to the original descriptions.

We are extremely grateful to Professor Alison Sharrock of the University of Manchester for sharing with us the online interactive exercises she has created for her students. We hope these might eventually be made available to all users of the course through Cambridge University Press.

Peter Jones
Newcastle upon Tyne, UK

Keith Sidwell,
Emeritus Professor of Latin and Greek, University College Cork, and Adjunct Professor, Department of Classics and Religion, University of Calgary

Notice

To avoid confusion, especially amongst users of *Reading Greek* (Cambridge 2nd edition 2008), it must be made clear that *Reading Latin* is the authors' private venture and has no connections with the Joint Association of Classical Teachers.

Notes

1 All dates are BC, unless otherwise specified.
2 Linking devices are used throughout the *Text* to indicate words that should be taken together. ⌢ links words next to each other, ⌐ ¬ links words separated from each other. Such phrases should be looked up under the first word of the group in the running vocabularies. Where verse passages appear, that is Sections 6A and 6D of the main text and sporadically in the Additional Readings (e.g. p. 287), the linking device for separated words is not necessarily backed up by an entry in the vocabularies.
3 All vowels should be pronounced short, unless they are marked with a macron (e.g. ē), when they should be pronounced long (see pronunciation guide, p. xiv of *Grammar and Exercises* volume).
4 Throughout the *Text* are slightly adapted extracts, relevant to the section in hand, drawn from *The World of Rome: An Introduction to Roman Culture* (Cambridge, 1997), edited by Peter Jones and Keith Sidwell.

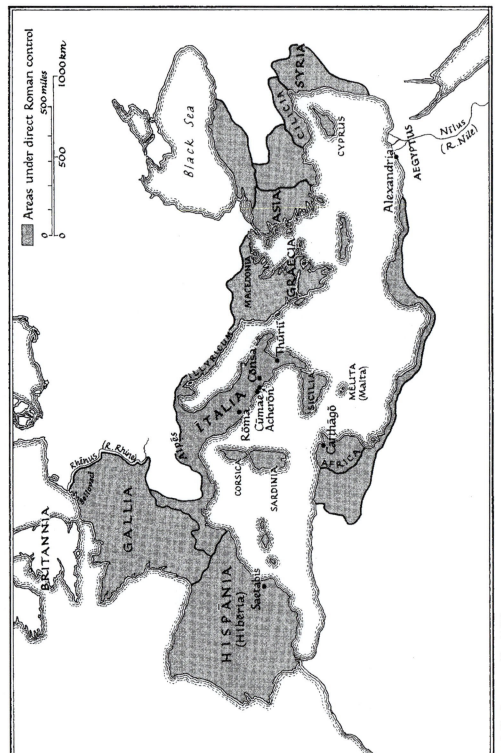

Map 1   The Roman world c. 44 BC

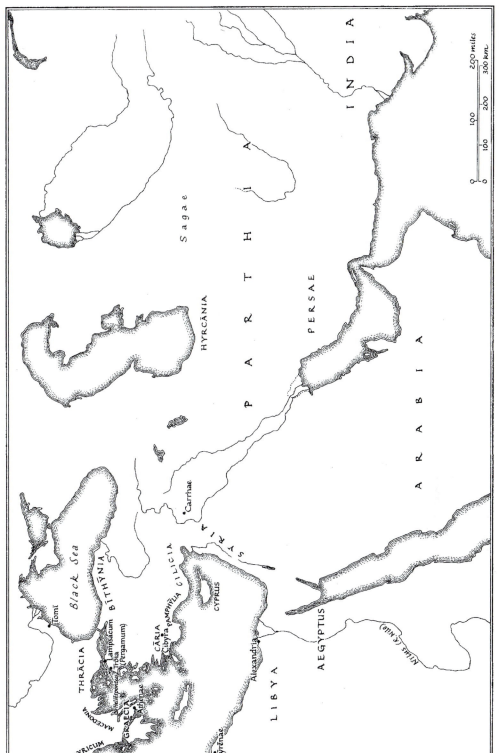

Map 2 Asia Minor and the East

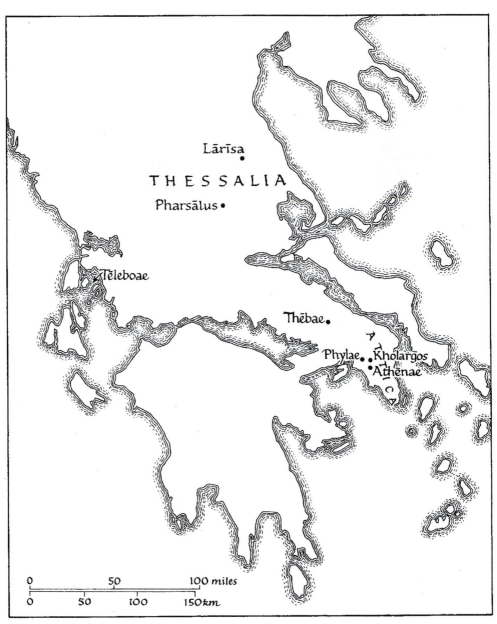

Lārīsa

THESSALIA

Pharsālus

Teleboae

Thēbae

Phylae Kholargos
Athēnae

A T T I C A

0   50   100 miles
0   50   100   150km

Map 3 Greece

Introduction

Greeks and Romans

1. Romulus and Remus

According to distant, heroic tradition, the Trojan prince Aeneas, fleeing from the destruction of Troy by the Greeks, settled in Italy and was the founding father of the Roman people. Rome itself was founded – tradition again – by Romulus on 21 April 753. He was the first of seven kings. In 509, the son of the last king Tarquinius Superbus – 'Tarquin the Proud' – raped the noble Roman woman Lucretia, and Rome rose up against and expelled the Tarquins for ever. It was then that Rome became a Republic. This was seen as the beginning of the age of freedom (*lībertās*). During this period of aristocratic government, Rome extended her power first through Italy and then, after two lengthy conflicts against North African Carthage (the Punic Wars), into the Western Mediterranean itself. As a result, Sicily, Sardinia, Corsica, Spain and North Africa (modern Tunisia) became Rome's first provinces. After Carthage was finally destroyed in 149, Rome moved into the Eastern Mediterranean (provincialising Greece, Asia (modern Turkey), Syria, Palestine and Egypt).

From the beginning Rome had been in contact with Greek culture, for Greek colonies had been established as early as the eighth century in Italy and Sicily. North of Rome lay another developed culture, that of the Etruscans (whose early kings ruled Rome till they were expelled in 509). Roman culture developed under these joint influences. When the Romans finally conquered Greece in 146, they found themselves in possession of the home of the most prestigious culture in the Mediterranean. Their reaction was very complex, but three main strands may be seen. They were proud of their military and administrative achievement and thus contemptuous of contemporary Greeks whom they had defeated. At the same time, they shared the reverence of contemporary Greeks for the great cultural achievements of earlier Greeks – Homer, Herodotus, Thucydides, the tragedians, comic poets and orators. The result of this ambivalent attitude was a more or less conscious decision to create for themselves a culture worthy of their position as the new dominant power. This culture was modelled on and emulated that of Greece in its heyday. Yet the Romans' pride in themselves ensured that the culture was Latin and its literature was written in Latin, not Greek. Horace's famous words illustrate Rome's debt to Greek culture:

Graecia capta ferum uictōrem cēpit, et artīs
intulit agrestī Latiō

Greece captured took as captive its wild foe
And brought the arts to rustic Italy

On the other hand, the poet Propertius, a contemporary of Virgil, describes Virgil's *Aeneid* in the following terms:

nescioquid māius nāscitur Īliade

A greater thing than Homer's *Iliad*
Is being born

Romans now felt their culture could stand comparison with the very best of the Greeks'. This veneration of the Greeks contrasts strongly with, for example, the Roman satirist Juvenal's constant attacks on the contemporary *Graeculus ēsuriēns* ('starving little Greek'), which reflected aristocratic contempt for 'modern' Greeks as the decadent descendants of a once great people. Yet at all periods individual Greeks (e.g. Polybius, Posidonius, Parthenius, Philodemus) were held in high esteem at Rome. And by the end of the first century Rome had become the cultural centre of the world, in the eyes not only of Romans but also of Greeks whose poets, scholars and philosophers now flocked there. It is part of the greatness of Rome that, when confronted with Greek culture, she neither yielded

2. Rome in the first century AD

completely nor trampled it under foot, but accepted the challenge, took it over, and transformed and transmitted it to Europe. Without the mediation of Rome, Western culture would be very different, and, arguably, much the poorer.

Here Cicero, one of Rome's most influential writers, reminds his brother Quintus (who was governor of Asia Minor, a Roman province heavily peopled by Greeks) just who he is in charge of and the debt Rome owes to them:

We are governing a civilised race, in fact the race from which civilisation is believed to have passed to others, and assuredly we ought to give civilisation's benefits above all to those from whom we have received it. Yes, I say it without shame, especially as my life and record leave no opening for any suspicion of indolence or frivolity: everything that I have attained I owe to those pursuits and disciplines which have been handed down to us in the literature and teachings of Greece. Therefore, we may well be thought to owe a special duty to this people, over and above our common obligation to mankind; schooled by their precepts, we must wish to exhibit what we have learned before the eyes of our instructors.

(Cicero, *Ad Quīntum* 1.1)

Part One **Plautus' comedies**

Titus Macc(i)us Plautus probably lived from *c.* 250 to *c.* 180. He is said to have written about 130 comedies of which nineteen survive. Like almost all Roman writers, he drew the inspiration for his work from earlier Greek models, which he freely translated and adapted to fit the Roman audience for which he was writing. For example, it is almost certain that he based *Aululāria*, the first play you will read, on a play by the Athenian Menander (*c.* 340 to *c.* 290). Plautus wrote comedies for production at Roman festivals (*fēriae*, *lūdī*), times devoted to worship of the gods and abstention from work. The originals were written in verse.

Actors in the Greek originals wore masks which covered the whole head (see p. 6). Though it is not absolutely certain that Plautus followed this convention, we have illustrated the Plautine characters in the Introduction with Greek mask-types from around the time of Menander.

Aululāria begins with the entry of the family Lar (household god), who sketches the history of the family in brief outline and alerts us to Euclio's miserliness. For the purposes of adaptation, we have filled out that brief family history with a number of scenes taken from elsewhere in Roman comedy. We start to follow Plautus at Section 1C. At the end of each section from here onwards we note the source we have adapted.

Introduction: familia Eucliōnis

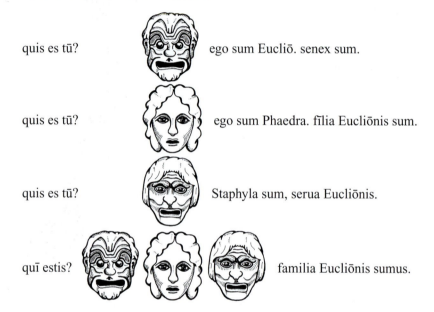

quis es tū?   ego sum Eucliō. senex sum.

quis es tū?   ego sum Phaedra. fīlia Eucliōnis sum.

quis es tū?   Staphyla sum, serua Eucliōnis.

quī estis?   familia Eucliōnis sumus.

drāmatis persōnae
Eucliō: Eucliō senex est, pater⁀Phaedrae.
Phaedra: Phaedra fīlia⁀Eucliōnis est.
Staphyla: serua⁀Eucliōnis est.
Eucliō senex est. Eucliō senex auārus est. Eucliō in⁀aedibus habitat
cum⁀fīliā. fīlia⁀Eucliōnis Phaedra est. est et serua in⁀aedibus.
seruae⁀nōmen est Staphyla.
Eucliōnis⁀familia in⁀aedibus habitat. sunt in⁀familiā⁀Eucliōnis
paterfamiliās, et Phaedra fīlia⁀Eucliōnis, et Staphyla serua. omnēs
in⁀aedibus habitant.

5

Running vocabulary for Introduction

auārus greedy
cum fīliā with (his) daughter
drāmatis the play's
ego I
es are you?
est is; he/she/it is; there is
estis? are you?
et also; and
Eucliō Euclio
Recliōnis of Euclio
Eucliōnis familia the household of Euclio
familia household
fīlia daughter

fīlia Eucliōnis (the) daughter of Euclio
habitat (he/she/it) lives
habitant (they) live
in aedibus in the house
in familiā Eucliōnis in Euclio's household
omnēs all (pl.)
pater Phaedrae father of Phaedra
paterfamiliās (the) head of the family
persōnae characters (lit. 'masks')
Phaedra Phaedra
quī who? (pl.)

quis who? (s.)
senex (an) old man
serua (the/a) (woman) slave
serua Eucliōnis (the) slave of Euclio
seruae nōmen the name of the slave-woman
Staphyla Staphyla
sum (I) am
sumus we are
sunt there are
tū? you (s.)

Grammar for Introduction

sum 'I am'

Learning vocabulary for Introduction

Nouns
Eucliō Euclio
famili-a household
fīli-a daughter
Phaedr-a Phaedra

seru-a slave-woman
Staphyl-a Staphyla

Verbs
habit-ō I dwell

Others
et and; also, too, even

The Roman family

Our word 'family' derives from the Latin *familia*, and that may lull us into thinking the two ideas are much the same. In fact *familia* has some significant differences. Strictly, it is a legal term, referring to those under the legal control of the head of household, the *paterfamiliās*. The *familia* covered the slaves of a household, but frequently did not include the wife; so that even if many Romans lived in groupings resembling the modern 'nuclear family', that was not what they referred to in talking about the *familia*. (*World of Rome*, **302**)

Section 1A

The scene moves back in time many years. Euclio's grandfather, Demaenetus, on the day of his daughter's wedding, fearful that his gold will be stolen amid the confusion of the preparations, entrusts it to the safe keeping of his household god (the Lar). He puts it in a pot and hides it in a hole near the altar.

drāmatis persōnae
Dēmaenetus: Dēmaenetus senex est, Eucliōnis⁀auus.   10
seruus: seruī⁀nōmen est Dāuus.
serua: seruae⁀nōmen est Pamphila.
coquus et tībīcina.
(*seruus in⁀scaenam intrat. ante⁀ iānuam⁀Dēmaenetī stat et clāmat. cūr*
clāmat? clāmat quod seruam uocat)   15
SERVVS   heus, Pamphila! ego Dāuus tē uocō!
SERVA   quis mē uocat? quis clāmat?
SERVVS   ego Dāuus tē uocō.
SERVA   quid est? cūr mē uocās?

3. aedēs (scaena)

Running vocabulary for 1A

ante‿iānuam‿Dēmaenetī before
  Demaenetus' door
clāmat (he/she/it) shouts, is
  shouting
coquus (nom.) (a/the) cook
cūr why?
Dāuus (nom.) Davus
Dēmaenetus (nom.) Demaenetus
drāmatis the play's
ego I
Ecliōnis‿auus (nom.) Euclio's
  grandfather

heus hey!
in‿scaenam onto the stage
intrat (he/she/it) enters
mē (acc.) me
Pamphila (nom., voc.) Pamphila,
  O Pamphila
persōnae characters
quid what?
quis who?
quod because
senex (nom.) an old man
seruae‿nōmen the slave's name

seruam (acc.) (the slave-woman
seruī‿nōmen the name of the
  slave
seruus (nom.) (a/the) slave
stat (he/she/it) stands
tē (acc.) you (s.)
tībīcina (nom.) (a/the) pipe-girl
uocās (do) you call, are you
  calling (s.)
uocat (he/she/it) calls, is calling
uocō I call, am calling

4. ego Dāuus tē uocō

(*seruus ad⁀iānuam appropinquat, sed iānua clausa est. seruus igitur iānuam*   20
pulsat)

SERVVS   heus tū, serua! ego iānuam pulsō, at tū nōn aperīs: iānua
                    clausa est.

SERVA   (*iānuam aperit*) cūr clāmās? ego hūc et illūc cursitō, tū autem
                    clāmās. ego occupāta sum, tū autem ōtiōsus es. seruus nōn es,   25
                    sed furcifer.

SERVVS   ego ōtiōsus nōn sum, Pamphila. nam hodiē Dēmaenetus,
                    dominus meus, fīliam in⁀mātrimōnium⁀dat : nūptiae⁀fīliae
                    sunt!

(*Dēmaenetus, dominus⁀serui⁀et⁀seruae, in⁀scaenam intrat*)   30

DĒMAENETVS   cūr clāmātis, Dāue et Pamphila? cūr stātis? cūr ōtiōsī
                    estis? nam hodiē nūptiae⁀fīliae⁀meae sunt. cūr nōn in⁀aedīs
                    intrātis et nūptiās parātis?

(*in⁀aedīs intrant seruus et serua, et nūptiās parant. in⁀scaenam intrant coquus*
et tībīcina. Dēmaenetus coquum et tībīcinam uidet)   35

DĒM.   heus uōs, quī estis? ego enim uōs nōn cognōuī.

COQVVS ET TĪBĪCINA   coquus et tībīcina sumus.
                    ad⁀nūptiās⁀fīliae⁀tuae uenīmus.

DĒM.   cūr nōn in⁀aedīs⁀meās intrātis et nūptiās parātis?

(*coquus et tībīcina in⁀aedīs⁀Dēmaenetī intrant*)   40

(*Dēmaenetus corōnam et unguentum portat. aulam quoque portat. aula*
aurī⁀plēna est)

DĒM.   heu! hodiē nūptiās⁀fīliae⁀meae parō. cūncta familia festīnat.
                    hūc et illūc cursitant puerī et puellae, ego coquōs et tībīcinās
                    uocō. nunc aedēs plēnae sunt coquōrum⁀et⁀tībīcinārum, et   45
                    cūnctī coquī et tībīcinae fūrēs sunt. heu! homo perditus sum,

A father's power

Stated at its most dramatic, the power of the *paterfamiliās* was absolute: the power of life and death over his *familia*, that is his legitimate children, his slaves, and his wife if married in a form that transferred paternal control (*manus*, lit. 'hand') to the husband. The *familia* could be seen as a state within a state: its members were subject to the judgement and absolute authority of the *pater* ('father') just as citizens were subject to the judgement and absolute authority of the citizen body. In exceptional circumstances sons or wives might be handed over by the state to paternal authority, as happened on the occasion of the scandal of the cult of Bacchus in 186 BC, or again under Augustus. But even if this awesome power was occasionally invoked, and its memory was kept alive, in practical terms it was not the most significant aspect of *potestās* ('power'). (*World of Rome*, **309**)

ad˘iānuam to the door
ad˘nūptiās˘fīliae˘tuae to the marriage-rites of your daughter
aedēs (nom. pl.) (the) house
aperīs you (s.) are opening (it)
aperit (he/she/it) opens
appropinquat (he/she/it) approaches
at but
aula (nom.) (the) pot
aulam (acc.) (a) pot
aurī˘plēna (nom.) full of gold
autem however
clāmās (do) you shout, are you shouting; you shout, you are shouting
clāmātis (do) you shout, are you shouting
clausa (nom.) closed, shut
cognōuī I know
coquī (nom.) cooks
coquōrum˘et˘tībīcinārum of cooks and pipe-girls
coquōs (acc.) cooks
coquum (acc.) (the) cook
coquus (nom.) (a/the) cook
corōnam (acc.) (a) crown, garland
cūncta (nom.) the whole
cūnctī (nom.) all
cūr why?
cursitant (they) run about, are running about
cursitō I run about
Dāue (voc.) O Davus
Dēmaenetus (nom.) Demaenetus
dominus (nom.) master

dominus˘seruī˘et˘seruae the master of the slave and slave-woman
ego I
enim for, because
festīnat (he/she/it) hurries about, is hurrying about
fīliam (acc.) (his) daughter
furcifer (nom.) (a) rascal
fūrēs (nom.) thieves
heu alas!
heus hey!
hodiē today
homo (a) fellow, man
hūc (to) here
iānua (nom.) (the) door
iānuam (acc.) (the) door
igitur therefore
illūc (to) there
in˘aedīs into the house
in˘aedīs˘Dēmaenetī into Demaenetus' house
in˘aedīs˘meās into my house
in˘mātrimōnium˘dat (he/she/it) is giving in marriage
in˘scaenam onto the stage
intrant (they) enter
intrat (he/she/it) enters
intrātis (do) you (pl.) enter
meus (nom.), my
nam for, because
nōn not
nunc now
nūptiae˘fīliae (the) marriage-rites of (his) daughter
nūptiae˘fīliae˘meae the marriage-rites of my daughter

nūptiās (acc.) (the) marriage-rites
nūptiās˘fīliae˘meae (acc.) (the) marriage-rites of my daughter
occupāta (nom.) busy
ōtiōsī (nom.) idle
ōtiōsus (nom.) idle
Pamphila (nom., voc.) Pamphila, O Pamphila
parant (they) prepare
parātis (do) you (pl.) prepare?; you (pl.) prepare
parō I prepare, am preparing
perditus (nom.) lost, done for
plēnae (nom. pl.) full
portat (he/she/it) carries, is carrying
puellae (nom.) girls
puerī (nom.) boys
pulsat (he/she/it) beats on, pounds
pulsō I beat on, am beating on, pound, am pounding
quī who?
quoque also, too
sed but
seruus (nom.) (a/the) slave
stātis (do) you stand, are you standing
tībīcina (nom.) (a/the) pipe-girl
tībīcinae (nom. pl.) pipe-girls
tībīcinam (acc.) (the) pipe-girl
tībīcinās (acc.) pipe-girls
tū (nom., voc.) you (s.)
uenīmus we come, are coming
uidet (he/she/it) sees
unguentum (acc.) ointment
uocō I call, am calling
uōs (nom., voc., acc.) you (pl.)

immō, perditissimus hominum. nam aulam habeō
aurī‿plēnam. ecce! aulam portō. (*senex aulam mōnstrat.*) nunc
aulam sub‿ueste cēlō. nam ualdē timeō. (*Sniffs air*) aurum
enim olet; et fūrēs aurum olfactant. aurum autem nōn olet, sī   50
sub‿terrā latet. sī aurum sub‿terrā latet, nūllum coquum
nūllam tībīcinam nūllum fūrem timeō. aulam igitur clam
sub‿terrā cēlō. ecquis mē spectat?

(*Dēmaenetus circumspectat. nēmo adest. Dēmaenetus igitur nēminem uidet*)
bene, sōlus sum. sed prius ad‿Larem appropinquō et   55
unguentum corōnamque dō, et supplicō.

(*ad‿Larem appropinquat. unguentum dat et corōnam. deinde Larī supplicat*)
ō Lar, tūtēla‿meae‿familiae, tē ōrō et obsecrō, ego tē semper
corōnō, semper tibi unguentum dō, semper sacrificium et
honōrem, tū contrā bonam Fortūnam dās. nunc ad‿tē aulam   60
aurī‿plēnam portō. sub‿ueste autem aulam cēlō. familia
dē‿aulā ignōrat, sed hodiē sunt nūptiae‿fīliae. plēnae sunt
aedēs coquōrum‿et‿tībīcinārum. immō, fūrum‿plēnae sunt.
aurum olet. ego igitur fūrēs timeō. ō Lar, tē ōrō et obsecrō,
aulam seruā!   65

(*senex ad‿focum appropinquat. prope‿focum fouea est. in‿foueā aulam cēlat.*)
ecce, saluum aurum est, saluus quoque ego. nunc enim tū
aulam habēs, Lar.

5. larārium

ad̑focum (to) the hearth
ad̑Larem (to) the Lar
ad̑tē to you (s.)
adest (he/she/it) is present
aedēs (nom.) house
appropinquō I approach, am approaching
appropinquat (he/she/it) approaches
aulam (acc.) (a/the) pot
aurī̑plēnam (acc.) full of gold
aurum (nom., acc.) (the) gold
autem however
bene good!
bonam (acc.) good
cēlat (he/she/it) hides
cēlō I hide, am hiding, conceal, am concealing
circumspectat (he/she/it) looks around
clam secretly
contrā in return
coquōrum̑et̑tībīcinārum of cooks and pipe-girls
coquum (acc.) cook
corōnam (acc.) (the) garland
corōnamque (acc.) and a (the) crown ('crown-and')
corōnō I garland
dās (you) give (s.)
dat (he/she/it) gives, offers
dē̑aulā about the pot
deinde then
Dēmaenetus (num.) Demaenetus
dō I give, offer
ecce look!

ecquis (nom.) anyone?
ego I
enim for, because
Fortūnam (acc.) Luck
fouea (nom.) (a/the) hole, pit
fūrem (acc.) thief
fūrēs (nom., acc.) thieves
fūrum̑plēnae (nom. pl.) full of thieves
habeō I have
habēs (you) have (s.)
hodiē today
hominum of men
honōrem (acc.) respect
igitur therefore
ignōrat (he/she/it) knows nothing
immō more precisely
in̑fouea in the hole, pit
Lar (voc.) Lar, household god
Larī (to) the Lar
latet (he/she/it) lies hidden
mē (acc.) me
mōnstrat (he/she/it) shows, reveals
nam for, because
nēminem (acc.) no one
nēmo (nom.) no one
nōn not
nūllam (acc.) no
nūllum (acc.) no
nunc now
nūptiaȇfīliae the marriage-rites of my daughter
ō O (addressing someone)
obsecrō I beseech
olet (it) gives off a smell
olfactant (they) sniff out

ōrō I beg
perditissimus (nom.) most lost, done for
plēnae (nom. pl.) full
portō I carry, am carrying
prius first, beforehand
propȇfocum near the hearth
quoque also, too
sacrificium (acc.) (a) sacrifice
saluum (nom.) safe
saluus (nom.) safe
sed but
semper always
senex (nom.) (the) old man
seruā save! protect!
sī if
sōlus (nom.) alone
spectat (he/she/it) is looking at
sub̑terrā beneath the earth
sub̑ueste under my clothes
supplicō I pray (to), make an entreaty (to)
supplicat (he/she/it) prays to, entreats
tē (acc.) you (s.)
tibi to you (s.)
tībīcinam (acc.) pipe-girl
timeō I fear, am afraid (of)
tū (s.) you
tūtēlȃmeaȇfamiliae (voc.) guardian of my household
ualdē very much
uidet (he/she/it) sees
unguentum (acc.) (the) ointment

From *Lar* to emperor

By including the place where they worked or lived in the relationship between themselves and the gods, Romans tried to confirm and maintain some stability and predictability in their lives from one day to the next. By worshipping the domestic deities of a household, the *Larēs*, in which slaves and freedmen joined with the free family, or by joining in the communal observances at the crossroads (the focus of any densely built-up neighbourhood), Romans helped define where they belonged in a perilous world. Further, the power of the patron, and behind that the power of the state, most easily recognised as the emperor himself, held the whole thing together. So it was perfectly natural to weave these too into the pattern of one's worship. Thus the slave honoured the personal *genius* of his master, the client that of his patron, and everyone that of their ultimate ruler, the emperor. (*World of Rome*, **261**)

Grammar for 1A

present indicative active of amō, habeō	**declension of *serua, seruus***	***in, ad***

Important notes

1 nom. is short for nominative and indicates the subject or complement of a sentence.
   acc. is short for accusative and indicates the object (direct) of a sentence. See *GE*, Glossary, p. xvii.
2 Where a 3rd s. verb is glossed '(he/she/it)', select the appropriate pronoun if there is no stated subject.
3 *uocās* would normally be translated 'you call/are calling', but after a question word like *cur*? 'why', English turns this round to '[why] are you calling/do you call?'

Learning vocabulary for 1A

Nouns
aul-a ae 1f. pot
aur-um ī 2n. gold
coqu-us ī 2m. cook
corōn-a ae 1f. garland
ego I
Lar Lar-is Lar (household god)
mē (acc.) me
scaen-a ae 1f. stage
seru-us ī 2m. male slave
tē (acc.) you (s.)
tū (nom.) you (s.)

Adjectives
plēn-us a um full (of) + gen.

Verbs
Numbers after the 1st p.s. form of the verb (here 1 or 2) refer to the conjugation.
cēl-ō 1 I hide
clām-ō 1 I shout
intr-ō 1 I enter
port-ō 1 I carry
uoc-ō 1 I call
habe-ō 2 I have
time-ō 2 1 fear, am afraid (of)

Others
ad (+ acc.) to(wards); at
autem but (2nd word in Latin, to be translated 1st word in English)
cūr why?

deinde next
enim for, because (2nd word in Latin, to be translated 1st word in English)
igitur therefore (usually 2nd word in Latin)
in (+ acc.) into, onto (+ abl.) in, on
nam for, because (1st word in Latin)
nōn not
nunc now
quoque also
sed but
semper always
sī if
sub (+ abl.) under, beneath

Section 1B

A very long time has passed. The old man Demaenetus has died without digging up the gold or revealing the secret to his son. Now, however, his grandson Euclio, an old man, is going to strike lucky. The Lar explains.

6. spectātōrēs, ego sum Lar familiāris

*(Eucliō in scaenā dormit. dum dormit, Lar in scaenam intrat et fābulam
explicat)*   70

LAR   spectātōrēs, ego sum Lar familiāris. deus sum familiae Ecliōnis.
        ecce Ecliōnis aedēs. est in‿aedibus Ecliōnis thēsaurus
        magnus. thēsaurus est Dēmaenetī, auī Ecliōnis. sed thēsaurus
        in aulā est et sub terrā latet. ego enim aulam clam in‿aedibus
        seruō. Ecliō dē thēsaurō ignōrat. cūr thēsaurum clam adhūc   75
        seruō? fābulam explicō. Ecliō nōn bonus est senex, sed auārus
        et malus. Ecliōnem igitur nōn amō. praetereā Ecliō mē nōn
        cūrat. mihi numquam supplicat. unguentum numquam dat,
        nūllās corōnās, nūllum honōrem. sed Ecliō fīliam habet
        bonam. nam cūrat mē Phaedra, Ecliōnis fīlia, et multum   80
        honōrem, multum unguentum, multās corōnās dat. Phaedram
        igitur, bonam fīliam Ecliōnis, ualdē amō. sed Ecliō pauper
        est. nūllam igitur dōtem habet fīlia. nam senex dē aulā auī
        ignōrat. nunc autem, quia Phaedra bona est, aulam aurī
        plēnam Ecliōnī dō. nam Ecliōnem in‿somniō uīsō et aulam   85
        mōnstrō. uidēte, spectātōrēs.

(Eucliō dormit. Lar imāginem auī in scaenam dūcit. Eucliō stupet)
EVCLIŌ dormiō an uigilō? dī magnī! imāginem uideō auī meī,
        Dēmaenetī. saluē, Dēmaenete! heu! quantum mutātus
        ab‿illō . . . ab‿īnferīs scīlicet in aedīs intrat. ecce! aulam   90
        Dēmaenetus portat. cūr aulam portās, Dēmaenete? ecce!
        circumspectat Dēmaenetus et sēcum murmurat. nunc ad āram
        Laris festīnat. quid facis, Dēmaenete? foueam facit et in foueā
        aulam collocat. mīrum hercle est. quid autem in aulā est? dī
        magnī! aula aurī plēna est.   95

DĒMAENETĪ IMĀGŌ   bene. nunc aurum meum saluum est.
EVC.   nōn crēdō, Dēmaenete. nūllum in‿aedibus aurum est.
        somnium falsum est. pauper ego sum et pauper maneō.

*(Euclio wakes up, and is angry that the gods torment him with what he feels
are false dreams of wealth)*
EVC.   heu mē miserum. ego sum perditissimus hominum. pauper   100
        sum, sed dī falsa somnia mōnstrant. auum meum in‿somniō
        uideō. auus aulam aurī plēnam portat, aulam sub terrā clam
        collocat iuxtā‿Larem. nōn tamen crēdō. somnium falsum est.
        quārē Lar mē nōn cūrat? quārē mē dēcipit?

Running vocabulary for 1B

ab˜illō from that (former self of his) [The whole phrase is a quotation from Virgil, *Aeneid* 2.274, used by Aeneas of the dead, mutilated ghost of Hector.]

ab˜īnferīs from the dead

adhūc so far

aedēs (nom.), *aedīs* (acc.) house

amō 1 I love, like

an? or?

ār-a ae 1f. altar

auārus (nom.) greedy

au-us ī 2m. grandfather

bene good! well

bon-a (nom. s.) good

bon-am (acc. s.) good

bon-us (nom. s.) good

circumspectō 1 I look around

clam secretly

collocō 1 I place

crēdō I believe

cūrō 1 I care for, look after, am concerned about

dē (+ abl.) concerning

de-us ī 2m. god

dēcipit (he/she/it) tricks, deceives

Dēmaenete (voc.) O Demaenetus

Dēmaenetī (gen.) of Demaenetus

dī 2m. (nom., voc. pl.) gods, O gods!

dō 1 I give offer

dormiō I sleep, am I asleep?

dormit (he/she/it) sleeps

dōtem (acc. s.) dowry

dūcit (he/she/it) leads

dum while

ecce look!

Eucliō (nom.) Euclio

Eucliōn-em (acc.) Euclio

Eucliōn-ī (dat.) to Euclio

Eucliōn-is (gen.) of Euclio

explicō 1 I tell, unfold

fābul-a ae 1f. story

facis are you (s.) doing

facit he/she/it is making

falsa (acc. pl.) false

falsum (nom. s.) false

familiāris (nom.) of the household

festīnō 1 I hurry

foue-a 1f. pit, hole

hercle by Hercules!

heu alas!

hominum (gen.) of men

honōrem (acc. s.) respect

ignōr-ō 1 I do not know

imāginem (acc.) vision

imāgō (nom.) vision

in˜aedibus in the house

in aedīs into the house

in˜somniō in a dream

iuxtā˜Larem next to the Lar

Laris (gen.) of the Lar

lateō 2 I lie hidden

magnī (voc. pl.) great, great amount of

magnus (nom. m. s.) great, great amount of

malus (nom. s.) evil, wicked

maneō 2 I remain

meī (gen. s.) my

meum (nom. s., acc. s.) my

mihi (to) me

mīrum (nom.) amazing

miserum (acc. s.) miserable, unhappy

mōnstrō 1 I reveal, show

mult-ās (acc. pl.) many

mult-um (acc. s.) much

murmurō 1 I mutter

mutātus (nom. s.) changed

nūllām (acc. s.) no

nūllās (acc. pl.) no, none

nūllum (nom. s., acc. s.) no

numquam never

pauper (nom.) poor (man)

perditissimus (nom. s.) most done for

praetereā moreover

quantum how (much)

quārē why?

quia because

quid what?

saluē welcome!

saluum (nom. s.) safe

scīlicet evidently

sēcum with himself

senex (nom.) (the) old man

seruō 1 I keep

somnia (acc. pl.) dreams

somnium (nom.) dream

spectātōrēs (voc. pl.) spectators, audience

stupeō 2 I am amazed, astonished

sub (+ abl.) under

supplicō 1 I make prayers to

tamen however, but

terr-a ae 1f. earth, land

thēsaur-us ī 2m. treasure

ualdē greatly

uideō 2 I see

uidēte see! look! (pl.)

uigilō 1 I am awake

uīsō 1 I visit

unguentum (acc.) ointment

(*Eucliō ad⌐Larem appropinquat, subitō autem foueam uidet. Eucliō celeriter*   105
multam terram ē foueā mouet. tandem aula appāret)

EVC.   quid habēs, ō Lar? quid sub⌐pedibus tenēs? hem. aulam uideō.
         nempe somnium uērum est.

(*Eucliō aulam ē foueā mouet. intrō spectat et aurum uidet. stupet*)

         euge! eugepae! aurum possideō! nōn sum pauper, sed dīues!   110
         (*suddenly crestfallen*) sed tamen hercle homo dīues cūrās semper
         habet multās, fūrēs in⌐aedīs clam intrant. ō mē miserum! nunc
         fūrēs timeō, quod multām pecūniam possideō. eheu! ut Lar
         mē uexat! hodiē enim mihi multam pecūniam, multās simul
         cūrās dat; hodiē igitur perditissimus hominum sum.   115
         quid tum? ā! bonum cōnsilium habeō. ecquis mē spectat?

(*Eucliō aurum sub⌐ueste cēlat et circumspectat. nēminem uidet. tandem*
ad⌐Larem appropinquat)

         ad tē, Lar, aulam aurī plēnam portō. tū aulam seruā et cēlā!

(*Eucliō aulam in⌐foueā iterum collocat; deinde multam terram super aulam*   120
aggerat)

         bene. aurum saluum est. sed anxius sum. quārē autem anxius
         sum? anxius sum quod thēsaurus magnus multās cūrās dat, et
         mē ualdē uexat. nam in⌐ dīuitum hominum ¬aedīs fūrēs multī
         intrant; plēnae igitur fūrum multōrum sunt dīuitum hominum   125
         aedēs. ō mē miserum!

ā! ha!
ad⌐Larem to the Lar
aedēs (nom. pl.), house
aggerō 1 I pile, heap up
anxius (nom. s.) worried
appāreō 2 I appear
appropinquō I approach
bene good! well
bon-um (acc. s.) good
cēlā hide!
celeriter quickly
circumspectō 1 I look around
clam secretly
collocō 1 I place
cōnsilium (acc. s.) plan
cūr-ā 1f. care, devotion, worry,
    concern
dīues (nom.) rich (man)
dīuitum (gen.) of rich (men)
dō 1 I give
ē (+ abl.) out of, from
ecquis (does) anyone?
Eucliō (nom.) Euclio
eheu what a pity! oh dear!
euge! eugepae! hoorah! yippee!
foue-a ae 1f. pit, hole
fūrēs (nom. pl., acc. pl.) thieves

fūrum (gen. pl.) of thieves
hem what's this?
hercle by Hercules!
hodiē today
hominum (gen.) (of) men
homo (nom. s.) fellow, man
in⌐aedīs into the house
in⌐foueā in the hole, pit
intrō inside
iterum again
magnus (nom. s.) great, great
    amount of
mihi (to) me
miserum (acc. s.) miserable,
    unhappy
moueō 2 I move
mult-am (acc. s.) much
mult-ās (acc. pl.) many
mult-ī (nom. pl.) many
mult-ōrum (gen. pl.) of much,
    many
nēminem (acc.) no one
nempe clearly, no doubt
ō O (addressing someone)
pauper (nom. s.) (a) poor (man)
pecūni-a ae 1f. money

perditissimus (nom. s.) most done
    for
possideō 2 I possess, have, hold
quārē why?
quid what?
quod because
saluum (nom. s.) safe
seruā keep safe!
simul at the same time
somnium (nom. s.) dream
spectō 1 I look at, see
stupeō 2 I am amazed, astonished
subitō suddenly
sub⌐pedibus under (your) feet
sub⌐ueste under my/his cloak
super (+ acc.) above
tamen however, but
tandem at length
teneō 2 I hold, possess, keep
terr-a ae 1f. earth, land
thēsaur-us ī 2m. treasure
tum then
ualdē greatly
uērum (nom. s.) true
uexō 1 I annoy, worry
uideō 2 I see
ut how!

Grammar for 1B

declension of *somnium, deus, fūr, aedis*	vocatives	1st and 2nd dedension adjectives apposition

Learning vocabulary for 1B

Nouns
cūr-a ae 1f. care, worry, concern
de-us ī 2m. god (nom. pl. *dī*)
thēsaur-us ī 2m. treasure
unguent-um ī 2n. ointment
aedis aed-is 3f. temple; pl. *aed-ēs ium* house
fūr fūr-is 3m. thief
honor honōr-is 3m. respect
senex sen-is 3m. old man

Adjectives
mult-us a um much, many
nūll-us a um no, none

Verbs
am-ō 1 I love
cūr-ō 1 I look after, care for
d-ō 1 I give
explic-ō 1 I tell, explain
supplic-ō 1 I make prayers (to)

posside-ō 2 I have, hold, possess
uide-ō 2 I see

Others
clam secretly
quārē why?
quod because
tamen however, but
tandem at length

Greeks and Romans

The Greek world had a distinctive way of life and a highly refined and rich culture. Some Roman aristocrats were bewitched by it. Scipio, the victor over Hannibal, was accused by his critics of adopting, while staying in Syracuse, the Greek city in Sicily, a dress and bearing 'which were un-Roman, and not even soldierly; he strolled about the gymnasium in a Greek cloak and sandals, and wasted his time over books and physical exercise' (Livy 29.19). Reading was not a suitable occupation for a man of action. However, by her victories, Rome became a centre of the Mediterranean-wide culture of which Greek was the principal medium. The great philosopher Poseidonius, from Apamea in Syria, found a place in the entourages of Roman generals, and drew his information and some of his preoccupations from them. The Greek historian Polybius, deported to Italy in 167 BC, worked entirely in a Roman context. This process of Hellenisation of Rome came at just the moment that Rome was developing its own truly Roman literature with the dramatist Plautus, the epic poet Q. Ennius, the first Roman historian Q. Fabius Pictor. The models were Greek (and so was the language used by Pictor), but their interests were distinctively Roman. (*World of Rome*, **43**)

Section 1C

(*Eucliō ex aedibus in scaenam intrat clāmatque*)

EVCLIŌ   exī ex aedibus! exī statim! cūr nōn exīs, serua mea?

STAPHYLA   (*ex aedibus exit et in scaenam intrat*) quid est, mī domine?
quid facis? quārē mē ex aedibus expellis? serua tua sum. quārē   130
mē uerberās, domine?

EVC.   tacē! tē uerberō quod mala es, Staphyla.

STAPH.   egone mala? cūr mala sum? misera sum, sed nōn mala,
domine. (*sēcum cōgitat*) sed tū īnsānus es!

EVC.   tacē! exī statim! abī etiam nunc . . . etiam nunc . . . ohē! stā!   135
manē! (*Eucliō sēcum cōgitat*) periī! occidī! ut mala mea serua
est! nam oculōs in occipitiō habet. ut thēsaurus meus mē
miserum semper uexat! ut thēsaurus multās cūrās dat! (*clāmat
iterum*) manē istīc! tē moneō, Staphyla!

STAPH.   hīc maneō ego, mī domine, tū tamen quō īs?   140

EVC.   ego in aedīs meās redeō (*sēcum cōgitat*) et thēsaurum meum
clam uideō. nam fūrēs semper in aedīs hominum dīuitum
ineunt . . .

EUC.   *Be quiet! Get out at once! Go away further now . . . further now.*
Whoa! Stop! Wait! [Euclio himself-with he-ponders]. I'm lost! I'm-done-for!
How evil my slave-woman she-is. For eyes in the-back-of-her-head she-has. How
treasure my me unhappy always it-troubles! How the-treasure many
worries it-gives! [He-shouts again] Wait there! You I-warn, Staphyla!

STAPH.   *Here I-wait I, my master.* You, *however, to-where you-go?*

EUC.   I *into house my I-return [himself-with he ponders] and treasure my*
secretly I see. For thieves always into the-house of-men rich they-enter . . .

7. quid est, mī domine: quid facis?
quārē mē ex aedibus expellis?

Running vocabulary for 1C

abī go away!
clāmatque and (he) shouts
cōgitō 1 I think, reflect, ponder
dīuitum (gen.) of rich (men)
domin-us ī 2m. lord, master
ē, ex (+ abl.) from, out of
egone am I?
etiam nunc further still
ex see *ē*
exī get out!
exīs are you (s.) going/coming out
exit (he/she/it) goes/comes out
expellis you (s.) are driving out
facis are you (s.), doing
hīc here

homo homin-is 3m. human; man, fellow
ineunt (they) enter
īnsān-us a um mad
īs are you (s.) going
istīc there
iterum again
mal-us a um evil, wicked, bad
manē! wait!
maneō 2 I wait, stay
me-us a um my, mine
mī (voc.)'O my'
miser miser-a um unhappy
moneō 2 I advise, warn
occidī I'm done for!
occipiti-um ī 2n. back of head

ocul-us ī 2m. eye
ohē stop!
periī I'm lost!
-que (added to a word) and (see *clamatque*)
quid (nom., acc.) what?
quō where?
redeō I am returning
sēcum with himself/herself
stā! stand (still)!
statim at once
tacē shut up!
tu-us a um your
uerberō 1 I flog, beat
uexō 1 I annoy, trouble
ut how!

Slaves in the family

Slaves, that is to say, belonged to the sentimental as well as the legal structure of the family. The universal bond that held the family together was power and authority, the ability to reward and punish. Within that was the potential for every type of emotional relationship: hatred and resentment, love and devotion. Slaves willingly died for their owners, as the Romans were anxious to advertise (there are no cases of masters dying for slaves). Slaves suckled, nursed, and brought up their future masters; attended and made love to them; assisted in their business ventures and catered for their pleasures. That close bonding took place in some cases was a welcome bonus, just as it was between husband and wife, or between parent and child. That does not mean that it was a normal or necessary condition of family life. (*World of Rome*, **354**)

(*Eucliō ē scaenā abit et in aedīs redit*)

STAPH.	ō mē miseram ! dominus meus īnsānus est. per⁀noctem	145
	numquam dormit, sed peruigilat; per⁀diem mē ex aedibus	
	semper expellit. quid in animō habet? quārē senex tam īnsānus	
	est?	

(*Eucliō tandem ex aedibus exit et in scaenam redit*)

EVC.	(*sēcum cōgitat*) dī mē seruant! thēsaurus meus saluus est! (*clāmat*)	150
	nunc, Staphyla, audī et operam⁀dā! ego tē moneō. abī intrō et	
	iānuam occlūde, nam ego nunc ad praetōrem abeō – pauper	
	enim sum. sī uidēs arāneam, arāneam seruā. mea enim arānea	
	est. sī uīcīnus adit et ignem rogat, ignem statim exstingue. sī	
	uīcīnī adeunt et aquam rogant, respondē 'aquam numquam in	155
	aedibus habeō.' sī uīcīnus adit et cultrum rogat, statim	
	respondē 'cultrum fūrēs habent.' sī Bona Fortūna ad aedīs it,	
	prohibē!	
STAPH.	Bona Fortūna numquam ad tuās aedīs adit, domine.	
EVC.	tacē, serua, et abī statim intrō.	160

Slaves and freedmen

Slavery played a crucial role in the reproduction of the Roman family, as well as in its structure. An extraordinary proportion of the funerary commemorations of Roman Italy under the Empire seem to be of freedmen, and they create our image of the Roman family as much as the freeborn or the nobility. The successful slave was the one who made him or herself thoroughly part of the owner's family: learning to speak Latin like a native, and to internalise Roman standards and values. This is where the legal equivalence of the father's power over children and slaves is important: though there was a world of difference between a free-born child and a slave, the family was a structure which treated a slave *like* a child, and could consequently give membership of society. Though the stigma of slavery lasted, there was nobody so anxious to be a good Roman as a freed slave ('freedman'). In this way, slavery and birth acted as alternative structures for reproducing the family: a freedman's freedman's freedman was as much of a Roman as a son's son's son, and a proud freeborn child (*ingenuus*) might himself be an ex-slave's child. (*World of Rome*, **355**)

abeō I am going away	*expellit* (he/she/it) drives out	*per noctem* by night
abī go away!	*exstingue* put out!	*peruigilō* 1 I stay awake
abit (he/she/it) goes away	*Fortūn-a ae* 1f. luck	*praetor praetōr-is* 3m. praetor
adit (he/she/it) approaches, comes up	*iānu-a ae* 1f. door	*prohibē* stop (her)!
	ignis ign-is 3m. fire	*quid* what?
adeunt (they) approach, come up	*īnsān-us a um* mad	*redit* (he/she/it) returns
anim-us ī 2m. mind	*intrō* inside (lines 151, 160)	*respondē* reply!
aqu-a ae 1f. water	*it* (she) comes	*rogō* 1 I ask (for)
arāne-a ae 1f. cobweb	*me-us a um* my, mine	*salu-us a um* safe
audī listen!	*miser miser-a um* unhappy	*sēcum* with himself/herself
bon-us a um good	*moneō* 2 I advise, warn	*seruā* keep! preserve!
cōgitō 1 I think, reflect, ponder	*numquam* never	*seruō* 1 I keep, preserve
cultrum (acc.) (a) knife	*ō* O (addressing someone)	*statim* at once
domin-us ī 2m. lord, master	*occlūde* shut!	*tacē* shut up!
dormit (he/she/it) sleeps	*operam dā!* pay attention!	*tam* so
ē, ex (+ abl.) from, out of	*pauper* (nom.) (a) poor (man)	*tu-us a um* your
exit (he/she/it) goes/comes out	*per diem* by day	*uīcīn-us ī* 2m. neighbour

A slave economy

For some historians, slavery was the defining characteristic of the Roman economy. The numbers of slaves were vast, but they were not to be found in equal numbers across the whole empire, nor at all periods. Further, a very high percentage of the total number of slaves was not employed directly in economic production, but in service in the houses of the great or as part of what passed for a civil service for government at local and imperial level. But those who participated in the chain of economic production are to be found everywhere, and their presence is taken for granted by our sources. They are there on the estates, whether as chained workers or supervisors. They are there in the hills, herding great flocks. They staff the offices of merchants. They provide the skilled craftsmanship of the potteries. Finally, as freedmen and women, they dominate the urban economy of Rome. But it needs to be remembered that slavery is only one of a number of ways of exploiting the labour-power of individuals and that it has costs which need to be taken into account. The slave, particularly a skilled one, was expensive. He or she had to be fed, clothed and housed. At the end of their productive life they had to be replaced. This did not make the employment of slaves automatic. It was an economic choice and in many circumstances was not seen as the inevitable one. This may in part explain why there is hardly any evidence of the free population protesting that work was being taken from them by the use of slaves. (*World of Rome*, **298**)

STAPH.　taceō et statim abeō. (*Staphyla abit et sēcum murmurat*) ō mē
　　　　miseram ! ut Phaedra, fīlia Eucliōnis, mē sollicitat! nam grauida
　　　　est Phaedra ē‿Lycōnidē,‿uīcīnō Eucliōnis. senex tamen
　　　　ignōrat, et ego taceō, neque cōnsilium habeō.
　　　　(*exit ē scaenā Staphyla*)　　　　　　　　　　　　　　　　165
　　　　(*Euclio now describes how, albeit reluctantly, he is going to the forum to collect
　　　　his praetor's free hand-out – to allay suspicions that he is wealthy.*)

EVC.　　nunc ad praetōrem abeō, nimis hercle inuītus. nam praetor
　　　　hodiē pecūniam in‿uirōs dīuidit. sī ad forum nōn eō, uīcīnī
　　　　meī 'hem!' inquiunt, 'nōs ad forum īmus, Eucliō ad forum
　　　　nōn it, sed domī manet. aurum igitur domī senex habet!' nam
　　　　nunc cēlō thēsaurum sēdulō, sed uīcīnī meī semper adeunt,　　170
　　　　cōnsistunt, 'ut‿ualēs, Eucliō ?' inquiunt, 'quid‿agis ?' mē
　　　　miserum! ut cūrās thēsaurus meus dat multās!

STAPH.　*I-am-silent and at-once I-go-away. (Staphyla she-goes-away and herself-with
　　　　she-mutters.) O me unhappy! How Phaedra, the-daughter of-Euclio, me
　　　　she-worries! For pregnant she-is Phaedra by Lyconides, the-neighbour
　　　　of-Euclio. The-old-man however he-does-not-know, and I I-am-silent, nor plan
　　　　I-have.*
　　　　(*She-goes-out from the-stage Staphyla*)

EUC.　　*Now to the-praetor I-go-away, too-much by-Hercules unwillingly. For
　　　　the-praetor today money among the-men he-divides. If to the-forum
　　　　not I-go, neighbours my 'Well!' they-say 'we to the-forum we-go, Euclio
　　　　to the-forum not he-goes, but at-home he-stays. Gold therefore at-home
　　　　the-old-man he-has!' For now I-hide the-treasure carefully, but neighbours
　　　　my always they-come-up, they-stand-around, 'How you-are, Euclio?' they-say,
　　　　'What you-are-up-to?' Me unhappy! How worries treasure my it-gives many
　　　　[=many worries]!*

　　　　　　　　　　　　　　　　　　　　　　　　(Plautus, *Aulularia* 40–119)

abeō I am going away	*hem* well!	*nimis* too (much)
abit (he/she/it) goes away	*hercle* by Hercules!	*nōs* (nom.) we
adeunt (they) approach, come up	*hodiē* today	*ō* O (addressing someone)
cōnsili-um ī 2n. plan	*ignōrō* 1 I do not know	*pecūni-a ae* 1f. money
cōnsistunt they stand around	*īmus* we are going	*praetor praetōr-is* 3m. praetor
dīuidit he is dividing	*inquiunt* (they) say	*quid agis?* what are you (s.) up to?
domī at home	*in uirōs* among the men	*sēcum* with himself/herself
ē, ex (+ abl.) from, out of	*inuīt-us a um* unwilling(ly)	*sēdulō* carefully
ē Lycōnidē, uīcīnō 'by Lyconides,	*it* (he) is going	*sollicitō* 1 I worry
the neighbour'	*maneō* 2 I wait	*taceō* 2 I am silent
eō I go	*me-us a um* my, mine	*uīcīn-us ī* 2m. neighbour
exit (he/she/it) goes out	*miser miser-a um* unhappy	*ut* how!
for-um ī 2n. forum	*murmurō* 1 I mutter	*ut ualēs?* how are you? (s.)
grauid-us a um pregnant	*neque* neither, and . . . not	

Grammar for 1C

1st and 2nd conj. imperatives	*miser*	*ā/ab* and *ē/ex*
eō	*ego, tū*	

Learning vocabulary for 1C

Nouns
aqu-a ae 1f. water
domin-us ī 2m. master, lord
ocul-us ī 2m. eye
uīcīn-us ī 2m. neighbour(ing)
ignis ign-is 3m. fire

Adjectives
mal-us a um bad, evil, wicked
me-us a um my, mine (m. voc. *mī*
  'O my')
salu-us a um safe
tu-us a um your(s)

Verbs
cōgit-ō 1 I ponder, reflect,
  consider
rog-ō 1 I ask
seru-ō 1 I save, keep

st-ō 1 *stet-ī stāt-um* I stand (This
  verb has irregular stems for
  other tenses ('principal parts')
  which you will be meeting
  later (**66, 82**). From now on
  these irregular stems will be
  listed. We suggest you learn
  them now. All verbs without
  such added stems listed are
  regular. You will be learning
  their stems later.)
uerber-ō 1 I flog, beat
uex-ō 1 I annoy, trouble, worry
mane-ō 2 *māns-ī māns-um* I
  remain, wait
mone-ō 2 I advise, warn
tace-ō 2 I am silent

Others
ē, ex (+ abl.) out of, from
neque neither; and . . . not; nor
numquam never
quid? what?
statim at once
ut how?

New forms: adjectives
miser miser-a um miserable,
  unhappy, wretched

New forms: verbs
e-ō I go, come; cf. *exeō*.
ab-eō I come, go out, go away
ad-eō I go, come to, approach
red-eō I return
The principal parts of *eō* are *īre iī
  itum*. So: *abeō abīre abiī
  abitum*, etc.

Slaves in the family

Slavery was embedded into family structure. Slaves could fulfil parallel functions to children and wives. If most Roman business was 'family business', the workforce and partners were supplied by slaves and freedmen. An archive of business records like the dossier of the Sulpicii from Murecine near Pompeii shows not only how slaves acted for their masters in important financial transactions, but also how difficult it is to distinguish freedmen from freeborn among the principal actors. A freedman, like a son, might inherit the family business; even a slave could be left his freedom together with an inheritance in a will, though this might be as a dirty trick to saddle him with a bankrupt estate. Equally, slave-women acted as concubines to the master, and might on acquiring freedom become their wives: that was a specific circumstance under which freedom could be granted below the legal age of 30, and gravestones suggest it was common. (*World of Rome*, **353**)

Section 1D

The scene changes. Enter a neighbour of Euclio's, Megadorus, with his sister,
Eunomia. (It is Eunomia's son, Lyconides, who has made Phaedra pregnant –
but no one knows this except Staphyla.) Eunomia is eager for Megadorus to
marry, and his thoughts turn to his neighbour's pretty daughter.

drāmatis persōnae
Megadōrus, uīcīnus Eucliōnis et frāter Eunomiae: uir dīues.
Eunomia, soror Megadōrī.
(Lycōnidēs fīlius Eunomiae est)   175
est uīcīnus Eucliōnis. nōmen uīcīnī Megadōrus est. Megadōrus
sorōrem habet. nōmen sorōris Eunomia est. Megadōrus igitur
frāter Eunomiae est, Eunomia soror Megadōrī. Eunomia fīlium
habet. nōmen fīlī Lycōnidēs est. amat Lycōnidēs Phaedram, Eucliōnis
fīliam. Lycōnidēs Phaedram amat, Phaedra Lycōnidem.   180

The-drama's characters
Megadorus, neighbour of-Euclio and brother of-Eunomia: a-man rich.
Eunomia, sister of-Megadorus.
(Lyconides son of-Eunomia he-is)
There-is a-neighbour of-Euclio. The-name of-the-neighbour
Megadorus it-is. Megadorus a-sister he-has. The-name of-the-
sister Eunomia it-is. Megadorus therefore brother of-Eunomia
he-is, Eunomia [is] sister of-Megadorus. Eunomia a-son she-has.
The-name of-the-son Lyconides it-is. He/she-loves Lyconides
Phaedra [= Lyconides loves Phaedra], Euclio's daughter.
Lyconides Phaedra he-loves, Phaedra Lyconides.

(*Eunomia Megadōrum ex aedibus in scaenam dūcit*)

MEGADŌRVS   optima fēmina, dā mihi manum tuam.
EVNOMIA   quid dīcis, mī frāter? quis est optima? fēminam enim
          optimam nōn uideō. dīc mihi.
MEG.   tū optima es, soror mea. tē optimam habeō.   185
EVN.   egone optima? tūne mē ita optimam habēs?
MEG.   ita dīcō.
EVN.   ut tū mē optimam habēs fēminam, ita ego tē frātrem habeō
          optimum. dā igitur mihi operam.
MEG.   opera mea tua est. iubē, soror optima, et monē: ego audiō.   190
          quid uīs? cūr mē ab aedibus dūcis? dīc mihi.
EVN.   mī frāter, nunc tibi dīco. uxōrem nōn habēs.
MEG.   ita est. sed quid dīcis?
EVN.   sī uxōrem nōn habēs, nōn habēs līberōs. sed uxōrēs uirōs
          semper cūrant seruantque et pulchrī līberī monumenta   195
          pulchra uirōrum sunt. cūr uxōrem domum nōn statim dūcis?
MEG.   periī, occidī! tacē, soror. quid dīcis? quid uīs? ego dīues sum;
          uxōrēs uirum dīuitem pauperem statim faciunt.

Running vocabulary for 1D

ab (+ abl.) away from
audiō I hear, am listening
dīc say! tell!
dīcis you (s.) say, are you (s) saying, do you (s) mean
dīcō I do say
dīues dīuit-is rich (man)
domum nōn dūcis do you (s.) not marry?
drāma drāmat-is 3n. play
dūcis are you (s.) leading, taking
dūcit (he/she/it) leads, takes
egone (am) I?
Eucliō Eucliōn-is m. Euclio
Eunomi-a ae 1f. Eunomia
faciunt (they) make

fēmin-a ae 1f. woman
fīli-us ī 2m. son
frāter frātr-is 3m. brother
habeō 2 I hold, regard X (acc.) as Y (acc.)
ita so, thus
iubeō 2 I order
līber-ī ōrum 2m. (pl.) children
Lycōnidēs Lycōnid-is 3m. Lyconides
manum (acc. s. f.) hand
Megadōr-us ī 2m. Megadorus
mihi (to) me
monument-a ōrum 2n. (pl.) memorial(s)
nōmen name
occidī I'm done for!

oper-a ae 1f. attention
optim-us a um best
pauper pauper-is poor (man/ woman)
periī I'm lost!
persōn-a ae 1f. actor
pulcher pulchr-a um beautiful
quis who?
seruantque 'and they protect'
soror sorōr-is 3f. sister
tibi to you
tūne 'do you?' (s.)
uir uir-ī 2m. man, husband
uir uir-ī 2m. man, husband
uīs do you (s.) wish, want
ut as
uxor uxōr-is 3f. wife

8. cūr uxōrem domum nōn statim dūcis?

EVN.	ut tū frāter es optimus, ita ego fēmina sum optima, sororque	
	optima tua. tē ita iubeō moneōque : dūc domum uxōrem!	200
MEG.	sed quam in animō habēs?	
EVN.	uxōrem dīuitem.	
MEG.	sed dīues sum satis, et satis pecūniae aurīque habeō.	

MEG.	praetereā uxōrēs dīuitēs domī nimis pecūniae aurīque rogant. nōn amō	
	uxōrum dīuitum clāmōrēs, imperia, eburāta uehicula, pallās,	205
	purpuram. sed . . .	
EVN.	dīc mihi, quaesō, quam uīs uxōrem?	
MEG.	(*sēcum cōgitat, tum* . . .) puella uīcīna, Phaedra nōmine, fīlia	
	Eucliōnis, satis pulchra est . . .	
EVN.	quam dīcis? puellamne Eucliōnis? ut tamen pulchra est, ita est	210
	pauper. nam pater Phaedrae pecūniam habet nūllam. Eucliō	
	tamen, quamquam senex est nec satis pecūniae aurīque habet,	
	nōn malus est.	
MEG.	sī dīuitēs uxōrēs sunt dōtemque magnam habent, post nūptiās	
	magnus est uxōrum sūmptus: stant fullō, phrygiō, aurifex,	215
	lānārius, caupōnēs, flammāriī; stant manuleāriī, stant propōlae,	
	linteōnēs, calceolāriī; strophiāriī adstant, adstant simul sōnāriī.	
	pecūniam dās, abeunt. tum adstant thȳlacistae in aedibus,	
	textōrēs limbulāriī, arculāriī. pecūniam dās, abeunt.	
	intolerābilis est sūmptus uxōrum, sī dōtem magnam habent.	220
	sed sī uxor dōtem nōn habet, in potestāte uirī est.	

MEG.	*Furthermore wives rich at-home too-much of-money of-gold/and they-ask-for.*
	Not I-like of-wives rich the-shouts, commands, ivory-adorned waggons,
	gar-ments, purple. But . . .
EUN.	*Tell to-me, I-ask, whom you-want wife? [= whom do you want as your wife?]*
MEG.	*(himself-with he-reflects, then . . .) A-girl neighbouring, Phaedra by-name,*
	daughter of-Euclio, enough beautiful she-is . . .
EUN.	*Whom you-say? The-daughter? of-Euclio? As, however, beautiful she-is,*
	so she-is poor. For the-father of-Phaedra money he-has none. Euclio, however,
	although an-old-man he-is nor enough of-money of-gold/and he-has, not evil
	he-is.
MEG.	*If rich wives they-are a-dowry/and great they-have, after the-wedding great it-is*
	wives' extravagance. They-stand-about fuller, embroiderer, goldsmith,
	wool-worker, shopkeepers, makers-of-bridal-veils [i.e. all these people stand
	about]; they-stand-about makers-of-sleeves, they-stand-about retailers,
	linen-weavers, shoemakers; sellers-of-breast-bands they-hang-about,
	they-hang-about at-the-same-time girdle-makers. Money you-give,
	they-go-away. Then they-hang-about [do] collectors-of-offerings in-the-house,
	weavers concerned-with-making-ornamental-hems, chest-makers. Money
	you-give, they-go-away. Unendurable it-is-the-expense of-wives, if a-dowry
	large they-have. But if a-wife a-dowry not she-has, in-the-power of-her-husband
	she-is.

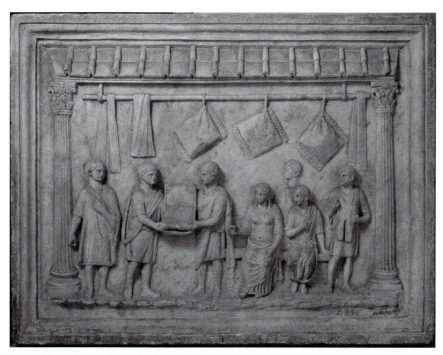

9. strophiāriī adstant, adstant simul sōnāriī

adstō (1) I hang about
anim-us ī 2m. mind
arculāri-us ī 2m. chest-maker
aurifex aurific-is 3m. goldsmith
aurīque and (of) gold
calceolāri-us ī 2m. shoemaker
caupō caupōn-is 3m. shopkeeper
clāmor clāmōr-is 3m. shout
dīc say! tell!
dīues dīuit-is rich (man/woman)
domī at home
domum (to) the home
dōs dōt-is 3f. dowry
dōtemque and a dowry
dūc domum marry! (lit. lead home)
eburāt-us a um adorned with ivory
fēmin-a ae 1f. woman
flammāri-us ī 2m. maker of bridal veils
frāter frātr-is 3m. brother
fullō fullōn-is 3m. fuller
imperi-um ī 2n. command, order
intolerābilis unendurable
ita so, thus

iube-ō 2 I order
lānāri-us ī 2m. woolworker
limbulāri-us a um concerned with making ornamental hems
linteō linteō-nis 3m. linen-weaver
magn-us a um great, large
manuleāri-us ī 2m. maker of sleeves
mihi (to) me
moneōque 'and I warn (you)'
nimis (+ gen.) too much (of)
nōmine by name
nūpti-ae ārum 1f. (pl.) marriage-rites
optim-us a um best
pall-a ae 1f. garment
pater patr-is 3m. father
pauper pauper-is poor (man/woman)
pecūni-a ae 1f. money
phrygiō phrygiōn-is 3m. embroiderer
post (+ acc.) after
potestās potestāt-is 3f. power
praetereā furthermore
propōl-a -ae 1m. retailer

puell-a ae 1f. girl
puellamne the girl?
pulcher pulchr-a um beautiful
purpur-a ae 1f. purple
quaesō please (lit. 'I ask')
quam (acc.) whom? what woman?
quamquam although
satis enough (of)
sēcum with himself
simul at the same time
sōnāri-us ī 2m. girdle-maker
soror sorōris 3f. sister
sororque and your sister
strophiāri-us ī 2m. seller of breast-bands
sūmptus (nom s.) extravagance, expense
textor textōr-is 3m. weaver
thȳlacist-a ae 1m. collector of offerings
tum then
uehicul-um ī 2n. waggon
uir uir-ī 2m. man, husband
uīs you (s.) wish, want
ut as
uxor uxōr-is 3f. wife

EVN.   rēctē dīcis, frāter. cūr nōn domum Eucliōnis adīs?

MEG.   adeō. ecce, Eucliōnem nunc uideō. ā forō redit.

EVN.   ualē, mī frāter.

(*exit ē scaenā soror Megadōrī*)   225

MEG.   et tū ualē, soror mea.

(Plautus, *Aulularia* 120–77)

ā (+ abl.) from
dīcis you (s.) are speaking
domum (to) the home

ecce look!
for-um ī 2n. forum
frāter frātr-is 3m. brother

rēctē rightly
soror sorōr-is 3f. sister
ualē! goodbye!

Grammar for 1D

present indicative active and imperative of *dīcō, audiō* puer, culter, uir	***quis/quī?*** ***domus***	***satis, nimis*** ***-que***

Learning vocabulary for 1D

Where a translation appears in brackets, the bracketed meaning of the word has already been learned (you can check the Total Vocabulary if you need to know where).

Nouns
fēmin-a ae 1f. woman
pecūni-a ae 1f. money
puell-a ae 1f. girl
fīli-us ī 2m. son
uir uir-ī 2m. man, husband
dīues dīuit-is 3m.f. rich (person)
frāter frātr-is 3m. brother
pater patr-is 3m. father
pauper pauper-is 3m.f. poor (person)
soror sorōr-is 3f. sister
uxor uxōr-is 3f. wife

Adjectives
magn-us a um great, large

optim-us a um best, very good

Verbs
habe-ō 2 I hold, regard X (acc.) as Y (acc.) (have)
iube-ō 2 *iuss-ī iussus* I order, command, tell
ualē goodbye!

Others
ā, ab (+ abl.) away from
ita so, thus; yes
nec and . . . not, neither; nor (= *neque*)
nimis too much (of) + gen.
-que and (added to end of word)

satis enough (of) + gen.
tum then
ut as, when (how!)

New forms: nouns
nōmen nōmin-is 3n. name
domum to home, homewards (see **30**)
domī at home (see **30**)

New forms: adjectives
pulcher pulchr-a um beautiful

New forms: verbs
dūc-ō 3 *dūx-ī, duct-us* I lead
domum dūc-ō I take home, marry
dīc-ō 3 *dīx-ī, dict-us* I speak, say
audi-ō 4 I hear, listen to

Luxury goods

Confirmation of the importance of the trade which Rome inspired throughout the empire comes from a startling source, the mystical vision of the *Revelation* of John, composed in Asia Minor towards the end of the first century AD. The author contemplates the end of earthly power and the destruction of the great city (*Revelation* 18.11): 'The merchants of the earth also will weep and mourn for her, because no one any longer buys their cargoes, cargoes of gold and silver, jewels and pearls, cloths of purple and scarlet, silks and fine linens; all kinds of scented woods, ivories, and every sort of thing made of costly woods, bronze, iron, or marble; cinnamon and spice, incense, perfumes and frankincense; wine, oil, flour, and wheat, sheep and cattle, horses, chariots, slaves, and the lives of men.' (*World of Rome*, **293**)

Imperial trade

Trade was not limited by the frontiers of the Roman empire. The most dramatic example was the trade in valuable exotic spices of the East, frankincense, myrrh, ivory, pearls, gemstones, and silk from as far afield as China, a trade which Pliny (*Natural History* 6.101) tells us drained coin on a huge scale from within the empire. Every year, about July, large ships would leave ports on the Red Sea bound either for the east coast of Africa or to catch the south-west monsoon off the coast of the Yemen to be blown across to near the mouth of the Ganges or to the Malabar coast of southern India. Having loaded up with their valuable cargoes, the ships caught the north-east monsoon in November to cross back to the Red Sea, up which they battled to return to port. Their cargoes were transferred to caravans of camels which carried them to Coptos on the Nile and then up to Alexandria and beyond. All this is documented in a handbook for traders, written in the mid first century AD, the *Periplūs Maris Erythraeī* ('Voyage round the Erythraean Sea'). The value of this trade is shown by a papyrus which documents a shipment of 4,700 pounds of ivory, nearly 790 of textiles, and a large quantity of nard, an aromatic resin; this cargo was worth some 131 talents, a considerable fortune. The figure is even more startling, when it is realised that just one of the large ships on the Red Sea run might carry over 100 such cargoes on its annual voyage. (*World of Rome*, **291**)

Section 1E

*Euclio, back from the forum, meets Megadorus, is highly suspicious of his
motives, but finally agrees to a dowry-less marriage for Phaedra. Staphyla is
horrified when she hears.*

(*abit ā forō in scaenam Eucliō*)

EVCLIŌ   (*sēcum cōgitat*) nunc domum redeō. nam ego sum hīc, animus
          meus domī est.

MEGADŌRVS   saluē Eucliō, uīcīne optime.   230

EVC.   (*Megadōrum uidet*) et tū, Megadōre. (*sēcum cōgitat*) quid uult
          Megadōrus? quid⁀cōnsilī habet? cūr homo dīues pauperem
          blandē salūtat? quārē mē uīcīnum optimum dīcit? periī!
          aurum meum uult!

MEG.   tū bene ualēs?   235

EVC.   pol ualeō, sed nōn ualeō⁀ā pecūniā. nōn satis pecūniae habeō, et
          paupertātem meam aegrē ferō.

MEG.   sed cūr tū paupertātem tuam aegrē fers? sī animus aequus est,
          satis habēs.

EVC.   periī! occidī! facinus Megadōrī perspicuum est: thēsaurum   240
          meum certē uult!

MEG.   quid tū dīcis?

EVC.   (*startled*) nihil. paupertās mē uexat et cūrās dat multās.
          paupertātem igitur aegrē ferō. nam fīliam habeō pulchram, sed
          pauper sum et dōtem nōn habeō.   245

MEG.   tacē. bonum habē animum, Eucliō, et dā mihi operam.
          cōnsilium enim habeō.

EVC.   quid cōnsilī habēs? quid uīs? (*sēcum cōgitat*) facinus nefārium!
          ō scelus! nōn dubium est! pecūniam uult meam! domum statim
          redeō. ō pecūniam meam!   250

(*exit ē scaenā in aedīs Eucliō*)

MEG.   quō abīs? quid uīs? dīc mihi.

EVC.   domum abeō . . .

(*Eucliō exit. mox in scaenam redit*)

          dī mē seruant, salua est pecūnia. redeō ad tē, Megadōre. dīc   255
          mihi, quid nunc uīs?

MEG.   ut tū mē, ita ego tē cognōuī. audī igitur. fīliam tuam uxōrem
          poscō. prōmitte!

EVC.   quid dīcis? cuius fīliam uxōrem uīs?

MEG.   tuam.   260

EVC.   cūr fīliam poscis meam? irrīdēsne mē, homo dīues hominem
          pauperem et miserum?

MEG.   nōn tē irrīdeō. cōnsilium optimum est.

Running vocabulary for 1E

aegrē hardly
aequ-us a um content
anim-us ī 2m. mind, heart, spirit
audī hear! listen!
bene well, thoroughly
blandē ingratiatingly
bon-us a um good
certē without doubt
cognōuī I know
cōnsili-um ī 2n. plan
cuius whose?
dōs dōt-is 3f. dowry
dubi-us a um in doubt
facinus (nom., acc.) deed, scheme
ferō I carry, endure
fers do you (s) endure

for-um ī 2n. forum
hīc here
homo homin-is 3m. (hu)man, fellow
irrīdeō 2 I laugh at (+ *ne* = ?)
mihi (to) me
mox soon
nefāri-us a um wicked
nihil nothing
occidī I'm done for!
oper-a ae 1f. attention
paupertās paupertāt-is 3f. poverty
periī I'm lost!
perspicu-us a um obvious
pol certainly (lit. 'by Pollux')

poscō 3 I demand, ask for (in marriage)
prōmitte promise!
quid cōnsilī what (of) plan?
quō to where?
saluē hail!
salūtō 1 I greet, welcome
scelus (nom., acc.) crime; criminal, villain
sēcum with himself
ualeō 2 I am well
ualeō ā (+ abl.) I am well from the point of view of
uīs do you (s.) wish, want
uult (he/she/it) wishes, wants

Roman marriage

One feature of Roman marriage that seems most surprising to us was the informality with which it could be both made and unmade. A legal marriage (*iūstum mātrimōnium*) was a union between two Roman citizens not otherwise legally disqualified from marriage. Simply to live together by consent as man and wife made a marriage, without any formalities, ceremonials before witnesses or signing of registers; and simply to separate constituted legal divorce. Either partner could leave the other, without discussion or consent; and though it was conventional to offer reasons for doing so (which ranged from failure to produce offspring to finding the partner's behaviour irritating), and it might be prudent to satisfy public opinion or the censor that you had not behaved irresponsibly, there were no legal formalities involved, nor courts to be satisfied.

Along with this remarkable freedom of consent went an equally remarkable arrangement about the problem of joint marital property. It simply did not exist. Either the wife was under the *manus* of her husband, in which case everything she had or acquired was his; or she was not, in which case there was a total separation of ownership. It was specifically disallowed for husband and wife to make donations to one another ('lest by mutual affection they despoil themselves'). The husband might provide his wife with a maintenance allowance, and certain expenses, but even these were reclaimable if beyond certain levels. If the wife's father was alive, she was in his power; but for the vast majority of wives of mature years whose fathers had died and who had become independent (*suī iūris*), their property was their own, with the proviso that they normally must have a male *tutor* ('guardian') with whose backing any legal contract would be made. By custom the wife brought with her to the marriage a dowry which passed to her husband's control; but it was not fully his since it was (with certain provisos) returnable in the case of divorce. (*World of Rome*, **316–17**)

EVC.   tū es homo dīues, ego autem pauper; meus ōrdō tuus nōn
       est. tū es quasi bōs, ego quasi asinus. sī bōs sīc imperat 'asine,   265
       fer onus', et asinus onus nōn fert, sed in lutō iacet, quid bōs
       facit? asinum nōn respicit, sed irrīdet. asinī ad bouēs nōn facile
       trānscendunt. praetereā, dōtem nōn habeō. cōnsilium igitur
       tuum nōn bonum est.

MEG.   sī uxōrem puellam pulchram habeō bonamque, satis dōtis habeō,   270
       et animus meus aequus est satis, satis dīues sum. quid opus
       pecūniae est? prōmitte!

EVC.   prōmittō tibi fīliam meam, sed nūllam dōtem. nūllam enim habeō
       pecūniam.

MEG.   ita est ut uīs. cūr nōn nūptiās statim facimus, ut uolumus? cūr   275
       nōn coquōs uocāmus? quid dīcis?

EUC.   *You you-are a-man rich, I, however, poor; my rank yours not it-is. You*
       you-are as-if an-ox, I as-if a-donkey. If the-ox thus he-orders
       'Donkey, carry the-load', and the-donkey the-load not he-carries, but in
       the-mud he-lies, what the-ox he-does? The-donkey not he-gives-a-
       second-glance-to, but he-laughs-at. Donkeys to oxen not easily
       they-cross-over. Furthermore, a-dowry not I-have. Plan therefore your
       not good it-is.

MEG.   *If [as] wife a-girl beautiful I-have good/and, enough of-a-dowry I-have,*
       and mind my content it-is enough, enough wealthy I-am. What need
       of-money there-is? Promise!

EUC.   *I-promise to-you daughter my, but no dowry. No for/because I-have*
       money.

MEG.   *Thus it-is as you-want. Why not marriage-rites at-once we-make, as*
       we-wish? Why not cooks we-call? What you-say?

EVC.   hercle, optimum est. ī, Megadōre, fac nūptiās, et fīliam meam
       domum dūc, ut uīs – sed sine dōte – et coquōs uocā. ego enim
       pecūniam nōn habeō. ualē.

MEG.   eō. ualē et tū.   280
(exit ē scaenā Megadōrus)

EVC.   dī immortālēs! pecūnia uērō ualet. nōn dubium est: pecūniam
       meam uult Megadōrus. heus tū, Staphyla! tē uolō! ubi es,
       scelus? exīsne ex aedibus? audīsne mē? cūr in aedibus manēs?

       (ex aedibus in scaenam intrat Staphyla)   285
       hodiē Megadōrus coquōs uocat et nūptiās facit. nam hodiē
       uxōrem domum dūcit fīliam meam.

STAPH. quid dīcis? quid uultis et tū et Megadōrus? ō puellam
       miseram! subitum est nimis. stultum est facinus!

[From the-house onto the-stage there-enters Staphyla]

EUC.   *Today Megadorus cooks he-calls and marriage-rites he-makes. For today (as) wife to-his-home he-leads daughter my.*

STAPH.   *What say-you? What you-want both you and Megadorus? O girl unhappy! Sudden it-is too-much. Stupid it-is the-scheme.*

aequ-us a um content
anim-us ī 2m. mind, heart, spirit
asin-us ī 2m. donkey
audīsne: ne turns *audīs* into a
    question
bon-us a um good
bōs bou-is 3m. ox
cōnsili-um ī 2n. plan
dōs dōt-is 3f. dowry
dubi-us a um in doubt
dūc bring! (*domum dūc* marry)
et . . . et both . . . and
fac make!
facile easily
facimus we make
facinus (nom.) deed, scheme
facit (he/she/it) is making, does
fer carry! bring!
fert (he/she/it) carries

hercle by Hercules!
heus hey!
hodiē today
homo homin-is 3m. (hu)man,
    fellow
iaceō 2 I lie
immortālēs (voc.) immortal
imperō 1 I order
irrīdeō 2 I laugh at
lut-um ī 2n. mud
nūpti-ae ārum 1f. (pl.)
    marriage-rites
onus (acc.) load, burden
opus (nom.) need
ōrdō ōrdin-is 3m. rank, class
praetereā moreover
prōmitte promise!
prōmittō 3 I promise
quasi as if

respiciō 3/4 I give a second glance
    to
sīc thus, as follows
sine (+ abl.) without
scelus (voc.) criminal, villain
stult-us a um stupid
subit-us a um suddenly
tibi to you
trānscendō 3 I cross over (to)
    (*ad* + acc.: = I become)
ualeō 2 I wield influence
ubi where?
uērō truly
uīs you (s.) wish, want
uolō I wish, want
uolumus we wish, want
uult (he/she/it) wishes, wants
uultis you (pl.) wish, want

Eating together

In many cultures one of the ways in which people express their sense of community is to eat food together. Ancient Greece and Rome were no exception. The people of a Greek city felt at one when they shared in the sacrificial meal, and the public festivals of the Romans continued that tradition. Because of the vast number of Roman citizens across the empire (5,000,000 by the death of Augustus in AD 14), however, it was small sub-groups of the citizen body that shared a meal or a commemoration. Here too the dependence of lower-status groups on the generosity of the rich could be seen on every occasion. From the emperor giving a feast to the Senate, or his wife hosting the *mātrōnae* (respectable married women) in the same way, down to a group of slaves meeting to honour the birthday of their owner, these occasions expressed a typical sense of communal order.

An inscription records a lavish benefaction given in Roman style at a small Greek country town, Acraephia in Boeotia. The benefactor here gives grain and wine to the country people and the landed proprietors, and distributes meat and sweetmeats with sweet wine, at breakfast (significantly) as well as dinner, while his wife gives a special breakfast to the children, the slaves, the wives, the female slaves and the maidens – an interesting pecking-order – and to the performers who had been hired for the part of the entertainments that the Romans would have called *lūdī*: the inscription specifies that that had never been done before. It is easy to see how such activity maintained people's dependence and interdependence while reinforcing everyone's position within the community. (*World of Rome*, **225–6**)

EVC.   et tacē et abī: et fac omnia, scelus, et fer omnia! ego ad forum abeō.   290
(*exit Eucliō*)

STAPH.   nunc et facinora et scelera Lycōnidis patent! nunc exitium
         fīliae Eucliōnis adest. nam hodiē grauidam domum dūcit
         uxōrem Megadōrus, neque cōnsilium habeō ego. periī!

(Plautus, *Aulularia* 178–279)

---

adsum I am near, at hand, present	*facinora* (nom.) schemes	*omnia* everything
cōnsili-um ī 2n. plan	*fer* carry! bring!	*pateō* 2 I am obvious, lie exposed
et . . . et both . . . and	*for-um ī* 2n. forum	*periī* I'm lost!
exiti-um ī 2n. destruction	*grauid-us a um* pregnant	*scelera* (nom.) crimes
fac do!	*hodiē* today	*scelus* (voc.) criminal, villain

Grammar for 1E

capiō, uolō, ferō   **onus; -ne**
imperatives   **quid + genitive**

Learning vocabulary for 1E

Nouns

nūpti-ae ārum 1f. pl. marriage-rites

oper-a ae 1f. attention; *operam dō* 1 *dedī datus* I pay attention

anim-us ī 2m. mind, spirit, heart

cōnsili-um ī 2n. plan; advice, judgment

dōs dōt-is 3f. dowry

homo homin-is 3m. human, man, fellow

Adjectives

bon-us a um good; brave; fit; honest

Verbs

irrīde-ō 2 *irrīs-ī irrīs-us* I laugh at, mock

saluē welcome!

posc-ō 3 *poposcī* I demand

prōmitt-ō 3 *prōmīs-ī prōmiss-us* I promise

Others

bene well; thoroughly; rightly

et . . . et both . . . and

hodiē today

-ne = ? (added to the first word of the sentence)

nihil nothing

occidī I'm done for!

periī I'm lost!

quasi as if, like

quid cōnsilī? what (of) plan?

quō (to) where

sēcum with/to himself/herself

ubi where (at)?

New forms: nouns

facinus facinor-is 3n. deed; crime; endeavour

onus oner-is 3n. load, burden

scelus sceler-is 3n. crime, villainy; criminal, villain

New forms: verbs

faci-ō 3/4 *fēcī factus* I make, do

ferō ferre tulī lātus I bear, lead

uol-ō uelle uolu-ī I wish, want

Section 1F

Pythodicus the head cook allots cooks to Euclio's and Megadorus' houses. The cook who goes to Euclio's house gets short shrift from the suspicious Euclio.

10. omnēs coquī intrant

Female freedom?

Women did not enjoy the sort of freedoms available in modern society; social convention ensured that on the whole women remained at least notionally subject to male authority, of the father, husband or *tūtor* (the justification offered for tutorship was the 'feebleness of the female sex'). But it does mean that the Roman family was virtually free of some of the typical traumas of modern Western marriages. No man or wife found themselves under a legal or religious compulsion to remain together. There was no need for painful and expensive divorce cases in the courts; there could be no arguments over the financial settlements of a divorce (except over the return of the dowry); there could not even be agonising suits for custody of the children, who were automatically in the *potestās* of the father, unless he had emancipated them, giving them total independence. One might say that it gave the wife far greater freedom; she could walk out of a disagreeable marriage at will. But it also left her more exposed: her husband could tell her at will to leave her home and her children. *Uxor, uāde forās*, 'Wife, get out of the house', was enough to terminate her marriage. (*World of Rome*, **318**)

(omnēs coquī intrant. nōmina coquōrum Pȳthodicus, Anthrax, Congriō   295
sunt. Pȳthodicus dux coquōrum est)

PȲTHODICVS   īte, coquī! intrāte in scaenam, scelera! audīte! dominus
             meus nūptiās hodiē facere uult. uestrum igitur opus est cēnam
             ingentem coquere.
CONGRIŌ   cuius fīliam dūcere uult?   300
PȲTH.   fīliam uīcīnī Eucliōnis, Phaedram.
ANTHRAX   dī immortālēs, cognōuistisne hominem? lapis nōn ita est
             āridus ut Eucliō.
PȲTH.   quid dīcis?
ANTH.   dē igne sī fūmus forās exit, clāmat 'mea pecūnia periit! dūc mē   305
             ad praetōrem!' ubi dormīre uult, follem ingentem in ōs
             impōnit, dum dormit.
PȲTH.   quārē?
ANTH.   animam āmittere nōn uult. sī lauat, aquam profundere nōn
             uult. et apud tōnsōrem praesegmina āmittere nōn uult, sed   310
             omnia colligit et domum portat.
PȲTH.   nunc tacēte et audīte, coquī omnēs. quid uōs facere uultis?
             cuius domum īre uultis, scelera? quid tū uīs, Congriō?
CON.   uolō ego domum uirī dīuitis inīre . . .
OMNĒS COQVĪ   nōs omnēs domum Megadōrī, uirī dīuitis, inīre   315
             uolumus, nōn domum Eucliōnis, uirī pauperis et trīstis.
PȲTH.   ut Eucliō uōs uexat! nunc tacēte uōs omnēs. (*to Anthrax*) tū abī
             domum Megadōrī; (*to Congriō*) tū, domum Eucliōnis.
CON.   ut uexat mē Eucliōnis paupertās! nam Eucliō, scīmus, auārus
             et trīstis est. in aedibus nīl nisi ināniae et arāneae ingentēs sunt.   320
             nihil habet Eucliō, nihil dat. difficile est igitur apud Eucliōnem
             cēnam coquere.

Running vocabulary for IF

āmittere to lose
Anthrax Anthrac-is 3m. Anthrax
anim-a ae 1f. breath
apud (+ acc.) at the home of
arāne-a ae 1f. cobweb
ārid-us a um dry
auār-us a um miserly
cēn-a ae 1f. dinner
cognōuistis do you (pl.) know?
colligō 3 I collect
Congriō Congriōn-is 3m. Congrio
coquere to cook
cuius whose?
dē (+ abl.) from
difficile (nom. s. n.) difficult
dormiō 4 I sleep
dormīre to sleep
dūcere to lead (in marriage)
dum while
dux duc-is 3m. leader

facere to make, do
follis foll-is 3m. bag
forās outside
fūm-us ī 2m. smoke
immortālēs (voc. pl.) immortal
impōnō 3 I place
ināni-a ae 1f. emptiness
ingentem (acc. s.) huge, large,
    massive.
ingentēs (nom. pl.) huge, large,
    massive
inīre to enter
īre to go (to)
lapis lapid-is 3m. stone
lauō 1 I wash
Megadōr-us ī 2m. Megadorus
nīl = nihil nothing
nisi unless, except
nōs (nom.) we

omnēs (nom., voc. pl.) all
omnia (acc. pl. n.) all, all things,
    everything
opus oper-is 3n. work, job
ōs ōr-is 3n. mouth
paupertās paupertāt-is 3f. poverty
periit (it) has disappeared
praesegmin-a 3 (n. pl.)
    nail-clippings
praetor praetōr-is 3m. praetor
    (state official who tried
    criminal cases)
profundere to pour away
Pӯthodic-us ī 2m. Pythodicus
sciō 4 I know
tōnsor tōnsōr-is 3m. barber
trīstis (nom.s. gen.s.) sad
ubi when
uester uestr-a um your(s)
uōs (nom., acc.) you (pl.)

An early guest

The satirist Martial mocked Caecilianus, who always came to lunch far too early: 'The slaveboy has still to announce the fifth hour to you, and out you come to lunch (*prandium*), Caecilianus. The courts are still in session, the morning-games of Flora are still going on. "Callistus! Quick! In with the slaves, never mind their bath! Spread the couches! Ah, Caecilianus, *do* come in and sit down!" You ask for hot water, but they haven't yet brought in any cold; the kitchen is closed and chilly, the hearth bare. Next time why not come really early, Caecilianus? No need to wait for the fifth hour – what you are after is clearly a late breakfast.' (Martial 8.67)

Amid the usual banter about the discourteously early guest of moneyed society, the beginnings of the Roman day emerge. Once again breakfast appears an indulgence, an extra meal for the privileged. Then there are the ablutions of the household, the need to fetch any water consumed from outside the house, the kitchen unused at the start of the day, and the public life of the city – including religious rites – going on well before the first planned meal, the *prandium*, at which wine might be served and guests invited. For most people the day began not with breakfast . . . but with the duties of the *salūtātiō* ('greeting of the patron'). (*World of Rome*, **224**)

PȲTH.   stultusne es, Congriō? facile enim est apud Eucliōnem cēnam
coquere. nam nūlla turba est. sī⌐quid uīs, ex aedibus tuīs tēcum
portā: nam nihil habet Eucliō! sed Megadōrus dīues est. apud   325
Megadōrum est ingēns turba, ingentia uāsa argentea, multae
uestēs, multum aurum. sī⌐quid seruī āmittunt, clāmant
statim 'coquī auferunt omnia bona! fūrēs sunt coquī omnēs!

11. coquī auferunt omnia bona!
fūrēs sunt coquī omnēs!

comprehendite coquōs audācīs! uerberāte scelera!' sed apud
Eucliōnem facile est nihil auferre: nihil enim habet! ī mēcum,   330
scelerum caput!

CON.   eō.

PȲTH.   *Stupid? you-are Congrio? Easy for/because it-is at Euclio's dinner to-cook. For*
no disturbance there-is. If anything you-want, from house your you-with
you-carry: for nothing he-has Euclio! But Megadorus rich he-is. At Megadorus'
there-is a-great disturbance, great pots silver, many clothes, much gold. If
anything slaves they-lose, they-shout at-once 'Cooks they-take-away all goods!
Thieves they-are cooks all! Seize the-cooks cocky! Flog the-rascals!' But at
Euclio's easy it-is nothing to-take-away: nothing for/because he-has! Come
me-with, of-crimes the-source!

CON.   *I-come.*

āmittō 3 I lose
apud (+ acc.) at the home of
argente-us a um silver
audācīs (acc. pl.) cocky, outrageous
auferō I take away
auferre to take away
bon-a -ōrum 2n. pl. goods
caput (voc.) head, fount, source
cēn-a ae 1f. dinner

comprehendō 3 I seize
Congriō Congriōn-is 3m. Congrio
coquere to cook
facile (nom. s. n.) easy
ingēns (nom. s.) ⎫ huge, large,
ingentia (acc. pl.) ⎭ massive.
mēcum with me
Megadōr-us ī 2m. Megadorus
omnēs (nom. pl.) all

omnia (acc. pl. n.) all, all things, everything
sī quid 'if. . . anything (acc.)'
stult-us a um stupid
tēcum with you
turb-a ae 1f. crowd, mob; disturbance
uās-um ī 2n. pot, vase
uerber-ō 1 I flog
uestis uest-is 3f. clothes

Showing off

'Have you had breakfast yet?' So the short-reigning emperor Vitellius on his way from Rome to the Rhine army to bid to become emperor, buttering up the servants of the public post, embracing the soldiers and muleteers and messengers at the posting-stations, and belching to show that *he* had started the day with some food (Suetonius, *Vitellius* 7.3). Gossip about this most hedonistic of emperors can help us to understand the precarious balance between riches and poverty so typical of life in Rome.

So short of money was his household that it is generally agreed that he had no money at all for the journey to Germany, and had to rent a garret for his wife and children whom he was leaving behind in Rome, and let out his own house for the remaining part of the year. He also took the pearl ear-ring from his mother's very ear to pawn it for the expenses of the journey. Nor could he get away from the crowd of creditors who waylaid him.

So the future emperor left the capital, in telling contrast with the usual lavish scenes of farewell or welcome at the gates which the great men usually received. But the money raised on the pledge of the ear-ring left plenty over for breakfasts. (*World of Rome*, **222**)

(*Congrio drags himself off grudgingly to Euclio's house, with his cooks. In seconds he comes rushing out again.*)

CON.   attatae! cīuēs omnēs, date uiam! periī, occidī ego miser!

12. attatae! cīuēs omnēs date uiam!
periī, occidī ego miser!

EVC.   (*calling to him from the house*) ō scelus malum! redī, coque! quō
          fugis tū, scelerum caput? quārē?   335
CON.   fugiō ego quod mē uerberāre uīs. cūr clāmās?
EVC.   quod cultrum ingentem habēs, scelus!
CON.   sed ego coquus sum. nōs omnēs coquī sumus. omnēs igitur cultrōs
          ingentīs habēmus.
EVC.   uōs omnēs scelera estis. quid‿negōtī est in aedibus meīs? uolō scīre   340
          omnia.
CON.   tacē ergō. ingentem coquimus cēnam. nūptiae enim hodiē fīliae
          tuae sunt.

EVC.   (*sēcum cōgitat*) ō facinus audāx! mendāx homo est: omne
          meum aurum inuenīre uult. (*out loud*) manēte, coquī omnēs.   345
          stāte istīc.

attatae aaaargh!

audācīs (acc. pl.) cocky,
   out-rageous

audāx (nom., acc. s.) cocky,
   outrageous

caput (voc.) head, fount,
   source

cēn-a ae 1f. dinner

coquō 3 I cook

cīuis cīu-is 3m.f. citizen

culter cultr-ī 2m. knife

fugiō 3/4 I flee

ingentem (acc. s.) ⎤ huge, large,
ingentīs (acc. pl.) ⎦ massive.

inuenīre to find

istīc there

mendāx (nom. s.) liar

nōs (nom.) we

omne (nom., acc. s.) all

omnēs (nom., voc. pl.) all

omnia (acc. pl. n.) all, all things,
   everything

quid negōtī what (of) business?

scīre to know

uerberāre to flog

ui-a ae 1f. road, way

uōs (nom.) you (pl.)

(*Eucliō domum intrat. tandem domō exit et in scaenam intrat. aulam in manibus fert*)

EVC.   (*sēcum cōgitat*) nunc omnem thēsaurum in hāc aulā fero. omne
      hercle aurum nunc mēcum semper portābō. (*out loud*) īte   350
      omnēs intrō. coquite, aut abīte ab aedibus, scelera!
      (*abeunt coquī. Eucliō sēcum cōgitat*)

EUC.   (*himself-with he-reflects*) O scheme audacious! Liar the-man he-is: all my gold
      to-find he-wants. Wait, cooks all. Stand there.
      (*Euclio his-house he-enters. At length from-the-house he-comes-out and onto*
      the-stage he-enters. A-pot in-his-hands he-carries)

EUC.   (*himself-with he-reflects*) Now all the-treasure in this pot I-carry. All
      by-Hercules the-gold now me-with always I-shall-carry. Go all inside. Cook, or
      depart from the-house, rascals!
      (*They-depart the-cooks. Euclio himself-with he-reflects*)

      facinus audāx est, ubi homo pauper cum dīuite negōt-
      ium‾habēre uult. Megadōrus aurum meum inuenīre et
      auferre uult. mittit igitur coquōs in meās aedīs. 'coquōs'   355
      dīcō, sed fūrēs sunt omnēs. nunc quid cōnsilī optimum est?
      mē miserum!

(Plautus, *Aulularia* 280–474)

---

audāx (nom. s.)	*intrō* inside	*omne* (acc. s.) all
auferre to take away	*inuenīre* to find	*omnem* (acc. s.) all
aut or	*manibus* (abl.) hands	*omnēs* (nom., voc. pl.) all
coquō 3 I cook	*mēcum* with me	*portābō* I will carry
cum (+ abl.) with	*Megadōr-us ī* 2m. Megadorus	*ubi* when
domō from the house	*mittō* 3 I send	
hāc (abl.) this	*negōtium habēre* to do business	

Grammar for 1F

present infinitive **nōs, uōs**	***omnis, ingēns, audāx***	***dīues, pauper***

Learning vocabulary for 1F

Nouns
cēn-a ae 1f. dinner
turb-a ae 1f. crowd, mob
cīuis cīu-is 3m. f. citizen
nihil (*nīl*) (indecl.) nothing

Verbs
āmittō 3 *āmīsī āmissus* I lose
auferō auferre abstulī ablātus I
  take away
coquō 3 *coxī coctus* I cook
mittō 3 *mīsī missus* I send
dormiō 4 I sleep

inueniō inuenīre inuēnī inuentum
  I find
sciō 4 I know
fugiō 3/4 *fugī fugitum* I escape,
  run off, flee
habeō negōtium I conduct
  business
in-eō inīre I enter, go in

Others
apud + acc. at the house of, in the
  hands of, in the works of
aut or
nīl = nihil nothing

quid negōtī? what (of) business,
  problem, trouble?
ubi when? (where (at)?)

New forms: adjectives
audāx audāc-is brave, bold,
  resolute
facil-is e easy
ingēns ingent-is huge, large,
  lavish
omn-is e all, every; *omnia*
  everything
trīst-is e sad, gloomy, unhappy

Section 1G

Euclio now looks around for a place to hide his gold safely outside the house. He settles on the shrine of Fidēs ('Trust', 'Credit') – but unknown to him, he is overheard by a neighbouring slave, Strobilus.

13. ecce! fānum uideō. quis deus fānī est?

EVCLIŌ   ecce! fānum uideō. quis deus fānī est? ā. Fidēs est. dīc mihi,
                   Fidēs, tūne uīs mihi custōs bona esse? nam nunc tibi ferō
                   omne aurum meum; aulam aurī plēnam bene custōdī, Fidēs!   360
                   prohibē fūrēs omnīs. nunc fānō tuō aurum meum crēdō.
                   aurum in fānō tuō situm est.
                   (*Eucliō in aedīs redit. in scaenam intrat Strobīlus seruus. omnia Eucliōnis*
                   uerba audit)
STROBĪLUS   dī immortālēs! quid audiō? quid dīcit homo? quid facit?   365
                   aurumne fānō crēdit? aurumne in fānō situm est? cūr in
                   fānum nōn ineō et aurum hominī miserō auferō?

EUCLIO   *Look! A-shrine I-see. Who god of-the-shrine he-is? Ah. Trust it-is. Say to-me,*
                   Trust, you? you-wish for-me a-guard good to-be? For now to-you I-bring all
                   gold my; the-pot of-gold full well guard, Trust! Stop thieves all. Now to-shrine
                   your gold my I-entrust. Gold in shrine your placed it-is.
                   (*Euclio into the-house he-returns. Onto the-stage he-enters Strobilus the-slave.*
                   All Euclio's words he-hears)
STROBILUS   *Gods immortal! What I-hear? What he-says the-man? What he-does? Gold?*
                   to-the-shrine he-entrusts? Gold? in the-shrine placed it-is? Why into the-shrine
                   not I-enter and the-gold from-the-man unhappy I-take-away?

                   (*Strobīlus in fānum init. Eucliō autem audit et domō exit. Strobīlum in fānō*
                   inuenit)
EVC.   ī forās, lumbrīce! quārē in fānum clam inrēpis? quid mihi ā   370
                   fānō aufers, scelus? quid facis?
(*Eucliō statim hominī plāgās dat*)
STRO.   quid tibi negōtī mēcum est? cūr mē uerberās?
EVC.   uerberābilissime, etiam mē rogās, fūr, trifūr? quid mihi ā fānō
                   aufers?   375
STRO.   nīl tibi auferō.
EVC.   age, redde statim mihi.
STRO.   quid uīs mē tibi reddere?
EVC.   rogās?
STRO.   nīl tibi auferō.   380
EVC.   age, dā mihi.
STRO.   nīl habeō. quid uīs tibi?
EVC.   ostende mihi manum tuam.
STRO.   tibi ostendō.
EVC.   age, manum mihi ostende alteram.   385
STRO.   em tibi.
EVC.   uideō. age, tertiam quoque ostende.
STRO.   homo īnsānus est!
EVC.   dīc mihi, quid ā fānō aufers?
STRO.   dī mē perdunt! nīl habeō, nīl ā fānō auferō!   390
EVC.   age rūrsum mihi ostende manum dextram.

Running vocabulary for 1G

ā aha!

age! come!

alter alter-a um one or other (of two)

auferō 3 I take X (acc.) away from Y (dat.)

crēdō 3 I believe X (dat.); entrust X (acc.) to Y (dat.)

custodi-ō 4 I guard

custōs custōd-is 3m.f. guard

dexter dextr-a a um right

ecce look!

em here you are! there!

fanō (dat. s.) to the/your shrine

fān-um ī 2n. shrine

Fidēs (nom. s., voc. s.) Faith

forās outside

hominī (dat. s.) from the fellow

immortāl-is e immortal

inrep-ō 3 I creep into

īnsān-us a um mad

lumbrīc-us ī 2m. worm

manum (acc. s. f.) hand

mēcum with me

mihi to/for me; from me

miserō (dat. s. m.) miserable

ostendō 3 I show

perdō 3 I lose, destroy

plāg-a ae 1f. blow; *plāgās dō* (+ dat.) I beat

prohibeō 2 I prevent, stop

reddō 3 I give back

rūrsum again

sit-us a um placed

Strobīl-us ī 2m Strobilus

terti-us a um third (hand)

tibi to/for you; from you

trifūr (voc. s.) triple thief

tuō (dat. s. m.) your

uerb-um ī 2n. word

uerberābilissim-us a um most floggable

Group worship

Many, maybe most, religious acts were performed by, in, or on behalf of, some sort of group. Group worship, of course, strengthened the sense of 'belonging' in the city. The cult places of the city, like the shrines at the heart of each city-district, were usually the preserve of an association of worshippers, and worship there expressed the inclusiveness and solidarity of the membership of the association. Through such bodies, the favour and patronage of the better-off could be gained and the dependent could try to improve their position. Many of the units which made up the city – associations of foreigners like the men from Tyre (Phoenicia – modern Lebanon) at Puteoli, groups of worshippers of *Bona Dea* or *Stata Māter* or of the Genius of the Emperor – were established within a religious setting. In such groups, people who lacked important patrons or a secure place in the life of the city could find some sort of stability and sense of identity. As members of groups they had a place, however humble, in relation to the powerful, and could echo the Alexandrian sailors hailing the emperor : 'through you we live . . . through you we enjoy liberty and our fortunes'.
(*World of Rome*, **262**)

STRO.   em.

EVC.   nunc laeuam quoque ostende.

STRO.   ecce ambās prōferō.

EVC.   redde mihi quod meum est!   395

STRO.   dīc mihi, quid mē uīs tibi reddere?

EVC.   certē habēs.

STRO.   habeō ego? quid habeō?

EVC.   nōn tibi dīcō. age, redde mihi.

STRO.   īnsānus es!   400

(*Euclio gives up*)

EVC.   periī. nīl habet homo. abī statim, scelus! cūr nōn abīs?

STRO.   abeō.

(*Eucliō in fānum init. aurum inuenit, et ē fānō portat, in alterō locō clam cēlat*)
(*But Strobilus, determined to get revenge on Euclio, has kept an eye on
Euclio, and this time steals the gold without giving himself away.*)

> Euclio enters in a paroxysm of grief and anger. After vainly appealing to the
> spectators for help, he is met by Lyconides, the young man responsible for
> Phaedra's pregnancy (though Euclio does not know it). Phaedra has, in fact,
> given birth, so the marriage with Megadorus is off, and Lyconides has decided it
> is time to confess all to Euclio and ask for Phaedra's hand in marriage. A
> misunderstanding arises as to who has 'laid his hands' on what . . .

EVC.   occidī, periī! quō currō? quō nōn currō? (*spectātōribus*) tenēte,   405
          tenēte fūrem! sed quī fūr est? quem fūrem dīcō? nesciō, nīl
          uideō, caecus eō. quis aulam meam aurī plēnam aufert mihi?
          (*spectātōribus*) dīcite mihi, spectātōrēs, quis aulam habet?
          nescītis? ō mē miserum!

(*in scaenam intrat Lycōnidēs, iuuenis summā͡ pulchritūdine, nūllā͡ continentiā*)   410

LYCŌNIDĒS   quī homo ante aedīs nostrās plōrat? edepol, Eucliō est,
          Phaedrae pater. certē ego periī. nam Eucliō uir summā͡ uirtūte
          est; certō omnia dē fīliā scit. quid mihi melius est facere?
          melius est mihi abīre an manēre? edepol, nesciō.

EUC.   *I-am-done-for, I-am-lost! To-where I-run? To-where not I-run?*
          (To-the-audience) Hold, hold the-thief! But who the-thief he-is? What
          thief I-say? I-do-not-know, nothing I-see, blind I-go. Who pot my of-gold
          full he-takes-away from-me? (To-the-audience) Say to-me, audience,
          who the-pot he-has? You-do-not-know? O me unhappy!
          (Onto the-stage there-enters Lyconides, a-young-man of/with-great
          beauty, of/with-no restraint)

LYC.   *What man before house our he-is-weeping? By-Pollux, Euclio*
          it-is, Phaedra's father. Without-doubt I-am-lost. For Euclio a-man
          of/with-great uprightness he-is; for-a-fact everything about his-daughter
          he-knows. What for-me better it-is to-do? Better it-is for-me to-depart or
          to-stay? By-Pollux, I-do-not- know.

age! come!

alter alter-a um one or other (of two)

amb-ō ae ō both

an or

ante (+ acc.) before

auferō 3 I take X (acc.) away from Y (dat.)

caec-us a um blind

certē without doubt

certō for a fact

currō 3 I run

dē (+ abl.) about, concerning

ecce look!

edepol by Pollux!

em here you are! there!

fān-um ī 2n. shrine

īnsān-us a um mad

iuuenis iuuen-is 3m. young man

laeu-a ae 1f. left (hand)

loc-us ī 2m. place, site

Lycōnidēs Lycōnid-is 3m. Lyconides

melius better

mihi to/for me; from me

nesciō 4 I do not know

noster nostr-a um our

nūllā continentiā (abl.) of no self-restraint

ostendō 3 I show

plōrō 1 I weep

prōferō 3 I show, hold out

quem (line 406) what, which (adjectival usage *GE* 1D, **29**)

quī (line 411) which, what (adjectival usage *GE* 1D, **29**)

quod (line 395) what, that which; which

reddō 3 I give back

spectātor spectātōr-is 3m. spectator audience-member

spectātōribus (dat. pl.) to the audience

summā pulchritūdine (abl.) of great beauty

summā uirtūte (abl.) of great uprightness

teneō 2 I hold

tibi to/for you

EVC.	heus tū, quis es?	415
LYC.	ego sum miser.	
EVC.	immō ego sum.	
LYC.	es bonō animō.	
EVC.	quid mihi dīcis? cūr mē animō bonō esse uīs?	
LYC.	facinus meum est, fateor, et culpa mea.	420
EVC.	quid ego ex tē audiō?	
LYC.	nīl nisi uērum. facinus meum est, culpa mea.	
EVC.	ō scelus, cūr tū tangis quod meum est?	
LYC.	nesciō. sed animō aequō es! mihi ignōsce!	
EVC.	uae tibi! iuuenis summā‿audāciā, nūllā‿continentiā es! cūr tū	425
	quod meum est tangis, impudēns?	
LYC.	propter uīnum et amōrem. animō aequō es! mihi ignōsce!	
EVC.	scelus, impudēns! nimis uīle uīnum et amor est, sī ēbriō licet	
	quiduīs facere.	
LYC.	sed ego iuuenis summā‿uirtūte sum, et habēre uolō quod	430
	tuum est.	
EVC.	quid dīcis mihi? impudēns, statim mihi refer quod meum	
	est.	
LYC.	sed quid uīs mē tibi referre?	
EVC.	id‿quod mihi aufers.	435
LYC.	sed quid est? nīl tibi auferō! dīc mihi, quid habeō quod	
	tuum est?	
EVC.	aulam aurī plēnam dīcō! redde mihi!	

(Plautus, *Aulularia* 580–764)

---

amor amōr-is 3m. love
animō aequō (abl.) in a calm frame of mind, i.e. cool, collected
animō bonō (abl.) in a cheerful frame of mind, i.e. cheerful
auferō 3 I take X (acc.) away from Y (dat.)
bonō animō see *animō bonō*
culp-a ae 1f. blame, guilt
ēbriō (dat. s. m.) (to) a drunkard
es! be! (s.)
fateor I confess
heus hey!

id quod that which
ignōscō 3 (+ dat.) I pardon
immō no, more precisely
impudēns (voc. s.) impudent, shameless (one)
iuuenis iuuen-is 3m. youth
licet it is permitted to (+ dat.)
mihi to/for me; from me; me
nesciō 4 I do not know
nisi except
nūllā continentiā (abl.) of no self-restraint
propter (+ acc.) on account of
quiduīs (acc.) whatever he likes

quod what, that which; which
reddō 3 I give back
referō 3 I hand back
summā audāciā (abl.) of great boldness
summā uirtūte (abl.) of great uprightness
tangō 3 I touch, lay hands on
tibi to/for you; from you; you
uae shame on (+ dat.)!
uēr-us a um true
uīl-is e cheap
uīn-um ī 2n. wine

Grammar for 1G

dative   **ablative of description**

Learning vocabulary for 1G

Nouns

audāci-a ae 1f. boldness, cockiness
continenti-a ae 1f. self-control, restraint
fān-um ī 2n. shrine
iuuenis iuuen-is 3m. young man
uirtūs uirtūt-is 3f. manliness, courage, goodness

Adjectives

aequ-us a um fair, balanced, equal
summ-us a um highest, top of
uēr-us a um true

Verbs

age! come!
crēdō 3 *crēdidī crēdit-us* or *um* I believe (+ dat.); I entrust X (acc.) to Y (dat.)

ostendō 3 *ostendī ostensus* I show, reveal
reddō 3 *reddidī redditus* I return, give back
tangō 3 *tetigī tāctus* I touch, lay hands on

Others

certē without doubt
certō for a fact

So the truth on both sides slowly creeps out. Lyconides gets his girl, and then recovers the gold from Strobilus (who is his servant). Here the manuscript breaks off, but from the few remaining fragments it looks as if the marriage with Lyconides is ratified, and Euclio has a change of heart and gives the happy couple the gold as a wedding gift.

Euclio is, in many ways, one of Plautus' finest characters. While we do not know on which play of Menander Plautus based his *Aululāria*, we do possess a play of Menander's which has a number of similarities. This play is *Dyskolos* (in Greek, Δύσκολος), 'The Bad-tempered Man'. Here is part of the introduction spoken by Pan, the local god of the neighbourhood in which the play is set. You may wish to identify common elements in Plautus and Menander and then look for contrasts.

(Enter Pan from the shrine)

PAN   Our scene is set in Attica at Phylae; I've just come out of the
           shrine of the Nymphs, a famous holy place belonging to the
           Phylasians and those who manage to cultivate the rocks here.
           In the farm here on the right lives an old man called Knemon,
           something of a recluse, always grumpy, hates crowds.
           'Crowds' indeed – he's getting on in years and has never in
           his life spoken a kind word to a soul. He never has a greeting
           for anyone, except for me, his neighbour, Pan; and he is
           bound to greet me as he passes, though I know he always
           wishes he didn't have to. The old man lives alone here with
           his daughter and an old servant. He's always at work fetching
           logs and digging away. He hates everyone from his
           neighbours here and his wife down to the villagers of
           Kholargos over there, the whole lot of them. The girl is as

sweetly simple as her upbringing, with never a thought of wrong. She serves the Nymphs, my companions, with devoted reverence, which makes us want to look after her.

Now there's a young man whose father farms some very valuable land around here. The young man lives in town, but came down with a sporting friend to hunt and happened to come to this very spot. So I made him fall madly in love with the girl.

Well, that's the plot in outline. You can see the details if you stay to watch, as I beg you to.

But I think I see our young lover and his sporting friend, coming along and talking together about the affair.

(Later on, a sacrifice is being prepared at Pan's shrine, and Getas, a cook, finds all his helpers drunk, and himself minus a saucepan. He knocks on Knemon's door – with predictable results)

GETAS   You say you've forgotten the saucepan? You've all got hangovers and are only half awake. Well, what are we to do now? It looks as if we must disturb the god's neighbours.

(He knocks at Knemon's door)

Hi there! They are the worst set of maids I know. Hullo there! They don't know about anything except sex – come on girls, be good – and of course a bit of blackmail if they're caught at it. What's wrong? Are none of the servants in? Ah! I think I hear someone hurrying to the door.

(Knemon opens the door)

KNEMON   What are you banging on the door for, damn you?

GET.   Don't bite my head off.

KNE.   By God I will, and eat you alive too.

GET.   No, for God's sake don't.

KNE.   Do I owe you anything, you scum?

GET.   Nothing at all. I haven't come to collect a debt or serve a subpoena. I want to borrow a saucepan.

KNE.   A saucepan?

GET.   Yes, a saucepan.

KNE.   You scoundrel, do you suppose that I sacrifice cattle and all the rest of it, like you?

GET.   I don't suppose you'd sacrifice so much as a snail. Goodbye, my dear chap. The women told me to knock at the door and ask. That's what I did. No result. I'll go back and tell them. God almighty, the man's a viper with grey hair.

(Exit Getas to shrine)

KNE.   They're man-eaters, the lot of them; knocking on the door as if I was a friend of theirs. Let me catch anyone coming to our door again and if I don't make an example of him to the

neighbours, you can call me a nobody. How that fellow got
away with it just now, I don't know.

(*Exit Knemon into his house: enter Getas from the shrine followed by Sikon*)

SIKON   Be damned to you. He was rude to you was he? I bet you
           talked like a stinker. Some people simply don't know how to
           manage these things. I've learned how to do it. I cook for
           thousands of people in town. I pester their neighbours and
           borrow cooking utensils from all of them. If you want to
           borrow from someone you must butter him up a bit. Suppose
           an old man opens the door; I call him 'Dad' or 'Grandad'. If
           it's a middle-aged woman I call her 'Madam'. If it's one of
           the younger servants I call him 'Sir'. To hell with you and all
           this stupid shouting 'boy!' I'd chat him up, like this. (*He
           knocks*) Here Daddy: I want you.

(*Knemon comes out*)

KNE.   What, you again!
SIK.   What's this?
KNE.   You are annoying me on purpose. Didn't I tell you to keep
           away? Pass me the strap, woman! (*Knemon beats Sikon*)
SIK.   Stop it: let me go.
KNE.   Not likely.
SIK.   Oh please, for God's sake.
KNE.   Just you try coming here again.
SIK.   Go and drown yourself.
KNE.   Still blathering?
SIK.   Listen – I came to ask you for a large saucepan.
KNE.   I haven't got one. And I haven't got a chopper either, or salt
           or vinegar or anything else. I've told all the neighbours quite
           simply to keep away from me.
SIK.   You didn't tell me.
KNE.   But I'm telling you now.
SIK.   Yes, curse you. But couldn't you tell me where I can borrow
           one?
KNE.   Don't you hear me? Must you go on blathering?
SIK.   Well, cheers for now.
KNE.   I won't be cheered by anyone.
SIK.   Get lost, then.
KNE.   What unbearable rogues. (*Exit*)
SIK.   Well, *he* cut me up nicely.

There is much that is reminiscent of *Aululāria* throughout *Dyskolos*. The figure
of the miser became a popular one in comedies of manners. Molière, writing for
the royal court in seventeenth-century Paris, took up the theme in his *L'Avare*,
on which Plautus' *Aululāria* had an obvious influence. In the following incident

the miser, Harpagon, chases out of the house his valet, La Flèche. Compare the scene with Euclio and Staphyla in *Aululāria* **1C**, and look for further points of contact between the three playwrights.

HARPAGON   Get out at once, and don't answer back. Be off, you professional swindler.

LA FLÈCHE   (*aside*) I've never seen anything worse than this damned crook. He's a real old devil and no mistake.

HARP.   What are you muttering to yourself?

LA FL.   Why are you after me?

HARP.   It's not for you to ask why; get out quickly or I'll bash you.

LA FL.   But what have I done to you?

HARP.   Enough to make me want to be rid of you.

LA FL.   Your son's my master and he told me to wait for him.

HARP.   Go and wait in the street then. And don't stick around in my house as if rooted to the spot, watching what goes on and taking advantage of everything. I don't want a perpetual spy watching my affairs, keeping a treacherous eye on all I do, eating up all I have, and poking about everywhere to see what he can steal.

LA FL.   And how the devil do you think anyone is going to steal from you? You don't give a thief much chance, locking everything up and standing guard day and night.

HARP.   I'll lock up what I please and stand guard when I like. Can't you see I'm surrounded by spies watching everything I do? (*aside*) I'm terrified that he may have some suspicions about my money. (*aloud*) You're just the sort of person to spread rumours that I've money hidden.

LA FL.   Well, have you money hidden?

HARP.   No, you impertinent rogue, I said nothing of the sort. (*aside*) How he infuriates me. (*aloud*) I insist that you don't spread malicious rumours that I have.

LA FL.   Bah! It's all the same to us whether you have or not.

HARP.   (*lifting a hand to hit him*) Don't you dare argue or I'll box your ears. I tell you again, get out.

LA FL.   Oh, all right: I'll go.

HARP.   Wait a minute. Are you taking anything of mine with you?

LA FL.   What could I be taking?

HARP.   Come here so that I can see. Show me your hands.

LA FL.   Here they are.

HARP.   Now turn them over.

LA FL.   Turn them over?

HARP.   Yes.

LA FL.   There you are.

HARP.   (*pointing to La Flèche's breeches*) Anything in there?

LA FL.   Look for yourself.

HARP.   (*feeling the bottom of his breeches*) These fashionable breeches are just the thing for hiding stolen property. I should like to see someone hanged for inventing them.

(*After more in this vein La Flèche leaves and Harpagon continues*)

This good-for-nothing valet is a great nuisance and I hate the sight of him limping about. It's a great worry having a large sum of money in the house and one is lucky if one has one's money well invested and keeps only what one needs for current expenses. It's difficult to find a safe hiding-place anywhere in the house. As far as I'm concerned I don't trust strong-boxes and have no faith in them. They are simply an invitation to thieves, the thing they go for first. However, I'm not sure whether I was wise to bury in the garden the ten thousand crowns I was paid yesterday. Ten thousand crowns in gold is the sort of sum – (*Enter Elise and Cleante talking in low voices*) Oh God! I must have given myself away! My anger must have got the better of me. I do believe I have been talking aloud to myself!

Amphitruo, leader of the Theban army, has left his home and his pregnant wife Alcumena, to fight the Teleboans (see map 3, p. xxii). He has taken his slave Sosia with him. Jupiter (*Iuppiter*) has fallen in lust with Alcumena, and in order to win her favours has disguised himself as Amphitruo; he has already impregnated her with another child. As the play starts, he is in bed with her, claiming to have taken a quick break from battle to be with her. To ensure that the liaison remains undetected, Jupiter has ordered Mercury (*Mercurius*) to disguise himself as Amphitruo's slave Sosia and make certain he is not interrupted; to prolong the liaison, he has ordered the sun to rise later than usual.

Section 2A

The cast is introduced

14. Comic heads

persōnae quīnque erunt.
duo hominēs rēgālēs erunt: alter erit Amphitruō, altera Alcumēna.
Amphitruō dux fortis est exercitūs Thēbānī, atque coniūnx Alcumēnae; uir summā uirtūte.
Alcumēna est coniūnx Amphitruōnis atque fēmina summā continentiā.　　　　5
ūnus seruus erit, Sōsia nōmine; seruus est Amphitruōnis, homo stultus et nūllā sapientiā.
duo dī erunt: alter erit Iuppiter, alter Mercurius. Iuppiter rēx deōrum est, amator Alcumēnae, ac Amphitruōnis similis.
Mercurius nūntius est deōrum, deus mendāx, ac Sōsiae similis.　　　　10

The extract opens with the disguised Mercury on guard in front of the house, awaiting Amphitruo's triumphant return from battle. He reminds the audience of what he had earlier said would happen: Amphitruo would leave the pregnant Alcumena for battle, and while he was away, Jupiter, disguised as Amphitruo, would impregnate her with a second child.

MERCVRIVS   nōmen Mercuriō ⌐ est ⌐ mihi; deus sum mendāx, deus sum multā sapientiā, dolīs multīs. ecce, hīc est oppidum Thēbae, hīc est domus Amphitruōnis, uirī summā uirtūte atque audāciā, dūcis exercitūs Thēbānī. uxor Alcumēna, fēmina summā continentiā, ex Ampitruōne grauida est.

MERCURY   *The name for me is Mercury. I am a lying god, I am a god of much intelligence, of many tricks. Look, here is the town Thebes, here is the house of Amphitruo, a man of great bravery and daring, general of the Theban army. His wife Alcumena, a woman of great modesty, is pregnant by Amphitruo.*

Running vocabulary for 2A

ac and (=*atque*)
Alcumēn-a ae 1f. Alcumena
alter alter-a um one *or* the other (of two)
amātor amātōr-is 3m. lover
Amphitruō -nis 3m. Amphitruō
atque and, also (also *ac*)
coniūnx coniug-is 3m./f. wife, husband
dol-us ī 2m. trick
domus nom. s. f. house
du-o ōrum two
dux duc-is 3m. leader, general
ecce look! see!

erit he/she/it/there will be (fut. of *sum*)
erunt they/there will be
exercitūs gen. s. 'of the army'
fort-is e brave, courageous
grauid-us a um pregnant
hīc here
Iuppiter Iou-is 3m. Jupiter, Jove
mendāx mendāc-is lying, cheating
Mercuriō ... mihi 'for me Mercury', i.e. my name is ...
Mercuri-us ī 2m. Mercury
nōmine 'by name'
nūnti-us ī 2m. messenger

oppid-um ī 2n. town
persōna -ae 1f. character, actor, mask
quīnque five
rēgāl-is e royal
rēx rēg-is 3m. king
sapienti-a ae 1f. wisdom, intelligence
simil-is e (+ gen.) like, similar to
Sōsi-a ae 1m. Sosia
stult-us a um stupid
Thēb-ae ārum 1f. pl. Thebes
Thēbān-us a um Theban
ūn-us a um one

sed Amphitruō, uir fortis, cum exercitū abīre uult. dīcet igitur Alcumēnae   15
'dum, uxor mea, domō nostrā cum exercitū absum, cum Tēleboīs bellum
ācre et difficile geram'. dum Amphitruō domō abest, pater meus, rēx
deōrum, imāginem capiet Amphitruōnis ac domum Alcumēnae intrābit.
Amphitruōnis similis, intus cum Alcumēnā domī cubābit atque clam
amābit. uobīs omnibus enim bene nōtus est Iuppiter noster; deus līber et   20
mendāx est. praetereā, quia Iuppiter amātor est ācer, noctem longam
faciet. nihil Iouī difficile est.

Mercury now brings the situation up to date.

utrimque igitur nunc grauida est Alcumēna – et ē uirō et ē summō Ioue.
mox tamen et Amphitruō et seruus ab exercitū per uiam domum redībunt.
intereā, ego hīc in uiā manēbō dum redeunt.   25

(The battle against the Teleboae is won, and Sosia is sent ahead to give Alcumena the good news. Mercury spots him coming)

ecce! Sōsia, seruus Amphitruōnis, nunc per uiam redit. omnia dē uictōriā
Alcumēnae nūntiāre uolet, at domum intrāre nōn poterit, quia ego seruum
dēcipiam et domō abigam. difficile mihi nōn erit, quia ego, Mercurius,   30
nūntius deōrum, imāginem Sōsiae, seruī Amphitruōnis, bene capiam: sīc
igitur Sōsiae similis erō.

(Sōsia, seruus Amphitruōnis, per uiam intrat)

SŌSIA   seruus quam ācer atque celer sum ego! at nox celeris nōn est. quam longa
et nigra est, uia quam longa!   35

MER.   (*clam*) ācer? atque celer? at nōn ācrem tē habeō neque celerem, sed
stultum.

SŌS.   ācer sum, quia nox nōn celeris sed longa ac nigra est, at ego, uir fortis et
audāx, sōlus per longam uiam, per longam noctem nigramque domum
redeō. sed quāre nox longa est? quid negōtī est? certē edepol, Nocturnus   40
dormit ēbrius, ut ego crēdō: nam Lūna nōn occidit neque diēs appārēre
potest. numquam iterum noctem uidēre poterō tam longam, tam nigram.

SOSIA: *I am keen, because the night is long and dark, but I, a brave and bold man,*
am returning home alone, along a long road and through a long, dark
night. But why is the night long? Surely, by heavens, the god of Night is
sleeping drunk, as I believe: for Moon is not setting nor can the day
appear. Never again shall I be able to see a night so long, so dark.

MER.   (*clam*) pergite, Nox et Lūna, ut nunc pergitis. numquam iterum dominō
meō et uestrō officium tam bonum facere poteritis. Iuppiter, dominus
uester, grātus erit.   45

SŌS.   noctem tam longam iterum uidēre nōlō. mālō noctem breuem esse. nam sī
dominus meus, ut solet, manūs meās uinciet atque mē uerberābit, nox ūna
appārēbit duo uel trēs. nōlō per noctem tam longam pendere.

15. pater meus, rēx deōrum . . . domum Alcumēnae intrābit

abigam I shall drive away (fut. of
    abigō 3)
absum I am absent
ācer (nom. s. m.) ⎤
ācre (acc. s. n.) ⎬ sharp, keen, hot
ācrem (acc. s. m.) ⎦
Alcumēn-a ae 1f. Alcumena
amātor amātōr-is 3m lover
amābit he will make love to (fut.
    of *amō* 1)
Amphitruō Amphitruōn-is 3m.
    Amphitruo
appārēbit (it) will appear (fut. of
    appāreō)
appāreō 2 I appear
at but
atque and
bell-um ī 2n. war
bene well, fine, thoroughly; good!
    right!
breu-is e short
capiam I shall take (fut. of *capiō*
    3/4)
capiet he/she/it will take (fut. of
    capiō 3/4)
celer (nom. s. m.) ⎤
celerem (acc. s. m.) ⎬ swift
celeris (nom. s. f.) ⎦
cubābit he will lie down (fut. of
    cubō 1)
cum (+ abl.) with
dēcipiam I shall deceive, trick
    (fut. of *dēcipiō* 3/4)
dīcet he/she will say (fut. of *dīcō*
    3)
diēs nom. s. day
difficil-is e difficult
domī at home (*domus*)
domō from home (abl. of
    domus f.)

domum (to) the home, house; acc.
    the house
dum while
duo two
ēbri-us a um drunk
ecce look!
edepol by heavens!
erit he/it will be (fut. of *sum*)
erō I shall be (fut. of *sum*)
exercitū abl. s. of *exercitus* 'army'
faciet he will make (fut. of *faciō*
    3/4)
fort-is e brave, courageous
geram I shall wage (fut. of *gerō* 3)
grāt-us a um grateful
grauid-us a um pregnant
hīc here
imāgō imāgin-is 3f. likeness,
    image
intereā meanwhile
intrābit he/she/it will enter (fut. of
    intrō)
intus inside
iterum again
Iuppiter Iou-is 3m. Jupiter
līber -a um free-wheeling
long-us a um long
Lūn-a ae 1f. Moon
mālō mālle I prefer
mānēbo I shall wait (fut. of *maneō*
    2)
man-ūs acc. pl. f. hand (*man-us*
    ūs)
mendāx mendāc-is lying
mox soon
niger nigr-a um black, dark
Nocturn-us ī 2m. god of the Night
nōlō nōlle I do not wish
noster nostr-a um our
nōt-us a um known

nox noct-is 3f. night
nūntiō 1 I tell, relate
nūnti-us ī 2m. messenger
occidō 3 I set
offici-um ī 2n. duty
pendō 3 I hang (a slave torture)
per along, through, by (+ acc.)
pergō 3 I go on, continue
poterit he will be able (fut. of
    possum)
poteritis you (pl.) will be able
    (fut. of *possum*)
poterō I shall be able (fut. of
    possum)
praetereā moreover
quam how
quia because, since
redībunt (they) will return (fut. of
    redeō)
rēx rēg-is 3m. king
sīc in this way
simil-is e (+ gen.) like, similar to
soleō 2 I am accustomed
sōl-us a um alone
stult-us a um stupid
tam so
Tēlebo-ae ārum 1m. pl. Teleboae
trēs tria tri-um three
uel or
uerberābit he will flog (fut. of
    uerberō 1)
uester uestr-a um your
ui-a ae 1f. road, way
uictōri-a ae 1f. victory, triumph
uinciet he will bind (fut. of *uinciō*
    4)
uolet he/she/it will want (fut. of
    uolō)
utrimque from two sources
uult he/she/it wishes (*uolō*)

MER.	(*clam*) sī nōn uīs per longam noctem pendere, tū faciēs quod ego uolō . . .	
SŌS.	ut crēdō, sōl uult dormīre, ēbrius bene.	50
MER.	(*clam*) ecce! hominem tam stultum numquam iterum uidēbō.	
SŌS.	nunc domum dominī meī adībō et intrābō. officium meum modo faciam	
	atque omnia dē uictōriā Alcumēnae bene nūntiābō. nam Alcumēna,	
	domina mea, dē uictōriā audīre certē uolet. sed ōrātiōnem meam paulīsper	
	cogitābō . . . quōmodō uictōriam nūntiābō Alcumēnae? atque quae uerba	55
	dē uictōriā dominae meae dīcam? dum domum adeō, cogitābō . . .	

MER.   *(aside): If do you do not wish to be hung-in-chains during the long night,*
       you will do what I want . . .

SOS.   *As I believe, the sun wants to sleep, well drunk.*

MER.   *(aside): Look! Never again shall I see a man so stupid!*

SOS.   *Now I shall approach and enter my master's house. I shall now carry out*
       my duty and will announce well to Alcumena everything about the victory.
       For Alcumena, my mistress, will definitely wish to hear about the victory.
       But I shall reflect on my speech for a while . . . how shall I announce the
       victory to Alcumena? And what words shall I say about the victory to my
       mistress? While I am approaching the house, I shall reflect . . .

(Plautus, *Amphitruo* 1–283)

---

adībō I shall approach (*ad-eō*)
Alcumēn-a ae 1f. Alcumena
atque and
bene thoroughly
cogitābō I shall reflect on, think
    about (fut. of *cogitō* 1)
dē (+ abl.) about, concerning
dīcam I shall say (fut. of *dīcō* 3)
domin-a ae 2f. mistress
domum (acc.) house
dum while
ēbri-us a um drunk
ecce look!

faciam I shall carry out (fut. of
    faciō 3/4)
faciēs you (s.) will do (fut. of
    faciō 3/4)
intrābō I shall enter (fut. of
    intrō 1)
iterum again
long-us a um long
modo now
nox noct-is 3f. night
nūntiābō I shall announce (fut. of
    nūntiō 1)
offici-um ī 2n. duty
ōrātiō ōrātion-is 3f. speech

paulīsper for a while
pendō 3 I hang (a slave torture)
quae (acc. pl. n.) what
quod what
quōmodō how?
sōl sōl-is 3m. sun
stult-us a um stupid
uerb-um ī 2n. word
uictōri-a ae 1f. victory, triumph
uidēbō I shall see (fut. of *uideō* 2)
uīs you (s) wish (*uolō*)
uolet (she) will wish (fut. of *uolō*)
uolō (I) wish
uult he/she/it wishes (*uolō*)

Grammar for 2A

future indicative active	**celer, ācer**	**3rd decl. monosyllables**
possum, nōlō, mālō	**1–1,000**	
noster, uester	**4th declension nouns; domus**	

Learning vocabulary for 2A

Nouns
lūn-a ae 1f. moon
sapienti-a ae 1f. wisdom, intelligence
uictōri-a ae 1f. victory
ui-a ae 1f. way, road
offici-um ī 2n. duty, job
oppid-um ī 2n. town
uerb-um ī 2n. word
Iuppiter Iou-is 3m. Jupiter, Jove (king of the gods)
nox noct-is 3f. night
rēx rēg-is 3m. king
sōl sōl-is 3m. sun
exercit-us ūs 4m. army
domō from home (*dom-us ūs* 4f.)

Adjectives
long-us a um long, lengthy
stult-us a um stupid, foolish
alter alter-a um one, another (of two: see Grammar **62**)
niger nigr-a um black
noster nostr-a -um our(s)
uester uestr-a um your(s) (more than one 'you', cf. *tuus*)

difficil-is e difficult
fort-is e brave, courageous; strong
simil-is e (+ gen. or dat.) resembling, like
mendāx mendāc-is lying, untruthful

Verbs
nūntiō 1 I announce
pergō 3 *perrexī perrrēctum* I proceed, continue
uinciō 4 *uīnxī uīnctus* I bind
capiō 3/4 *cēpī captus* I take, capture
dēcipiō 3/4 *dēcēpī dēceptus* I deceive

Others
ac (*atque*) and
at but (often introduces a supposed objection)
atque and, also
bene good! fine! (well, thoroughly, rightly)
cum (+ abl.) (in company) with
dē (+ abl.) about, concerning

dum while
ecce look! see!
hīc here
iterum again
modo now
mox soon
quia because
sīc thus, so
tam so

New forms: nouns
dom-us ūs 4f. house, home
domum to home; *domī* at home; *domō* from home
man-us ūs 4f. hand

New forms: adjectives
ācer ācr-is e keen, sharp, hot
celer celer-is -e swift

New forms: verbs
mālō mālle māluī I prefer
nōlo nōlle nōluī I refuse, am unwilling
possum posse potuī I am able, can

Tavern culture

The tavern is (as we think) a common feature of the medieval and early modern city. But that is wrong. A semi-public place where poorer inhabitants of the city can go to eat and drink, mix socially and enjoy other pleasures such as gambling or bought sex is not something that the economic and social circumstances of every urbanised civilisation produce. And though, at first sight, they may not look like another favour from the rich, that is in fact what the taverns of a Roman city amounted to. The property market which made the necessary building available, the customers' cash which paid for the services, the sources of production and supply which made food and drink (especially wine) available at affordable prices – all these were spin-offs from the working of the system of keeping the urban elite in the style to which they were accustomed. (*World of Rome*, **227**)

Section 2B

Sosia rehearses the Teleboan assault that triggered the battle; Amphitruo's arrival in enemy territory; his peace offer; its rejection; the preparation on both sides for battle; the conflict; Amphitruo's victory; and the surrender of the enemy envoys next day.

SŌSIA   'ut recordor – nam nihil oblīuīscor – nōs in ōtiō et pāce sumus, sed
Tēleboae, uirī saeuī, uirī summā ferōciā, ut cognōscimus, nōs
adgrediuntur. pugna ācris est, et multam praedam multāsque rēs
adipīscuntur, nūllamque rem relinquunt. deinde ex agrō domum   60
regrediuntur. at ciuēs nostrī, ut recordor, Tēleboās ulcīscī et capita
excīdere uolunt, quia Tēleboae, hostēs saeuī et iniūstī, omnīs rēs nostrās
fūrantur, nūllāsque relinquunt. mīlitēs igitur nostrī, fortēs uirī et iūstī, ad
terram Tēleboārum in nāuibus prōgrediuntur. nam altera causa bellī, ut
opīnāmur, iūsta est, altera iniūsta.   65

ubi ē nāuibus ēgrediuntur atque castra pōnunt, Amphitruō statim hostīs
per lēgātōs sīc adloquitur: "cauēte, ō Tēleboae! nōlīte nōs adgredī! sī
omnem praedam nostram nōbīs reddere uultis, Amphitruō sīc pollicētur:
exercitum nostrum sine proeliō domum redūcemus nostram; ab agrō
abībimus, pācem et ōtium uōbīs dābimus. at sī nōn uultis neque omnia   70
nōbīs reddētis, exercitus noster oppidum uestrum oppugnābit et in proeliō
dēlēbit. pugna ācris erit." sīc loquuntur Amphitruōnis lēgātī.

at Tēleboae sīc respondent: "nōlīte nōs adloquī, Thēbānī, sed statim abīte
ex agrīs et cauēte. nostrī mīlitēs uirī sunt, uirtūte magnā, summā ferōciā.
bellum gerēmus per tōtam diem, sī necesse erit, et nōs nostrōsque rēsque   75
nostrās tūtārī possumus. tu igitur, Amphitruō, ex agrō nostrō ēgredere! uōs
omnēs nostrō ex agrō ēgrediminī, exercitumque uestrum dēdūcite. nōlīte
hīc manēre. at sī manēbitis, pugna ācris erit, et diēs proeliī uōbīs erit
longa. sīc nōs pollicēmur."

sīc Tēleboae loquuntur, multaque nostrō exercituī minantur, et   80
Amphitruōnem exercitum dē agrō statim dēdūcere iubent. Amphitruō
igitur, quia hostīs ulcīscī uult, ē castrīs omnem exercitum ēdūcit
legiōnēsque īnstruit nostrās. deinde imperātōrēs, ubi in medium exeunt et
extrā turbam ōrdinum colloquuntur, mox cōnsentiunt: "uictī post proelium
uictōribus urbem, ārās, rēs omnīs dēdent." tālis est condiciō proeliī et sīc   85
imperātōrēs pollicentur.

clāmor ad caelum it. Amphitruō Iouem precātur et exercitum hortātur,
deinde in proelium inruit. cōpiae utrimque in proelium inruunt. dēnique,
ut uolumus, nostra manus superat, sed hostēs nōn fugiunt. Amphitruō, ut
hoc cōnspicātur, equitēs in proelium inruere iubet. in proelium igitur   90
inruunt, cōpiaeque hostium fugiunt. hostīs igitur sequimur et prōterimus.

Running vocabulary for 2B

adgredī to attack, approach
(*adgredior* 3/4 dep.)
adgrediuntur they approach, go
up to, attack (*adgredior*
3/4 dep.)
adipīscuntur they get, gain
(*adipīscor* 3 dep.)
adloquī to address (*adloquor*
3 dep.)
adloquitur he/she/it addresses
(*adloquor* 3 dep.)
ager agr-ī 2m. field, territory
Amphitruō Amphitruōn-is 3m.
Amphitruo
ār-a ae 1f. altar
bell-um ī 2n. war
bellum gerō 3 I wage war
cael-um ī 2n. sky
caput capit-is 3n. head
castr-a ōrum 2n. pl. camp
caueō 2 I beware, am wary of
caus-a ae 1f. reason, justification
clāmor clāmor-is 3m. cry, shout
cognōscō 3 I get to know, examine
colloquuntur they discuss
(*colloquor* 3 dep.)
condiciō condiciōn-is 3f.
condition
cōnsentiō 4 I agree
cōnspicātur he sees, observes
(*conspicor* 1 dep.)
cōpi-ae ārum 1f. pl. forces, troops
dēdō 3 I hand over
dēdūcō 3 I lead down/away
dēleō 2 I destroy
dēnique finally
diem acc. s. f. day (*diēs* 5f./m.)
diēs nom s. f. day
ēdūcō 3 I lead out
ēgredere leave! get out! (s.)
(*ēgredior* 3/4)
ēgrediminī leave! get out! (pl.)
(*ēgredior* 3/4)

ēgrediuntur they get out of
(*ēgredior* 3/4 dep.)
eques equit-is 3m. cavalry
excīdō 3 I cut off
extrā (+ acc.) outside
ferōci-a ae 1f. ferocity, insolence
fūrantur they steal (*furor* 1 dep.)
gerō see *bellum gerō*
hortātur (he) encourages, urges
on (*hortor* 1 dep.)
hostis host-is 3m. enemy
imperātor imperātor-is 3m.
general
iniūst-us a um unjust
in medium into the middle
inruō 3 I rush, charge
īnstruō 3 I draw up
iūst-us a um just
lēgāt-us ī 2m.envoy, ambassador,
official
legiō legiōn-is 3f. legion
loquuntur (they) say (*loquor*
3 dep.)
manus nom. s. f. band (*man-us -ūs*
4f. hand, band)
mīles mīlit-is 3m. soldier
minantur (+ dat.) they threaten
(*minor* 1 dep.)
nāuis nāu-is 3f. boat, ship
necesse necessary
ō O (addressing someone)
oblīuīscor 3 dep. I forget
opīnāmur we think (*opinor* 1 dep.)
oppugnō 1 I attack
ōrdō ōrdin-is 3m. rank, row
ōti-um ī 2n. leisure
pāx pāc-is 3f. peace
per (+ acc.) through, along
pollicēmur we promise (*polliceor*
2 dep.)
pollicentur they promise
(*polliceor* 2 dep.)
pollicētur he promises (*polliceor*
2 dep.)

pōnō 3 I pitch, place
post (+ acc.) after, behind
praed-a ae 1f. booty, plunder
precātur (he) prays to (*precor*
1 dep.)
proeli-um ī 2n. battle
prōgrediuntur they march
forward, advance (*prōgredior*
3/4 dep.)
prōterō 3 I tread down
pugn-a ae 1f. fight
recordor 1 dep. I remember
redūcō 3 I bring/lead back
regrediuntur I return (*regredior*
3/4 dep.)
relinquō 3 I leave behind, abandon
rem acc. s. f. thing; (*rēs rēī* 5f.
thing, matter, business,
property, affair)
rēs acc. pl. f. property (*rēs rēī* 5f.
thing, matter, business,
property, affair)
respondeō 2 I reply
saeu-us a um savage, fierce
sequimur we follow, pursue
(*sequor* 3 dep.)
sine (+ abl.) without
superō 1 I overcome
tāl-is e such
Tēlebo-ae ārum 1m. the Teleboae
terr-a ae 1f land
Thēbān-us ī 2m Theban
tōt-us a um (the) whole
tūtārī to guard, protect (*tūtor*
1 dep.)
uictī nom. pl. m. the conquered,
losers
uictor victor-is 3m. victor, winner
ulcīscī to take revenge on
(*ulcīscor* 3 dep.)
urbs urb-is 3f. city
utrimque on both sides

per tōtam diem usque ad uesperum pugnāmus. postrēmō nox uenit et
proelium dirimit. sīc hostīs nostrōs uincimus et opus perficimus.

Amphitruō, ubi illūstrem adipīscitur uictōriam, lēgātōs hostium in castra
postrīdiē uenīre iubet. lēgātī hostium ex urbe proficīscuntur, et nōs   95
precantur; posteā dēdunt urbem, līberōs, omnīsque rēs dīuīnās
hūmānāsque in arbitrium Amphitruōnis.'

*'A shout goes to the sky. Amphitruo prays to Jove and encourages the
army, then rushes into battle. Troops from both sides rush into battle. At
last, as we wish, our band prevails, but the enemy does not flee.
Amphitruo, as he observes this, orders the cavalry to charge into battle.
They therefore charge into battle, and the troops of the enemy flee. So we
pursue the enemy and trample over them. Throughout the whole day right
up to the evening we fight. Eventually night comes and breaks off the
battle. In this way we conquer our enemy and finish the job.*

*Amphitruo, when he gains this famous victory, next day orders the enemy's
ambassadors to come to the camp. The enemy's ambassadors set out from
the city and implore us; afterwards, they surrender the city, children, and
all things human and divine into Amphitruo's authority.'*

(*Sosia has finished his practice speech*)

ut bellum recordor, sīc capita rērum mox meae dīcam dominae. nunc
in aedīs intrābō et omnia Alcumēnae dīcam – nam, ut opīnor, nihil   100
oblīuīscor.

(Plautus, *Amphitruo* 186–263)

---

adipīscitur he gains, gets
  (*adipīscor* 3 dep.)
agō 3 I do, act; drive, lead
Alcumen-a ae 1f Alcumena
Amphitruō Amphitruōn-is 3m.
  Amphitruo
arbitri-um ī 2n. power, authority,
  judgment
bell-um ī 2n. war
caput capit-is 3n main point
castr-a ōrum 2n. pl. camp
dēdō 3 I hand over
diem acc. s. f. day
dirimō 3 I break off
dīuīn-us a um divine, sacred
domin-a ae 1f. mistress
host-is is 2m. enemy

hūmān-us a um human
illūstr-is e famous
imperi-um ī 2n. orders
lēgāt-us ī 2m. envoy, ambassador,
  official
līber-ī ōrum 2m. pl. children
oblīuīscor 3 dep. I forget
opīnor 1 dep. I think, am of the
  opinion
opus oper-is 3n. job, business
perficiō 3/4 I finish, complete,
  carry out
posteā later, afterwards
postrēmō at last
postrīdiē next day
precantur they pray to (*precor*
  1 dep.)

proeli-um ī 2n. battle
proficīscuntur they set out
  (*proficīscor* 3 dep.)
pugnō 1 I fight
recordor 1 dep. I remember
rērum gen. pl. f. of affairs, matters
  (*rēs rēī* 5f. thing, matter,
  business, property, affair)
rēs acc. pl. f. things (*rēs rēī* 5f.
  thing, matter, business,
  property, affair)
tōt-us a um (the) whole (of)
ueniō 4 I come
uesper uesper-ī 2m. evening
uincō 3 I conquer, defeat
urbs urb-is 3f. city
usque ad right up to

16. pusteā dēdunt urbem, līberōs omnīsque rēs dīuīnās hūmānāsque in arbitrium Amphitruōnis
(= p. 64 lines 96–97)

Grammar for 2B

present deponent	rēs	nūllus, alter
nōlī	caput	

Learning vocabulary for 2B

Nouns

praed-a ae 1f. booty, plunder
ager agr-ī 2m. land, field, territory
lēgāt-us ī 2m. ambassador, army
    official
castr-a ōrum 2n. pl. camp
proeli-um ī 2n. battle
hostis host-is 3m. enemy
opus oper-is 3n. job, work, task

Adjectives

saeu-us a um wild, angry

Verbs

pugnō 1 I fight
caueō 2 *cāuī cautus* I am wary
respondeō 2 *respondī respōnsum* I
    reply
agō 3 *ēgī āctus* I do, act
cognōscō 3 *cognōuī cognitus* I get
    to know, examine

dēdūcō 3 *dēdūxī dēductus* I lead
    away, down
nesciō 4 I do not know
īnspiciō 3/4 *īnspexī īnspectus* I
    look into; inspect, examine
perficiō 3/4 *perfēcī perfectus* I
    finish, complete; carry out

Others

ō (+ voc.) O

New forms: nouns

caput capit-is 3n. head; source
diēs diē-ī 5m. or f. day
rēs rē-ī 5f. thing, matter, business,
    property, affair

New forms: verbs

hortor 1 dep. I encourage
minor 1 dep. I threaten (+ dat.)
opīnor 1 dep. I think

precor 1 dep. I beg, pray
recordor 1 dep. I remember
polliceor 2 dep. I promise
adipīscor 3 *adeptus* I gain, get
adloquor 3 *adlocūtus* I address,
    talk to
loquor 3 dep. *locūtus* I talk,
    speak, say
oblīuīscor 3 dep. *oblītus* I forget
proficīscor 3 *profectus* I set out
sequor 3 dep. *secūtus* I follow
mentior 4 dep. I lie, deceive
adgredior 3/4 dep. *adgressus* I
    approach
ēgredior 3/4 *ēgressus* I go/come
    out
prōgredior 3/4 *prōgressus* I
    advance

Section 2C

Mercury determines to use his Sosia disguise to out-Sosia Sosia and drive him away from the house. He utterly outwits the bewildered slave and, with the help of a few well-timed punches, almost convinces him that he is someone else.

MERCURIUS   quid faciet ille seruus? intrābitne per iānuam in hās aedīs? dīcetne
mulierī Amphitruōnis omnia dē illā uictōriā? ego ad illum citō adībō et ab
hīs aedibus abigam. numquam illum hominem ad hās aedīs peruenīre
hodiē sinam. quandō mea fōrma illīus fōrmae similis esse uidētur, mōrēs   105
similēs habēbō. ego igitur scelestus et mendāx erō. hanc iānuam igitur
dēfendam et illum ab hīs aedibus citō abigam.

(Sōsia Mercurium cōnspicātur)

SŌSIA   iam ego domum intrābō et capita rērum mulierī Amphitruōnis
nūntiābō . . . sed quis est hic homo? quem uideō ante domum? mīlitemne   110
uideō? nam ille certē iānuam dēfendere uidētur, ut mīles. obsecrō hercle,
quam fortis est! nōn placet . . . certē hospitium meum pugneum erit. miser
sum! iam ille mē opprimet et necābit.

(Mercury limbers up with his fists, pretending not to see Sōsia)

MER.   quam magnum est pondus huic pugnō, et quam magnum illī . . .   115

SŌS.   periī! quam īrātus est! pugnōs plānē ponderat, ut arbitror.

MER.   sī quis hūc ueniet, pugnōs edet.

SŌS.   sed iam plēnus cēnae sum! mālō illum mē nōn uidēre . . . plānē īrāscitur.

MER.   sī hic pugnus ōs tanget, exossātum erit . . .

SŌS.   nōlō illum mē exossāre. ō mē miserum! tantī erō quantī mūrēna!   120

MER.   nescioquis hīc loquitur.

SŌS.   saluus sum! mē nōn uidet! nam nōmen mihi nōn nescioquis sed Sōsia est.

(Mercurius Sōsiam cōnspicātur)

MER.   quō abīre uīs, miser? dīc mihi, quis es? seruusne es, an
liber? loquere, furcifer!   125

SŌS.   seruus sum, et hanc domum dominī et mulieris iam per iānuam inīre uolō.

MER.   cuius seruus es? cūr in hās aedīs inīre cōnāris? cūr tēcum loqueris? quid
nūntiābis? dīc, furcifer.

SŌS.   mēcum nōn loquor sed uictōriam mulierī dominī meī nūntiāre cōnor. nam
haec iubet dominus meus. illīus enim seruus sum.   130

MER.   mentīris! abī, scelerum caput! homo nihilī es! ualdē īrāscor! nisi statim
abībis, ego tē, sceleste, exossābō! tantī eris quantī mūrēna!

SŌS.   īrātus plānē est. sī in mē pugnōs exercēre uīs, cūr in parietem illōs haud
prīmō domās?

SOS.   *But I am already full of dinner! I prefer him not to see me . . . he is
obviously getting angry.*

MER.   *If this fist touches his face, it will be de-boned.*

SOS.   *I don't want him to de-bone me! Misery me! I shall be worth as much as
an eel!*

MER.   *Someone or other is talking here.*

SOS.   *I'm saved! He doesn't see me! For my name is not 'Someone or other' but Sosia.*

(*Mercury observes Sosia*)

MER.   *Where do you want to go, wretch? Tell me, who are you? Are you slave, or free? Speak, scoundrel!*

SOS.   *I am a slave, and I wish to go through the door into the home of my master and his wife.*

MER.   *Whose slave are you? Why are you trying to go into this house? Why are you speaking with yourself? What will you announce? Speak, scoundrel.*

SOS.   *I am not talking with myself but trying to announce the victory to the wife of my master. For my master orders me [to do] this. I am that man's slave.*

MER.   *You're lying! Off with you, fount of iniquity! You are a worthless being. I am getting extremely angry! Unless you leave at once, I shall de-bone you, villain! You'll be worth as much as an eel!*

SOS.   *He is clearly annoyed. If you want to exercise your fists on me, why do you not first break them in on the wall?*

Running vocabulary for 2C

abigō 3 I drive away
Amphitruō Amphitruōn-is 3m. Amphitruo
ante (+ acc.) in front of, before
arbitror 1 dep. I think, consider, judge
citō quickly
cōnor 1 dep. I try, attempt
cōnspicor 1 dep. I catch sight of
dēfendō 3 I defend
domō 1 I tame, habituate, 'break in'
edō 3 I eat, consume
exerceō 2 I exercise
exossāt-us a um de-boned
exossō 1 I de-bone
fōrm-a ae 2f. shape, form
furcifer furcifer-ī 2m. scoundrel, ratbag
haec (nom./acc. pl. n.) these things (pron.)
hanc (acc. s. f.) this (adj.)
hās (acc. pl. f.) this (adj.)
haud no(t)
hercle by Hercules
hic (nom. s. m.) this (adj.); this man, he (pron.)
hīs (dat./abl. pl. m./f./n) this (adj.)
hospiti-um ī 2n. reception

huic (dat. s. m.) to/for this (adj.), to this man, to him (pron.)
iam now, by now; already; presently
iānu-a ae 1f. door
illā (abl. s. f.) that (adj.)
ille (nom. s. m.) that (adj.); he (pron.); that man
illī (dat. s. m./f.) to/for that (adj.), to/for him, that man (pron.)
illīus (gen. s. m.) of him, his (pron.)
illōs (acc. pl. m.) them (pron.); those (adj.)
illum (acc. s. m.) him (pron.), that man; that (adj.)
īrāscor 3 dep. I grow angry
īrāt-us a um angry, enraged
liber liber-a um free
mēcum to/with myself/me
Mercuri-us ī 2m. Mercury
mīles mīlit-is 3m. soldier
mōs mōr-is 3m. way, habit, custom; (pl.) character
mulier mulier-is 3f. wife, woman
mūrēn-a ae 1f. eel
necō 1 I kill
nescioquis (nom. s. m.) someone or other

nihilī of no worth, value
nisi unless
obsecrō 1 I implore, beg (i.e. you, the audience)
opprimō 3 I surprise, catch, crush
ōs ōr-is 3n. face
pariēs pariet-is 3m. wall
per (+ acc.) through, by
perueniō 4 I reach
placet it is pleasing
plānē clearly
ponderō 1 I weigh (up)
pondus ponder-is 3n. weight
prīmō first
pugne-us a um fisty
pugn-us ī 2m. fist
quam how!
quandō since, because
scelest-us a um wicked, villainous, criminal
sinō 3 I allow
sī quis if anyone
Sōsi-a ae 1m. Sosia
tantī . . . quantī worth as much as
tēcum to/with yourself/you
ualdē extremely, greatly
ueniō 4 I come
uideor 2 dep. I seem

MER.   sī haud abībis statim . . .   135
SŌS.   abīre haud poterō.
MER.   cūr abīre nōn poteris?
SŌS.   abīre haud poterō quod hīc habitō, atque huius familiae seruus sum.
MER.   quis est dominus tibi?
SŌS.   Amphitruō et mulier illīus, Alcumēna.   140
MER.   et quid est nōmen tibi, scelerum caput?
SŌS.   (*grandly*) Sōsiam mē uocant Thēbānī, Dāuī filium.

17. Sōsia ego sum, nōn tū

MER.   quid tū loqueris? mentīris, furcifer. tū Sōsia es? ego sum Sōsia.
(*Mercurius Sōsiam uerberat*)
SŌS.   periī! mē necāre uult!   145
MER.   etiam clāmās, homo nihilī? cui seruus nunc es?
SŌS.   sum Amphitruōnis Sōsia et mulieris illīus.
MER.   nescius etiam es. nōlī mentīrī. Sōsia ego sum, nōn tū.
(*iterum illum uerberat Mercurius*)
SŌS.   periī, occidī.   150
MER.   etiam clāmās, homo nihilī? tacē.
SŌS.   tacēbō.
MER.   quis dominus tuus est? cui nunc seruus es?
SŌS.   nesciō. quem uīs?
MER.   bene loqueris. quid igitur? quid nunc tibi est nōmen?   155
SŌS.   nesciō. quid iam uīs?
MER.   bene dīcis. nescius nōn es. at respondē: esne Amphitruōnis Sōsia? estne
       mulier illīus domina tua?
SŌS.   at nōlī, precor, mē Sōsiam uocāre.
MER.   bene respondēs. nūllus enim est seruus Amphitruōnis nisi ego.   160

sōs.   (*clam loquitur*) nūllus est homo tam scelestus quam hic. quis est seruus
            Amphitruōnis Sōsia nisi ego? egone iam stō domum ante nostram? quis
            loquitur nisi ego? quis hīc habitat nisi ego? nesciusne nōminis meī sum?
            domum igitur inībō nostram.

(*Sōsia domum inīre per iānuam cōnātur sed Mercurius prohibet*)   165

MER.   quae uerba loqueris? tuamne dīcis hanc domum? sed haec domus mea est,
            nōn tua, homo nihilī. nōlī mentīrī.

(*iterum uerberat Mercurius Sōsiam*)

sōs.   periī! nam ego nōn mentior. quis ego sum, sī nōn Sōsia? per Iouem iūrō,
            Sōsia sum ego!   170

MER.   at ego per Mercurium iūrō, Iuppiter tibi non crēdit. ubi ego Sōsia nōlō
            esse, tū Sōsia eris. nunc, quandō ego sum Sōsia, mālō tē Sōsiam nōn esse.
            abī, scelerum caput.

(Plautus, *Amphitruo* 264–462)

*(To prove that he is 'Sosia', Mercury tells Sosia fully and accurately everything
that happened in the battle, to Sosia's utter amazement.)*

Alcumen-a ae 1f Alcumena
Amphitruō Amphitruōn-is 3m.
   Amphitruo
ante (+ acc.) in front of, before
cōnor 1 dep. I try, attempt
Dāu-us ī 2m. Davus
domin-a ae 1f. mistress
etiam still, even, as well; actually,
   then!; yes indeed
furcifer furcifer-ī 2m. scoundrel,
   ratbag
habitō 1 I live, dwell

haec (nom. s. f.) this (adj.)
hanc (acc. s. f.) this
haud not
hic nom. s. m. this
huius (gen. s. f.) of this
illīus gen. s. m. of him
iūrō 1 I swear
Mercuri-us ī 2m. Mercury
mulier mulier-is 3f. wife
necō 1 I kill
nesciō 4 I do not know

nesci-us a um knowing nothing,
   ignorant (of + gen.)
nihilī of no value
nisi except
per (+ acc.) through, by
prohibeō 2 I prevent, stop
quandō since
tam . . . quam as . . . as
Thēbān-us a um Theban
tibi line 171: *crēdō* takes the
   dative
uerberō 1 I beat up

18. at ego per Mecurium iūrō

Grammar for 2C

hic, ille

Learning vocabulary for 2C

Nouns

fōrm-a ae 1f. shape, looks, beauty
mīles mīlit-is 3m. soldier
mōs mōr-is 3m. way, habit, custom; (pl.) character
mulier mulier-is 3f. woman; wife

Pronouns

mēcum with/to me (myself) (= *mē* + *cum*); pl. *nōbīscum*
tēcum with/to you(rself); pl. *uōbīscum*

Adjectives

īrāt-us a um angry
nesci-us a um knowing nothing, ignorant (of + gen.)
scelest-us a um criminal, wicked

Verbs

necō 1 I kill
dēfendō 3 *dēfendī dēfēnsus* I defend
opprimō 3 *oppressī oppressus* I surprise, catch; crush
sinō 3 *sīuī situs* I allow, permit
arbitror 1 dep. I think, consider; give judgment
cōnor 1 dep. I try
uideor 2 dep. *uīsus* I seem
īrāscor 3 dep. *īrātus* I grow angry

Others

citō quickly
etiam still, even, as well; actually, then! yes indeed
haud not

iam now, by now, already; presently
nihilī of no worth, value
nisi unless, if . . . not; except
per (+ acc.) through, by
plānē clearly
quam how! (+ adj. or adv.)
quandō since, when

New forms: adjectives and pronouns

hic haec hoc this, pl. these; (as pron.) this man/woman/thing; he/she/it
ill-e ill-a ill-ud that, pl. those; (as pron.) that man/woman/thing; he/she/it

---

Husband and wife

Some of the arrangements of the Roman marriage appear to us heartless and unfeeling. In particular many now find marriage arrangements for political and financial ends alien and shocking. In theory, *patria potestās* meant that a father could hand over his daughter in marriage to anyone he liked to construct an alliance. The young Pompey's first marriage was to the daughter of his trial judge; the bystanders are supposed to have sung the wedding hymn when he was acquitted. Several marriages later, his union with Caesar's daughter sealed their alliance in the triumvirate. In law, a girl could be married at the onset of puberty, or even before, and there are numerous cases of girls married as young as 12. Cicero betrothed his daughter Tullia at 9; when she died aged 30, she had been married three times. No less cynical seems the casual way in which happy unions might be dissolved for political purposes. A notable victim of this was the future emperor Tiberius: when his son-in-law Agrippa died, Augustus made his stepson Tiberius divorce Agrippa's daughter Vipsania, to marry his widow Julia. The story goes that Tiberius was particularly fond of Vipsania (and suspicious of Julia), and missed her so badly that Augustus took steps to prevent them meeting again. (*World of Rome*, **341**)

Section 2D

Meanwhile Jupiter-Amphitruo has had his fun with Alcumena and prepares, as he says, to go back to the fighting. She is disconsolate, but he gives her a golden dish he claims to have been presented with after killing the Teleboan king in battle (in fact Amphitruo had been given it, and Sosia was bringing it back from the battle-field in a sealed box).

By now Sosia has gone back to tell Amphitruo what has happened. Amphitruo angrily refuses to believe him. He lovingly greets Alcumena but finds that she cannot understand why he has come back so soon – why, he only ate and slept with her last night (and Sosia had returned with him as well) and he gave her that golden dish. The shocked Amphitruo demands she produce this dish, at the same time asking Sosia if the seal on the box is still unbroken . . .

illā⌒nocte Iuppiter Alcumēnam iterum amāuit. longum post tempus nox
longa fīnīuit et sōl appāruit. Alcumēna grauiter tulit quod Iuppiter uincere   175
Tēleboās et ante lūcem abīre māluit quam manēre. Iuppiter ergō illī
dōnum dedit, pateram auream rēgis Tēleboārum; et ubi Alcumēna Iouī
grātiās ēgit, Iuppiter discessit. nihilōminus Alcumēna, trīstis quod Iuppiter
multās post hōrās abiit, 'ēheu' inquit 'uoluptātem unā⌒nocte habēre potuī,
dum uir meus domī adfuit. sed ille subitō hinc ā mē abiit ante lūcem. sōla   180
hīc mihi nunc uideor, quia ille nōn adest sed hinc discessit.'

Running vocabulary for 2D

abiit (he/she/it [has] left, went away (perf. of *abeō*); with *quod*, often 'had —ed . . . '
adfuit he/she/it [has] was present, here (perf. of *adsum*)
Alcumēn-a ae 1f. Alcumena
amāuit he/she/it has made love to (perf. of *amō* 1)
ante (+ acc.) before
appāruit he/she/it [has] appeared (perf. of *appāreō* 2)
aure-us a um golden
dedit he/she/it gave, has given (perf. of *dō*)
discessit he/she/it [has] departed, left (perf. of *discēdō* 3)
dōn-um ī 2n. present, gift

ēheu alas!
ergō therefore
fīnīuit he/she/it [has] finished (perf. of *fīniō* 4)
grātiās ēgit he/she/it gave, has given, thanks (perf. of *agō* 3); with *ubi*, often 'had —ed . . . '
grauiter ferō 3 I take it badly
hinc from here
hōr-a ae 1f. hour
illā nocte on that night
inquit he/she/it says (*inquam*)
lūx lūc-is 3f. light
māluit he/she/it [has] preferred (perf. of *mālō*)
nihilōminus nevertheless
pater-a ae 1f. plate

post (+ acc.) after
potuī I was able, could (perf. of *possum*)
quam than
sōl-us a um alone, lonely
subitō suddenly
Tēlebo-ae ārum 1m. pl. the Teleboae
tempus tempor-is 3n. time
tulit he/she/it took it, has taken it [badly] (perf. of *ferō*)
uincō 3 I conquer
ūnā nocte in one night (abl.)
uoluptās uoluptāt-is 3f. agreeable experience, pleasure

intereā Sōsia ad Amphitruōnem rediit et omnia dē Sōsiā alterō nūntiat. ille
ergō īrātus fit, quod Sōsia 'ego etiam' inquit 'deciēs dīxī: uērō tēcum
adsum Sōsia, et uērō domī ego sum. sum ergō et hīc et illīc'. Amphitruō
crēdere nōluit, sed Sōsiam castigāre māluit. Sōsia iterum dīxit 'mīrum   185
mihi est et tibi, inquam. nam Sōsia ille, ut ego, omnia nūntiāuit dē proeliō,
et omnia scīuit. nam ille "bellum gessimus" inquit "in Tēleboās.
hāc⁀nocte nāuis nostra ē portū discessit et longum post tempus cōpiae
nostrae dēlēuērunt urbem et legiōnēs Tēleboārum. post, Amphitruō rēgem
in proeliō necāuit et pateram auream rēgis Tēleboārum cēpit".'   190

uērum Amphitruō īrātus nōn crēdidit sed rem inuestīgāre uoluit. tertiā⁀
hōrā ad iānuam appropinquāuit et Alcumēnam cōnspexit.

AMPHITRUŌ   ecce! longum post tempus, Alcumēnam cōnspexī ego, et illa mē.
             quam laeta rēs est, et mihi et illī, quod domī aderō!
ALCUMĒNA   (*to herself*) ecce! meus uir hīc quidem adest! sed cūr tam subitō rediit? 195
AMPH.   Amphitruō, longum post tempus, adest et uxōrem salūtat laetus, ūnam
             optimam Thēbārum omnium. ualēsne?
ALC.   quid dīxistī, mī uir? quid tū mē sīc salūtāuistī? nam tē hāc⁀nocte
             sine⁀dubiō uīdī.
AMPH.   immō, tē nisi nunc nōn uīdī.   200
ALC.   cūr negās?
AMPH.   (*īrātus fit*) quia uēra didicī dīcere.

adsum I am present, here
Alcumēn-a ae 1f. Alcumena
Amphitruō Amphitruōn-is 3m. Amphitruo
appropinquāuit he/she/it [has] approached (perf. of appropinquō 1)
aure-us a um golden
bell-um gessimus we [have] waged war (perf. of gerō 3)
castigō 1 I rebuke
cēpit he/she/it [has] captured, taken; took (perf. of capiō 3/4)
cōnspexī I [have] caught sight of (perf. of cōnspiciō 3/4)
cōnspexit he/she/it [has] caught sight of (perf. of cōnspiciō 3/4)
cōpi-ae ārum 1f. troops, forces
crēdidit he/she/it [has] believed, trusted (perf. of crēdō 3)
deciēs ten times
dēlēuērunt they [have] destroyed (perf. of dēleō)
didicī I [have] learned (perf. of discō 3)
discessit he/she/it [has] departed (perf. of discēdō 3)
dīxī I [have] said (perf. of dīcō 3)
dīxistī you (s.) [have] said (perf. of dīcō 3)
dīxit he/she/it (has) said (perf. of dīcō 3)

ergō therefore
fīō fierī I become, am made (3s. fit)
gessimus see bellum
hāc nocte (on) this night
hōr-a ae 1f. hour
iānu-a ae 1f. door
illīc (at) there
immō more precisely (i.e. yes, or no, expressing strong agreement or disagreement)
in (+ acc.) against
inquam I say
inquit he/she/it says (inquam)
intereā meanwhile
inuestīgō 1 I look into
īrāt-us a um angry, furious
laet-us a um happy, joyful
legiō legiōn-is 3f. legion
māluit he/she/it [has] preferred (perf. of mālō)
mīr-us a um wonderful, amazing
nāuis nāu-is 3f. ship
necāuit he/she/it [has] killed (perf. of necō 1)
negō 1 I deny, say no
nōluit he/she/it [has] refused, has not wished/wanted (perf. of nōlō)
nūntiāuit he/she/it [has] announced (perf. of nūntiō 1)
pater-a ae 1f. plate
port-us ūs 4m. port, harbour

post afterwards, later
post (+ acc.) after
quid (line 198) why?
quidem certainly, in fact, admittedly
rediit he/she/it [has] returned (perf. of redeō)
salūtāuistī you (s) [have] greeted (perf. of salūtō 1)
salūtō 1 I greet
scīuit he/she/it has known, knew (perf. of sciō 4)
sine dubiō without doubt, most certainly
Sōsi-a ae 1m. Sosia
subitō suddenly
Tēlebo-ae ārum 1m. pl. the Teleboae
tempus tempor-is 3n. time
tertiā hōrā at the third hour (abl.)
Thēb-ae ārum 1f. pl. Thebes
ualeō 2 I am well, flourishing
uēra the truth (n. pl. of uēr-us a um)
uērō indeed, truly
uērum but
uīdī I have seen, saw (perf. of uideō 2)
uoluit he/she/it [has] wanted (perf. of uolō)
urbs urb-is 3f. city

Love matches

A good range of sources attest marital affection in action. When Cicero writes to his wife Terentia as 'light of my life' or 'most faithful and best of wives' and expresses his longing to see her (Letters to Friends 14.4) or when Pliny writes to his Calpurnia in even more gushing terms ('I am seized by unbelievable longing for you . . . I spend the greater part of the night haunted by your image', Letters 7.5), it makes little difference whether they really meant it, or were just putting it on. This was an appropriate way of addressing a Roman wife. Similarly the hundreds of gravestones that celebrate a wife's long fidelity, and address her as cārissima, 'dearest', dulcissima, 'sweetest', rārissima, 'rarest', and the like, however conventional and stilted the sentiments expressed, demonstrate at least the envisaged possibility of strong affection in marriage: 'To Urbana, the sweetest, chastest and rarest of wives, who certainly has never been surpassed, and deserves to be honoured for living with me to her last day in the greatest pleasantness and simplicity, with equal conjugal affection and hard work. I added these words so that readers should understand how much we loved each other.' (CIL VI.29580, Rome) (World of Rome, 344)

ALC.	immō tū uēra nōn dīxistī. cūr hūc tū et Sōsia rediīstis tam citō? cūr nōn abiīstis ad legiōnēs, ut hāc‿nocte dīxistī, et hostēs uīcistī? nōlī mē sīc castigāre! nōlī īrātus fierī! 205
AMPH.	(*tacitus fit*) at nōn intellegō. quō‿in‿locō hoc dīxī?
ALC.	hīc, in aedibus ubi tū habitās.
AMPH.	tacē, mulier! numquam edepol hoc dīxī. stultane es, uxor mea? cūr mē nōn salūtāuistī, ut uxōrēs pudīcae uirōs salūtāre dēbent?
ALC.	tē sine‿dubiō heri, ubi aduēnistī, salūtāuī, ut dēbuī; post, manum prehendī 210 et ōsculum dedī tibi.
SŌSIA	tūne heri hunc salūtāuistī?
ALC.	et tē quoque etiam, Sōsia.
AMPH.	(*tacitus iterum fit*) sed nōn adfuimus ego et Sōsia. dēlīrat uērō uxor. suspicor et hanc et illum mendācēs esse. 215

AMPH.	*Look! After a long time I have caught sight of Alcumena, and she of me. How happy the situation is, both for me and her, since I shall be here at home!*
ALC.	*(to herself) Look! My husband is certainly present here! But why has he returned so suddenly?*
AMPH.	*Amphitruo, after a long time, is here and joyful[ly] greets his wife, the single best [woman] of all Thebes. Are you well?*
ALC.	*What did you say, my husband? Why did you greet me in this way? For without doubt I saw you this night.*
AMPH.	*But I certainly did not see you except now.*
ALC.	*Why do you deny [it]?*
AMPH.	*(becomes angry) Because I have learned to tell the truth.*
ALC.	*No, you have not told the truth. Why have you and Sosia returned here so quickly? Why did you not depart for the legions, as you said last night, and conquer the enemy? Don't rebuke me in this way! Don't become angry!*
AMPH.	*(falls silent) But I don't understand. In what place did I say this?*
ALC.	*Here, in the house where you live.*
AMPH.	*Silence, woman! Never, by Pollux, did I say this. Are you stupid, my wife? Why did you not welcome me, as chaste wives ought to greet their husbands?*
ALC.	*I undoubtedly welcomed you yesterday, when you came, as I ought; afterwards, I took your hand and gave you a kiss.*
SOS.	*You welcomed this man yesterday?*
ALC.	*And you too, Sosia.*
AMPH.	*(again he falls silent) But Sosia and I were not here. My wife really is mad. I suspect she and that man to be liars.*

ALC.	ēcastor sāna et salua sum. ergō tacē! nōn dēbet uir mulierem castigāre.
AMPH.	sed cūr tū 'tē heri uīdī' inquis? nam illā‿nocte in portum sine dubiō aduēnī; ibi cēnāuī; post, ibi dormīuī in nāue, neque intrāuī in aedīs nostrās, sed Tēleboās oppugnāuī et uīcī, urbemque dēlēuī rēgemque necāuī.

abiīstis you (pl) [have] departed, left (perf. of *abeō*)

adfuimus we were present (per. of *adsum*)

aduēnī I [have] arrived, came (perf. of *adueniō* 4)

aduēnistī you (s) [have] arrived, come; came (perf. of *adueniō* 4)

castigō 1 I rebuke

cēnāuī I [have] dined, had dinner (perf. of *cēnō* 1)

dēbeō 2 I ought

dēbuī I ought to have (perf. of *dēbeō* 2, + inf.)

dedī I gave, have given (perf. of *dō* 1)

dēlēuī I [have] destroyed (perf. of *dēleō* 2)

dēlīrō I am mad, crazy

dīxī I (have) said (perf. of *dīcō* 3)

dīxistī you (s) [have] said (perf. of *dīcō* 3)

dormīuī I [have] slept (perf. of *dormiō* 4); after *ubi*, often 'had —ed . . .'

ēcastor by Castor (a Roman god)

edepol by Pollux!

ergō therefore

fīō fierī I become, am made (3s. fit; inf. fierī)

habitō 1 I live, dwell

hāc nocte (on) this night

heri yesterday

hūc (to) here

ibi there

illā nocte (on) that night

immō more precisely (i.e. yes, or no, expressing strong agreement or disagreement)

inquis you (s) say (*inquam*)

intellegō 3 I understand

intrāuī I [have] entered (perf. of *intrō* 1)

legiō legiōn-is 3f. legion

loc-us-ī 2m. place

nāu-is is 3f. ship

necāuī I [have] killed (perf. of *necō*)

oppugnāuī I [have] attacked (perf. of *oppugnō* 1)

ōscul-um ī 2n. kiss

port-us ūs 4m. port, harbour

post afterwards

prehendī I took, have taken (perf. of *prehendō* 3)

pudīc-us a um chaste, honest

quō in locō in what place?

rediīstis you (pl) [have] returned (perf. of *redeō*)

salūtāuī I [have] greeted (perf. of *salūtō* 1)

salūtāuistī you (s.) [have] greeted (perf. of *salūtō* 1) salūtō 1 I greet

sān-us a um sane, healthy

sine dubiō without doubt, most certainly

suspicor 1 dep. I suspect

tacit-us a um silent

uēra the truth (n. pl. of *uēr-us a um*)

uērō indeed, truly

uīcī I [have] conquered, defeated (perf. of *uincō*)

uīcistī you (s) [have] conquered (perf. of *uincō* 3)

uīdī I saw, I have seen (perf. of *uideō* 2)

urbs urb-is 3f. city

Paternal power

The most persistent, and in the eyes of the Romans the most quintessentially Roman, feature of the family was the power of the father, *patria potestās*. Not only were they aware that the Roman father had powers over his family, and especially his adult children, that were exceptional, but it was a proud tradition to which they clung tenaciously. The second-century AD lawyer Gaius commented that 'this right is peculiar to Roman citizens, for there are virtually no other men who have such power over their sons as we have', and cited the views of the emperor Hadrian in support. (*World of Rome*, **308**)

ALC.	immō post mēcum illā˘nocte cenāuistī et cubuistī et . . .	220
AMPH.	quid est?! periī, Sōsia!	
ALC.	. . . et post sine˘dubiō omnia dē proeliō dīxistī. praetereā, dōnum mihi dedistī auream pateram rēgis Tēleboārum. tum ante lūcem abiīstī.	
AMPH.	uērum pateram auream tibi nōn dedī! quis dē paterā aureā dīxit?	
ALC.	ego quidem ē tē audīuī, et ē tuā manū accēpī pateram et grātiās⌐ tibi ⌐ēgī! uīsne pateram illam uidēre?	225
AMPH.	uolō equidem.	
ALC.	heus tū, serua, pateram illam hūc portā.	

(*serua exit*)

SŌS.	nōlī crēdere. (*Sosia nods knowingly at the box he is carrying*) nam in hāc cistā pateram illam sine dubiō posuī.	230
AMPH.	saluum signum est?	
SŌS.	īnspice.	
AMPH.	saluum est. uxor mea sine dubiō mentītur.	

(*serua cum paterā redit*)   235

ALC.	ecce, patera aurea.	
AMPH.	summe Iuppiter, quid ego uideō? haec illa est patera aurea! periī, Sōsia. age, Sōsia, solue signum et aperī cistam.	
SŌS.	(*signum soluit et cistam aperit. omnēs tacitī fīunt*) Iuppiter! prō Iuppiter! hīc patera nūlla in cistā est!	240

(Plautus, *Amphitruo* 499–854)

---

abiīstī you (s) went away, [have] left (perf. of *abeō*)

accēpī I [have] received (perf. of *accipiō* 3/4)

ante (+ acc.) before

aperiō 4 I open

audīuī I [have] heard (perf. of *audiō* 4)

aure-us a um golden

cenāuistī you (s) [have] dined (perf. of *cēnō* 1)

cist-a ae 1f. chest

cubuistī you (s) [have] gone to bed (perf. of *cubō* 1)

dedī I gave, have given (perf. of *dō* 1)

dedistī you (s) gave, have given (perf. of *dō* 1)

dīxistī you (s) [have] said (perf. of *dīcō* 3)

dīxit he/she/it has said (perf. of *dīcō* 3)

dōn-um ī 2n. gift

equidem for my part

fīō fierī I become, am made (3 pl. *fīunt*)

grātiās ēgī I gave, have given, thanks (perf. of *grātiās agō* 3)

heus hey!

hūc (to) here

illā nocte (on) that night

immō more precisely (i.e. yes, or no, expressing strong agreement or disagreement)

īnspiciō 3/4 I inspect, look closely at

lūx lūc-is 3f. right

pater-a ae 1f. plate

periī I have been destroyed, I'm dead! (perf. of *pereō*)

post afterwards

posuī I [have] placed, put (perf. of *pōnō*)

praetereā besides

prō in the name of!

sign-um 2n. (wax) seal

sine dubiō without doubt, most certainly

soluō 3 I release, undo, break

Sōsi-a ae 1m. Sosia

tacit-us a um silent

Tēlebo-ae ārum 1m. pl. the Teleboae

tum then

uērum but

Grammar for 2D

---

perfect indicative active   **irregular verbs**   **ablative of time**

Learning vocabulary for 2D

Nouns

grāti-ae ārum 1f. pl. thanks, recompense

hōr-a ae 1f. hour

sign-um ī 2n. seal; signal, sign

tempus tempor-is 3n. time

uoluptās uoluptāt-is 3f. agreeable experience; pleasure; desire

urbs urb-is 3f. city

Adjectives

aure-us a um golden

tacit-us a um silent

Verbs

castigō 1 I rebuke, chasten

salūtō 1 I greet

suspicor 1 dep. I suspect

dēbeō 2 I ought (+ inf.); owe

dēleō 2 *dēlēuī dēlētus* I destroy

gerō 3 *gessī gestus* I do, conduct; *bellum gerō* I wage war

grātiās agō 3 *ēgī āctus* I give thanks

inquam I say (*inquam inquis inquit*, 3 pl. *inquiunt*)

soluō 3 *soluī solūtus* I release, undo

uincō 3 *uīcī uictus* I conquer

adsum adesse adfuī adfutūrus I am present, am at hand

fīō fierī factus I become, am done, am made

Others

ante (+ acc.) before, in front of

ergō therefore

ibi there

immō more precisely, i.e. no or yes (a strong agreement or disagreement with what precedes)

in (+ acc.) against (into, onto)

post (adv.) later, afterwards; (+ acc.) after, behind

sine (+ abl.) without; *sine dubiō* without doubt, certainly

subitō suddenly

uērō indeed

uērum but

Section 2E

*(Merry confusion reigns and gets even worse when Jupiter re-appears, still
disguised as Amphitruo, and he and Amphitruo meet. Amphitruo is outraged
because a friend summoned to tell the difference has not been able to
distinguish between the two.)*

*When Jupiter has gone in to help Alcumena give birth to twins – his son
Hercules and Amphitruo's son Eurystheus – Amphitruo explodes with fury onto
the stage, threatening to kill this other-Amphitruo. But the maidservant Bromia
interrupts him to announce the birth of twins, in extraordinary circumstances.
Jupiter then emerges in person to foretell Hercules' heroic life and labours and
to reconcile Amphitruo to his wife.*

IUPPITER   (*in aedīs exit*) hinc in aedīs ingrediar; nam Alcumēna intrō mox parturiet
et duo filiī nāscentur.

AMPHITRUŌ   (*intrat et Amphitruōnem alterum propter scelera castigat, nescius
dolōrum Iouis.*) periī miser! quid ego faciam? Amphitruō ille homo nihilī
est! numquam edepol dē hāc rē mentiētur inultus. nam ad rēgem   245
prōgrediar et rem tōtam ēloquar; ego pol Amphitruōnem illum ulcīscar
hodiē! numquam illum effugere patiar! sed ubi est ille? nescius ego – nisi
intrō abiit ille hūc ad uxōrem meam. quid nunc agam nisi illum hāc sequar
in aedīs et necābō? sī illum cōnspicābor, mortī statim propter scelera
dabō! neque mē Iuppiter neque dī omnēs prohibēre illum ad mortem   250
statim mittere audēbunt, etiam sī uolent. nunc iam hāc ingrediar in aedīs.
tantī Amphitruō alter erit quantī fungus putidus!

(*Enter Bromia with news of the dramatic birth of the children*)

BROMIA   ō mē miseram! uae miserae mihi! caput dolet, neque audiō, nec uītam nec
uōcem habeō, nec quicquam cōnspicor. nam ubi Alcumēna intrō parturīuit   255
et deōs inuocāuit, subitō fuit strepitus, crepitus, sonitus, tonitrus! ibi uōx
nescioquis exclāmāuit 'Alcumēna, quamquam timēs, adest auxilium. ergō
nōlī timēre! nōlī tē sollicitāre! prō continentiā tuā, Iuppiter propitius hūc
aduēnit et tibi et tuīs.' mīrum est: nōn mentior. uōx Iouis fuit! tum
Alcumēna inuocāuit deōs immortālīs et sine dolōre peperit.   260

AMPH.   quamquam īrātus sum et uxōrem meam propter impudīcitiam castigō,
gaudeō tamen, sī uērō Iouis uōx fuit et dolus nōn fuit.

BROM.   immō uōcis deī similis fuit. tum geminōs puerōs cōnspicor. sed, ubi
parturīuit uxor tua, puerōs lauāre iussit nōs. uērum puer alter, ubi lāuī,
quam magnus est! ut multum ualet! ut similis fīliī Iouis!   265

AMPH.   mīrum est!

BROM.   'magis mīrum' loquēris! subitō duo anguēs intrō appāruērunt et capita
subleuāuērunt.

AMPH.   eī mihi!

BROM.   nōlī timēre, nōlī tē sollicitāre. ubi anguēs puerōs cōnspexērunt, in illōs   270
statim irruērunt. sed ubi cōnspexit anguēs ille alter puer, impetum in

Running vocabulary for 2E

adueniō 4 *aduēnī* I come, arrive
Alcumēn-a ae 1f. Alcumena
Amphitruō Amphitruōn-is 3m.
    Amphitruo
anguis angu-is 3m. snake
appāreō 2 *appāruī* I appear
audeō I dare
auxili-um ī 2n. help
Bromi-a ae 1f Bromia (lit
    'roaring', a title of the Greek
    god Dionysus)
cōnspicābor I shall catch sight of
    (fut. of *cōnspicor* 1 dep.)
cōnspiciō 3/4 *cōnspexī* I catch
    sight of
cōnspicor 1 dep. I catch sight of
crepit-us ūs 4m. smash
doleō 2 I hurt
dolor dolōr-is 3m. pain
dol-us ī 2m. trick
edepol by Pollux!
effugiō 3/4 I escape, run off
eī alas!
ēloquar I shall unfold (fut. of
    ēloquor 3 dep.)
exclāmō 1 I shout out
fung-us ī 2m. mushroom
gaudeō 2 I rejoice
gemin-us a um twin
hāc this way
hinc from here
hūc (to) here
immortāl-is e immortal
impet-us ūs 4m attack
impudīciti-a ae 1f. faithlessness
ingrediar I shall enter, go in (fut.
    of *ingredior* 3/4 dep.)
intrō inside
inult-us a um unpunished
inuocō 1 I call on
irruō 3 *irruī* I rush at, charge
lauō lauāre lāuī I wash
loquēris you (s.) will say (fut. of
    loquor 3 dep.)
magis more
mentiētur he/she/it will lie (fut. of
    mentior 4 dep.)
mīr-us a um wonderful, amazing
mors mort-is 3f. death
multum (adv.) much, very
nāscentur they will be born (fut.
    of *nāscor* 3 dep.)
nescioquis nom. s. of someone or
    other

19. subito fuit strepitus, crepitus, sonitus, tonitrus!

nihilī of no worth
pariō 3/4 *peperī* I bear, give birth
parturiō 4 I am in labour, give
    birth
patiar I shall allow (fut. of *patior*
    3/4 dep.)
pol by Pollux!
prō (+ abl.) in return for
prōgrediar I shall make my way,
    advance (fut. of *prōgredior*
    3/4 dep.)
prohibeō 2 I prevent
propiti-us a um well-disposed,
    favourable
propter (+ acc.) on account of
puer puer-ī 2m. boy
putid-us a um rotten
quamquam although

quicquam (acc. n.) anything
sequar I shall follow, pursue (fut.
    of *sequor* 3 dep.)
sollicitō 1 I worry
sonit-us ūs 4m. loud noise
strepit-us ūs 4m. din, turmoil
subleuō 1 I raise, lift
tantī . . . quantī worth as
    much . . . as . . .
tonitr-us ūs 4m. crash of thunder
tōt-us a um the whole
uae (+ dat.) alas!
ualeō 2 I am strong, fit, healthy
uīt-a ae 1f. life
ulcīscar I shall take revenge on
    (fut. of *ulcīscor* 3 dep.)
uōx uōc-is 3f. voice

	anguēs subitō fēcit et ambōs necāuit. clārum est: alter puer, quī illōs anguēs necāuit, Iouis est, alter tuus.	
AMPH.	pol, dē hāc rē nōn mē sollicitābō, sī poterō rēs meās dīuidere cum Ioue. abī, Bromia, domum intrō; nam Iouem precābor et sacrificābor.	275

BROM. *Misery me! Alas for miserable me! My head hurts, I do not see, nor do I have life nor voice, nor can I catch sight of anything. For when Alcumena had begun her labour inside and had called on the gods, suddenly there was a tremendous din, smash, noise, and crash of thunder! There someone or other's voice shouted 'Alcumena, though you are afraid, help is at hand. So don't be afraid! Don't worry yourself! Because of your chastity, Jupiter has come here to favour both you and yours.' It's a miracle: I'm not lying. It was the voice of Jove! Then Alcumena called on the immortal gods and gave birth without pain.*

AMPH. *Although I am angry and reprimand my wife because of her faithlessness, still I rejoice, if truly it was the voice of Jove and not a trick.*

BROM. *Yes, it certainly resembled the voice of a god. Then I catch sight of the boys – twins! But when your wife had given birth, she ordered us to wash the boys. Truly, the one boy, when I washed him – how big he was! How strong! How like a son of Jove!*

AMPH. *It's a miracle!*

BROM. *'More than a miracle' you will say! For suddenly two snakes appeared inside and raised their heads.*

AMPH. *Alas for me!*

BROM. *Don't be afraid! Don't worry yourself! When the snakes caught sight of the boys, they immediately rushed at them. But when that one boy saw the snakes, he suddenly lauched an attack on them and killed both. It's clear: the one boy who killed the snakes is Jove's, the other yours.*

ALC. *Heavens, I won't worry myself on this matter, if I shall be able to divide my wealth with Jove's! Off you go, Bromia, inside the house; for I shall pray to Jove and sacrifice.*

(*intrat Iuppiter*)

IUPP.	nōlī timēre, Amphitruō, neque tē sollicitāre! prō uirtūte tuā, tē tuōsque malum accipere nōn patiar. tē et uītam tuōrum tuēbor, et futūra tibi ēloquar. Herculēs cum leōne Nemaeō luctābitur, pellem illīus adipīscētur et prō tegumentō ūtētur. ad Lernam prōgrediētur, Hydram cum capitibus nouem adgrediētur, et mortī dabit. tum aprum Erymanthium sequētur et occīdet. cum ceruō ferōcī ex Arcadiā regrediētur. auīs Stymphālidēs in īnsulā Martis uēnābitur et necābit. Augeae rēgis stabula ūnō die pūrgāre cōnābitur; flūmen in stabula uertet et rem bene geret. in Crētam īnsulam proficīscētur et cum Mīnōtaurō in Graeciam regrediētur. Diomēdem, Thrāciae rēgem, et equōs quattuor illīus (hī enim carnem hūmānam edunt)	280 285

20. impetum in anguēs subitō fēcit et ambōs necāuit

accipiō 3/4 *accēpī* I receive
adgrediētur he/she/it will attack
    (fut. of *adgredior* 3/4 dep.)
adipīscētur he/she/it will get, win
    (fut. of *adipīscor* 3 dep.)
amb-ō ae both
Amphitruō Amphitruōn-is 3m.
    Amphitruo
angu-is is 3m. snake
aper apr-ī 2m. boar
Arcadi-a ae 1f. Arcadia
Augeae gen. s. Augeas (a king)
au-is is 3f. bird
Bromi-a ae 1f Bromia (lit.
    'roaring', a title of the Greek
    god Dionysus)
carō carn-is 3f. flesh
ceru-us ī 2m. stag, hart
clār-us a um clear, obvious
cōnābitur he/she/it will try (fut. of
    cōnor 1 dep.)
Crēt-a ae 1f. Crete
Diomēdem acc. s. m. Diomedes, a
    Greek king
dīuidō 3 I divide
edō 3 I eat
ēloquar I shall unfold (fut. of
    ēloquor 3 dep.)
equ-us ī 2m. horse
Erymanthi-us a um from
    Erymanthus
ferōx ferōc-is wild, fierce
flūmen flūmin-is 3n. river
futūr-a ōrum 2n. pl. the future

Graeci-a ae 1f. Greece
Herculēs nom. s. m. Hercules
    (Heracles in Greek)
hūmān-us a um human
Hydr-a ae 1f. Hydra, a
    many-headed snake
impetem faciō in (+ acc.) I launch
    an attack upon
īnsul-a ae 1f. island
intrō inside
leō leōn-is 3m. lion
Lern-a ae 1f. Lerna
luctābitur he/she/it will wrestle,
    struggle (fut. of *luctor* 1 dep.)
mal-um ī 2n. bad, evil
Mars Mart-is 3m. Mars (god of
    War)
Mīnōtaur-us ī 2m. Minotaur
    (half-man, half-bull)
mors mort-is 3f. death
Nemae-us a um from Nemea
nouem nine
occīdō 3 I kill
patiar I shall allow (fut. of *patior*
    3/4 dep.)
pell-is is 3f. skin, hide
pol by Pollux!
precābor I shall pray to (fut. of
    precor 1 dep.)
prō (+ abl.) in return for; as, for
proficīscētur he/she/it will set out
    (fut. of *proficīscor* 3 dep.)

prōgrediētur he/she/it will
    advance, move on (fut. of
    prōgredior 3/4 dep.)
puer puer-ī 2m. boy
pūrgō 1 I clean
quattuor four
quī who (nom. s. m.)
regrediētur he/she/it will return
    (fut. of *regredior* 3/4 dep.)
rem bene gerō 3 I do things well,
    am successful
sacrificābor I shall offer sacrifice
    (fut. of *sacrificor* 1 dep.)
sequētur he/she/it will follow,
    pursue (fut. of *sequor* 3 dep.)
sollicitō 1 I worry
stabul-um ī 2n. stable
Stymphālidēs acc. pl. f. from
    Stymphalia, home of
    man-eating birds
tegument-um ī 2n. covering,
    protection
Thrāci-a ae 1f. Thrace (northern
    Greece)
tuēbor I shall protect (fut. of *tueor*
    2 dep.)
tum then
uēnābitur he/she/it will hunt (fut.
    of *uēnor* 1 dep.)
uertō 3 I divert
uīt-a ae 1f. life
ūnō diē in one day
ūtētur he/she/it will use (sc. the
    hide) (fut. of *ūtor* 3 dep.)

mortī mittet. et ad aliōs quattuor labōrēs nītētur et tandem, nescius mortis, in caelum ingrediētur. propter fīlium meum igitur, Amphitruō, tū glōriam immortālem accipiēs. tū pacīscēris cum Alcumēnā uxōre et nōn īrāscēris; ingredere igitur illī et amplexāre. ego in caelum regrediar.

AMPH.   faciam ita ut iubēs. haud timēbō, haud mē sollicitābō. ingrediar hūc ad   290
uxōrem intrō et amplexābor. nunc, spectātōrēs, plaudite.

(Plautus, *Amphitruo* 861–1146)

---

accipiō 3/4 I receive
Alcumen-a ae 1f Alcumena
ali-us a um other
Amphitruō Amphitruōn-is 3m.
    Amphitruo
amplexābor I shall embrace (fut.
    of *amplexor* 1 dep.)
amplexor 1 dep. I embrace
cael-um ī 2n. heaven, sky
glōri-a ae 1f. glory
immortāl-is e immortal

ingrediar I shall enter (fut. of
    ingredior 3/4 dep.)
ingrediētur he/she/it will enter
    (fut. of *ingredior* 3/4 dep.)
intrō inside
īrāscēris you (s) will grow angry
    (fut. of *īrāscor* 3 dep.)
labor labōr-is 3m. labour, toil
mors mort-is 3f. death
nītētur he/she/it will direct his
    efforts to (fut. of *nītor* 3 dep.)

pacīscēris you will make your
    peace (fut. of *pacīscor* 3 dep.)
plaudō 3 I applaud
propter (+ acc.) on behalf of
quattuor four
regrediar I shall return (fut. of
    regredior 3/4 dep.)
sollicitō 1 I worry
spectātor spectātor-is 3m.
    spectator

Grammar for 2E

future deponent   **genitive of value**

Learning vocabulary for 2E

Nouns
uīt-a ae 1f. life
dol-us ī 2m. trick, fraud, deception
mal-um ī 2n. trouble; evil
mors mort-is 3f. death
uōx uōc-is 3f. voice; word

Adjectives
amb-ō ae ō both (like *duo*: see **54**)
pūtid-us a um rotten

Verbs
sollicitō 1 I bother, worry
amplexor 1 dep. I embrace
cōnspicor 1 dep. I catch sight of
audeō 2 semi-dep. *aus-us* I dare
accipiō 3/4 *accēpī, accept-us* I
    receive, welcome, learn,
    obtain
ingredior 3/4 dep. *ingress-us* I
    enter

patior 3/4 dep. *pass-us* I endure,
    suffer; allow

Others
hāc this way
hūc (to) here
intrō inside
prō (+ abl.) for, in return for; on
    behalf of; in front of
propter (+ acc.) on account of
quamquam although

The Amphitruo theme has been a fruitful one in Western literature. It has interesting theatrical, theological and psychological possibilities: the effect of Jupiter's intervention in a happy marriage, the theme of the 'wronged' wife/husband – but what happens when a god is responsible for the wrong? – the emotions of Alcumena, the 'justification' for it all in the birth of Hercules. There is a pleasing complexity about the plot, with much scope for mistaken identity. Molière's *Amphitryon* (1688) has a major innovation, in that Sosia is given a wife, Cleanthis, with whom Mercury–Sosia can become embroiled in the same way as Amphitruo–Jupiter is embroiled with Alcumena. Dryden's *Amphitryon, or The Two Sosias* (1690), based on Molière's, goes yet further and, while keeping Sosia's wife, introduces a maid for Alcumena called Phaedra. Mercury–Sosia, inevitably, falls in love with Phaedra and has the irate Mrs Sosia to deal with. Neither play is psychologically very complex, unlike Kleist's German version of 1807, which concentrates powerfully on the conflict of emotions within Alcumena. The Frenchman Jean Giraudoux wrote *Amphitryon 38* (i.e. the 38th version!) in 1929, and this play is remarkable for the brilliant wit and irony of the conversations between Jupiter and Alcumena (when Jupiter teasingly asks Alcumena what the night with him was like and suggests a variety of epithets, including 'divine', she, to his great fury, rejects them all and when he indignantly demands know what it *had* been like, she replies 'so . . . domestic').

Shakespeare used the theme of the twin servants in *A Comedy of Errors*. This play is largely based on Plautus' *Menaechmi*, the story of twins separated at birth who find themselves brought together as adults, but Shakespeare increases the possibilities for havoc by introducing twin servants too. Rogers and Hart's *The Boys from Syracuse*, a Broadway hit of 1938, is a further development of Shakespeare's idea.

Acknowledging Greek literature

'Their race is quite worthless and unteachable, and I speak as a prophet that when it gives us its literature, it will ruin everything.' (Cato the Elder writing about Greeks to his son: Pliny, *Natural History* 29.13)

'Conquered Greece took her uncultivated conqueror captive and invaded rustic Latium with the arts.' (Horace, *Epistles* 2.1.156–7)

These two quotations neatly set out the paradox. For Cato, Greek literature was dangerous. It was foreign. It undermined the Roman ideals set out in the preceding section. So, we are told, when the future general Agricola enthused over philosophy 'beyond what was allowed a Roman and a senator', his sensible mother took him in hand (Tacitus, *Agricola* 4) and he ended up as the doyen of Roman military aristocrats.

Yet the quotation from Horace shows that the Greeks won a cultural war to match the Romans' military conquest. Romans accepted Greek literature's historical primacy (and often enough paid lip-service to its aesthetic superiority) and were open about their enjoyment of Greek material. Plautus and Terence, for example, recycled Greek 'New Comedy' (late fourth–third century BC) in Latin. Since it retained its Greek setting, Greek names and *mōrēs*, and the characters got into terrible scrapes, it gave Romans a chance to feel superior to Greeks: but they still recognised brilliant comedy when they saw it. Indeed, elsewhere Cato remarks: 'it is a good idea to dip into their [Greek] literature, but not to learn it thoroughly'. Even Cato was not totally opposed to it. So, in time, Greek literature was incorporated into *Rōmānitās*, the sense of what it meant to be Roman. (*World of Rome*, **435**)

Part Two Early Roman history: from Aeneas to Hannibal

Section 3A **Aeneas and the Trojan War**

Aeneas was a great Trojan hero, destined (Homer tells us) to survive the Trojan War and rule Troy (*Iliad* 20.294–308; see map 2, p. xxi). The early Roman epic poet Naevius, however, picked up the tradition (reported in Greek historians in the fifth century BC) that Aeneas came to Italy and was the 'founding father' of the Roman race (though not of the city of Rome). This suited Romans well: Aeneas linked Rome with the gods and myths of early Greek epic, especially Homer – a sort of Roman passport to civilisation – and since he was the son of Venus, he was also the distant ancestor of the first emperor Augustus, who presented himself as the second founder of Rome after the horrors of the civil wars and collapse of the Republic at the end of the first century BC.

Aeneas, however, did bring with him a slight technical problem. While the Greek geographer Eratosthenes had dated the fall of Troy to 1184 BC, Roman tradition had it that Romulus and Remus founded Rome in 753 BC. But myth was ever flexible. Later juggling of dates resulted in the story of Aeneas settling down and dying in Lavinium south of Rome; his son Ascanius subsequently moving to Alba Longa; and over 300 years later, *his* descendants Romulus and Remus founding Rome itself.

Section 3A(i)

Jupiter decides to exclude the goddess Discordia from the wedding feast of Peleus and Thetis. This leads to a beauty contest on Mount Ida, judged by the Trojan Paris; and the result of this is that Paris abducts Greek Helen and starts the Trojan War.

ubi Pēleus Thetin in mātrimōnium dūxit, Iuppiter ad epulās deōs plūrimōs conuocāuit, sed nōn Erida (id est, Discordiam). ea īrātissima in mālō aureō scrīpsit 'fōrmōsissimae'. deinde ad iānuam uēnit et per eam id mālum mīsit in medium. et propter hoc mālum – malum minimum – maxima discordia Iūnōnī, Venerī, Mineruae fuit. deae eae igitur propter eam discordiam Iouī dīxērunt:

5

21. The judgement of Paris

Running vocabulary for 3A(i)

conuocō 1 I summon
de-a ae 1f. goddess
Discordi-a ae 1f. the goddess
    Discord; (without capital
    letter) discord, strife, quarrel
ea (nom. s. f.) she
eae those (nom. pl. f.)
eam line 3 (i.e. the door: acc. s. f.)
    it
eam line 5 (acc. s. f.) that
epul-ae ārum 1 f. pl. feast,
    banquet

Erida acc. s. of *Eris Erid-os* 3 f.
    the Goddess Strife
fōrmōsissim-us a um most
    beautiful (from *fōrmōsus*)
iānu-a ae 1f. door
id (nom. s. n. acc s. n.) that
īrātissim-us a um very angry
    (from *īrātus*)
Iūnō Iūnōn-is 3f. Juno
→ *māl-um ī* 2n. apple
mātrimōni-um ī 2n. marriage
maxim-us a um very large, very
    big

medi-us a um middle (of)
Minerv-a ae 1f. Minerva
minim-us a um very small
Pēle-us ī (or Greek form -*eos*)
    2m. Peleus
plūrim-us a um very many
scrībō 3 *scrīpsī* I write
Thetin acc. s of *Thetis Thetid-is*
    (or *Thetid-os*) 3f. Thetis
ueniō 4 *uēnī* I come
Venus Vener-is 3f. Venus

'tū, rēx deōrum, iūdicā; quis nostrī pulcherrima est?'
Iuppiter breue⁀tempus sēcum meditātur. tum eīs respondit:
'nōlīte mē rogāre! mālō iūdicium meum solitum retinēre. nam uōs omnīs
amō pariter, et omnēs mihi pulcherrimae uidēminī. alia uestrī numquam   10
mihi uidētur pulchrior esse quam alia. egō arbiter uestrī pessimus, nōn
optimus sum. sed est iuuenis Trōiānus, Paris nōmine. is fōrmōsissimus est
et arbiter uestrī multō melior quam egō erit. recipite iūdicium eius potius
quam iūdicium meum.'

Iuppiter igitur Mercuriō dīxit: 'deās eās in Īdam montem ad Paridem   15
dēdūc, et eī dīc: 'quis deārum eārum tibi uidētur pulcherrima esse? tū
pulchritudinem deārum iūdicā!'
ubi deae in Īdam uēnērunt, Mercurius Paridī dīxit: 'quis, pāstor, hārum
deārum tibi fōrmōsissima uidētur? quis plūs pulchitūdinis praestat?'
meditātur Paris breue⁀tempus. tum: 20
'cūr mē rogās? nōn sum dignus. nam pāstor sum et arbiter melior
capellārum quam deārum erō. hae omnēs mihi pulcherrimae uidentur. sed
dīc mihi, eās iūdicābō ut sunt? nam melius mihi uidētur eās iūdicāre
nūdās, quod ita eae plūs pulchritūdinis praestabunt'.
respondit Mercurius: 'fac ut uīs, pāstor'.   25
ubi nūdae sunt, dea quaeque prīuātim eī loquitur.
Iūnō eī dīxit: 'potentissimus eris et in omnibus terrīs plūrimōs⁀annōs
rēgnābis.'
Minerua eī: 'fortissimus inter mortālīs eris et omnem⁀uītam artificia
optima sciēs.'   30
Venus autem eī: 'fēmina Graeca est, Helena nōmine, et pulcherrima
omnium. sī in mē plūs pulchritūdinis uidēs et mē pulcherrimam iūdicābis,
eam dabō tibi. uxōrem eam habēbis pulchriōrem quam omnīs aliās.'
Paris igitur breue⁀tempus meditātur. tum Venerem pulchriōrem quam deās
aliās esse iūdicāuit; et ob id iūdicium, inuīsī fuērunt Trōiānī et Iūnōnī et 35
Mineruae. post, Paris Helenam rapuit et laetissimus eam abdūxit et cum eā
Īlium uēnit et uxōrem habuit multōs⁀annōs.

(Hyginus, *Fabulae*: '*Paridis Iūdicium*'; Lucian, *Iūdicium Deārum*)

Outdoing the Greeks

The Roman attitude to Greek literature can be compared with the way Romans successfully managed
to control a diverse empire over such a long period – i.e. they acknowledged and used the strengths
of the people they had subdued. The Greeks, powerful and unconquerable as a cultural force, were
accepted for what they were and made to work for Rome. Roman writers both acknowledged the
Greek inspiration for their work and struggled to outdo it, even while ostensibly accepting Greek
superiority . . . Very occasionally, a writer even makes a claim for Roman superiority. For example,
Propertius writes of the as yet unfinished *Aeneid* of Virgil: 'Make way, Roman writers, make way you
Greeks! Something greater than the *Iliad* is being born.' (*World of Rome*, **438**)

abdūcō 3 *abdūxī* I lead away
alia . . . alia nom. s. f. one . . .
    another (from *alius a ud* other)
ali-us a ud other (cf. ūnus **54**)
ann-us ī 2m. year
arbiter arbitr-ī 2m. judge
artifici-um ī 2n. skill, craft
breue tempus for a short time
capell-a ae 1f. she-goat ←—
de-a ae 1f. goddess
dign-us a um worthy
eā (abl. s. f.) her
eae (nom. pl. f.) they
eam (acc. s. f.) her
eārum (gen. pl. f.) (of) those
eās line 23 (acc. pl. f.) them
eās line 15 (acc. pl. f.) those
eī lines 29, 31 (dat. s. m.) (sc.
    said) to him
eī lines 16, 26 (dat. s. m.) to him
eis (dat. pl. f.) to them
eius (gen. s. m.) of him, his
fōrmōsissim-us a um most
    beautiful (from *fōrmōsus*) ←—
fortissim-us a um bravest (from
    fortis)
Graec-us a um Greek
Helen-a ae 1f. Helen
id acc. s. n. that
Īd-a ae 1f. Mt Ida

Īli-um ī 2n. Troy (tr. to Troy)
inter (+ acc.) among
inuīs-us a um hateful to (+ dat.)
is (nom. s. m.) he
iūdici-um ī 2n. judgement
iūdicō 1 I judge
Iūnō Iūnōn-is 3f. Juno
laetissim-us a um very happy (tr.
    very happily) (from *laetus*)
meditor 1 dep. I think
melior nom. s. m. better (from
    bonus)
melius (nom. s. n.) better (from
    bonus)
Mercuri-us ī 2m. Mercury
Mineru-a ae 1f. Minerva
mōns mont-is 3m. mountain
mortālis mortāl-is 3m. mortal
multō much (lit. by much)
multōs annōs for many years
nūd-us a um naked
ob (+ acc.) because of
omnem uītam for all of (your) life
Paris Parid-is 3m. Paris
pariter equally
pāstor pāstōr-is 3m. shepherd
pessim-us a um very bad (from
    malus)
plūrimōs annōs for very many
    years

plūrim-us a um very many
plūs more (X gen.)
potentissim-us a um very
    powerful, most powerful (from
    potēns)
potius rather
praestō 1 I display
prīuātim privately
pulcherrim-us a um most
    beautiful (from *pulcher*)
pulchrior more beautiful (nom.
    s. f.: from *pulcher*)
pulchriōrem more beautiful (acc.
    s. f.: from *pulcher*)
pulchritūdō pulchritūdin-is 3f.
    beauty
quaeque (nom. s. f.) each (from
    quisque)
quam than
rapiō 3/4 *rapuī* I snatch
recipiō 3/4 *recēpī* I accept
rēgnō 1 I rule
retineō 2 *retinuī* I retain
solit-us a um usual
terr-a ae 1f. land
Trōiān-us a um Trojan
Trōiān-us ī 2m. Trojan
ueniō 4 *uēnī* I come
Venus Vener-is 3f. Venus

Grammar for 3A

is
accusative of time

comparative and superlative
adjectives

Learning vocabulary for 3A(i)

Noun
de-a ae 1f. goddess
discordi-a ae 1f. discord, strife,
    quarrel (with capital letter, the
    goddess Discord)
iānu-a ae 1f. door
Mineru-a ae 1f. Minerva, goddess
    of crafts and wisdom
terr-a ae 1f. land, earth
arbiter arbitr-ī 2m. judge
Mercuri-us ī 2m. Mercury,
    messenger of Jupiter
iūdici-um ī 2n. judgment

māl-um ī 2n. apple
mātrimōni-um ī 2n. marriage
Iūnō Iūnōn-is 3f. Juno, wife of
    Jupiter, goddess of marriage
Paris Parid-is 3m. Paris
pāstor pāstōr-is 3m. shepherd
pulchritūdō pulchritūdin-is 3f.
    beauty
Venus Vener-is 3f. Venus, goddess
    of love

Adjectives
ali-us a ud other (note n. s. *aliud*;
    gen. s. *-ius* dat. s. *aliī*, [like

ūnus **54**]; other cases like
    bonus)
breu-is e short, brief
fōrmōs-us a um beautiful,
    handsome, graceful, shapely

Verbs
iūdicō 1 I judge
meditor 1 dep. I think
ueniō 4 *uēnī uentum* I come

Others
plūs more (of in gen.)
quam than

Section 3A(ii)

*The Greeks in anger at Paris' behaviour send an expeditionary force to Troy,
which succeeds after ten years in capturing and destroying the stronghold by the
famous ruse of the 'Wooden Horse'. The remnants of the Trojans, now exiled
from their homeland, are led by Aeneas. His destined arrival in Italy to found
Rome is delayed for a long time by the opposition of Juno. She wants her
favourite city Carthage to rule the world. But Jupiter decrees that Rome will be
founded by Aeneas' distant descendants, go on to defeat Carthage (the Punic
Wars) and become the ruler of the whole world.*

Graecī īrātissimī bellum gerere et Īlium dēlēre et Helenam referre
cōnstituērunt; sed quamquam plūs quam nouem‾annōs ante eam urbem
mānsērunt, Īlium capere nōn potuērunt. Vlixēs igitur eōs līgneum equum   40
maximum facere iussit, hominum optimōrum plēnum. in eō scrīpsērunt
DANAĪ EQVVM MINERVAE DANT. equum eum in lītore posuērunt et
castra relīquērunt. Trōiānī laetissimī per portās equum in arcem Mineruae
dūxērunt.

> '... scandit fātālis māchina mūrōs,   45
> fēta armīs. puerī circum innūptaeque puellae
> sacra canunt.'

sed dum Trōiānī per illam noctem dormiunt, mīlitēs Graecī statim ex eō
equō exiērunt et portārum custōdēs occīdērunt; deinde portās aperuērunt,
et ubi mīlitēs plūrēs urbem intrāuērunt, Īlium cēpērunt. id fātum   50
Trōiānōrum fuit.

*The Greeks, very angry, decided to wage war and to destroy Troy and bring back
Helen. But although they remained for more than nine years before that city,
they were unable to capture Ilium. Ulysses therefore ordered them to make a
very large wooden horse, full of the best men. Upon it they wrote THE GREEKS
GIVE THE HORSE TO MINERVA. They placed that horse upon the shore and
left their camp. The Trojans very joyful(ly) brought the horse through the gates
into the citadel of Minerva.*

> '... The fateful engine climbs upon their walls,
> Pregnant with weapons. Round it boys and girls
> Unwed sing sacred songs.'

*But while the Trojans were asleep through that night, the Greek soldiers at once
came out of that horse and killed the guards of the gates; then they opened the
gates and when more soldiers had entered the city, they captured Troy. That was
the fate of the Trojans.*

Running vocabulary for 3A(ii)

ann-us ī 2m. year
aperi-ō 4 *aperuī* I open
arm-a ōrum 2n. pl. arms
arx arc-is 3f. citadel
bell-um ī 2n. war
can-ō 3 I sing
circum around
cōnstitu-ō 3 *cōnstituī* I decide
custōs custōd-is 3m. guard
Dana-ī ōrum 2m. pl. the Danaans
   (Greeks)
eam (acc. s. f.) that
eō line 41 (abl. s. m.) it
eō line 48 (abl. s. m.) that
eōs (acc. pl. m.) them
equ-us ī 2m. horse
eum (acc. s. m.) that
fātāl-is e fateful

fāt-um ī 2n. fate
fēt-us a um pregnant (with)
Graec-ī ōrum 2m. pl. the Greeks
Graec-us a um Greek
Helen-a ae 1f. Helen
id that (nom. s. n.)
Īli-um ī 2n. Ilium, Troy
innūpt-us a um unmarried
īrātissim-us a um very angry
   (from *īrātus*)
laetissim-us a um very happy (tr.
   very happily) (from *laetus*)
līgne-us a um wooden
lītus lītor-is 3n. shore
māchin-a ae 1f. machine
maxim-us a um very large (from
   magnus)
Mineru-a ae 1f. Minerva

mūr-us ī 2m. wall
nouem nine
nouem annōs for nine years
occīd-ō 3 *occīdī* I kill
plūrēs a more
pōnō 3 *posuī* I place
port-a ae 1f. gate
puer puer-ī 2m. boy
refer-ō referre rettulī I bring back
relinqu-ō 3 *relīquī* I leave
sacr-a ōrum 2 n. pl. sacred songs
scand-ō 3 I climb
Trōiān-ī ōrum 2 m. pl. the Trojans
Vlixēs Vlix-is 3m Ulysses
   (Odysseus)

Literature to serve Rome's needs

Aeneas, the founding figure of the Roman people, was the mythological embodiment of Roman family values. The standard image of Aeneas escaping from Troy is of a man with his old father on his shoulders and his young son in his hand. As developed by Virgil, this becomes the icon of Roman *pietas* ('respect'): the family man who looks back respectfully to the past generation and fights to secure the hope of the next. With his family, he carries the sacred symbols of its continuity, the Penates. Even if we find *pius Aenēās* ('pious Aeneas') a dull hero, his message comes through clearly enough: for the Roman, family values lay at the heart of respect for the gods and for the Roman community that was itself a family, the *patria* ('fatherland') . . .

The poet Ennius (2nd C BC) took Homer, composer of the great epic *Iliad*, as his model for a great epic history of Rome in the same style and form. Plautus staged comedies which look at first sight to be merely translations of Greek originals, but in fact fed all sorts of Roman elements into them. For example, in his speech in *Amphitruo* (p. 22), Sosia accurately describes Roman ways of justifying warfare and imposing terms on a defeated enemy. Virgil, on the other hand, in his *Aeneid*, took characters from Greek myth (e.g. Trojan Aeneas) and suffused them with the Roman ethos, turning them into heroes who would found Rome. (*World of Rome*, **301, 437**)

dux gentis Trōiānae Aenēas fuit. is fīlius Veneris et Anchīsae fuit (illa dea,
hic mortālis fuit). ubi mīlitēs Graecī Īlium dēlēuērunt, Aenēas profugus
ōrās Trōiae relinquit et plūrimōs‿annōs multa patitur ob īram Iūnōnis,
Iouis uxōris. nam, quod Iūnō amāuit Carthāginem, urbem Libyae dīuitem   55
et asperam et ferōcem futūram – immo dītiōrem et asperiōrem et
ferōciōrem quam omnīs aliās urbēs – nōluit Trōiānōs Rōmam condere,
urbem dītiōrem, ferōciōrem, meliōrem quam Carthāginem. sīc autem
Parcae uoluērunt: 'id fātum futūrum est: Trōiānī Rōmam condent, et
Carthāginem, urbem pēiōrem, in tribus bellīs asperrimīs et ferōcissimīs   60
uincent.' Iūnō tamen Aenēan ab Ītaliā multōs‿annōs, maria omnia circum,
arcēre uoluit.
'tantae mōlis erat Rōmānam condere gentem.'

sed Iuppiter nōluit Aenēan longē ab Ītaliā plūrēs‿annōs errāre. melius eī
uidētur Venerem cōnsōlārī, quod ea Aenēan amāuit. sīc igitur Iuppiter eī   65
dīxit:
'nōlī umquam timēre. meliōra tempora uenient. manent immōta fāta tibi.
uidēbis Rōmam futūram urbem dītiōrem, ferōciōrem, meliōrem quam
Carthāginem. et Aenēas, fīlius tuus, nunc mortālis, dīuīnus fīet. Aenēas in
Ītaliam ingrediētur. illīc bellum maximum geret. in eō bellō populōs   70
ferōcissimōs uincet et moenia Lāuīniī pōnet, urbis multō minōris quam
Rōmae futūrae. fīlius eius Iūlus trīgintā‿annōs rēgnābit. sed moenia
Lāuīniī relinquet et rēgnum in Albam Longam trānsferet, urbem māiōrem
quam Lāuīnium, sed multō minōrem quam Rōmam futūram. post
trecentōs annōs, Rōmulus nāscētur. hic Rōmam condet, urbem maximam   75
et dītissimam. hic moenia Rōmae pōnet et in urbe eā rēgnābit et dē
nōmine suō gentem "Rōmānam" appellābit. Rōmānī bella plūrima gerent
et per orbem tōtum plūrimōs‿annōs rēgnābunt.'

*But Jupiter did not want Aeneas to wander far from Italy for more years. It
seems better to him to console Venus, because she loved Aeneas. Therefore
Jupiter spoke to her thus:*
*'Do not ever be afraid. Better times will come. For you the fates remain
unmoved. You will see Rome about to become a city richer, more ferocious and
better than Carthage. And Aeneas, your son, now mortal, will become divine.
Aeneas will enter Italy. There he will fight a very great war. In that he will defeat
very ferocious peoples and will set up the walls of Lavinium, a city much
smaller than the future Rome. His son Iulus will reign for thirty years, but he
will abandon the walls of Lavinium and transfer his kingdom to Alba Longa, a
city larger than Lavinium, but much smaller than the future Rome. After three
hundred years, Romulus will be born. He will found Rome, a very large and
very rich city. He will set up the walls of Rome and will reign in that city and
will call his race "Roman" from his own name. The Romans will wage very
many wars and throughout the whole world will rule for very many years.'*

22. Aeneas arrives in Italy

Aenē-as ae 1m. (acc. *Aenēan*)
Aeneas
Alb-a Long-a ae 1f. Alba Longa
ali-us a ud other (cf. *ūnus* **54**)
Anchīs-es ae Anchises
ann-us ī 2m. year
appell-ō 1 I call
arce-ō 2 I keep away (from)
asper asper-a um harsh, cruel,
dangerous
asperiōrem (acc. s. f.: from *asper*)
harsher, crueller, more
dangerous
asperrim-us a um very harsh
(from *asper*)
bell-um ī 2n. war
Carthāgō Carthāgin-is 3f.
Carthage
circum (+ acc.) around (placed
after the noun and adjective it
governs here)
cond-ō 3 *condidī* I found
cōnsōlor 1 dep. I console,
comfort, encourage
dē (+ abl). from
dītiōrem (acc. s. f.: from *dīues*)
richer
dītissim-us a um very wealthy
(from *dīues*)
dīuīn-us a um divine
dux duc-is 3m leader
ea (nom. s. f.) she
eā (abl. s. f.) that
eī line 65 (dat. s. f.) to her
eī line 64 (dat. s. m.) to him
eius (gen. s. m.) of him, his
eō (abl. s. n.) that
erat it was
err-ō 1 I wander
fāt-um ī 2n. fate

ferōciōrem (acc. s. f.: from *ferōx*)
fiercer
ferōcissim-us a um very fierce
(from *ferōx*)
ferōx ferōc-is fierce
futūr-us a um future, to come,
destined to be
gēns gent-is 3f. race
Graec-us a um Greek
hic (line 53) the latter
id (nom. s. n.) that (thing)
Īli-um ī 2n. Ilium, Troy
illa (line 52) the former
illīc there
immōt-us a um unmoved,
unchanged
īr-a ae 1f. anger
is he (nom. s. m.)
Ītali-a ae 1f. Italy
Iūl-us ī 2m. Iulus
Lāuīni-um ī 2n. Lavinium
Liby-a ae 1f. Libya
longē far
māiōrem (acc. s. f.: from *magnus*)
greater, bigger
mare mar-is 3n. sea
maxim-us a um very large (from
magnus)
meliōra (nom. pl. n.: from *bonus*)
better
meliōrem (acc. s. f.: from *bonus*)
better
melius (nom. s. n.: from *bonus*)
better
minōrem (acc. s. f.: from *paruus*)
smaller
minōris (gen. s. f.: from *paruus*)
smaller
moeni-a um 3 n. pl. walls,
ramparts

mōlēs -is 3f. difficulty (here gen.,
'at the cost of . . . ')
mortālis mortāl-is 3m. (or
mortāl-is e adj.) mortal
multō (by) much
multōs annōs for many years
nāsc-or 3 I am born
ob (+ acc.) because of
ōr-a ae 1f. shore
orb-is is 3m world
Parc-ae ārum 1f. pl. the Fates
pēiōrem (acc. s. f.: from *malus*)
worse
plūrēs annōs for more years
plūrimōs annōs for very many
years
plūrim-us a um very many (from
multus)
pōnō 3 I set up, place
popul-us ī 2m. people
profug-us a um in flight, in exile
rēgn-ō 1 I reign, rule
rēgn-um ī 2n. kingdom
relinqu-ō 3 I leave
Rōm-a ae 1f. Rome
Rōmān-us a um Roman
Rōmul-us ī 2m. Romulus
su-us a um his
tant-us a um so great
tōt-us a um the whole (of)
trānsfer-ō trānsferre I transfer
trecent-ī ae a three hundred
trīgintā thirty
trīgintā annōs for thirty years
Trōi-a ae 1f. Troy
Trōiān-ī ōrum 2m. pl. the Trojans
Trōiān-us a um Trojan
umquam ever

'hīs ego nec mētās rērum nec tempora pōnō:
imperium sine fīne dedī. quīn aspera Iūnō   80
cōnsilia in melius referet, mēcumque fouēbit
Rōmānōs, rērum dominōs gentemque togātam.'

(Hyginus, *Fabulae*: '*Equus Troiānus*'; Virgil, *Aeneid* 2.237–9, 1.1–282)

asper a um cruel, dangerous
fīn-is 3m (or f.) end
foue-ō 2 *fōuī* I cherish, look after
gens gent-is 3f. race
imperi-um ī 2n. power

in melius (acc. s. n.: from *bonus*)
    for the better
mēt-a ae 1f. limit, turning-post
pōnō 3 I place
quīn anyhow

referō I alter
Rōmān-ī ōrum 2m. pl. the Romanr
togāt-us a um wearing the toga

Learning vocabulary for 3A(ii)

Nouns
Helen-a ae 1f. Helen
Ītali-a ae 1f. Italy
port-a ae 1f. gate
Rōm-a ae 1f. Rome
Aenē-ās ae 1m. (acc. *Aenēan*)
    Aeneas
ann-us ī 2m. year
equ-us ī 2m. horse
Graec-ī ōrum 2m. pl. the Greeks
Trōiān-ī ōrum 2m. pl. the Trojans
bell-um ī 2n. war
fāt-um ī 2n. fate
Īli-um ī 2n. Ilium, Troy
Lāuīni-um ī 2n. Lavinium

Carthāgō Carthāgin-is 3f.
    Carthage
dux duc-is 3m. leader, general
gēns gent-is 3f. race; tribe; clan;
    family; people
moeni-a um 3 n. pl. walls,
    ramparts
mortāl-is mortāl-is 3m.

Adjectives
asper -a um harsh, cruel,
    dangerous
ferōx ferōc-is fierce
futūr-us a um future, to come,
    destined to be
mortāl-is e mortal

Rōmān-us a um Roman
Trōiān-us a um Trojan

Verbs
rēgnō 1 I reign, rule
condō 3 *condidī conditus* I found
occīdō 3 *occīdī occīsus* I kill
pōnō 3 *posuī positus* I set up,
    place, position, put
relinquō 3 *relīquī relictus* I leave,
    abandon

Others
multō (by) much
ob (+ acc.) on account of,
    because of
umquam ever

Romulus and Remus

The Roman foundation myth was a very complex one. It was also different from the Greek ones in the way in which it did not point up positive elements like good order or natural advantages. Far from it. It focused instead on things which were agreed to be bad – wildness, exile, rootlessness, brutality and killing. Romulus and Remus were the miraculous sons of Mars, the god associated with the pointless fury of war. Turned out of their household, they were exposed to the savagery of nature, only to be rescued and suckled by a she-wolf, the animal that in the ancient countryside most commonly embodied ferocity. Wolves were a terrible and common threat, with none of the grand dignity attributed, alongside violence, to the lion. Later the twins were reared by shepherds, who of all people were considered to be outsiders and uncivilised. When they grew up they decided to found a city in the region where they had been exposed; but in a quarrel over who should have the right to found the city, Romulus killed his brother. He went on to establish Rome by encouraging the homeless and vagabonds of Italy to come to the city and take refuge at the Asylum. The son of his father, he added to these resources by pillaging his neighbours, and abducting from the neighbouring Sabines the womenfolk that his community needed. That the Romans said all this about their early days tells us much about their view of the world in the late Republic and early Empire. (*World of Rome*, **6**)

Section 3B **Romulus and Remus**

No less mythical than the story of Aeneas is the account Romans gave of the foundation of Rome itself. If the Romans wanted the Trojan story to tie Roman history closely to that of the Greeks, the Romulus and Remus legend seems designed to portray the Romans as inherently warlike and wild, with a close relationship to the countryside of Italy. In the first place, the twins are the offspring of the illicit union of the war god Mars with a Vestal virgin, Rhea Silvia. Secondly, they are suckled by a wolf and then discovered and brought up by a shepherd. Further, it will emerge that the fledgling Roman state, lacking man- and woman-power, needed to bring outsiders into Rome in order to grow, by treachery and *force majeure* in the case of women. Throughout Roman literature, these themes continue to be repeated and elaborated.

Section 3B(i)

Amulius drove out his brother Numitor and became king of Latium. But Numitor's sister, Rhea Silvia (a priestess of Vesta), is seduced by Mars and produces twins. Afraid of this development, Amulius decides to get rid of them. His plan does not succeed and the boys end up founding the city of Rome, though with the unfortunate loss in the process of Remus.

prīmus conditor et urbis et imperiī Rōmulus fuit, Marte nātus et Rheā
Siluiā, Vestae sacerdōte. sacerdōs, grauida facta ex Marte, nōn mentīta est,
sed hoc dē sē cōnfessa est et mox puerōs peperit geminōs. Fāma nōn   85
morāta est, sed rem statim dīuulgāuit. rēx Amūlius autem, dē sē et rēgnō
suō magnopere ueritus, geminōrum uītae statim minātus est; nam
Rōmulum cum Remō frātre necāre uoluit. eōs igitur in flūmen audācter

Running vocabulary for 3B(i)

Amūli-us ī Amulius
audācter boldly (from *audāx*)
conditor conditōr-is 3m. founder
cōnfessa est (she) confessed, acknowledged (from *cōnfiteor*)
dīuulg-ō 1 I make public
facta (nom. s. f.: from *fīō*) having been made
Fām-a ae 1f. the goddess Rumour
flūmen flūmin-is 3n. river
gemin-ī ōrum 2m. pl. twins
grauid-us a um pregnant (by: *ex* + abl.)

imperi-um ī 2n. rule, command; empire
magnopere very much
Mars Mart-is 3m. the god Mars
mentīta est (she) lied (from *mentior*)
minātus est (he) threatened, made threats against
morāta est (she) delayed (from *moror*)
nātus (nom. s. m.: from *nāscor*) born from X (abl.)
pariō 3/4 *peper-ī* I bear, give birth to

prīm-us a um first
puer puer-ī 2m. boy
rēgn-um ī 2n. kingdom
Rem-us ī 2m. Remus
Rhe-a ae Silui-a ae 1f. Rhea Silvia
Rōmul-us ī 2m. Romulus
sacerdōs sacerdōt-is 3f. priestess
sē line 85 herself (abl.)
sē line 86 himself (abl.)
su-us a um his; her; their
ueritus (nom. s. m. from *uereor*) fearing
Vest-a ae 1f. the goddess Vesta

abiēcit. sed mortuī nōn sunt, quod Tiberīnus flūmen suum repressit, et
lupa, secūta uāgītum eōrum puerōrum, ūbera sua īnfantibus obtulit.   90
Faustulus, pāstor rēgius, eōs repperit. tum cum geminīs in casam suam
celeriter sē tulit atque eōs bene ēducāuit.
ubi adulēscentes factī sunt, geminī Amūlium interfēcērunt et Numitōrī,
auō suō, rēgnum restituērunt. sed Rōmulus moenia urbis nouae aedificāre
uoluit. Rōmulus sīc frātrem suum adlocūtus est: 95
'Reme, uīsne urbem nouam aedificāre?'
respondit eī Remus:
'ita uērō. sed uter nostrī urbem reget?'
Rōmulus, frātrem suum adlocūtus, respondit:
'cūr nōn augurāmur?'   100
Remus igitur in montem Auentīnum, Romulus in Pālatīnum sē tulit; ille
sex uulturēs, hic duodecim cōnspicātus est. quod uictor fuit, Rōmulus
urbem suam 'Rōmam' appellāuit, ut dīcunt. propter augurium laetī, cīuēs
moenia aedificāre coepērunt, et mox fundāmenta nouī mūrī facta sunt.
Rōmulus Celerem, custōdem suum, adlocūtus sīc iussit: 105
'nōlō quemquam mūrōs trānsīre; nam minimī sunt. sī quis trānsīre audet,
interfice eum!' Celer, hoc pollicitus, iuxtā mūrōs morātus est.
hoc mandātum autem Remus ignōrāuit. ad fundāmenta sē tulit. ibi murōs
minimōs conspicatus contempsit. 'sic populus tutus erit?' locutus, nec
morātus, mūrōs trānsīre stultē ausus est. Celer Remum, hoc stultē ausum, 110
celeriter interfēcit.

(Florus, *Epitome*: *A Romulo Temporum Regum Septem*, 1.1; Aurelius Victor, *De Viris*
Illustribus Urbis Romae 1; Ovid, *Fasti* 4.835–43)

---

abiciō 3/4 *abiēcī* I throw, cast
  away
adlocūtus (nom. s. m.) addressing
adlocūtus est (nom. s. m.) he
  addressed (from *adloquor*)
adulēscēns adulēscent-is 3m.
  youth
aedificō 1 I build
Amūli-us ī 2m Amulius
appell-ō 1 I call
Auentīn-us a um Aventine
auguri-um ī 2n. augury
auguror 1 dep. I take the auguries
ausum (acc. s. m.) having dared
  (from *audeō*)
ausus est (nom. s. m.) he dared
  (from *audeō*)
au-us ī 2m. grandfather
cas-a ae 1f. cottage
Celer Celer-is 3m. Celer
celeriter quickly (from *celer*)
coep-ī I have begun

cōnspicātus (nom. s. m.) having
  caught sight of (from
  cōnspicor)
cōnspicātus est (nom. s. m.) (he)
  saw (from *cōnspicor*)
contemnō 3 *contempsī* I despise,
  scorn
custōs custōd-is 3m. guardian
duodecim twelve
ēduc-ō 1 I bring up, educate
facta sunt (nom. pl. n.) (they)
  were made (from *fīō*)
factī sunt (nom. pl. m.: from *fīō*)
  (they) became
Faustul-us ī 2m. Faustulus
flūmen flūmin-is 3n. river
fundāment-um ī 2n. foundation
gemin-ī ōrum 2m. pl. twins
hic (l.102) the latter
ignōr-ō 1 I do not know (of)
ille (l.101) the former
īnfāns īnfant-is 3m. infant

interficiō 3/4 *interfēcī* I kill,
  murder
iuxtā (+ acc.) near
laet-us a um happy, joyful
locūtus (nom. s. m.: from *loquor*)
  having spoken
lup-a ae 1f. she-wolf
mandāt-um ī 2n. command
mōns mont-is 3m. hill
morātus (nom. s. m.) delaying,
  having delayed (from *moror*)
morātus est (nom. s. m) (he)
  stayed (from *moror*)
mortuī sunt (nom. pl. m) they died
  (from *morior*)
mūr-us ī 2m. wall
nou-us a um new
Numitor Numitōr-is 3m. Numitor
offerō offerre obtulī I offer
Palātīn-us a um (sc. *mōns*)
  Palatine
pāstor pāstōr-is 3m. shepherd

pollicitus (nom. s. m.: from
    polliceor) having promised
popul-us ī 2m. people
puer puer-ī 2m. boy
quemquam (acc. s. m.) anyone
quis (nom. s. m.) (after *sī*) anyone
rēgi-us a um of the king
rēgn-um ī 2n. kingdom
reg-ō 3 I rule
Rem-us ī 2m. Remus

reperiō 4 *repperī* I find
reprimō 3 *repressī* I hold back
restitu-ō 3 *restituī* I restore
Rōm-a ae 1f. Rome
Rōmul-us ī 2m. Romulus
secūta (nom. s. f.) having
    followed (from *sequor*)
sē tulit (he) betook himself (*ferō
    ferre tulī*)
stultē foolishly (from *stultus*)

su-us a um his; their
Tiberīn-us ī 2m. the river god
    Tiber
trānse-ō trānsīre I cross
tūt-us a um safe
uāgīt-us ūs 4m. wailing, crying
ūber ūber-is 3n. dug, teat, udder
uictor uictōr-is 3m. victor
uter (nom. s. m.) which of the two
uultur uultur-is 3m. vulture

Grammar for 3B

**perfect deponents active
semi-deponents**

**deponent perfect participle
adverbs**

sē, suus

23. Romulus and Remus are taken in by the shepherd Faustulus and his wife

Learning vocabulary for 3B(i)

Nouns
au-us ī 2m. grandfather
mūr-us ī 2m. wall
puer puer-ī 2m. boy
Rōmul-us ī 2m. Romulus
fundāment-um ī 2n. foundation
imperi-um ī 2n. command; order;
    empire
rēgn-um ī 2n. kingdom
custōs custōd-is 3m. guardian
Mars Mart-is 3m. the god Mars

flūmen flūmin-is 3n. river

Adjectives
grauid-us a um pregnant
laet-us a um joyful, happy
nou-us a um new
su-us a um his; her; their

Verbs
aedificō 1 I build
nāscor 3 dep. *nāt-us* I am born

interficiō 3/4 *interfēcī interfectus*
    I kill, murder
sē fert, sē tulit (s)he betakes
    (her)himself, (s)he betook
    (her)himself (*ferō ferre tulī
    lātus*)
trānseō trānsīre trānsiī trānsitum
    I cross

Others
audācter boldly (from *audāx*)

Section 3B(ii)

The new city lacks people and more especially women. After vain attempts to persuade neighbours to offer marriage contracts, Romulus concocts a plan to stage an entertainent in Rome, invite the local Sabines and kidnap their unmarried women.

sed imāgō urbis magis quam urbs facta est: nam incolae dēfuērunt. lūcus
tamen fuit in‿proximō; Rōmulus hunc lūcum 'asÿlum' facit, et hūc statim
plūrimī hominēs adgressī sunt. ibi Latīnī, Tuscī, trānsmarīnī, Trōiānī et
multī aliī celeriter congregātī sunt. ita ex uariīs elementīs factus est   115
populus Rōmānus.
sed nūllae mulierēs adgressae sunt et in asÿlum congregātae sunt. tum ex
cōnsiliō patrum, Rōmulus lēgātōs circā uīcīnās gentēs mīsit. eī igitur in
urbēs uariās sē tulērunt et societātem cōnūbiumque nouī populī suī petere
ausī sunt. nusquam autem uīcīnī benīgnē audīuērunt, nec societātem nec   120
cōnūbium pollicitī sunt; nōn enim uoluērunt populum Rōmānum,
māiōrem factum, potentiōrem quam sē esse.

But the image of a city rather than an (actual) city was created: for inhabitants were lacking. However, there was a grove in the neighbourhood; Romulus made this grove 'an asylum' [place of refuge] and hither at once very many men came. There Latins, Etruscans, people from overseas, Trojans and many others, quickly gathered. Thus the Roman people was created out of differing elements. But no women came and gathered in the asylum. Then, upon the advice of the fathers [senators], Romulus sent envoys around the neighbouring tribes. They therefore betook themselves to different cities and dared to ask for alliance and marriage of [i.e. with] the new people. Nowhere, however, did their neighbours hear them kindly, nor did they promise alliance and marriage; for they did not wish the Roman people, when it had become bigger, to be more powerful than themselves.

Rōmulus igitur, breue tempus sēcum meditātus, spectāculum gentibus
uīcīnīs parāuit. plūrimī Rōmam adgressī conuēnērunt, maximē Sabīnōrum
līberī ac coniugēs. ubi spectāculī tempus uēnit, tum orta est uīs, et iuuenēs   125
Rōmānī, nōn multum morātī, uirginēs Sabīnōrum celeriter rapuērunt.
parentēs uirginum miserē profūgērunt, īrātīque deōs magnopere
inuocāuērunt; uirginibus tamen Rōmulus sīc benīgnē locūtus est:
'nōlīte nōbīs magnopere īrāscī, sed potius patribus tuīs īrāsciminī. illī
enim, hominēs superbissimī, cōnūbium nōbīs nōn pollicitī sunt. uōs tamen   130
in mātrimōnium dūcere maximē uolumus et coniugēs habēre. mollīte īrās
et benīgnē date nōbīs animōs tuōs, ut coniugēs cārissimae. saepe, ex
iniūriā, grātia orta est.'
hīs uerbīs suīs mollīuit paulum animōs uirginum.

nam cupiditās et amor ad muliebre ingenium maximē efficācēs precēs sunt.   135

For desire and love are the most effective prayers to the female intellect.

(Livy 1.9)

Running vocabulary for 3B(ii)

adgressae sunt (nom. pl. f.: from
  adgredior) (they) came
adgressī (nom. pl. m.: from
  adgredior) having come to
adgressī sunt (nom. pl. m.: from
  adgredior) (they) came
amor amōr-is 3m. love
asÿl-um ī 2n. sanctuary, place of
  refuge
ausī sunt (nom. pl. m.: from
  audeō) they dared
benīgnē kindly, favourably
cār-us a um dear (sup. *cārissimus*)
celeriter quickly (from *celer*)
circā (+ acc.) around
congregatae sunt (nom. pl. f.:
  from *congregor*) (they)
  gathered together
congregātī sunt (nom. pl. m.:
  from *congregor*) (they)
  gathered together
coniūnx coniug-is 3f. wife
cōnūbi-um ī 2n. marriage
conueniō 4 *conuēnī* I come
  together
cupiditās cupiditāt-is 3f. desire
dēsum dēesse dēfuī I am lacking
efficāx efficāc-is effective
element-um ī 2n. element,
  beginning
facta est (nom. s. f. (from *fīō*)) (it)
  was made, came into being
factum (acc. s. m.: from *fīō*)
  having become

factus est (nom. s. m.: from *fīō*)
  (it) was made, came into
  existence
grāti-a ae 1f. friendship
imāgō imāgin-is 3f. appearance
incol-a ae 1m. and f. inhabitant
ingeni-um ī 2n. mind
iniūri-a ae 1f. injury, wrongdoing
in proximō nearby
inuocō 1 I invoke, pray to
īr-a ae 1f. anger
īrāscor 3 dep. *īrātus* I become
  angry with X (dat.)
Latīn-ī ōrum 2m. pl. Latins
līber-ī ōrum 2m. pl. children
locūtus est (nom. s. m.: from
  loquor) (he) spoke (to)
lūc-us ī 2m. grove, wood
magis more
magnopere earnestly, very much,
  greatly
maximē especially, most of all
meditātus (nom. s. m.: from
  meditor) having thought,
  having considered
miserē wretchedly
molliō 4 I soften
morātī (nom. pl. m.: from *moror*)
  having delayed
muliebr-is e of a woman
multum much, for long
nusquam nowhere
orta est (nom. s. f.: from *orior*)
  there arose, there began;

there has arisen, there has
  begun
parēns parent-is 3m. and f. parent
parō 1 I get ready, prepare,
  organise
pater patr-is 3m. senator
  (= father of the city)
paulum a little
petō 3 *petīuī* I seek, ask for
pollicitī sunt (nom. pl. m.: from
  polliceor) (they) promised
popul-us ī 2m. people
potēns potent-is powerful
potius rather
prec-ēs um 3f. pl. prayer, entreaty
profugiō 3/4 *profūgī* I flee, run
  away
rapiō 3/4 *rapuī* I seize, snatch
  away
Sabīn-ī ōrum 2m. pl. Sabines
saepe often
sē line 122 themselves
societās societāt-is 3f.
  partnership, political alliance
spectācul-um ī 2n. public
  entertainment, show
superb-us a um haughty, arrogant
trānsmarīn-ī ōrum 2m. pl. people
  from overseas
Tusc-ī ōrum 2m. pl. Etruscans
uari-us a um diverse, various
uirgō uirgin-is 3f. unmarried
  woman
uīs f. violence

Wandering heroes

A common thing to say about your beginnings in antiquity was that your ancestors had made a long journey from elsewhere to found your community. In Italy, ancient connections with the Greek world were often given a background in the myth of Herakles (= Hercules) and his wanderings, or of the stories of the wanderings of heroes and their followers which followed the Trojan war – tales made famous in the epics of Homer. The Romulus story did not fit easily into this type of myth. Hercules made an appearance in the original stories, and was worshipped at a Great Altar, appropriately in the part of Rome where the river-harbour on the Tiber encouraged the settlement of people from overseas. But the Romans found a way of tying themselves into the world of Greece and its history in the story of Aeneas, the Trojan hero, who wandered the world after the sack of Troy, before settling in central Italy to found the community into which Romulus and Remus were later to be born. By the fourth century BC there was a cult to Aeneas at the sacred centre of Lavinium, in which Roman magistrates were involved. It is likely that the Aeneas myth became popular at the very time when Rome started to be of significance in the wider world of the Mediterranean, and it took its definitive form in the epic, the *Aeneid*, which Virgil wrote to glorify the Rome of the first emperor, Augustus. (*World of Rome*, **7**)

24. The rape of the Sabine women

Learning vocabulary for 3B(ii)

Nouns

grāti-a ae 1f. friendship (*grātiae* thanks)
līber-ī ōrum 2m. pl. children
lūc-us ī 2m. grove, wood
popul-us ī 2m. people
cōnūbi-um ī 2n. marriage
spectācul-um ī 2n. public entertainment, show
amor amōr-is 3m. love

coniūnx coniug-is 3f. wife; 3m. husband
imāgō imāgin-is 3f. appearance; ghost; idea
pater patr-is 3m. senator (*patrēs* = fathers of the city) (father)
uirgō uirgin-is 3f. unmarried woman

Adjectives

benīgn-us a um kind, favourable
uari-us a um diverse, various

Verbs

inuocō 1 I invoke, call upon
rapiō 3/4 *rapuī raptus* I seize, snatch away, carry away, plunder
orior 4 dep. *ortus* I arise, begin; spring from, originate

Others

celeriter quickly (from *celer*)
potius rather

Additional revision vocabulary

Revise the following irregular deponent verbs with their principal parts, paying special attention to the perfect participles:

adgredior 3/4 dep. *adgressus* I approach; I attack (note also *ēgredior* I go/come out, *ingredior* I enter, *prōgredior* I advance, have the same principal parts)
adipīscor 3 dep. *adeptus* I gain, get

īrāscor 3 dep. *īrātus* (+ dat.) I grow angry with
loquor 3 dep. *locūtus* I speak (note also *adloquor* I address, speak to, has the same principal parts)
oblīuīscor 3 dep. *oblītus* I forget

patior 3 dep. *passus* I endure, suffer, allow
proficīscor 3 dep. *profectus* I set out
sequor 3 dep. *secūtus* I follow
uideor 2 dep. *uīsus* I seem

Section 3C **Sextus Tarquinius and Lucretia, 509 BC**

Tradition had it that there were seven kings of Rome. These were Romulus, Numa Pompilius, Tullius Hostilis, Ancus Martius, Tarquinius Priscus, Servius Tullius and Tarquinius Superbus.

A striking feature of the way Romans told their history is the appearance of women at important turning points (e.g. the Sabine women at the very start of their city's evolution). This tale of Lucretia's rape by Sextus Tarquinius, son of the King, Tarquinius Superbus, is another example. Her rape and suicide trigger a moment of high historical importance: the expulsion of monarchy from Rome and start of the Republic. The story pinpoints a central Roman belief about how their state should be governed: not by one man, who could use his monarchic power to override with impunity traditional Roman virtues such as chastity and frugal living, but by constitutional, Republican consensus. Not for nothing did *rēs pūblica* mean '*public* property/business/matter'.

Section 3C(i)

509 BC. Rome was ruled by the Etruscan king Tarquinius Superbus (and 'haughty, contemptuous' is indeed how Roman historians saw him). His son Sextus Tarquinius was a true son of his father. One evening, while besieging the town of Ardea, he and his companions fall into discussing the virtues of their wives. One of his companions, Collatinus, Lucretia's husband, claims the prize when on a surprise visit his wife outdoes the other matrons in her virtuous lifestyle. But her virtue arouses Sextus Tarquinius' lust, and he plots to usurp Collatinus' marital rights.

dum forte cēnant, Sextus Tarquinius et Collātīnus, coniūnx Lucrētiae, et
aliī iuuenēs, dē uxōribus loquī coepērunt. suam quisque uxōrem
magnopere laudāuit; et inde certāmen ortum est. 'uxor mea,' dīxit quīdam
'honestius uīuit quam uestrae omnēs. nam lānam dīligentius facit, domum
impigrius cūrat, līberōs seuērius ēducat.' alius autem respondit 'immō   140
uxor mea dīligentius, impigrius, seuērius uīuit quam aliae. ego certō uictor
futūrus sum.' tum Collātīnus eīs sīc locūtus est:

Running vocabulary for 3C(i)

cēnō 1 I dine
certāmen certāmin-is 3n. contest, competition
coepī I have begun, I began
Collātīn-us ī 2m. L. Tarquinius Collatinus
dīligentius more carefully (from *dīligēns*)
ēducō 1 I bring up, educate

forte by chance
honestius more honourably (from *honestus*)
impigrius more energetically (from *impiger*)
inde thence, from this
lān-a ae 1f. wool
laudō 1 I praise
Lucrēti-a ae 1f. Lucretia

quīdam (nom. s. m.) one
quisque (nom. s. m.) each
seuērius more strictly (from *seuērus*)
Sext-us ī Tarquini-us ī 2m. Sextus Tarquinius (son of the king Tarquinius Superbus)
uictor uictōr-is 3m. victor
uīuō 3 I live

'nōlīte plūs loquī. nēmō honestius uīuit quam uxor mea. nēmō Lucrētiam
meam uictūrus est. cūr nōn cōnscendimus equōs? mox oculīs melius quam
uerbīs cognitūrī sumus mulierum nostrārum ingenia.'   145

Rōmam igitur equīs celerrimē prōgressī sunt. quō ubi peruēnērunt, aliae
mulierēs in conuīuiō luxūque cum aequālibus tempus terunt; Lucrētia
autem inter seruās in mediō aedium sedet et lānam facit. 'ut uidētis,'
inquit Collātīnus 'uxor mea semper eadem est. ego certissimē uictor sum.'
Lucrētia coniugem et aliōs iuuenīs benīgnē excēpit. uictor marītus etiam   150
benīgnius domum inuītāuit aliōs iuuenīs. ibi Tarquinium mala libīdō stuprī
cēpit; nam Lucrētiae et pulcherrima fōrma et castitās admīrābilis eum
incitāuit.

*Therefore on their horses they quickly advanced to Rome. When they had
arrived there, the other women were wasting their time with their friends in
dining and extravagance; but Lucretia was sitting among her slave-women in
the middle of the house and making wool. 'As you see,' said Collatinus, 'my wife
is always the same. Most surely, I am the winner.' Lucretia received her
husband and the other young men kindly. Her victorious husband more kindly
still invited the other young men to his house. There a gross lust for adultery
gripped Tarquinius; for Lucretia's most beautiful form and her admirable
chastity spurred him on.*

ubi rediērunt in castra iuuenēs, etiam magis incendit libīdō eadem animum
Tarquiniī. sēcum meditātus 'nōnne uultus eī pulcherrimus?' inquit 'nōnne   155
uerba optima? nōnne color ēlegantissimus? nōnne faciēs fōrmosissima?
magis magisque in⌐diēs amōre ārdeō. sed quid futūrum est? nōnne
Lucrētia mē amātūra est? nesciō. difficillimum erit, sed nihilōminus
ausūrus sum ultima; ausūrōs forsque deusque maximē iuuat.'

---

admīrābil-is e astonishing,
  wonderful
aequāl-is 1f. contemporary, friend
amātūra est (she) is destined to
  love (from *amō*)
amōre with love (abl. of *amor*)
ārdeō 2 I burn
ausūrōs (acc. pl. m.) people who
  will dare
ausūrus sum I am going to dare
  (from *audeō*)
benīgnius more kindly (from
  benīgnus)
castitās castitāt-is 3f. chastity
celerrimē very quickly (from
  celer)

certissimē for absolute certain
  (from *certus*)
cognitūrī sumus we are destined
  to find out
Collātīn-us ī 2m. L. Tarquinius
  Collatinus
color colōr-is 3m. colouring,
  complexion
cōnscendō 3 I mount
conuīui-um ī 2n. feasting
eadem (nom. s. f.) the same
ēlegāns ēlegant-is elegant, refined
equīs on (their) horses (abl. pl.
  equus)
excipiō 3/4 *excēpī* I receive
faci-ēs ēī 5f. face

fors f. chance
honestius more honourably (from
  honestus)
incendō 3 *incendī* I inflame
incitō 1 excite
in diēs as the days go by, day by
  day
ingeni-um ī 2n. mind
inuītō 1 I invite
iuuō 1 I help
lān-a ae 1f. wool
libīdō libīdin-is 3f. desire
Lucrēti-a ae 1f. Lucretia
lux-us ūs 4m. extravagance
magis more (from *magnus*)
marīt-us ī 2m. husband

maximē most, very much (from *magnus*)

medium ī 2n. the middle

melius better (adverb from *melior*)

nēmō (nom. s.) no one

nihilōminus nevertheless

nōnne surely?, not?

oculīs with (our) eyes (abl. pl. of *oculus*)

peruenio 4 *peruēnī* I arrive

quō to where (tr. 'there')

sedeō 2 I sit

seru-a ae 1f. female slave

stupr-um ī 2n. (illicit) sexual intercourse

Tarquini-us ī 2m. Sextus Tarquinius

terō 3 I waste

uerbīs with (our) words (abl. pl. of *uerbum*)

uictor uictōr-is 3m. victor

uictūrus est is destined to beat (from *uincō*)

uīuō 3 I live

ultim-us a um most extreme, utmost, greatest

uult-us ūs 4m. appearance

Grammar for 3C

future participle active and deponent principal parts	**ablative of means** *nōnne? īdem, nēmō*	**comparative and superlative adverbs**

Learning vocabulary for 3C(i)

Nouns

lān-a ae 1f. wool

fors f. chance (only nom., and abl. *forte* 'by chance')

uictor uictōr-is 3m. victor

Adjectives

dīligēns dīligent-is careful

honest-us a um honourable

impiger impigr-a impigrum energetic

seuēr-us a um strict, stern

Verbs

cēnō 1 I dine

ēducō 1 I bring up, educate

uīuō 3 *uīxī uīctum* I live

Others

in diēs day by day, as the days go by

magis more

nōnne doesn't/don't? surely not?

Lucretia

It is a curiosity of early Roman history that at some key turning-points we find stories about women. Perhaps the most famous of these was of Lucretia, whose cynical rape by a son of the king, Tarquinius Superbus, and subsequent suicide enraged a noble, Lucius Junius Brutus, and drove him to expel the king and his family from Rome about 510/509 BC. The romantic stories of the expulsion of the Tarquins were greatly elaborated in the literary tradition. But there is no need to doubt that a revolution took place and that its leaders came from within the Roman aristocracy. Similar tussles between powerful aristocrats and hereditary one-man rule were taking place at much this time in South Italy, Sicily and Greece. What is important is the way in which later Roman historians characterised the political change which came about in 510/509 BC. For centuries to come, hatred of the idea of domination by one man was central to the way in which the institutions of the Republic developed. When the monarchy was overthrown, the question became: who now was to exercise the *imperium* which the kings had had? For Livy (2.1) 'you could reckon the origins of freedom as lying more in the fact that the *imperium* held by the consuls lasted only a year than in any diminution of the powers which the kings once held'. (*World of Rome*, **12**)

Section 3C(ii)

Tarquin arrives at Lucretia's house on a surprise visit and is received with great friendliness. But during the night, he sneaks into Lucretia's room and blackmails her into submission.

tālia sēcum ārdentissimē meditātus, Sextus Tarquinius Collātiam uēnit.   160
Lucrētia īgnāra eum etiam benīgnius quam anteā excēpit et parāuit etiam
dīligentius epulās hostī suō. ille post epulās in cubiculum suum intrat. ubi
omnēs dormīuērunt, surrēxit et cum gladiō uēnit in cubiculum Lucrētiae.
sinistrā manū pectus Lucrētiae oppressit et:
'tacē, Lucrētia' inquit; 'Sextus Tarquinius sum; ferrum in manū est. nisi   165
tacēbis, eōdem‿gladiō moritūra es.'
illa, pauida ex somnō, respondēre nōn potuit, sed tremit et sē rogat:
'quid factūra sum? pugnābō? at uir fēminam facillimē uictūrus est.
clāmābō? at in dextrā gladius est. sī clāmābō, eōdem‿gladiō moritūra sum.
effugiam? at mē manibus‿suīs crūdēlissimē oppressit. nēmō mē   170
dēfēnsūrus est.'
etiam magis īnstat Tarquinius precibus pretiōque minīsque; nec prece nec
pretiō nec minīs eam mōuit ille.
Tarquinius eī dīxit:
'nīl agis; nisi mihi cessūra es, fāmam tuam crīminibus‿falsīs crūdēlissimē   175
dēlēbō. ita enim patrem et coniugem tuum certiōrēs‿faciam: "Lucrētiam
et seruum in eōdem‿lectō in sordidō adulteriō dēprehendī; ambōs igitur
eōdem‿gladiō interfēcī" '.
eīs minīs Tarquiniī libīdō pudīcitiam Lucrētiae uīcit. inde profectus
Tarquinius celerrimē domum redit.   180

Running vocabulary for 3C(ii)

adulteri-um ī 2n. adultery
anteā before
ārdentissimē in a very impassioned way (from *ārdēns*)
benīgnius more kindly (from *benignus*)
celerrimē very quickly (from *celer*)
certiōrem faci-ō I inform X (acc.)
cessūra es you (f. s.) are going to yield (from *cēdō*)
Collāti-a ae 1f. Collatia (home of L. Tarquinius Collatinus and Lucretia)
Collātiam to Collatia
crīminibus falsīs by false accusations (abl. pl. of *crīmen falsum*)

crūdēlissimē most cruelly (from *crūdēlis*)
cubicul-um ī 2n. bedroom
dēfēnsūrus est (nom. s. m.) (he) is going to defend (from *dēfendō*)
dēprehendō 3 *dēprehendī* I catch
dextr-a ae 1f. right hand
dīligentius more carefully (from *dīligēns*)
effugiō 3/4 I escape, run away
eōdem gladiō by/with the same sword (abl. s.)
eōdem lectō the same bed (abl. s.)
epul-ae ārum 1 f. pl. meal
excipiō 3/4 *excēpī* I receive
facillimē very easily (from *facilis*)
factūra sum (nom. s. f.: from *faciō*) I am going to do

fām-a ae 1f. reputation
ferr-um ī 2n. sword
gladi-us ī 2m. sword
īgnār-us a um ignorant (sc. of Tarquinius' intentions)
inde thence
īnstō 1 I urge, press my case
libīdō libīdin-is 3f. lust
Lucrēti-a ae 1f. Lucretia
manibus suīs with his hands (abl. pl. of *manus sua*)
minīs with threats (abl. pl. of *minae*)
moritūra es (nom. s. f.: from *morior*) you are destined to die
moritūra sum (nom. f. s.: from *morior*) I shall die
moueō 2 *mōuī* I move
nēmō no one (nom. s.)

opprimō 3 *oppressī* I press down (on)
parō 1 I prepare
pauid-us a um terrified
pectus pector-is 3n. breast
prece by prayers (abl. of *prex*)
precibus with prayers (abl. of *precēs*)

pretiō with bribery (abl. s. of *pretium*)
pudīciti-a ae 1f. chastity
Sext-us Tarquini-us 2m. Sextus Tarquinius (son of the king Tarquinius Superbus)
sinistrā manū with his left hand (abl. of *sinistra manus: sinister sinistr-a um* left)

somn-us ī 2m. sleep
sordid-us a um filthy
surgō 3 *surrēxī* I arise
tāl-is e such
tremō 3 I tremble
uictūrus est (nom. s. m.) (he) is going to defeat (from *uincō*)

25. The rape of Lucretia

Learning vocabulary for 3C(ii)

Nouns
epul-ae ārum 1f. pl. meal; feast
min-ae ārum 1f. pl. threats
gladi-us ī 2m. sword

preti-um ī 2n. price, value, reward
libīdō libīdin-is 3f. lust, desire
prec-ēs um 3 f. pl. (occasionally *prex prec-is* 3f.) prayer(s)

Verbs
opprimō 3 *oppressī oppressus* I press down (on)
morior 3/4 dep. *mortuus* I die

Section 3C(iii)

Lucretia summons her father and her husband, explains what has happened, demands justice against the rapist and then kills herself. Brutus swears vengeance and ends the rule of kings at Rome.

inde Lucrētia maesta et ad patrem et ad uirum nūntium eundem mīsit:
'uenīte cum fidēlibus amīcīs; festināte; rēs atrōx facta est.'
uēnērunt celerrimē pater Sp. Lucrētius et Collātīnus cum L. Iūniō Brūtō.
Lucrētiam maestam in cubiculō inuēnērunt. quaesīuit uir:
'satin saluē?'   185
Lucrētia 'minimē' inquit. 'nēmō salua esse potest, sī pudīcitiam āmīsit.
uestīgia uirī aliēnī, Collātīne, in lectō sunt tuō; ille corpus tantum uiolāuit,
animus meus tamen īdem est et īnsōns; mors testis erit. adulterum
ferōcissimē pūnīte: Sextus Tarquinius est.'
dedērunt omnēs eandem fidem et ueniam eandem. sīc enim Lucrētiam   190
cōnsōlātī sunt:
'nōnne Tarquinius maximē noxius est? mēns hominum peccat, nōn
corpus; nēmō noxius est sī cōnsilium abest.'
sed illa:
'quamquam noxiam mē nōn habeō, supplicium tamen grātius acceptūra   195
sum quam uīuere. nēmō impudīca exemplō Lucrētiae uīuet.'
nec morāta, suum pectus ferrō celerrimē fīxit, prōlāpsaque in uulnus
moribunda cecidit. conclāmāuērunt uir paterque. Brūtus tamen ferrum ex
uulnere Lucrētiae extraxit et prae sē tenuit:
'per hunc castissimum sanguinem, ego Tarquinium Superbum uī et armīs   200
exsecūtūrus sum, nec illum nec alium quemquam rēgem esse Romae
passūrus sum.'
Brūtus clāmōre Quirītēs maximē concitāuit; Tarquinius cum suīs
celerrimē fūgit: diēs rēgibus illa suprēma fuit.

*Then Lucretia sad(ly) sent the same message to her father and her husband:
'Come with trusted friends; make haste; an appalling deed has been done.' They
came very quickly, her father, Spurius Lucretius and Collatinus, with Lucius
Iunius Brutus. They found the sad Lucretia in her bedroom. Her husband asked:
'Are you all right?' Lucretia replied, 'Not at all. No one can be "all right", if she
has lost her chastity. The traces of another man, Collatinus, are upon your bed;*

26. Brutus, accompanied by two lictors and accensus (attendant)

he violated only my body, but my mind is the same and innocent; death shall be
my witness. Punish the adulterer most ferociously: it is Sextus Tarquinius.'
Everyone gave the same promise and the same pardon. For they consoled
Lucretia thus: 'Tarquinius is most guilty, is he not? It is the mind of men that
sins, not the body; no one is guilty if intention is absent.' But she (replied):
'Although I do not hold myself guilty, nonetheless I shall be inclined more
gratefully to receive punishment than to live. No unchaste woman shall live
because of Lucretia's example.'

Not delaying, she very swiftly stabbed her breast with a sword, and collapsing
upon the wound fell dying. Her father and husband let out a cry together. But
Brutus pulled the sword from Lucretia's wound and held it before him (saying):
'By this most chaste blood, I intend to pursue Tarquin the Proud by force and by
arms, nor shall I suffer him or anyone else to be a king at Rome.' Brutus stirred
up the Quirites (Romans) very greatly with his cry; Tarquinius fled very quickly
with his followers: that day was the last one for kings.

(Livy 1.57–9; Ovid, Fasti 2.721–852)

Running vocabulary for 3C(iii)

absum I am absent
acceptūra sum (nom. f. s) I shall receive (from *accipiō*)
adulter adulter-ī 2m. adulterer
aliēn-us a um strange
amīc-us ī 2m. friend
armīs with arms (abl. of *arm-a ōrum* 2n. pl.)
atrōx atrōc-is appalling
Brūtus see L. Iūnius Brūtus
cadō 3 *cecidī* I fall
cast-us a um chaste
celerrimē very quickly (from *celer*)
clāmōre with a shout (abl. s. of *clāmor clāmōr-is* 3m.)
Collātīn-us ī 2m. L. Tarquinius Collatinus (Lucretia's husband)
concitō 1 I stir up
conclāmō 1 I shout together, bewail
cōnsōlor 1 dep. I console, comfort
corpus corpor-is 3n. body
cubicul-um ī 2n. bedroom
eandem (acc. s. f.) the same
eundem (acc. s. m.) the same
exemplō by the example (abl. of *exempl-um ī* 2n.)
exsecūtūrus sum (nom. s. m.) I shall pursue/punish (from *exsequor*)
extrahō 3 *extraxī* I pull out

ferōcissimē most fiercely
ferrō with a sword (abl. of *ferr-um ī* 2n.)
ferr-um ī 2n. sword
festīnō 1 I hurry
fidēl-is e faithful, loyal
fidēs fidē-ī 5f. pledge
fīgō 3 *fīxī* I pierce
grātius with more pleasure (from *grātus*)
īdem (nom. s. m.) the same
impudīc-us a um unchaste
inde for that reason
īnsōns innocent
L. (= *Lūci-us i*) *Iūni-us ī Brūt-us ī* 2m. Lucius Iunius Brutus
lect-us ī 2m. bed
Lucrēti-a ae 1f. Lucretia
maest-us a um sad
maximē very greatly, most of all (from *magnus*)
mēns ment-is 3f. mind
minimē not at all (lit. very little)
moribund-us a um dying
nēmō (nom. s.) no one
noxi-us a um guilty
nūnti-us ī 2m. message
passūrus sum (nom. s. m.) I shall allow (from *patior*)
peccō 1 I do wrong
pectus pector-is 3n. breast
prae (+ abl.) in front of

prōlābor 3 dep. *prōlāpsus* I fall down
pudīciti-a ae 1f. chastity
pūniō 4 punish
quaerō 3 *quaesīuī* I enquire, ask
quemquam (acc. s. m.) anyone
Quirīt-ēs ium 3m. pl. Romans
Rōmae at Rome
saluē with everything in order (adverb) (*satin saluē* = Is everything OK?)
sanguis sanguin-is 3m. blood
satin = *satisne*
Sext-us Tarquini-us 2m. Sextus Tarquinius (son of the king Tarquinius Superbus)
Sp. (= *Spuri-us i*) *Lucrēti-us i* 2m. Spurius Lucretius (father of Lucretia)
supplici-um ī 2n. punishment
suprēm-us a um last
tantum only
Tarquini-us ī Superb-us ī 2m. Tarquinius Superbus (king of Rome)
teneō 2 *tenuī* I hold
test-is is 3m. witness
ueni-a ae 1f. pardon
uestīgi-um ī 2n. trace
uī by force (abl. of *uīs*)
uiolō 1 I violate, defile
uulnus uulner-is 3n. wound

Learning vocabulary for 3C(iii)

Nouns
pudīciti-a ae 1f. chastity
nūnti-us ī 2m. messenger;
    message; news
ferr-um ī 2n. sword, iron
nēmō nēmin-is m. or f. no one,
    nobody (see **86**)
uulnus uulner-is 3n. wound

Adjectives
īdem eadem idem the same
    (see **86**)
maest-us a um sad
noxi-us a um guilty; harmful

Verbs
teneō 2 *tenuī tentus* I hold

Others
celerrimē very quickly (from
    celer: see **87**)
inde thence, from there; for that
    reason; from that time
maximē very greatly, most of all
    (from *magnus*: see **87**)
Rōmae at Rome

27. Lucretia's suicide

28. Hannibal's oath

Section 3D **Hannibal**

The first Punic War between Rome and Carthage was fought over Sicily, a land close to Italy, and therefore a possible base from which to attack it, and rich in agricultural wealth. It lasted from 264 to 241 BC, and Rome emerged as the victor, making Sicily its first province. Carthage, faced with a huge indemnity, moved into silver-rich southern Spain to help pay it off. From there, Hannibal decided to launch a second assault against Rome (218 BC). His subsequent successes, at the river Trebia (218 BC), at Lake Trasimene (217 BC) and in southern Italy at Cannae (216 BC) pushed Rome to the very brink of defeat. The city did not make peace, however, and eventually Hannibal was recalled to Carthage in 203 BC to face the Roman army with which Publius Cornelius Scipio was threatening Carthage. He was defeated by the Roman at Zama in 202 BC and the success of the Romans in the war led directly to their annexation of Spain. But Hannibal remained an important political figure in Carthage, and (according to Nepos) Romans remained deeply suspicious of him. So Hannibal fled, first to King Antiochus III's Syria (195 BC), then to King Prusias' Bithynia (190 BC), where he preferred suicide to capture.

Section 3D(i) Oath

Desire for revenge against Rome had been instilled in Hannibal from an early age by his father, as he here explains, late in his life, to Antiochus III, king of Syria, whom he is trying to persuade to declare war against Rome.

'ubi puer fuī,' inquit Antiochō Hannibal 'pater meus Hamilcar, in   205
Hispāniam imperātor profectūrus, Iouī optimō maximō hostiās immolāre
et dīs aliīs supplicāre uoluit. mihi dīxit: "placetne tibi mēcum in castra
proficīscī?" ego eī respondī: "mihi maximē placet". tum ille "et mihi
placet", inquit "sī placēbit tibi fidem mihi dare." simul mē ad āram
addūxit et sīc iūrāre iussit: "numquam in amīcitiā cum Rōmānīs futūrus   210
sum". id ego iūs iūrandum patrī dedī. mihi crēde. nēminī licet dubitāre
mentem meam; et semper eādem mente sum futūrus. quārē, sī placet tibi
dē Rōmānīs amīcē cōgitāre, nihil tibi obstat; sī tamen bellum Rōmānīs
parābis, melius erit uōbīs mihi fauēre et mē imperātōrem facere.'

(Nepos, *Hannibal* 2)

Running vocabulary for 3D(i)

addūcō 3 *addūxī* I lead to
amīcē in a friendly manner
amīciti-a ae 1f. friendship,
        alliance

Antioch-us ī 2m. Antiochus
        (Antiochus the Great, king of
        Syria)
ār-a ae 1f. altar
dubitō 1 I doubt

faue-ō 2 I favour (+ dat.)
fid-ēs ēī 5f. oath
Hamilcar Hamilcar-is 3m.
        Hamilcar (father of Hannibal)

Hannibal Hannibal-is 3m.
    Hannibal (son of Hamilcar,
    leader of the Carthaginians)
Hispāni-a ae 1f. Spain
hosti-a ae 1f. (sacrificial) victim
immolō 1 I sacrifice
imperātor imperātōr-is 3m.
    general
iūrō 1 I swear

iūs iūrand-um iūr-is iūrand-ī
    3m/2n. oath
licet it is permitted to X (dat.) to
    Y (inf.); X (dat.) is allowed to
    Y (inf.)
mēns ment-is 3f. mind, purpose
obstō 1 I stand in the way of
    (+ dat.)
parō 1 I prepare

placet it pleases X (dat.) to Y
    (inf.); X (dat.) wants/decides
    to Y (inf.)
quārē therefore
simul at the same time
supplicō 1 I make prayers to
    (+ dat.)

Grammar for 3D

more datives

Learning vocabulary for 3D(i)

Nouns
amīc-us ī 2m. friend, ally
Hannibal Hannibal-is 3m.
    Hannibal (son of Hamilcar,
    leader of the Carthaginians)
mēns ment-is 3f. mind, purpose

Adjectives
amīc-us a um friendly

Verbs
parō 1 I prepare, get ready,
    provide; obtain; I am about
    (to)

supplicō 1 I make prayers to
    (+ dat.)
placet it pleases X (dat.) to
    Y (inf.); X (dat.) decides to
    Y (inf.)

Their finest hour

Whenever Romans wanted to pinpoint their 'finest hour', they could highlight the war against Hannibal, and with some justification. The Roman spirit was remarkable. Even at the moment when Hannibal was at the gates of Rome, there was no sign of a peace party. When affairs were at their lowest ebb in Italy, Rome still kept, indeed reinforced, armies in the field in Spain to engage the Carthaginians there. Rome's basically amateurish military command system was adapted to counter the strategic genius of Hannibal. Hannibal came into Italy with the proclaimed aim of freeing the communities of Italy from the yoke of Rome. Although in the south he gained some defections, the vast majority remained loyal. Here lies the more mundane, but most important, reason for Rome's success. Year after year Rome was able to mobilise the resources and manpower of Italy on an enormous scale. From the time of the Hannibalic war onwards, Rome maintained large numbers of troops in the field around the Mediterranean and beyond in a way that no other ancient state could have even contemplated. Rome's success in the Second Punic War proved that she was no longer in any sense a conventional city-state. (*World of Rome*, **33**)

Section 3D(ii) The Barcas and the opposition faction of Hanno

Hannibal is a member of the Barca family, to which the general Hasdrubal was attached by marriage. When Hannibal was a young boy, as Livy tells us, Hasdrubal wanted to initiate him into the army in Spain, with a view to his eventually taking over the generalship; but there was opposition in the Carthaginian senate from the anti-Barcans, led by Hanno. Hanno's arguments, however, prove ineffective. In this episode, Livy hints at the suspicion which could attach to over-powerful individuals because of their popular appeal.

placuit Hasdrubalī, imperātōrī Carthāginiēnsium, Hannibalem puerum ad   215
sē in Hispāniam uocāre. sed Hannō, alterīus factiōnis prīnceps, in senātū
sīc locūtus est:
'Hasdrubal seruīuit libīdinī Hamilcaris, patris Hannibalis; Hasdrubalī
igitur nunc placet idem ab Hannibale petere. minimē autem nōbīs licet patī
iuuenīs nostrōs seruīre libīdinī imperātōrum. praetereā, nōlumus   220
Hannibalem parum mātūrē nōbīs imperāre. mihi placet igitur eum domī
tenēre. ita nōbīs licēbit eum cōgere lēgibus magistrātibusque pārēre et
uīuere aequō iūre cum cēterīs. alioquīn paruus hic ignis incendium
maximum exsuscitābit et Hannibal lībertātī nostrae maximē obstābit.'
paucīs et optimīs Hannōnis opiniō placuit; sed, ut plērumque fit, māior   225
pars partem meliōrem uīcit.

Hasdrubal, commander of the Carthaginians, decided to summon Hannibal, still a boy, to him to Spain. But Hanno, the leader of the other faction, spoke as follows in the senate: 'Hasdrubal was a slave to the lust of Hamilcar, Hannibal's father; therefore Hasdrubal now decides to seek the same thing from Hannibal. However, we are not in the least allowed to suffer our young men to serve the lust of our generals. Besides, we do not wish Hannibal to rule over us too soon. I vote therefore to keep him at home. In this way we will be allowed to force him to obey the laws and the magistrates and to live on an equal footing with the rest. Otherwise, this small fire will arouse a great conflagration, and Hannibal will be a very great obstruction to our freedom.' Hanno's opinion pleased the few and the best; but, as often happens, the greater part (majority) defeated the better part.

(Livy 21.3–4)

Running vocabulary for 3D(ii)

aequō iūre on equal terms
 (*aequ-us a um* equal; *iūs iūr-is*
 3n. rights, law, privilege)
alioquīn otherwise
Carthāginiēns-ēs ium 3m.
 Carthaginians
cēter-ī ōrum 2m. pl. the others,
 the rest

cōgō 3 I compel
exsuscitō 1 I stir up, arouse
factiō factiōn-is 3f. faction
Hamilcar Hamilcar-is 3m.
 Hamilcar (father of Hannibal)
Hannō Hannōn-is 3m. Hanno
Hasdrubal Hasdrubal-is 3m.
 Hasdrubal

Hispāni-a ae 1f. Spain
imperātor imperātōr-is 3m.
 general
imperō 1 I give orders to,
 command (+ dat.)
incendi-um ī 2n. fire, blaze
lēx lēg-is 3f. law
lībertās lībertāt-is 3f. freedom

licet it is allowed to X (dat.) to
Y (inf.); X (dat.) is allowed to
Y (inf.)
magistrāt-us ūs 4m. magistrate
mātūrē soon, early
obstō 1 I stand in the way of
(+ dat.)

opīniō opīniōn-is 3f. opinion,
view
pāreō 2 I obey (+ dat.)
pars part-is 3f. party, portion
parum too
pauc-ī ōrum 2m. pl. the few
petō 3 I seek, ask for

plērumque for the most part,
mostly
praetereā besides, moreover
prīnceps prīncip-is 3m. leader
senāt-us ūs 4m. senate
seruiō 4 I serve (+ dat.)

Learning vocabulary for 3D(ii)

Nouns	**Adjectives**	**Verbs**
imperātōr imperātōr-is 3m. general; commander; ruler; leader	*aequ-us a um* level; calm; impartial	*seruiō* 4 I serve (+ dat.)

War against Hannibal

What the Romans had not anticipated was what sort of war it was going to be. They expected to fight it in Spain and Africa. But Hannibal pre-empted them and in a remarkable march transferred an army from Spain, through southern France, and over the Alps into Italy. Here he proceeded to inflict a series of increasingly serious defeats on the Romans at the Trebia (218 BC), Lake Trasimene (217 BC), and with most devastating effect in southern Italy at Cannae (216 BC). Such was the scale of the Roman defeat at Cannae that everyone must have expected them to negotiate what terms they could. Indeed, in 215 BC Philip, king of Macedon, signed an agreement with Carthage in the hope of gaining a seat at the peace negotiations and picking up some advantage for himself.

However, Rome would not give in. She created new armies. Very slowly events swung in Rome's favour. In 205 BC, the Roman general, Publius Cornelius Scipio (Scipio), was able to invade Africa. With Carthage itself now under threat, Hannibal was at last recalled from Italy in 203 BC and in the following year was defeated by Scipio at the battle of Zama. In the settlement of the war Carthage was permitted to survive, but no longer as an international power, and was forced to pay a huge indemnity. As with Sicily after the First Punic War, so now Rome took over Spain. From 197 BC Spain became two *prōuinciae* of two new praetors, although the conquest and pacification of the whole peninsula was to take another two centuries. It is no surprise, however, to find the Romans exploiting the mineral wealth, particularly the silver, from an early date. (*World of Rome*, **32**)

Section 3D(iii) Character of Hannibal

*Romans acknowledged Hannibal's military prowess, but they had their
prejudices about him too, especially because the Punic Wars featured so large in
their historical memory and understanding of themselves. 'Punic treachery'
became a by-word in Rome. Here Hannibal's enormous military talents are
listed, but his virtues are balanced by as many faults.*

ingenium habilissimum fuit: nam eī placuit uel imperātōrī pārēre uel
imperāre mīlitibus. itaque et imperātōrī suō et exercituī cordī fuit
Hannibal; et ubi rem fortiter ac strēnuē agere necesse fuit, Hasdrubal
nēminem alium exercituī praeficere māluit, neque mīlitēs aliī ducī plūs   230
cōnfīsī sunt, quod semper eīs in pugnā salūtī fuit. maxima in perīculīs
audācia fuit, cōnsilium inter ipsa perīcula optimum. nūllus labor potuit
aut corpus fatīgāre aut animum uincere. calōrem ac frīgus aequē passus
est; cibus pōtiōque nōn uoluptātī eī fuit sed necessitātī; noctēs atque diēs
uigilāre potuit; requiēuit ubi ōtium eī fuit. saepe humī iacuit et inter mīlitēs 235
dormīuit; uestis eadem‿ac mīlitum fuit, arma atque equī praeclāriōrēs.
equitum peditumque longē optimus fuit; eī ōtium semper odiō fuit. prīmus
in proelium iit, ultimus excessit. nihil eī unquam impedīmentō fuit.
hās tantās uirtūtēs ingentia uitia aequāuērunt: inhūmāna crūdēlitās,
perfidia plūs quam Pūnica, nihil uērī, nihil sānctī, nūllus deum metus,   240
nūllum iūs iūrandum, nūlla religiō. sed in bellō etiam uitia eī auxiliō
fuērunt.

*His disposition was most adaptable: for it pleased him either to obey his
commander or to give orders to his soldiers. Therefore Hannibal was beloved
both of his commanding-officer and of his army; and when it was necessary to
perform a task bravely and quickly, Hasdrubal would rather place no one else in
charge of the army, nor did the soldiers trust more in another leader. His
boldness in dangers was very great, and his counsel amidst those very dangers
excellent. No amount of hard work could either tire his body or vanquish his
spirit. He put up equally (well) with heat and cold; food and drink were not as a
pleasure for him, but as a necessity; he could stay awake night and day; his
clothing was the same as that of the soldiers, (but) his arms and horses (were)
more distinguished. He was far the best of the cavalry and infantry; he always
hated leisure. He was the first to go into battle, the last to leave. Nothing ever
stood in his way.
Such great virtues as these massive faults equalled; inhuman cruelty, treachery
more than Carthaginian (Punic), nothing true, nothing holy, no fear of the gods,
no oath, no religious scruples. But in war even his faults were a help to him.*

(Livy 21.4)

Running vocabulary for 3D(iii)

aequō 1 I balance
arm-a ōrum 2n. pl. arms
auxiliō est (it) is of help to X
　(dat.), X (nom.) helps Y (dat.)
calor calōr-is 3m. heat
cib-us ī 2m. food
cōnfīdō 3 semi-dep. cōnfīsus I
　trust, rely on (+ dat.)
cordī est (he) is beloved by X
　(dat.); X (nom.) is beloved by
　Y (dat.)
corpus corpor-is 3n. body
crūdēlitās crūdēlitāt-is 3f. cruelty
deum gen. pl. of deus
eadem ac the same as
eques equit-is 3m. horseman
excēdō 3 excessī I leave, go out of
fatīgō 1 I tire
frīgus frīgor-is 3n. cold
habil-is e adaptable
Hasdrubal Hasdrubal-is 3m.
　Hasdrubal
humī on the ground
iaceō 2 iacuī I lie
impedīmentō est (it) is an
　impediment to X (dat.),
　X (nom.) hinders Y (dat.)

imperō 1 I give orders to,
　command (+ dat.)
ingeni-um ī 2n. disposition,
　character, talents
inhūmān-us a um savage
inter (+ acc.) among
itaque therefore
iūs iūr-is iūrand-um ī 3n./2n. oath
labor labōr-is 3m. toil, hard work
longē by far
met-us ūs 4m. fear
necesse est it is necessary (+ inf.)
necessitātī est (it) acts as a
　necessity for X (dat.), (it) is
　necessary for X (dat.)
odiō est (it) is hateful to X (dat.),
　X (dat.) hates Y (nom.)
ōti-um ī 2n. leisure (× 2)
pāreō 2 I obey (+ dat.)
pedes pedit-is 3m. foot-soldier,
　infantry
perīcul-um ī 2n. danger
perfidi-a ae 1f. treachery
pōtiō pōtiōn-is 3f. drink
praeclār-us a um distinguished
praeficiō 3/4 I put X (acc.) in
　charge of Y (dat.)

prīm-us a um first
pugn-a ae 1f. battle
Pūnic-us a um Punic,
　Carthaginian
religiō religiōn-is 3f. religion,
　reverence for the gods
requiēscō 3 requiēuī I rest
saepe often
salūtī est (he) acts as a safeguard
　to X (dat.), (he) provides
　salvation for X (dat.)
sanct-um ī 2n. piety
strēnuē quickly, actively
tant-us a um (so) great
uel... uel either... or
uēr-um ī 2n. truth
uest-is is 3f. clothing
uigilō 1 I stay awake
uirtūs uirtūt-is 3f. virtue
uiti-um ī 2n. vice
ultim-us a um last
unquam ever
uoluptātī est (it) acts as a pleasure
　to X (dat.), (it) brings pleasure
　to X (dat.)

Learning vocabulary for 3D(iii)

Nouns
ōti-um ī 2n. cessation of conflict;
　leisure, inactivity
corpus corpor-is 3n. body

iūs iūr-is 3n. rights, law, privilege,
　justice
iūs iūr-is iūrand-um ī oath
uirtūs uirtūt-is 3f. virtue

Adjectives
imperō 1 I give orders to,
　command (+ dat.)

Others
longē far

After Hannibal

The Roman army was a citizen militia rather than a professional army, and in theory a new army was conscripted to serve with the new magistrates each year. For this reason, the *stīpendium* that they were paid was not high, since it was intended only to be enough money to cover the expenses of citizens who were taken away from their normal livelihood. Indeed, it remained low until Julius Caesar, as consul in 59 BC, doubled the amount they were paid (Suetonius, *Julius* 26.3). In practice, though, the long campaigns against Hannibal, followed by the no less demanding overseas wars of the second century, led to longer and longer periods of service becoming necessary. It was possible, if a man had a taste for the military life, to string together a series of campaigns, and even look forward to re-enlisting after he had returned home to his farmstead. (*World of Rome*, **174**)

Section 3D(iv) Aemilius Paullus

The battle of Cannae (216 BC) was a crucial moment in the war against Hannibal. The Romans suffered a massive defeat, which threatened to make the city of Rome itself vulnerable to Carthaginian attack. In this account of part of the battle, the courage and obstinacy of the consul, Lucius Aemilius Paulus, are highlighted. Quintus Fabius (Maximus) was nick-named cunctator 'delayer' because he took on Hannibal with guerilla tactics, delaying any final resolution in pitched battle. But Romans tired of these tactics. Cannae was the result, with 50,000 Roman dead, 4,500 captured and 17,000 surrendered. Winning a big battle outright usually brought a war to an end. Winning a big battle against the Romans guaranteed that the war would continue.

Poenī Paulum cōnsulem in prīmo proeliō fundā grauiter uulnerāuērunt.
hoc autem uulnus eī nūllī͡impedīmentō fuit. saepe occurrit Hannibalī et,
hostibus ferōciter minātus, proelium restituere cōnātus est. sed tandem   245
placuit equitibus eum prōtegere, quod eī auxiliō esse uoluērunt. ad pedēs
igitur dēscendērunt.

   multās hōrās equitēs fortiter pugnāuērunt; aliī mortuī sunt, aliī fūgērunt.
sed placuit Paulō, uulneribus fessō, manēre et hostibus resistere. tandem
cōnsul uulnerātus in saxō sēdit. ubi Lentulus, tribūnus mīlitum, eum uīdit,   250
'L. Aemilī' inquit, 'īnsōns es huius clādis. tibi auxiliō esse uolō. cape hunc
equum, dum tibi uīrēs supersunt, et comes ego tibi aderō ac prōtegam.
mihi crēde. nōlī facere funestiōrem hanc pugnam morte cōnsulis. etiam
sine hōc, satis lacrimārum lūctūsque nōbīs est. hic diēs semper Rōmānīs
odiō erit.' ad ea cōnsul: 'Cn. Cornēlī, frūstrā mihi salūtī esse uīs. nōlī   255
morārī; minimum est tempus ē manibus hostium ēuādere; nunc mihi pārē:
abī, et nūntiā hoc pūblicē patribus: "nunc uōbīs necesse est salūtī esse
cīuibus nostrīs. urbem Rōmānam mūnīte ac praesidiīs firmāte; uictor
hostis mox aduentūrus est. obstāte eī et dīs omnibus supplicāte." hoc
prīuātim dīc Q. Fabiō "L. Aemilius, praeceptōrum eius memor, et uīxit et   260
mortuus est, cīuibus Rōmānīs salūtī esse conatus." nunc igitur, nōlī mihi
adesse et mē in hāc strāge mīlitum meōrum patere exspīrāre.'

(Livy 22.49.1–11)

Running vocabulary for 3D(iv)

adsum adesse I am present with
   (+ dat.)
aduenio 4 *aduēnī aduentum* I
   arrive, arrive at
aliī . . . aliī some . . . others
auxiliō est (it) is of help to X
   (dat.), X (nom.) helps Y (dat.)
clād-ēs is 3f. defeat, disaster

Cn. Cornēli-us ī 2m. Gnaeus
   Cornelius (the *praenomen* and
   nomen gentilicium of Cn.
   Cornelius Lentulus)
comes comit-is 3m. companion
cōnsul cōnsul-is 3m. consul
dēscendō 3 *dēscendī* I descend, go
   down

eques equit-is 3m. horseman
ēuādō 3 *ēuāsī ēuāsum* I escape
exspīrō 1 I die
fess-us a um weary, wearied by
   X (abl.)
firmō 1 I strengthen
frūstrā in vain
fund-a ae 1f. sling

fūnest-us a um deadly
grauiter grievously, seriously
impedīmentō est (it) is an impediment to X (dat.), X (nom.) hinders Y (dat.)
īnsōns īnsont-is innocent
lacrim-a ae 1f. tear
L. Aemili-us 2m. Lucius Aemilius Paul(l)us
Lentul-us ī 2m. Gnaeus Cornelius Lentulus
lūct-us ūs 4m. grief, mourning
memor memor-is mindful of, remembering (+ gen.)
mūniō 4 I fortify, defend
necesse est it is necessary for X (dat.) to Y (inf.)
nūllī impedīmentō est (it) is no impediment to X (dat.), X (nom.) does not hinder Y (dat.)

obstō 1 I stand in the way of, obstruct, hinder (+ dat.)
occurrō 3 *occurrī* I attack, oppose, resist (+ dat.)
odiō est (it) is hateful to X (dat.), X (dat.) hates Y (nom.)
pāreō 2 I obey (+ dat.)
Paul-us ī 2m. L. Aemilius Paul(l)us
pes ped-is 3m. foot
Poen-ī ōrum 2m. pl. Carthaginians
praecept-um ī 2n. teaching
praesidi-um ī 2n. garrison, protection
prīm-us a um first
prīuātim in private
prōtegō 3 I protect
pūblicē in public
pugn-a ae 1f. battle

Q. Fabi-us ī 2m. Quintus Fabius Maximus
resistō 3 I resist (+ dat.)
restitu-ō 3 I revive, repair
saepe often
salūtī est (it/he) is a source of salvation to X (dat.), X (nom.) saves Y (dat.)
sax-um ī 2n. rock
sede-ō 2 *sēdī* I sit
strāg-ēs is 3f. defeat, slaughter
supersum superesse ī I survive
tribūn-us ī 2m. tribune
tribūn-us mīlitum military tribune
uīr-ēs uīr-ium f. (pl. of *uīs*) strength
uulnerāt-us a um wounded
uulnerō 1 I wound

Learning vocabulary for 3D(iv)

Nouns
cōnsul cōnsul-is 3m. consul
eques equit-is 3m. horseman; cavalry
uīr-ēs uīr-ium f. (pl. of *uīs*) strength, military forces
uīs f. force (acc. *uim*, abl. *uī*: no other cases)

Adjectives
prīm-us a um first

Verbs
obstō 1 *obstitī* (*obstātum*) I stand in the way of, obstruct, hinder (+ dat.)
pāreō 2 I obey (+ dat.)
adsum adesse adfuī I am present with (+ dat.) (learned at 2D without + dat.)
necesse est it is necessary for X (dat.) to Y (inf.)

Others
saepe often
salūtī est (it/he) is a source of salvation to X (dat.), X (nom.) saves Y (dat.)

29. Site of the Battle of Cannae

Section 3D(v) Death of Hannibal

After fleeing Carthage in 196 BC, Hannibal went to Antiochus III in Syria and helped him during an unsuccessful war on Rome. Upon Antiochus' defeat, he made his way via Crete to King Prusias in Bithynia. He helped Prusias in his successful war against Eumenes, king of Pergamum. But his luck was about to run out. His whereabouts were reported in Rome, and the Romans sent envoys to pressure Prusias into betraying Hannibal. Nepos tells the final chapter in the tale of Rome's greatest adversary.

If you wanted to be a real Roman you had to know about Hannibal. He helped the Romans understand themselves – and he became a key figure in Roman historical memory. So there were three statues of him in Rome. At antique markets it always raised the price to say that Hannibal had owned the item for sale. Mothers were said to bring to heel unruly chidren with the words Hannibal ad portās!

True, he ended up as part of someone else's story – the 'other man' in the Scipio Africanus legend – rather as the British tend to think of Rommel as part of Montgomery's story and Napoleon as part of Wellington's. But as a later Scipio (Aemilianus) once observed, Carthage was the whetstone of the Romans – it kept them sharp.

dum lēgātī Prūsiacī Rōmae apud T. Quīntium Flaminīnum cōnsulārem
cēnant, dē Hannibale mentiō facta est. ex hīs lēgātīs quīdam dīxit 'is in
Prūsiae rēgnō est'. id Flaminīnus senātuī dētulit. quia senātōribus Hannibal   265
uīuus odiō et impedīmentō⁀maximō fuit, lēgātōs in Bīthȳniam mīsērunt,
in hīs Flaminīnum. hic rēgem iussit inimīcissimum suum Hannibalem
sēcum nōn diūtius habēre, sed sibi dēdere. 'Hannibal Rōmānīs odiō est et
impedīmentō⁀maximō, dum uīuit, mihi crēde. sī tibi placet, licet cīuitātī
Rōmānae maximō⁀auxiliō esse. nōlī diūtius Hannibalem prōtegere, sed   270
nōbīs dēde.' hoc Prūsias negāre ausus nōn est: illud tamen recūsāuit:
'nōlī ā mē id postulāre. nam aduersus iūs hospitiī est. uōbīs tamen licet
eum comprehendere. refugium eius facile inuentūrī estis.'
Hannibal enim in castellō sē tenuit (hoc dōnum rēgis fuit et ūsuī⁀maximō
Hannibalī). nam aedificium in omnibus partibus exitūs habuit, quia   275
Hannibal oppugnātiōnem hostium magnopere ueritus est. sed tandem
castellum eī salūtī nōn fuit, sed maximō⁀impedīmentō.

nam hūc lēgātī Rōmānōrum uēnērunt ac multitūdine domum eius
circumdedērunt. puer ab iānuā prōspicit et Hannibalī dīxit:
'plūrēs uirī armātī, praeter cōnsuētūdinem, appāruērunt et aedificiō adsunt.' 280
Hannibal igitur dīxit:
'obsidentne omnīs portās? aedificium circumī ac celeriter mihi nūntiā.'
puer ubi circumiit celeriter renūntiāuit:
'omnēs exitūs occupātī sunt.'

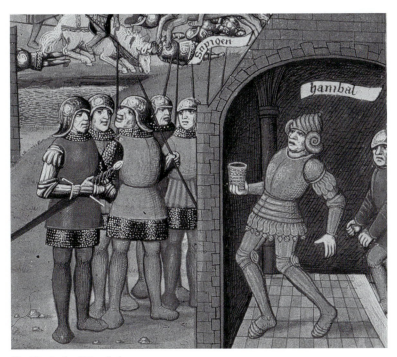

30. The death of Hannibal

Running vocabulary for 3D(v)

aduersus (+ acc.) against
aedifici-um ī 2n. building
appāreō 2 *appāruī* I appear
armāt-us a um armed
Bīthȳni-a ae 1f. Bithynia
castell-um ī 2n. fort
circumdō 1 *circumdedī* I surround
circumeō cirumīre circumiī I go
around
cīuitās cīuitāt-is 3f. state
comprehendō 3 I capture, arrest
cōnsuētūdō cōnsuētūdin-is 3f.
custom, what is usual
cōnsulār-is is 3m. ex-consul
dēdō 3 I surrender
dēfer-ō dēferre dētulī I report
diūtius any longer
dōn-um ī 2n. gift
exit-us ūs 4m. exit
Flaminīn-us see *T. Quīntius
Flaminīnus*
hospiti-um ī 2n. guest-friendship,
hospitality
impedīmentō maximō est X
(nom.) is a very great
hindrance to Y (dat.)

inimīc-us ī 2m. enemy
(*inimīcissimus* is the
superlative: 'greatest enemy')
licet it is permitted (+ dat. and
inf.); X (dat.) is permitted to Y
(inf.)
maximō auxiliō est (it) is of very
great help to X (dat.),
X (nom.) helps Y (dat.) very
greatly
maximō impedīmentō est (it) is a
very great impediment to X
(dat.), X (nom.) hinders Y
(dat.) very greatly
mentiō mentiōn-is 3f. mention
multitūdō multitūdin-is 3f. a large
number
negō 1 I deny
obsideō 2 *obsēdī obsessus* I
besiege
occupāt-us a um blocked
odiō est (he) is hateful to X (dat.),
X (dat.) hates Y (nom.)
oppugnātiō oppugnātiōn-is 3f.
assault, attack
pars part-is 3f. part

postulō 1 I ask X (acc.) for Y
(acc.)
praeter (+ acc.) contrary to
prōspiciō 3/4 *prōspexī* I look out
prōtegō 3 I protect
Prūsiac-us a um of Prusias (king
of Bithynia)
Prūsi-as ae m. Prusias (king of
Bithynia)
puer puer-ī 2m. slave
quīdam (nom. s. m) one
recūsō 1 I refuse
refugi-um ī 2n. hiding-place,
refuge
renūntiō 1 I report back
senātor senātōr-is 3m. senator
senāt-us ūs 4m. senate
T. Quīnti-us ī Flaminīn-us ī 2m.
Titus Quintius Flamininus
uereor 2 dep. *ueritus* I fear
uīu-us a um alive
ūsuī maximō of the greatest
usefulness to X (dat.)

Hannibal igitur, quia tantae multitūdinī resistere nōn potuit, fīnem uītae   285
suae praeuīdit. sibi locūtus est:
'id nōn fortuitō factum est, sed mē hostēs petunt. nihil mihi salūtī esse
potest, neque mihi diūtius licet uītam retinēre.'
quod autem fātō suō praeesse uoluit et uītam suam aliēnō arbitriō
dīmittere nōluit, memor prīstinārum uirtūtum, uenēnum (nam hoc solitus   290
est sēcum semper habēre) sūmpsit.

*For hither the envoys of the Romans came and encircled his house with a large
number (of soldiers). A slave-boy saw (them) from the doorway and said to
Hannibal: 'Rather a lot of armed men have appeared, against what is normal,
and are at the building.' Hannibal therefore said: 'Are they besieging all the
gates? Go around the building and tells me quickly.' When the slave-boy had
gone around, he quickly reported back: 'All the exits are blocked.' Hannibal,
therefore, because he could not stand up to such a number, foresaw the end of
his life. He said to himself: 'This has not happened by chance, but my enemies
are after me. Nothing can save me, nor can I keep my life any longer.' But
because he wished to be in command of his own fate and did not wish to
abandon his life to the will of someone else, mindful of his former virtues, took
poison (for he was accustomed always to have this with him).*

(Nepos, *Hannibal* 12)

---

aliēn-us a um belonging to
    someone else, another's
arbitri-um ī 2n. judgement
dīmittō 3 I release, abandon
diūtius any longer
fīn-is is 3m. end
fortuitō by chance
licet it is permitted (+ dat. and
    inf.); X (dat.) is permitted to
    Y (inf.)

memor memor-is mindful of,
    remembering (+ gen.)
multitudo multitūdin-is 3f. a large
    number
petō 3 I seek, look for
praesum praeesse I am in charge
    of (+ dat.)
praeuideō 2 *praeuīdī* I foresee
prīstin-us a um former, original
resistō 3 I resist (+ dat.)

retineō 2 I retain, hold onto
tant-us a um so great
soleō 2 semi-dep. *solitus* I am
    accustomed (+ inf.)
sūmō 3 *sūmpsī* I consume
uenēn-um ī 2n. poison

Learning vocabulary for 3D(v)

Nouns
puer puer-ī 2m. slave (boy)
aedifici-um ī 2n. building
auxili-um ī 2n. help, aid
impedīment-um ī 2n. hindrance
pars part-is 3f. part; faction party
senāt-us ūs 4m. senate

Adjectives
tant-us a um so great; so much; so
    important

Verbs
licet 2 *licuit* it is permitted (+ dat.
    and inf.); X (dat.) is permitted
    to Y (inf.)
dēdō 3 *dēdidī dēditus* I hand over,
    surrender
prōtegō 3 *prōtexī prōtectus* I
    protect

Others
auxiliō est (it) is of help to X
    (dat.), X (nom.) helps Y (dat.)
diū for a long time: comparative:
    diūtius for longer: superlative
    diūtissimē for a very long time
impedīmentō (maximō) est X
    (nom.) is a (very great)
    hindrance to Y (dat.)
odiō est (he/it/she) is hateful to X
    (dat.), X (dat.) hates Y (nom.)

Part Three The demise of the Roman Republic

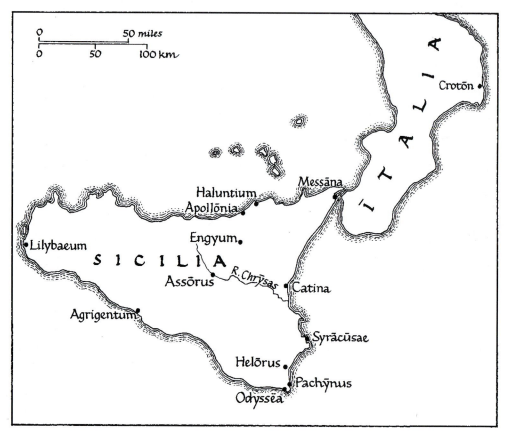

31. The province of Sicily

Sicily became the first Roman province in 241, immediately after the Romans had defeated the Carthaginians in the First Punic War. Sicily had been at the heart of that dispute, for besides its position, Sicily's grainfields were a desirable acquisition. By 146 the Romans were to acquire and administer as provinces Sardinia, Corsica, Spain, Macedonia and Africa (roughly modern Tunisia). Soon Asia was added (133–129), and then Gaul (after 121, especially during Julius Caesar's campaigns (58–50)), Cilicia (from 102), Bithynia (74), Syria (64–63), Cyprus (58), Egypt (30) and other places east. Roman control over the Mediterranean was virtually complete.

The Romans in general preferred to control the province within the existing provincial structure rather than impose a brand new system of their own. A consul or praetor was elected for a one-year term of office, and kept his consular or praetorian *imperium* ('right to give orders/rule') for the duration of that year.

32. Grainfields of Sicily (Selinus hinterland)

Once he had completed his duties in Rome, he could leave for the province assigned to him, where he was expected to remain until his successor arrived. It usually happened that his consular or praetorian *imperium* would have expired by then, so he was given proconsular or propraetorian *imperium* (*prō-* 'in the place of', 'standing for') until he was replaced. Tenure was generally one year, but it could be renewed. His authority over provincials was virtually unlimited, but Roman citizens in the provinces had a right of appeal against him (*prōuocātiō*). The governor was mainly responsible for defence, internal order and jurisdiction, and at the end of his term of office could be called to give a financial account of his governorship. Each governor took a relatively small staff (*cohors*) of men with him – a *quaestor* (his right-hand man, usually in charge of finance), *lēgātī* (usually *senātōrēs*), friends and relatives of semi-official status (*comitēs*), *praefectī* (men in charge of special jobs), and other minor officials, e.g. *līctōrēs* and *scrībae* (clerks).

The problem was that the temptation of graft and corruption appears to have been virtually irresistible. Since winning office in Rome was an expensive business, a wealthy province gave the politician a chance to recoup. He could sell justice; he could sell exemptions from state duties (such as, for example, supplying ships and men for external defence); he could work hand in glove with tax collectors (*pūblicānī*, men who bought the right to collect taxes in a province). Indeed, so serious was this problem that the very first standing court in Rome was a court *dē repetundīs*, 'on provincial extortion' (*repetō* = 'I demand back what is mine'), established in 149 in an effort to check these abuses.

In 75 Cicero had gone to Sicily as *quaestor* and boasted that he had made not a penny out of it and indeed that he had checked abuses against the locals. This is why Cicero claims that the provincials turned to him for the prosecution of the notorious Gaius Verres. As *praetor* of Sicily from 73 to 71, Verres had by all accounts mismanaged and abused the province on a grand scale. Despite efforts at Rome by Verres' friends to delay the trial, and for all Verres' influential backers, the young Cicero was victorious. Verres' counsel Hortensius abandoned the case and Verres went into exile. Cicero now became one of Rome's leading advocates.

Not all provincial governors were as bad as Verres. Besides, the system of empire that Rome imposed on its subjects lasted in the West from 241 until (traditionally) AD 476 – a period of some 650 years. It must have been seen by the provincials to have had advantages, since Rome's military strength was simply not enough to keep under permanent subjection such vast areas of territory. One of the secrets of empire was surely Rome's tolerance. As long as states paid their taxes and toed the line when it came to foreign policy, Rome was generally happy to leave well alone. Roman protection, the purpose of which was the maintenance of the *pāx Rōmāna*, must have been seen as a great blessing by vulnerable states, and trading advantages across the expanding empire were considerable. But there was always a price to pay.

Here Cicero, in a letter to his brother Quintus, who was about to enter a third year of tenure as governor of Asia, outlines his views of the ideal governor.

A *On self-restraint*

You will no doubt continue to resist the temptations of money, of pleasure and of desires of all kinds; there will therefore not be much risk of your being unable to restrain the dishonest man of business or the over-rapacious tax-collector, while the Greeks,[1] when they see you living as you do, will think that some famous man from their own history, or perhaps even a godlike human from the sky, has dropped into their province.

I say all this not by way of advice to you on how to act, but to make you glad that you have so acted and are so acting. It is indeed a splendid thing that you should have spent three years in supreme command in Asia without being deflected from the path of honour and self-restraint by any of the temptations your province offers – statues, pictures, vases, dress, slaves, beautiful women or financial deals. What could be more eminently desirable than that your excellence, your restraint and self-control should not be hidden in some obscure corner, but be displayed in Asia before the eyes of our most famous province, for the ears of all tribes and nations to hear of. Your official visits cause no fear, your advent no panic, you demand no exhausting expenditure. Wherever you go you give pleasure both in public and private, for you come to the community as protector, not as tyrant, to the home as guest not as plunderer.

1. Greek settlers had populated the west coast of Asia Minor (modern Turkey) since the tenth century.

B *On a governor's cohors*

In these matters, however, your own experience has no doubt taught you that it is not enough that you should have these qualities yourself, but that you must keep your eyes open and do all you can to make it clear that the responsibility you bear for your province to allies, to citizens, and to the Roman state is not yours alone but is shared by all your subordinates.

C *On bribery*

In short, let it be recognised by your whole province that the lives, the children, the good name and the property of all those whom you govern are very near your own heart. Finally, ensure that everyone believes that, if word of a bribe reaches your ear, you will take action against the giver as hostile as against the taker. No one will give a bribe when it has been made clear that, generally, those who claim to have your confidence can achieve nothing.

D *On tax-farmers*

But of course the great obstacle to your goodwill and sense of duty are the tax-farmers. If we stand in their way we alienate from ourselves and from the state a class which has deserved very well of us and which we have brought into close association with public affairs; but if we give way to them in everything, we shall acquiesce in the ruin of those for whose security and indeed interests we are in duty bound to care . . . To manage the tax-farmers to their satisfaction – especially if they took on the job at a loss[2] – and at the same time to avoid ruining the provincials requires a touch of genius out of this world; but I'm sure that's just what you have.

Let us start with the Greeks. Their most bitter grievance is that they are subject to taxation at all; they should not feel such a grievance since they were already in that position under their own freely adopted institutions . . . At the same time Asia ought to remember that if she were not governed by us she would hardly have been spared the disasters of external war or internal discord. But our government cannot be maintained without taxes, and she ought without resentment to pay over some of her wealth as the price of permanent peace and quiet.

(Cicero, *Ad Quīntum* 1.1)

We follow the story of Verres' mismanagement of Sicily through a number of incidents adapted from the published version of Cicero's prosecution speech against him. Verres in fact fled the country after an earlier hearing. Since Sicily contained many Greek communities (old Greek colonies), there are many Greek names in the text.

References are given at the end of each section to Cicero's original text.

---

2. I.e. because 'tax-farmers' had purchased the right to collect ('farm') provincial taxes at too high a price to make it easy for them to make a profit.

Section 4A(i)

Verres ruthlessly seized from the provincials whatever took his fancy. Here, he breaks into the temple of Hercules at Agrigentum to steal a particularly fine statue. (On thieving governors, see Introduction to this section, Cicero letter A. See p. xix Note 2 for significance of ⌐⌐·*)*

Herculis templum apud Agrigentīnōs est nōn longē ā forō. ibi est
simulācrum ipsīus Herculis pulcherrimum. quamquam plūrima
simulācra uīdī, iūdicēs, pulchrius simulācrum quam illud numquam
cōnspicātus sum. ad hoc templum Verrēs nocte seruōs quōsdam
armātōs repente mīsit.   5

There is among the people of Agrigentum a temple of Hercules not far from the forum. There is there a very beautiful statue of Hercules himself. Although I have seen very many statues, judges, I have never seen a statue more beautiful than that one. It was to this temple that Verres sent by night some of his slaves, armed.

hī concurrērunt et templum expugnābant, sed custōdēs templī clāmāuēre,
et seruīs obsistere templumque dēfendere cōnābantur. sed seruī Verris eōs
clāuīs et pugnīs reppulērunt, et ubi ualuās templī effrēgērunt, simulācrum
commouēbant. intereā fāma per tōtam urbem percrēbrēscēbat; fāma erat
seruōs ⌐ templum ⌐ expugnāre.   10

subitō nūntius quīdam, in forum celerrimē ingressus, nūntiāuit seruōs ⌐
quōsdam simulācrum Herculis ⌐ commouēre. omnēs Agrigentīnī, ubi
surrēxērunt tēlaque arripuērunt, breuī tempore ad templum ex tōtā
urbe accurrērunt. ubi ad templum peruēnērunt, uīdērunt seruōs ⌐

33. Herculis templum

simulācrum summā uī commouēre ⌐ cōnārī. tum Agrigentīnī, maximē   15
īrātī, impetum ⌐ repente ⌐ fēcērunt; fīēbat magna lapidātiō; seruī Verris
fūgērunt.

num scelera pēiōra umquam audīuistis, iūdicēs? num facinora
scelestiōra umquam accēpistis? audīte, iūdicēs, operamque dīligentius
date: mox et pēiōra et scelestiōra audiētis.   20

(In Verrem II 4.43.94–5)*

Running vocabulary for 4A(i)

accurrō 3 *accurrī* I run up
Agrigentīn-us ī 2m. person from
  Agrigentum (town in Sicily)
apud (+ acc.) among
armāt-us a um armed
arripiō 3/4 *arripuī* I seize, snatch
clāu-a ae 1f. club
commouēbant 'they began to
  shift' (impf. of *commoueō*)
commoueō 2 I shake free, shift
cōnābantur 'they tried' (impf. of
  cōnor)
concurrō 3 *concurrī* I make a
  charge, rush
effringō 3 *effrēgī* I break open
expugnābant 'they began to
  storm' (impf. of *expugnō*)
expugnō 1 I storm
fām-a ae 1f. rumour, report

fīēbat 'there occurred' (impf. of
  fīō)
Herculēs Hercul-is 3m. Hercules
impetum faciō 3/4 *fēcī* I make an
  attack
intereā meanwhile
ips-e a um (him/her/it)self (gen. s.
  ipsīus)
iūdex iūdic-is 3m. judge
lapidātiō lapidātiōn-is 3f. stoning
longē ā/ab (+ abl.) far from
num surely . . . not?
obsistō 3 (+ dat.) I resist, obstruct
percrēbrēscēbat 'it began to
  spread' (impf. of
  percrēbrēscō)
perueniō 4 *peruēnī (ad)* I reach,
  arrive at, come to
pugn-us ī 2m. fist

quīdam quaedam quoddam a, a
  certain, some (92)
repellō 3 *reppulī* I drive back,
  drive out
repente suddenly
seruōs . . . commouēre 'that
  slaves . . . were shifting'
seruōs . . . cōnārī 'that
  slaves . . . were trying'
seruōs . . . expugnāre 'that
  slaves . . . were storming'
simulācr-um ī 2n. image
surgō 3 *surrēxī* I arise, rise up
tēl-um ī 2n. weapon, missile
templ-um ī 2n. temple
tōt-us a um (like *ūnus* (see **54**):
  gen. s. *tōt-īus*, dat. s. *tōt-ī*)
  whole, complete
ualu-a ae 1f. folding door
Verr-ēs is 3m. Verres

Grammar for 4A

imperfect indicative active and dep.	*iste, quīdam, num* perfect and future infinitive	**accusative and infinitive** negō

Learning vocabulary for 4A(i)

From now on items are listed alphabetically in each category.

Nouns
Agrigentīn-us ī 2m. person from
  Agrigentum (town in Sicily)
fām-a ae 1f. rumour, report;
  reputation
impet-us -ūs 4m. attack
pugn-us ī 2m. fist
simulācr-um ī 2n. image, copy
templ-um ī 2n. temple
Verr-ēs is 3m. Verres

Adjectives
quīdam quaedam quoddam a, a
  certain, some
tōt-us a um (gen. s. *totīus*) whole,
  complete

Verbs
expugnō 1 I storm
impetum faciō 3/4 *fēcī factus*
  I make an attack

perueniō 4 *peruēnī peruentum*
  (ad) I reach, arrive at, come to
repellō 3 *reppulī repulsus* I drive
  back, drive out

Others
apud (+ acc.) among; (at the
  house of, in the hands of, in
  the works of)
intereā meanwhile
repente suddenly

Section 4A(ii)

*Verres orders two henchmen to seize an image of a river-god from a temple.
Though this fails, he has more success with some bronze-work dedicated by
Scipio in a shrine of the Great Mother.*

Assōrīnī posteā, uirī summā fortitūdine, hanc uirtūtem Agrigentīnōrum
imitātī sunt. Chrȳsas fluuius est quī per agrōs Assōrīnōrum fluit.
Assōrīnī hunc fluuium deum habent coluntque et multōs honōrēs eī
dant. in eius templō simulācrum Chrȳsae est ē marmore factum, at
Verrēs, propter singulārem eius templī religiōnem, id poscere nōn ausus   25
est. Tlēpolemō dedit et Hierōnī negōtium. illī nocte uēnēre, ualuās
aedis effrēgēre et intrāuēre. sed custōdēs mātūrē sēnsērunt hominēs ⌐
quōsdam aedem ⌐ intrāre (uīcīnīs signum būcinā dedēre), et Assōrīnī ex
agrīs concurrēbant. fūgērunt Tlēpolemus Hierōque.

Mātris Magnae fānum apud Enguīnōs est. in hōc fānō erant lōrīcae   30
galeaeque aēneae hydriaeque magnae. eās in illō fānō Scīpiō posuit,
nōmenque suum īnscrīpsit. quid plūra dīcam? omnia illa, iūdicēs,
Verrēs abstulit; nihil in illō religiōsissimō fānō relīquit. tū uidēlicet
sōlus, Verrēs, haec monumenta intellegis et iūdicās, Scīpiō, homo
summā doctrīnā et hūmānitāte, haec nōn intellegēbat!   35

*Later the Assorini, men of the highest bravery, imitated this courage of the
people of Agrigentum. The Chrysas is the river which flows through the territory
of the Assorini. The Assorini regard this river as a god and worship it and give it
many honours. In its temple there is a statue of Chrysas made of marble, but
Verres did not dare to ask for it, because of the exceptional religious importance
of that temple. He passed the business over to Tlepolemus and Hiero. They came
by night, broke down the temple doors and entered. But the guardians early
enough realised that some men were entering the shrine (they gave the signal to
neighbours on a trumpet) and the Assorini ran together from the fields.
Tlepolemus and Hiero fled.*

*Among the Enguini there is a shrine of the Great Mother. In this shrine were
breastplates and helmets of bronze and great water-jars. Scipio placed them in
that shrine, and inscribed his own name upon them. Why should I say more? All
of them, judges, Verres made off with; he left nothing in that most holy shrine. It
seems that you alone, Verres, understand and can judge these monuments, while
Scipio, a man of the highest learning and humanity, did not understand them!*

(*In Verrem* II 4.44.96–8)

34. Māter Magna

Running vocabulary for 4A(ii)

aēne-us a um bronze
Assōrīn-us ī 2m. person from
  Assorus
būcin-a ae 1f. trumpet
Chrȳs-as ae m. River Chrysas
colō 3 I worship
concurrēbant 'they began to rush'
  (impf. of *concurrō*)
dīcam line 32 'should I say'
doctrīn-a ae 1f. learning
effringō 3 *effrēgī* I break down
Enguīn-us ī 2m. person from
  Engyum
erant 'there were' (impf. of *sum*)
fact-us a um made, constructed
fluō 3 I flow
fluui-us ī 2m. river
fortitūdō fortitūdinis 3f. bravery

gale-a ae 1f. helmet
Hierō Hierōn-is 3m. Hiero
hominēs . . . intrāre 'that men
  were entering'
hydri-a ae 1f. jar
hūmānitās hūmānitāt-is 3f.
  culture
imitor 1 *imitātus* I copy
īnscrībō 3 *īnscrīpsī* I inscribe
intellegēbat '(he) understood'
  (impf. of *intellegō*)
intellegō 3 I understand
iūdex iūdic-is 3m. judge
lōrīc-a ae 1f. breastplate
marmor marmor-is 3n. marble
Māter Magna Mātris Magnae
  Great Mother (i.e. the goddess
  Cybele)

mātūre early, in time
monument-um ī 2n. monument
negōti-um ī 2n. business, job
posteā afterwards
quī 'which' (nom. s. m.)
quid line 32 why?
religiō religiōn-is 3f. sanctity
religiōs-us a um sacred, revered,
  holy, awesome
Scīpiō Scīpiōnis 3m. Scipio
sentiō 4 *sēnsī* I perceive, realise
singulār-is e peculiar, unique
sōl-us a um alone
Tlēpolem-us ī 2m. Tlepolemus
ualu-a ae 1f. folding door
uidēlicet apparently (sarcastic)

Learning vocabulary for 4A(ii)

Adjectives
colō 3 *coluī cultus* I worship;
  cultivate, till; inhabit
iūdex iūdic-is 3m. judge

negōti-um ī 2n. business, work,
  duty

Verbs
sentiō 4 *sēnsī sēnsus* I feel,
  understand, perceive, realise

Others
posteā afterwards
quid why?
religiōs-us a um sacred, revered,
  holy, awesome

Section 4A(iii)

Verres orders slaves to remove a statue from the shrine of Ceres in Catina, and gets a friend to accuse someone else of the act. But the priestesses of the shrine were witnesses to the deed.

est apud Catinēnsīs sacrārium Cereris. sed nōn licet uirīs in sacrārium illud intrāre. mulierēs et uirginēs sacra cōnficere solent. in eō sacrāriō signum Cereris erat perantīquum. hoc signum seruī Verris ex illō religiōsissimō atque antīquissimō locō nocte sustulērunt.

Among the people of Catina there is a shrine of Ceres, but men are not allowed to enter that shrine. Women and girls are accustomed to complete the sacred rites. In that shrine is a very ancient statue of Ceres. This statue the slaves of Verres removed by night from that most holy and ancient place.

postrīdiē sacerdōtēs Cereris rem ad magistrātūs suōs dētulērunt; omnibus   40
rēs atrōcissima uidēbātur. tum iste, quod suspīciōnem ā sē dēmouēre uolēbat, amīcum quendam suum iussit aliquem reperīre et accūsāre.

nōlēbat enim Verrēs in crīmine esse. amīcus igitur ille nōmen seruī cuiusdam dētulit; tum hunc seruum accūsāuit, testīsque fictōs in eum dedit. senātus Catinēnsium rem lēgibus suīs iūdicāre cōnstituit et   45
sacerdōtēs uocāuit.

For Verres did not wish to be under accusation. Therefore that friend reported the name of a certain slave; then he accused that slave and brought false witnesses against him. The senate of Catina decided to judge the affair by its own laws and called the priests together.

ubi senātus dē omnibus rēbus rogāuit, sacerdōtēs respondērunt seruōs ⌐ Verris in templum nocte ¬ intrāuisse et signum locō ¬ sustulisse; affirmārunt sē ⌐ omnīs omnia ¬ cōnspicātās⁻esse. senātus igitur negāuit illum⁻seruum ⌐ in templum nocte ¬ ingressum⁻esse et signum ¬ sustulisse, et cōnfirmāuit eum ⌐ innocentem ¬ esse. opīnor, iūdicēs, uōs ⌐   50
scelera pēiōra numquam ¬ audīuisse. sed operam mihi date; nam et pēiōra putō uōs ⌐ mox ¬ audītūrōs⁻esse.

(*In Verrem* II 4.45.99–100)

Running vocabulary for 4A(iii)

accūsō 1 I accuse
affirmō 1 I state strongly, assert
aliquis someone (decl. like *quis*)
antīqu-us a um old
atrōx atrōc-is appalling, shocking

audītūrōs esse 'to be about to hear' (fut. inf. of *audiō*)
audīuisse 'to have heard' (perf. inf. of *audiō*)

Catinēns-is is 3m. person from Catina
Cerēs Cerer-is 3f. Ceres (goddess of corn)
cōnficiō 3/4 I carry out

cōnfirmō 1 I state clearly, confirm
cōnspicātās esse 'to have seen'
   (perf. inf. of *cōnspicor*)
cōnstituō 3 *cōnstituī* I decide
crīmen crīmin-is 3n. charge
dēferō dēferre dētulī I report
dēmoueō 2 I remove
dētul- see *dēferō*
erat 'there was' (impf. of *sum*)
eum . . . esse 'that he was'
fict-us a um false
illum seruum . . . ingressum
   esse . . . sustulisse 'that that
   slave had entered . . . (and)
   removed'
ingressum esse 'to have entered'
   (perf. inf. of *ingredior*)
innocēns innocent-is guiltless
intrāuisse 'to have entered' (perf.
   inf. of *intrō*)
iste that person (i.e. Verres)

lēx lēg-is 3f. law
loc-us ī 2m. place
magistrāt-us ūs 4m. magistrate,
   state official
negō 1 I deny, say that X is not the
   case
nōlēbat '(he) did not want' (impf.
   of *nōlō*)
perantīqu-us a um very old
postrīdiē next day
putō 1 I think
reperiō 4 I find
sacerdōs sacerdōt-is 3f. priestess
sacr-a ōrum 2n. pl. rites
sacrāri-um ī 2n. shrine
sē . . . cōnspicātās esse 'that they
   had seen'
seruōs . . . intrāuisse . . . sustulisse
   'that the slaves had
   entered . . . (and) removed'

sign-um ī 2n. statue
soleō 2 I am accustomed, used
suspiciō suspiciōn-is 3f. suspicion
sustulērunt see *tollō*
sustulisse 'to have removed' (perf.
   inf. of *tollō*)
test-is testis 3m. witness
tollō 3 *sustulī* I remove, take away
uidēbātur '(it) seemed' (impf. of
   uideor)
uirgō uirgin-is 3f. young girl,
   virgin
uolēbat 'he wished' (impf. of
   uolō)
uōs . . . audītūrōs esse 'that you
   will hear'
uōs . . . audīuisse 'that you have
   heard'

Learning vocabulary for 4A(iii)

Nouns
ist-e a ud that over there/of yours
   (used especially when
   referring to opponents at a
   trial: *iste* here is always used
   to mean Verres)
loc-us ī 2m. place, region (pl.
   loc-a ōrum 2n. pl.)
magistrāt-us ūs 4m. magistrate,
   state official
sacerdōs sacerdōt-is 3m.f.
   priest(ess)

sacr-a ōrum 2n. pl. rites
sign-um ī 2n. statue (seal; signal,
   sign)

Adjectives
innocēns innocent-is guiltless
sacer sacr-a um holy, sacred

Verbs
accūsō 1 I accuse X (acc.) of Y
   (gen.)
affirmō 1 I state strongly, assert
cōnfirmō 1 I state clearly, confirm

dēferō dēferre dētulī dēlātus I
   report, bring news of; accuse,
   denounce; transfer
negō 1 I deny, say that X is not the
   case
putō 1 I think
reperiō 4 *repperī repertus* I find
soleō 2 *solitus* (semi-dep.) I am
   accustomed, used
tollō 3 *sustulī sublātus* I lift;
   remove, take away

Temple sanctity

Roman self-consciousness about their religion was enhanced by the extraordinary growth of Roman power (the phenomenon that Polybius had set out to explain in his *History*). By the early second century BC the Romans could say to a Greek city: 'that we are people who set quite the highest store on reverence towards the gods, one might surmise especially from the favour vouchsafed to us by the divine power on that account; indeed, we are persuaded also by many other considerations that our high regard for the divine power has been manifest'. The Romans might, not unreasonably, believe that their stupendous success was due to their peculiar piety towards the gods. (*World of Rome*, **362**)

Section 4A(iv)

Three 'tribes' elected one man each to go forward to a final drawing of lots for the priesthood of Jupiter. Verres ensured that his man, Theomnastus, got through to the last three, but how was he to ensure that Theomnastus emerged triumphant from the lottery?

Syrācūsīs lēx est dē sacerdōtiō Iouis (nam id sacerdōtium Syrācūsānī
putant amplissimum esse). haec lēx Syrācūsānōs iubet trīs uirōs ex
tribus generibus per suffrāgia creāre; tunc illōs trīs necesse est sortīrī.   55
ita ūnus ex tribus sacerdōs Iouis fit. Theomnāstus quīdam, amīcus
Verris, istīus imperiō in tribus illīs renūntiātus est. necesse
igitur erat illōs trīs sortīrī. Syrācūsānī, opīnātī Verrem ⌐ sortem sollicitāre
numquam ¬ ausūrum⌐esse, ēuentum laetī exspectābant; spērābant enim
Verrem ⌐ rem nōn ¬ perfectūrum⌐esse. quid fēcit Verrēs? prīmō iste uetuit   60
sortīrī, et iussit Syrācūsānōs extrā sortem Theomnāstum renūntiāre.
Syrācūsānī negābant id ⌐ fierī ¬ posse; praetereā, fās ⌐ negābant ¬ esse.

iussit igitur iste Syrācūsānōs sibi lēgem dē sacerdōtiō recitāre. lēgem ita
recitārunt 'quot hominēs per suffrāgia renūntiāuimus, tot sortīs in
hydriam conicimus. is sacerdōs fit, cuius nōmen ex hydriā exit.' tum   65
Verrēs 'quot hominēs renūntiāuistis?' Syrācūsānī respondēre 'trīs.'
Verrēs 'oportetne igitur trīs sortīs inicere, ūnam ēdūcere?' Syrācūsānī
'ita oportet.' Verrēs igitur Syrācūsānōs iussit trīs sortīs, omnīs nōmine
Theomnāstī īnscrīptās, in hydriam conicere. fīēbat clāmor maximus;
Syrācūsānī negāuēre fās⌐esse. omnibus id scelestissimum uidēbātur. quid   70
plūra dīcam? illō⌐modō Verrēs amplissimum illud Iouis sacerdōtium
Theomnāstō dedit.

So he ordered the Syracusans to read out aloud to him the law about the priesthood. They recited the law as follows: 'As many men as we return by votes, this many lots we throw into the water-jar. That man becomes a priest whose name comes out of the jar.' Then Verres (asked): 'How many men have you returned?' The Syracusans replied: 'Three.' Verres (said): 'So you must throw in three lots and draw out one?' The Syracusans (replied): 'Yes, we must.' And so Verres ordered the Syracusans to throw into the jar three lots, all inscribed with the name of Theomnastus. There was a mighty clamour; the Syracusans said that it was not right. To everybody this appeared a most criminal act. Why should I say more? In that way Verres managed to give that very prestigious priesthood of Jupiter to Theomnastus.

(*In Verrem* II 2.50.126–7)

35. Great Altar of Zeus Eleutherios, Syracuse

Running vocabulary for 4A(iv)

ampl-us a um important,
  prestigious
ausūrum esse 'to be about to dare'
  (fut. inf. of *audeō*)
clāmor clāmōr-is 3m. outcry
coniciō 3/4 I throw
creō 1 I choose
cuius 'whose'
dīcam l.71 'should I say'
ēdūcō 3 I pick out
erat 'it was' (impf. of *sum*)
ēuent-us ūs 4m. outcome, result
exspectābant 'they awaited'
  (impf. of *exspectō*)
extrā (+ acc.) outside
fās indecl. n. right
fās . . . esse 'that it was right'
fīēbat 'there arose' (impf. of *fīō*)
genus gener-is 3n. tribe

hydri-a ae 1f. jar
id . . . posse 'that it could'
illō modō 'in that way'
iniciō 3/4 I throw in
īnscrīpt-us a um inscribed
lēx lēg-is 3f. law
negābant '(they) denied' (impf. of
  negō)
nōmine 'with the name'
oportet it is right, proper,
  necessary
perfectūrum esse 'to be about to
  achieve' (fut. inf. of *perficiō*)
praetereā besides, moreover
prīmō at first
quot however many; how many?
recitō 1 I read out
renūntiātus est '(he) was returned,
  selected'

renūntiō 1 I return, select, appoint
sacerdōti-um ī 2n. priesthood
sors sort-is 3f. lot-drawing; lot
sortior 4 dep. I draw lots
spērābant 'they were hoping'
  (impf. of *spērō*)
suffrāgi-um ī 2n. vote
Syrācūsān-us ī 2m. person from
  Syracuse, Syracusan
Syrācūsīs 'at Syracuse'
Theomnāst-us ī 2m. Theomnastus
tot so many
Verrem . . . ausūrum esse 'that
  Verres . . . would dare'
Verrem . . . perfectūrum esse 'that
  Verres would achieve'
uetō 1 *uetuī* I forbid
uidēbātur '(it) seemed' (impf. of
  uideor)

Learning vocabulary for 4A(iv)

Nouns
clāmor clāmōr-is 3m. shout;
  outcry; noise
lēx lēg-is 3f. law

Syrācūsān-us ī 2m. person from
  Syracuse, Syracusan

Verbs
coniciō 3/4 *coniēcī coniectus*
  I throw

uetō 1 *uetuī uetitus* I forbid

Others
prīmō at first
praetereā besides, moreover

Section 4B(i)

Verres' passion for beautiful objects was matched by his lust. Here, on a mission to King Nicomedes, king of Bithynia in northern Asia Minor (modern Turkey), Verres arrives at Lampsacum, and is put up at the house of Ianitor, while his entourage is lodged elsewhere. He orders his men to find him a woman. (Cf. Introduction, Cicero letter A, B.)

oppidum est in Hellēspontō Lampsacum, iūdicēs. hoc oppidum clārius
et nōbilius est quam ūllum Asiae oppidum, et ipsī Lampsacēnī
quiētiōrēs omnibus‿aliīs‿hominibus. mālunt enim ut Graecī ōtiō ūtī et   75
pāce fruī, quam tumultum excitāre. Verrēs ōlim peruēnit Lampsacum,
cum magnā calamitāte et prope perniciē cīuitātis. Lampsacēnī istum
dēdūxērunt ad Iānitōrem quendam hospitem, comitēsque eius omnīs
apud cēterōs hospitēs collocārunt. ut mōs fuit istīus, statim iussit
comitēs suōs, uirōs pēiōrēs omnibus‿aliīs turpiōrēsque, reperīre   80
mulierem cēterīs pulchriōrem. uōs omnēs scītis, iūdicēs, Verrem
fēminās cēterīs pulchriōrēs semper cupīuisse.

(In Verrem II 1.24.63)

Running vocabulary for 4B(i)

Asi-a ae 1f. Asia Minor
calamitās calamitāt-is 3f. disaster, calamity
cēter-ī ae a the rest; the others
cēterīs 'than the others'
cīuitās cīuitāt-is 3f. state
clār-us a um famous, well-known
collocō 1 I lodge
comes comit-is 3m. companion, friend; (pl.) retinue
cupiō 3/4 I desire, yearn for, want desperately
excitō 1 I raise, arouse
fruor 3 dep. (+ abl.) I enjoy
Hellēspont-um ī 2n. Hellespont

hospes hospit-is 3m. host
Iānitor Iānitōr-is 3m. Ianitor
ips-e a um (him/her/it)self, (them)selves
Lampsac-um ī 2n. Lampsacum (or Lampsacus)
Lampsacum line 76 to Lampsacum
Lampsacēn-us ī 2m. person from Lampsacum (or Lampsacus)
nōbil-is e renowned, distinguished
ōlim once
omnibus aliīs 'than all the others'
omnibus aliīs hominibus 'than all other men'

pāx pāc-is 3f. peace
perniciēs perniciē-ī 5f. destruction
prope almost
quiēt-us a um peaceful, law-abiding
tumult-us ūs 4m. riot, outcry, disorder
turp-is e disgusting, filthy, outrageous
ūll-us a um any
ūtor 3 dep. (+ abl.) I use, make use of

Grammar for 4B

ablative usages   **genitive of description**   *alius, aliquis, ipse*

Provincial governors

The staff that accompanied a governor was basically the same as that which served with an army commander. One of the quaestors elected each year looked after the governors' financial dealings, and one or more *lēgātī*, assigned by the Senate, acted as his immediate subordinates. Again, commander and governor both made use of groups of advisers which made up a *cōnsilium* of the type normally consulted by any Roman who had important decisions to make. There is a famous inscription recording the grant of citizenship to a group of Spanish cavalrymen by Pompey's father, Cnaeus Pompeius Strabo, during his campaign in the war against the Italian allies in 89 BC. This lists a *cōnsilium* which includes, on the one hand, men who had already held the praetorship, and on the other, his own son, then only seventeen (*ILS* 8888). (*World of Rome*, **178**)

Learning vocabulary for 4B(i)

Nouns
Asi-a ae 1f. Asia Minor
calamitās calamitāt-is 3f. disaster, calamity
comes comit-is 3m. companion, friend; (pl.) retinue
hospes hospit-is 3m. host; friend; guest; connection
Lampsacēn-us -ī 2m. person from Lampsacum
pāx pāc-is 3f. peace

Adjectives
cēter-ī ae a the rest; the others
clār-us a um famous, well-known
Graec-us a um Greek
nōbil-is e renowned, distinguished; wellborn, noble
turp-is e disgusting, filthy, outrageous; ugly
ūll-us a um any (gen. *ūllīus*, dat. *ūllī* – cf. *nūllus* 62)

Verbs
cupiō 3/4 *cupīuī cupītus* I desire, yearn for, want desperately
fruor 3 dep. *frūctus* (+ abl.) I enjoy
ūtor 3 dep. *ūsus* (+ abl.) I use, make use of; adopt

Others
prope (adv.) almost; (prep., + acc.) near

Section 4B(ii)

Verres' henchman Rubrius tells him of a rare beauty at Philodamus' house. Verres demands to stay there; when refused, he lodges Rubrius there despite Philodamus' protests.

erat comes istīus Rubrius quīdam, homo factus ad eius libīdinēs. is
homo, quī mīrō artificiō haec omnia inuestīgāre solēbat, ad eum dētulit
uirum esse Philodāmum meliōrem omnibus‿aliīs‿Lampsacēnīs; esse   85
hominem apud eōs multī honōris, magnae exīstimātiōnis; eum fīliam
habēre eximiae pulchritūdinis; sed illam uirginem esse summā
integritāte, pudīcitiā, modestia. Verrēs, ut haec audīuit, summā
cupiditāte exārsit. statim dīxit sē ad Philodāmum migrātūrum esse.
hospes Iānitor, nihil suspicātus, sed opīnātus sē Verrem offendisse,   90
hominem summā uī retinēre coepit. Verrēs igitur, alterō cōnsiliō ūsus,
Rubrium ad Philodāmum migrāre iussit. Philodāmus, ubi haec audīuit,
summā‿celeritāte ad istum uēnit. negāuit hoc mūnus suum esse,
negāuit sē eum receptūrum esse; sē praetōrēs et cōnsulēs recipere solēre,
nōn eōrum amīcōs. quid plūra dīcam? iste tōtum illīus postulātum   95
neglēxit, et seruōs suōs dēdūcere Rubrium ad Philodāmum iussit,
quamquam ille Rubrium recipere nōn dēbēbat.

(In Verrem II 1.25.63–5)

Running vocabulary for 4B(ii)

artifici-um ī 2n. skill, ingenuity
coepī (perf.) I began
cōnsul cōnsul-is 3m. consul
cupiditās cupiditāt-is 3f. lust, desire
dīcam (line 95) 'should I say'
exārdeō 2 *exārsī* I burn, am on fire
eximi-us a um outstanding
exīstimātiō exīstimātiōn-is 3f. reputation
factus ad made for
Iānitor Iānitōr-is 3m. Ianitor

integritās integritāt-is 3f. integrity
inuestīgō 1 I look into, search out
migrō 1 I move
mīr-us a um wonderful, amazing
modesti-a ae 1f. discretion
mūnus mūner-is 3n. job, duty
neglegō 3 *neglēxī* I ignore
offendō 3 *offendī* I offend
omnibus aliīs Lampsacēnīs 'than all other men of Lampsacum'
Philodām-us ī 2m. Philodamus
postulāt-um ī 2n. demand

praetor praetōr-is 3m. praetor (state official)
quī (nom. s. m.) 'who'
recipiō 3 *recēpī receptus* I welcome, receive, take in
retineō 2 I hold back
Rubri-us ī 2m. Rubrius
summā celeritāte 'with the utmost speed'
suspicor 1 dep. I suspect

36. sed illam uirginem esse summā integritāte, pudīcitiā, modestiā

Learning vocabulary for 4B(ii)

Nouns

cupiditās cupiditāt-is 3f. lust, greed, desire

Verbs

coepī (perf. in form) I began

neglegō 3 *neglēxī neglēctus* I ignore, overlook, neglect

recipiō 3/4 *recēpī receptus* I welcome, receive, take in

retineō 2 *retinuī retentus* I hold back, detain, restrain; maintain

Section 4B(iii)

*Philodamus feels in duty bound to show respect to Rubrius, so lays on a party –
at which Verres instructs Rubrius to abduct the girl. As the evening progresses,
things get out of hand.*

Philodāmus, uir aliīs⁻prōuinciālibus semper multō hospitālior
amīciorque, ipsum illum Rubrium domum suam recēpit; et quod
nōluit inuītus uidērī, magnum conuīuium comparāuit. nōn sōlum   100
Rubrium comitēs omnīs inuītāre iussit, sed etiam fīlium suum forās ad
propinquum quendam mīsit ad cēnam. sed Verrēs Rubrium fīliam
Philodāmī auferre iussit. Rubrius igitur cum comitibus suis summā⁻
celeritāte ad conuīuium uēnit; discubuēre; factus est sermō inter eōs;
Graecō mōre bibērunt; et hōc tempore sermōne laetitiāque conuīuium   105
celebrābant. postquam rēs satis calēre uīsa est, Rubrius 'quaesō' inquit
'Philodāme, cūr ad nōs fīliam tuam nōn uocās?' Philodāmus, uir
summā grauitāte, maximē īrātus est; uehementer negābat mulierēs
oportēre in conuīuiō cum uirīs accumbere. tum alius ex aliā parte
'uocā mulierem' inquit; et simul seruōs suōs Rubrius iussit iānuam   110
claudere. haec ubi Philodāmus intellēxit, seruōs suōs ad sē uocāuit et
iussit eōs sē ipsum neglegere, fīliam summā uī dēfendere, rem fīliō
summā⁻celeritāte nūntiāre.

Running vocabulary for 4B(iii)

accumbō 3 I lie down, recline
aliīs prōuinciālibus 'than the
  other provincials'
alius ex aliā parte 'different
  people from different parts'
bibō 3 *bibī* I drink
caleō 2 I am warm/hot
celebrō 1 I fill X (acc.) with
  Y (abl.)
claudō 3 I close
comparō 1 I prepare, get ready
conuīui-um ī 2n. party
discumbō 3 *discubuī* I lie down,
  spread myself about

forās out
grauitās grauitāt-is 3f.
  seriousness, solemnity
hospitāl-is e welcoming
inter (+ acc.) among
intellegō 3 *intellēxī* I perceive,
  understand
inuītō 1 I invite
inuīt-us a um unwilling
ips-e a um (him/her/it) self
laetiti-a ae 1f. merriment,
  festivity, joy
multō (by) much
oportēre 'ought'

Philodām-us ī 2m. Philodamus
postquam after
propinqu-us ī 2m. relative
quaesō 'I say', 'please'
Rubri-us ī 2m. Rubrius
sermō sermōn-is 3m.
  conversation, discussion
sōlum only
summā celeritāte 'with the utmost
  speed'
uehementer strongly

37. postquam rēs satis calēre uīsa est

clāmor intereā factus est per tōtās aedīs. Rubrius ipse Philodāmum aquā
feruentī perfūdit. haec ubi seruī Philodāmī fīliō nūntiārunt, statim domum   115
festīnāuit. omnēs Lampsacēnī, simul‿ut haec audīuēre, eōdem animō
fuērunt et ad aedīs Philodāmī nocte conuēnērunt. iste, ubi uīdit sē suā
cupiditāte et libīdine tantōs tumultūs concitāuisse, effugere uolēbat.

*Meanwhile there was a clamour throughout the whole house. Rubrius himself
drenched Philodamus with boiling water. When the slaves of Philodamus had
reported these events to his son, he immediately hurried home. All the people of
Lampsacum, as soon as they heard these things, were of the same mind and
gathered by night at the house of Philodamus. When the defendant saw that he
had aroused such a great brouhaha by his cupidity and lust, he wanted to get
away.*

(*In Verrem* II 1.26.65–7)

concitō 1 I stir up	*festīnō* 1 I hurry	*Rubri-us ī* 2m. Rubrius
conueniō 4 *conuēnī* (*ad*) I meet (at)	*ips-e a um* (him/her/it) self	*simul ut* as soon as
effugiō 3 I escape	*nūntiārunt = nūntiāuērunt*	*tumult-us ūs* 4m. riot, outcry
feruēns feruent-is boiling	*perfundō* 3 *perfūdī* I drench, soak	
	Philodām-us ī 2m. Philodamus	

Note

lines 110–13. Roman custom allowed free citizen women at *conuīuia,* but Greek custom did not. The only
women at Greek parties were slaves or *hetairai* ('courtesans').

Learning vocabulary for 4B(iii)

Nouns
conuīui-um ī 2n. party
grauitās grauitāt-is 3f.
   seriousness, solemnity;
   importance, authority
laetiti-a ae 1f. merriment,
   festivity, joy
sermō sermōn-is 3m.
   conversation, discussion

Adjectives
ali-us a ud other (see **102**)

sōl-us a um alone (gen. s. *sōlīus,*
   dat. s. *sōlī*)

Verbs
bibō 3 *bibī* I drink
comparō 1 I prepare, provide, get
   ready; get
conueniō 4 *conuēnī conuentum*
   (*ad*) I meet (at)
effugiō 3 *effūgī effugitum* I escape
festīnō 1 I hurry

intellēgō 3 *intellēxī intellēctus*
   I perceive, understand,
   comprehend, grasp
inuītō 1 I invite
oportet 2 *oportuit* X (acc.) ought
   (to + inf.); it is right, fitting
   for X (acc.) to Y (inf.)

Others
inter (+ acc.) among, between
simul at the same time
sōlum (adv. of *sōlus*) only

Section 4B(iv)

The Lampsaceni, all agreeing on their feelings about the behaviour of Verres'
men at the party, attack Verres' house to get at him. They are restrained by some
passing Romans, who suggest they consider the consequences.

haec ubi omnēs Lampsacēnī eōdem⌢sēnsū⌢et⌢dolōre locūtī sunt, ferrō
et saxīs iānuam caedere coepērunt, et eōdem tempore igne circumdare.   120
cīuēs Rōmānī quīdam, quī Lampsacī negōtiābantur, summā⌢celeritāte
concurrērunt. ōrābant obsecrābantque Lampsacēnōs; assēnsērunt
Verrem esse pessimum et omnibus⌢aliīs multō turpiōrem; sed dīxērunt
Lampsacēnōs hominī scelerātō parcere oportēre, potius quam
praetōrem Rōmānum necāre; hōc ⌐ enim ⌐ modō peccātum eōrum minus   125
fore. hīs uerbīs ūsī, tandem Lampsacēnōs ā uī retinuērunt.

When the people of Lampsacum had said these things with the same sentiment
and anguish, they began to beat down the door with iron implements and rocks
and at the same time to encircle it with fire. Some Roman citizens, who were
doing business in Lampsacum, ran up with the greatest speed. They begged and
besought the Lampsacenes; they agreed that Verres was a very bad man and
worse than all others; but they said that the men of Lampsacum ought to spare a
wicked man rather than kill a Roman praetor; for in this way their crime would
be the lesser. Using these words, they finally held the Lapsacenes back from
violence.

(*In Verrem* II 1.27.68–9)

Running vocabulary for 4B(iv)

assentiō 4 *assēnsī* I agree
caedō 3 I cut (down); beat (down)
circumdō 1 I surround
concurrō 3 *concurrī* I run together
dolor dolōr-is 2m. pain, anguish
eōdem sēnsū et dolōre (abl.) 'with
   the same sentiment and
   anguish'
hōc modō 'in this way'

Lampsacī 'at Lampsacum'
multō (by) much, far
negōtior 1 dep. I do business
obsecrō 1 I beg, beseech
omnibus aliīs 'than all others'
ōrō 1 I beg, pray
parcō 3 (+ dat.) I spare
peccāt-um ī 2n. crime, error

praetor praetōr-is 3m. praetor
   (Roman state official; here
   Verres)
quī (nom. pl. m.) 'who'
sax-um ī 2n. stone, rock
scelerāt-us a um wicked
sēns-us ūs 4m. sentiment
summā celeritāte 'with the utmost
   speed'

Learning vocabulary for 4B(iv)

Nouns
celeritās celeritāt-is 3f. speed
praetor praetōr-is 3m. praetor
   (Roman state official)

Verbs
caedō 3 *cecīdī caesus* I cut
   (down); flog, beat; kill
concurrō 3 *concurrī concursum*
   I run together

obsecrō 1 I beg, beseech
ōrō 1 I beg, pray
parcō 3 *pepercī parsum* (+ dat.)
   I spare

Section 4C(i)

Diodorus lived in the Sicilian town of Lilybaeum, and possessed some very fine silver cups. Here, Diodorus finds out that Verres is after them, so he claims a relative in Malta has them; when Verres looks for the relative, Diodorus writes to the relative telling him to say to Verres' men that he has just sent the cups back to Lilybaeum. Diodorus then tactfully leaves Sicily for Rome.

Diodōrus, quī Melitēnsis erat, Lilybaeī multōs annōs habitābat. hic
homo, quem dīcō, erat nōbilī genere nātus et splendidus et grātiōsus
propter uirtūtem, quam omnēs Lilybītanī cognōuerant. at Verre⁻
praetōre, prope āmissūrus erat omnia quae domī collēgerat. nam   130
comitēs, quōs Verrēs Lilybaeum dēdūxerat, Diodōrum pōcula quaedam
habēre nūntiāuērunt; ea pōcula omnibus aliīs pulchriōra esse. (quae
pōcula, ut posteā audīuī, Mentōr summō artificiō fēcerat.) quod ubi
Verrēs audīuit, cupiditāte īnflammātus, Diodōrum ad sē uocāuit et
pōcula, quōrum mentiōnem comitēs fēcerant, poscēbat. ille sē Lilybaeī   135
ea pōcula nōn habēre respondit, sed Melitae apud propinquum
quendam relīquisse. tum iste mittēbat hominēs Melitam, scrībēbat ad
quōsdam Melitēnsīs, pōcula rogābat, iubēbat Diodōrum ad illum
propinquum suum dare litterās. quod ubi audīuit, Diodōrus, quī sua
seruāre cōnstituerat, ad propinquum suum litterās mīsit; quibus in   140
litterīs scrībere ausus⁻erat propinquum oportēre negāre sē pōcula
habēre, sed affirmāre sē ea paucīs illīs diēbus mīsisse Lilybaeum. quās
ubi propinquus perlēgit, ita fēcit. intereā Diodōrus ipse, quī abesse
domō paulisper cōnstituerat potius quam argentum āmittere, Lilybaeō
abiit.   145

(In Verrem II 4.18.38–9)

Running vocabulary for 4C(i)

absum abesse I am away from, I am absent
argent-um ī 2n. silver; silver-plate
artifici-um ī 2n. skill
ausus erat 'he had dared' (plupf. of *audeō*)
cognōuerant '(they) had become acquainted with', '(they) knew' (plupf. of *cognōscō*)
collēgerat 'he had collected' (plupf. of *colligō* 3 *collēgī*)
cōnstituerat '(he) had decided' (plupf. of *cōnstituō* 3 *cōnstituī*)
dēdūxerat 'he had brought (down)' (plupf. of *dēdūcō*)

Diodōr-us ī 2m. Diodorus
fēcerant '(they) had made' (plupf. of *faciō*)
fēcerat '(he) had made' (plupf. of *faciō*)
genus gener-is 3n. family, stock
grātiōs-us a um popular
habitābat : tr. 'had been living'
īnflammāt-us a um inflamed, on fire
Lilybaeī (locative) at Lilybaeum
Lilybaeō (abl.) from Lilybaeum
Lilybaeum (acc.) to Lilybaeum
Lilybītān-us ī 2m. person from Lilybaeum
litter-ae ārum 1f. pl. letter

Melitae (locative) in Malta
Melitam (acc.) to Malta
Melitēns-is Melitēnsis 3m. person from Malta, Maltese
mentiō mentiōn-is 3f. mention
mentiōnem facere to make mention of X (gen.)
Mentōr Mentōr-is 3m. Mentor
nāt-us a um (+ abl.) born of, from
pauc-ī ae a few
paulisper for a while
perlegō 3 *perlēgī* I read through, peruse
pōcul-um ī 2n. cup
propinqu-us ī 2m. relative

quae (line 132 acc. pl. n.) (and) these (lit. 'which')
quam (acc. s. f.) which
quās (acc. pl. f.) line 142 (and) this (sc. letter) (lit. 'which')
quem (acc. s. m.) whom

quī (nom. s. m.) who
quibus (abl. pl. f.) line 140 (and) this (lit. 'which')
quod (acc. s. n.) lines 133, 139 (and) this (lit. 'which')
quōrum (gen. pl. n.) of which

quōs (acc. pl. m.) whom
seruō 1 I keep safe, preserve
splendid-us a um fine, excellent
Verre praetōre 'with Verres (as) praetor' (abl.)

Grammar for 4C

pluperfect indicative active and dep.
quī, quae, quod

uses of ablative, including ablative absolute

locative

38. *pōcula quaedam*

Learning vocabulary for 4C(i)

Nouns

argent-um ī 2n. silver; silver-plate; money
genus gener-is 3n. family, stock; tribe
litter-ae ārum 1f. pl. letter
pōcul-um ī 2n. cup

Adjectives

īnflammāt-us a um inflamed, on fire
nāt-us a um (+ abl.) born of, from

Verbs

absum abesse āfuī āfutūrus I am away from, I am absent

cōnstituō 3 *cōnstituī cōnstitūtus* I decide
perlegō 3 *perlēgī perlēctus* I read through, peruse
seruō 1 I keep safe, preserve (save, keep)

Section 4C(ii)

Verres, enraged that he can no longer simply steal the cups from Diodorus'
relation, dreams up a way of summoning Diodorus back to Sicily – on a
trumped-up charge. Verres' relations in Rome warn him that he has gone too far.

quae ubi iste audīuit, nōn mediocrī īnsāniā et furōre sē gerere omnibus
uidēbātur; hōc modō agēbat, quia nōn potuerat argentum Diodōrō
auferre. Diodōrō igitur absentī minābātur, clāmābat pālam,
lacrimābātur. postrēmō seruōs suōs iussit Diodōrum tōtā prōuinciā
conquīrere; sed ille iam castra commōuerat et pōcula collēgerat; illō   150
tempore Rōmae habitābat. Verrēs igitur, quī aliquō modō Diodōrum
in prōuinciam reuocāre uolēbat, hanc ratiōnem excōgitābat: cōnstituit
Diodōrum, quem absentem esse sciēbat, fīctī cuiusdam crīminis
accūsāre. rēs clāra erat tōtā Siciliā, Verrem argentī cupiditāte hominem
absentem accūsāuisse.   155

intereā Diodōrus Rōmae sordidātus circum patrōnōs atque hospitēs
quōs cognōuerat circumībat, et rem omnem nārrābat. quae ubi pater
amīcīque Verris audiērunt, litterās uehementīs istī mittēbant rem clāram
esse tōtā Rōmā et inuidiōsam; perspicuum esse omnia illa propter
argentum fierī; īnsānīre eum; cauēre oportēre; peritūrum esse hōc   160
ūnō crīmine. quās ubi Verrēs perlēgit, sēnsit sē stultē fēcisse; nam
prīmum annum prōuinciae sibi esse; sē nūllam pecūniam hōc tempore
habēre. furōrem suum igitur nōn pudōre, sed metū et timōre repressit;
Diodōrum absentem condemnāre nōn ausus est. Diodōrus intereā,
Verre praetōre, prope triennium prōuinciā domōque caruit.   165

Meanwhile at Rome, Diodorus was going around his patrons and the
guest-friends he knew, dressed in dirty clothing, and reporting the whole affair.
When Verres' father and friends heard this, they sent a strongly worded letter to
the defendant (saying) that the whole business was well known and unpopular at
Rome; it was obvious that all this was being done for money; he was crazy; he
should watch out; he would be done for because of this one charge. When Verres
had read the letter, he realised that he had acted foolishly; for it was his first
year of provincial governorship; he had no money at this time. So he held his
madness in check not out of a sense of shame, but through fear and
apprehension; he did not dare to condemn Diodorus in his absence. Meanwhile
Diodorus, under Verres' praetorship, had to do without the province and his
home for nearly three years.

quid plūra dīcam? nihil hōc clārius esse potest, iūdicēs. eō tempore,
Verre praetōre, tōtā Siciliā, nēmo poterat cōnseruāre aut domī retinēre
eās rēs quās Verrēs magis concupīuerat.

(In Verrem II 4.19.40–2)

Running vocabulary for 4C(ii)

absēns absent-is absent, away
careō 2 (+ abl.) I do without, lack, stay away from
caueō 2 I am wary, am on guard, take care
circum (+ acc.) around
circumeō circumīre I go round
cognōuerat 'he had got to know' 'he knew' (plupf. of *cognōscō*)
collēgerat 'he had collected' (plupf. of *colligō* 3 *collēgī*)
commōuerat '(he) had moved' (plupf. of *commoueō* 2 *commōuī*) *castra commōuerat* '(he) had moved camp'
concupīuerat '(he) had desired' (plupf. of *concupīscō* 3)
condemnō 1 I find guilty, condemn
conquīrō 3 I look for, search out
cōnseruō 1 I save, keep safe
crīmen crīmin-is 3n. charge, accusation
dīcam line 166 'should I say'
Diodōr-us ī 2m. Diodorus
excōgitō 1 I think up, devise
fīct-us a um trumped up

furor furōr-is 3m. passion, anger, rage
gerere: sē gerere lit. 'to conduct himself, i.e. 'to behave'
hōc ūnō crīmine 'as a result of this single accusation' (abl.)
īnsāni-a ae 1f. madness, lunacy
īnsāniō 4 I am mad
inuidiōs-us a um unpopular
lacrimor 1 dep. I burst into tears, cry
mediocr-is e moderate, ordinary
met-us ūs 4m. fear
metū 'from fear' (abl.)
mod-us ī 2m. way, fashion, manner
palam openly, publicly
patrōn-us ī 2m. patron (see p. 166)
pereō perīre periī peritum I perish, am done for
perspicu-us a um clear, obvious
postrēmō finally
potuerat 'he had been able' (plupf. of *possum*)
prōuinci-a ae 1f. province
pudor pudōr-is 3m (sense of) shame
pudōre 'from shame' (abl.)

quae (acc. pl. n.) lines 146, 157 (and) these (sc. things) (lit. 'which')
quās (acc. pl. f.) which
quās (acc. pl. f.) line 161 (and) this (sc. letter) (lit. 'which')
quem (acc. s. m.) whom
quī (nom. s. m.) who
quōs (acc. pl. m.) whom
ratiō ratiōn-is 3f. plan, reason
reprimō 3 *repressī* I restrain, keep a grip on
reuocō 1 I call back
Sicili-a ae 1f. Sicily
sordidāt-us a um poorly dressed (a sign of mourning or of being on a charge)
stultē stupidly
timōre 'from apprehension' (abl.)
tōtā prōuinciā 'over the whole province' (abl.)
tōtā Rōmā 'all over Rome' (abl.)
tōtā Siciliā 'all over Sicily' (abl.)
trienni-um -ī 2n. a period of three years
uehemēns uehement-is strongly worded
Verre praetōre 'with Verres (as) praetor' (abl.)

Learning vocabulary for 4C(ii)

Nouns
mod-us ī 2m. way, fashion, manner
prōuinci-a ae 1f. province
ratiō ratiōn-is 3f. plan, method; reason; count, list; calculation
Sicili-a ae 1f. Sicily

Adjectives
absēns absent-is absent, away

Verbs
circumeō circumīre circumiī circumitum I go around
colligō 3 *collēgī collēctus* I collect, gather; gain, acquire

commoueō 2 *commōuī commōtus* I move; remove; excite, disturb
excōgitō 1 I think up, devise
reuocō 1 I call back

Others
circum (+ acc.) around
postrēmō finally
stultē stupidly

Governor as judge

Although the origin of the provinces was military and the perception of them remained so to a considerable extent, the work done by a provincial governor had always included tasks which we would consider civilian. These became progressively more important as the empire expanded. One of the major functions of the governor in a province not under military threat was jurisdiction. As an *imperium*-holder, he was able to conduct cases between Roman citizens, but, simply because he was the representative of the power of Rome, he also dealt with those involving non-Romans. The extent of such jurisdiction varied from province to province, because it depended on the type and number of the provincial communities themselves. (*World of Rome,* **180**)

Section 4D(i)

*Verres made a habit of accepting bribes from cities in Sicily which wanted to
avoid contributing money, men or ships to the defence of the province (see
Introduction, Cicero letter C). Consequently, while Verres became very rich, the
Sicilian defences were almost non-existent and the province was wide open for
pirates to loot almost at will. Here one of Verres' ships manages to capture a
pirate ship, but Verres uses the captives for his own purposes.*

P. Caesētiō et P. Tadiō praefectīs, decem nāuēs sēmiplēnae, quae ē
portū ēgressae erant, nāuem quandam pīrātīs refertam cēpērunt. sed quid   170
dīxī? nāuem nōn cēpērunt, sed inuēnērunt et abdūxērunt. erat ea nāuis
plēna iuuenum fōrmōsissimōrum, plēna argentī, plēna uestium. quae
nāuis, ut dīxī, ā classe nostrā nōn capta est, sed inuenta est et abducta
est. quibus‿rēbus‿nūntiātīs, Verrēs, quamquam in actā cum mulierculīs
quibusdam iacēbat ēbrius, ērēxit sē tamen et statim iussit omnia quae in   175
nāue abductā erant exhibērī. P. Caesētiō et P. Tadiō ducibus, nāuis
pīrātārum Syrācūsās ā nautīs appellitur. naue ⌜ eō ⌝ appulsā, exspectātur ab
omnibus supplicium. eī praedōnēs, quī senēs et dēfōrmēs erant, ā Verre ut
hostēs habitī, secūrī percussī sunt; hīs‿senibus‿necātīs, illī, quī fōrmōsī
uidēbantur aut quī artificēs erant, ab eō abductī, amīcīs datī sunt. aliī ab eō   180
cohortī et fīliō distribūtī sunt, aliī, quī symphōniacī erant, amīcīs
quibusdam Rōmam missī sunt. quibus‿omnibus‿distribūtīs, archipīrāta
ipse ā nūllō uīsus est. hodiē, iūdicēs, omnēs arbitrantur pecūniam Verrī
clam ā pīrātīs datam esse, et archipīrātam līberātum esse.

(*In Verrem* II 5.25.63–4)

39. nāuis

Running vocabulary for 4D(i)

ā/ab (+ abl.) by (after passive verbs)
abdūcō 2 *abdūxī abductus* I appropriate, withdraw, remove
abducta est '(it) was appropriated' (perf. passive of *abdūcō*)
abduct-us a um having been removed (perf. participle passive of *abdūcō*)
act-a ae 1f. shore
appellitur lit. '(it) is brought to shore' (pres. passive of *appellō* 3 *appulī appulsus*) [Translate as *past* tense. Since Latin often uses the present tense 'vividly' in this way, do not hesitate to translate a Latin present tense into the past in English if it suits the context better.]
archipīrāt-a ae 1m. pirate chief
artifex artific-is 3m. craftsman
Caesēti-us ī 2m. Caesetius
capta est '(it) was captured' (perf. passive of *capiō*)
classis class-is 3f. fleet
cohors cohort-is 3f. governor's retinue
datam esse 'to have been given' '(that) (it) had been given' (perf. passive inf. of *dō* 1)
datī sunt '(they) were given' (perf. passive of *dō*)
dēfōrm-is e misshapen, ugly

distribūtī sunt '(they) were divided up among' (+ dat.) (perf. passive of *distribuō* 3 *distribuī distribūtus*)
ēbri-us a um drunk
eō to that place, thither
ērigō 3 *ērēxī* I draw up, lift up
exhibērī 'to be put on display' (pres. inf. passive of *exhibeō* 2)
exspectātur lit. '(it) is awaited' (pres. passive of *exspectō* 1) [Translate as *past* tense]
habit-us a um held, regarded (perf. passive participle of *habeō*)
hīs senibus necātīs 'with these old men having been killed' (abl. absolute)
iaceō 2 I lie
inuenta est '(it) was found' (perf. passive of *inueniō*)
līberātum esse 'to have been freed' '(that) (he) had been freed' (perf. passive inf. of *līberō* 1)
missī sunt '(they) were sent' (perf. passive of *mittō* 3 *mīsī missus*)
muliercul-a ae 1f. woman (with sneering tone)
naue . . . appulsā 'with the ship having been brought to shore' (abl. absolute)
nāuis nāu-is 3f. ship
naut-a ae 1m. sailor

P. = Pūbliō (*Pūbli-us ī* 2m.) Publius
percussī sunt '(they) were struck' (perf. passive of *percutiō* 3/4 *percussī percussus*)
pīrāt-a ae 1m. pirate
port-us ūs 4m. harbour
praedō praedōn-is 3m. pirate
praefect-us ī 2m. captain, prefect
quibus omnibus distribūtīs 'with all whom having been distributed' (abl. absolute)
quibus rēbus nūntiātīs 'with which things having been announced' (ablative absolute)
refert-us a um filled (with: abl.) (perfect participle passive of *referciō* 4 *refersī refertus* I fill up)
secūr-is secūris 3f. axe (abl. s. *secūrī*)
sēmiplēn-us a um half-full; undermanned
supplici-um ī 2n. punishment; death penalty
symphōniac-us ī 2m. musician
Syrācūs-ae ārum 1f. Syracuse
Tadi-us ī 2m. Tadius
uestis vest-is 3f. clothes
uidēbantur '(they) seemed' (impf. passive of *uideō:* lit. 'they were seen' (sc. 'as'))
uīsus est '(he) was seen' (perf. passive of *uideō*)

Grammar for 4D

the passive
all tenses, imperative,
infinitive, participle

ferō and eō

Learning vocabulary for 4D(i)

Nouns
classis class-is 3f. fleet
cohors cohort-is 3f. governor's retinue; cohort
nāuis nāu-is 3f. ship
naut-a ae 1m. sailor
pīrāt-a ae 1m. pirate

port-us ūs 4m. harbour
praedō praedōn-is 3m. pirate; robber
praefect-us ī 2m. captain, prefect; (adj.) in charge of (+ dat.)

Adjectives
ēbri-us a um drunk

Verbs
exspectō 1 I await, wait for
iaceō 2 I lie
līberō 1 I free, release

Others
ā/ab by (usually a person, after passive verbs); (away from)

Section 4D(ii)

*The Syracusans, however, kept a count of the pirates executed. Verres, to make
up numbers, executed Roman citizens who, he claimed, had been involved in
Sertorius' revolt or had joined up with pirates.*

Syrācūsānī, hominēs perītī et hūmānī, habēbant ratiōnem cotīdiē   185
praedōnum secūrī percussōrum. sed praedōnum magnum numerum
dēesse mox sēnsērunt (nam ratiō eōrum habita erat ex numerō
rēmōrum quī cum nāue captī erant). nam ā Verre omnēs quī aliquid
aut artificī aut fōrmae habuerant remōtī atque abductī erant. quibus⌐
abductīs, iste homo nefārius, clāmōrem populī fore suspicātus, in   190
praedōnum locum substituere coepit cīuīs Rōmānōs, quōs in carcerem
anteā coniēcerat (eōs Sertōriānōs mīlitēs fuisse aut suā uoluntāte cum
praedōnibus coniūnctōs esse arguēbat). hōc modō cīuēs Rōmānī, quī ā
multīs cīuibus Rōmānīs cognōscēbantur et ab omnibus dēfendēbantur,
secūrī feriēbantur.   195

haec igitur est gesta rēs, haec erat uictōria praeclāra: Verre praetōre,
nāue ⌐ praedōnum ⌐ captā, dux praedōnum līberātus est, symphōniacī
Rōmam missī, fōrmōsī hominēs et artificēs domum Verris abductī, et in
eōrum locum cīuibus⌐Rōmānīs ⌐ secūrī⌐ percussīs, omnis uestis ablāta, omne
aurum et argentum ablātum atque āuersum.   200

(In Verrem II 5.28.71–3)

40. argentum

Running vocabulary for 4D(ii)

abductī (sc. *sunt*) '(they were) removed' (perf. passive of *abdūcō* 3 *abdūxī abductus*)

abductī erant '(they) had been removed' (plupf. pass. of *abdūcō* 3 *abdūxī abductus*)

ablāt-a/um (sc. *est*) '(it was) taken away' (perf. passive of *auferō auferre abstulī ablātus*)

anteā formerly, previously

arguō 3 I claim, charge

artifex artific-is 3m. craftsman

artificī-um ī 2n. skill: the gen. *artificī* depends on *aliquid*, 'some [of] skill', cf. *satis*, *nimis* with gen. (**31** and **102**)

āuersum (sc. *est*) '(it was) stolen' (perf. passive of *āuertō* 3 *āuertī āuersus*)

aut . . . aut either . . . or

captī erant '(they) had been captured' (plupf. passive of *capiō*)

carcer carcer-is 3m. prison

cīuibus Rōmānīs . . . percussīs 'with Roman citizens having been executed' (abl. absolute)

cognōscēbantur 'they were recognised' (impf. passive *of cognōscō*)

coniūnctōs esse 'to have been linked' '(that they) were linked' (perf. passive inf. of *coniungō* 3 *coniūnxī coniūnctus*)

cotīdiē daily

dēfendēbantur '(they) were defended' (impf. passive of *dēfendō*)

dēsum dēesse I am missing, lacking

feriēbantur '(they) were being struck' (impf. passive of *feriō* 4)

fōrmae [gen. follows *aliquid*: cf. note on *artificium*]

gesta (*est*) '(it) was achieved' (perf. passive of *gerō*)

habita erat '(it) had been had' (plupf. passive of *habeō*) tr. 'had been made'

hūmān-us a um considerate, civilised

līberātus est '(he) was freed' (perf. passive of *līberō*)

missī (sc. *sunt*) '(they were) sent' (perf. passive of *mittō*)

nāue . . . captā 'with a ship having been captured' (abl. absolute)

nefāri-us a um wicked, vile, criminal

numer-us ī 2m. number

percuss-us a um executed (perf. participle passive of *percutiō* 3/4 *percussī percussus*)

perīt-us a um knowledgeable, skilful

praeclār-us a um very famous, outstanding, brilliant

quibus abductīs 'with whom having been removed' (abl. absolute)

remōtī (erant) '(they) had been got out of the way' (plupf. pass. of *remoueō* 2 *remōuī remōtus*)

rēm-us ī 2m. oar

secūr-is secūris 3f. axe

Sertōriān-us a um of Sertorius (Roman who led a revolt against the Roman dictator Sulla from Spain in 83 and gained some support. See Text 4F(ii))

substituō 3 I substitute

symphōniac-us ī 2m. musician

uestis uest-is 3f. clothing

uoluntās uoluntāt-is 3f. will, wish

Learning vocabulary for 4D(ii)

Nouns

numer-us ī 2m. number

secūris secūr-is 3f. axe

uestis uest-is 3f. clothes, clothing, dress

Adjectives

nefāri-us a um wicked, vile, criminal

praeclār-us a um very famous, outstanding, brilliant

Verbs

desum dēesse dēfuī dēfutūrus I am missing, lacking; fail; abandon (+ dat.)

feriō 4 I strike, beat; kill (no 3rd or 4th principal parts – these

tenses are supplied by *percussī, percussus*, from *percutiō* 3/4 I strike, beat; kill)

Others

aut . . . aut either . . . or

cotīdiē daily

Piracy

The Mediterranean had been troubled for decades by groups of pirates who disrupted trade and the corn supply. Some headway was made in the eastern Mediterranean by Rome's generals in the 70s; but the problem was not eradicated. In 67 BC the tribune A. Gabinius, against fierce senatorial opposition, proposed a bill directly to the people that Pompey should be given *imperium* against them, covering the whole Mediterranean. With brilliant organisation and strategy Pompey cleared first the western and then the eastern Mediterranean in a single season of campaigning. (*World of Rome*, **64**)

Section 4E(i)

Verres took a fancy to the wife of a certain Syracusan, Cleomenes. In order to get Cleomenes out of the way, Verres put him, a Syracusan, in charge of what there was of the fleet. Here Verres, living it up as usual, sees Cleomenes off from the harbour. Cleomenes, fancying himself as a second Verres, hears that a pirate ship is nearby – and runs for it. The rest of the fleet follows.

ēgreditur Cleomenēs ē portū. ēgredientem eum sex nāuēs sēmiplēnae
sequuntur. Verrēs tamen, quī multīs diēbus nōn erat uīsus, tum
Cleomenem ēgredientem nāuīsque sequentīs īnspiciēbat: quibus vīsīs,
homo ille, praetor populī Rōmānī, stetit soleātus, cum palliō purpureō,
mulierculā quādam nīxus in lītore. cum classis quīntō diē Pachȳnum   205
dēnique appulsaˉesset, nautae, coāctī fame, rādīcēs palmārum agrestium
colligere coepērunt. Cleomenēs, quī putābat sē mox alterum Verrem
fore, tōtōs diēs in lītore manēbat pōtāns atque amāns.

ecce autem repente, ēbriō Cleomenē, nautīs cibō egentibus, nūntiātur
nāuīs praedōnum esse in portū Odyssēae. nostra autem classis erat,   210
Cleomenē pōtante et ēbriō, in portū Pachȳnī. quōs praedōnēs cum
uīdisset adeuntīs, prīnceps Cleomenēs in nāue suā mālum ērigī, praecīdī
ancorās imperāuit et cēterās nāuīs sē sequī iussit. cum nāuis Cleomenis,
cuius celeritās incrēdibilis erat, breuī tempore Helōrum aduolāuisset
fugiēns, cēterī tamen, ut poterant, paulō tardius Helōrum nāuigābant,   215
nōn praedōnum impetum fugientēs sed imperātōrem sequentēs. tum
nāuēs postrēmae fugientēs in perīculō prīncipēs erant; postrēmās enim
nāuīs prīmās aggrediēbantur praedōnēs. cum prīma ā praedōnibus
captaˉesset nāuis Haluntīnōrum, cuius praefectus Phȳlarchus erat, mox
Apollōniēnsis nāuis capta est, cuius praefectus Anthrōpinus occīsus est.   220

(*In Verrem* II 5.33.86–34.90)

41. postrēmas enim nāuīs prīmās aggrediēbantur
praedōnēs

Running vocabulary for 4E(i)

adeuntīs (acc. pl. m.) '(as they were) approaching' (pres. part. of *adeō*)

aduolāuisset '(it) had flown' (plupf. subj. of *aduolō* 1)

aggredior 3/4 dep. I attack (lit. 'I go up to')

agrest-is e wild

amāns (nom. s. m.) 'making love' (pres. part. of *amō* 1)

ancor-a ae 1f. anchor-cable

Anthrōpin-us ī 2m. Anthropinus

Apollōniēns-is e from Apollonia (a town in Sicily)

appulsa esset 'had landed' (plupf. subj. passive of *appellor* 3 *appulī appulsus*)

capta esset '(it) had been captured' (plupf. subj. pass. of *capiō* 3/4 *cēpī captus*)

cib-us ī 2m. food

Cleomen-ēs is 3m. Cleomenes

cōgō 3 *coēgī coāctus* I force, compel

cuius (gen. s.) 'whose', 'of which'

cum although (line 213)

cum when (lines 205, 211, 218)

dēnique finally

egentibus (abl. pl. m.) '(as they were) lacking, needing' (pres.

part. of *egeō* 2 (+ abl.) I need, lack)

ēgredientem (acc. s. m.) '(as he was) leaving' (pres. part of *ēgredior*)

ērigō 3 I erect

fam-ēs is 3f. hunger

fugiēns (nom. s. f.) 'fleeing' (pres. part. of *fugiō* 3/4)

fugientēs (nom. pl. m./f.) 'fleeing', 'as they were fleeing' (pres. part. of *fugiō* 3/4)

Haluntīn-us ī 2m. person from Haluntium (a town in northern Sicily)

Helōr-us ī 2f. Helorus (city on east coast of Sicily)

incrēdibil-is e amazing, unbelievable

lītus lītor-is 3n. shore

māl-us ī 2m. mast

muliercul-a ae 1f. woman (sneering tone)

nāuigō 1 I sail

nītor 3 dep. *nīxus* (+ abl.) I lean on

Odyssē-a ae 1f. Odyssea (a promontory on the southern extremity of Sicily)

Pachȳn-us ī 2m./f. Pachynus (the southeastern promontory of Sicily)

palli-um ī 2n. Greek cloak

palm-a ae 1f. palm-tree

paulō slightly, rather

Phȳlarch-us ī 2m. Phylarchus

postrēm-us a um last

pōtāns (nom. s. m.) 'drinking' (pres. part. of *pōtō* 1)

pōtante (abl. s. m.) 'drinking' (pres. part. of *pōtō* 1)

praecīdō 3 I cut

prīnceps prīncip-is 3m. leader; (adj.) first

purpure-us a um purple; crimson

quīnt-us a um fifth

rādīx rādīc-is 3f. root

sēmiplēn-us a um half-full; under-manned

sequentēs (nom. pl. m.) 'following' (pres. part. of *sequor* 3 dep.)

sequentīs (acc. pl. f.) 'following', 'as they were following' (pres. part. of *sequor* 3 dep.)

soleāt-us a um beslippered, in slippers

tard-us a um slow

uīdisset 'he had seen' (plupf. subj. of *uideō* 2 *uīdī*)

Grammar for 4E

present participle	***cum* + subj.**	**genitive of relative pronoun**
pluperfect subjunctives	***mare***	

Learning vocabulary for 4E(i)

Nouns

cib-us ī 2m. food

Cleomen-ēs is 3m. Cleomenes

lītus lītor-is 3n. shore

prīnceps prīncip-is 3m. leader, chieftain; (adj.) first

Adjectives

postrēm-us a um last

quīnt-us a um fifth

Verbs

aggredior 3/4 dep. *aggressus* I attack (go up to)

egeō 2 *eguī* – (+ abl. or gen.) I lack, need, am in want of

nāuigō 1 I sail

nītor 3 dep. *nīsus* or *nīxus* (+ abl.) I lean on; I strive, exert myself

Others

dēnique finally; in a word

paulō slightly (cf. *multō*)

Section 4E(ii)

Things go from bad to worse. Cleomenes reaches Helorus, disembarks, and hides. The pirates set fire to the fleet and the whole population comes out to watch.

quibus rēbus, Cleomene⌐īnsciō, factīs, Cleomenēs, cum Helōrum
peruēnisset, sē in terram ē nāue ēiēcit, nāuemque fluctuantem in marī
relīquit. reliquī praefectī nāuium, cum imperātōrem in terram exeuntem
uīdissent, secūtī sunt; nam ipsī, quōrum nāuēs tardiōrēs nāue Cleomenis
erant, marī nūllō modō praedōnēs effugere poterant. tum praedōnum dux,   225
cuius nōmen Hēracleō erat, Rōmānōs ita facile uictum īrī nōn opīnātus,
classem pulcherrimam populī Rōmānī, in lītus expulsam et ēiectam,
īnflammārī incendīque iussit. Cleomenēs, cum in pūblicō esse nōn ausus
esset, quamquam nox erat, inclūserat sē domī. hōc modō, Cleomenē domī
manente, classis cuius Cleomenēs prīnceps erat ā praedōnibus incēnsa est.   230

ō tempus miserum prōuinciae Siciliae! ō rem calamitōsam! ō istīus
nēquitiam! ūnā atque eādem nocte, iūdicēs, uidēre licēbat Verrem
amōre, classem Rōmānam incendiō praedōnum cōnflagrantem. quārum
rērum grauium nūntius Syrācūsās peruēnit ad praetōrium, quō istum ē
conuīuiō redūxerant paulō ante mulierēs cum cantū et symphōnia. sed   235
(ita seuēra erat domī Verris disciplīna) in rē tam grauī nēmo ad
Verrem admittēbātur, nēmo audēbat Verrem dormientem excitāre.
calamitās tamen breuī tempore ab omnibus cognita est; nam nāuīs
cōnflagrantīs cōnspicātī, Syrācūsānī magnam calamitātem acceptam esse
et mox perīculum sibi maximum fore statim intellēxērunt. concursābat   240
igitur ex urbe tōtā maxima multitūdō.

O unhappy time for the province of Sicily! O disastrous affair! O the wickedness of the defendant! On one and the same night, judges, one could see Verres burning from love, and a Roman fleet burning from the fires of pirates. A messenger (bringing news of) these grave matters arrived at the governor's residence in Syracuse, to where women had a little earlier brought back the defendant from a feast accompanied by singing and a band. But (so strict was the discipline of Verres' house) in such a serious situation no one was admitted to see Verres, no one dared to wake up Verres as he slept. But the calamity was soon known about by all; for having seen the ships blazing, the Syracusans realised at once that a great disaster had been sustained and that soon they would be in the greatest danger. Therefore a very large crowd began to assemble from the whole city.

(*In Verrem* II 5.35.91–3)

Running vocabulary for 4E(ii)

accipiō 3/4 *accēpī acceptus* I
  sustain, meet with
admittō 3 I let in
ante earlier, before (adv.)
ausus esset 'he had dared' (plupf.
  subj. of *audeō* 2 semi dep.)
calamitōs-us a um disastrous
cant-us ūs 4m. song, singing
Cleomene īnsciō 'with Cleomenes
  not knowing' (abl. absolute)
concursō 1 I rush together
cōnflagrantem (acc. s. m./f.) '(as
  he/it was) burning' (pres. part.
  of *cōnflagrō* 1)
cōnflagrantīs (acc. pl. f.)
  'burning' (pres. part. of
  cōnflagrō 1)
cuius (gen. s. m.) 'whose'
  (line 226)
cuius (gen. s. f.) 'of which'
  (line 230)
cum when (line 221)
cum since (lines 223 and 228)
disciplīn-a ae 1 f. order, control

dormientem (acc. s. m.) '(while he
  was) sleeping' (pres. part. of
  dormiō 4)
ēiciō 3/4 *ēiēcī ēiectus* I throw out;
  mē ēiciō I throw myself out
excitō 1 I rouse
exeuntem (acc. s. m.) 'departing'
  (pres. part. of *exeō*)
expellō 3 *expulī expulsus* I drive
  out
fluctuantem (acc. s. f.) 'tossing
  about' (pres. part. of *fluctuō* 1)
grau-is e serious, important,
  weighty
Helōr-us ī 2f. Helorus (city on
  east coast of Sicily)
Hēracleō Hēracleōn-is 3m.
  Heracleo
incendi-um ī 2n. fire
incendō 3 *incendī incēnsus* I burn
inclūdō 3 *inclūsī* I shut up
īnflammō 1 I set on fire
īnsci-us a um not knowing
manente (abl. s. m.) 'remaining'
  (pres. part. of *maneō*)

mare mar-is 3n. sea (abl. s. *marī*)
marī (abl. s.) line 225 on the sea
multitūdō multitūdin-is 3f. crowd,
  number
nēquiti-a ae 1f. wickedness
ō oh! (exclamation: followed by
  acc.)
peruēnisset 'he had reached'
  (plupf. subj. of *peruēniō* 4
  peruēnī)
praetōri-um ī 2n. governor's
  residence
pūblic-um ī 2n. public place
quārum (gen. pl. f.) 'of which',
  '(and) of these'
quō to where
quōrum (gen. pl. m.) 'whose'
redūcō 3 *redūxī reductus* I bring
  back, lead back
reliqu-us a um remaining, left
symphōni-a ae 1f. band
Syrācūs-ae ārum 1f. pl. Syracuse
tard-us a um slow
uīdissent 'they had seen' (plupf.
  subj. of *uideō* 2 *uīdī*)

Learning vocabulary for 4E(ii)

Nouns

incendi-um ī 2n. fire
mare mar-is 3n. sea (*marī* (abl. s.)
  'on the sea')
multitūdō multitūdin-is 3f. mob,
  crowd, number
nēquiti-a ae 1f. wickedness

Adjectives

grau-is e serious, important,
  weighty

reliqu-us a um remaining, left
tard-us a um slow

Verbs

accipiō 3/4 *accēpī acceptus* I
  sustain, meet with; (receive,
  welcome; learn; obtain)
cōnflagrō 1 I burn (intrans.)
incendō 3 *incendī incēnsus* I set
  fire to, burn (trans.)

redūcō 3 *redūxī reductus* I bring
  back, lead back

Others

ante (adv.) earlier, before;
  ([+ acc.] before, in front of)
quō to where, whither (in direct
  q. = whither? to where?)

Section 4E(iii)

The pirates, after their brief but unhindered stay at Helorus, decide to go on an uninterrupted tour of the harbour at Syracuse – an unparalleled happening.

praedōnēs, cum ūnam illam noctem Helōrī commorātī̄ essent,
cōnflagrantīs nāuīs iam relīquerant et accēdere coepērunt Syrācūsās. quī
praedōnēs uidēlicet saepe audierant nihil esse pulchrius quam
Syrācūsānōrum moenia ac portūs et statuerant sē numquam ea uīsūrōs   245
esse nisi Verre praetōre. statim igitur sine ūllō metū in ipsum portum
penetrāre coepērunt.

prō dī immortālēs! pīrātica nāuis, tē praetōre, Verrēs, usque ad
forum Syrācūsānōrum accessit! quō numquam Carthāginiēnsēs nāuēs
(dum marī plūrimum̄ poterant), numquam classis Rōmāna tot Pūnicīs   250
Siciliēnsibusque bellīs accēdere potuērunt, hīc, tē praetōre, praedōnum
nāuēs peruagātae sunt. ō spectāculum miserum atque acerbum! ō
factum turpius omnibus quōrum mentiōnem fēcī! huic nāuī pīrāticae
lūdibriō erat urbis glōria, lūdibriō erat populī Rōmānī nōmen, lūdibriō
erat nostrōrum hominum multitūdō quae Syrācūsīs habitat.   255

In the name of the immortal gods! A pirate ship in your praetorship, Verres, reached right as far as the Syracusan forum! To where the ships of the Carthaginians (while they had very great power at sea) were never able to approach, (to where) a Roman fleet in so many Punic and Sicilian wars (was) never (able to approach), here, under your praetorship, the ships of brigands wandered. O spectacle unhappy and bitter! O deed baser than all those which I have mentioned! The glory of the city (of Rome) was a laughing-stock to this pirate vessel, the name of the Roman people was a laughing-stock, the crowd of our men which lives in Syracuse was a laughing-stock.

(*In Verrem* II 5.36.95–38.100)

Running vocabulary for 4E(iii)

accēdō 3 *accessī* I approach, reach
acerb-us a um bitter
Carthāginiēns-is e Carthaginian, Punic
commorātī essent 'they had waited' (plupf. subj. of *commoror* 1 dep.)
cōnflagrantīs (acc. pl. f.) 'burning' (pres. part. of *conflagrō*)
cum when (line 242)
fact-um ī 2n. achievement
glōri-a ae 1f. glory, renown, fame
Helōrī (locative) at Helorus

immortāl-is e everlasting, immortal
lūdibriō esse to be a laughing-stock/joke to X (dat.) [*lūdibriō* is predicative dative from *lūdibri-um ī* 2n.]
mentiō mentiōn-is 3f. mention
met-us ūs 4m. fear
moenia moen-ium 3n. pl. walls
ō oh! (exclamation followed by acc.)
penetrō 1 I penetrate, reach into
peruagor 1 dep. I rove freely about

pīrātic-us a um (of a) pirate
plūrimum possum I am very powerful
prō! in the name of!
Pūnic-us a um Punic, Carthaginian
quōrum (gen. pl. n.) 'of which'
Siciliēns-is e Sicilian
statuō 3 *statuī* I decide, determine
Syrācūs-ae ārum 1f. pl. Syracuse
Syācūsīs at Syracuse
tot so many (indecl.)
uidēlicet presumably
usque right up as far as

Learning vocabulary for 4E(iii)

Nouns

glōri-a ae 1f. glory, renown, fame
mentiō mentiōn-is 3f. mention
met-us ūs 4m. fear, terror

Adjectives

tot so many (indecl.)

Verbs

accedō 3 *accessī accessum*
    I approach, reach
commoror 1 dep. I delay, wait

possum posse potuī + adv. I am
    powerful, have power; (am
    able, can)

Others

cum (+ subj.) when; since;
    although; (+ abl. with)

42. Syrācūsānōrum moenia

Plundering art

One of the first symptoms of a Roman admiration for Greek art was the plunder of statues and paintings from captured cities. The plunder of statues had already characterised the conquest of Etruria: cult-statues had been taken from the temples of Veii and Praeneste, and in 264 a Roman general took 2,000 statues from Volsinii. Such depredations were partly inspired by religious motives: the spoils were deposited as thank-offerings in temples. But, with the conquest of Greek cities, other motives began to prevail: a desire to beautify the city, a concern for self-advertisement on the part of the victorious generals, ultimately a genuine passion for Greek art. A turning-point was the capture, in 212 and 209, of Syracuse and Tarentum, the artistic capitals of Sicily and Magna Graecia, which started a huge flow of art-treasures to Rome. Further acquisitions followed the defeat of the Aetolians in 188, that of the Macedonians in 167, and, most spectacularly, the sack of Corinth by L. Mummius in 146. (*World of Rome*, **461**)

Section 4F(i)

There follow the final horrors perpetrated by Verres, which Cicero saves up for the climax of his speech. They involve innocent Roman citizens being put to death. Here Servilius, whose only crime was to complain a little too freely about Verres' disgraceful behaviour, is publicly beaten – and dies.

reliqua causa, iūdicēs, quam nunc agō, nōn ad sociōrum salūtem sed ad
cīuium Rōmānōrum uītam et sanguinem pertinet. quā⌢in⌢causā hortor
uōs, quibus loquor, hortor precorque ut operam dīligentissimē dētis,
nēue argūmenta exspectētis. nam, sī uultis, facillimē tōtī Siciliae
persuādēbō ut testis sit.   260

nam in forō Lilybaeī cīuis Rōmānus, cui nōmen C. Seruīliō erat,
uirgīs et uerberibus ante pedēs Verris abiectus est.

num potes negāre, Verrēs, tē hoc fēcisse? audē hoc prīmum negāre, sī
potes: ab omnibus Lilybaeī uīsum est, ab omnibus tōtā Siciliā audītum.
dīcō cīuem Rōmānum, cum ā līctōribus tuīs caesus esset, ante oculōs tuōs   265
concidisse. at quam ob causam, dī immortālēs!

Surely you cannot deny, Verres, that you did this? Dare first of all to deny this: it was witnessed by all the people of Lilybaeum, and heard about by all of Sicily. I say that a Roman citizen, when he had been beaten by your lictors, fell down before your eyes. But for what reason, in the name of the immortal gods!

accidit⌢ut Seruīlius loquerētur līberius dē istīus nēquitiā. quod istī cum
nūntiātum esset, Seruīliō imperāuit ut Lilybaeum uenīret (accidit⌢ut
Verrēs Lilybaeī adesset). Seruīlius igitur, cum Verrēs imperāsset ut adīret,
Lilybaeum uēnit.   270

(In Verrem II 5.53.139–54.141)

(When Servilius arrived, Verres challenged him to prove that he [Verres] had been guilty of crime, and offered to set up a 'court' to hear the 'case'. Servilius naturally refused, saying it was quite wrong to charge him in this way.)

Faced with Servilius' refusal to accept the 'challenge' and his insistence that he was innocent, Verres has him flogged till he agrees.

quae cum Seruīlius uehementer affirmāsset, Verrēs sex līctōribus
imperāuit ut eum circumsisterent multaque ōrantem uerberibus
caederent. dēnique proximus līctor, cui Sextiō nōmen erat, oculōs

Running vocabulary for 4F(i)

abiciō abicere abiēcī abiectus I
    throw down
accidit ut (+ subj.) it happened
    that
adesset (impf. subj. of *adsum*
    adesse) '(he) was present'
adīret (impf. subj. of *adeō adīre*)
    '(to) come (sc. to him)' '(that)
    he should come (sc. to him)'
agō 3 *causam* I plead a case,
    conduct a case before (+ dat.)
argūment-um ī 2n. proof
C. = *Gāiō: Gāi-us ī* 2m. Gaius
caederent (impf. subj. of *caedō* 3)
    '(to) beat', '(that) they should
    beat'
caus-a ae 1f. case; reason
    (line 266)
circumsisterent (impf. subj. of
    circumsistō 3) '(to) stand
    round' '(that) they should
    stand round'

concidō 3 *concidī* I fall down,
    collapse
cui (nom. s. m.) 'to whom',
    'whose'
dētis (pres. subj. of *dō*) '(to) give'
    '(that) you (pl.) should give'
exspectētis (pres. subj. of
    exspectō) '(not to) await',
    '(and that) you (pl.) should
    (not) await'
immortāl-is e immortal
līberius 'too freely' (comparative
    adverb of *līber*)
līctor līctōr-is 3m. magistrate's
    attendant, lictor
Lilybae-um ī 2n. Lilybaeum
    (locative *Lilybaeī*)
loquerētur (impf. subj. of *loquor*
    3 dep.) '(he) talked'
nēue 'and (that X should) not . . .'
persuādeō 2 *persuāsī* I persuade
    X (dat.) (to: *ut* + subj.; not to
    nē + subj.)

pertineō (*ad*) 2 I am relevant (to)
pēs ped-is 3m. foot
proxim-us a um nearest
quā in causā (abl.) and in this case
quibus (dat. pl. m.) 'to whom',
    'before whom'
salūs salūt-is 3f. safety
sanguis sanguin-is 3m. blood
Seruīli-us ī 2m. Servilius
Sexti-us ī 2m. Sextius
sit (pres. subj. of *sum*) '(to) be'
    '(that) it should be'
soci-us ī 2m. ally
testis test-is 3m. witness
uehementer strongly
uenīret (impf. subj. of *ueniō* 4)
    '(to) come' '(that) he should
    come'
uerber uerber-is 3n. blow
uirg-a ae 1f. rod (symbol of a
    lictor's authority when bound
    in a bundle, also called *fascēs*)
ut (+ subj.) 'to . . .', 'that . . .
    should'

43. līctōrēs

clāmitantī tundere coepit. itaque ille, oculīs sanguine complētīs,
concidit; nihilōminus Verrēs Sextium hortābātur ut iacentī 275
latera tunderet. quibus‿modīs tandem prope morientī persuāsit ut
respondēret nēue tacēret. ille, cum ita respondisset ut Verrēs uoluerat
sēmimortuus sublātus, breuī tempore posteā est mortuus.

iste autem homo Venereus, adfluēns omnī lepōre et uenustāte, dē bonīs
Seruīlī in aede Veneris argenteum Cupīdinem posuit. sīc etiam fortūnīs 280
hominum abūtēbātur ad nocturna uōta cupiditātum suārum.

But this man, a devotee of Venus, dripping with all charm and elegance, set up
in the temple of Venus a silver Cupid from the goods of Servilius. For so did he
abuse the fortunes of men for the nocturnal vows of his lusts.

(*In Verrem* II 5.54.142)

abūtor 3 dep. (+ abl.) I misuse
ad (+ acc.) for the purpose of, to
    fulfil (line 281)
adfluō 3 I flow, drip
argente-us a um (of) silver
bon-a ōrum 2n. pl. goods
clāmitantī (dat. s. m. present
    participle of *clāmitō* 1) 'to the
    disadvantage of him, as he
    kept shouting': tr. 'as he
    shouted'
compleō 2 *complēuī complētus*
    I fill
Cupīdō Cupīdin-is 3m. (statue of)
    Cupid

dē (+ abl.) from
fortūn -a ae 1f. fortune
iacentī (dat. s. m. present
    participle of *iaceō* 2) 'to the
    disadvantage of him as he
    lay': tr. 'as he lay'
latus later-is 3n. side
lepōs lepōr-is 3m. charm
morientī (dat. s. m. present
    participle of *morior* 3/4 dep)
nihilōminus nevertheless
nocturn-us a um night-time,
    nocturnal
quibus modīs (abl. pl. m.) '(and)
    by these means'

respondēret (impf. subj. of
    respondeō 2) '(to) reply',
    '(that) he should reply'
sēmimortu-us a um half-dead
tacēret (impf. subj. of *taceō* 2)
    '(and not to) be silent' '(and
    that) he should (not) be silent'
tunderet (impf. subj. of *tundō* 3)
    '(to) beat' '(that) he should
    beat'
tundō 3 I beat
uenustās uenustāt-is 3f. elegance,
    desirability
uōt-um ī 2n. vow
Venere-us a um devoted to Venus

Grammar for 4F

present and imperfect subjunctives **indirect commands**	***accidit/perficiō ut*** **pres. part. as noun**	**dative and ablative of relative pronoun**

Learning vocabulary for 4F(i)

Nouns
caus-a ae 1f. cause; reason
līctor līctōr-is 3m. magistrate's
    attendant, lictor
pēs ped-is 3m. foot
salūs salūt-is 3f. safety
sanguis sanguin-is 3m. blood
testis test-is 3m. witness
uerber uerber-is 3n. blow; whip

Adjectives
līber līber-a um free
proxim-us a um nearest; next

Verbs
abiciō 3/4 *abiēcī abiectus* I throw
    down/away
accidit 3 *accidit* (*ut/ut nōn* +
    subj.) it happens (that/that not)
concidō 3 *concidī* I fall, collapse;
    am killed
persuādeō 2 *persuāsī persuāsum*
    I persuade X (dat.) (*ut/nē* +
    subj. 'that/that . . . not',
    'to . . . /not to')

Others
ad (+ acc.) for the purpose of
    (towards; at)
dē (+ abl.) from; down from
    (about, concerning)
nēue 'and (that X should)
    not . . . ', 'and not to'
uehementer strongly
ut (+ subj.) 'to . . . ', 'that should'
    (negative *nē* 'not to . . . ',
    'that . . . should not')

44. lautumiae

A governor's staff

The variety of treatment that the provinces received, with different systems of taxation and different patterns of jurisdiction, came about because the Roman Empire itself was not, at this stage, based on any imperial system. It was simply the aftermath of a series of military involvements, which had turned into longer-term commitments. The size of the governor's staff was really very small, if it is thought of as intended to administer a whole province. In addition to the staff, the governor might appoint military commanders at a lower level than his *lēgātī*, known as *praefectī*; and he was accompanied by a group of assistants (scribes, attendants and, of course, his lictors). He also often took younger men, who might help with various tasks and at the same time gain some experience of Roman rule overseas, called *comitēs* ('companions').

All these people, however, seem very few compared with the task of governing large areas like Sicily, or half of Spain, or the province of Asia (the Aegean coast of modern Turkey), with its numerous and highly sophisticated Greek cities. The answer is that they did not 'govern' these areas in the modern sense. They took no interest in or responsibility for the day-to-day life of the people there. That was the task of the local provincial communities themselves, who looked after the upkeep of the cities, raised local taxes and provided the courts which judged the ordinary cases between their own citizens. To a large extent, the work of a governor was still that of the commander of an occupying army, even if, as in the case of peaceful provinces like Sicily or Asia, the number of soldiers under his command was small. (*World of Rome*, **182**)

Section 4F(ii)

*Cicero's final charge relates to Gavius from Consa who, escaping from Verres'
prison in the mines in Syracuse, was thought to complain a little too loudly.*

Gauius hic, quem dīcō, Cōnsānus erat. ab istō in uincula Syrācūsīs
coniectus erat, sed perfēcit ut clam ē lautumiīs profugeret, Messānamque
peruenīret. quō cum peruēnisset, loquī et querī coepit sē, cīuem
Rōmānum, in uincla coniectum esse; sē nunc Rōmam itūrum et Verrem   285
dēlātūrum. quem in nāuem ingredientem, seruī Verris retraxēre. itaque
Gauius statim ad magistrātum dēdūcitur. eō ipsō diē, accidit ut Verrēs
Messānam uenīret. quō cum uēnisset, imperāuit ut rēs tōta sibi dēferrētur.

seruī igitur dētulērunt Gauium, cīuem Rōmānum, questum esse sē
Syrācūsīs in uinculīs fuisse; quem iam ingredientem in nāuem et Verrī   290
minitantem ā sē retractum esse. Verrēs, scelere et furōre īnflammātus, in
forum uēnit; ārdēbant oculī, tōtō ex ōre crūdēlitās ēminēbat.

*Therefore the slaves reported that Gavius, a Roman citizen, had complained
that he had been in chains in Syracuse; as he was returning to his ship and
threatening Verres, he had been dragged back by the man. Verres, inflamed with
criminality and madness, came into the forum; his eyes were ablaze, and cruelty
stood out from his whole visage.*

in forum ingressus, repente imperat ut Gauius mediō in forō nūdētur et
dēligētur et caedātur. cum ille miser sē cīuem Rōmānum esse clāmāret, et
Lūcium Raecium equitem Rōmānum cognitōrem nōmināret, tum iste eum   295
ā Sertōriō in Siciliam missum esse dīcit. deinde imperat seruīs ut
hominem nūdent, dēligent, caedant. quae cum iste imperāuisset, seruī ita
fēcēre, et accidit ut mediō in forō Messānae uirgīs caederētur cīuis
Rōmānus, iūdicēs, et nūlla alia uōx illīus miserī audīrētur nisi haec – 'cīuis
Rōmānus sum.' quibus⁀uerbīs ūsus, persuāsitne Gauius Verrī, ā⁀quō tam   300
atrōciter caedēbātur, ut sibi parceret nēue caederet? minimē, iūdicēs. is
enim perfēcit ut nōn modo caederētur, sed etiam crux (crux! inquam) illī
miserō comparārētur. in crucem ausus est Verrēs hominem agere quī sē
cīuem Rōmānum esse dīcēbat.

(*In Verrem* II 5.61.160–62.162)

Running vocabulary for 4F(ii)

ā quō (abl. s. m.) by whom
agō 3 I drive
ārdeō 2 I blaze
atrōciter appallingly

audīretur (impf. subj. pass. of
  audiō 4) '(it) was heard'
caedant (pres. subj. of *caedō* 3)
  '(to) beat' '(that) they should
  beat'

caedātur (pres. subj. pass. of
  caedō 3) 'should be beaten'
caederet (impf. subj. of *caedō* 3)
  '(not to) beat' '(that) he
  should (not) beat'

caederētur (impf. subj. pass, of *caedō* 3) '(he) was beaten'

clāmāret (impf. subj. of *clāmō* 1) '(he) was shouting'

cognitor cognitōr-is 3m. one who would know him, a referee

comparārētur (impf. subj. pass. of *comparō* 1) '(it) was obtained/prepared'

Cōnsān-us a um from Consa [see map 1]

crūdēlitās crūdēlitāt-is 3f. cruelty

crux cruc-is 3f. cross

dēlātūrum sc. *esse*

deferrētur (impf. subj. pass. of *dēferō dēferre*) '(it) should be reported'

dēligent (pres. subj. of *dēligō* 1) '(that) they should bind' '(to) bind'

dēligētur (pres. subj. pass. of *dēligō* 1) '(that) he should be bound'

ēmineō 2 I project, stand out

eques equit-is 3m. 'knight' (Roman business class)

furor furōr-is 3m. rage, fury

Gaui-us ī 2m. Gavius

itūrum sc. *esse*

lautumi-ae ārum 1f. pl. stone quarries (see Illustration 44 p. 157)

Lūci-us Raeci-us ī 2m. Lucius Raecius (a Roman *eques*)

medi-us a um middle (of)

Messān-a ae 1f. Messana (city on east coast of Sicily)

minitor 1 dep. I threaten (+ dat.)

modo only

nōmināret (impf. subj. of *nōminō* 1) '(he) was naming'

nūdent (pres. subj. of *nūdō* 1) '(to) strip' '(that) they should strip'

nūdētur (pres. subj. pass. of *nūdō* 1) '(that) he should be stripped'

ōs ōr-is 3n. face

parceret (impf. subj. of *parcō* 3) '(to) spare' '(that) he should spare'

perficiō 3/4 *perfēcī ut* + subj. I bring it about that

peruenīret (impf. subj. of *perueniō* 4) 'arrived'

profugeret (impf. subj. of *profugiō* 3/4) 'he escaped'

queror 3 dep. *questus* I complain

quibus (abl. pl. n.) *uerbīs* 'and these words' (object of *ūsus*)

retrahō 3 *retraxī retractus* I drag back

Sertōri-us ī 2m. Sertorius (opponent of Sulla [the former dictator] who led resistance to the regime from Spain and attracted Romans and local Spaniards to his cause)

Syrācūsīs at Syracuse

uenīret (impf. subj. of *ueniō* 4) '(he) came'

uinc(u)l-um ī 2n. chain, bond

uirg-a ae 1f. rod

Learning vocabulary for 4F(ii)

Nouns

furor furōr-is 3m. rage, fury; madness

ōs ōr-is 3n. face; mouth

uinc(u)l-um ī 2n. chain, bond

Adjectives

medi-us a um middle (of)

Verbs

agō 3 *ēgī āctus* I drive, lead, direct (do, act)

nūdō 1 I strip

perficiō 3/4 *perfēcī perfectus ut/ut nōn* (+ subj.) I bring it about that/that not (finish, complete, carry out)

profugiō 3/4 *profūgī* I escape, flee away

Others

modo only (now)

nōn modo . . . sed etiam not only . . . but also (also *nōn sōlum . . . sed etiam*)

Cīvis Rōmānus sum

Paul, the early Christian missionary, was arrested by the Roman authorities in Jerusalem in, perhaps, AD 58, because his presence had caused his opponents to riot against him. The commander of the Roman garrison ordered Paul to be detained and flogged: 'But when they tied him up for the lash, Paul said to the centurion who was standing there, "Can you legally flog a man who is a Roman citizen, and moreover has not been found guilty?" When the centurion heard this, he went and reported it to the commandant. "What do you mean to do?" he said. "This man is a Roman citizen." The commandant came to Paul. "Tell me, are you a Roman citizen?" he asked. "Yes", said he. The commandant rejoined, "It cost me a large sum to acquire this citizenship." Paul said, "But it was mine by birth."' (*Acts of the Apostles* 22.25ff.) (*World of Rome*, **1**)

Section 4G(i)

Cicero wonders what Verres' father would say if he were judging the case. He points out the unique protection afforded by the claim to be a Roman citizen, which Verres has abused – and thus closed the world to Roman travellers, who have relied upon it.

45. hoc teneō, hīc haereō, iūdicēs

sī pater ipse Verris nunc adesset et sī nunc iūdicāret, per deōs immortālīs,   305
quid facere posset? quid dīceret? sī audīret ā tē cīuīs Rōmānōs secūrī
percussōs, ā tē archipīrātam līberātum, propter tuam neglegentiam
classem Rōmānam captam atque incēnsam, ā tē dēnique Gauium in
crucem āctum, possēs ab eō ueniam petere, possēs ut tibi ignōsceret
postulāre? ō nōmen dulce lībertātis! ō iūs eximium nostrae cīuitātis!   310
acciditne ut cīuis Rōmānus in prōuinciā populī Rōmānī ab eō quī praetor
esset in forō uirgīs caederētur? quid? in crucem tū agere ausus es eum quī
sē cīuem Rōmānum esse dīceret? at⁀enim Gauium speculātōrem fuisse
dīcis et clāmitāsse sē cīuem Rōmānum esse quod moram mortī quaereret.
hoc tū, Verrēs, dīcis, hoc tū cōnfitēris, illum clāmitāsse sē cīuem   315
Rōmānum esse, hoc teneō, hīc haereō, iūdicēs, hōc sum contentus ūnō,
omittō ac neglegō cētera, cīuem Rōmānum sē esse dīcēbat. sī tū, Verrēs,
apud Persās aut in extrēmā Indiā ad supplicium dūcāris, quid aliud clāmēs
nisi tē cīuem esse Rōmānum? sī cīuem tē esse Rōmānum dīcās, nōnne
putēs tē aut effugium aut moram mortis assecūtūrum? hominēs tenuēs,   320
obscūrō locō nātī, nāuigant, adeunt ad ea loca quae numquam anteā
uīdērunt, arbitrātī sē tūtōs fore et hanc rem sibi praesidiō futūram. nam sīc
opīnantur: 'sī ad loca numquam anteā ā nōbīs uīsa nāuigāuerimus, tūtī
erimus, quod cīuēs sumus Rōmānī. sī ad fīnīs orbis terrārum adierimus,
cīuitās Rōmāna nōs prōteget.' sī tollās hanc spem, sī tollās hoc praesidium   325
cīuibus Rōmānīs, sī cōnstituās nihil esse opis in hāc uōce 'cīuis Rōmānus
sum', iam omnīs prōuinciās, iam omnia rēgna, iam omnīs līberās cīuitātēs,
iam omnem orbem terrārum cīuibus Rōmānīs praeclūdās.

(*In Verrem* II 5.63.163–65.168)

Running vocabulary for 4G(i)

āctum [understand *esse*: perf. inf.
  pass. of *ago* 3]
adesset '(he) were present' (impf.
  subj. of *adsum adesse*)
adierimus we go to (lit: we shall
  have gone to: future perfect of
  adeō adīre)
anteā before (adv.)
assecūtūrum [understand *esse*:
  fut. inf.]
assequor 3 *assecūtus* I achieve,
  gain
archipīrāt-a ae 1m. chief pirate
at enim 'but, one may object'
audīret 'he were hearing' (impf.
  subj. of *audiō* 4)
captam [understand *esse*: perf.
  inf. pass.]
cīuitās cīuitāt-is 3f. state,
  citizenship
clāmēs 'would you shout' (pres.
  subj. *of clāmō* 1)
clāmitō 1 I keep on shouting
cōnfiteor 2 dep. I confess,
  acknowledge
cōnstituās 'you (s.) were to
  decide' (pres. subj. of
  cōnstituō 3)
content-us a um happy, satisfied
crux cruc-is 3f. cross
dīcās 'you (s.) were to say' (pres.
  subj. of *dīcō* 3)

dīceret 'would he be saying'
  (impf. subj. of *dīcō* 3)
dūcāris '(you) (s.) were to be led'
  (pres. subj. pass. of *dūcō* 3)
dulc-is e sweet
effugi-um ī 2n. escape
eximi-us a um excellent
extrēm-us a um farthest
fīn-ēs fīn-ium 3m.pl. boundary
futūram [understand *esse*: fut. inf.]
Gaui-us ī 2m. Gavius
haereō 2 I stick
ignōscō 3 (+ dat.) I forgive
immortāl-is e immortal
incēnsam [understand *esse*: perf.
  inf. pass.]
Indi-a ae 1f. India
iūdicāret 'he were judging' (impf.
  subj. of *iūdicō* 1)
līberātum [understand *esse*; perf.
  inf. pass.]
lībertās lībertāt-is 3f. freedom
mor-a ae 1f. delay
nāuigāuerimus we sail (lit: we
  shall have sailed: future
  perfect of *nāuigō* 1)
neglegenti-a ae 1f. carelessness
ō oh! [exclamation]
obscūr-us a um undistinguished,
  mean
omittō 3 I pass over
ops op-is 3f. help

orbis (*orb-is* 3m.) *terrārum* the
  world
per (+ acc.) in the name of
percussōs [understand *esse*: perf.
  inf. pass.]
Pers-ae ārum 1m. pl. the Persians
petō 3 I seek
possēs? 'would you (s.) be able?'
  (impf. subj. of *possum posse*)
posset? 'would he be able?'
  (impf. subj. of *possum posse*)
praeclūdās 'you (s.) would shut
  off' (pres. subj. of *praeclūdō*
  3)
praesidi-um ī 2n. protection,
  defence [*praesidiō* predicative
  dat., lit. 'for a protection']
putēs 'you (s.) would think' (pres.
  subj. of *putō* 1)
quaerō 3 I seek, look for
speculātor speculātōr-is 3m. spy
supplici-um ī 2n. punishment
tenu-is e small, humble
tollās 'you (s.) were to remove'
  (pres. subj. of *tollō* 3)
tūt-us a um safe
ueni-a ae 1f. pardon
uirg-a ae 1f. lictor's rod

Note

lines 312–13. *eum qui… dīceret* 'the sort of person who said' (see **145.1**).

Grammar for 4G

future perfects
uses of subjunctives
  (conditionals, relatives,

cum, quamuīs, reported
speech)

infinitives without esse

Learning vocabulary for 4G(i)

Nouns
lībertās lībertāt-is 3f. freedom,
  liberty
mor-a ae 1f. delay
neglegenti-a ae 1f. carelessness
praesidi-um ī 2n. protection,
  defence, guard

Adjectives
immortāl-is e immortal
tūt-us a um safe

Verbs
clāmitō 1 I keep on shouting
  (= *clāmō* + *it-*)
cōnfiteor 2 dep. *cōnfessus* I
  confess, acknowledge
ignōscō 3 (+ dat.) *ignōuī ignōtum*
  I forgive
petō 3 *petīuī petītus* I seek, beg
quaerō 3 *quaesīuī quaesītus* I
  seek, look for; ask

Others
anteā before (adv.: cf. *ante*)
per (+ acc.) in the name of
  (through, by)

Section 4G(ii)

Cicero asks why Verres did not consult Raecius, and gives a sarcastic picture of what Verres' response would have been to each of Raecius' two possible replies. Verres has been an enemy to the whole civilised Roman world: his crime is indescribable, and would move even the dumb beasts to pity.

quid? cum Gauius Lūcium Raecium equitem Rōmānum quī tum in
Siciliā erat ut cognitōrem nōmināret, cūr litterās ad eum nōn mīsistī? sī   330
Raecius cognōsceret hominem, aliquid dē summō suppliciō remitterēs;
sī ignōrāret, tum, sī ita tibi uidērētur, nouum iūs cōnstituerēs, et eum
quī cognitōrem nōn daret, quamuīs cīuis Rōmānus esset, in crucem
tollerēs.

sed quid ego plūra dē Gauiō? nōn sōlum Gauiō tum fuistī īnfestus,   335
Verrēs, sed etiam nōminī, generī, iūrī populī Rōmānī hostis; nōn illī
hominī, sed causae commūnī lībertātis inimīcus fuistī. nam facinus est
uincīre cīuem Rōmānum, scelus uerberāre, prope parricīdium necāre:
quid dīcam in crucem tollere? uerbō satis dignō tam nefāria rēs
appellārī nūllō modō potest. sī haec nōn ad cīuīs Rōmānōs, sī nōn ad   340
aliquōs amīcōs nostrae cīuitātis, sī nōn ad hominēs, sed ad bēstiās
conquerī et dēplōrāre uellem, tamen omnia mūta atque inanima
commouērentur. nisi Verrem pūnīueritis, iūdicēs, cīuitās Rōmāna
uōx nihilī erit. nisi hominis istīus inaudīta atque singulāria facinora
damnāueritis, nēmō usquam tūtus erit.   345

(*In Verrem* II 5.65.168–67.171)

Running vocabulary for 4G(ii)

appellō 1 I call
bēsti-a ae 1f. beast
caus-a ae 1f. cause
cīuitās cīuitāt-is 3f. state
cognitor cognitōr-is 3m. one who
  would support (him), referee
cognōsceret '(he) had recognised'
  (impf. subj. of *cognōscō* 3)
commouērentur '(they) would be
  moved' (impf. subj. of
  commoueō 2)
commūn-is e common
cōnstituerēs 'you would have
  established' (impf. subj. of
  cōnstituō 3)
conqueror 3 dep. I complain of
crux cruc-is 3f. cross
damnāueritis you (pl.) condemn
  (lit: you shall have
  condemned, future perfect of
  damnō 1 I condemn)

dēplōrō 1 I denounce
dīcam (line 339) 'should I say'
  (pres. subj. of *dīcō*)
dign-us a um worthy
eques equit-is 3m. 'knight'
  (member of Roman business
  class)
Gaui-us ī 2m. Gavius
ignōrāret 'he had not known', 'he
  had been unacquainted with'
  (impf. subj. of *ignōrō* 1)
inanim-us a um inanimate
inaudīt-us a um unheard of
īnfest-us a um hateful, hostile
inimīc-us a um hostile, enemy
Lūci-us ī 2m. Lucius
mūt-us a um mute, dumb
nōminō 1 I name
parricīdi-um ī 2n. parricide;
  treason

pūnīueritis you (pl.) punish (lit.
  you shall have punished:
  future perfect of *pūniō* 4 I
  punish)
quamuīs (+ subj.) although
Raeci-us ī 2m. Raecius
remitterēs 'you would have
  remitted' X (acc.) from Y
  (*dē* + abl.) (impf. subj. of
  remittō 3)
singulār-is e peculiar (sc. to
  Verres), remarkable
supplici-um ī 2n. punishment;
  summum supplicium the death
  penalty
tollerēs 'you would have lifted'
  (impf. subj. of *tollō* 3)
uellem 'I were wishing' (impf.
  subj. of *uolō uelle*)
uidērētur 'it had seemed right'
  (impf. subj. pass. of *uideō* 2)

Notes

lines 332–3 *eum quī … nōn daret* 'the sort of the person who did not give' (see **145.1**)

line 335 *sed quid ego plūra dē Gauiō?* sc. *dīcam* (pres. subj.); tr. 'But why should I say more …'

Learning vocabulary for 4G(ii)

Nouns

caus-a ae 1f. cause (case; reason)

cīuitās cīuitāt-is 3f. state

eques equit-is 3m. 'knight'
   (member of Roman business
   class; horseman; pl. cavalry)

supplici-um ī 2n. punishment;
   summum supplicium the death
   penalty

Adjectives

inimīc-us a um hostile, enemy

46. Cicero

Section 4H

Cicero's peroration returns to the crimes Verres committed against the gods and their statues. In a direct appeal to the deities affected by his depredations, the orator lists the series of thefts and calls upon the gods to direct the minds of the judges to producing a result which fits the heinousness of the crime.

dēnique ad Verrem redeō et ad scelera, quae contrā deōs commīsit. nam
sānctissimum et pulcherrimum simulācrum tuum, Iuppiter Optime
Maxime, iste Syrācūsīs sustulit, ut domī suae tenēret, omnī religiōne
rēiectā. duo fāna tua, Iūnō Rēgīna, īdem iste omnibus dōnīs nūdāuit, ut sē
dītāret, domum suam ōrnāret. tē, Minerua, ita expīlāuit, ut Athēnīs et   350
Syrācūsīs ē religiōsissimīs templīs aurī grande pondus auferret. uōsque,
Lātōna et Apollō et Diāna, sīc iste sprēuit, ut Dēlī fānum nocturnō
latrōciniō compīlāret, nēmine obstante. etiam tē, Diāna, spoliāuit, cuius
simulācrum sānctissimum Segestae tollendum⌢et⌢asportandum⌢cūrāuit.
nam fūrēs suōs Segestam mīsit, quī templum tuum compīlārent. tē,   355
Mercurī, tantum dēspexit, ut imāginem tuam in domō et prīuātā palaestrā
pōneret. tē, Herculēs, tam arroganter iste contempsit, ut Agrigentī seruōs
īnstrueret, quī simulācrum tuum conuellere suīs sēdibus et auferre
cōnārentur. tēque, sānctissima māter⌢Īdaea, augustissimō in templō sīc
spoliātam relīquit, ut nihil maneat, nihil exstet. tēque, Cerēs et Lībera, iste 360
ūnus sīc polluit et uiolāuit, ut simulācrum Cereris ūnum, quod ā uirō aspicī
fās nōn est, sacrāriō Catinae conuellendum⌢auferendumque⌢cūrāret,
alterum autem, quod tāle erat ut nōn hūmānā manū factum uidērētur,
Hennā ex suā sēde ac domō tolleret.

implōrō atque obtestor uōs deōs deāsque omnīs, quōrum templīs iste,   365
furōre mōtus, bellum sacrilegum indīxit, ut iūdicēs eandem mentem
habēre cōgātis ad⌢iūdicandam⌢causam, quam in⌢suscipiendā⌢causā ego
habuī. nam ideō causam suscēpī, iūdicēs, et ad⌢Siciliam⌢prōtegendam, et
ad⌢sociōs⌢dēfendendōs, et ad⌢dignitātem ⌈ reī pūblicae ⌉ retinendam. uōs
igitur precor, iūdicēs, ut C. Verrem exitus, uitā et factīs dignus, uestrō   370
iūdiciō cōnsequatur.

Running vocabulary for 4H

ad dignitātem . . . retinendam to
  maintain the dignity
ad iūdicandam causam for
  judging the case
ad Siciliam prōtegendam to
  protect Sicily
ad sociōs dēfendendōs to defend
  our allies

Agrigent-um ī 2n. Agrigentum
  (Acragas) (locative *Agrigentī*)
Apollō Apollin-is 3m. Apollo
arroganter arrogantly
aspici-ō 3/4 *aspexī aspectus* I
  look upon
asport-ō 1 I carry off
Athēn-ae ārum 1f. pl. Athens
august-us a um august, venerated

Catin-a ae 1f. Catina (= Catania)
Cerēs Cereris 3f. Ceres (goddess
  of agriculture)
cōg-ō 3 *coēgī coāctus* I force,
  compel
committ-ō 3 *commīsī commissus* I
  commit
compīl-ō 1 I despoil, rob

cōnsequ-or 3 dep. *cōnsecūtus* I
catch up with
contrā (+ acc.) against
contemn-ō 3 *contempsī*
contemptus I show contempt
for
conuellendum auferendumque
cūrāret (he) saw to the tearing
down and carrying off of (sc.
the statue)
conuell-ō 3 *conuellī conuulsus* I
tear away
cūr-ō 1 I see to the —ing
(gerundive) of
Dēl-os ī 2f. (the island of) Delos
dēspici-ō 3/4 *dēspexī dēspectus* I
despise, look down on
Diān-a ae 1f. Diana (= Artemis,
goddess of hunting)
dignitās dignitāt-is 3f. dignity;
distinction, position; honour;
rank; high office
dign-us a um (+ abl.) worthy (of)
dīt-ō 1 I enrich
dōn-um ī 2n. gift, offering
exit-us ūs 4m. outcome
expīl-ō 1 I despoil, rob
exst-ō 1 *exstitī exstātum* I exist,
am extant
fact-um ī 2n. deed; fact (line 370;
compare and contrast *factum*
line 363)
fās n. indecl. right
grand-is e large
Henn-a ae 1f. Enna
Hercul-ēs is 3m. Hercules

hūmān-us a um human
ideō for this reason
imāgō imāgin-is 3f. image, statue
implōrō 1 I beg
in suscipiendā causā In
undertaking the case
indīc-ō 3 *indīxī indictus* I declare
X (acc.) on Y (dat.)
īnstru-ō 3 *īnstrūxī īnstructus* I
draw up, prepare
Lātōn-a ae 1f. Leto (mother of
Artemis and Apollo)
latrōcini-um ī 2n. robbery
Līber-a ae 1f. Libera (Italian
goddess of agriculture,
sometimes identified with
Proserpina or Ariadne)
māter Īdaea mātr-is Īdae-ae 3f. +
1f. adj. Mother of Mount Ida
(= Cybele)
nocturn-us a um night-time,
nocturnal
obtestor 1 dep. I call to witness
ōrn-ō 1 I adorn
palaestr-a ae 1f.
wrestling-ground, palaestra
pollu-ō 3 *polluī pollūtus* I pollute,
defile
pondus ponder-is 3n. weight
prīuāt-us a um private
quī (+ subj.) in order to (lit. 'who
would . . .', i.e. with a view to
him . . .) (lines 355, 358)
rēgīn-a ae 1f. queen
rēici-ō 3/4 *rēiēcī rēiectus* I
discard, renounce

religiō religiōn-is 3f. sense of
reverence, religious scruples
rēs pūblica reī pūblicae 5f. + 1f.
republic, state
sacrāri-um ī 2n. shrine
sacrileg-us a um sacrilegious,
impious
sānct-us a um holy
sēd-ēs is 3f. base, foundation
Segest-a ae 1f. Segesta (locative
Segestae)
soci-us ī 2m. ally
spern-ō 3 *sprēuī sprētus* I disdain
spoli-ō 1 I strip
suscipi-ō 3/4 *suscēpī susceptus* I
undertake
Syrācūs-ae ārum 1f. pl. Syracuse
tāl-is e of such a kind
tantum so much
tollendum et asportandum cūrāuit
saw to the lifting and carrying
off of (sc. the statue)
uiol-ō 1 I violate
ut (+ subj. after *ita, sīc, tantum,
tam, talis*) so that, with the
result that (lines 350, 352,
356, 357, 360, 361, 363)
[remember that *ut* (+ subj.)
after words expressing
command, requests or prayer
means 'to']
ut (+ subj.) in order to/that (lines
348, 349) [remember that *ut*
(+ subj.) after words
expressing command, requests
or prayer means 'to']

Grammar for 4H

result and purpose clauses   **gerundives**

Learning vocabulary for 4H

Nouns
dignitās dignitāt-is 3f. dignity;
distinction, position; honour;
rank; high office
dōn-um ī 2n. gift, offering
fact-um ī 2n. deed
fās n. indecl. right
rēgīn-a ae 1f. queen
imāgō imāgin-is 3f. image, statue
(appearance, ghost, idea)
religiō religiōn-is 3f. sense of
reverence, religious scruples
rēs pūblica reī pūblicae 5f. + 1f.
republic, state

sēd-ēs is 3f. base, foundation
soci-us ī 2m. ally, friend

Adjectives
dign-us a um worthy, (+ abl.)
worthy (of)
hūmān-us a um human
sānct-us a um holy
tāl-is e of such a kind

Verbs
aspici-ō 3/4 *aspexī aspectus*
I look upon
cōg-ō 3 *coēgī coāctus* I force,
compel, gather

committ-ō 3 *commīsī commissus*
I commit
conuell-ō 3 *conuellī conuulsus*
I tear away
cūr-ō 1 I see to the —ing of X
(acc.) (look after, care for)
īnstru-ō 3 *īnstrūxī īnstructus*
I draw up, prepare, equip
suscipi-ō 3/4 *suscēpī susceptus*
I undertake

Others
contrā (+ acc.) against

The Roman Republic (*rēs pūblica*) traditionally began in 509 (see Introduction p. 1). The Republic lasted until the dictatorship of Julius Caesar (46–44). In that time, Rome rose from obscurity to undisputed domination of the whole Mediterranean.

By the first century power resided with the highest ranks (*ōrdinēs*) in Roman society, the senators (*senātōrēs* or *patrēs cōnscrīptī*), recruited indirectly by popular election via the censors, and the *equitēs* ('knights') who qualified for their rank by wealth.

The Republic was governed by its annually elected officers of state (*magistrātūs*). For the aspiring politician the first rung on the *cursus honōrum* ('course of public office' or 'race of honours') was to be elected *quaestor* (minimum age 30), then *praetor* (minimum age 39) and finally, with luck, one of the two consuls (*cōnsulēs*) (minimum age 42). Along the way it might suit him to hold one or more of the other posts available, such as tribune of the plebs (*tribūnus plebis*) or aedile (*aedīlis*). During their year of office, the consuls were virtual rulers of Rome (see pp. 122–3). The power which they and provincial governors wielded was called *imperium*. All magistrates worked in conjunction with the senate (*senātus*), an advisory body which consisted of all ex-magistrates.

The pursuit of prestige (*glōria*) and status (*dignitās*) was the aim of the ambitious Roman. To this end, he assiduously cultivated political alliances (*amīcitiae*) and personal dependants who could be relied upon to help him (his *clientēs* – 'clients') and whom he could help in turn in his role as their *patrōnus*. The race to the top was fiercely competitive. While twenty quaestors were elected every year, there were only two consuls. In the chase for the tiny number of consulships, *nōbilēs* ('nobles' – men from families which had previously produced a consul) constantly claimed a distinct advantage. Men from families which had produced only lower-ranking magistrates in the past would find it more difficult, while those, like Cicero, whose families had never before held any office, would have to overcome that disadvantage to win any of the lower magistracies and only rarely would succeed in getting as far as the consulship. A man from either of these two backgrounds could be described as a *nouus homo* ('new man').

Lucius Sergius Catilina, a noble, was following the normal *cursus honōrum*. Praetor in 68, then governor in Africa in 67, he planned to stand for the consulship in 66, but was charged with extortion (see p. 124). Cicero toyed with the idea of defending him. Finally, acquitted, Catiline stood in 64 for the consulship of 63. For whatever reason – possibly his shady past, possibly prejudice created against him by Cicero – the nobles withdrew their support and Cicero was elected, although he was a *nouus homo* (a fact of which Cicero constantly boasted, together with the fact that he became consul *suō annō*, 'in his year', i.e. at the youngest possible age for becoming consul). This incident and its aftermath are the subjects of the next section.

Gaius Sallustius Crispus the historian

Sallust wrote his history of the Catilinarian conspiracy between 44 (the death of Caesar) and 35 (his own death). Among his Latin sources, some perhaps at first hand, others written, he probably relied heavily upon Cicero, who had published his own speeches against Catiline in 60. The two writers were both *nouī hominēs* and had in common a loathing for Catiline, whom they portray as the archetypal villain. But their motives were different. In 63–62 Cicero must have felt it to his advantage to make as much of the conspiracy as possible, so that he could be portrayed (and portray himself) as the saviour of his country. Sallust is without this personal political bias. Like most Roman historians after him, Sallust was interested in reflecting upon the lessons which the past could offer and particularly on the way society had degenerated to its contemporary level. This approach often leads him into inaccuracies about the chronology of events, which are often, it seems, almost secondary to the main aim. His analyses of Roman decadence are, however, of great interest. Like the reflections of the poet Virgil, they spring from the experience of the disastrous civil wars of the 40s and early 30s. In the text, you will find that we follow the main line of the story. But it is worth your while reading in translation some of the more philosophical passages. S. A. Handford's Penguin translation is handiest for this purpose.

The strong moral line which Sallust takes about the corruption of Roman society appealed greatly to St Augustine, who called him 'an historian noted for his truthfulness'. Indeed, 'moral truthfulness' of this kind abounds in Roman literature and ensured its survival in the Christian world. The story of Catiline itself has also fascinated later authors. Ben Jonson (1573–1637), a contemporary of Shakespeare, first produced his play *Catiline* in 1611, the year the King James Bible (the so-called 'Authorised Version') was published. Like Shakespeare's *Julius Caesar* and *Coriolanus*, it is an example of Roman historical drama. But whereas Shakespeare used translations as his sources (North's *Plutarch* for these plays), it is clear that Jonson knew and used his sources at first hand.

Note on sources

References are given at the end of each section to Sallust's original text, although the passages still contain much which has been adapted or inserted.

Reference list of characters

NB Most Roman citizens had three names, a *praenōmen* 'forename', a *nōmen* 'gēns (tribe) name' and a *cognōmen* 'family name'. There was a limited number of *praenōmina*, which were abbreviated to initials, as in English. Thus P. = Pūblius, C. = Gāius, L. = Lūcius, Q. = Quīntus, T. = Titus, M. = Mārcus. The name used in the Latin text is here printed in capitals.

A *Conspirators*

Lūcius Sergius CATILĪNA	Noble and *senātor*; *praetor* 68; governor of Africa 67–66; candidate for consulship in 64 and 63; leader of the conspiracy.
P. Cornēlius LENTULUS Sura	*senātor*; he had risen to the consulship, but had been thrown out of the senate in 70 BC. He made a comeback and was *praetor* in 63; chief conspirator at Rome after Catiline's departure.
P. GABĪNIUS Capitō	*eques*; used by Lentulus as an intermediary with the Allobroges; in the plot to take over Rome, he and Statilius were to start fires.
C. Cornēlius CETHĒGUS	*senātor*; bloodthirsty and impatient; in the plot to take over Rome, he was sent to kill Cicero.
L. STATILIUS	*eques*; in the plot to take over Rome, he and Gabinius were to start fires.
L. CASSIUS Longīnus	*senātor*; only major conspirator not to give incriminating oath to the Allobroges.
L. Calpurnius BĒSTIA	*senātor*; tribune of the plebs 62; in the plot to take over Rome, his speech to an assembly, in which he was to complain of Cicero's measures, was to be the signal for action.
C. MĀNLIUS	Catiline's chief lieutenant; leading an army of debtors in Etruria.
C. CORNĒLIUS	*eques*; with Vargunteius, involved in a foiled plot to kill Cicero.
L. VARGUNTĒIUS	*senātor*; with C. Cornelius, involved in a foiled plot to kill Cicero.
P. UMBRĒNUS	Former businessman in Gaul; tried to induce Allobroges to join the conspiracy.
FAESULĀNUS	Unknown soldier from Faesulae; in charge of Catiline's left wing in the final battle.
SEMPRŌNIA	Wife of Decimus Iunius Brutus (consul 77); mother of D. Brutus, one of Caesar's assassins in 44; along with several other noblewomen involved in the conspiracy.

B *Informers against the conspirators*

FULVIA	Lover of Q. Curius; induced him to betray the conspiracy.
Q. CURIUS	Ex-*senātor* (removed by the censors for immoral behaviour); lover of Fulvia; betrayed the conspiracy.
ALLOBROGĒS	Ambassadors from this Gallic tribe, whose territory was in Gallia Transalpina (see map p. 209); in Rome to make a complaint to the senate of extortion by Roman officials; Lentulus used P. Umbrenus to induce them to join the conspiracy, but instead they extracted damning evidence and betrayed the plot.
T. VOLTURCIUS	From Croton, a coastal town in southern Italy; sent by Lentulus with the Allobroges to Catiline, bearing a letter and verbal instructions; captured at the Mulvian bridge, he gave information against the conspirators.

C *Roman authorities and their supporters*

Mārcus Tullius CICERŌ	*cōnsul* 63 (a *nouus homo*); chief architect of the conspiracy's failure.
C. ANTŌNIUS	*cōnsul* with Cicero in 63; handed over command to Petreius in the final battle because of gout.
Q. Caecilius METELLUS CELER	*praetor* 63; sent to Picenum to keep the peace; cut off Catiline's retreat to Gaul.
M. PETRĒIUS	A *lēgātus* under the command of C. Antonius in Etruria; commanded the army in the final battle against Catiline.
Q. FABIUS SANGA	*patrōnus* of the Allobroges; used by them as an intermediary with Cicero in the betrayal of the plot.
L. Valerius FLACCUS	*praetor* 63; one of the *praetōrēs* in charge of the operation at the Mulvian bridge, where the letter from Lentulus to Catiline was captured along with Volturcius.
M. Porcius CATŌ	Tribune of the plebs 62; his firm advocacy of the death penalty for the conspirators won the day.

Sallust's introduction to Catiline

Sallust introduces us to Catiline, outlines his character and shady past, and relates the early history of the conspiracy:

In writing about Catiline's conspiracy I will try to be as brief and accurate as I can. It is an affair which I regard as particularly memorable because of the unprecedented nature of the crime and of the danger it caused. Before I begin my narrative I must say a few words about the character of the man himself. Lucius Catiline was born of an aristocratic family. He had enormous mental and physical energy, but his character was evil and depraved. Even when quite young he enjoyed internal wars, murder, robbery, and civil strife, and in these he spent his early manhood. Physically he could endure hunger, cold, and lack of sleep to an incredible degree. He was reckless, cunning, devious, and capable of any kind of pretence or dissimulation; he hankered after other people's property and was lavish with his own; his passions were violent, he had a ready enough tongue but little sense. His desires were immoderate and always directed to the extravagant, the incredible and what was out of reach.

47. Sulla

After the period of Sulla's dominance he was taken with an overwhelming ambition to get his hands on public affairs, and provided he could do so was careless of the means to be used. His fierce ambition was continually stirred by his poverty and sense of guilt, both of which he had fed by the practices of which I have spoken. He was driven on also by the corruption of public morals, which were being disturbed by the two complementary evils of extravagance and meanness.

(*Catilīnae coniūrātiō* 4–5.8)

In a city so large and so corrupt Catiline found it very easy to surround himself with a gang given to every vice and crime. There were shameless gluttons and gamblers who had wasted their family fortunes on gaming or on their stomachs or on sex; there were those convicted of murder or sacrilege, or fearing conviction for other crimes committed; there were those who relied for their support on hand and tongue prepared to commit perjury or shed their fellows' blood; there were in a word all those haunted by disgrace, poverty or bad conscience. To Catiline they were all close friends. And any innocent man who happened to become friendly with him was easily assimilated to the rest by the attraction which regular contact brought. But it was chiefly the familiarity with the young that he sought. Their characters were still unformed and easily moulded, and they were readily ensnared. He adjusted his approach to the follies of their age, finding prostitutes for some, buying hounds and horses for others, and in the end sparing neither expense nor modesty to make them submit to his influence. I know there are some who think that the young men who frequented Catiline's household had very little respect for decency [sexual deviancy is the charge here]; but this opinion gained currency for reasons other than knowledge of its truth.

When he was quite a young man Catiline had had many disgraceful affairs; there was one with a young woman of noble birth, and another with a priestess of Vesta, as well as many similar illegal and sacrilegious relationships. In the end he fell in love with Aurelia Orestilla, in whom no honest man found anything to admire except her good looks; she hesitated to marry him because she did not want a stepson who was already grown up, and it is generally believed that Catiline murdered the young man and so made way for the marriage by crime. This act was in my opinion a prime cause of his forming his conspiracy. His guilty conscience, with crimes against gods and men weighing on it, allowed neither sleep nor rest, and wrought his mind into a state of devastating tension. His face lost its colour, he became pale, with bloodshot eyes and restless gait, and in short showed in every look all the signs of madness. But he taught the young men, whom he had ensnared as I have described, every kind of wickedness. From their number he provided himself with false witnesses and signatories; he taught them to make light of honour, fortune and danger, and when they had no reputation or shame left urged them to still greater crimes. If there was no immediate motive for wrong-doing they waylaid and murdered at random whether there was reason or not; indeed he preferred the cruelty of motiveless crime to the enervation of mind and hand by lack of practice.

These were the friends and accomplices on whom Catiline relied in making his plans to overthrow the government. His own debts in all parts of the world were huge, and most of Sulla's soldiers had wasted their means and were led to long for civil war by memories of their former plunder and victory.[1] There was no army in Italy; Gnaeus Pompeius was waging a war in a distant part of the world;[2] he himself had great hopes of his candidacy for the consulship; the senate was not alerted, and the general peace and quiet provided the opportunity Catiline needed. Accordingly about the first of June in the consulship of Lucius Caesar and Gaius Figulus[3] he started to approach his followers individually,

1. Sulla had been dictator at Rome 82–79. The veterans of his campaigns were provided with land obtained by massacres and proscriptions of enemies.
2. Pompey the Great, later to contest the Civil War with Julius Caesar. At this time he was fighting Mithradates, king of Pontus, in the East.
3. 64.

48. Rome

Cicero, Catiline and Rome

Cicero (Marcus Tullius Cicero), from Arpinum, the home-town of Marius, achieved the rare feat of rising from a non-senatorial family to win the consulship of 63 BC at the first attempt and at the minimum age. Early in his year as consul, he demonstrated his credentials by leading successful campaigns against a series of popular tribunician bills, including a bill to deal with the chronic problem of debt and a bill for settling people on the land, which was one of the most enlightened pieces of legislation of the era. His campaigns centred largely around arousing fears of renewed disruption and ascribing personal motives to the bills' proposers. Nowhere does he acknowledge the existence of the social and economic problems which the bills were designed to settle.

No surprise then to find a growing centre of open discontent in Etruria, the same region that had been the focus of the troubles led by Lepidus in 78 BC. Men oppressed by 'the savagery of the money-lenders and of the Roman courts' (Sallust, *Catiline* 33) found a local leader in a certain C. Manlius and a vocal and forceful champion at Rome in the senator L. Sergius Catilina, who was making his second, and again unsuccessful, attempt to be elected consul. Frustration in Etruria threatened to, and eventually did, boil over into open revolt. The Senate responded with the usual declaration of the *senātūs cōnsultum ultimum*. (*World of Rome*, **66**)

encouraging some and trying out others. He spoke of his own resources, of the unreadiness of the public authorities, and of the great rewards the conspiracy would bring. When his enquiries were complete he called a meeting of the boldest and most desperate.

(Catilīnae coniūrātiō 14–17.2)

When Catiline saw that those to whom I have referred had assembled, though he had had many meetings with them individually he thought a general address of encouragement would be timely, and led them to a private part of the house, and after removing all witnesses addressed them in the following terms.

'If I had not already assured myself of your courage and loyalty, the present opportunity would have presented itself to no purpose. The high hopes of power which are now mine would have been vain, and with none but cowards and faint-hearts to rely on I would not now be running these risks. But you have proved yourselves in many a crisis to be my brave and faithful friends. I have made up my mind to embark on this great and glorious enterprise, knowing well that your ideas of right and wrong coincide with mine. The firmest base for friendship is to share likes and dislikes. I have told you all individually what I have in mind. But my purpose is inflamed still further as time passes by the thought of what our future will be unless we strike a blow to secure our freedom. Public affairs are now in the jurisdiction and control of a few powerful men; it is to them that kings and rulers pay tribute and that peoples and races pay their taxes. The rest of us, energetic and admirable as we are, nobles and commons, are reduced to a vulgar mob, without influence or authority and subservient to those who in a true democracy would stand in awe of us. The consequence is that all influence, power, prestige and wealth is in their hands or in the hands of those they choose; while to us there remain danger, defeat, prosecution and poverty. How long will men of your courage put up with all this? Is it not better to die bravely than to live in misery and dishonour, despised and ridiculed, and die in ignominy? I swear faithfully – by all I hold sacred – that victory is in our grasp. We are young and in good heart; they are physically and financially past their prime. All we need is to act; the result will bring success. How can anyone with any spirit put up with their having an overabundance of riches which they pour away on building in the sea and levelling mountains, while we lack the means to procure the bare necessities of life? They acquire house after house, we have nowhere for our domestic hearth. They buy pictures, statues, embossed silver; they pull down new houses to build still others; they make every conceivable use and misuse of their wealth as it suits them, and still cannot exhaust it. We have poverty in the home, debt outside it, present misery and a hopeless future, nothing left in short except our miserable lives. Wake up, then; there before your very eyes are the liberty, the wealth, the honour and the glory you long for; Fortune offers them all if you succeed. The very enterprise, its opportunity and dangers, your need, the spoils of war, are all beyond the power of my words to describe. Let me lead you or serve in your ranks; my heart and body are yours to command. These are the plans I shall with your help follow as consul, unless I am mistaken in you and you prefer slavery to command.'

His audience were in the depths of misfortune, without hope or means, and thought they would profit greatly from public disorder. None the less, many of them asked him to explain the conditions on which war would be waged, what profit they would get from victory, what their prospects and resources would be. Catiline proceeded to promise cancellation of all debt and proscription of the rich, as well as magistracies, priesthoods, plunder and everything else which war and the licence of victory can offer. He went on to remind them that Piso was in Nearer Spain,[4] and Publius Sittius of Nuceria with an army in Mauretania,[5] both of them being in his plot; that Gaius Antonius was a candidate for the consulship, and he hoped would be his colleague; he added that Antonius was an intimate friend of his and under many pressures; Catiline hoped to initiate his programme when they became joint consuls. He finished with lavish abuse of all good citizens, and flattering commendation of his own gang, mentioning each by name; he recalled the poverty and ambitions of individuals, the danger and disgrace threatening many of them, and the profits many others had made out of Sulla's victory. When he saw he had them sufficiently excited, he urged on them the importance of his candidacy and dismissed the meeting.

There were those who said that Catiline, after he had finished speaking, compelled his accomplices in crime to swear an oath, and carried round bowls containing a mixture of human blood and wine which they had to taste, binding themselves by a solemn oath as if it was a religious rite, before he finally revealed his plan; and his purpose, they added, was to knit them more closely together because of mutual consciousness of their dreadful crime. There were others who believed that these and many other details were invented by people who thought that the prejudice against Cicero which subsequently arose would be moderated by stressing the appalling nature of the crime committed by those whom he had put to death. I have too little evidence to give judgement in a matter of such moment.

(Catilīnae coniūrātiō 20–22)

4. As governor. He was killed while journeying through the province.
5. North Africa.

49. libīdinibus adeō dēditus

The world's workshop

Even when the city was at its most crowded, it depended for survival on people on the move to bring
in the staples for the food of the masses, and the luxuries of life for the wealthy – a good deal of
which filtered out in the different ways, direct and indirect, that we have examined, into the life of the
community as a whole. The materials for all this came from all over the Roman world. Praising the
city in the second century AD, the Greek orator Aelius Aristides called it 'the common workshop of the
world'. He did not mean that Rome was experiencing an early Industrial Revolution, but that it was
the place where raw produce from all over the world was transformed into the stuff of civilisation.
One might even say that supplying Rome, like paying tribute to imperial Persia or to the Athenian
empire of the fifth century BC, was one of the things that defined the empire. (*World of Rome*, **228**)

Section 5A(i)

Summer 64. Curius, one of Catiline's backers for the consulship of 63, tells his lover Fulvia about Catiline's plans. She spreads the news and the result is a defeat in the elections for Catiline, a victory for the 'new man' Cicero. This does not stop Catiline's revolutionary plans. He places arms in strategic locations and supplies Manlius (whom he will eventually join) with money.

sed in eā coniūrātiōne fuit Q. Curius, nātus haud obscūrō locō,
libīdinibus adeō dēditus, ut eum cēnsōrēs senātū mouērent. huic hominī
tanta uānitās inerat ut nōn posset reticēre quae audierat; tanta īnsolentia
ut numquam sua ipse scelera cēlāret: tanta audācia ut semper dīceret
faceretque quaecumque uolēbat. erat eī cum Fuluiā, muliere nōbilī,   5
stuprī uetus cōnsuētūdō sed Curius tam pauper factus est ut eī minus
grātus fieret. repente autem adeō glōriārī coepit ut maria montīsque
Fuluiae pollicērētur. et tam īnsolēns ferōxque fīēbat ut eī mortem
interdum minārētur, nisi sibi obnoxia esset. at Fuluia, īnsolentiae Curī
causā cognitā, rem reī pūblicae tam perīculōsam esse putābat, ut,   10
omnia, quae dē Catilīnae coniūrātiōne audierat, multīs nārrāret. eae rēs,
ā Fuluiā nārrātae, in prīmīs effēcērunt ut cōnsulātus M. Tulliō Cicerōnī
mandārētur. namque anteā plēraque nōbilitās tam inuida erat ut
cōnsulātum nouō hominī mandāre nōllent. nam 'polluātur cōnsulātus',
inquiēbant, 'sī eum quamuīs ēgregius homo nouus adipīscātur.' sed ubi   15
perīculum aduēnit, inuidia atque superbia post fuēre. igitur, comitiīs
habitīs, cōnsulēs dēclārantur M. Tullius et C. Antōnius; quod
factum prīmō coniūrātōrēs concusserat. neque tamen Catilīnae furor
minuēbātur, sed in diēs plūra agitāre, arma per Italiam locīs
opportūnīs parāre, pecūniam Faesulās ad Mānlium quendam   20
portāre.

(*Catilīnae coniūrātiō* 23–24.2)

Notes

1 From now on you will find notes on new grammar at the end of each running vocabulary. Consult these as you read the chapter.
2 Names are given only on their first occurrence in this section. Consult the list on *Text and Vocabulary* pp. 168–9 if you forget them.

Running vocabulary for 5A(i)

adeō to such an extent
agitō 1 I stir up, discuss [see note line 19]
Antōni-us ī 2m. Gaius Antonius
arm-a ōrum 2n. pl. arms; armed men
C. = *Gāi-us ī* 2m. Gaius

Catilīn-a ae 1m. Catiline
cēnsor cēnsōr-is 3m. censor (official appointed every five years to vet senate)
Cicerō Cicerōn-is 3m. Cicero
comiti-a ōrum 1 n. pl. elections

concutiō 3/4 *concussī concussus* I shake, alarm
coniūrātiō coniūrātiōn-is 3f. conspiracy
coniūrātor coniūrātōr-is 3m. conspirator

cōnsuētūdō cōnsuētūdin-is 3f. amorous association (+ gen. 'involving')

cōnsulāt-us ūs 4m. consulship

Curi-us ī 2m. Quintus Curius

dēclārō 1 I declare

dēdit-us a um devoted to (+ dat.)

efficiō 3/4 *effēcī effectus* I bring (it) about (that: *ut* + subj.)

ēgregi-us a um outstanding

fact-um ī 2n. deed, happening

Faesul-ae ārum 1f. pl. Faesulae (Fiesole)

ferōx ferōc-is savage, wild

Fului-a ae 1f. Fulvia

glōrior 1 dep. I boast

grāt-us a um pleasing to X (dat.)

in prīmīs especially

īnsolēns īnsolent-is arrogant

īnsolenti-a ae 1f. arrogance

īnsum inesse īnfuī (+ dat.) I am in

interdum sometimes

inuid-us a um envious

inuidi-a ae 1f. envy, hatred

M. = Mārc-us ī 2m. Marcus

mandō 1 I entrust X (acc.) to Y (dat.)

Mānli-us ī 2m. Manlius

minuō 3 I diminish, weaken

mōns mont-is 3m. mountain

moue-ō 2 *mōuī mōtus* i remove X (acc.) from Y (abl.)

namque for, in fact

nārrātae (nom. pl. f.) 'told'

nārrō 1 I tell, relate

nōbilitās nōbilitāt-is 3f. nobility

obnoxi-us a um servile to X (dat.) [see note on line 9]

obscūr-us a um ignoble (lit. 'dark')

opportūn-us a um strategic

parāre [see note line 20]

perīculōs-us a um dangerous

plērusque plēraque plērumque the majority of

polluō 3 I pollute

portāre [see note line 21]

post '(put) behind (them)'

Q. = Quīnt-us ī 2m. Quintus

quaecumque (acc. pl. n.) whatever (things)

quamuīs however [see note line 15]

reticeō 2 I keep quiet (about)

stupr-um ī 2n. sexual intercourse [outside marriage, and frowned upon because of Fulvia's status]

superbi-a ae 1f. pride, arrogance

Tulli-us ī 2m. Tullius

uānitās uānitāt-is 3f. vanity, boasting

uetus ueter-is old, long-established (like *dīues*. See **47**)

Grammar for 5A

historic infinitive　　　　　**ablative of respect**

Notes

line 9 *nisi...esset* reports his conditional statement 'if you don't lick my boots, I'll...'; translate 'if she *were* not...'

line 10 *causā cognitā* 'with the reason having been found out' (ablative absolute)

line 14 *nouus homo* i.e. a man whose family had not previously held a consulship, *nōllent* is pl. because *plēraque nōbilitās* = 'most of the *nobles*'.

line 15 *quamuīs* qualifies *ēgregius*: 'a *homo nouus* however *ēgregius*'.

lines 16–17 *comitiīs habitīs* 'with the elections having been held' (ablative absolute).

line 19 *agitāre*: infinitive, but used as main verb: translate 'he stirred up'.

line 20 *parāre*: infinitive but used as main verb: translate 'he got ready'.

line 21 *portāre*: infinitive but used as main verb: translate 'he conveyed'.

Learning vocabulary for 5A(i)

Nouns

arm-a ōrum 2n. pl. arms; armed men

coniūrātiō coniūrātion-is 3f. conspiracy

coniūrātor coniūrātōr-is 3m. conspirator

cōnsulāt-us ūs 4m. consulship

mōns mont-is 3m. mountain

Adjectives

grāt-us a um pleasing to X (dat.)

uetus ueter-is (like *dīues*, **47**) old; long-established

Verbs

agitō 1 I stir up, incite (*agō* + *-it-*)

efficiō 3/4 *effēcī effectus* I bring about (often followed by *ut* + subj.); cause, make; complete

īnsum inesse īnfuī īnfutūrus I am in X (dat.)

mandō 1 I entrust X (acc.) to Y (dat.)

moueō 2 *mōuī mōtus* I remove X (acc.) from Y (abl.) (move, cause, begin)

nārrō 1 I tell, relate X (acc.) to Y (dat.)

Others

adeō to such an extent

in prīmīs especially

quamuīs however, ever such a (qualifying an adj.; cf. *quamuīs* + subj. 'although')

Section 5A(ii)

63. Catiline gathers more supporters, among them some women, whose desire for a new order is closely related to their vast debts. Sempronia, an extremely accomplished noblewoman, is one recruit.

eō tempore plūrimōs hominēs adiūnxisse sibi Catilīna dīcitur, mulierēs
etiam aliquot, quae prīmō ingentīs sūmptūs stupro tolerāuerant, posteā,
cum propter aetātem quaestum sīc facere nōn possent, in aes⁀aliēnum
maximum inciderant. igitur sē Catilīnae adiūnxērunt ut sē aere⁀aliēnō   25
līberārent, et Catilīna eās in coniūrātiōnem laetus accēpit ut per eās
seruōs urbānōs sollicitāret atque urbem incenderet. uirōs eārum sē uel
adiūnctūrum sibi uel interfectūrum putābat.

50. cantū et saltātiōne docta

sed in eīs erat Semprōnia, quae multa saepe uirīlis audāciae facinora
commīserat. haec mulier genere atque fōrmā, praetereā uirō atque   30
līberīs satis fortūnāta fuit; litterīs Graecīs et Latīnīs docta, cantū et
saltātiōne magis docta quam necesse est mātrōnae. sed eī cāriōra semper
omnia quam decus atque pudīcitia fuit; libīdō sīc accēnsa, ut saepius
peteret uirōs quam peterētur. uērum ingenium eius haud absurdum;
posse uersūs facere, iocum mouēre, sermōne ūtī uel modestō uel mollī   35
uel procācī. prōrsus multae facētiae multusque lepōs inerat.

(*Catilīnae coniūrātiō* 24.3–25)

Running vocabulary for 5A(ii)

absurd-us a um foolish, silly
accēns-us a um on fire, aroused
adiungō 3 adiūnxī adiūnctus I
  join X (acc.) to Y (dat.)
aes aliēn-um aer-is aliēn-ī (3n. +
  1/2 adj.) debt (lit. 'someone
  else's bronze')
aetās aetāt-is 3f. age
aliquot several
cant-us ūs 4m. singing
cār-us a um dear
committō 3 commīsī I commit
decus decor-is 3n. honour
doct-us a um skilled in X (abl.)
facēti-ae ārum 1f. pl. wit

fortūnāt-us a um fortunate in X
  (abl.)
ioc-us ī 2m. joke (*iocum mouēre*
  = 'to crack a joke')
incidō 3 incidī I fall into (*in* +
  acc.)
ingeni-um ī 2n. intellect
Latīn-us a um Latin
lepōs lepōr-is 3m. charm
litter-ae ārum 1f. pl. literature
mātrōn-a ae 1f. lady, wife and
  mother
modest-us a um chaste
moll-is e gentle
petō 3 I proposition, court
posse (line 35): see note

procāx procāc-is bold, forward
prōrsus in a word
quaest-us ūs 4m. living
saltātiō saltātiōn-is 3f. dancing
Semprōni-a ae 1f. Sempronia
sollicitō 1 I stir up
stupr-um ī 2n. prostitution
sūmpt-us ūs 4m. expenses,
  expenditure
tolerō 1 I sustain
uel... uel... uel either...
  or... or
uers-us ūs 4m. verse; (pl.) poetry
uirīl-is e of a man
urbān-us a um of the city

Notes

lines 30–1 *genere atque fōrmā... uirō atque līberīs*: ablatives (of respect) – await *fortūnāta* to solve them.
lines 31–2 *litterīs Graecīs et Latīnīs* and then *cantū et saltātiōne*: ablatives of respect – await *docta* to solve
  them.
line 33 Supply *erat* with *accēnsa*.
line 34 *uērum... absurdum*: no verb, so supply *erat* or *fuit*.
line 35 *posse*: infinitive, but used as main verb, so translate 'she could'.
line 36 *inerat* is governed by *both facētiae* and *lepōs*, but it is singular by attraction to the last-mentioned
  nominative noun. A common phenomenon.

Learning vocabulary for 5A(ii)

Nouns
aes aer-is 3n. bronze
aes aliēn-um aer-is aliēn-ī 3n. +
  1/2 adj. debt (lit. 'someone
  else's bronze')
aetās aetāt-is 3f. age; lifetime;
  generation
litter-ae ārum 1f. pl. literature
  (letter)
mātrōn-a ae 1f. wife, mother; lady
uers-us ūs 4m. verse; (pl.) poetry

Adjectives
aliēn-us a um someone else's
doct-us a um skilled in X (abl.),
  learned
fortūnāt-us a um fortunate, lucky
  in X (abl.)
Latīn-us a um Latin
modest-us a um chaste, modest,
  discreet

Verbs
adiungō 3 adiūnxī adiūnctus I
  join X (acc.) to Y (dat.)
petō 3 petīuī petītus I proposition,
  court; attack, make for (beg;
  seek)

Others
aliquot several
uel... uel either... or

Section 5A(iii)

*Summer 63. Catiline tries for the consulship of 62, but is again defeated. He
stations his troops throughout Italy. Manlius is stationed at Faesulae. Catiline
plots tirelessly, but gets nowhere. At a night-time meeting (6 November), he
suggests his readiness to depart for the army, if Cicero is done away with first.
C. Cornelius and L. Vargunteius attempt this task (early on the morning of
7 November), but are foiled.*

hīs rēbus comparātīs, Catilīna nihilōminus in proximum annum
cōnsulātum petēbat. neque intereā quiētus erat, sed omnibus modīs
īnsidiās parābat Cicerōnī. sed Cicerō, ut hās īnsidiās ēuītāret, per
Fuluiam effēcerat ut Q. Curius cōnsilia Catilīnae sibi prōderet. igitur   40
Catilīna postquam diēs comitiōrum uēnit et repulsam tulit, cōnstituit
bellum facere. deinde, ut sociōs in dīuersīs partibus Ītaliae habēret, C.
Mānlium Faesulīs aliōs aliīs locīs per Ītaliam posuit. intereā Rōmae
multa simul agere; cōnsulibus īnsidiās collocāre, parāre incendia,
opportūna loca armātīs hominibus obsidēre, ipse cum tēlō esse, sociōs   45
hortārī ut semper intentī parātīque essent; diēs noctīsque festīnāre,
uigilāre, neque īnsomniīs neque labōre fatīgārī. postrēmō cum nihil
prōcessisset, coniūrātiōnis prīncipēs nocte conuocat et 'praemīsī' inquit
'Mānlium ad exercitum, item aliōs in alia loca opportūna, quī initium
bellī faciant. ego nunc ipse ad exercitum proficīscerer, nisi Cicerō etiam   50
uīueret, sed prius Cicerōnem necārī uolō, nē mea cōnsilia impediat.'
quae cum dīxisset, perterritīs cēterīs coniūrātōribus, C. Cornēlius eques
Rōmānus operam suam pollicitus et cum eō L. Varguntēius senātor
cōnstituēre eā nocte paulō post cum armātīs hominibus ad Cicerōnem
introīre ut eum dē imprōuīsō interficerent. Curius, ubi intellegit tantum   55
perīculum cōnsulī impendēre, properē per Fuluiam Cicerōnī dolum quī
parābātur ēnūntiat. nē igitur Cicerō dē imprōuīsō interficerētur, illī
iānuā prohibitī sunt, itaque tantum facinus frūstrā suscēperant.

(*Catilīnae coniūrātiō 26–28.3*)

Running vocabulary for 5A(iii)

agere [see note on line 44]
armāt-us a um armed
C. = Gāi-us ī 2m. Gaius
collocō 1 I place [for *collocāre*
  see note on line 44]
comiti-a ōrum 2n. pl. elections
conuocō 1 I call together, summon
Cornēli-us ī 2m. Gaius Cornelius
dē imprōuīsō: see *imprōuīsō*
dīuers-us a um different

ēnūntiō 1 I declare, announce X
  (acc.) to Y (dat.)
esse [see note on line 45]
ēuītō 1 I avoid
Faesul-ae ārum 1f. pl. Faesulae
  (Fiesole)
fatīgō 1 I tire [for *fatīgārī* see note
  on line 47]
festīnāre [see note on line 46]
frūstrā in vain
hortārī [see note on line 46]

impediō 4 I impede, hinder
impendeō 2 I hang over, threaten
  X (dat.)
imprōuīsō: *dē imprōuīsō*
  unexpectedly
initi-um ī 2n. beginning
īnsidi-ae ārum 1f. pl. ambush,
  trap
īnsomni-a ae if. sleeplessness
  (pl. = bouts of sleeplessness)
intent-us a um vigilant

intro-eō (-īre) I go in
itaque and so, therefore
item likewise
L. = Lūci-us ī 2m. Lucius
labor labōr-is 3m. toil, hard work
nihilōminus nevertheless
obsideō 2 I besiege [see note on line 45 for *obsidēre*]
oper-a ae 1f. service
opportūn-us a um strategic
parāre [see note on line 44]
parāt-us a um prepared
perterrit-us a um terrified

petō 3 I stand for
postquam after (+ indic; usually perfect: tr. 'after had —ed')
praemittō 3 *praemīsī* I send in advance
prius first
prōcēdō 3 *prōcessī* I go forward, succeed
prōdō 3 I betray, reveal
prohibeō 2 *prohibuī prohibitus* I keep X (acc.) away from Y (abl.)
properē hastily

quiēt-us a um quiet
repuls-a ae 1f. defeat
repulsam ferō ferre tulī I am defeated (lit. 'I bear a defeat')
senātor senātōr-is 3m. senator
suscipiō 3/4 *suscēpī* I undertake
tēl-um ī 2n. weapon
uigilō 1 I stay awake [for *uigilāre* see note on line 47]
Varguntēi-us ī 2m. Lucius Vargunteius

Notes

line 44 *agere*: infinitive but used as main verb: translate 'he did'. Similarly *collocāre* 'he placed', *parāre* 'he prepared'.
line 45 *obsidēre* 'he besieged', *esse* 'he was' (i.e. 'went around').
line 46 *hortārī* 'he urged', *festīnāre* 'he hurried'.
line 47 *uigilāre* 'he stayed awake'. *fatīgārī* 'he was made weary'.

Learning vocabulary for 5A(iii)

Nouns
īnsidi-ae ārum 1f. pl. trap, ambush
oper-a ae 1f. service (attention)
tēl-um ī 2n. weapon

Adjectives
armāt-us a um armed
dīuers-us a um different
opportūn-us a um strategic, suitable, favourable

Verbs
collocō 1 I place, station
conuocō 1 I summon, call together
impediō 4 I prevent, impede, hinder
petō 3 *petīuī petītus* I stand for (public office); (beg; seek; proposition, court; make for, attack)

prohibeō 2 I prevent, hinder, keep X (acc.) away from Y (abl. or *ā (ab)* + abl.)

Others
frūstrā in vain
itaque and so, therefore
postquam (conj. + indicative) after
prius before, previously, first

Manlius' revolutionary activities in Etruria had induced Cicero to take official action. On 21 October the senate passed the *senātūs cōnsultum ultimum,* decreeing that the consuls 'should see to it that the republic comes to no harm'. On 27 October Manlius led an army into the field. The consuls reacted by sending out four commanders to take defensive measures in various regions. One of these, Q. Metellus Celer, was sent to Picenum (see map p. 209: *Ager Pīcēnus*). At Rome rewards were offered for information leading to the arrest of conspirators and night-watches were set. There was an atmosphere of great trepidation among the people.

Catiline, undeterred by the preparations for defence or by threat of prosecution, continued plotting. On 8 November (the day after Cornelius' and Vargunteius' attempt on Cicero's life) Catiline attended the senate. Cicero delivered his speech *In Catilīnam I* ('Against Catiline'), a savage attack on Catiline, urging him to leave Rome, along with his band of thugs. Catiline's defence was rebuffed by the senate,

51. Cicero attacking Catiline in the senate

and the same night he voluntarily left Rome. According to letters he sent to influential men, he was heading for exile in Marseilles. But Sallust portrays his intention at that moment as being to join Manlius, which is in fact what he eventually did.

Meanwhile, in Etruria, Manlius was leading a deputation to the Roman commander who had been sent against him. He complained of the avarice of usurers and of the bondage to which many of his 'soldiers' had been reduced. It

was poverty, not treachery, which urged them to revolt. The Roman commander replied that they should lay down their arms and approach the senate.

By mid-November, the news had reached Rome of Catiline's arrival at Manlius' camp. The senate promptly declared them *hostēs* – 'public enemies' – and offered an amnesty by a fixed date to their supporters. The consuls were to enrol troops. Cicero was to take charge of guarding Rome. C. Antonius was to pursue Catiline with an army. At this point Sallust digresses to comment on the great popular support there was for the conspiracy in the city, before he continues with his narrative.

Section 5B(i)

On Catiline's instructions, Lentulus approaches the ambassadors of the Allobroges, a Gallic tribe, via P. Umbrenus (who has done business in Gaul) and tries to draw them into the revolution.

īsdem temporibus Rōmae Lentulus, sīcutī Catilīna praecēperat,
quōscumque nouīs⁀rēbus idōneōs esse crēdēbat, aut per sē aut per aliōs   60
sollicitābat. igitur P. Vmbrēnō cuidam negōtium dat ut lēgātōs
Allobrogum requīrat eōsque impellat ad societātem bellī, sciēbat enim
Lentulus Allobrogēs pūblicē prīuātimque aere aliēnō oppressōs et nātūrā
gentem Gallicam bellicōsam esse. exīstimābat igitur fore⁀ut facile ad
tāle cōnsilium addūcerentur. Vmbrēnus, quod in Galliā negōtiātus erat,   65
plērīsque prīncipibus cīuitātum nōtus erat atque eōs nōuerat; itaque sine
morā, ubī⁀prīmum lēgātōs in forō cōnspexit, rogāuit pauca dē statū
cīuitātis et miserō eius cāsū. postquam illōs uīdit querī dē auāritiā
magistrātuum, accūsāre senātum quod in eō nihil auxilī esset, miseriīs
suīs remedium mortem exspectāre, 'at ego' inquit, 'uōbīs, sī modo uirī   70
esse uultis, ratiōnem ostendam quā tanta ista mala effugiātis.' haec ubi
dīxit, Allobrogēs, in maximam spem adductī, ōrāre Vmbrēnum ut suī
miserērētur; nihil tam difficile esse quod nōn factūrī essent, ut cīuitātem
aere aliēnō līberārent. ille eōs in domum quandam perdūcit quae forō
propinqua erat. praetereā Gabīnium arcessit, quō māior auctōritās   75
sermōnī inesset et quō facilius eīs persuādēret. Gabīniō praesente
coniūrātiōnem aperit, nōminat sociōs, praetereā multōs innoxiōs, quō
lēgātīs animus amplior esset. persuāsit eīs ut operam pollicērentur,
deinde pollicitōs operam suam domum dīmittit.

(*Catilīnae coniūrātiō* 39.6–40)

Running vocabulary for 5B(i)

addūcō 3 addūxī adductus I lead
  to, draw to
Allobrogēs Allobrog-um 3m. pl.
  Allobroges [Gallic tribe, see
  name list, *Text and Vocabulary*
  p. 169 and map]
ampl-us a um large, great
aperiō 4 I reveal
arcessō 3 I summon
auāriti-a ae 1f. avarice, greed
auctōritās auctōritāt-is 3f.
  weight, authority
bellicōs-us a um warlike
cās-us ūs 4m. fortune
cōnspiciō 3/4 cōnspexī I catch
  sight of
dīmittō 3 I send away
exīstimō 1 I think, consider

fore ut (+ subj.) 'that it would
  happen that . . .'
Gabīni-us ī 2m. P. Gabinius
  Capito
Galli-a ae 1f. Gaul
Gallic-us a um Gallic
idōne-us a um qualified (for),
  suitable (for) (+ dat.)
impellō 3 I urge, persuade
innoxi-us a um innocent
Lentul-us ī 2m. P. Cornelius
  Lentulus Sura
misereor 2 dep. I take pity on
  (+ gen.)
miseri-a ae 1f. misery, distress
nātūr-a ae 1f. nature
negōtior 1 dep. I do business
nōminō 1 I name

nōscō 3 nōuī nōtus I get to know
  (nōuī = I know)
nōt-us a um known to X (dat.)
nouae rēs nouārum rērum
  (1/2 adj. + 5f. noun)
  revolution (lit. 'new things')
P. = Pūbliō: Pūbli-us ī 2m.
  Publius
pauc-ī ae a a few
perdūcō 3 I bring to
plērīque plēraeque plēraque the
  majority of
praecipiō 3/4 praecēpī I instruct,
  order
praesēns praesent-is present
prīuātim individually
propinqu-us a um near to X (dat.)
pūblicē publicly, as a state

52. Allobrox

queror 3 dep. I complain
quīcumque quaecumque
    quodcumque whoever,
    whatever (declines like *quī*
    quae quod)
quō + comparative + subjunctive
    'in order that . . . more' [see
    notes on lines 75–76]

remedi-um ī 2n. cure
requīrō 3 I seek out
sīcutī (+ indicative) just as
societās societāt-is 3f. alliance,
    partnership (+ gen. expressing
    sphere of alliance; tr. 'in X')
sollicitō 1 I rouse up, incite to
    revolt

spēs spē-ī 5f. hope
stat-us ūs 4m. state
ubi prīmum as soon as
Vmbrēn-us ī 2m. Publius
    Umbrenus

Grammar for 5B

purpose with *quō*   ***fore ut* + subjunctive**

Notes

line 62 *bellī* governed by *societās* and completing the idea of partnership by expressing what the partners
    will share in.
line 63 *oppressōs*: sc. *esse* (see **148** for the suppression of *esse* in reported speech).
line 69 *quod . . . esset*: subjunctive within reported speech (see **147**)
line 71 *quā . . . effugiātis*: note the mood of the verb. See **150³**.
line 72 *ōrāre*: historic infinitive.
line 73 *quod . . . factūrī essent*: subjunctive within reported speech (see **142**). There is strong emphasis on
    the future, hence the composite future subjunctive (= fut. participle + subj. of *sum*)
lines 75–6, 77–8 *quō maior . . . inesset* ⎤ All express purpose, with a comparative
                quō facilius . . . ⎟ idea: 'in order the more
                persuādēret ⎬ –ly to–' (adv.); 'in order that
                quo . . . amplior esset ⎦ more –' (adj.)

Learning vocabulary for 5B(i)

Nouns
auctōritās auctōritāt-is 3f.
    weight, authority
nātūr-a ae 1f. nature
spēs spē-ī 5f. hope(s); expectation

Adjectives
ampl-us a um large, great
idōne-us a um suitable (for),
    qualified (for) (+ dat.)
nōt-us a um known, well-known

pauc-ī ae a (pl.) a few, a small
    number of
plērīque plēraeque plēraque the
    majority of

Verbs
aperiō 4 *aperuī apertus* I open;
    reveal
dīmittō 3 *dīmīsī dīmissus* I send
    away (*dis-* + *mittō*)
exīstimō 1 I think, consider (*ex* +
    aestimō = I value)

nōscō 3 *nōuī nōtus* I get to know
    (perfect tenses = I know etc.)
queror 3 dep. *questus* I complain
requīrō 3 *requīsīuī requīsītus* I
    seek out; ask for (*re-* +
    quaerō)
sollicitō 1 I stir up, arouse; incite
    to revolt (bother, worry)

Others
ubi prīmum as soon as (with
    perfect indicative)

Section 5B(ii)

The Allobroges decide to betray the conspiracy, not to join it. They use Q.
Fabius Sanga, a patrōnus *of their tribe, as an intermediary with Cicero. Cicero*
urges them to pretend loyalty to the conspirators.

sed Allobrogēs, quippe quī nōndum coniūrātiōnī sē adiungere
cōnstituissent, rem diū cōnsīderābant. in alterā parte erat aes aliēnum,   80
studium bellī, magna mercēs in spē uictōriae; at in alterā, maiōrēs opēs
cīuitātis Rōmānae, tūta cōnsilia, prō incertā spē certa praemia. haec illīs
uoluentibus, tandem uīcit fortūna reī pūblicae. itaque Q. Fabiō Sangae,
cīuitātis suae patrōnō, rem omnem, utī cognōuerant, aperiunt. Cicero,   85
per Sangam cōnsiliō cognitō, lēgātīs Allobrogum praecipit ut studium
coniūrātiōnis uehementer simulent, cēterōs adeant, bene polliceantur,
dentque operam ut coniūrātōrēs quam⁻maximē manifestōs faciant.

(Catilīnae coniūrātiō 41)

Running vocabulary for 5B(ii)

cert-us a um sure, certain
cōnsīderō 1 I ponder, consider
Fabi-us ī 2m. Fabius [Quintus
    Fabius Sanga]
fortūn-a ae 1f. fortune
incert-us a um uncertain
manifest-us a um in the open,
    caught in the act, plainly guilty
mērcēs mercēd-is 3f. profit,
    reward

nōndum not yet
opēs op-um 3f. pl. resources
patrōn-us ī 2m. patron
praecipiō 3 I give instructions to
    X (dat.) to do Y: *ut* + subj.
praemi-um ī 2n. reward, prize
prō (+ abl.) instead of
Q. = Quīntō: Quīnt-us ī 2m.
    Quintus
quam maximē as much as possible

quippe quī see GE **145.2**
Sang-a ae 1m. Q. Fabius Sanga
simulō 1 I feign
studi-um ī 2n. enthusiasm (for)
    (+ gen.)
uoluō 3 I turn over, reflect on
utī = ut

Notes

line 81 *at in alterā*: supply *parte* and *erant.*
lines 87–8 *simulent… adeant… polliceantur dentque*: all verbs in the *ut* clause introduced by *praecipit*
    (line 86).
line 87 *bene polliceantur*: tr. 'make fine promises'.

Learning vocabulary for 5B(ii)

Nouns
fortūn-a ae 1f. fortune, luck; (pl.)
    wealth
opēs op-um 3f. pl. resources;
    wealth (s. *ops op-is* help, aid)
praemi-um ī 2n. prize, reward
studi-um ī 2n. enthusiasm, zeal

Adjectives
cert-us a um sure, certain

manifest-us a um in the open;
    obvious, clear; caught in the
    act

Verbs
cōnsīderō 1 I consider, ponder
praecipiō 3/4 *praecēpī praeceptus*
    I instruct, give orders to X
    (dat.) to do/not to do Y: *ut/nē*
    + subj. (*prae + capiō*)

simulō 1 I feign

Others
nōndum not yet
prō (+ abl.) instead of (for, in
    return for; on behalf of; in
    front of)
quam + superlative adv. as … as
    possible
utī = ut

Meanwhile, elsewhere, both in Gaul and in Italy, there were other stirrings of
revolt by agents of Catiline, all firmly handled by the Roman authorities.

Section 5B(iii)

At Rome, Lentulus and the others fix the final plans. L. Bestia, tribune of the plebs, is to make a speech attacking Cicero, when Catiline is near enough to the city. This will be the signal for Statilius and Gabinius to start fires, Cethegus to kill Cicero, and the rest to commit other murders.

at Rōmae Lentulus, cum cēterīs quī prīncipēs coniūrātiōnis erant,	
parātīs (ut uidēbātur) magnīs cōpiīs, cōnstituerant utī, cum Catilīna	90
propius cum exercitū uēnisset, L. Bēstia contiōne habitā quererētur dē	
āctiōnibus Cicerōnis; cōnstituerant utī, eā contiōne habitā, cētera	
multitūdō coniūrātiōnis negōtia exsequerētur. quae negōtia dīuidere	
hōc modō cōnstituerant; Statilius et Gabīnius utī cum magnā manū	
duodecim simul opportūna loca urbis incenderent, quō facilior aditus	95
ad cōnsulem fieret; Cethēgus utī Cicerōnis iānuam obsidēret eumque,	
iānuā frāctā, uī aggraderētur; utī fīliī familiārum, quōrum ex nōbilitāte	
maxima pars erat, parentīs interficerent; postrēmō utī urbe incēnsā,	
Cicerōne necātō, caede et incendiō perculsīs omnibus, ad Catilīnam	
ērumperent.	100

(Catilīnae coniūrātiō 43.1–2)

Running vocabulary for 5B(iii)

āctiō āctiōn-is 3f. public action
adit-us ūs 4m. approach
Bēsti-a ae 1m. Lucius Bestia
caedēs caed-is 3f. carnage, slaughter
Cethēg-us ī 2m. C. Cornelius Cethegus
contiō contiōn-is 3f. public meeting; *contiōnem habēre* to hold a public meeting

cōpi-ae ārum 1f. pl. forces
dīuidō 3 I divide
duodecim twelve
ērumpō 3 I break out, rush out
exsequor 3 dep. *exsecūtus* I carry out
frangō 3 *frēgī frāctus* I break (down)
L. = Lūci-us ī 2m. Lucius
man-us ūs 4f. band

nōbilitās nōbilitāt-is 3f. nobility
obsideō 2 I besiege
parēns parent-is 3m. parent
percellō 3 *perculī perculsus* I scare, unnerve
propius nearer (comp. of *prope*)
quō + comp. + subj. 'in order that . . . more' [see note on lines 95–96]
Statili-us ī 2m. L. Statilius

Notes

lines 95–6 *quō facilior . . . fieret*: 'in order that there might be . . . an easier . . .' (purpose with comparative idea).
line 97 *fīliī familiārum* i.e. sons subject to *patria potestās*. The power of a father over his children was absolute: he could even kill them with impunity.

Learning vocabulary for 5B(iii)

Nouns
caedēs caed-is 3f. slaughter, carnage
man-us ūs 4f. band (hand)

parēns parent-is 3m. father, parent; f. mother

Adjectives
duodecim twelve

Verbs
frangō 3 *frēgī frāctus* I break
obsideō 2 *obsēdī obsessus* I besiege (*ob* + *sedeō*)

Section 5C(i)

The Allobroges through Gabinius meet the other conspirators. They demand an oath from Lentulus, Cethegus, Statilius and Cassius (and receive one from all except Cassius). With this incriminating evidence on them, they are sent off by Lentulus with T. Volturcius, to formalise their compact with Catiline, who is now with Manlius near Faesulae. Lentulus sends a letter to Catiline by Volturcius, which contains some words of exhortation for Catiline.

sed Allobrogēs, ex praeceptō Cicerōnis, per Gabīnium cēterōs
coniūrātōrēs conueniunt. ab Lentulō, Cethēgō, Statiliō, item Cassiō
postulant iūs iūrandum, quod signātum ad cīuīs perferant; aliter haud
facile fore ut ad tantum negōtium impellantur. cēterī nihil suspicantēs
dant, Cassius sē eō breuī uentūrum pollicētūr, ac paulō ante lēgātōs ex   105
urbe proficīscitur. quō iūre iūrandō datō, Lentulus Allobrogēs ad
Catilīnam cum T. Volturciō quōdam dīmīsit, ut illī, prius‿quam
domum pergerent, cum Catilīnā societātem cōnfirmārent. Lentulus ipse
Volturciō litterās ad Catilīnam dat, quārum exemplum īnfrā scrīptum
est: 110

'tē hortor utī cōgitēs tuum perīculum. intellegās tē uirum esse.
cōnsīderēs tua cōnsilia. auxilium petās ab omnibus, etiam ab īnfimīs.'

ad‿hoc mandāta uerbīs dat:

'ab senātū hostis iūdicātus es. cūr tamen seruōs repudiās? seruōs
accipiās. in urbe parāta sunt quae iussistī. hīs rēbus parātīs, proficīscāris.   115
nōlī cūnctārī ipse propius accēdere.'

(Catilīnae coniūrātiō 44)

53. West end of Forum Rōmanum

Running vocabulary for 5C(i)

ad hoc in addition (lit. to this)
aliter otherwise
breuī (sc. *tempore*) shortly, soon
Cassi-us ī 2m. L. Cassius
    Longinus
cūnctor 1 dep. I delay, hesitate
    (+ inf.)
eō to that place (i.e. to the
    Allobroges' territory)

exempl-um ī 2n. copy
impellō 3 I drive to, persuade
īnfim-us a um lowest
īnfrā below
item likewise
mandāt-um ī 2n. order
perferō perferre I carry to
praecept-um ī 2n. instruction
prius quam before (+ subj.)

propius nearer
repudiō 1 I reject
signāt-us a um sealed (*signō* 1)
societās societāt-is 3f. alliance
T. = Titō: Tit-us ī 2m. Titus
Volturci-us ī 2m. Titus Volturcius

Grammar for 5C

jussive subjunctives   **subjunctives of wishes and possibility**   **impersonal verbs cardinals and ordinals**

Notes

line 103 *quod…perferant*: note mood of verb (*quī* + subj. expressing purpose).
line 104 *fore ut*: assume a verb of saying before this, 'they said'.
line 105 *uentūrum*: esse has been suppressed.
line 111 *intellegās*: subjunctive 'you should understand', 'understand'.
line 112 *cōnsīderēs*: subjunctive 'you should consider', 'consider'; *petās*: subjunctive 'you should seek', 'seek'.
line 115 *accipiās*: subjunctive 'you should take on', 'take on'; *proficīscāris*: subjunctive 'you should set out', 'set out'.

Learning vocabulary for 5C(i)

Nouns
exempl-um ī 2n. copy; example

Verbs
cūnctor 1 dep. I delay, hesitate
    (+ inf.)

Others
breuī shortly, soon (sc. *tempore*)
eō to that place
item likewise
propius nearer

54. litterās ad Catilīnam dat

Section 5C(ii)

2 December (night). Cicero arranges for the praetōrēs *to catch the Allobroges and Volturcius with the evidence on the Mulvian bridge (which carries the road to Gaul over the Tiber to the north of the ancient city). Volturcius in terror yields.*

hīs rēbus ita āctīs, cōnstitūtā nocte quā proficīscerentur Allobrogēs,
Cicerō, ā lēgātīs cūncta ēdoctus, praetōribus imperat ut in ponte
Muluiō per īnsidiās Allobrogum comitātūs dēprehendant. sine morā ad
pontem itum est. praetōrēs, hominēs mīlitārēs, sine tumultū praesidiīs   120
collocātīs, sīcutī eīs praeceptum erat, occultē pontem obsident.
postquam ad id locī lēgātī cum Volturciō peruēnērunt et simul
utrimque clāmor exortus est, Gallī, citō cognitō cōnsiliō, sine morā
praetōribus sē trādunt; Volturcius prīmō, cohortātus cēterōs, gladiō sē ā
multitūdine dēfendit. deinde, ubi ā lēgātīs dēsertus est, timidus ac uītae   125
diffīdēns, uelut hostibus sēsē praetōribus dēdit.

(*Catilīnae coniūrātiō* 45)

55. pōns Muluius

Running vocabulary for 5C(ii)

citō quickly
cohortor 1 dep. I encourage
comitāt-us ūs 4m. retinue
cūnct-us a um the whole (of)
dēprehendō 3 I capture, arrest
dēserō 3 *dēseruī dēsertus* I desert
diffīdō 3 I distrust, despair of (+ dat.)

ēdoct-us a um having been informed of X (acc.)
exorior 4 dep. *exortus* I arise
Gall-ī ōrum 2m. pl. the Gauls
itum est 'they went' (pf. pass. of *eō*) [see note]
mīlitār-is e military
Mului-us a um Mulvian
occultē secretly, in hiding

pōns pont-is 3m. bridge
sēsē = sē
sīcutī just as
timid-us a um frightened
trādō 3 I hand over
tumult-us ūs 4m. noise
uelut as, just as
utrimque on both sides

Notes

line 117 *quā proficīscerentur*: note mood of verb (*quī* + subj. indicating purpose).
line 118 *cūncta ēdoctus*: verbs which take two accusatives in the active (like *doceō* 'I teach X Y') often retain one of them in the passive: here it expresses the thing taught.
line 120 *itum est*: lit. 'it was gone'; tr. 'they went', 'there was a general movement to the bridge'.
line 121 *praeceptum erat*: note the gender of the part.
line 122 *ad id locī*: 'to that [of] place' (cf. *quid cōnsilī*).

Learning vocabulary for 5C(ii)

Nouns
pōns pont-is 3m. bridge

Pronouns
sēsē = sē

Adjectives
mīlitār-is e military
timid-us a um frightened, fearful

Verbs
cohortor 1 dep. I encourage, exhort (*con-* + *hortor*)
exorior 4 dep. *exortus* I arise (*ex* + *orior*)
trādō 3 *trādidī trāditus* I hand over; hand down, relate (*trāns* + *dō*)

Others
sīcutī or *sīcut* (just) as
uelut as, just as
utrimque on both sides

Historical importance of the Mulvian bridge

The civil wars culminated in the success of Constantine at the battle of the Mulvian Bridge in AD 312. This was truly one of the most important moments in the history of Europe, because Constantine chose to fight the battle under the banner of the Christian God. From that moment Christianity was transformed from an intermittently persecuted religion first into the personal religion of the Roman emperor, the recipient of imperial patronage and favour, and then by the end of the fourth century into the religion of the Roman state. When artists came to depict Christ in this period, more and more he appears as a Roman emperor, sitting in judgement on his people. So the emperor became Christ-like and Christ became a Roman emperor writ large. (*World of Rome*, **116**)

Section 5C(iii)

3 December (morning). Cicero receives the news. But, with so many important citizens implicated, he has mixed feelings about it. He ponders what to do with the conspirators. He decides that he is in favour of uncompromising action. He has the culprits arrested and brought to the temple of Concord, where he has summoned a senate meeting. Flaccus the praetor *is ordered to bring the incriminating evidence.*

quibus rēbus cōnfectīs, omnia properē per nūntiōs Cicerōnī dēclārantur.
at illum ingēns cūra atque laetitia simul occupāuēre. nam laetābātur
intellegēns, coniūrātiōne patefactā, cīuitātem perīculīs ēreptam esse;
porrō autem anxius erat, tantīs cīuibus dēprehēnsīs. igitur sīc sēcum   130
loquēbātur:

'cīuīs, quī maximum scelus commīsērunt, iūdicātūrī sumus, ubi eōs
in senātum uocāuerimus. sententiam dīcere mē oportēbit. ego eōs
pūnīrī uolō. nam sī eīs ā nōbīs parcātur, magnō sit reī pūblicae
dēdecorī. immō, nisi pūnītī erunt, putō fore ut reī pūblicae uehementer   135
noceātur. quod⁓sī summum supplicium postulāuerō et cīuēs Rōmānī
iussū cōnsulis morientur, poena illōrum mihi onerī erit. nihilōminus mē
decet rem pūblicam salūtī meae praepōnere. sī hanc sententiam dederō
et hominēs scelestī interfectī erunt, saltem rem pūblicam ab hīs tantīs
perīculīs seruāuerō. sīc placet. mē decet in hāc sententiā mē ipsum   140
cōnstantem praebēre. nec putō fore ut mē huius cōnstantiae umquam
paeniteat.'

igitur Cicerō, cōnfirmātō animō, uocārī ad sēsē iubet Lentulum
coniūrātōrēsque cēterōs. sine morā ueniunt. cōnsul Lentulum, quod
praetor erat, ipse manū tenēns in senātum perdūcit; reliquōs cum   145
custōdibus in aedem Concordiae uenīre iubet. eō senātum aduocat et
Volturcium cum Allobrogibus intrōdūcit. Flaccum praetōrem litterās,
quās ā lēgātīs accēperat, eōdem afferre iubet.

(*Catilīnae coniūrātiō* 46)

Running vocabulary for 5C(iii)

aduocō 1 I summon
affer-ō afferre attulī allāt-us
    I bring to
anxi-us a um worried, anxious
Concordi-a ae 1f. Concord
cōnficiō 3/4 *cōnfēcī cōnfectus*
    I finish
cōnstāns cōnstant-is resolute,
    steady
cōnstanti-a ae 1f. resolution,
    steadiness
decet it is fitting for X (acc.) to do
    Y (inf.)

dēclārō 1 I declare, report
dēdecorī est it is a disgrace to X
    (dat.)
dēprehendō 3 *dēprehendī*
    dēprehēnsus I catch, detect
eōdem to the same place
ēripiō 3/4 *ēripuī ēreptus* I rescue
    X (acc.) from Y (dat.)
Flacc-us ī 2m. L. Valerius Flaccus
intrōdūcō 3 I bring in, lead in
iussū by the order of X (gen.)
laetor 1 dep. I rejoice, am happy
nihilōminus nevertheless

noceō 2 I harm (+ dat.)
occupō 1 I seize
onerī est it is a burden to X (dat.)
paenitet 2: *mē paenitet* I regret X
    (gen.)
patefaciō 3/4 *patefēcī patefactus*
    I reveal, expose
perdūcō 3 I lead
poen-a ae 1f. penalty
porrō furthermore, besides
praebeō 2 I show (*mē*: myself
    [to be] Y acc.)

praepōnō 3 I put X (acc.) before
  Y (dat.)
properē hastily

pūniō 4 I punish
quod sī but if
saltem at least

sententi-a ae 1f. opinion

Notes

lines 134–5 *sī eīs ā nōbīs parcātur, magnō sit reī pūblicae dēdecorī*: remember the rule for *sī* + pres. subj.
  (if X were to happen, Y would happen). *eīs ā nōbīs parcātur*: *parcō* takes dative in active forms; in
  passive 'it' is the subject; *eīs* the people to be spared, *ā nōbis* the agent (the people sparing), *dēdecorī* is
  further defined by *magnō*.
line 136 *noceātur*: passive of a verb which takes dative object in active. 'It' is subject (cf. *parcātur*), *reī*
  pūblicae the thing to be harmed (line 135).
lines 141–2 *ut huius cōnstantiae mē umquam paeniteat*: *mē paenitet* = I regret, taking a genitive of what is
  regretted.

Learning vocabulary for 5C(iii)

Nouns

poen-a ae 1f. penalty
sententi-a ae 1f. opinion;
  judgement; sentence; maxim

Verbs

affer-ō afferre attulī allāt-us
  (or *adfer-ō adferre adtulī*
  adlāt-us) I bring to
cōnficiō 3/4 *cōnfēcī cōnfectus*
  I finish
decet it befits X (acc.) to Y (inf.)

ēripiō 3/4 *ēripuī ēreptus* I snatch
  away, rescue X (acc.) from Y
  (dat.)
noceō 2 I harm (+ dat.)
occupō 1 I seize
patefaciō 3/4 *patefēcī patefactus*
  I reveal, expose, throw open
praebeō 2 I show, display (myself
  to be X: *mē* + acc. adj. or
  noun)
pūniō 4 I punish

Others

dēdecorī est it is a disgrace for X
  (dat.)
iussū by the order of X (gen.)
nihilōminus nevertheless
onerī est it is a burden to X (dat.)
porrō besides, moreover

Concrete

A crucial contribution of Italy and the Romans was the invention of concrete. This happened towards
the end of the third century, probably as the outcome of experiments with a *pisé* (rammed clay)
technique of the type familiar in North Africa, knowledge of which may have reached Italy at the
time of the Hannibalic Wars. It was found that a mixture of lime, water and a gritty substance, such
as sand, produces on setting a strongly cohesive and durable material which can be used either to
bond masonry or in its own right as a building material. Once discovered, concrete construction was
gradually perfected during the following three centuries as, by trial and error, builders came to
appreciate its potential. Greek architecture had depended essentially upon carefully shaped
stonework assembled without mortar and upon 'trabeated' (post and lintel) construction, techniques
which were prodigal of material, which required a high degree of skill at all stages, and which
severely restricted the size of interiors. The concrete used by builders in Roman Italy was far less
wasteful (the debris of stone-cutters was absorbed as an aggregate), it was much more effective for
the construction of vaults, and once properly set it created a homogeneous mass which was less
vulnerable to collapse than dry stone construction. Moreover it required less skilled labour: most of
the skill came in the planning stage, and the actual execution was a mechanical process, so could be
carried out by the slaves who were available in abundance after Rome's Eastern conquests. This
opened the way to large-scale building projects. Among the earliest examples was a massive vaulted
warehouse near the river-port in Rome, the Porticus Aemilia (193), needed for the imports of grain
required to feed the new metropolis. Another was the quay at Puteoli, where it was discovered that
an admixture of the local volcanic sand (*puluis puteolānus*, or pozzolana) gave the concrete
'hydraulic' properties, which enabled it to set even under water. (*World of Rome*, **465**)

56. aedis Concordiae

Volturcius, turning 'state's evidence' (or had he been an innocent 'dupe' all along?), betrayed the conspirators. The Allobroges described Lentulus' delusions of grandeur: he used to cite a Sibylline prophecy that one of his family (the Cornelii) would rule Rome. The senate, after authenticating the incriminating letter, ordered Lentulus to resign his office and the others with Lentulus to be held in open custody. Popular support for the plot evaporated.

The next day (4 December), a plot to free Lentulus and the others was discovered. Cicero convened the senate on 5 December and asked their advice about what he should do with the prisoners, who had in a recent session already been pronounced guilty of treason. Senate procedure demanded that speakers be called in a strict order. The consul designate (i.e. next year's consul) was the first to be asked and so on. Sallust reports the speeches of Caesar (who advocated an unheard-of penalty of 'life imprisonment') and Cato, a man well known for his strictness and moral rectitude (who was in favour of the death penalty). In Sallust's view the issue was decided by Cato's speech.

But as a matter of fact, it was the consul's responsibility to make this decision, and Cicero was trying at this meeting to bolster up an unconstitutional measure. It was illegal to execute Roman citizens without trial. It was on this occasion that Cicero made the speech later published as *In Catilinam* IV (the 'fourth Catiline'), in which he spoke in support of the view of the consul designate, D. Iunius Silanus (who recommended the death penalty), as if the matter really were in the hands of the senate.

Here we interrupt Sallust's narrative to see how Cicero justified this severity in the 'fourth Catiline'.

57. Cato

Section 5D(i)

*My view is based on kindness – towards Rome. You would not think a father
kind, if he failed to punish a slave who had killed his family. So we will be
deemed kind, if we are severe to these men. For Lentulus handed everything we
hold dear over to his cronies Catiline, Cethegus, Gabinius and Cassius to be
destroyed.*

in hāc causā, nōn atrōcitāte animī moueor – quis enim est mē
mītior? – sed singulārī quādam hūmānitāte et misericordiā. uideor enim   150
mihi uidēre hanc urbem, lūcem orbis terrārum atque arcem omnium
gentium, subitō ūnō incendiō concidentem. uersātur mihi ante oculōs
aspectus et furor Cethēgī in uestrā caede bacchantis, Lentulī rēgnantis,
Catilīnae cum exercitū uenientis. cum haec mihi prōpōnō, tum
lāmentātiōnem mātrum familiās, tum fugam uirginum et puerōrum,   155
tum uexātiōnem uirginum Vestālium perhorrēscō, et, quia mihi
uehementer haec uidentur misera atque miseranda, idcircō in eōs, quī
ea perficere uoluērunt, mē seuērum uehementemque praebēbō. etenim
quaerō, sī quis pater familiās, līberīs suīs ā seruō interfectīs, uxōre
occīsā, incēnsā domō, supplicium dē seruīs nōn quam acerbissimum   160
sūmat, utrum is clēmēns ac misericors an inhūmānissimus et
crūdēlissimus esse uideātur? mihi uērō ille importūnus ac ferreus esse
uideātur, nisi dolōre nocentis suum dolōrem lēniat. sīc nōs misericordēs
habēbimur, sī uehementissimī in hīs hominibus fuerimus quī nōs, quī
coniugēs, quī līberōs nostrōs trucīdāre uoluērunt, quī singulās domōs et   165
hoc ūniuersum reī pūblicae domicilium dēlēre cōnātī sunt; sīn
remissiōrēs esse uoluerimus, crūdēlissimī habēbimur.

nam Lentulus attribuit nōs necandōs Cethēgō et cēterōs cīuīs
interficiendōs Gabīniō; urbem incendendam Cassiō attribuit, tōtam
Ītaliam uāstandam dīripiendamque Catilīnae. Lentulus ad ēuertenda   170
fundāmenta reī pūblicae Gallōs arcessit, ad incendendam urbem seruōs
concitat, ad dūcendum contrā urbem exercitum Catilīnam uocat. quid
hōc facinore magis timendum? quid hōc scelere minus neglegendum?

(*In Catilīnam* IV 11–13)

Running vocabulary for 5D(i)

acerb-us a um bitter
an: see *utrum*
arcessō 3 I summon
arx arc-is 3f. citadel
aspect-us ūs 4m. appearance
atrōcitās atrōcitāt-is 3f. harshness
attribuō 3 I assign, give X (acc.)
    to Y (dat.) (as his share)
bacchor 1 dep. I rave, revel, act
    like a Bacchant
clēmēns clēment-is merciful
concitō 1 I incite
crūdēl-is e cruel
dīripiō 3/4 I tear apart
dolor dolōr-is 3m. pain, anguish
domicili-um ī 2n. dwelling
etenim for in fact, and indeed
ēuertō 3 I overturn
ferre-us a um made of iron,
    unfeeling
fug-a ae 1f. flight
fundāment-um ī 2n. foundation
Gall-ī ōrum 2m. pl. Gauls

hūmānitās hūmānitāt-is 3f.
    humanity, kindness
idcircō for this reason, therefore
importūn-us a um cruel, savage
inhūmān-us a um cruel, savage
lāmentātiō lāmentātiōn-is 3f.
    lamentation
lēniō 4 I soothe
lūx lūc-is 3f. light
māter familiās mātr-is familiās 3f.
    mother (of the household)
miserand-us a um to be pitied
misericordi-a ae 1f. pity
misericors misericord-is
    compassionate
mīt-is e gentle, mild
orbis terrārum orb-is terrārum
    3m. the world (lit. the circle of
    lands)
pater familiās patr-is familiās 3m.
    father (head of the household)
perhorrēscō 3 I shudder greatly
    at, have a great fear of

prōpōnō 3 I imagine (*mihi
    prōpōnō* = I set before my
    mind's eye)
remiss-us a um mild, slack
sīn but if
singulār-is e unparalleled,
    extraordinary
singul-ī ae a individual
sūmō 3 I take
supplicium sūmere to exact the
    penalty (from X: *dē* + abl.)
trucīdō 1 I butcher
uāstō 1 I lay waste
uehemēns uehement-is violent
uersor 1 dep. I stay
uexātiō uexātiōn-is 3f.
    ill-treatment
ūniuers-us a um whole, entire
utrum . . . an = double question,
    i.e. A? or B?
Vestāl-is e Vestal (belonging to
    the goddess Vesta)

Grammar for 5D

more uses of gerundive   **verbs of fearing**

Notes

line 153 *in uestrā caede* 'in your slaughter' = 'in slaughter of you'. Possessive adjectives are often used in
    this way.
lines 159–61 *sī . . . sūmat . . . uideātur*: note mood of verbs, and remember *sī* + pres. subj., pres. subj. = 'if X
    were to happen, Y would happen'.
line 160 *quam acerbissimum* 'as bitter as possible'. See Learning vocabulary 5B(iii).
lines 163 *uideātur . . . nisi . . . lēniat*: see note on lines 159–61. *nocentis*: 'of the person who harmed him':
    pres. part. used as a noun.

Learning vocabulary for 5D(i)

Nouns
arx arc-is 3f. citadel
dolor dolōr-is 3m. pain, anguish
fug-a ae 1f. flight
lūx lūc-is 3f. light

Adjectives
crūdēl-is e cruel
miserand-us a um to be pitied
misericors misericord-is
    compassionate
uehemēns uehement-is impetuous,
    violent

Vestāl-is e Vestal (belonging to
    the goddess Vesta)

Verbs
arcessō 3 *arcessīuī arcessītus*
    I summon
attribuō 3 *attribuī attribūtus*
    I assign, give (*ad* + *tribuō*)
prōpōnō 3 *prōposuī prōpositus*
    I set before; imagine; offer
    (*prō* + *pōnō*)
sūmō 3 *sūmpsī sūmptus* I take; put
    on; eat; *supplicium sūmere dē*

(+ abl.) to exact the penalty
from X

Others
idcircō for this/that reason,
    therefore
utrum . . . an = double question,
    i.e. A or B? (negative: *annōn*,
    i.e. A or not?)

Section 5D(ii)

*You must not be afraid of seeming too strict. The opposite is more to be feared.
Help is at hand to protect Rome – namely, the whole population.*

quae cum ita sint, nōlīte timēre nē in hōc scelere tam nefandō
seuēriōrēs fuisse uideāminī. multō magis est timendum nē, remissiōne   175
poenae, crūdēlēs in patriam fuisse uideāmur. hoc, inquam, magis est
uerendum quam nē nimis uehementēs in acerbissimōs hostīs fuisse
uideāmur. sed audiō, patrēs cōnscrīptī, uōcēs eōrum quī uererī uidentur
ut habeam satis praesidī ad cōnsilia uestra trānsigenda. omnia et prōuīsa
et parāta et cōnstitūta sunt, patrēs cōnscrīptī, cum meā summā cūrā   180
atque dīligentiā, tum maximā populī Rōmānī uoluntāte ad summum
imperium retinendum et ad commūnīs fortūnās cōnseruandās. omnēs
adsunt omnium ōrdinum hominēs, omnium generum, omnium
dēnique aetātum; plēnum est forum, plēna templa circum forum, plēnī
omnēs aditūs huius templī ac locī.   185

(*In Catiīnam* IV 13–14)

Running vocabulary for 5D(ii)

acerb-us a um bitter
adit-us ūs 4m. entrance
commūn-is e shared, in common
cōnscrīpt-us a um chosen, elected
cōnseruō 1 I preserve
cum . . . tum both . . . and
dīligenti-a ae 1f. diligence
genus gener-is 3n. kind, type
imperi-um ī 2n. power, authority,
    dominion

nē (+ subj.) that, lest (after *timeō,
    uereor*)
nefand-us a um impious,
    execrable
ōrdō ōrdin-is 3m. rank
patrēs cōnscrīptī = senātōrēs
    senators
patri-a ae 1f. fatherland
prōuideō 2 *prōuīdī prōuīsus*
    I take care of

remissiō remissiōn-is 3f.
    remission, relaxation
trānsigō 3 I accomplish
uereor 2 dep. I fear, am afraid
    ('that': *nē* + subj.; 'that not':
    ut + subj.)
uoluntās uoluntāt-is 3f. will, wish
ut (+ subj.) (after *uereor*)
    'that . . . not'

Notes

lines 174, 175, 177 *nē*: following *timeō* or *uereor* – '(I am afraid) that X will happen'.
line 175 *seuēriōrēs*: remember that comparatives may mean 'rather' and 'too' as well as 'more'.
lines 178–9 *uererī . . . ut*: 'be afraid that X will *not* happen'.
lines 180–1 *cum . . . tum*: 'both . . . and' – a favourite construction in Cicero.

Learning vocabulary for 5D(ii)

Nouns

genus gener-is 3n. type, kind (family; stock; tribe)

imperi-um ī 2n. power, authority, dominion (command, order)

ōrdō ōrdin-is 3m. rank (i.e. section of society or line of soldiers)

patrēs cōnscrīptī = senātōrēs senators

patri-a ae 1f. fatherland

uoluntās uoluntāt-is 3f. will, wish

Adjectives

acerb-us a um bitter

commūn-is e shared in, common, universal

Verbs

cōnseruō 1 I keep safe, preserve (*con + seruō*)

prōuideō 2 *prōuīdī prōuīsus* I take care (often followed by *nē* + subj.) (*prō + uideō*)

uereor 2 dep. *ueritus* I fear, am afraid (usually followed by *nē/ut* + subj.)

Others

cum . . . tum both . . . and (especially common in Cicero)

58. plēnum est forum

Rhetoric

Rhetoric generally has a bad name today. We value 'sincerity' over 'artifice', and our modern preference poses real problems for our appreciation both of Latin and of Renaissance English literature. As C. S. Lewis once said, 'Rhetoric is the greatest barrier between us and our ancestors ... Nearly all our older poetry was written and read by men to whom the distinction between poetry and rhetoric, in its modern form, would have been meaningless.' Some Romans too questioned the details of rhetorical education and considered whether, with the death of political freedom under the Empire, rhetoric still had an important role. And yet a good case can be made in favour of rhetoric.

There were two main types of rhetorical exercise: *suāsōriae* and *contrōuersiae*. In *suasoriae* pupils took incidents from myth or history and argued over them: Should Scipio cross to Africa? Should Caesar accept the kingship? These exercises obviously helped to develop boys' skills in constructing arguments. In *contrōuersiae*, pupils argued difficult cases in law, many of which were clearly fictitious.

Pliny's teacher Quintilian gave an example familiar in his day (*An Orator's Education* 7.2.17). A son banished from home studies medicine. When his father falls ill, and all the other doctors despair of saving him, the son is summoned and says that he can cure him, if the father drinks the medicine he gives him. The father, having drunk part of the medicine, says that he has been poisoned. The son drinks the rest, but the father dies, and the son is accused of parricide. The pupil had to devise arguments for and against the accused.

Pliny himself in middle age attended lectures by a visiting Greek rhetorician and noted the relative unreality of the cases, but he still defended the practice. 'The imaginary cases in the schools and lecture-halls do no harm with their blunted foils and are none the less enjoyable, especially to the old, who like nothing so much as to witness the joys of their youth' (*Letters* 2.3). And some could be less irrelevant than they seemed at first sight. Rome saw many cases of alleged poisoning, and Cicero, facing the rise to power of Caesar, took his mind off the current crisis by composing arguments, in Greek and Latin, about whether a man should remain in his country under a tyranny (*Letters to Atticus* 9.4).

The apparently artificial world of the rhetorical school did positively prepare its pupils for both the law courts and political life. The value of this educational system gradually received official recognition. At Rome from the time of Julius Caesar onwards, there were privileges for teachers who were also Roman citizens, and the emperor Vespasian founded two chairs for the teaching of Greek and Latin rhetoric (Quintilian was the first holder of the Latin chair). Outside Rome, teachers of grammar and rhetoric were granted exemption from civic obligation, again by Vespasian. The point is that the emperors wanted to provide access to education, which they hoped would help to integrate local elites into the Roman elite. They also hoped that their patronage of rhetoric, a fundamental characteristic of Roman civilisation, would help to legitimate their rule. (*World of Rome*, **371**)

Section 5D(iii)

This is the only issue which brings all classes together. What eques, tribūnus
aerārius *or even slave is there who does not want to defend the state?*

haec est causa sōla in quā omnēs eadem sentiant. quis enim est quī nōn
studiō et dīligentiā ad salūtem patriae dēfendendam dignitātemque
cōnseruandam cōnsentiat? quis eques est, quem haec causa nōn ad
concordiam cīuitātis coniungat? quis tribūnus aerārius, quī nōn parī
studiō dēfendendae reī pūblicae conueniat? quis dēnique est cui nōn   190
haec templa, aspectus urbis, possessiō lībertātis cum cārissima sit, tum
dulcissima et iūcundissima? seruus est nēmo quī nōn audāciam cīuium
perhorrēscat, quī nōn hanc cīuitātem stāre cupiat, quī nōn ad salūtem
reī pūblicae dēfendendam parātus sit, quantum audet et potest.

(*In Catilīnam* IV 14–16)

Running vocabulary for 5D(iii)

aspect-us ūs 4m. appearance
cār-us a um dear, valued
concordi-a ae 1f. harmony
coniungō 3 I bring X (acc.) to
    support Y (*ad* + acc.)
cōnsentiō 4 I agree

dīligenti-a ae 1f. care, diligence
dulc-is e sweet
iūcund-us a um pleasant
pār par-is equal
parāt-us a um prepared (to: *ad* +
    acc. from *parō* 1)

perhorrēscō 3 I shudder greatly at
possessiō possessiōn-is 3f.
    possession
quantum as much as
tribūn-us ī aerāri-us ī 2m. citizen
    of the class below *equitēs*

Notes

line 186 *in quā...sentiant*: the subjunctive is generic (see **145.1**).
lines 186–8 *quī nōn...cōnsentiat*: the subjunctive is generic (see **145.1**).
lines 188–9 *quis eques: quis tribūnus aerārius: quis* is used here as an adjective (cf. **102³**).
lines 188–9 *quem...nōn...coniungat*: the subjunctive is generic (see **145.1**).
lines 189–90 *quī nōn...conueniat*: the subjunctive is generic (see **145.1**).
lines 190–1 *cui nōn...sit*: the subjunctive is generic (see **145.1**).
line 192 *nēmo*: here used as an adjective (= *nūllus*).
lines 192–4 *quī nōn...perhorrēscat, quī nōn...cupiat, quī nōn...sit*: generic statements, using the
    subjunctive (see **145.1**).

Learning vocabulary for 5D(iii)

Nouns	Adjectives	Others
concordi-a ae 1f. harmony	*dulc-is e* sweet	*quantum* as much as
dīligenti-a ae 1f. care, diligence	*iūcund-us a um* pleasant	

Section 5D(iv)

You have the Roman people behind you. Take care you do not fail them. Our very native land begs you, and you have to consider the lives and fortunes of all. Beware of allowing such crimes to be repeated or even considered again.

quae cum ita sint, patrēs cōnscrīptī, uōbīs populī Rōmānī praesidia nōn   195
dēsunt; prōuidendum est nē uōs populō Rōmānō dēesse uideāminī.
habētis cōnsulem parātum nōn ad uītam suam dēfendendam, sed ad
uestram salūtem cūrandam. omnēs ōrdinēs ad cōnseruandam rem
pūblicam mente, uoluntāte, uōce cōnsentiunt. patria commūnis, obsessa
facibus et tēlīs impiae coniūrātiōnis, uōbīs supplex manūs tendit, uōbīs   200
sē, uōbīs uītam omnium cīuium, uōbīs ārās Penātium, uōbīs illum
ignem Vestae sempiternum, uōbīs omnium deōrum templa
commendat. praetereā dē uestrā uītā, dē coniugum uestrārum atque
līberōrum animā, dē fortūnīs omnium hodiē uōbīs iūdicandum est.
habētis ducem memorem uestrī, oblītum suī. habētis omnīs ōrdinēs,   205
omnīs hominēs, ūniuersum populum Rōmānum ūnum atque idem
sentientem. cōgitāte! imperium tantīs labōribus fundātum, lībertātem
tantā uirtūte stabilītam, fortūnās tantā deōrum benignitāte auctās ūna
nox paene dēlēuit. id nē umquam posthāc cōnficī possit ā cīuibus, hodiē
prōuidendum est. immō˘uērō hodiē uōbīs prōuidendum est nē id   210
umquam posthāc uel cōgitārī possit ā cīuibus.

(*In Catilīnam* IV 18–19)

Running vocabulary for 5D(iv)

anim-a ae 1f. soul, life
ār-a ae 1f. altar
augeō 2 *auxī auctus* I increase
benignitās benignitāt-is 3f. kindness
commendō 1 I entrust X (acc.) to Y (dat.)
cōnsentiō 4 I agree
fax fac-is 3f. torch, firebrand
fundō 1 I establish
immō uērō nay rather
impi-us a um with no respect for gods, parents or fatherland

iūdicandum est it is to be judged (*iūdicō* 1)
labor labōr-is 3m. toil, hard work, trouble
memor memor-is mindful of X (gen.)
nē (+ subj.) after *prōuideō* 'in case', 'lest'
oblīuīscor 3 dep. *oblītus* I forget (+ gen. of person)
paene almost
parāt-us a um prepared (to: *ad* + acc., from *parō* 1)

Penātēs Penāt-ium 3m. pl. gods of the household
posthāc after this time, hereafter, in future
prōuidendum est care must be taken (*prōuideō* 2)
sempitern-us a um eternal
stabiliō 4 I make firm
supplex supplic-is suppliant
tendō 3 I stretch forth
uel even
ūniuers-us a um whole
Vest-a ae 1f. Vesta (goddess of the hearth)

59. ignis Vestae

Notes

line 196 *prōuidendum est nē*: lit. 'it is to be taken care about lest...'.

lines 200–01 *uōbīs sē...* : not solved until *commendat* in line 203. Tr. 'to you herself (obj.)...' etc.

line 204 *uōbīs iūdicandum est*: tr. 'you ought to judge' (lit. 'it is to-be-judged as-far-as-you-are-concerned').

lines 209–10 *nē...* : 'that', 'lest', picked up *by prōuidendum est*, lit. 'it is to be taken care about'.

line 210 *uōbīs prōuidendum est nē...* : tr. 'you must take care, lest...' (lit. 'it is to-be-taken-care-about as-far-as-you-are-concerned').

Learning vocabulary for 5D(iv)

Nouns

ār-a ae 1f. altar

labor labōr-is 3m. toil, hard work; trouble

Adjectives

impi-us a um with no respect for gods, parents or fatherland

memor memor-is remembering X (gen.), mindful of X (gen.)

supplex supplic-is suppliant (also a noun)

Verbs

augeō 2 *auxī auctus* I increase (trans.)

oblīuīscor 3 dep. *oblītus* I forget (+ gen. of person)

tendō 3 *tetendī tēnsus* or *tentus* I stretch (out); offer; direct; travel

Others

paene almost

uel even (either... or)

The 'sincerity gap'

The problem was that rhetoric was at the very heart of Roman education, and its purpose was to prepare students both to use and to recognise plausible (i.e. not true) arguments in every situation. Any orator, for example, was out to persuade the audience of the truth of his case, whatever the actual truth of the matter. This did not worry Romans. They were trained in rhetoric and could spot a rhetorical device a long way off. And writers knew this. Caesar, for example, had no difficulty in composing accounts of his campaigns in Gaul (*The Gallic War*) and against Pompey (*The Civil War*) with a heavy bias towards his own interest. It would seem true not only because it was rhetorically persuasive, but also because he himself had witnessed the events. It was, in other words, real.

But the 'sincerity gap' could upset a later generation of readers for whom 'reality', 'truth' and 'the writer's life' were indissociable from each other. Petrarch, a central figure in the Italian Renaissance of the fourteenth century, rediscovered the lost *Letters* of Cicero. When he compared these with the lofty thoughts of Cicero's well-known rhetorical and philosophical works, he wrote a letter of his own to his dead ex-hero, bidding him farewell for ever (*Letters to Friends* 24.3)! (*World of Rome*, **443**)

Section 5E(i)

We now rejoin Sallust's narrative. 5 December (night). Cicero, fearful of delay, gives orders for the executions. Lentulus, Cethegus, Statilius and Gabinius are taken to the Tullianum, a vile subterranean dungeon, and garotted.

postquam senātus in Catōnis sententiam discessit, Cicerō, ueritus nē
quid eā nocte nouārētur, triumuirōs omnia, quae ad supplicium
postulābantur, parāre iubet. dum triumuirī, ab eō iussī, haec parābant,
cōnsul praesidia dispōnēbat. ipse praesidiīs dispositīs Lentulum in   215
carcerem dēdūcit. cēterī carcerem intrant ā praetōribus dēductī. est in
carcere locus, Tulliānum appellātus, circiter duodecim pedēs humī
dēpressus, cuius faciēs incultū, tenebrīs, odōre foedāta, terribilis est. in
eum locum dēmissus Lentulus ibi manēbat, dum uindicēs rērum
capitālium, quibus praeceptum erat, laqueō gulam frangerent; quod   220
tandem fēcērunt. ita ille patricius, ex gente clārissimā Cornēliōrum, quī
cōnsulāre imperium Rōmae habuerat, dignam mōribus factīsque suīs
mortem inuēnit. dē Cethēgō, Statiliō, Gabīniō eōdem modō supplicium
sūmptum est.

(*Catilīnae coniūrātiō* 55)

Running vocabulary for 5E(i)

appellō 1 I call
capitāl-is e involving a capital
  charge, punishable by death
carcer carcer-is 3m. prison
Catō Catōn-is 3m. M. Porcius
  Cato
circiter about
cōnsulār-is e consular
Cornēli-ī ōrum 2m. pl. the
  Cornelii
dēmittō 3 *dēmīsī dēmissus* I send
  down
dēprimō 3 *dēpressī dēpressus*
  I sink

discēdō 3 *discessī* I depart;
  discēdō in sententiam X (gen.)
  I go over to X's view
dispōnō 3 *disposuī dispositus*
  I place, station
dum (+ indicative) while;
  (+ subjunctive) until
faciēs faciē-ī 5f. appearance
foedō 1 I make foul
gul-a ae 1f. throat (tr. 'neck')
humī in the ground
incult-us ūs 4m. neglect
laque-us ī 2m. garotte
nouō 1 I make changes

odor odōr-is 3m. smell, stench
patrici-us ī 2m. patrician (member
  of a select group of families)
tenebr-ae ārum 1f. pl. darkness
terribil-is e frightful, dreadful
triumuir-ī ōrum 2m. pl. triumvirs
  (a commission responsible for
  prisons and executions)
Tulliān-um ī 2n. Tullianum
uindex uindic-is 3m. punisher

60. The Tullianum (today the Chapel of St Peter in Prison)

Grammar for 5E

participle summary	*dum, antequam/priusquam*	*utpote quī*

Notes

lines 212–13 *nē quid... nouārētur*: *quid* is accusative of respect. Tr. 'in any respect', *nouārētur* impersonal passive 'changes might be made' (with the overtone of 'revolution', the expression for which was *rēs nouae*).

lines 219–20 *dum... frangerent*: 'until... they should break', 'for... to break', *uindicēs rērum capitālium*: i.e. the executioners.

line 222 *cōnsulāre*: he had been consul in 71.

Learning vocabulary for 5E(i)

Nouns

carcer carcer-is 3m. prison; barrier

faciēs faciē-ī 5f. appearance; face

hum-us ī 2f. ground (NB *humum* (acc.) to the ground; *humī* (locative) on or in the ground)

Adjectives

terribil-is e dreadful, frightening

Verbs

discēdō 3 *discessī discessum* I depart; (with *in sententiam* +

gen.) I go over to X's view (*dis-* + *cēdō*)

dispōnō 3 *disposuī dispositus* I set, place (in different places) (*dis-* + *pōnō*)

Section 5E(ii)

*Late December 63 to early January 62. Catiline meanwhile marshals his poorly
equipped army into two legions. He avoids an encounter with the consul
Antonius' army (which is approaching from Rome) since he hopes any day to
receive reinforcements from the city. When news of Lentulus' execution comes,
and despite desertions, Catiline marches across the mountains (the Apennines),
heading for Gaul. But Q. Metellus Celer cuts off his escape route. Catiline
decides to fight Antonius' army.*

dum ea Rōmae geruntur, Catilīna ex omnī cōpiā, quam et ipse   225
addūxerat et Mānlius habuerat, duās legiōnēs īnstituit. sed ex
omnī cōpiā circiter pars quārta erat mīlitāribus armīs īnstructa, cēterī
sparōs aut lanceās aut praeacūtās sudīs portābant. sed postquam
Antōnius cum exercitū aduentābat, Catilīna, perīculō perturbātus, per
montīs iter facere. modo ad urbem modo ad Galliam castra mouēre,   230
hostibus occāsiōnem pugnae nōn dare. spērābat breuī tempore magnās
cōpiās sēsē habitūrum, dum Rōmae sociī cōnsilia perficerent. intereā
seruōs repudiābat, ueritus nē uidērētur causam cīuium cum seruīs
fugitīuīs commūnicāuisse. sed postquam in castra nūntius peruēnit,
Rōmae coniūrātiōnem patefactam esse et dē Lentulō coniūrātōribusque   235
cēterīs supplicium sūmptum, plērīque quī sē rapīnārum causā Catilīnae
coniūnxissent, dīlābuntur. reliquōs Catilīna, agmine īnstructō, per
montīs asperōs magnīs itineribus in agrum Pistōriēnsem abdūcit, eō
cōnsiliō ut occultē perfugeret in Galliam Trānsalpīnam. at Q. Metellus
Celer, ā senātū missus, cum tribus legiōnibus in agrō Pīcēnō   240
exspectābat dum Catilīna castra in Galliam mouēret. nam ex difficultāte
rērum exīstimābat fore ut Catilīna perfugeret in Galliam Trānsalpīnam,
antequam legiōnibus Rōmānīs interclūderētur.

igitur Metellus, ubi iter eius ex perfugīs cognōuit, castra properē
mōuit, ac sub ipsīs rādīcibus montium cōnsēdit, quā Catilīnae   245
dēscēnsus erat in Galliam properantī. neque tamen Antōnius procul
aberat, utpote quī locīs aequiōribus sequerētur. sed Catilīna, postquam
uidet sēsē montibus et cōpiīs hostium clausum esse et in urbe rēs
aduersās, neque fugae neque praesidī ūllam spem, cōnstituit in tālī rē
fortūnam bellī temptāre et cum Antōniō quam prīmum cōnflīgere.   250

(*Catilīnae coniūrātiō* 56–57.5)

Running vocabulary for 5E(ii)

abdūcō 3 I lead away
absum abesse i am distant
addūcō 3 *addūxī* I bring
aduentō 1 I approach, advance
aduers-us a um unfavourable
aequ-us a um level
agmen agmin-is 3n. column
antequam (+ subj.) before
asper asper-a um rough
Celer Celer-is 3m. (Q. Metellus)
    Celer
circiter about
claudō 3 *clausī clausus* I shut in
commūnicō 1 I share X (acc.) with
    Y (*cum* + abl.)
cōnflīgō 3 I fight (with X: *cum* +
    abl.)
coniungō 3 *coniūnxī* I join (I join
    X: *mē coniungō* + dat.)
cōnsīdō 3 *cōnsēdī* I take up
    position, encamp
cōpi-a ae 1f. multitude, crowd
cōpi-ae ārum 1f. pl. forces, troops
dēscēns-us ūs 4m. descent

difficultās difficultāt-is 3f.
    difficulty
dīlābor 3 dep. I slip away
dum (+ ind.) while
dum (+ subj.) until [see note on
    line 241]
dum provided that (line 232)
fugitīu-us a um runaway
Galli-a ae 1f. Gaul
īnstituō 3 *īnstituī* I draw up
interclūdō 3 I cut off
iter itiner-is 3n. journey; route
lance-a ae 1f. lance, spear
legiō legiōn-is 3f. legion
magnum iter = a forced march
Metell-us ī 2m. Q. Metellus Celer
modo . . . modo at one time . . . at
    another
occāsiō occāsiōn-is 3f.
    opportunity for X (gen.)
occultē secretly
perfug-a ae 1m. deserter
perfugiō 3/4 I flee for refuge
perturbō 1 I worry, disturb

Pīcēn-us a um of Picenum
Pistōriēns-is e of Pistoria
praeacuō 3 *praeacuī praeacūtus*
    I sharpen to a point
procul far off
properē hastily
properō 1 I hurry
pugn-a ae 1f. battle
Q. = *Quīnt-us ī* 2m. Quintus
quā where [see **139.3**]
quam prīmum as soon as possible
rādix rādīc-is 3f. foot (lit. 'root')
rapīn-a ae 1f. plunder
repudiō 1 I reject
spar-us ī 2m. hunting-spear
spērō 1 I hope, expect
sub (+ abl.) beneath
sudis sud-is 3f. stake
temptō 1 I test, try
Trānsalpīn-us a um across the
    Alps, Transalpine
utpote (quī) (+ subj.) inasmuch
    as, since (he)

Notes

line 227 *pars quārta* i.e. a quarter.
lines 230–1 *facere . . . mouēre . . . dare*: see **153.**
line 232 *habitūrum*: *esse* suppressed.
lines 234ff. *nūntius*: remember that a noun may generate an indirect statement quite as easily as a verb, i.e.
    'a messenger (with a message to the effect that . . .)'.
line 236 *sūmptum*: *esse* suppressed.
lines 236–7 *quī sē . . . coniūnxissent*: causal clause, see **145.2.**
line 241 *dum . . . mouēret*: 'until', 'for . . . to . . .' (purpose).
lines 245–6 Note *properantī* agreeing with *Catilīnae,* dat. of advantage or possession.
line 248 *in urbe* i.e. in Rome (often known simply as *urbs*).

Learning vocabulary for 5E(ii)

Nouns

agmen agmin-is 3n. column
cōpi-a ae 1f. multitude, crowd
cōpi- ae ārum 1f. pl. forces, troops
iter itiner-is 3n. journey; route
legiō legiōn-is 3f. legion
occāsiō occāsiōn-is 3f.
    opportunity
pugn-a ae 1f. battle, fight

Adjectives

asper asper-a um rough

Verbs

absum abesse āfuī āfutūrus I am
    distant (am absent, away)
cōnsīdō 3 *cōnsēdī* I settle down;
    encamp
properō 1 I hurry, make haste

spērō 1 I hope, expect
temptō 1 I try, test, attempt; attack

Others

circiter about (adv.)
modo . . . modo at one time . . . at
    another
quam prīmum as soon as possible

The changing face of the Roman army

173. The theory was that all the citizens of the Republic were liable for conscription into the army. Cicero says that anyone who avoided conscription was liable to be sold as a slave, on the grounds that he was not facing up to danger as a free man should (Cicero, *In Defence of Caecina* 34.99) In practice though, through the early and middle Republic, the only people who were called up for army service were those who had a census qualification down to and including the fifth *classis*. The reason for this was that during this period, soldiers had to provide their own equipment, of which the *prōletāriī* (the group below the fifth *classis*) were reckoned incapable. It is no doubt for this reason that the property-level that gave access to the fifth *classis* was progressively lowered, so that from 11,000 *assēs* (a standard unit of coinage) before the Hannibalic War, it had fallen to 1,500 *assēs* by the last quarter of the second century. This last represents a very small amount of property indeed, almost certainly insufficient to maintain an average-sized family. (For **174**, see above, p. 115)

175. The reduction in the qualification for the fifth *classis*, shows that, however keen the people may have been to serve, there were not enough of them to provide the forces needed to sustain Rome's military activity around the Mediterranean. Matters came to a head when in 107 BC Gaius Marius, who had been elected consul with much opposition from the established noble families in Rome, was allotted the *prōuincia* of Numidia, where a war was being carried on against King Jugurtha. [But Marius needed more troops. So he threw open the levy to all, taking volunteers from the very poorest members of the state, who had hitherto been excluded …]

176. In some ways this was simply the logical extension of what had been happening over the previous hundred years, as the lower limit for membership of the fifth classis had been systematically reduced. It did, however, make quite clear what had apparently been concealed hitherto, that when the soldiers had completed their tour of duty and went home, they would need support from somewhere. This was more obviously true for Marius' volunteers than had been the case before, because Marius' men would not have a farm to go back to once they had been discharged. As a result, Marius tried to ensure that those soldiers who served with him in his three-year campaign in Numidia and subsequent campaigns were given land to go to when they returned.

177. It does seem that Marius' opening of service in the army to volunteers from among the *prōletāriī* created a different relationship between a commander and his troops from what had been the case before. When in 88 BC, Sulla marched against Rome to regain the command against Mithridates which Marius had taken from him, he apparently had little difficulty in persuading his newly recruited army to follow him; and through the period of the civil wars, down to the victory of Octavian over Mark Antony at Actium in 31 BC, a series of army commanders led troops which were prepared to follow their own general against the city itself. Sulla in 88 and 82 BC, Marius in 87, Caesar in 49 and Octavian in 43 all marched with Roman armies to seize the city which had not been taken since the Gallic sack of 390. It is, of course, too simplistic to put this down simply to Marius' change of recruitment policy in 107. The tradition of the independent power of a holder of *imperium* and the growth in the importance and extent (both in area and time) of the great commands also play a part. But there does also seem to be a change in the atmosphere, almost in the psychology of the armies of the last century of the Republic. It is as if the soldiers who had previously reckoned on getting land and booty for themselves by fighting the enemies of Rome on the instructions of the Senate had now decided that they were more likely to achieve this by backing one general against another.

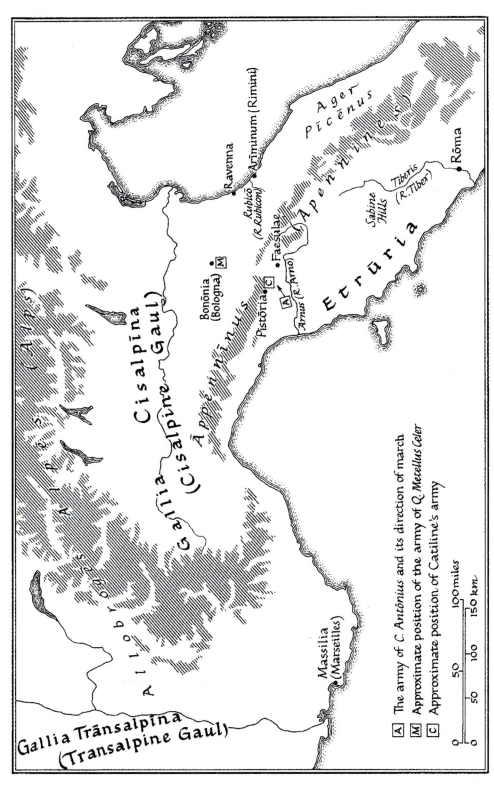

61. Catiline: the final phase

Section 5F(i)

Catiline speaks to his troops before the battle, reminds them what situation they are in and that they have no choice but to fight, if they are to retain their country, liberty and lives.

itaque contiōne aduocātā huiuscemodī ōrātiōnem habuit.
'nōuī, mīlitēs, uerba uirtūtem nōn addere, neque exercitum fortem
ex timidō fierī ōrātiōne imperātōris. sed dīcam cūr uōs conuocāuerim
et cūr ōrātiōnem habeam. idcircō uōs aduocāuī, quō pauca monērem,
simul utī causam meī cōnsilī aperīrem. scītis equidem, mīlitēs, dē   255
ignāuiā Lentulī. igitur scītis nōn sōlum quam ignāuus Lentulus fuerit,
sed etiam quantum perīculī haec ignāuia nōbīs attulerit. nunc uērō quō
locō rēs nostrae sint, omnēs intellegitis. nam uidētis nōn sōlum quot
hostēs nōs persecūtī sint, sed etiam quantī exercitūs, ūnus ab urbe, alter
ā Galliā, nōbīs obstent. frūmentī egestās nōs impedit quōminus in hīs   260
locīs maneāmus. quōcumque īre placet, nōn dubium est quīn ferrō iter
aperiendum sit. quae cum sciātis, uōs moneō utī fortī et parātō animō
sītis, et cum proelium inībitis, utī meminerītis quantam spem in hōc
proeliō posuerītis. oportet uōs meminisse nōs dīuitiās, decus, glōriam,
praetereā lībertātem atque patriam in dextrīs nostrīs portāre, sī   265
uīcerimus, nōn dubium est quīn omnia nōbīs tūta sint. sī metū
cesserimus, eadem illa aduersa fīent. praetereā, mīlitēs, nōn eadem nōbīs
et illīs necessitūdō impendet. nam nōs prō patriā, prō lībertāte, prō uītā
certāmus, illī prō potentiā paucōrum. nēmō igitur uestrum est quīn
sciat causam nostram iūstam esse. ergō audācius aggrediminī, memorēs   270
prīstinae uirtūtis.'

(*Catilīnae coniūrātiō* 57.6–58.12)

Running vocabulary for 5F(i)

ā/ab (+ abl.) from (the direction of)
addō 3 I add, increase
aduers-us a um hostile
aduocō 1 I summon
attulerit '(it) has brought' (perf. subj. of *adferō*)
cēdō 3 *cessī* I yield
certō 1 I contend, fight
contiō contiōn-is 3f. meeting, assembly
conuocāuerim 'I have called together' (perf. subj. of *conuocō* 1)
decus decor-is 3n. honour
dextr-a ae 1f. right hand

dīuiti-ae ārum 1f. pl. riches
dubi-us a um doubtful
egestās egestāt-is 3f. lack
equidem at any rate
ex [line 253 = instead of]
frūment-um ī 2n. corn
fuerit '(he) has been' (pf. subj. of *sum*)
Galli-a ae 1f. Gaul
huiuscemodī of this kind
ignāu-us a um idle; cowardly
ignāui-a ae 1f. laziness; cowardice
impendeō 2 I threaten, overhang (+ dat.)
iūst-us a um just

meminerītis '(you) remember' (subj. of *meminī* 'I remember' – perfect in form)
meminī I remember (perfect in form)
necessitūdō necessitūdin-is 3f. necessity
ōrātiō ōrātiōn-is 3f. speech; *ōrātiōnem habeō* I make a speech
persecūtī sint '(they) have pursued' (perf. subj. of *persequor*)
posuerītis 'you (pl.) have placed' (perf. subj. of *pōnō* 3)
potenti-a ae 1f. power

prīstin-us a um former
quant-us a um how much, how big
quīn (+ subj.) (lines 261, 266
    after *nōn dubium est*) that

quīn (+ subj.) (line 269)
    'who . . . not' [see **174.2**]
quō (+ subj.) (line 254) in order to
quōcumque wherever

quōminus (+ subj.) from (—ing)
quot how many

Grammar for 5F

**perfect subjunctives and
    usages**

**indirect questions
conditionals**

quōminus, quīn

Notes

line 254 *quō pauca monērem*: 'in order to give advice on a few points' lit. 'advise a few things'.
line 257 *quantum perīculī*: see **31**.

Learning vocabulary for 5F(i)

Nouns
contiō contiōn-is 3f. meeting,
    assembly
decus decor-is 3n. honour; beauty
dextr-a ae 1f. right hand
dīuiti-ae ārum 1f. pl. riches
frūment-um ī 2n. corn
ignāui-a ae 1f. laziness;
    cowardice
ōrātiō ōrātiōn-is 3f. speech
potenti-a ae 1f. power

Adjectives
aduers-us a um hostile; opposite;
    unfavourable
ignāu-us a um lazy; cowardly
quant-us a um how much, how
    great

Verbs
addō 3 *addidī additus* I add;
    increase
aduocō 1 I summon

cēdō 3 *cessī cessum* I yield; go
certō 1 I struggle, fight; vie
meminī meminisse (defective:
    perfect form only) I remember
persequor 3 dep. *persecūtus* I
    pursue, follow after

Others
ōrātiōnem habēre to make a
    speech
quōcumque (to) wherever
quot how many

Section 5F(ii)

'Had you not taken this course, most of you would have lived out your lives in exile. But you all opted for this course. Now it will take courage to succeed. There is no safety in running away. But I have good hopes of victory, since necessity is driving you. Even if you lose, take some of the enemy with you!'

'plērīque uestrum, nisi coniūrātiōnis participēs factī essētis, cum summā turpitūdine in exsiliō aetātem ēgissētis. nōn‿nūllī uestrum Rōmae uīuere potuistis; quod‿sī ibi mānsissētis āmissīs bonīs, nīl nisi aliēnās opēs exspectāuissētis; illa fēcissētis, nisi foeda atque intoleranda uōbīs uīsa   275
essent. mē potius sequī cōnstituistis. sī rem‿bene‿gerere uultis, audāciā opus‿est. nam in fugā salūtem spērāre, ea uērō dēmentia est.

'cum uōs cōnsīderō, mīlitēs, magna mē spēs uictōriae tenet. sī enim sociī ignāuī fuissētis, hoc cōnsilium ⌐ numquam ¬ cēpissem. animus, aetās, uirtūs uestra mē impediunt quōminus dēspērem, praetereā necessitūdō,   280
quae etiam timidōs fortīs facit. nam saepe mīlitēs metus superāuisset, nisi eōs necessitūdō pugnāre coēgisset. quod‿sī uirtūtī uestrae fortūna inuīderit, cauēte inultī animam āmittātis, neu captī sīcutī pecora trucīdēminī! nīl uōs impedit quīn, mōre uirōrum pugnantēs, cruentam atque lūctuōsam uictōriam hostibus relinquātis!   285

'scītis cūr uōs conuocāuerim. postquam in proelium inieritis, sciam utrum frūstrā locūtus‿sim necne.'

(*Catilīnae coniūrātiō* 58.13–21)

Running vocabulary for 5F(ii)

agō 3 *ēgī* I spend, pass
anim-a ae 1f. life
bon-a ōrum 2n. pl. goods
cauēte (+ subj. or *nē* + subj.) beware of —ing
cōnsilium capere to make a plan
conuocāuerim 'I have summoned' (pf. subj. of *conuocō* 1)
cruent-us a um bloody
dēmenti-a ae 1f. madness
dēspērō 1 I lose hope
exsili-um ī 2n. exile
foed-us a um disgraceful
intolerand-us a um unbearable

inuideō 2 *inuīdī* I begrudge, envy (+ dat.)
inult-us a um unavenged
locūtus sim 'I have spoken' (pf. subj. of *loquor*)
lūctuōs-us a um grief-stricken, mournful
mōre in the manner of X (gen.)
necessitūdō necessitūdin-is 3f. necessity
necne or not (following *utrum* 'whether')
neu = *nēue* and that . . . not
nōn nūllī some

opus est there is need of X (abl.)
particeps particip-is sharer in (+ gen.)
pecus pecor-is 3n. sheep; cattle
quīn (+ subj.) from (—ing)
quod sī but if
quōminus (+ subj.) from (—ing)
rem bene gerere to succeed
superō 1 I overcome
trucīdō 1 butcher
turpitūdō turpitūdin-is 3f. disgrace, dishonour
utrum . . . necne whether . . . or not

Note

lines 272–3 *nisi... factī fuissētis... ēgissētis*: 'if... had not... would have'. There are several other examples of this construction. *sī/ nisi* + pluperfect subjunctive, pluperfect subjunctive. The basic formula is 'if X had/had not happened, Y would not have happened'. Other examples are in lines 274–5, 275–6, 278–9, 281–2. See **173**, cf. **144**[3].

Learning vocabulary for 5F(ii)

Nouns

bon-a ōrum 2n. pl. goods

exsili-um ī 2n. exile

necessitūdō necessitūdin-is 3f. necessity

Verbs

agō 3 *ēgī āctus* I spend, pass (do, act; drive, lead, direct)

inuideō 2 *inuīdī inuīsum* I envy, begrudge (+ dat.)

trucīdō 1 I butcher, slaughter

Others

mōre in the manner of, like X (gen.)

opus est there is need of X (abl.)

Section 5G(i)

The two sides prepare for battle. Catiline takes precautions so that his soldiers have equal chances of survival. Manlius is put in charge of the conspirators' right wing, a Faesulan of the left. On the Roman side Antonius' gout forces him to give command to M. Petreius, an experienced soldier, who knows the men and encourages them accordingly.

quae cum dīxisset, paulum commorātus Catilīna signa canere iubet
atque ōrdinēs in locum aequum dēdūcit. deinde remōtīs omnium equīs,
quō mīlitibus, exaequātō perīculō, animus amplior esset, ipse pedes   290
exercitum prō locō atque cōpiīs īnstruit, octō cohortīs īn fronte posuit,
reliquārum signa īn subsidiō collocat. ab eīs centuriōnēs, ex mīlitibus
optimum‾quemque armātum, in prīmam aciem dūcit. quibus rēbus
factīs, Mānlium dextrō cornū, Faesulānum quendam sinistrō cornū
praeficit.   295

at ex alterā parte C. Antōnius pedibus aeger M. Petrēiō lēgātō
exercitum permittit. ille cohortīs ueterānās in fronte, post eās cēterum
exercitum in subsidiīs locat. ipse equō circumiēns unum‾quemque
nōmināns appellat atque hortātur; rogat ut meminerint sē contrā
latrōnēs inermīs prō līberīs, prō ārīs atque focīs certāre. homo mīlitāris,   300
quod amplius annōs trīgintā in exercitū fuerat, mīlitem quemque et
facta cuiusque fortia nōuerat. igitur circumeundō et ūnum‾quemque
nōminandō et facta cuiusque nārrandō, mīlitum animōs accendēbat.
cum omnīs circumīsset, mīlitēs ad pugnandum, ad interficiendum, ad
moriendum erant parātī.   305

(Catilīnae coniūrātiō 59)

Running vocabulary for 5G(i)

accendō 3 I fire
aciēs aciē-ī 5f. battle-line
aeger aegr-a um ill
amplius more than
appellō 1 I address
canō 3 I sound (lit. 'sing')
centuriō centuriōn-is 3m. centurion (commander of a century – actually less than 100 men)
circumeundō by going round (abl. gerund of *circumeō*)
corn-ū ūs 4n. wing (dat. s. *cornū*)
cuiusque (gen. s. m.) of each (man)
dexter dextr-a um right

exaequō 1 I make equal
Faesulān-us ī 2m. man from Faesulae
foc-us ī 2m. hearth
frōns front-is 3f. front
inerm-is e unarmed
interficiendum killing (acc. gerund of *interficiō*)
latrō latrōn-is 3m. bandit
lēgāt-us ī 2m. commander
locō 1 I place
M. = Mārcō: Mārc-us ī 2m. Marcus
moriendum dying (acc. gerund of *morior*)

nārrandō by relating (abl. gerund of *nārrō*)
nōminandō by naming (abl. gerund of *nōminō*)
nōminō 1 I name
optimum quemque = all the best men (line 293)
parāt-us a um prepared (to: *ad* + gerund)
pedes pedit-is 3m. foot-soldier
permittō 3 I entrust X (acc.) to Y (dat.)
Petrēi-us ī 2m. M. Petreius
praeficiō 3/4 *praefecī praefectus* I put X (acc.) in charge of Y (dat.)

prō (+ abl.) (line 291) in
accordance with
pugnandum fighting (acc. gerund
of *pugnō*)
quemque (acc. s. m.) (line 301)
each

remoueō 2 *remōuī remōtus* I
remove
sign-um ī 2n. (line 292) standard
sign-um ī 2n. (line 288)
trumpet-call
sinister sinistr-a um left

subsidi-um ī 2n. (or pl.) reserve
ueterān-us a um veteran
ūnum quemque = each individual
(lines 298, 302)

Grammar for 5G

gerunds	**uterque**	**comparative clauses,**
quisque, quisquam	**cornū**	**correlatives, unreal**
		comparisons

Notes

line 290 *quo ... esset* see **155**.
line 292 *reliquārum*: sc. '(of the) cohorts'.

Learning vocabulary for 5G(i)

Nouns

aciēs aciē-ī 5f. battle-line; sharp
edge, point; keenness (of
sight)
centuriō centuriōn-is 3m.
centurion
corn-ū ūs 4n. wing (of army);
horn
latrō latrōn-is 3m. robber, bandit
lēgāt-us ī 2m. commander
(ambassador, official)

sign-um ī 2n. standard,
trumpet-call (seal; signal,
sign; statue)
subsidi-um ī 2n. reserve; help

Adjectives

aeger aegr-a um ill
dexter dextr-a um right,
favourable
sinister sinistr-a um left;
unfavourable

Verbs

appellō 1 I name, call; address

cūrō 1 I am in command (look
after, care for; see to the —ng
of X (acc.) + gerundive)
nōminō 1 I name
praeficiō 3/4 *praefēcī praefectus*
I put X (acc.) in charge of Y
(dat.)

Others

amplius more than (from *ampl-us
a um* great)
prō (+ abl.) in accordance with
(for, in return for; on behalf
of; in front of; instead of)

Section 5G(ii)

The battle begins and is ferociously contested. Catiline displays astounding activity, both as soldier and general. Petreius breaks the centre. Manlius and the Faesulan die in the front line. Catiline, seeing the position is hopeless, plunges into the thick of the fighting and is stabbed.

sed ubi, omnibus rēbus explōrātīs, Petrēius tubā signum dat, cohortīs
paulātim incēdere iubet. idem facit hostium exercitus. postquam eō
uentum est unde ā ferentāriīs proelium committī posset, exercitus
uterque maximō clāmōre cum īnfestīs signīs concurrunt. pīla omittunt,
gladiīs rēs geritur. ueterānī, prīstinae uirtūtis memorēs, comminus   310
ācriter īnstāre, illī haud timidī resistunt. maximā uī certātur. intereā
Catilīna, cum expedītīs in prīmā aciē uersārī, labōrantibus succurrere,
integrōs prō sauciīs arcessere, omnia prōuidēre, multum ipse pugnāre,
saepe hostem ferīre; strēnuī mīlitis et bonī imperātōris officia simul
exsequēbātur. Petrēius, ubi uidet Catilīnam, contrā⁀ac ratus erat,   315
magnā uī tendere, cohortem praetōriam in mediōs hostīs indūcit,
eōsque perturbātōs atque aliōs alibī resistentīs interficit. deinde utrōque
ex latere cēterōs aggreditur. Mānlius et Faesulānus in prīmīs pugnantēs
cadunt. Catilīna, postquam fūsās cōpiās sēque cum paucīs relictum
uidet, memor generis atque prīstinae suae dignitātis, in cōnfertissimōs   320
hostīs incurrit, ibīque pugnāns cōnfoditur.

(*Catilīnae coniūrātiō* 60)

Running vocabulary for 5G(ii)

alibī (with *aliōs*) in different
  places [see **102¹**]
cadō 3 I fall, die
comminus to close quarters
cōnfert-us a um close-packed
cōnfodiō 3/4 I stab
contrā ac (+ indic.) contrary to
  what
expedīt-us ī 2m. light-armed
  soldier
explōrō 1 I investigate,
  reconnoitre
exsequor 3 dep. I carry out,
  perform
ferentāri-us ī 2m. light-armed
  soldier (armed only with
  missiles)
fundō 3 *fūdī fūsus* I rout
incēdō 3 I advance
incurrō 1 I run into

indūcō 3 I lead X (acc.) into Y (*in*
  + acc.)
īnfest-us a um hostile; *cum īnfestīs
  signīs* = 'with standards set
  for attack'
īnstō 1 I press on, approach
integer integr-a um fresh, not
  wounded
labōrō 1 I am in difficulties
latus later-is 3n. flank
omittō 3 I leave out, leave aside;
  let fall
paulātim little by little, gradually
perturbō 1 I disturb, confuse
pīl-um ī 2n. heavy javelin
  (normally thrown by soldiers
  before hand-to-hand fighting
  began)
praetōri-us a um praetorian (i.e.
  the best fighters)

prīstin-us a um former
proelium committere to join battle
ratus see *reor*
reor 2 dep. *ratus* I think, believe,
  suppose
resistō 3 I resist
sauci-us a um wounded
strēnu-us a um energetic
succurrō 3 I run to help (+ dat.)
tendō 3 I struggle, fight
tub-a ae if. trumpet
uersor 1 dep. I am occupied
ueterān-us ī 2m. veteran
unde from where
uterque (nom. s. m.) each (of two)
  [note the pl. verb]
utrōque (abl. s. n.) each (of the
  two)

62. utrōque ex latere cēterōs aggreditur

Notes

line 307 *eō*: *'to that place ...'* picked up by *unde* 'from where'.

line 308 *uentum est*⎫
line 311 *certātur* ⎬ impersonal passives (see **160**).

line 311 *īnstāre*
line 312 *uersārī, succurrere*
line 313 *arcessere, prōuidēre, pugnāre,* ⎬ historic infinitives.
line 314 *ferīre*

line 319 *fūsās ... relictum: sc. esse.*

Learning vocabulary for 5G(ii)

Nouns
latus later-is 3n. side; flank
pīl-um ī 2n. heavy javelin

Adjectives
integer integr-a um whole,
    untouched
prīstin-us a um former; original
sauci-us a um wounded

Verbs
cadō 3 *cecidī cāsum* I fall, die

īnstō 1 *īnstitī* – I press upon; urge;
    pursue; am at hand, approach;
    strive after (*in* + *stō*)
omittō 3 *omīsī omissus* I give up;
    let fall; omit, leave aside
    (*ob* + *mittō*)
reor 2 dep. *ratus* I think, believe,
    suppose
resistō 3 *restitī* (+ dat.) I resist;
    stand back, halt; pause (*re* +
    sistō)

succurrō 3 *succurrī succursum*
    I run to help, assist (+ dat.)
    (*sub* + *currō*)
tendō 3 *tetendī tēnsus* or *tentus*
    I strive, fight; (stretch (out);
    offer; direct; (intrans.) travel)
uersor 1 dep. I am occupied; stay,
    dwell; am in a certain
    condition

Others
paulātim little by little, gradually
unde from where, whence

Section 5G(iii)

*Aftermath. The mettle of Catiline's troops is now clear. There has been no
retreat, no wounds in the back. Catiline is found deep in the enemy lines, still
breathing. No free man has been taken alive. But the victory is a sour one, as the
best soldiers are dead or wounded and visitors to the battlefield find friends and
relatives among the dead.*

sed cōnfectō proeliō, tum uērō cernerēs quanta audācia quantaque
animī uīs fuisset in exercitū Catilīnae. nam ferē quem quisque uīuus
pugnandō locum cēperat, eum āmissā animā corpore tegēbat. nec
quisquam nisi aduersō uulnere conciderat. Catilīna uērō longē ā suīs   325
inter hostium cadāuera repertus est, paululum etiam spīrāns,
ferōciamque animī, quam habuerat uīuus, in uultū retinēns. postrēmō
ex omnī cōpiā neque in proeliō neque in fugā quisquam cīuis ingenuus
captus est.

neque tamen exercitus populī Rōmānī laetam aut incruentam   330
uictōriam adeptus erat. nam strēnuissimus˜quisque aut occiderat in
proeliō aut grauiter uulnerātus discesserat. multī autem quī ē castrīs
uīsendī aut spoliandī grātiā prōcesserant, uoluentēs hostīlia cadāuera,
amīcum aliī, pars hospitem aut cognātum reperiēbant. fuēre item quī
inimīcōs suōs cognōscerent. ita uariē per omnem exercitum laetitia,   335
maeror, lūctus atque gaudia agitābantur.

(Catilīnae coniūrātiō 61)

Running vocabulary for 5G(iii)

aduers-us a um in front
anim-a ae 1f. soul, life
cadāuer cadāuer-is 3n. corpse
cernō 3 I see
cognāt-us ī 2m. kinsman,
  blood-relative
ferē almost
ferōci-a ae 1f. ferocity
gaudi-um ī 2n. joy
hostīl-is e of the enemy
incruent-us a um bloodless
ingenu-us a um free-born
lūct-us ūs 4m. mourning
maeror maerōr-is 3m. grief

occidō 3 *occidī* I die, fall
paululum a very little
prōcēdō 3 *prōcessī* I advance,
  proceed, come forth
pugnandō by fighting (abl. gerund
  of *pugnō*)
quisquam (nom. s. m.) (line 328)
  any (adj.)
quisquam (nom. s. m.) (line 325)
  anyone (pronoun)
quisque (nom. s. m.) (line 323)
  each person
spīrō 1 I breathe

spoliandī of stripping (corpses)
  (gen. gerund of *spoliō* 1)
strēnuissimus quisque all the most
  energetic men
strēnu-us a um energetic
tegō 3 I cover
uariē in different ways
uīsendī of visiting/viewing (gen.
  gerund of *uīsō* 3)
uīu-us a um living, alive
uoluō 3 I turn (over) (trans.)
uulnerō 1 I wound
uult-us ūs 4m. face, expression

Notes

line 322 *cernerēs*: referring to the past (see **158.2**).
line 323 *quem* with *locum*: *locum* picked up by *eum*.
line 334 *aliī... pars*: 'some...others'. A variant of *aliī... aliī*.

Learning vocabulary for 5G(iii)

Nouns

anim-a ae if. soul, life, breath
ferōci-a ae 1f. ferocity
gaudi-um ī 2n. joy
lūct-us ūs 4m. grief, mourning
uult-us ūs 4m. face, expression

Adjectives

aduers-us a um in front (i.e.
   facing the enemy) (hostile;
   opposite; unfavourable)
uīu-us a um alive, living

Verbs

occidō 3 *occidī occāsum* I fall, die
   (*ob* + *cadō*)
tegō 3 *tēxī tēctus* I cover
uoluō 3 *uoluī uolūtus* I roll, turn
   (over) (trans.)
uulnerō 1 I wound

Section 6A **High life and high society: Catullus (*c.* 84–*c.* 54 BC)**

I DINNERS, FRIENDS AND POETRY

All Roman literature that we have from the Republican period reflects Roman high society, and its moral and political values. But the *grauitās* of the great has been counterbalanced by the frivolity of the young. In Cicero's day, a group of young poets within this social milieu was cultivating a lighter, though learned, style of writing. These poets included Gaius Valerius Catullus and Licinius Calvus. Cicero called them *neōteroi,* a Greek word meaning 'the younger set', or 'revolutionaries', but he did not mean it to be complimentary. Their subjects ranged from obscene lampoon through love poetry to 'epyllion', a short and intensely learned epic which they modelled on works by Greek writers based in Alexandria (third to first century).

Section 6A(i)

Catullus promises his friend Fabullus a wonderful meal – as long as Fabullus brings all the necessaries. But Catullus can offer one thing.

cēnābis bene, mī Fabulle, apud mē
paucīs ⌐, sī tibi dī fauent, ⌐ diēbus,
sī tēcum attuleris bonam atque magnam
cēnam, nōn sine candidā puellā
et uīnō et sale et omnibus cachinnīs.   5
haec sī, inquam, attuleris, uenuste noster,
cēnābis bene; nam tuī Catullī
plēnus sacculus est arāneārum.
sed contrā accipiēs merōs amōrēs
seu quid suāuius ēlegantiusue est: 10
nam unguentum dabo, quod meae puellae
dōnārunt Venerēs Cupīdinēsque,
quod tū cum olfaciēs, deōs rogābis,
tōtum ⌐ ut ⌐ tē faciant, Fabulle, nāsum.

(Catullus 13)

63. cēnābis bene

Running vocabulary for 6A(i)

amor amōr-is 3m. love [see note
  for meaning of pl.]
arāne-a ae 1f. cobweb
cachinn-us ī 2m. laugh
candid-us a um beautiful
cēnō 1 I have dinner, dine
contrā in return
Cupīdō Cupīdin-is 3m. Cupid
  (god of desire)
dōnō 1 I give; dōnārunt =
  dōnāuērunt [see Reference
  Grammar **A4**]

ēlegāns ēlegant-is elegant
Fabull-us ī 2m. Fabullus
faueō 2 fāuī fautum I am
  favourable to (+ dat.)
mer-us a um unmixed, pure
mī vocative of meus
nās-us ī 2m. nose
noster = mī (vocative)
olfaciō 3/4 I smell
saccul-us ī 2m. little purse
sal sal-is 3m. salt; wit
seu or if [see note]

suāu-is e sweet
ue or
uenust-us a um charming, smart
  [used as a noun here]
uīn-um ī 2n. wine
unguent-um ī 2n. perfume
Venus Vener-is 3f. Venus (goddess
  of love)

Grammar for 6A

poetry and metre   **hexameter, hendecasyllables,**
rhetoric   **scazons, sapphics**

Notes

line 2 Hold *paucīs* (which is solved by *diēbus*).
line 8 *plēnus*: placed early to set up a surprise: remember it takes gen. *sacculus*: diminutive. See **GE** p. 188.
line 9 The pl. *amōrēs* in Catullus usually means 'girl-friend': but it can mean 'sexual intercourse' or 'passion';
    'the gods of love' or 'an object arousing love' are other suggestions you may like to consider.
line 10 *seu quid*: after *sī, nē* and *num, quis* = anyone/anything (see **144**[1]). *seu* = *sīue*. Tr. 'or something
    that...'
line 11 *meae puellae*: dative, solved by *dōnārunt*.
line 14 *tōtum*: with *tē*: the joke is held back until the last word.

Learning vocabulary for 6A(i)

Nouns
amor amōr-is love; (pl.)
  girl-friend; sexual intercourse

uīn-um ī 2n. wine

Adjectives
mer-us a um unmixed, pure

Verbs
dōnō 1 I give

Section 6A(ii)

Catullus warns Asinius to stop stealing the napkins. It is unsophisticated, and the last napkin he stole holds special memories for Catullus.

Marrūcīne Asinī, manū sinistrā
nōn bellē ūteris: in iocō atque uīnō
tollis lintea neglegentiōrum.
hoc salsum esse putās? fugit tē, inepte:
quamuīs sordida rēs et inuenusta est.   5
nōn crēdis mihi? crēde Pōlliōnī
frātrī, quī tua fūrta uel talentō
mūtārī uelit: est enim lepōrum
differtus puer ac facētiārum.
quārē aut hendecasyllabōs trecentōs   10
exspectā, aut mihi linteum remitte,
quod mē nōn mouet aestimātiōne,
uērum est mnēmosynum meī sodālis.
nam sūdāria Saetaba ex Hibērīs
mīsērunt mihi mūnerī Fabullus   15
et Vērānius: haec amem necesse est
ut Vērāniolum meum et Fabullum.

(Catullus 12)

Running vocabulary for 6A(ii)

aestimātiō aestimātiōn-is 3f. value
Asini-us ī 2m. Asinius [see note]
bellē nicely, properly
differt-us a um crammed with (+ gen.)
Fabull-us ī 2m. Fabullus
facēti-ae ārum 1f. pl. wit
fūrt-um ī 2n. theft
hendecasyllab-us ī 2m. hendecasyllable [the Greek metre used for poems of personal abuse: the metre also of this poem: see **181**]
Hibēr-ī ōrum 2m. pl. Spaniards
inept-us a um stupid
inuenust-us a um not smart, charmless

ioc-us ī 2m. joke, joking, fun
lepōs lepōr-is 3m. charm
linte-um ī 2n. table-napkin
Marrūcīn-us ī 2m. Marrucinus [see note]
mnēmosyn-um ī 2n. keepsake (a Greek word Latinised)
mūnus mūner-is 3n. gift [*mūnerī* 'as a gift': predicative dative, see **L(e)2**]
mūtō 1 I change
neglegēns neglegent-is careless [note the comparative form]
Pōlliō Pōlliōn-is 3m. (C. Asinius) Pollio
quamuīs ever such a
quārē therefore

remittō 3 I send back
Saetab-us a um from Saetabis (a Spanish town famous for its linen goods)
sals-us a um witty, smart
sodālis sodāl-is 3m. friend
sordid-us a um cheap, low, dirty
sūdāri-um ī 2n. handkerchief, napkin
talent-um ī 2n. talent [a huge sum, see note]
Vērāniol-us ī 2m. dear Veranius
Vērāni-us ī 2m. Veranius

Notes

line 1 Marrūcīnus may be this man's *cognōmen*, normally the last of three – *praenōmen* (e.g. Gāius), *nōmen* (e.g. Valērius, the family name), *cognōmen* (e.g. Āfrīcānus, sometimes from some exploit or ancestor's exploit). Asinius will be the *nōmen*. *manū sinistrā*: the abl. is solved in line 2 by *ūteris*.

line 2 *in iocō atque uīnō* i.e. *in conuīuiō*.
line 3 *neglegentiōrum*: comp. adj. used as a noun. Tr. 'rather...' (not 'more').
line 4 *fugit tē*: lit: 'it escapes you'. Tr. 'you're wrong'.
line 7 *talentō*: abl. of the price Pollio would be willing to pay. Tr. 'for a talent'. Reference Grammar **L(f)4(v)**.
line 8 *uelit*: 'he would like': potential subjunctive, see **158.2**.
lines 8–9 *lepōrum*: hold: it is solved by *differtus* (which also governs *facētiārum*).
lines 16–17 *haec amem necesse est*: *ut* has been left out before the clause *haec amem*. This is common:
   see 6A(iii), lines 18, 19. Tr. 'that I should...' The *ut* in line 17 means 'as' sc. 'I love'.
line 17 *Vērāniolum*: diminutive. See **GE** p. 188.

Learning vocabulary for 6A(ii)

Nouns	Verbs	Others
facēti-ae ārum 1f. pl. wit	*mūtō* 1 I change, alter, exchange (trans.)	*quārē* therefore (lit. (abl.) 'from which thing' = wherefore; as question = why?)
ioc-us ī 2m. joke, joking, fun		
lepōs lepōr-is 3m. charm		
mūnus mūner-is 3n. gift; duty		
sodālis sodāl-is 3m. friend		

Catullus and Greek poetry

Since the late second century BC, some Roman love-poets had been tentatively experimenting with the work of Greek love-poets of the third century and after. These were the so-called 'Hellenistic' poets, sometimes called 'Alexandrians', because Alexandria in Egypt was a hotbed of Hellenistic poetic experiment (at any rate, the terms distinguish them from the 'Classical' Greek poets of the fifth–fourth century BC). One of the main features of Hellenistic poetry was *doctrīna* – its commitment to poetry full of learning and allusions to other poets and poetry. In 73 BC, the Hellenistic poet Parthenius, a Greek from Nicaea (in what is now Turkey), arrived as a prisoner-of-war in Rome. He was freed, and it was thanks largely to him that the ideal of poetic *doctrīna* caught on in Rome too, being taken up seriously by the *neōteroi* ('the younger set', a Greek name given by Cicero), the trendy younger poets like Catullus, before becoming characteristic of all subsequent poetry.

   Sometimes this feature can seem like mere learning for learning's sake. At other times, it seriously elevates the poetry. Catullus, wondering how many of his mistress Lesbia's kisses will satisfy him, answers: 'as many as the grains of Libyan sand that lie in silphium-bearing Cyrene between the oracle of sweating Jove and the holy tomb of ancient Battus' (7.4–6). He takes us to a far country (North Africa), and mentions some details associated with it: an important and expensive medicinal herb (silphium), a desert shrine (Jove's oracle at Siwa in the south-east, famous all over the world, consulted by Alexander the Great) and the ancient King Battus, who had founded Cyrene in the north-west, home of Callimachus, most famous of the Alexandrian poets whom Catullus was imitating. This site and these names do poetic work, flattering Lesbia by associating her kisses with a romantic, distant country which has a lush and suggestive past, in which she too, thanks to Catullus, now has a share. (*World of Rome*, **446–7**)

Section 6A(iii)

After spending yesterday in poetic play with you, Licinius, I could hardly sleep.
So I have written this poem for you.

hesternō, Licinī, diē ōtiōsī
multum lūsimus in meīs tabellīs,
ut conuēnerat esse dēlicātōs:
scrībēns uersiculōs uterque nostrum
lūdēbat numerō modo hōc modo illōc,   5
reddēns mūtua per iocum atque uīnum.
atque illinc abiī tuō lepōre
incēnsus, Licinī, facētiīsque,
ut nec mē miserum cibus iuuāret
nec somnus tegeret quiēte ocellōs,   10
sed tōtō ⌐ indomitus ⌐ furōre lectō
uersārer, cupiēns uidēre lūcem,
ut tēcum loquerer simulque ut essem.
at dēfessa ⌐ labōre ⌐ membra ⌐ postquam
⌐ sēmimortua lectulō iacēbant,   15
hoc, iūcunde, tibī poēma fēcī,
ex quō perspicerēs meum dolōrem.
nunc audāx caue sīs, precēsque nostrās,
ōrāmus, caue dēspuās, ocelle,
nē poenās Nemesis reposcat ā tē.   20
est uēmēns dea: laedere hanc cauētō.

(Catullus 50)

Running vocabulary for 6A(iii)

caue + subjunctive, 'beware of -ing' [see note]
cauētō beware of (+ inf.)
conuenit 4 *conuēnit* it is agreed
dēfess-us a um tired out
dēlicāt-us a um sophisticated, decadent, gay
dēspuō 3 I spit out, reject completely
hestern-us a um yester- (with *diē*)
indomit-us a um uncontrollable
iūuō 1 I help, delight, please
laedō 3 I harm, do down
lectul-us ī 2m. bed [diminutive of *lectus*: see **GE** p. 188]

Licini-us ī 2m. Licinius [see note]
lūdō 3 *lūsī* I play, have a good time, make jokes
membr-um ī 2n. limb
mūtu-us a um in return, reciprocal [sc. 'verses']
Nemesis f. (Greek word) Nemesis, goddess of revenge
numer-us ī 2m. metre
ocell-us ī 2m. (line 10) eye; (line 19) apple of my eye
ōtiōs-us a um at leisure, enjoying oneself
perspiciō 3/4 I see clearly, understand fully [see note]

poēma n. poem (from the Greek *poieō* 'I make', the equivalent of *faciō*)
quiēs quiēt-is 3f. sleep, rest
reposcō 3 I exact (in return)
sēmimortu-us a um half-dead
simul together (sc. with you)
somn-us ī 2m. sleep
tabell-ae ārum 1f. pl. writing-tablets
uēmēns = *uehemēns*
uersicul-us ī 2m. scrap of verse, epigram [diminutive *of uersus*: see **GE** p. 188]
uersor 1 (passive) I toss and turn

Notes

line 1 *Licinī*: C. Licinius Calvus Macer, orator and poet.
line 5 *illōc* = *ilō*. Cf. *hōc* – in earlier Latin both words had the suffix -*ce*.
line 6 *per iocum atque uīnum*: cf. *in iocō atque uīno* in 6A(ii) line 2.
line 9 *ut*: 'with the result that'.
line 11 *tōtō*: hold – it is solved by *lectō*, not *furōre*, which is abl. of cause after *indomitus*.
line 16 *iūcunde*: the adjective is used in the vocative as a noun; cf. *uenuste noster* in 6A(i).
line 17 *ex quō perspicerēs*: purpose clause introduced by relative pronoun (see **150**).
lines 18, 19 *caue sīs* and *caue dēspuās*: 'beware of -ing'. Here you would normally expect *nē* (see
    Reference Grammar **S2(d)** 'verbs of fearing'), but as with *haec amem necesse est* in 6A(ii) line 16, the
    conjunction has been omitted. This is a common idiom with certain words.
line 21 *cauētō*: future imperative, i.e. 'beware (in future)'. Reference Grammar **A2 Note 1**.

Learning vocabulary for 6A(iii)

Nouns
membr-um ī 2n. limb
quiēs quiēt-is 3f. sleep, rest
somn-us ī 2m. sleep

Adjectives
ōtiōs-us a um at leisure

Verbs
iūuō 1 *iūuī iūtus* I help, delight,
    please
laedō 3 *laesī laesus* I harm
lūdō 3 *lūsī lūsum* I play

64. in meīs tabellīs

Making use of Greek literature

It quickly became the standard practice for those Romans who had completed their education in
Rome to go to Athens to study. But Roman acceptance of Greek literature was never uncritical. Their
passion for *ūtilitās* saw to that. Consequently they took Greek literature and used it for their own,
Roman purposes. The story of Roman literature is at one level the vast enterprise of naturalising, or
'Romanising', this impressive Greek heritage. Much later St Augustine adopted the same principle in
recommending that Christians should regard pagan literature as the Jews had regarded the riches of
Egypt – take what is good and put it to your own uses. (*World of Rome*, **436**)

2 CATULLUS AND LESBIA

A fairly large number of Catullus' poems either are addressed to or refer to Lesbia. It is widely believed that this name was a pseudonym for Clodia, a prominent member of high society and wife of an ex-consul Q. Metellus Celer, and that Catullus had had an adulterous affair with her at some time before her husband died in 59. When the affair ended, Catullus was bitter and attacked Lesbia vehemently.

The following four poems are taken from different stages of the relationship: 5 and 7 come before the break-up, 8 and 11 after it.

Section 6A(iv)

Let us love and store up kisses while we can, and ignore what the envious say about us.

uīuāmus mea Lesbia, atque amēmus,
rūmōrēsque senum seuēriōrum
omnīs ūnius aestimēmus assis!
sōlēs occidere et redīre possunt:
nōbīs cum semel occidit breuis lūx,   5
nox est perpetua ūna dormienda.
dā mī bāsia mīlle, deinde centum,
dein mīlle altera, dein secunda centum,
deinde usque altera mīlle, deinde centum,
dein, cum mīlia multa fēcerīmus,   10
conturbābimus illa, nē sciāmus,
aut nē quis malus inuidēre possit,
cum tantum ⌐ sciat esse ⌐ bāsiōrum.

(Catullus 5)

Running vocabulary for 6A(iv)

aestimō 1 I value [see note]
as ass-is 3m. as (a coin of small value) [tr. 'penny', 'dime'; see note]
bāsi-um ī 2n. kiss
conturbō 1 I confuse; wreck the account of

dein = deinde
Lesbi-a ae 1f. Lesbia [see Intro, to 6A]
mī = mihi
occidō 3 *occidī* I set (other meanings: I fall, die)
perpetu-us a um unending

rūmor rūmōr-is 3m. (piece of) gossip, unfavourable report
semel once; *cum semel =* as soon as
sōlēs (pl. of *sōl*) = 'light of the sun', 'the sun each day'
usque continually, without a break

65. dā mi bāsia mīlle

Notes

line 2 *rūmōrēs*: acc. – hold until solved (by *aestimēmus*). *seuēriōrum*: cf. *neglegentiōrum* in 6A(ii) line 3. Tr. 'rather...' (not 'more').

line 3 *ūnius... assis*: genitive of price or value after *aestimēmus*. Tr. 'at one penny/dime'.

line 5 *nōbīs*: hold until solved (by *dormienda*).

line 10 *fēcerīmus*: future perfect (not perf. subj.), despite the long *-ī* of *-īmus*.

line 13 *tantum... bāsiōrum*: cf. *satis/nimis* + gen. (31). Tr. 'so many...' (lit. 'such and such an amount of...').

Learning vocabulary for 6A(iv)

Nouns

rūmor rūmōr-is 3m. rumour, (piece of) gossip, unfavourable report

Verbs

aestimō 1 I value; estimate

occidō 3 *occidī occāsum* I set (intrans.); (I fall; die)

Others

dein = deinde then, next

mī = mihi [NB *mī* is also vocative of *meus*]

semel once (*cum semel* = as soon as)

usque continually, without a break (often used with *ad* = right up to)

Section 6A(v)

How many of your kisses will satisfy me? An infinite number.

quaeris, quot mihi bāsiātiōnēs
tuae, Lesbia, sint satis superque.
quam magnus numerus Libyssae harēnae
lāsarpīciferīs iacet Cyrēnīs
ōrāclum Iouis ⌐ inter ⌐ aestuōsī   5
et Battī ueteris sacrum sepulcrum;
aut quam sīdera multa, cum tacet nox,
fūrtīuōs ⌐ hominum uident ⌐ amōrēs:
tam tē bāsia multa bāsiāre
uēsānō satis et super Catullō est,   10
quae nec pernumerāre cūriōsī
possint nec mala fascināre lingua.

(Catullus 7)

Running vocabulary for 6A(v)

aestuōs-us a um sweltering, hot
bāsiātiō bāsiātiōn-is 3f. kiss [see note]
bāsiō 1 I kiss
bāsi-um ī 2n. kiss
Batt-us ī 2m. Battus (first king of Cyrene)
Catull-us ī 2m. Catullus
cūriōs-us a um inquisitive, prying

Cyrēn-ae ārum 1f. pl. Cyrene (city in NW Libya, or the territory of Cyrene)
fascinō 1 I bewitch, cast a spell on
fūrtīu-us a um stolen
harēn-a ae 1f. sand
lāsarpīcifer lāsarpīcifer-a um silphium-bearing
Libyss-a ae f. adj. African

lingu-a ae 1f. tongue [see note]
ōrācl-um ī 2n. oracle
pernumerō 1 I tally up
sepulcr-um ī 2n. tomb
sīdus sīder-is 3n. star
super more than enough (adv.)
uēsān-us a um crazed, maddened

Notes

line 1 *bāsiātiō*: a sort of abstract noun (!) formed from the usual word *bāsium*.
line 3 *quam magnus*: lit. 'how great...', picked up eventually by *tam... multa* (line 9) 'so many'.
line 5 *inter*: the preposition governs *ōrāclum*: notice the word pattern in lines 5–6.
line 7 *quam... multa*: lit. 'how many', picked up by *tam... multa* (line 9) 'so many'. Cf. *quam magnus* (line 3).
line 8 *fūrtīuōs*: hold until solved (by *amōrēs*).
line 9 *bāsia bāsiāre*: cf. *pugnam pugnāre* 'to fight a fight'. Note that here *tē* is the object, *bāsia* is an internal or cognate accusative. Eng. 'to give you... kisses'.
line 10 *uēsānō*: hold until solved (by *Catullō*).
line 11 *possint*: potential subjunctive (see **158.2**).
line 12 *mala lingua*: another subject *of possint.*

Learning vocabulary for 6A(v)

Nouns
harēn-a ae 1f. sand
lingu-a ae 1f. tongue; language
ōrāc (u)l-um ī 2n. oracle

sepulc (h)r-um ī 2n. tomb
sīdus sīder-is 3n. star

Others
super (adv.) more than enough; above, over; (prep. + acc./abl.) over, above; (+ abl.) about

Section 6A(vi)

For all the pleasure she once gave, she has gone, Catullus, for good. So abandon her – despite the pain.

miser Catulle, dēsinās ineptīre,
et quod ⌐ uidēs perīsse ⌐ perditum dūcās.
fulsēre quondam candidī tibī sōlēs,
cum uentitābās quō puella ⌐ dūcēbat
⌐ amāta nōbīs quantum amābitur nūlla.   5
ibi illa multa cum iocōsa fīēbant,
quae tū uolēbās nec puella nōlēbat,
fulsēre uērē candidī tibī sōlēs.
nunc iam illa nōn uolt: tū quoque inpotēns nōlī,
nec quae fugit sectāre, nec miser uīue,   10
sed obstinātā mente perfer, obdūrā.
ualē, puella. iam Catullus obdūrat,
nec tē ⌐ requīret nec rogābit ⌐ inuītam.
at tū dolēbis, cum rogāberis nūlla.
scelesta, uae tē, quae tibī manet uīta?   15
quis nunc tē adībit? cūī uidēberis bella?
quem nunc amābis? cuius esse dīcēris?
quem bāsiābis? cūī labella mordēbis?
at tū, Catulle, dēstinātus obdūrā.

(Catullus 8)

Running vocabulary for 6A(vi)

bāsiō 1 I kiss
bell-us a um beautiful
candid-us a um bright
dēsinō 3 I cease from X (inf.) [see note]
dēstināt-us a um stubborn, obstinate
doleō 2 I grieve, feel anguish
dūcō 3 (line 2) I consider, think [see note]
fulgeō 2 *fulsī* I shine
ineptiō 4 I play the fool, am silly
inpotēns inpotent-is powerless (sc. 'as you are')

inuīt-us a um unwilling [see note]
iocōs-us a um full of fun
labell-um ī 2n. lip
mordeō 2 I bite
nōbīs line 5 tr. 'by me' [see note line 5]
nūlla (line 5) 'no woman'; (line 14) 'not at all'
obdūrō 1 I am firm, hold out
obstināt-us a um resolute, stubborn
perdō 3 *perdidī perditus* I lose, destroy
pereō perīre periī I pass away, die

perferō perferre I endure (to the end)
quondam once
sector 1 dep. I keep pursuing (= *sequor* + *-it-*)
sōlēs (pl. of *sōl*) 'light of the sun'
uae (+ acc.) alas for
uentitō 1 I keep coming (= *ueniō* + *-it-*)
uērē truly
uolt = *uult*

Notes
line 1 *dēsinās*: jussive subjunctive (see **157**).
line 2 *quod*: tr. 'that which', picked up by *perditum. dūcās*: jussive subjunctive, cf. *dēsinās* (see **157**).
line 5 *nōbīs*: pl. for s. is very common in poetry, especially with personal pronouns. The dative expresses the agent (usually expressed by *ā/ab* + abl.).

line 6 *illa*: n. pl. 'those things (sc. I am reflecting on)'. Note *cum* is postponed, though it introduces the
    clause, *iocōsa* is used as a noun.
line 10 *quae fugit*: the clause is introduced by the next word *sectāre*: sc. *eam* to make sense of it.
line 13 *inuītam*: agrees with *tē*: sc. 'since you are...'
line 18 *cūī*: sympathetic dative (!); see Reference Grammar **L(e)5**.

Learning vocabulary for 6A(vi)

Adjectives
candid-us a um white; bright,
    beautiful
inuīt-us a um unwilling

Verbs
doleō 2 I suffer pain, grieve
dūcō 3 *dūxī ductus* I think,
    consider (lead)
fulgeō 2 *fulsī* I shine
obdūrō 1 I am firm, hold out,
    persist

pereō perīre periī peritum I
    perish, die; (*periī* I am lost)
perferō perferre pertulī perlātus I
    endure (to the end); complete;
    carry to; announce

Arretine pottery

One of the most travelled products and one which was at times produced on something approaching
an industrial scale was pottery. One of the most interesting results of Augustus' settlement of the
empire and making the sea-ways safe was the sudden dominance throughout the empire and
beyond of the red gloss pottery (known as Arretine or *terra sigillāta*) produced at Arretium (Arezzo)
in Umbria. For a short period in the reigns of Augustus and Tiberius there was an extraordinary
fashion for this pottery and it was transported in large quantities over great distances.

At first sight this is surprising. Pottery is not a product of such value that it could easily carry the
costs of long-distance transport. Although wrecks have been discovered with whole cargoes of
pottery, more normally pottery formed part-loads along with primary products. It should also be
remembered that ships bringing wine, oil or corn needed to find cargoes for the return voyage.

However, it also needs to be noted that by the middle of the first century, the pottery produced at
Arretium had just as quickly lost its widespread market. The technology of producing red gloss
pottery moved to southern and central Gaul, and later to eastern Gaul, and North Africa. It can be
demonstrated that workshop owners from Arretium were responsible for bringing their skills to the
new regions. Cn. Ateius, who had a workshop in Arretium, seems to have opened branches in Lyons
and southern Gaul. Further, the potters of southern Gaul occasionally stamped their pottery
'Arretine', thus acknowledging the origins of the style. The quantities of pottery produced at these
centres were on an industrial scale; but this does not presuppose organisation as a modern industry.
Study of the stamps of workshop owners and craftsmen suggests the pottery was produced by large
numbers of independent potteries which rarely employed more than about twenty slave craftsmen.
(*World of Rome*, **297**)

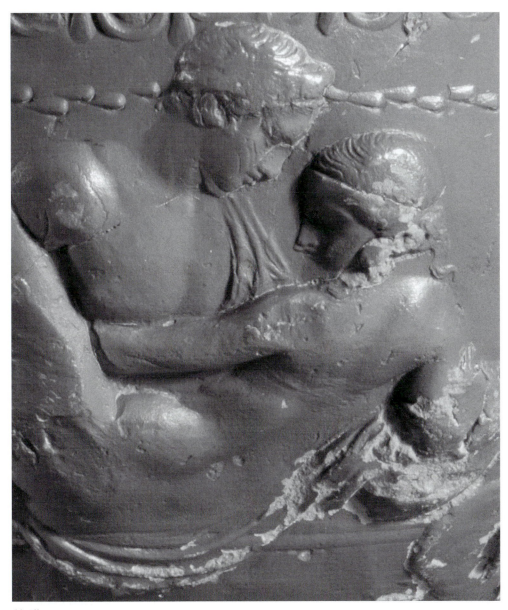

66. Īlia rumpēns

Section 6A(vii)

Furius and Aurelius, prepared to go wherever Catullus goes, take this brief message to Lesbia: let her live with her lovers and forget my love.

Fūrī et Aurēlī, comitēs Catullī,
sīue in extrēmōs penetrābit Indōs,
lītus ut longē resonante Eōā ⌐
       tunditur ⌐ undā,
sīue in Hyrcānōs Arabasue mollīs,   5
seu Sagās sagittiferōsue Parthōs,
sīue quae septemgeminus colōrat
       aequora Nīlus,
sīue trāns altās gradiētur Alpēs,
Caesaris ⌐ uīsēns monimenta ⌐ magnī,   10
Gallicum Rhēnum horribile aequor ulti-
       mōsque Britannōs,
omnia haec, quaecumque feret uoluntās
caelitum, temptāre simul parātī,
pauca nūntiāte meae puellae   15
       nōn bona dicta.
cum suīs uīuat ualeatque moechīs,
quōs ⌐ simul complexa tenet ⌐ trecentōs,
nūllum amāns uērē, sed identidem omnium
       īlia rumpēns;   20
nec meum ⌐ respectet, ut ante, ⌐ amōrem,
quī illius culpā cecidit uelut prātī
ultimī flōs, praetereunte ⌐ postquam
       tāctus ⌐ arātrō est.

(Catullus 11)

Running vocabulary for 6A(vii)

aequor aequor-is 3n. line 8 plain; line 11 sea
Alpēs Alp-ium 3f. pl. Alps
alt-us a um high
Arabs Arab-is 3m. Arab (Greek acc. pl. *Arabas*)
arātr-um ī 2n. plough
Aurēli-us ī 2m. Aurelius
Britann-ī ōrum 2m. pl. Britons
caelit-ēs um 3m. pl. gods (lit. 'dwellers in heaven')
Caesar Caesar-is 3m. (C. Julius) Caesar [see note]
colōrō 1 I dye, stain [See note]

complector 3 dep. *complexus* I embrace
culp-a ae 1f. fault (often used of sexual misconduct)
dict-um ī 2n. word
Eō-us a um Eastern, oriental
extrēm-us a um furthest
flōs flōr-is 3m. flower
Fūri-us ī 2m. Furius
Gallic-us a um Gallic, of Gaul
gradior 3/4 dep. I go
horribil-is e terrible, dreadful [see note]

Hyrcān-ī ōrum 2m. pl. the Hyrcani (a people dwelling to the south-east of the Caspian sea)
identidem again and again
īlia īl-ium 3n. pl. groin, private parts
Ind-ī ōrum 2m. pl. the Indians
moech-us ī 2m. adulterer
moll-is e soft, luxurious, effeminate
moniment-um ī 2n. testimonial
Nīl-us ī 2m. the River Nile

Parth-ī ōrum 2m. pl. the Parthians
(a people on Rome's eastern
boundaries)
penetrō 1 I make my way,
penetrate as far as
praetereō praeterīre I pass by [see
note]
prāt-um ī 2n. meadow, field
*quīcumque quaecumque
quodcumque* whoever,
whatever
resonō 1 I re-echo
respectō 1 I look for, count on

Rhēn-us ī 2m. the River Rhine
[see note]
rumpō 3 I burst
Sag-ae ārum 1m. pl. the Sacae (a
Scythian people: dwelling to
the north-east of Rome's
borders)
sagittifer sagittifer-a um
arrow-bearing
septemgemin-us a um sevenfold
(i.e. with seven mouths)
seu or (if) [= *sīue*: see note on
structure]

simul together
sīue... sīue (seu) whether... or
[see note on structure]
trāns (+ acc.) across
tundō 3 I beat, pound
ualeō 2 lit. 'I am well' [see note]
-ue (added to the end of a word) or
uērē truly
uīsō 3 I go and look at, view, visit
ultim-us a um (lines 11–12)
furthest; (line 23) the edge of
und-a ae 1f. water, wave
ut (line 3, + indic.) where

Notes

Structure: in line 1, Furius and Aurelius are addressed as friends of Catullus, and in lines 2–12, their
friendship is shown by the number of places they are prepared to go to with Catullus – whether (*sīue*)
Catullus will go to X or (*sīue/seu*) Y or (*sīue*) Z. Lines 13–14 summarise the past twelve lines, describing
Furius and Aurelius as *parātī* (ready) to do all this (*omnia haec* (13)). At 15, we find out what they
should in fact do: *nūntiāte* 'give a message' to Lesbia. Lines 17–24 describe the content of the message,
in subjunctives (*uīuat... ualeat... respectet*) – 'let her...'
line 2 *extrēmōs*: hold until solved (by *Indōs*).
lines 3–4 *lītus*: subject of the *ut* clause. Take *longē* closely with *resonante* and hold *longē resonante Eōā*
until solved (by *undā*: the function of the abl. phrase is revealed by the passive form of *tunditur*). NB
here *ut* means 'where'.
lines 7–8 *quae*: n. pl. – hold until solved (by *aequora*: 'the plains which...' obj. of *colōrat*); *colōrat*: possibly
refers to the silt left by the Nile after its annual flood.
line 9 *altās*: hold until solved (by *Alpēs*).
line 10–12 Caesar was engaged in the conquest of Gaul from 58 until 49. In 55 he crossed the Rhine and
made an expedition into Germany. In the same year came the first of his two forays across the Channel
to Britain. The words in lines 11–12 are in apposition to *monimenta*. The *horribile aequor* may refer to
the English Channel (which caused Caesar many problems). But it is a scholar's correction, not the
version preserved by the MSS.
line 17 *cum suīs*: hold until solved (by *moechīs*). *ualeat*: a 3rd person form of *ualē* 'farewell' (but see also
the basic meaning of the verb).
line 18 *trecentōs*: agreeing with *quōs* – '300 of them' (!) – held back for effect.
line 21 *meum*: hold until solved (by *amōrem*).
lines 23–4 The word-order is complex: hold *praetereunte* until solved by *arātrō* – the abl. is not absolute,
but instrumental after the passive verb *tāctus... est*. As often, *postquam*, which introduces the clause, is
postponed. The subject is *flōs*.

Learning vocabulary for 6A(vii)

Nouns
aequor aequor-is 3n. plain; sea
culp-a ae 1f. fault; blame (often
of sexual misconduct)

Adjectives
alt-us a um high; deep
extrēm-us a um furthest
*quīcumque quaecumque
quodcumque* whoever,
whatever [declines like *quī*
106 + *cumque*]

ultim-us a um furthest; last;
greatest

Verbs
gradior 3/4 dep. *gressus* I step,
walk, go (cf. compounds in
-*gredior*)
*praetereō praeterīre praeteriī
praeteritum* I pass by; neglect,
omit

ualeō 2 I am strong; am well; am
powerful; am able (cf. *ualē*
'Farewell!')

Others
simul together (at the same time)
sīue (seu)... sīue (seu)
whether... or
trāns (+ acc.) across
-*ue* (added on to the end of a
word: cf. -*ne* and -*que*) or

Section 6B 49: **Cicero, Caelius and the approach of civil war**

In 51 Cicero was sent out with proconsular power to govern Cilicia (see map p. xxi). He was going to be out of Rome during a crucial period. Soon after his consulship of 63, the men whose ambition was threatening to crush the Republic – Pompey (*Pompēius*) and Caesar notably – had combined in an uncharacteristic alliance to get a securer grip on power. In 59 Caesar, as consul, arranged a special command for himself, which gave him control of Illyricum and the province of Gaul, and from 58 to 49 he proceeded to pacify and conquer Gaul, and made a first incursion into Britain. Pompey, who had already won many victories in the East in the 60s, had these conquests ratified. In 55, he was given command of the armies in Spain. The third member of this so-called 'triumvirate', Crassus, was given a command against the Parthians, but died in battle against them at Carrhae in 53. Cicero had suffered directly from this combination of ambitious men. He had spent 58–57 in exile. He was well aware that Rome was in the grip of Pompey and Caesar. So when he left Rome to take up his position in Cilicia, he charged his protégé Marcus Caelius Rufus, whom he had successfully defended on a charge of attempting to poison Clodia, to report on developments there. This selection of letters concentrates on the developing crisis of 49, as Pompey and Caesar headed towards civil war. The question for politically active people was – with whom should they throw in their lot?

67. uolūmen

Section 6B(i)

Caelius tells Cicero of the arrangements he has made for keeping him abreast of events in Rome.

CAELIVS CICERŌNĪ S. (alūtem dīcit)
RŌMAE A.(b) V.(rbe) C.(onditā) 703 (= 51), *c.* 26 May

discēdēns pollicitus sum mē omnīs rēs urbānās dīligentissimē tibi
perscrīptūrum. data tanta opera est ut uerear nē tibi nimium argūta
haec sēdulitās uideātur; tametsī sciō tū quam sīs cūriōsus, et quam
omnibus peregrīnantibus grātum sit minimārum quoque rērum quae
domī gerantur fierī certiōrēs. tamen in hōc tē dēprecor nē meum hoc   5
officium adrogantiae condemnēs; nam hunc labōrem alterī dēlēgāuī,
nōn quīn mihi suāuissimum sit tuae memoriae operam dare, sed ipsum
uolūmen, quod tibi mīsī, facile (ut ego arbitror) mē excūsat, nesciō
cuius ōtī esset nōn modo perscrībere haec, sed omnīnō animaduertere;
omnia enim sunt ibi senātūs⌒cōnsulta, ēdicta, fābulae, rūmōrēs. quod   10
exemplum sī forte minus tē dēlectārit, nē molestiam tibi cum impēnsā
meā exhibeam, fac mē certiōrem. sī quid in rē pūblicā māius āctum
erit, quod istī operāriī minus commodē persequī possint, et
quem⌒ad⌒modum āctum sit, et quae exīstimātiō secūta quaeque dē eō
spēs sit, dīligenter tibi perscrībēmus. ut nunc est, nūlla magnopere   15
exspectātiō est.

(Ad familiārēs 8.1)

Running vocabulary for 6B(i)

adroganti-a ae 1f. conceit, presumption
animaduertō 3 I observe, take note of
argūt-us a um verbose, wordy
A.V. C. = ab urbe conditā 'from the city having been founded', 'from the city's foundation'
certior fīō I am informed (lit. 'I am made more certain')
certiōrem faciō I inform X (acc.) (lit. 'make X more certain')
commod-us a um satisfactory, convenient
condemnō 1 I condemn X (acc.) for Y (gen.)
cūriōs-us a um curious
dēlectārit = dēlectāuerit
dēlectō 1 I please

dēlēgō 1 I entrust
dēprecor 1 dep. I pray earnestly
dīligēns dīligent-is careful
ēdict-um ī 2n. edict
excūsō 1 I excuse
exhibeō 2 I cause
exīstimātiō exīstimātiōn-is 3f. view
exspectātiō exspectātiōn-is 3f. expectation
fābul-a ae 1f. story
forte by chance, perchance
impēns-a ae 1f. expense
memori-a ae 1f. remembering, memory
molesti-a ae 1f. annoyance
nimium = nimis
omnīnō altogether, completely
operāri-us ī 2m. hireling

peregrīnō 1 I am abroad, travel
perscrībō 3 *perscrīpsī perscrīptus* I write in detail
quem ad modum how
quīn 'that . . . not'
S. = salūtem dīcit 'greets' (+ dat.)
sēdulitās sēdulitāt-is 3f. zeal, earnestness
senātūs cōnsult-um ī 2n. decree of the senate
suāu-is e delightful, sweet, pleasant
tametsī however, though
uolūmen uolūmin-is 3n. volume (i.e. papyrus roll)
urbān-us a um of the city, city

Notes

line 1 *discēdēns*: Caelius had gone with Cicero as far as Pompeii, it seems.

line 3 *sciō tū: tū* belongs with *sīs*, within the *quam* clause, *quam*: solved by *grātum* (cf. *quam . . . cūriōsūs* line 3). Now await an infinitive phrase to complete *quam . . . grātum sit* (*fierī certiōrēs* line 5).

lines 8–9 *nesciō cuius ōtī esset*: 'I don't know of what leisure it would be (sc. the job)' i.e. 'I don't know what amount of spare time it would take . . .' The subjunctive is potential (see **158.2**).

line 11 *nē*: purpose clause (explained by *fac mē certiōrem*).

line 12 *sī quid . . . māius*: i.e. 'if anything more important'.

line 13 *quod . . . possint*: the subjunctive is potential (see **158.2**).

lines 14–15 *secūta*: sc. *sit*.

Learning vocabulary for 6B(i)

Nouns

fābul-a ae 1f. story; play

memori-a ae 1f. remembering, memory, recollection; record

Adjectives

commod-us a um satisfactory, convenient

suāu-is e sweet, pleasant, delightful

Verbs

animaduertō 3 *animaduertī animaduersus* I observe, take note of

condemnō 1 I condemn X (acc.) for Y (gen.)

excūsō 1 I excuse

perscrībō 3 *perscrīpsī perscrīptus* I write in detail

Phrases

certiōrem faciō I inform X (acc.)

certior fīō I am informed

salūtem dicit 'he greets' (+ dat.) (at the head of letters, abbreviated to *S.* or *S.D.*)

Others

forte by chance, perchance

omnīnō altogether, completely

quem ad modum (often written as one word) how

Securing the province

It was not only senatorial procedure that made the provincial governor resemble the provincial commander in the republican period. When Cicero was governor of Cilicia in southern Asia Minor in 51 BC, his letters to the Senate, reporting what he had achieved (Cicero, *Letters to Friends* 15.2 and 15.14) are entirely taken up with military matters, even though most of his time was spent on administration and the law courts. In other words, the primary responsibility of the governor was still seen as ensuring the military security of the area to which he had been sent. (*World of Rome*, **179**)

Section 6B(ii)

Caelius requests information about Pompey (at this time in Greece) and gives some reports on Caesar's position in Gaul, following the Gallic revolt of 52.

tū sī Pompēium, ut uolēbās, offendistī, fac mihi perscrībās quī tibi uīsus
sit, et quam ōrātiōnem habuerit tēcum, quamque ostenderit uoluntātem
(solet enim aliud sentīre et loquī). quod ad Caesarem, crēbrī et nōn
bellī dē eō rūmōrēs, sed susurrātōrēs dumtaxat ueniunt. alius dīcit   20
Caesarem equitem perdidisse (quod, ut opīnor, certē fīctum est); alius
septimam legiōnem uāpulāsse, ipsum apud Bellouacōs
circumsedērī interclūsum ab reliquō exercitū; neque adhūc certī
quicquam est, neque haec incerta tamen uulgō iactantur, sed inter
paucōs, quōs tū nōstī, palam sēcrētō nārrantur.   25

(Ad familiārēs 8.1)

Running vocabulary for 6B(ii)

adhūc up to now
Bellouac-ī ōrum 2m. pl. Bellovaci
   (a tribe living in north-west
   Gaul)
bell-us a um pretty
circumsedeō 2 I besiege, blockade
crēber crēbr-a um frequent
dumtaxat only, merely

fingō 3 *fīnxī fīctus* I make up,
   fabricate
iactō 1 I discuss
incert-us a um uncertain
interclūdō 3 *interclūdī interclūsus*
   I cut off
nōstī = nōuistī
offendō 3 *offendī* I meet
palam openly

perdō 3 *perdidī* I lose
Pompēi-us ī Cn. Pompeius
   Magnus
sēcrētō secretly
susurrātor susurrātōr-is 3m.
   whisperer, tale-bearer
uāpulō 1 I am beaten (*uāpulāsse*
   = uāpulāuisse)
uulgō generally

Notes

line 17 *fac* + subjunctive: 'make sure you...' (cf. *caue* + subj. in **6A(iii)** 18, 19).
lines 17–18 *quī... sit*: 'how he seemed to be' (old abl. of *quī*: see **14³**) i.e. 'what you thought of him'.
line 19 *aliud sentīre et loquī*: 'to think one thing and say another', *quod ad Caesarem*: 'as (lit. 'as to that
   which') regards Caesar'. The verb *attinet =* 'concerns' is omitted.
line 20 *rūmōrēs*: sc. *sunt.*
line 21 *alius*: sc. *dīcit. ipsum*: i.e. Caesar.
lines 23–4 *certī quicquam*: 'anything (of) certain'; cf. *satis* + gen. 'enough (of)' **31**.

Learning vocabulary for 6B(ii)

Adjectives
bell-us a um beautiful, pretty
crēber crēbr-a um frequent; thick,
   close
incert-us a um uncertain

Verbs
circumsedeō 2 *circumsēdī*
   circumsessus I besiege,
   blockade
fingō 3 *fīnxī fīctus* I make up,
   fabricate
iactō 1 I discuss; throw; boast;
   toss about

offendō 3 *offendī offēnsus* I meet
   with; offend
perdō 3 *perdidī perditus* I lose;
   destroy

Others
adhūc up to now
palam openly

Section 6B(iii)

Cicero rebukes Caelius for not telling him what he really wants to know about events in Rome, and reports (circumspectly) on his meeting with Pompey.

M. CICERŌ PRŌCŌS. S.D. M. CAELIŌ
Athens, 6 July 51

quid? tū mē hoc tibi mandāsse exīstimās, ut mihi perscrībēs
gladiātōrum compositiōnēs, et uadimōnia dīlāta et ea quae nōbīs, cum
Rōmae sumus, nārrāre nēmo audeat? nē ⌐ illa ⌐ quidem cūrō mihi scrībās
quae maximīs in rēbus reī pūblicae geruntur cotīdiē, nisi quid ad mē
ipsum pertinēbit; scrībent aliī, multī nūntiābunt, perferet multa etiam   30
ipse rūmor. quārē ego nec praeterita nec praesentia abs tē, sed
(ut ab homine longē in posterum prospiciente) futūra exspectō, ut, ex
tuīs litterīs cum fōrmam reī pūblicae uīderim, quāle aedificium
futūrum sit scīre possim.

cum Pompēiō complūrīs diēs nūllīs in aliīs nisi dē rē pūblicā   35
sermōnibus uersātus sum; quae nec possunt scrībī nec scrībenda sunt.
tantum habētō, cīuem ēgregium esse Pompēium, ad omnia quae
prōuidenda sunt in rē pūblicā et animō et cōnsiliō parātum. quārē dā tē
hominī; complectētur, mihi crēde, iam īdem Pompēiō et bonī et malī
cīuēs uidentur quī nōbīs uidērī solent.   40

(Ad familiārēs 2.8)

68. gladiātōrum compositiōnēs

Running vocabulary for 6B(iii)

abs = *ab*
aedifici-um ī 2n. building
complector 3 dep. I embrace
complūr-ēs a several
compositiō compositiōn-is 3f. pairing, match
cūrō 1 I want [see note]
differō differe distulī dīlātus I put off, postpone
ēgregi-us a um outstanding, excellent

gladiātor gladiātōr-is 3m. gladiator
habētō 'be sure' [see note]
M. = *Mārcus* (*Mārcō* with *Caeliō*)
mandō 1 I order X (dat.) to (*ut* + subj.)
nē... quidem not even (emphasising the word enclosed)
pertineō 2 I affect, relate to (*ad* + acc.)
poster-um ī 2n. future

praesēns praesent-is present
praeterit-us a um past (perf. part. pass. of *praetereō*)
PRŌCŌS. = *prōcōnsul*
prōcōnsul-is 3m. proconsul (i.e. governor of a province)
prōspiciō 3/4 I look forward, see ahead
quāl-is e what sort of
tantum (just) so much
uadimōni-um ī 2n. court appearance (lit. 'bail')

Notes

lines 27–8 *ea quae... audeat*: generic subjunctive (see **145.1**).
line 28 (*cūrō*)... *scrībās*: 'you to write' cf. *caue* + subj. in **6A(iii)** 18, 19 and *fac* + subj. in **6B(ii)** 17. *illa* is the object of *scrībās*.
line 32 *ut*: purpose, solved (eventually) by *scīre possim*.
line 37 *habētō*: future imperative, cf. *cauētō* in **6A(iii)**. The force may not be strongly future, since this is a common form with *habeō*. See Reference Grammar **A2 Note 1**.
lines 39–40 *īdem... quī*: 'the same people... as'.

Learning vocabulary for 6B(iii)

Adjectives	Verbs	Others
complūr-ēs a several	*complector* 3 dep. *complexus* I embrace	*nē... quidem* not even (emphasising the word enclosed)
ēgregi-us a um outstanding, excellent	*mandō* 1 I order X (dat.) to/not to Y (*ut/nē* + subj.); entrust X (acc.) to Y (dat.)	
praesēns praesent-is present		
quāl-is e what sort of		

Later in 51 Caelius was elected curule aedile, an important step on the *cursus honōrum*. One of his new duties was to stage public games. Caelius became very anxious about the animals to appear in the *uēnātiōnēs* (wild animal hunts). He was eager to increase his prestige by putting on an extravagant show. So he wrote to Cicero requesting help. He had already made several mentions of these animals in earlier letters.

The next letter was written soon after his election victory.

Section 6B(iv)

Caelius urges Cicero to supply him with wild beasts, and promises to make arrangements for their transportation.

69. uēnātiō

CAELIVS CICERŌNĪ S.
Rome, 2 September 51

ferē litterīs omnibus tibi dē panthērīs scrīpsī. turpe tibi erit Patiscum
Cūriōnī decem panthērās mīsisse, tē nōn multīs partibus plūrīs; quās
ipsās Cūriō mihi et aliās Āfricānās decem dōnāuit. tū, sī modo
memoriā tenueris et Cibyrātās arcessieris itemque in Pamphȳliam
litterās mīseris (nam ibi plūrīs panthērās capī aiunt), quod uolēs, efficiēs.   45
hoc uehementius labōrō nunc, quod seorsus ā collēgā putō mihi omnia
paranda. amābō tē, imperā tibi hoc. in hōc negōtiō nūlla tua nisi
loquendī cūra est, hoc est, imperandī et mandandī. nam,
simulatque erunt captae, habēs eōs quī alant eās et dēportent; putō
etiam, sī ūllam spem mihi litterīs ostenderis, mē istō missūrum aliōs.   50

(Ad familiārēs 8.9)

Running vocabulary for 6B(iv)

Āfricān-us a um African
aiō irr. I say
alō 3 I tend, feed
Cibyrāt-a ae from Cibyra [see map p. xxi]
collēg-a ae 1m. colleague
Cūriō Cūriōn-is 3m. C. Scribonius Curio: tribune in

50, friend and correspondent of Cicero
dēportō 1 I transport
ferē almost
istō to the place where you are
labōrō 1 I am concerned with
Pamphȳli-a ae 1f. Pamphylia [see map p. xxi]

panthēr-a ae 1f. panther
Patisc-us ī 2m. Patiscus, a Roman businessman in Asia
seorsus apart
simulatque as soon as

Notes

line 42 *multīs partibus*: 'by many parts' i.e. 'many times' (abl. of measure of difference, **100B.5**).
line 44 *Cibyrātās*: understand *panthērās*.
line 46 *collēgā*: M. Octavius was the other curule aedile with Curio.
line 47 *paranda*: understand *esse. amābō tē*: 'please' (lit. 'I shall love you'). *imperā tibi hoc*: *hoc* is direct object (in the place usually taken by *ut* + subj.). *nūlla tua*: hold until solved (by *cūra*).
line 49 *habēs eōs*: Caelius had sent some men to deal with a financial transaction in the vicinity, *quī alant... dēportent*: subjunctive, to indicate purpose (see **150.3**).
line 50 *missūrum*: sc. *esse*.

Learning vocabulary for 6B(iv)

Nouns	Verbs	Others
collēg-a ae 1m. colleague	*aiō* irr. I say *alō* 3 *aluī altus* or *alitus* I feed, nourish, rear; support; strengthen	*ferē* almost *simulatque* as soon as (also *simulac* or *simul*)

A taste of the good life

Undoubtedly the best-known feature of Roman 'daily life' is the games, *lūdī*. These took place on those special occasions, in a complicated calendar, when holidays occurred. The *lūdī*, like the 'circuses' in the satirist Juvenal's famous phrase *pānem et circēnsēs* ('bread and chariot-races'), were part of the 'pay-off' for dependence. What the élite offered the masses in *lūdī* was not simply 'entertainment' in a modern sense, or even distraction from the awfulness of precarious city life: rather it was a small and momentary taste of the world that the rich permanently enjoyed.

There was a repertoire of these 'perks' (the Latin term was *commoda*). All of them were timeless ingredients of their own aristocratic lifestyle watered down for mass consumption. Take literary, musical, cultural entertainments. Their main purpose was the amusement of the rich. Take the competitive games. The masses could share in the exciting activities of aristocrats as they fought and hunted. Take the baths. Hot water and fine oil had been the reward of a hero as far back as Homer's *Odyssey*, and the minstrels and the competitions at games belonged in a Homeric setting too (*Odyssey* 4.39–51, 8.62–130). Dependency made these features of aristocratic life briefly available to the whole Roman people.

But the reason was not altruism. It was a truly remarkable city in which the poor were able to share in some of the goodies of the rulers, and the culture of the *commoda*, through promoting dependence and advertising the wealth and felicity of the state, helped the wealthy to go on living in a self-congratulatory cocoon. (*World of Rome*, **218**)

Section 6B(v)

(The imperātor *in the title is explained by Cicero's success in a minor engagement against some mountain tribes, for which his troops hailed him by that very flattering appellation.)*

The panthers seem to have got wind of your plans for them.

M. CICERŌ IMPERĀTOR S.D. M. CAELIŌ AEDĪLĪ CVRVLĪ
Laodicea, 4 April 50

dē panthērīs per eōs, quī uēnārī solent, agitur mandātū meō dīligenter;
sed panthērārum mira paucitās est, et eās quae sunt ualdē aiunt querī,
quod nihil cuiquam īnsidiārum in meā prōuinciā nisi sibi fīat, itaque
panthērae cōnstituisse dīcuntur in Cāriam ex nostrā prōuinciā dēcēdere,
sed tamen sēdulō fit et in prīmīs ā Patiscō. quicquid erit, tibi erit; sed   55
quid esset, plānē nesciēbāmus.

tū uelim ad mē dē omnī reī pūblicae statū quam dīligentissimē
perscrībās. ea enim certissima putābō, quae ex tē cognōrō.

(Ad familiārēs 2.11)

Running vocabulary for 6B(v)

aedīlis aedīl-is 3m. aedile [see explanation at **6B(iii)**]
agitur impersonal 'it is being done' (i.e. 'things are being done')
Cāri-a ae 1f. Caria [see map p. xxi]
cognōrō = cognōuerō
curūl-is e curule

dēcēdō 3 I leave
fit: impersonal 'it is being done' (i.e. 'action is being taken')
mandāt-us ūs 4m. order
mīr-us a um amazing
panthēr-a ae 1f. panther
Patisc-us ī 2m. Patiscus (see previous letter)

paucitās paucitāt-is 3f. paucity, lack
quisquis quicquid whoever, whatever
sēdulō assiduously
stat-us ūs 4m. position
ualdē very much, strongly
uēnor 1 dep. I hunt

Notes

line 52 *ualdē*: hold – it qualifies *querī*.
line 53 *nihil cuiquam īnsidiārum*: tr. 'no (of) ambushes for anyone'.
line 56 *esset*: lit. 'was going to be'. Cicero writes as if the time of the letter were when Caelius was actually reading it. Hence *nesciēbāmus* and *esset*. Tr. 'we (= I) don't know, what it is (going to be)'.
lines 57–8 *tū uelim…perscrībās*: 'I would like you to write'; *uelim* is potential subjunctive (see **158.2**). For *perscrībās*, subjunctive without a conjunction, cf. *caue* + subj. **6A(iii)** lines 18, 19, *fac* + subj. **6B(ii)** line 17 and *cūrō* + subj. **6B(iii)** line 28.

Learning vocabulary for 6B(v)

Adjectives
mīr-us a um amazing, wonderful
quisquis quicquid whoever, whatever (declines like *quis* +

quis, but it is not found in all forms)

Others
ualdē very much, strongly

The crisis was looming larger and getting nearer. The alliance between Pompey and Caesar had been getting shakier ever since the death of Julia, Pompey's wife and Caesar's daughter, in 54, and the death of Crassus in Parthia in 53. The confrontation finally came in 50. Caesar was on the point of returning from his extended command in Gaul. In normal circumstances, he would surrender his armies and return as a private citizen. But he knew that Pompey and many senators would take advantage of this loss of *imperium*, and Caesar demanded protection in the shape of either a continuation of his *imperium* in Gaul, an unconditional offer of the consulship, or some other compromise (e.g. Pompey giving up the control over his armies as well).

70. Cn. Pompēius

Section 6B(vi)

Caelius reports that Pompey is backing a move to make Caesar relinquish his imperium *before he re-enters Italy, as the condition of taking up the consulship. He foresees war, and a difficult choice for himself and Cicero to make.*

CAELIVS CICERŌNĪ S.

Rome, *c.* 8 August 50

dē summā rē pūblicā saepe tibi scrīpsī mē in annum pācem nōn uidēre
et, quō propius ea contentiō accēdit (quam fierī necesse est), eō clārius   60
id perīculum appāret. prōpositum est hoc, dē quō eī quī rērum
potiuntur sunt dīmicātūrī. nam Gn. Pompēius cōnstituit nōn patī
C. Caesarem cōnsulem aliter fierī, nisi exercitum et prōuinciās
trādiderit; Caesarī autem persuāsum est sē saluum esse nōn posse, sī ab
exercitū recesserit. fert illam tamen condiciōnem, ut ambō exercitūs   65
trādant. sīc illī amōrēs et inuidiōsa coniūnctiō nōn ad occultam recidit
obtrectātiōnem, sed ad bellum sē ērumpit. neque quid cōnsilī capiam,
reperiō; neque dubitō quīn tē quoque haec dēlīberātiō sit perturbātūra.

in hāc discordiā uideō Gn. Pompēium senātum quīque rēs iūdicant
sēcum habitūrum, ad Caesarem omnīs accessūrōs quī cum timōre aut   70
malā spē uīuant; exercitum cōnferendum nōn esse. omnīnō satis spatī
est ad cōnsīderandās utrīusque cōpiās et ēligendam partem.

ad summam, quaeris quid putem futūrum esse. sī alter uter eōrum
ad Parthicum bellum nōn eat, uideō magnās impendēre discordiās, quās
ferrum et uīs iūdicābit; uterque et animō et cōpiīs est parātus. sī sine   75
tuō perīculō fierī posset, magnum et iūcundum tibi Fortūna
spectāculum parābat.

(Ad familiārēs 8.14)

Running vocabulary for 6B(vi)

aliter for a second time
alter uter one or the other
appāreō 2 I appear
C. = Gāium: Gāi-us ī 2m. Gaius
clār-us a um clear
condiciō condiciōn-is 3f.
    condition, term
condiciōnem ferre to propose a
    condition
cōnferō cōnferre I compare
coniūnctiō coniūnctiōn-is 3f.
    union
contentiō contentiōn-is 3f.
    struggle

dēlīberātiō dēlīberātiōn-is 3f.
    question
dīmicō 1 I fight
dubitō 1 I doubt
ēligō 3 I choose
eō [see note on line 60]
ērumpō 3 I break out (with *sē*)
Gn. (line 62) = *Gnaeus ī* 2m.
    Gnaeus; (line 69) = *Gnaeum*
impendeō 2 I impend, threaten,
    am at hand
inuidiōs-us a um odious
obtrectātiō obtrectātiōn-is 3f.
    backbiting
occult-us a um secret, covert

pars part-is 3f. side (part)
Parthic-us a um Parthian
perturbō 1 I disturb
potior 4 dep. I control (+ gen.)
prōposit-um ī 2n. question
quō (line 60) [see note]
recēdō 3 *recessī* I leave (*ab* + abl.)
recidō 3 I come to, issue in
    (*ad* + acc.)
spati-um ī 2n. time
spectācul-um ī 2n. show
summ-a ae 1f. (line 73) total; *ad*
    summam to sum up
timor timōr-is 3m. fear

Notes

line 59 *summā*: i.e. 'high politics'. *in annum*: 'in a year's time'.

line 60 *quō* (+ comp.)...*eō* (+ comp.): 'the...-er, the...-er' (lit. 'by how much the more...by so much the more'). (Watch for comparative adverbs in *-ius*.)

line 64 *Caesarī persuāsum est*: impersonal passive: lit. 'it has been persuaded to Caesar' i.e. 'Caesar has been persuaded' (see **160**).

line 65 *fert*: subject is Caesar.

line 66 *occultam*: hold until solved (by *obtrectātiōnem*).

line 67 *capiam*: the subjunctive is deliberative (indirect); see **157²**.

line 69 *quīque*: 'and those who' (i.e. senators and men of equestrian rank – rich and respectable).

line 70 *habitūrum*: understand *esse*, *accessūrōs*: understand *esse*.

lines 70–1 *quī...uīuant*: subjunctive in indirect speech, but probably generic. *exercitum...esse*: still in indirect statement after *uideō*.

lines 74–5 *sī...nōn eat*: note mood of verb – the main clause, unusually, has an indicative verb, *uideō*.

lines 75–6 *sī...posset*: see note on lines 74–5. The main verb is *parābat* – see next note for its tense.

line 77 *parābat*: Caelius writes as if the time of the letter were when Cicero was actually reading it. See previous letter; tr. 'is preparing'. This usage is known as 'epistolary tense'.

Learning vocabulary for 6B(vi)

Nouns

condiciō condiciōn-is 3f. condition, term; *condiciōnem ferre* to make terms

pars part-is 3f. side; (part)

spati-um ī 2n. space; time

timor timōr-is 3m. fear

Adjectives

clār-us a um clear (famous, well-known)

Verbs

dīmicō 1 I fight

dubitō 1 I doubt; hesitate (+ inf.)

potior 4 dep. I control (+ gen.)

Others

quō + comparative...*eō* + comparative 'the more...the more...'

Caelius was right. The senate forced the issue and demanded that Caesar surrender his armies before he enter Italy. Caesar advanced from Ravenna to Ariminum, crossing the Rubicon (the boundary of his province and Italy) and so technically beginning the war. Negotiations, in which Cicero played a part, continued, but failed. In 49 Caelius chose his destiny and went over to Caesar. He was rewarded with the next step on the *cursus honōrum*, the praetorship.

Caelius wrote the following letter to Cicero when he (Caelius) was on his way with Caesar's army to Spain, conquest of which was seen as essential to success in the war. Caelius had received a letter from Cicero indicating that Cicero was thinking of joining Pompey's side. Caelius' reply urges him to rethink and not to turn his back on Caesar.

Section 6B(vii)

CAELIVS CICERŌNĪ S.
Liguria (?), *c.* 16 April 49

exanimātus tuīs litterīs, quibus tē nihil nisi trīste cōgitāre ostendistī, hās
ad tē īlicō litterās scrīpsī.

per fortūnās tuās, Cicerō, per līberōs tē ōrō et obsecrō nē quid   80
grauius dē salūte et incolumitāte tuā cōnsulās. nam deōs hominēsque
amīcitiamque nostram testificor mē tibi praedīxisse neque temere
monuisse sed, postquam Caesarem conuēnerim sententiamque eius
quālis futūra esset partā uictōriā cognōrim, tē certiōrem fēcisse. sī
exīstimās eandem ratiōnem fore Caesaris in dīmittendīs aduersāriīs et   85
condiciōnibus ferendīs, errās. nihil nisi atrōx et saeuum cōgitat atque
etiam loquitur. īrātus senātuī exiit, hīs intercessiōnibus plānē incitātus
est; nōn meherculēs erit dēprecātiōnī locus.

sī tōtum tibi persuādēre nōn possum saltem dum quid dē Hispāniīs
agāmus scītur exspectā; quās tibi nūntiō aduentū Caesaris fore nostrās. 90
quam istī spem habeant āmissīs Hispāniīs nesciō; quod porrō tuum
cōnsilium sit ad dēspērātōs accēdere nōn medius˜fidius reperiō.

hoc quod tū nōn dīcendō mihi significāstī Caesar audierat ac, simul
atque 'hauē' mihi dīxit, statim quid dē tē audīsset exposuit. negāuī mē
scīre, sed tamen ab eō petiī ut ad tē litterās mitteret quibus maximē ad 95
remanendum commouērī possēs. mē sēcum in Hispāniam dūcit; nam
nisi ita faceret, ego, prius quam ad urbem accēderem, ubicumque essēs,
ad tē percurrissem et hoc ā tē praesēns contendissem atque omnī uī tē
retinuissem.

etiam˜atque˜etiam, Cicerō, cōgitā nē tē tuōsque omnīs funditus   100
ēuertās, nē tē sciēns prūdēnsque eō dēmittās unde exitum uidēs nūllum
esse. quod˜sī tē aut uōcēs optimātium commouent aut nōn˜nūllōrum
hominum īnsolentiam et iactātiōnem ferre nōn potes, ēligās cēnseō
aliquod oppidum uacuum ā bellō dum haec dēcernuntur; quae iam
erunt cōnfecta. id sī fēceris, et ego tē sapienter fēcisse iūdicābō et   105
Caesarem nōn offendēs.

(Ad familiārēs 8.16)

Running vocabulary for 6B(vii)

aduent-us ūs 4m. arrival
aduersāri-us ī 2m. enemy
amīciti-a ae 1f. friendship
atrōx atrōc-is fierce, unyielding
cēnseō 2 I propose; think [see note]
cognōrim = cognōuerim
cōnsulō 3 I take measures
contendō 3 contendī I strive for
dēcernō 3 I decide
dēmittō 3 I let fall, cast down
dēprecātiō dēprecātiōn-is 3f. asking for pardon
dēspērāt-us a um hopeless
ēligō 3 I choose
errō 1 I am wrong
etiam atque etiam again and again
ēuertō 3 I upset, overturn
exanimāt-us a um upset

exit-us ūs 4m. way out
expōnō 3 exposuī I relate
funditus utterly
hauē greetings, hello
Hispāni-a ae 1f. Spain (there were two provinces)
iactātiō iactātiōn-is 3f. vanity
īlicō at once
incitō 1 I rouse
incolumitās incolumitāt-is 3f. safety
īnsolenti-a ae 1f. insolence
intercessiō intercessiōn-is 3f. veto
medius fidius I call heaven to witness; so help me God
meherculēs by Hercules
nōn nūll-ī ae a some
optimātēs optimāt-ium 3m. pl. optimates

pariō 3/4 peperī partus I obtain
partā see pariō
percurrō 3 percurrī I run along
praedīcō 3 praedīxī I foretell, tell in advance
prūdēns prūdent-is foreseeing
quod sī but if
remaneō 2 I remain
saltem at least
sapienter wisely
scītur: impersonal passive 'it is known'
significō 1 I make clear to
temere casually, thoughtlessly
testificor 1 dep. I call to witness
tōtum (adv.) completely
uacu-us a um free (from) (ā + abl.)
ubicumque wherever

Notes

line 79 scrīpsī: epistolary perfect 'I am writing'.
line 81 grauius: tr. 'too serious'.
lines 83–4 conuēnerim... cognōrim: subjunctives in a subordinate clause in indirect speech.
line 87 hīs intercessiōnibus: vetoes moved by the tribune L. Metellus to obstruct Caesar.
lines 89–90 quid... agāmus: i.e. whether we win there or not.
line 91 istī: i.e. Pompey's supporters ('those people of yours').
line 101 eō... unde: 'to that point... from where'.
line 102 optimātium: the supporters of the senate.
line 103 ēligās cēnseō: 'I propose that you should...' For subjunctive without conjunction, cf. **6A(iii)** lines 18, 19 (cauē), **6B(ii)** line 17 (fac), **6B(iii)** line 28 (cūrō) and **6B(v)** lines 57–8 (uelim).

Learning vocabulary for 6B(vii)

Nouns
amīciti-a ae 1f. friendship

Adjectives
atrōx atrōc-is fierce, unyielding
nōn nūll-ī ae a some (lit. 'not none' – often written as one word)

uacu-us a um empty; free (from) (+ abl. or ā + abl.)

Verbs
errō 1 I am wrong; wander
pariō 3/4 peperī partus I bring forth, bear, produce; obtain, acquire

Others
etiam atque etiam again and again
quod sī but if
saltem at least
ubicumque wherever

It is probably true that, despite all, Cicero still had hopes of mediating in the dispute between Pompey and Caesar, so in his reply Cicero concentrates on his refusal to get involved in the civil war. We know that, after a letter from Caesar, he had thought seriously about leaving Italy for Malta, thus making reconciliation with Caesar a distinct possibility. But we do not know whether the following letter to Caelius represents the wavering of a pragmatist, or the concern of a responsible citizen for peace, even at the cost of his own future.

Section 6B(viii)

M. CICERŌ IMP. S.D. M. CAELIŌ
Cumae, 2 or 3 May 49

uelim tū crēdās hoc, mē ex hīs miseriīs nihil aliud quaerere nisi ut
hominēs aliquandō intellegant mē nihil māluisse quam pācem, eā
dēspērātā nihil tam fūgisse quam arma cīuīlia. huius mē cōnstantiae
putō fore ut numquam paeniteat. etenim meminī in hōc genere glōriārī
solitum esse familiārem nostrum Q. Hortēnsium, quod numquam bellō   110
cīuīlī interfuisset. hōc nostra laus erit illūstrior quod illī tribuēbātur
ignāuiae, dē nōbīs id exīstimārī posse nōn arbitror.

nec mē ista terrent quae mihi ā tē ad timōrem fīdissimē atque
amantissimē prōpōnuntur. nūlla est enim acerbitās quae nōn omnibus
hāc orbis terrārum perturbātiōne impendēre uideātur. quam quidem   115
ego ā rē pūblicā meīs prīuātīs et domesticīs incommodīs libentissimē
redēmissem.

itaque neque ego hunc Hispāniēnsem cāsum exspectō neque
quicquam astūtē cōgitō. sī quandō erit cīuitās, erit profectō nōbīs locus;
sīn autem nōn erit, in eāsdem solitūdinēs tū ipse, ut arbitror, ueniēs in   120
quibus nōs cōnsēdisse audiēs. sed ego fortasse uāticinor et haec omnia
meliōrēs habēbunt exitūs. recordor enim dēspērātiōnēs eōrum quī senēs
erant adulēscente mē. eōs ego fortasse nunc imitor et ūtor aetātis uitiō.
uelim ita sit; sed tamen.

extrēmum illud erit: nōs nihil turbulenter, nihil temere faciēmus. tē   125
tamen ōrāmus, quibuscumque erimus in terrīs, ut nōs līberōsque
nostrōs ita tueāre ut amīcitia nostra et tua fidēs postulābit.

(Ad familiārēs 2.16)

Running vocabulary for 6B(viii)

acerbitās acerbitāt-is 3f. anguish,
     affliction, bitterness
adulēscēns adulēscent-is 3m.
     youth
aliquandō at some time
astūtē craftily, cunningly
cās-us ūs 4m. outcome
cīuīl-is e civil [see note]
cōnstanti-a ae 1f. constancy,
     steadfastness
dēspērātiō dēspērātiōn-is 3f.
     hopelessness, despair

dēspērō 1 I lose hope of
domestic-us a um domestic,
     personal
etenim for; and indeed
exit-us ūs 4m. outcome
extrēm-us a um final, last (i.e.
     word)
familiāris familiār-is 3m. friend
fidēs fidē-ī 5f. loyalty, honour
fīd-us a um faithful, loyal
fortasse perhaps
glōrior 1 dep. I boast

Hispāniēns-is e Spanish, in Spain
Hortēnsi-us ī 2m. Q. Hortensius
     Hortalus, consul in 69; Rome's
     leading forensic orator before
     Cicero; they were not always
     on the best of terms
illūstr-is e famous, renowned
imitor 1 dep. I imitate
impendeō 2 I threaten (+ dat.)
incommod-um ī 2n.
     inconvenience, misfortune

intersum interesse interfuī I take
part in (+ dat.) [see note]
laus laud-is 3f. praise
libentissimē very gladly
miseri-a ae 1f. misery
orbis terr-ārum orb-is terrārum
3m. the world (lit. 'the circle
of the lands')
perturbātiō perturbātiōn-is 3f.
disturbance

prīuat-us a um private
profectō undoubtedly, assuredly
Q. = Quīntum: Quīnt-us ī 2m.
Quintus
quandō (line 119) at any time
quidem indeed
redimō 3 *redēmī* I buy off X (acc.)
from Y (*ā* + abl.)
sīn but if

solitūdō solitūdin-is 3f. deserted
place
temere rashly, thoughtlessly
terreō 2 I make afraid, frighten
tribuō 3 I put down [see note]
tueor 2 dep. I look after, stand by
turbulenter violently, seditiously
uāticinor 1 dep. I prophesy; rave,
talk wildly
uiti-um ī 2n. defect, fault

Notes

line 106 *uelim* + subj: 'I would like (you to…)'. See line 124 (and cf. **6A(iii)** lines 18, 19 (*caué*), **6B(ii)**
line 17 (*fac*), **6B(iii)** line 28 (*cūrō*), **6B(v)** lines 57–8 (*uelim*), **6B(vii)** line 103 (*cénseō*).
line 108 *tam…quam*: 'so much…as' (see **179.2**). *arma cīuīlia = bellum cīuīle* (lines 110–11). *huius mē*
cōnstantiae: huius…cōnstantiae gen. and *mē* acc. with *paeniteat* '(of) this…I…regret'.
line 111 *interfuisset*: subjunctive in a subordinate clause in indirect speech (see **147**). *hōc…quod*: 'in this
respect…that', *illī*: 'in his case'. *tribuēbātur*: impersonal – the subject is 'Hortensius' refusal to take part
in the Civil War'.
line 113 *ad timōrem*: i.e. 'to make me afraid'.
lines 114–15 *omnibus*: dat. – hold until solved (by *impendēre*).
line 115 *hāc…perturbātiōne*: locative–temporal abl. *uideātur*: generic subjunctive (see **145.1**). *quam*: i.e.
acerbitātem.
line 116 *meīs prīuātīs et domesticīs incommodīs*:… 'at the cost of…' abl. of price. Cf. *talentō*, **6A(ii)** line 7.
line 124 *uelim* + subj: 'I would like (it to)'. See line 106 and note.
line 126 *quibuscumque*: hold until solved (by *in terrīs*).

Learning vocabulary for 6B(viii)

Nouns
adulēscēns adulēscent-is 3m.
youth
cās-us ūs 4m. outcome; event,
occurrence; disaster, death;
cāsū by accident, by chance
fidēs fidē-ī 5f. loyalty, honour;
trust, faith; promise;
protection

Adjectives
fīd-us a um faithful, loyal

Verbs
imitor 1 dep. I imitate
terreō 2 I frighten
tueor 2 dep. *tuitus* or *tūtus* I look
after, protect; look at

Others
aliquandō at some time
fortasse perhaps
quidem indeed (places emphasis
on the preceding word)
sīn but if

In June 48, two months before the battle of Pharsalus at which Pompey was
defeated, Cicero was in Pompey's camp. Even then he was an uncomfortable
supporter. His sharp tongue constantly rebuked Pompey, and Pompey is said
to have remarked 'I wish Cicero would go over to the enemy: then he might
fear us !'

Meanwhile Caelius was having some misgivings about being on Caesar's side.
In the same year, as *praetor*, he tried to move an abolition of debts (he was
himself heavily in debt), but this was unsuccessful and he was forced from office.
He joined a rebellion against Caesar and was soon after killed at Thurii.

Section 6C: **The end of the civil war: the battle of Pharsalus**

Pompey had long been diffident of his chances in a pitched battle against Caesar. This diffidence had caused him to abandon Italy in the face of Caesar's advance in 49 and make for Greece. In 48 Caesar finally caught up with him in Thessaly and, rather surprisingly, Pompey offered battle.

These extracts are from Caesar's own account of the battle taken from his Dē bellō cīuīlī. *You should pay careful attention to the 'colouring' Caesar gives his account.*

Section 6C(i)

Caesar encourages his troops immediately before the battle, reminding them of his constant search for peace. A trooper, Crastinus, sets an example for the others to follow. (See map on p. 252.)

exercitum cum mīlitārī mōre ad pugnam cohortārētur, in prīmīs
commemorāuit testibus sē mīlitibus ūtī posse, quantō studiō pācem
petīsset; neque sē umquam abūtī mīlitum sanguine neque rem
pūblicam alterutrō exercitū prīuāre uoluisse. hāc habitā ōrātiōne,
exposcentibus mīlitibus et studiō pugnandī ārdentibus, tubā signum   5
dedit.

erat Crāstinus ēuocātus in exercitū Caesaris, uir singulārī uirtūte. hic,
signō dato, 'sequiminī mē', inquit, 'et uestrō imperātōrī quam
cōnstituistis operam date. ūnum hoc proelium superest; quō cōnfectō,
et ille suam dignitātem et nōs nostram lībertātem reciperābimus.' simul,   10
respiciēns Caesarem, 'faciam' inquit 'hodiē, imperātor, ut aut uīuō
mihi aut mortuō grātiās agās'. haec cum dīxisset, prīmus ex dextrō
cornū prōcucurrit, multīs mīlitibus sequentibus.

(*Dē bellō cīuīlī* 3.90–1)

Running vocabulary for 6C(i)

abūtor 3 I misuse (+ abl.)
alteruter alterutr-a um one or the
　　other (declines like *alter*)
ārdeō 2 I burn (intrans.)
commemorō 1 I mention, recall
Crāstin-us ī 2m. Crastinus
exposcō 3 I entreat
ēuocāt-us ī 2m. recalled veteran

faciō ut (+ subj.) I bring it about
　　that (line 11)
prīuō 1 I deprive X (acc.) of Y
　　(abl.)
prōcurrō 3 *prōcucurrī* I run
　　forward, advance
reciperō 1 I regain, recover

respiciō 3/4 I turn my gaze upon,
　　look round at
singulār-is e outstanding,
　　remarkable
supersum superesse I am left,
　　remain
tub-a ae 1f. trumpet

Notes

line 1 Caesar is subject throughout the first paragraph.
line 2 *testibus*: 'as witnesses' (predicative with *mīlitibus*).
lines 8–9 *quam . . .*: hold until picked up (by *operam*).
lines 11–12 *uīuō mihi aut mortuō*: solved by *grātiās agās*.

Learning vocabulary for 6C(i)

Verbs
ārdeō 2 *ārsī ārsum* I burn; am in love

faciō 3/4 *ut* + subj. I bring it about that . . . (cf. *efficiō/perficiō ut*)
prōcurrō 3 *prōcucurrī prōcursum* I run forward, advance

respiciō 3/4 *respexī respectus* I look round (back) at, turn my gaze upon; reflect upon; care for

71. Caesar

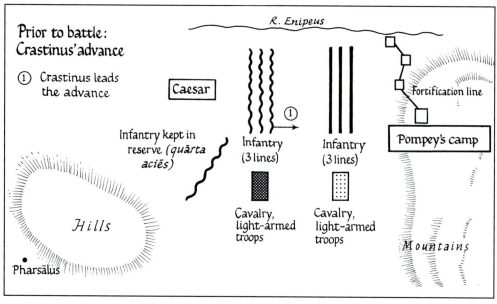

Prior to battle: Crastinus' advance

① Crastinus leads the advance

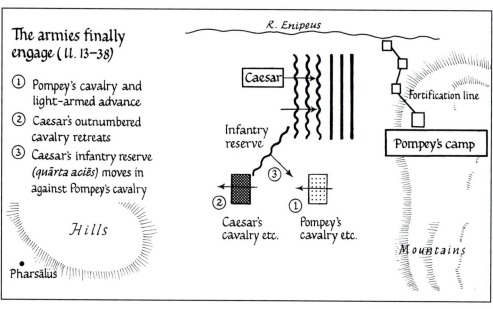

The armies finally engage (ll. 13–38)

① Pompey's cavalry and light-armed advance

② Caesar's outnumbered cavalry retreats

③ Caesar's infantry reserve (*quārta aciēs*) moves in against Pompey's cavalry

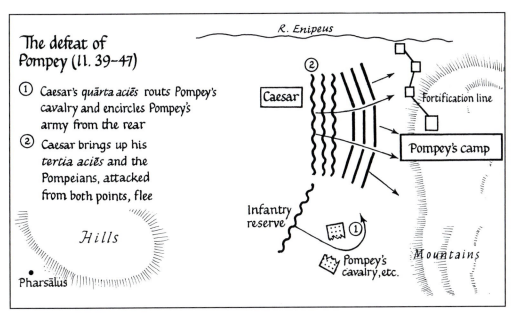

The defeat of
Pompey (ll. 39–47)

① Caesar's *quārta aciēs* routs Pompey's
cavalry and encircles Pompey's
army from the rear

② Caesar brings up his
tertia aciēs and the
Pompeians, attacked
from both points, flee

Hills

Pharsālus

R. Enipeus

Caesar

Fortification line

Pompey's camp

Infantry
reserve

Pompey's
cavalry, etc.

Mountains

72. The battle of Pharsālus 48 BC

Section 6C(ii)

Caesar's troops advance, but Pompey's hold their ground. Their aim is to exhaust Caesar's troops, but Caesar's men are too experienced to fall into that trap. Battle is joined. When Pompey's cavalry look like causing trouble, Caesar's fourth line is brought into action; the third line completes the rout.

inter duās aciēs tantum erat relictum spatī ut satis esset ad concursum
utrīusque exercitūs. sed Pompēius suīs praedīxerat ut Caesaris   15
impetum exciperent nēue sē locō mouērent aciemque eius distrahī
paterentur; ita enim spērābat fore ut prīmus excursus uīsque mīlitum
īnfringerētur, aciēsque distenderētur; simul fore ut, duplicātō cursū,
Caesaris mīlitēs exanimārentur et lassitūdine cōnficerentur. hoc, ut
nōbīs uidēbātur, nūllā ratiōne factum est. nam est quaedam animī   20
incitātiō atque alacritās, nātūrāliter innāta omnibus, quae studiō
pugnandī incenditur. hanc nōn reprimere sed augēre imperātōrēs
dēbent.

sed nostrī mīlitēs signō datō cum īnfestīs pīlīs prōcucurrissent atque
animum͞aduertissent nōn concurrī ā Pompēiānīs, ūsū perītī ac   25
superiōribus pugnīs exercitātī suā sponte cursum repressērunt et ad
medium ferē spatium cōnstitērunt, nē cōnsūmptīs uīribus
appropinquārent, paruōque intermissō temporis spatiō ac rūrsus
renouātō cursū pīla mīsērunt celeriterque, ut erat praeceptum ā
Caesare, gladiōs strīnxērunt. neque uērō Pompēiānī huic reī dēfuērunt.   30
nam et tēla missa excēpērunt et impetum legiōnum tulērunt et ōrdinēs
cōnseruārunt pīlīsque missīs ad gladiōs rediērunt. eōdem tempore
equitēs ab sinistrō Pompēī cornū, ut erat imperātum, ūniuersī
prōcucurrērunt, omnisque multitūdō sagittāriōrum sē profūdit. quōrum
impetum noster equitātus nōn tulit sed paulātim locō mōtus cessit,   35
equitēsque Pompēī hōc ācrius īnstāre et sē turmātim explicāre aciemque
nostram ā latere apertō circumīre coepērunt. quod ubi Caesar animum͞,
aduertit quārtae aciēī dedit signum.

illae celeriter prōcucurrērunt īnfestīsque signīs tantā uī in Pompēī
equitēs impetum fēcērunt ut eōrum nēmō cōnsisteret omnēsque   40
conuersī nōn sōlum locō excēderent, sed prōtinus incitātī fugā montīs
altissimōs peterent. quibus summōtīs omnēs sagittāriī funditōrēsque
dēstitūtī inermēs sine praesidiō interfectī sunt. eōdem impetū cohortēs
sinistrum cornū, Pompēiānīs etiam tum in aciē pugnantibus et
resistentibus, circumiērunt eōsque ā tergō adortī sunt. eōdem tempore   45
tertiam aciem Caesar prōcurrere iussit; quōrum impetum sustinēre
Pompēiānī nōn potuērunt atque ūniuersī terga uertērunt.

(*Dē bellō cīuīlī* 3.92–4)

Running vocabulary for 6C(ii)

adorior 4 dep. *adortus* I attack
alacritās alacritāt-is 3f.
    enthusiasm, liveliness
animum aduertō = animaduertō
appropinquō 1 I approach
concurs-us ūs 4m. attack,
    engagement
cōnficiō 3/4 *cōnfēcī cōnfectus*
    I weaken
cōnsistō 3 *cōnstitī* I stop, stand
    my ground
cōnsūmō 3 *cōnsūmpsī cōnsūmptus*
    I use up
conuertor 3 dep. *conuersus* I turn
    round
curs-us ūs 4m. distance to run;
    running
dēstituō 3 *dēstituī dēstitūtus*
    I leave, abandon
distrahō 3 I pull apart
distendō 3 I stretch out
duplicō 1 I double
equitāt-us ūs 4m. cavalry
exanimō 1 I deprive of breath,
    exhaust

excēdō 3 I depart, leave (+ abl. of
    separation 'from')
excipiō 3/4 *excēpī* I sustain,
    receive
excurs-us ūs 4m. attack
exercitō 1 I train
explicō 1 I unfold; *mē explicō*
    I deploy
funditor funditōr-is 3m. slinger
incitātiō incitātiōn-is 3f. energy
incitō 1 I set in motion; (passive)
    I rush
inerm-is e unarmed
īnfest-us a um hostile (with
    pīlum = 'at the ready'; with
    signa = 'indicating attack')
īnfringō 3 I break
innāt-us a um innate in X (dat.)
intermittō 3 *intermīsī intermissus*
    I leave, let pass
lassitūdō lassitūdin-is 3f.
    weariness
mittō 3 *mīsī missus* I throw
nātūrāliter by nature, naturally
perīt-us a um skilled

Pompēiān-ī ōrum 2m. pl. the
    followers of Pompey
praedīcō 3 *praedīxī* I tell X (dat.)
    beforehand
profundō 3 *profūdī* I pour out; *sē
    profundere* to pour forth
prōtinus at once
renouō 1 I renew, start again
reprimō 3 *repressī* I hold back,
    check
rūrsus again
sagittāri-us ī 2m. archer
sponte of one's own accord; *suā
    sponte* of their own accord
stringō 3 *strīnxī* I draw
summoueō 2 *summōuī summōtus*
    I dislodge
superior superiōr-is earlier
sustineō 2 I withstand
terg-um ī 2n. back
turmātim in squadrons
uertō 3 *uertī* I turn (trans.)
ūniuers-us a um all together
ūs-us ūs 4m. experience

Notes

line 14 *tantum* governs *spatī*.
line 24 *cum*: 'when' (not governing *īnfestīs pīlis*).
line 25 *nōn concurrī ā*: impersonal passive (indirect speech) – 'that it was not being rushed together by…'
    i.e. 'that…were not making a charge' (see **160²**).
line 30 *neque… dēfuērunt*: i.e. they were equal to the situation.
line 36 *hōc*: 'at this', 'because of this' (abl.).
line 37 *ā latere apertō*: i.e. from the left (the sword was in the right hand).

Learning vocabulary for 6C(ii)

Nouns
curs-us ūs 4m. running; course;
    direction; voyage
equitāt-us ūs 4m. cavalry
terg-um ī 2n. back

Adjectives
inerm-is e unarmed
īnfest-us a um hostile; at the
    ready; indicating attack

ūniuers-us a um all together,
    whole, entire

Verbs
adorior 4 dep. *adortus* I attack,
    rise up against
animum aduertō = animaduertō
appropinquō 1 I approach (+ dat.)
cōnsistō 3 *cōnstitī* – I stop, stand
    my ground

excēdō 3 *excessī excessum*
    I depart, go out; surpass
excipiō 3/4 *excēpī exceptus*
    I sustain, receive, welcome;
    catch; make an exception of
mittō 3 *mīsī missus* I throw; (send)
reprimō 3 *repressī repressus*
    I hold back, check
sustineō 2 *sustinuī sustentus*
    I withstand; support
uertō 3 *uertī uersus* I turn (trans.)

73. equitātus

The influence of Greek art

The influx of Greek art-works promoted a fashion for them: people did not merely want to look at them in temples and public places, they wanted to acquire them for their houses and villas. But while generals and provincial governors could get statues, silver plate, paintings and so forth by plunder, others had to buy them on the art-market. Greek artists were not slow to appreciate the advantages of the situation; they rapidly adapted to producing works for sale to Roman collectors. Among the most successful were the so-called Neo-Attic workshops which emerged in Athens and elsewhere during the second century BC to create a nice line in up-market garden furniture decorated with conventional reliefs of Greek mythological subjects broadly based on models of the fifth and fourth centuries, and even battle: note the Roman soldier on the far left, above. (*World of Rome*, **462**)

Pompey saw that his cavalry were routed and that the part of his forces in which he had placed his greatest confidence was in panic, and mistrusting the rest of his army, he left the field and rode straight to his camp. There he shouted, in a voice loud enough for all the troops to hear, 'Keep an eye on the camp, and if anything goes wrong see to its defence. I am going round to the other gates to encourage the garrison.' Having said this he retired to his headquarters to await the outcome, but with little hope of success.

The retreating Pompeians were driven back inside the rampart and Caesar, thinking that they should be given no respite in their panic, urged his men to take advantage of their good luck and storm the camp. They were exhausted by the great heat (for the action had been prolonged till midday), but were ready for anything and obeyed his orders. The camp was being vigorously defended by the cohorts left to guard it, and even more fiercely by the Thracian and barbarian auxiliaries. For the troops who had retreated from the battlefield were terrified and exhausted, and most of them threw away their arms and military standards, with their minds on further flight rather than the defence of the camp. Those who had taken up their positions on the rampart were unable to hold out against the shower of javelins and the exhaustion from the wounds they inflicted, and left their position; and led by their centurions and tribunes they fled straight to the shelter of the heights of the hills that adjoined the camp.

In Pompey's camp one could see shelters newly built, a great weight of silver plate displayed, and quarters laid out with freshly cut turf, those of Lucius Lentulus and some others being covered with ivy. There were many other indications too of excessive luxury and confidence in victory, which prompted the thought that they were sure enough of the outcome to provide themselves with unnecessary comforts. Yet they had continually taunted Caesar's unhappy and long-suffering army with luxury, though it was always short even of bare necessities. When our men were already circulating inside the rampart Pompey secured a horse, tore off his general's insignia, rode precipitately out of the rear gate and spurred at speed straight to Larisa. Nor did he stop there, but with a few of his men whom he had picked up in flight rode on through the night in the same haste, and finally reached the sea with about thirty cavalrymen. There he embarked on a grain-ship, often complaining, it is said, of the misjudgement which had led him to be betrayed by the part of the force which he had hoped would bring him victory but had in fact started the rout.

(*Dē bellō cīuīlī* 3.94–6)

Section 6C(iii)

Since the hilltops had no water, Pompey's men moved on. Caesar, splitting up his forces, pursued, and surrounded the hill and cut off the water supply where the Pompeians had taken up position. The Pompeians prepared to surrender.

Caesar castrīs potītus ā mīlitibus contendit nē in praedā occupātī
reliquī negōtī gerendī facultātem dīmitterent. quā rē impetrātā montem
opere circummūnīre īnstituit. Pompēiānī, quod is mōns erat sine aquā,   50
diffīsī eī locō relictō monte ūniuersī iugīs eius Lārīsam uersus sē
recipere coepērunt. quā spē animaduersā Caesar cōpiās suās dīuīsit
partemque legiōnum in castrīs Pompēī remanēre iussit, partem in sua
castra remīsit, quattuor sēcum legiōnēs dūxit commodiōreque itinere
Pompēiānīs occurrere coepit et prōgressus mīlia passuum sex aciem   55
īnstruxit. quā rē animaduersā Pompēiānī in quōdam monte
cōnstitērunt. hunc montem flūmen subluēbat. Caesar mīlitēs cohortātus,
etsī tōtīus diēī continentī labōre erant cōnfectī noxque iam suberat,
tamen mūnitiōne flūmen ā monte sēclūsit, nē noctū aquārī Pompēiānī
possent. quō perfectō opere illī dē dēditiōne missīs lēgātīs agere   60
coepērunt. paucī ōrdinis senātōriī, quī sē cum hīs coniūnxerant, nocte
fugā salūtem petīuērunt.

(Dē bellō cīuīlī 3.97)

Running vocabulary for 6C(iii)

agō 3 (*dē* + abl.) I discuss
aquor 1 dep. I fetch water
circummūniō 4 I fortify, enclose
    (by a wall)
cōnficiō 3/4 *cōnfēcī cōnfectus*
    I weaken
coniungō 3 *coniūnxī* I join
    (trans.); *mē coniungō* (+ dat.)
    I join X
contendō 3 *contendī* I demand of
    X (*ā* + abl.) that Y (*ut* + subj.)
continēns continent-is continual
dēditiō dēditiōn-is 3f. surrender
diffīdō 3 semi-dep. *diffīsus* I
    distrust (+ dat.)
dīuidō 3 *dīuīsī* I divide
etsī although, even though

facultās facultāt-is 3f. opportunity
impetrō 1 I obtain by request
īnstituō 3 *īnstituī* I begin
iug-um ī 2n. ridge
Lārīs-a ae 1f. Larisa
mūnitiō mūnitiōn-is 3f.
    fortification
noctū by night
occupāt-us a um busy with X (*in*
    + abl.)
occurrō 3 I intercept (+ dat.)
opus oper-is 3n. earthwork,
    fortification
pass-us ūs 4m. pace, step; *mīlle*
    passūs = 1 Roman mile (pl.
    mīlia passuum)

Pompēiān-ī ōrum 2m. pl. the
    followers of Pompey
potior 4 dep. I gain control of
    (+ abl.)
recipiō 3/4: *mē recipiō* I retreat
remaneō 2 I remain
remittō 3 *remīsī* I send back
sēclūdō 3 *sēclūsī* I cut off X (acc.)
    from Y (*ā* + abl.)
senātōri-us a um senatorial
subluō 3 I flow at the foot of
subsum subesse I am close at hand
uersus (placed after an acc.) in the
    direction of

Note

line 51 *iugīs*: 'on . . .', 'by means of . . .'

Learning vocabulary for 6C(iii)

Nouns

opus oper-is 3n. fortification; (job, work, task)

Verbs

agō 3 *ēgī āctus* I discuss (*dē +* *abl.*); (do, act; drive, lead; spend, pass; direct)

cōnficiō 3/4 *cōnfēcī cōnfectus* I weaken; (finish)

diffīdō 3 semi-dep. *diffīsus* I distrust (+ dat.)

impetrō 1 I obtain by request

īnstituō 3 *īnstituī īnstitūtus* I begin; construct; resolve

potior 4 dep. I gain control of (+ abl.); (control (+ abl.))

recipiō 3/4: *mē recipiō* I retreat; (welcome, receive, take in)

remaneō 2 *remānsī remānsum* I remain

remittō 3 *remīsī remissus* I send back; remit

Others

etsī although, even though, even if

noctū by night

After Pharsalus

For much of the next three years Caesar was engaged in facing and defeating his opponents in many parts of the Roman world. During this time he had himself appointed to several consulships and also to the post of dictator, culminating in 44 BC with his appointment as perpetual dictator (*dictātor perpetuus*).

The period also saw an unprecedented legislative activity. Caesar sponsored nearly forty pieces of legislation which tackled all the problems which had bedevilled the previous era: debt, the corn supply, land settlements, government of the provinces, corruption at home, a revision of the calendar. There were grandiose building schemes, large-scale civil engineering projects, grants of citizenship to some provincials, and gifts to all sorts and conditions of men. In this way he 'bound himself to many men' (Cicero, *Letters to Friends* 9.17.2). In return he was himself piled high with honours, many of them unprecedented in Rome but familiar from the Hellenistic world, some befitting the gods.

Julius Caesar should be counted the first Roman emperor. In practice the world treated him as a monarch, though he rejected in public the title of 'king'. He was well aware of the resentment such behaviour might arouse among the aristocracy. He deliberately sought to avoid the harshness which Sulla had shown to his defeated opponents. 'Let this be a new way of conquering, to make mildness (*misericordia*) and generosity (*līberālitās*) our shield' (Caesar in Cicero, *Letters to Atticus* 9.7C.1). This was the show of clemency (*clementia*) for which Caesar became famed. But this was a double-edged virtue. To forgive was the prerogative of the king or tyrant. Roman nobles resented the idea that their careers depended on any other person's whim.

There were those who were not prepared to accept Caesar's gesture. The Younger Cato, hunted down in Africa in 46 BC, chose suicide rather than accept Caesar's forgiveness, and in so doing established a model of behaviour, empty gesture though it was, for some in future generations who could not bring themselves to live quietly under a monarchy. There was of course another way of opposing Caesar. On 15 March (the Ides in the Roman calendar) 44 BC Caesar was assassinated at a meeting of the Senate by members of a large conspiracy, which included many who had benefited from his favour. (*World of Rome*, **73**)

Section 6C(iv)

Caesar accepts the Pompeians' surrender, assures them of his leniency, enjoins his soldiers to treat them well and moves on.

Caesar prīmā lūce omnīs eōs quī in monte cōnsēderant ex
superiōribus locīs in plānitiem dēscendere atque arma prōicere iussit.
quod ubi sine recūsātiōne fēcērunt passīsque palmīs prōiectī ad terram   65
flentēs ab eō salūtem petīuērunt, cōnsōlātus cōnsurgere iussit et pauca
apud eōs dē lēnitāte suā locūtus, quō minōre essent timōre, omnīs
cōnseruāuit mīlitibusque suīs commendāuit, nē quī eōrum uiolārentur
neu quid suī dēsīderārent. hāc adhibitā dīligentiā ex castrīs sibi legiōnēs
aliās occurrere et eās quās sēcum dūxerat inuicem requiēscere atque in   70
castra reuertī iussit eōdemque diē Lārīsam peruēnit.

(Dē bellō cīuīlī 3.98)

Running vocabulary for 6C(iv)

adhibeō 2 I show, use
commendō 1 I charge X (dat.)
    that Y should not happen
    (*nē* + subj.)
cōnsōlor 1 dep. I reassure
cōnsurgō 3 I get up
dēscendō 3 I descend
dēsīderō 1 I lose, find missing
fleō 2 I weep

inuicem in turn
Lārīs-a ae 1f. Larisa
lēnitās lēnitāt-is 3f. clemency
neu = nēue ('and that . . . not')
occurrō 3 I come to meet (+ dat.)
palm-a ae 1f. palm, hand
pandō 3 *pandī passus* I spread out
    (trans.)
plānitiēs plānitiē-ī 5f. plain

prōiciō 3/4 *prōiēcī prōiectus*
    I throw down
recūsātiō recūsātiōn-is 3f.
    objection, refusal
requiēscō 3 I rest
reuertor 3 dep. I return
superior superiōr-is higher
uiolō 1 I maltreat

Notes

line 63 *prīmā lūce*: i.e. at dawn.
line 66 *cōnsōlātus*: the subject is Caesar.
line 67 *quō minōre essent timōre*: purpose clause (see **155**). For the abl., cf. *bonō animō esse*.
line 68 *nē quī*: 'that none . . .'
line 69 *quid suī*: 'anything of his own (i.e. possessions)'.
lines 70–1 The infinitives are solved by *iussit.*

Learning vocabulary for 6C(iv)

Adjectives
superior super-ius (gen.
    superiōr-is) higher; earlier

Verbs
dēscendō 3 *dēscendī dēscēnsum*
    I descend
fleō 2 *flēuī flētum* I weep
occurrō 3 *occurrī occursum* I run
    to meet, meet; attack (+ dat.)

prōiciō 3/4 *prōiēcī prōiectus*
    I throw down
reuertor 3 dep. *reuersus* I return

Others
neu = nēue and that . . . not

Pompey had fled, but found few places willing to take him in. Eventually he arrived in Egypt, where the young King Ptolemy was waging war on his sister Cleopatra. He made approaches to Ptolemy, and then:

When the friends of the King, who were administering the kingdom for him because of his youth, heard the news, they were afraid (so they said later) that Pompey might suborn the royal army and seize Alexandria and Egypt, or else they despised him for his misfortunes, in the way their friends so often turn against those in adversity. Whatever their motives, they gave a generous reply in public to his messengers and bade him come to the King; but meanwhile they formed a secret plot with Achillas, one of the King's officers and a man to stick at nothing, and with L. Septimius, a military tribune, and sent them to kill Pompey. They addressed him courteously, and he was induced by his previous knowledge of Septimius, who had served as a centurion with him during the war against the pirates, to embark with a few companions on a small boat; whereupon Achillas and Septimius assassinated him.

(*Dē bellō cīuīlī* 3.104)

Such was the end of Pompey the Great; such, effectively, was the end of the civil war.

Section 6D: **Four Roman poets**

Introduction

From the very beginning of Roman literature, Greek models had been a primary inspiration. We have already seen how Pḷautus 'translated' plays from Greek New Comedy. The situation was similar in later centuries. Catullus' 'learned' style was developed with inspiration from the Alexandrian Greek poets, such as Callimachus (third century). The Latin poets mostly employed Greek metres, such as the hexameter and pentameter. By and large they followed, too, the literary genres (e.g. epic, didactic, epigram etc.) which the Greeks had developed. So *imitātiō* ('imitation') was the literary rule. But despite this dependence on the Greeks, Roman poets did not simply copy. They spoke with their own distinctive voices about things which concerned them. For these poets, as for their later European successors, the availability of a tradition stretching back centuries meant that their work could be richer and more sophisticated. It did not make their poetry any less Roman.

Of the four poets represented here, Lucretius is a poet of the late Republic, but Virgil and Horace span the period from the late Republic to Augustus' principate and Ovid is a wholly Augustan poet. For the historical background to this period, see the sections on Augustus and Virgil pp. 302 and 312 below.

Section 6D(i) Titus Lucrētius Cārus (Lucretius) (c. 94–c. 55)

The six books of *Dē rērum nātūrā* ('On the nature of the universe') are in the tradition of 'didactic' ('teaching') poetry, which goes back ultimately to the eighth- to seventh-century Greek poet Hesiod's *Works and Days*, a manual on farming and the ritual calendar. Lucretius' poem is an attempt to summarise and to argue out for the Roman reader the philosophy of the Greek Epicurus (342–271), who held the following doctrines: (1) the world and all it contains is made up from minute particles called atoms; (2) everything, including the soul, is material, and living things simply dissolve into their constituent atoms after death; (3) the gods, though they exist, live in utter bliss, and take no part in influencing events in the universe; (4) the combinations of atoms (and therefore all events) occur by chance.

Lucretius' most fervently expressed aim was to convince his reader that religion and the superstition which it fostered, particularly the fear of punishments after death, were not based on reason. The follower of Epicurus could finally be free of irrational dread.

In this passage from the fifth book, Lucretius explains how men came to have their false ideas of the gods' power.

praetereā caelī ratiōnēs ōrdine certō
et uaria ⌐ annōrum cernēbant ⌐ tempora uertī
nec poterant quibus ⌐ id fieret cognōscere ⌐ causīs.
ergō perfugium sibi habēbant omnia dīuīs
trādere et illōrum nūtū facere omnia flectī.   5
in caelōque deum sēdīs et templa locārunt,
per caelum uoluī quia nox et lūna uidētur,
lūna diēs et nox et noctis signa seuēra
noctiuagaeque facēs caelī flammaeque uolantēs,
nūbila sōl imbrēs nix uentī fulmina grandō   10
et rapidī fremitūs et murmura magna minārum.

ō genus īnfēlix hūmānum, tālia ⌐ dīuīs
cum tribuit ⌐ facta atque īrās adiūnxit acerbās!
quantōs tum gemitūs ipsī sibi, quantaque ⌐ nōbīs
⌐ uulnera, quās lacrimās peperēre minōribu' nostrīs!   15
nec pietās ūllast uēlātum saepe uidērī
uertier ad lapidem atque omnīs accēdere ad ārās
nec prōcumbere humī prōstrātum et pandere palmās
ante deum dēlūbra nec ārās sanguine multō
spargere quadrupedum nec uōtīs nectere uōta,   20
sed mage plācātā ⌐ posse omnia ⌐ mente tuērī.

Running vocabulary for 6D(i)

adiungō 3 *adiūnxī* I join, add
cael-um ī 2n. heaven, sky
cernō 3 I discern, perceive, see
dēlūbr-um ī 2n. temple, shrine
dīu-us ī 2m. god
faciō 3/4 I suppose, imagine
  (line 5)
fax fac-is 3f. torch
flamm-a ae 1f. flame
flectō 3 I steer, guide, control
fremit-us ūs 4m. roar
fulmen fulmin-is 3n. lightning,
  thunderbolt
gemit-us ūs 4m. groan
grandō grandin-is 3f. hail
hūmān-us a um human
imber imbr-is 3m. rain, storm
īnfēlix īnfēlīc-is unhappy
īr-a ae 1f. anger
lacrim-a ae 1f. tear
lapis lapid-is 3m. stone
locārunt = locāuērunt

locō 1 I place
mage = magis
min-ae ārum 1f. pl. threats
minōrēs minōr-um 3m. pl.
  descendants
murmur murmur-is 3n. murmur
nectō 3 I link, string together X
  (acc.) to Y (dat.)
nix niu-is 3f. snow
noctiuag-us a um wandering in
  the night
nūbil-a ōrum 2n. pl. clouds
nūt-us ūs 4m. nod, command
ōrdō ōrdin-is 3m. order
palm-a ae 1f. palm, hand
pandō 3 I spread out, extend
perfugi-um ī 2n. refuge
pietās pietāt-is 3f. respect for the
  gods
plācāt-us a um calm, tranquil
prōcumbō 3 I bow down
prōstrāt-us a um prostrate

quadrupēs quadruped-is 3m.
  (four-footed) beast
rapid-us a um rapid, swift
ratiōnēs 'workings'
sēdēs sēd-is 3f. abode
spargō 3 I sprinkle
templ-um ī 2n. region (inhabited
  by particular beings), quarter
tempor-a um 3n. pl. seasons
tribuō 3 I assign
uēlāt-us a um veiled, with covered
  head [see note]
uent-us ī 2m. wind
uertier: passive infinitive
  (present) of *uertō* 3 (passive
  means 'I turn' intrans.)
uertor 3 passive = *reuertor*
  (line 2)
uolō 1 I fly
uōt-um ī 2n. vow, prayer

74. pietās

Notes

For the metre, GE **180.4** and **184**.

line 1 *praetereā*: Lucretius has noted that men have an inborn knowledge of the gods' existence, but
misinterpret the evidence of their senses so as to think the gods responsible for phenomena in the
world. *caelī ratiōnēs*: part of an indirect statement introduced by *cernēbant* (verb *uertī*).

line 2 *uaria*: acc. pl. n. – hold until solved (by *tempora*) – second subject of *uertī*.

line 3 *quibus*: abl. pl. f. – solved by *causīs*; normal order would be: *nec poterant cognōscere quibus causīs
id fieret.*

line 5 *trādere et... facere*: these two infinitives are in apposition to *perfugium*, i.e. 'handing
over... supposing...'. *omnia flectī*: indirect statement depending on *facere* (*illōrum nūtū* also belongs
to this indirect statement).

line 6 *-que*: postponed – it joins this line to the previous one. *deum*: gen. pl. (see line 16).

line 7 *quia*: postponed – it introduces the clause which begins *per caelum uoluī*.

line 8 *noctis signa seuēra*: i.e. the stars.

line 9 *noctiuagae... facēs, flammae... uolantēs*: i.e. shooting-stars or meteors.

line 11 The two phenomena referred to in this line are probably both the same: thunder. *minārum*: i.e. the
threats of the gods (as men imagine these noises signify).

line 13 *cum*: postponed – it introduces the clause beginning *tālia dīuīs*.

lines 14–15 This sentence is arranged as a *tricolon* with *anaphora* (see **GE** p. 271(f) and (g)). The verb
(*peperēre*) is held back until the third limb. The subject is *ipsī* (i.e. early men), the exclamatory words
(*quantōs... quanta... quās*) are all acc. agreeing with the objects. The verb constructs with acc. and dat.
to mean 'I produce X for Y'. *minōribu'* = *minōribus* (the s is cut off to make the syllable light).

line 16 *ūllast* = *ūlla est. ūelātum*: sc. 'for a person (to...)'. It was the Roman custom to pray with the head
veiled.

line 17 *uertier ad lapidem*: Romans approached statues of the gods from the right, then, after praying,
turned right to face them, and prostrated themselves (see line 18). Apart from stone statues, though,
there were boundary-stones (*terminī*) and other sacred rocks which were venerated by the placing of
garlands on them, or the pouring of oil. *omnīs*: acc. pl. f. – hold until solved (by *ad ārās*).

line 18 *pandere palmās*: i.e. to stretch out the arms with the hands palm uppermost.

line 19 *deum*: gen. pl. (see above line 6).

line 21 *plācātā*: abl. s. f. – hold until solved (by *mente*).

nam cum suspicimus magnī caelestia mundī

For when we look up at the vast tracts of the sky

templa super stellīsque micantibus aethera fīxum,

and the ether above us studded with twinkling stars

et uenit in mentem sōlis lūnaeque uiārum,

and there comes into our minds the thought of the paths of the sun and the moon,

tunc aliīs oppressa malīs in pectora cūra

then in our hearts, oppressed as they are   25 with other sorrows,

illa quoque expergēfactum caput ērigere īnfit,

a new anxiety stirs and starts to rear its head

nē quae forte deum nōbīs immēnsa potestās

and we wonder if it is some divine power beyond our measuring

sit, uariō mōtū quae candida sīdera uerset.

which is turning the bright stars in their various courses.

temptat enim dubiam mentem ratiōnis egestās,

Our minds are shaken and begin to doubt. This is a failure of reason.

ecquaenam fuerit mundī genitālis orīgō,

We ask ourselves   30 if there was once a day on which the world was born

et simul ecquae sit fīnis, quoad moenia
                                        mundī
	and at the same time if there is a limit
	beyond which its walls will not be able to
	                                        endure

sollicitī mōtūs hunc possint ferre labōrem,	the drudgery of this anxious motion
an dīuīnitus aeternā dōnāta salūte	or whether they are blessed with eternal security
perpetuō possint aeuī lābentia tractū	and can glide through the infinite tracts of time
immēnsī ualidās aeuī contemnere uīrīs.	and mock its mighty power. 35 Besides
praetereā cūi nōn animus formīdine dīuum	do not all men find their hearts contracting with fear of the gods
contrahitur, cūi nōn corrēpunt membra pauōre,	and their limbs creeping with fright
fulminis horribilī cum plāgā torrida tellūs	when the earth is scorched by the shuddering stroke of lightning
contremit et magnum percurrunt murmura caelum?	and murmurs run all round the sky?

nōn populī gentēsque tremunt, rēgēsque
                                        superbī
	Do not the nations tremble and all the 40
	                                        peoples of the earth?

corripiunt dīuum percussī membra timōre,	Do not the limbs of proud kings crawl with fear
	and are they not stricken by the thought
nē quid ob admissum foedē dictumue superbē	that the time has come for them to pay for some foul deed they have done
poenārum graue sit soluendī tempus adāctum?	or some proud word they have spoken? Then, too,

summa etiam cum uīs uiolentī per mare
                                        uentī
	when a great gale comes upon the sea and
	                                        sweeps

induperātōrem classis super aequora uerrit	the general and his fleet over the face of 45 the water

cum ualidīs pariter legiōnibus atque
                                        elephantīs,
	with all his mighty legions, elephants and
	                                        all,

nōn dīuum pācem uōtīs adit ac prece
                                        quaesit
	does he or does he not go and offer up
	                                        vows to the gods

	and beg them to send him their peace?

uentōrum pauidus pācēs animāsque secundās,	And does he not in his fright pray to the winds to send him their peace too and their favouring breath?
nēquīquam, quoniam uiolentō turbine saepe	Little good it does him: as often as not there comes a fierce squall
correptus nīlō fertur minus ad uada lētī?	and snatches him up and carries him away, 50 even as he prays, to the shallow waters of death.
usque adeō rēs hūmānās uīs abdita quaedam	There is always a mysterious force which tramples upon the affairs of men
obterit et pulchrōs fascīs saeuāsque secūrīs	grinding the emblems of their power under its heel
prōculcāre ac lūdibriō sibi habēre uidētur.	and making a mockery of the splendid rods and the pitiless axes. Lastly
dēnique sub pedibus tellūs cum tōta uacillat	when the whole earth trembles under our feet
concussaeque cadunt urbēs dubiaeque minantur,	when cities are shaken and fall 55 or totter and threaten to fall
quid mīrum sī sē temnunt mortālia saecla	is it any wonder if the children of men despise themselves and leave
atque potestātēs magnās mīrāsque relinquunt	the great powers and the wonderful strength
in rēbus uīrīs dīuum, quae cūncta gubernent?	of the gods in the world to rule everything?

(Lucretius, *Dē rērum nātūrā* 5.1183–1240)

Grammar for 6D

hexameter in Lucretius	archilocheans	elegiac couplets

Learning vocabulary for 6D(i)

Nouns
cael-um ī 2n. sky, heaven
dīu-us ī 2m. god
flamm-a ae 1f. flame
nix niu-is 3f. snow
ōrdō ōrdin-is 3m. order (rank)

pietās pietāt-is 3f. respect for the gods (also for one's family, home and native land)
uent-us ī 2m. wind
uōt-um ī 2n. vow, prayer

Verbs
pandō 3 *pandī passus* I spread out, extend; throw open, disclose

Section 6D(ii) Pūblius Vergilius Marō (Virgil) (70–19 BC)

For Virgil's life, works and connections with Augustus, see below p. 312.

These two passages are taken from Aeneid *6. Aeneas, as ordered by his dead father Anchises in a dream, has landed at Cumae in Italy, and is now making the journey to Hades, guided by the Sibyl (a prophetess). There he will meet Anchises, who will show his son the future greatness of Rome.*

Aeneas and the Sibyl journey through the darkness of the Underworld, past personified evils of the world above and various other monsters. They come to the ferry, on which the souls are conveyed to Hades by Charon. He and the shades are described.

ībant obscūrī sōlā sub nocte per umbram
perque domōs Dītis uacuās et inānia rēgna:
quāle per incertam lūnam sub lūce malignā
est iter in siluīs, ubi caelum condidit umbrā
Iuppiter, et rēbus nox ⌐ abstulit ¬ ātra colōrem.   5

Running vocabulary for 6D(ii), 1–5

āter ātr-a um black	*inān-is e* empty, insubstantial	*quāle just as* (see note)
color colōr-is 3m. colour	*malign-us a um* niggardly,	*silu-a ae* 1f. wood
condō 3 *condidī* I hide	grudging	*sōl-us a um* lonely
Dīs Dīt-is 3m. Dis (= Pluto, god	*obscūr-us a um* dark (tr. 'in	*umbr-a ae* 1f. shadow, darkness
of the Underworld)	darkness')	

Notes

line 1 For the metre, see **GE 180.4**, p. 274. *ībant*: the subjects are Aeneas and the Sibyl. *sōlā*: with *sub nocte*. The adjectives are, in a sense, both with the wrong noun (a figure called *hypallage*) – *obscūrus* would describe *nox* well, and *sōlus* the travellers.
line 2 *inānia rēgna*: also governed by *per*.
line 3 *quāle ... iter*: lit. 'what sort of journey (there is)'. Understand 'they were going on' from line 1, and tr. 'the sort of journey one makes...'
line 4 *caelum*: object – hold until solved (by *condidit ... Iuppiter*).
line 5 *Iuppiter*: Jupiter controls the weather (along with much else). *rēbus*: dat. of disadvantage (solved by *abstulit*). Tr. 'the world'.

uestibulum ante ipsum prīmīsque in faucibus Orcī	Before the entrance, in the very throat of Hell,
Lūctus et ultrīcēs posuēre cubīlia Cūrae,	Grief and Care and Revenge had made their beds.
pallentēsque habitant Morbī trīstisque Senectūs,	Pale disease lived next crabbed Old Age.
et Metus et malesuāda Famēs ac turpis Egestās,	There too were Fear and Hunger that stops at nothing and squalid Poverty
terribilēs uīsū fōrmae, Lētumque Labōsque;	and Drudgery and Death, all fearful things 10 to look upon.
tum cōnsanguineus Lētī Sopor et mala mentis	Then there were Sleep the sister of Death and all
Gaudia, mortiferumque aduersō in līmine Bellum,	the Evil Pleasures of the heart and War the murderer
	standing before them on the threshold.
ferrēīque Eumenidum thalamī et Discordia dēmēns	There too were the iron-clad sleeping quarters of the Furies
uīpereum crīnem uittīs innexa cruentīs.	and raging Discord with vipers for hair bound up with blood-soaked ribbons.
in mediō rāmōs annōsaque bracchia pandit	In the middle a huge dark elm spread out 15 its ancient branching arms.
ulmus opāca, ingēns, quam sēdem Somnia uulgō	This, they say, is the nesting place of foolish dreams
uāna tenēre ferunt, foliīsque sub omnibus haerent.	each clinging beneath its own leaf.
multaque praetereā uariārum mōnstra ferārum,	Here too by the doors are stabled many strange kinds of creature
Centaurī in foribus stabulant Scyllaeque biformēs	Centaurs – man and horse, Scyllas – maiden and dogs,
et centumgeminus Briareus ac bēlua Lernae	Briareus with his hundred hands and the 20 Hydra of Lerna
horrendum strīdēns, flammīsque armāta Chimaera,	hissing horribly and the Chimera armed in fire,
Gorgones Harpyiaeque et fōrma tricorporis umbrae.	Gorgons and Harpies and the three-bodied shade of Geryon.
corripit hīc subitā trepidus formīdine ferrum	Here Aeneas felt sudden fear and took hold of his sword

75. Scyllaeque bifōrmēs

Aenēās strictamque aciem uenientibus offert,	and met them with naked steel as they came at him.
et nī docta comes tenuīs sine corpore uītās	If his wise mentor had not warned him 25 that they were spirits,
admoneat uolitāre cauā sub imāgine fōrmae	frail and bodiless existences fluttering in an empty semblance
inruat et frūstrā ferrō dīuerberet umbrās.	of substance, he would have charged them and to no purpose have parted shadows with his steel.

hinc uia Tartareī ⌐ quae fert ⌐ Acherontis ad undās.
turbidus hīc caenō uāstāque uorāgine gurges
aestuat atque omnem ⌐ Cōcȳtō ēructat ⌐ harēnam.   30
portitor hās horrendus aquās et flūmina seruat
terribilī squālōre Charōn, cuī plūrima ⌐ mentō
⌐ cānitiēs inculta iacet, stant lūmina flammā,
sordidus ⌐ ex umerīs nōdō dēpendet ⌐ amictus.
ipse ratem contō subigit uēlīsque ministrat   35
et ferrūgineā ⌐ subuectat corpora ⌐ cumbā,
iam senior, sed crūda deō uiridisque senectūs.
hūc omnis turba ad rīpās effūsa ruēbat,
mātrēs atque uirī dēfūnctaque corpora uītā
magnanimum hērōum, puerī innūptaeque puellae,   40
impositīque rogīs iuuenēs ante ōra parentum:
quam multa ⌐ in siluīs autumnī frīgore prīmō
⌐ lāpsa cadunt folia, aut ad terram gurgite ab altō
quam multae glomerantur auēs, ubi frīgidus annus
trāns pontum fugat et terrīs immittit aprīcīs.   45

Running vocabulary for 6D(ii), 28–49

Acherōn Acheront-is 3m. Acheron
(one of the rivers of the
Underworld)
aestuō 1 I boil, seethe
amict-us ūs 4m. cloak
ann-us ī 2m. season
aprīc-us a um sunny
autumn-us ī 2m. autumn, fall
auis au-is 3f. bird
caen-um ī 2n. mud
cānitiēs cānitiē-ī 5f. white hair
Charōn Charont-is 3m. Charon
(the ferryman of the dead)
Cōcȳt-us ī 2m. Cocytus ('the
wailing river') [see note]
cont-us ī 2m. pole
crūd-us a um (lit. 'unripe')
youthful, vigorous
cumb-a ae 1f. boat
dēfungor 3 dep. *dēfūnctus* I have
done with, finish (+ abl.)
dēpendeō 2 I hang down
effūs-us a um hurrying, rushing
(lit. 'poured out')
ēructō 1 I belch forth, spout up
ferō ferre I lead (intrans.)
ferrūgine-us a um dark (lit.
'rust-coloured')

foli-um ī 2n. leaf
frīgid-us a um cold
frīgus frīgor-is 3n. cold
fugō 1 I put to flight
glomeror 1 (passive) I gather,
assemble
gurges gurgit-is 3m. torrent,
flood, sea, river
hērōs hērō-is 3m. hero (human
being of divine parentage)
horrend-us a um dreadful, terrible
(lit. 'to be shuddered at')
immittō 3 I send X (acc.) to Y
(dat.)
impōnō 3 *imposuī impositus* I put
on (to X: dat.)
incult-us a um neglected,
disordered
innūpt-us a um unmarried
lābor 3 dep. *lāpsus* I fall
lūmin-a um 3n. pl. eyes
magnanim-us a um great-hearted
[*magnanimum* is gen. pl. Cf.
deum in **6D(i)** line 6]
ment-um ī 2n. chin
ministrō 1 I attend to (+ dat.)
nōd-us ī 2m. knot
pont-us ī 2m. sea

portitor portitōr-is 3m.
harbour-officer, exciseman
ratis rat-is 3f. boat
rīp-a ae 1f. bank
rog-us ī 2m. funeral pyre
ruō 3 I rush
senectūs senectūt-is 3f. old age
senior seniōr-is very old
(comparative of *senex*)
seruō 1 I guard
silu-a ae 1f. wood
sordid-us a um dirty, filthy
squālor squālōr-is 3m. filth,
squalor (lit. 'stiffness')
subigō 3 I push on, thrust forward
subuectō 1 I convey, transport
Tartare-us a um of Tartarus,
Tartarean
turbid-us a um thick, murky
(with: + abl.)
uāst-us a um huge, vast
uēl-um ī 2n. sail
uirid-is e green
umer-us ī 2m. shoulder
und-a ae 1f. water
uorāgō uorāgin-is 3f. abyss, gulf

stābant ōrantēs prīmī trānsmittere cursum
tendēbantque manūs rīpae ulteriōris amōre.
nāuita sed trīstis nunc hōs nunc accipit illōs,
ast aliōs longē summōtōs arcet harēnā.

(Virgil, *Aeneid* 6.268–316)

---

arceō 2 I keep away X (acc.) from
   Y (abl.)
ast = *at*
nāuit-a ae 1 m. sailor (= *nauta*)

rīp-a ae 1f. bank
summoueō 2 *summōuī summōtus* I
   drive away, move along

trānsmittō (*cursum*) 3 I make a
   crossing [See note]
ulterior ulteriōr-is further

Notes

line 28 *hinc uia*: sc. *est. Tartareī*: gen. s. m. – hold (until solved by *Acherontis*). It belongs in the clause introduced by *quae*.

line 29 *turbidus*: with abl. of respect *caenō*. Used predicatively with *gurges* (i.e. 'a torrent, murky...' not 'a murky torrent'). *uāstā... uorāgine*: abl. of description (qualifying *gurges*). The prose order of this line would be: *hīc gurges, turbidus caenō, uāstāque uorāgine, aestuat...*

line 30 *omnem*: acc. s. f. – hold (solved by *harēnam*). *Cōcȳtō*: = *in Cōcȳtum.*

line 31 *portitor*: in apposition to the subject *Charōn*. Tr. 'as harbour-officer' (since he, like similar people in the Roman world, collects tolls and controls access to the harbour where his boat stands). *hās*: acc. pl. f. Hold until solved (by *aquās*); the phrase is the object of *seruat.*

line 32 *terribilī squālōre*: abl. of description, *cuī... mentō*: lit: 'for whom on the chin'. Tr. 'on whose chin'. Dative is commonly used in poetry for genitive in such expressions. *plūrima*: nom. s. f. – hold until solved (by *cānitiēs*).

line 33 *stant flammā*: lit. 'stand with flame' i.e. 'are staring and ablaze'.

line 34 *sordidus*: nom. s. m. – hold until solved (by *amictus*). *nōdō*: abl. of means 'by –'. Charon is wearing a cloak knotted (not fastened with a pin) over his left shoulder, leaving his right arm and shoulder bared for his work.

line 36 *ferrūgineā*: abl. s. f. – hold until solved (by *cumbā*: the abl. expresses place), *corpora*: i.e. the dead.

line 37 *sed crūda deō uiridisque senectūs*: sc. *est. deō* 'the god's'.

lines 39–41 All these people make up the *turba* of line 38; the nominatives (*mātrēs, uirī, corpora, puerī, puellae* and *iuuenēs*) are in apposition to *turba*.

line 39 *dēfūncta*: nom. pl. n. governs *uītā*, and is used predicatively with *corpora* (i.e. 'bodies finished with...' not 'finished-with bodies'. Cf. *turbidus* in line 29).

line 40 *magnanimum hērōum*: depends on *corpora*.

line 41 *impositī*: nom. pl. m. – cf. *dēfuncta... corpora* (line 39). Used predicatively with *iuuenēs*, i.e. 'youths placed...' not 'placed youths...'

lines 42, 44 *quam multa... quam multae*: 'as many as (the... which)'.

line 42 *autumnī frīgore prīmō*: *autumnī* depends on *frīgore*. The abl. phrase expresses time.

line 43 *cadunt*: here tr. 'die' (or *lāpsa* as 'having slipped' (sc. 'off the tree') and *cadunt* as 'fall' (sc: 'to the ground')). *aut ad terram gurgite ab altō*: this belongs in the new simile, introduced by *quam multae* in line 44.

line 45 *fugat*: sc. *eās* (= 'the birds').

line 46 *trānsmittere*: infinitive of indirect command (poetic use of a Greek construction instead of the normal *ut* + subj.; see **136**). *prīmī* belongs with *trānsmittere cursum*.

line 47 *amōre*: abl. of cause 'from desire (for)'.

line 48 *sed*: postponed (normally first word in a clause), *nunc hōs*: sc. *accipit.*

line 49 *harēnā*: = *rīpīs* (where the boat is standing and where access is gained to it). This line is the cue for Aeneas to ask the Sibyl why some people are allowed to sail, while others are kept on the shore. The answer is that only the buried may cross; the unburied, quite apart from the religious taboo on their crossing, have no coin with which to pay for their passage. Among the unburied, Aeneas meets his steersman Palinurus, who was lost overboard before the Trojans arrived in Italy.

76. uīuōs dūcent dē marmore uultūs

Aeneas has reached the Elysian Fields, where Anchises explains to him the workings of the universe, then shows him a parade of the Roman leaders who will spring from his line. In this tailpiece to the long revelation, Anchises reminds the Roman that others may cultivate the arts to a higher degree, but that his task, government of the world, can also be classified as an 'art'.

'excūdent aliī spīrantia mollius aera   50
(crēdō equidem), uīuōs ⌐ dūcent dē marmore ⌐ uultūs,
ōrābunt causās melius, caelīque meātūs
dēscrībent radiō et surgentia sīdera dīcent:
tū regere imperiō populōs, Rōmāne, mementō
(hae tibi erunt artēs), pācīque impōnere mōrem,   55
parcere subiectīs et dēbellāre superbōs.'

(Virgil, *Aeneid* 6.847–53)

Running vocabulary for 6D(ii), 50–56

aes aer-is 3n. bronze statue
ars art-is 3f. skill, art, accomplishment
dēbellō 1 I subdue, conquer
dēscrībō 3 I delineate
equidem indeed; for my part
excūdō 3 I beat out, fashion

impōnō 3 I add X (acc.) to Y (dat.)
marmor marmor-is 3n. marble
meāt-us ūs 4m. motion, revolution
mementō remember, be sure (to: + inf.) (imperative of *meminī*)
moll-is e soft, pliant, flexible
mōs mōr-is 3m. civilisation

radi-us ī 2m. rod
regō 3 I govern, direct
spīrō 1 I breathe
subiect-ī ōrum 2m. pl. the conquered
superb-us a um proud, arrogant
surgō 1 I rise

Notes

line 50 *aliī* i.e. the Greeks (also for the other things mentioned in lines 50–3).

lines 50–2 *mollius… melius*: the comparison is with the Romans, sc. 'than you Romans'. *mollius*: qualifies
   spīrantia. Tr. 'in more flowing (i.e. lifelike) lines'.

line 51 *uīuōs*: acc. pl. m. – hold until solved (by *uultūs*: possibly the adjective is used predicatively
   [cf. lines 39 and 41 above], i.e. 'faces which live', not 'living faces'), *dūcent*: in the sense 'bring forth'.

line 52 *caelī*: i.e. 'of the heavenly bodies'. The phrase *caelī meātūs* is object of *dēscrībent*.

line 54 *surgentia sīdera*: i.e. 'the risings of the stars'. Cf. **119** note.

Learning vocabulary for 6D(ii)

Nouns

ars art-is 3f. skill, art,
   accomplishment
autumn-us ī 2m. autumn, fall
frīgus frīgor-is 3n. cold; pl. cold
   spells
lūmen lūmin-is 3n. light; (pl.) eyes
rīp-a ae 1f. bank
silu-a ae 1f. wood

umbr-a ae 1f. shadow, darkness;
   shade, ghost
umer-us ī 2m. shoulder
und-a ae 1f. water, wave

Adjectives

obscūr-us a um dark; obscure;
   mean, ignoble
sōl-us a um lonely (alone)
superb-us a um proud, haughty,
   arrogant

Verbs

fugō 1 I put to flight
impōnō 3 *imposuī impositus* I put
   X (acc.) on Y (dat.)
lābor 3 dep. *lāpsus* I slip, glide,
   fall down; make a mistake
surgō 3 *surrēxī surrēctum* I rise,
   arise, get up

Section 6D(iii) Quīntus Horātius Flaccus (Horace) (65–8)

Horace's father was a freedman. Yet he had enough money and ambition to enable
his son to study in Rome and Athens. In about 38 or 37 Horace was introduced
by Virgil to Maecenas, whose *clientēla* ('circle of dependants') he joined soon
after. Maecenas gave him a farm in the Sabine hills which allowed him a retreat
from Rome and a return to the simple life of the country landowner which he
often praised. After Virgil's death, he became close to Augustus (a letter survives
in which Augustus makes fun of his paunch), but refused an appointment as his
personal secretary.

   His most celebrated achievement (he himself called them 'a monument more
lasting than bronze') was the first three books of *Carmina* ('The Odes'), written
between the battle of Actium (31) and 23. His last work was a fourth book of
Carmina, published *c.* 13. It contains much poetry celebrating Augustus and his
achievements, and includes other pieces like the following, which the poet and
scholar A. E. Housman thought the most beautiful poem in ancient literature.

77. Grātia cum Nymphīs

Art and propaganda

The coming to power of Augustus ushered in an age when the propaganda of the individual became synonymous with the propaganda of the state. The emperor, learning from the example set by the power-brokers of the late Republic, made visual propaganda one of the bulwarks of his regime.

There were various aspects to this propaganda. One was the emphasis on Roman legends. Augustus' efforts to affirm a Roman historical identity and specifically to stress the links between the Julian family and the legendary founders of the city automatically promoted the popularity of artistic representations of the foundation legends. That such representations were not wholly new is attested by the Basilica Aemilia frieze and the painted frieze of a small late-Republican tomb on the Esquiline; but they received an extra boost from the publication of Virgil's *Aeneid* in 19 BC. The importance of Roman legend to Augustus' political programme was clearly demonstrated in the emperor's *Forum Augustum*, dedicated in 2 BC, which contained a gallery of statues of the heroes of Rome's past. The types of Romulus with the spoils won in single-handed combat with the king of Caenina and of Aeneas saving his father and son from the ruins of Troy became famous symbols: they were reproduced, for example, in statues and paintings of the following years at Pompeii. (*World of Rome*, **475**)

Torquatus, spring has returned. But the seasons have a lesson to teach about hopes of immortality. All things change for the worse. Men are more badly off still, since death is final. What point is there in denying yourself? Once you are dead, no quality that you possess can change your condition. The examples of Hippolytus and Theseus prove the point.

diffūgēre niuēs, redeunt iam grāmina campīs
    arboribusque comae;
mūtat terra uicēs, et dēcrēscentia ⌜ rīpās
    ⌝ flūmina praetereunt;
Grātia ⌜ cum Nymphīs geminīsque sorōribus audet   5
    dūcere ⌝ nūda chorōs.
immortālia nē spērēs, monet annus et almum ⌜
    quae rapit hōra ⌝ diem:
frīgora mītēscunt Zephyrīs, uēr prōterit aestās
    interitūra simul   10
pōmifer Autumnus frūgēs effūderit, et mox
    brūma recurrit iners.
damna tamen celerēs ⌜ reparant caelestia ⌝ lūnae:
    nōs ubi dēcidimus
quō pater Aenēās, quō Tullus dīues et Ancus,   15
    puluis et umbra sumus.
quis scit an adiciant hodiernae crāstina ⌜ summae
    ⌝ tempora dī superī?
cūncta manūs auidās fugient hērēdis, amīcō ⌜
    quae dederīs ⌝ animō.   20
cum semel occiderīs et dē tē splendida Mīnōs
    fēcerit arbitria,
nōn, Torquāte, genus, nōn tē fācundia, nōn tē
    restituet pietās;
īnfernīs neque enim tenebrīs Diāna pudīcum   25
    līberat Hippolytum,
nec Lēthaea ⌜ ualet Thēseus abrumpere cārō
    ⌝ uincula Pērithoō.

(Horace, *Odes* 4.7)

Running vocabulary for 6D(iii)

abrumpō 3 I break
adiciō 3/4 I add
Aenēās (Greek nom.) Aeneas (Trojan hero, mythical founder of Roman race)
aestās aestāt-is 3f. summer
alm-us a um bountiful, nourishing [see note]

amīc-us a um friendly [see note]
an whether
Anc-us ī 2m. Ancus (third king of Rome)
arbitri-um ī 2n. judgement
arbor arbor-is 3f. tree
auid-us a um greedy
brūm-a ae 1f. winter

caelest-is e in the heavens
camp-us ī 2m. field, plain
cār-us a um dear
chor-us ī 2m. dance
com-a ae 1f. foliage
crāstin-us a um tomorrow's
cūnct-us a um all, the whole of
damn-um ī 2n. loss

dēcidō 3 I go (lit. 'fall') down
dēcrēscō 3 I decrease
Diān-a ae 1f. Diana [see note]
diffugiō 3/4 *diffūgī* I disperse, scatter (intrans.)
effundō 3 *effūdī* I pour out
fācundi-a ae 1f. eloquence
frūgēs frūg-um 3f. pl. produce, fruits
gemin-us a um twin
grāmen grāmin-is 3n. grass
Grāti-a ae 1f. Grace (one of the three Graces)
hērēs hērēd-is 3m. heir
Hippolyt-us ī 2m. Hippolytus [see note]
hodiern-us a um today's
iners inert-is sluggish, motionless
īnfern-us a um of the Underworld

intereō interīre interiī interitum I die
Lēthae-us a um of Lethe [see note]
Mīnōs Mīnō-is 3m. Minos (one of the judges in the Underworld)
mītēscō 3 I grow mild
nūd-us a um naked
Nymph-a ae 1f. Nymph
Pēritho-us ī 2m. Perithous [see note]
pōmifer pōmifer-a um apple-bearing
prōterō 3 I trample on
pudīc-us a um chaste
puluis puluer-is 3m. dust
recurrō 3 I run back, return
reparō 1 I make good
restituō 3 I bring back, revive

simul = simulatque
splendid-us a um splendid, brilliant
summ-a ae 1f. total
super-ī ōrum 2m. pl. the gods above
tenebr-ae ārum 1f. pl. shadows, darkness
Thēseus (Greek nom.) Theseus [see note]
Torquāt-us ī 2m. Torquatus
Tull-us ī 2m. Tullus (second king of Rome)
uēr uēr-is 3n. spring
uic-ēs 3f. pl. successive forms/conditions
Zephyr-us ī 2m. West Wind

Notes

For the metre, see **185**.

line 3 *dēcrēscentia*: nom. pl. n. – solved by *flūmina praetereunt*: i.e. flow between.

line 7 *immortālia*: 'immortality', *almum*: acc. m. s. – hold (solved by *diem*). *hōra* and *annus* are both subjects *of monet*. The prose order would be: *hōra quae diem almum rapit.*

line 9 *Zephyrīs*: abl. of cause.

line 13 *celerēs . . . lūnae*: i.e. months passing quickly.

line 15 *quo*: '(to) where': understand *decidērunt* with *Aenēās, Tullus* and *Ancus* as subject.

lines 17–18 *hodiernae*: dat. s. f. – solved by *summae. crāstina*: acc. pl. n. solved by *tempora*: the subject of *adiciant* is *dī superī*.

lines 19–20 *amīcō . . . animō*: dat. 'to your friendly heart' (imitating a Greek expression meaning 'to your dear heart'). The clause means 'whatever you have gratified your dear heart with'.

line 21 *occiderīs*: future perfect, despite the long vowel in *-īs. splendida*: acc. pl. n. –hold until solved (by *arbitria*).

lines 23–4 *genus, fācundia* and *pietās* are all subjects of *restituet*. Note the anaphora (*nōn . . . nōn tē . . . nōn tē*): see *GE* p. 271(g).

line 25 *īnfernīs . . . tenebrīs*: abl. of separation 'from'. *pudīcum*: acc. s. m. – hold until solved (by *Hippolytum*).

lines 25–6 Diana, goddess of the hunt and of chastity, could not save her dearest devotee Hippolytus (whose death was devised by Aphrodite, whom he had spurned).

line 27 *Lēthaea*: acc. pl. n. – hold until solved (by *uincula*). Lethe was the River of Forgetfulness.

lines 27–8 *cārō . . . Pērithoō*: abl. of separation 'from'. See Reference Grammar **L(f)1**. Theseus had gone down to Hades with his friend Perithous, to bring back Persephone, with whom Perithous was in love, and who had been abducted by Pluto. Both had been enchained, but Theseus had been rescued by Heracles, and returned to the world above. Now dead, and back in Hades for ever, he is unable to rescue his friend.

Learning vocabulary for 6D(iii)

Nouns	**Adjectives**	**Others**
arbor arbor-is 3f. tree	*caelest-is e* in the heavens	*an* whether (in indirect questions,
camp-us ī 2m. field, plain	*cūnct-us a um* all, the whole of	+ subj.: = *num*); = *ne* (= ?)
com-a ae 1f. hair; foliage	*nūd-us a um* naked	(in direct question)
tenebr-ae ārum 1f. pl. shadows, darkness		

78. Autumnus

Section 6D(iv) Pūblius Ovidius Nāsō (Ovid) (43 BC–AD 17)

Ovid, educated, like Horace, at Rome and then Athens, was intended by his father for a public career. But by the time he reached the age of qualification for the quaestorship (twenty-five) he had decided to follow a literary career instead. He was extraordinarily prolific. He wrote love-elegy (*Amōrēs*, published in 20), ironic 'didactic' poetry on how to succeed with the opposite sex (*Ars amātōria*, AD 1), tragedy (he wrote a *Mēdēa*), epic (*Metamorphōsēs*, myths of the 'changes of shape' which men and gods took on), learned aetiology (i.e. the reasons why modern practices, institutions etc. take the form they do – *Fastī*) and verse epistles (*Hērōides, Trīstia, Epistulae ex Pontō*). He was a brilliantly witty and sophisticated poet, whose spirit was much at odds with contemporary authority. His *Ars amātōria* was especially frowned on by Augustus since it seemed to encourage a laxity of sexual *mōrēs* which was the reverse of that desired by the emperor. Indeed, it was partly this poem, and more significantly what Ovid calls mysteriously an *error* (probably some sort of scandal surrounding the emperor's daughter Julia) which led to his sudden banishment to Tomis, a remote settlement on the Black Sea, in AD 8. His verse epistles were written from there. He was never allowed to return to Rome.

Love-elegy, the genre to which the *Amōrēs* belong, though it has Greek roots (Menander's New Comedy and Hellenistic love epigram), appears to have been a peculiarly Roman development. The chief innovator seems to have been Cornelius Gallus (*c.* 70–26), of whose poetry very little remains. Two older contemporaries of Ovid, Propertius and Tibullus, men in whose circle Ovid moved, wrote books of poems which centre around a love-affair. Ovid took over many of their themes, but treated them in a less serious way. It is never safe to assume that this poet writes with his hand on his heart.

Ovid is taking a siesta in his room. Corinna enters, and her appearance arouses the poet's ardour. He strips her clothes off, despite her feigned resistance. He praises her body – and wishes for many such days.

aestus erat, mediamque diēs exēgerat hōram;
   adposuī mediō membra leuanda torō.
pars adaperta fuit, pars altera clausa fenestrae,
   quāle ⌐ ferē siluae ¬ lūmen habēre solent,
quālia ⌐ sublūcent fugiente ¬ crepuscula Phoebō   5

Running vocabulary for 6D(iv)

adapert-us a um open
adpōnō 3 *adposuī* I lay
aest-us ūs 4m. (lit. 'heat') hot part of the day
claus-us a um closed

crepuscul-um ī 2n. twilight [pl. used for s.]
exigō 3 *exēgī* I complete
fenestr-a ae 1f. window
leuō 1 I relieve, rest

Phoeb-us ī 2m. (lit. Phoebus, god of the sun) the sun
quālia/quāle [see note]
sublūceō 2 I glow faintly
tor-us ī 2m. bed, couch [see note]

79. lassī requiēuimus ambō

aut ubi nox abiit nec tamen orta diēs.
illa uerēcundīs ⌐ lūx est praebenda ¬ puellīs,
   quā timidus ⌐ latebrās spēret habēre ¬ pudor.
ecce, Corinna uenit tunicā uēlāta recīnctā,
   candida ⌐ dīuiduā ¬ colla tegente comā,   10
quāliter in thalamōs fōrmōsa Semīramis īsse
   dīcitur et multīs Lāis amāta uirīs.
dēripuī tunicam; nec multum rāra nocēbat,
   pugnābat tunicā sed tamen illa tegī;
quae, cum ita pugnāret tamquam quae uincere nōllet,   15
   uicta est nōn aegrē prōditiōne suā.
ut stetit ante oculōs positō uēlāmine nostrōs,
   in tōtō nusquam corpore menda fuit:
quōs umerōs, quālīs ⌐ uīdī tetigīque ¬ lacertōs!
   fōrma ⌐ papillārum quam fuit ¬ apta premī!   20
quam castīgātō plānus sub pectore uenter!
   quantum et quāle latus! quam iuuenāle femur!
singula quid referam? nīl nōn laudābile uīdī,
   et nūdam pressī corpus ⌐ ad usque ¬ meum.
cētera quis nescit? lassī requiēuimus ambō.   25
   prōueniant mediī sīc mihi saepe diēs.

(Ovid, *Amōrēs* 1.5)

aegrē with difficulty
apt-us a um fit
castīgāt-us a um well-formed (lit. 'well-disciplined')
coll-um ī 2n. neck [pl. used for s.]
Corinn-a ae 1f. Corinna
dēripiō 3/4 *dēripuī* I tear off
dīuidu-us a um parted
femur femor-is 3n. thigh
iuuenāl-is e youthful
lacert-us ī 2m. arm
Lāis Lāid-is 3f. Lais (a famous Corinthian courtesan)
lass-us a um weary, tired out
latebr-ae ārum 1f. pl. hiding-place
laudābil-is e worthy of praise

mend-a ae 1f. blemish
nusquam nowhere
papill-a ae 1f. breast [See note]
pectus pector-is 3n. breast
plān-us a um flat
pōnō 3 *posuī positus* I lay aside
praebeō 2 I provide, offer
premō 3 *pressī* I press
prōditiō prōditiōn-is 3f. betrayal
prōueniō 4 I turn out, am successful
pudor pudōr-is 3m. modesty, sense of shame
quāliter just as, just the way in which
rār-us a um thin [see note]

recingō 3 *recīnxī recīnctus* I unfasten, unbelt
referō referre I relate [See note]
requiēscō 3 *requiēuī* I take a rest, relax
Semīramis Semīramid-is 3f. Semiramis (legendary queen of Assyria)
singūl-ī ae a individual, one by one
thalam-us ī 2m. bedroom [pl. used for s.]
tunic-a ae 1f. tunic
uēlāmen uēlāmin-is 3n. clothing
uēlō 1 I clothe
uenter uentr-is 3m. stomach
uerēcund-us a um shy, modest

Notes

For the metre, see **186**.

line 1 *mediam*: acc. s. f. – hold until solved (by *hōram*).

line 2 *mediō*: dat. s. m. – hold until solved (by *torō*). *torō*: dat. of motion towards. Tr. 'on...' Cf. **6D(ii)** line 30 *omnem Cōcÿtō ēructat harēnam* 'belches forth all its sand into Cocytus'.

line 3 *pars... pars altera*: the window had two shutters, *clausa*: sc. *fuit*.

line 4 *quāle... lūmen*: lit: 'what sort of light'. Tr. 'the sort of light which...'

line 5 *quālia... crepuscula*: lit. 'what sort of twilight...'. Tr. 'the sort of twilight which...'. *fugiente*: abl. s. m. – hold until solved (by *Phoebō* – abl. abs.).

line 6 *orta*: sc. *est*.

line 7 *illa*: nom. s. f. – *lūx* is the complement. Tr. 'that is the (sort of) light...'. *uerēcundīs*: dat. pl. f. – hold until solved (by *puellīs*). (The dat. means 'to'.)

line 8 *timidus*: nom. s. m. – hold until solved (by *pudor*). *spēret*: generic subjunctive (see tr. for *illa*, line 7). (See **145.1**.)

line 10 *candida*: acc. pl. n. – hold (solved by *colla* – but await a verb still). *dīuiduā*: abl. s. f. Hold until solved (by *comā*) – *tegente* is also abl. s. f., and provides the verb governing *candida... colla*. The phrase is abl. abs.

line 12 *multīs*: dat. pl. m. – hold until solved (by *uirīs*). The dative expresses agent 'by', after the passive participle *amāta*. Cf. **6A(vi)** line 5 *amāta nōbīs* 'loved by me'. See *Reference Grammar* **L(e)(iv)**. *Lāis*: second subject (with *Semīramis*) of *dīcitur*. Carry over also *in thalamōs... īsse*.

line 13 *multum... nocēbat*: adverbial acc. (or internal). Tr. 'did it do much harm', *rāra*: i.e. *tunica*. Tr. 'being thin'.

line 14 *tunicā*: abl. of instrument 'with', 'by'. Solved by *tegī*. *sed tamen*: postponed – normally one would expect these words at the beginning of a clause. *illa*: i.e. Corinna

line 15 *ita... tamquam quae... nōllet*: 'just like one who did not want...' Generic subjunctive (see above, line 8). Note elision of *cum* and *ita*.

line 17 *ut* = 'when'.

line 18 *in tōtō*: await a solving noun (*corpore*).

lines 19–22 *quōs... quālis... quam... quam... quantum... quāle... quam*: all exclamatory. Cf. **6D(i)** lines 14–15.

line 19 *quōs umerōs, quālis... lacertōs*: obj. of *uīdī tetigīque*. Hold *quālis* as obj. until solved by *lacertōs*.

line 20 *fōrma papillārum = papillae fōrmōsae*. The subject of the exclamation here precedes the introductory words *quam... apta*. *premī*: explanatory (epexegetic) inf. after *apta*. Tr. *premō* here as 'caress'.

line 21 *quam*: qualifies *plānus*. *castīgātō*: abl. s. n. – hold until solved (by *sub pectore*).

line 23 *referam*: deliberative subj.: see **157²**. Cf. *quid plūra dīcam?* 'Why should I say more?'

line 24 *nūdam*: acc. s. f, adj. used as a noun. It refers to Corinna, *corpus ad usque meum*: normal order
would be *usque ad corpus meum*.

line 26 *prōueniant*: subjunctive expressing a wish for the future. See Reference Grammar **L–V Intro.(a)4**.
mediī: nom. pl. m. – hold until solved (by *diēs*).

Learning vocabulary for 6D(iv)

Nouns
coll-um ī 2n. neck
lacert-us ī 2m. arm, upper arm
latebr-ae ārum 1f. pl.
hiding-place, lair
pudor pudōr-is 3m. modesty,
sense of shame
thalam-us ī 2m. chamber,
bedchamber

tor-us ī 2m. couch; bed
tunic-a ae 1f. tunic

Adjectives
plān-us a um level, flat; plain,
distinct
singul-ī ae a individual, one by
one

Verbs
pōnō 3 *posuī positus* I lay aside (=
dēpōnō); (place, position, put)
praebeō 2 I provide, offer; (show,
display)
premō 3 *pressī pressus* I press;
oppress

Others
aegrē with difficulty

The Latin language

'The Latin language has been accepted by almost everyone as though by public consent as the
common tongue of all the Christian peoples. I recall that at times there have been some who wrote
to our king even in their own language and that it was in turn proposed that they should receive a
reply in our Slavonic tongue, so that when they seemed too conscious of their own position and
importance, we should not seem altogether negligent of our own. But in this, as in other matters,
one should look to the agreement of the majority of the Christian rulers and peoples and use Latin.'
(Rainold Heidenstein, 1553–1620)

The main reason why Rome's ghosts have been able to walk so freely since the end of the ancient
world is because Latin became the medium through which the world was educated, at least in
Western Europe, and then beyond that in those areas colonised from it (the Americas, Africa etc.).
This tradition was due to the fact that the universal Church adopted the universal language as its own.
In the monasteries of the medieval world, the worship of God through the liturgy went on in Latin.
Latin texts (Christian and pagan) were studied (though a poem like Virgil's *Aeneid* was read both for
style and as an allegory of the journey of the human soul, rather than for its Roman content). All
commentaries, hymns, poems, dramas, annals, letters, laws and saints' lives were written in Latin.

As a result, Latin remained the language of education, and it was not until the nineteenth century
that scholarly and theological works were normally produced in vernacular languages. Newton's
epoch-making *Philosophiae Nātūrālis Prīncipia Mathēmatica* ('Mathematical Principles of Natural
Philosophy') appeared in 1687. The parliaments of Croatia and Hungary used Latin until 1847 and
1848 respectively. And Latin remains an important subject in the secondary-school curriculum. It is
the history of Latin, then, which explains both the occurrence of Roman ghosts and the survival of
interest in the language and Roman culture. (*World of Rome*, **496**)

Part Four Additional Reading for Sections 1B to 5G

Beginning at section 1B, we provide a series of additional passages of real Latin (and one adapted medieval Latin passage) with running vocabulary and notes, adapted to the level reached in the sections to which they are appended. The glossaries for these passages contain both vocabulary and hints on how to read each sentence as it comes. The instruction 'hold' suggests that the meaning of the word cannot be finally decided at that point in the sentence; you are asked to keep information about the word in mind until it is 'solved' by later developments. Note that there is no extra reading for sections 3A or 4H.

1B   *1. The Vulgate*

This passage is taken from the Vulgate, Jerome's fourth–fifth-century AD translation of the Bible into Latin. It is called 'Vulgate' from its title *ēditiō uulgāta* 'popular edition'. Cf. 'vulgar' in English.

et (*Deus*) *ait* (said) '*ego sum Deus patris tuī, Deus* (of) *Abraham, Deus* (of) *Isaac, et Deus* (of) *Jacob.*' (Exodus 3.6)

---

patris tuī of your father

'*ego sum quī* (who) *sum*'. (Exodus 3.14)

2. Conversational Latin

Contrary to popular belief, Latin always has been a spoken as well as a written language. Most of our texts from ancient times, of course, reflect the literary, written, form. But in Plautus, Terence and the letters of Cicero we do hear the voice of Romans. Here are some common conversational gambits:

saluē or *saluus sīs* or *auē* (or *hauē*) 'Hello!' (lit. 'Greetings', 'May you be safe', 'Hail!')

ualē 'Goodbye!' (lit. 'Be strong')

sīs or *sī placet* or *nisi molestum est* or *grātum erit sī* . . . or *amābō tē* 'Please' (lit. 'If you will', 'If it pleases', 'If it's no trouble', 'It would be nice if . . .', 'I will like you (if you . . .)')

grātiās tibi agō 'Thank you' (lit. 'I give thanks to you')

ut ualēs? or *quid agis?* or *quid fit?* 'How are you?' (lit. 'Are you strong?', 'What are you doing?', 'What is happening?')

est or *est ita* or *etiam* or *ita* or *ita uērō* or *sānē* or *certē* 'Yes' (lit. 'It is', 'It is so', 'Even', 'Thus', 'Thus indeed', 'Certainly', 'Surely')

nōn or *nōn ita* or *minimē* 'No' (lit. 'Not', 'Not so', 'Least')

age or *agedum* 'Come on'

rēctē 'Right' (lit. 'Correctly')

malum 'Damn!' (lit. 'A bad thing')

dī tē perdant! 'Damn you!' (Lit. 'May the gods destroy you')

īnsānum bonum 'Damned good' (Lit. 'A crazy good thing')

Latin conversation did not die out with the end of the Roman Empire. Erasmus of Rotterdam, the great Dutch humanist, originally wrote his *Colloquia Familiāria* (first published in 1518) partly as an aid to teaching Latin conversation. The first 'Colloquy' introduces the pupil to various modes of greeting. These are the formulae recommended to lovers ('Greetings my . . .'):

	mea Cornēliola	('little Cornelia')
	mea uīta	('life')
	mea lūx	('light')
	meum dēlicium	('darling', 'delight')
	meum suāuium	('sweetheart', lit. 'kiss')
saluē	*mel meum*	('honey')
	mea uoluptās ūnica	('only joy')
	meum corculum	('sweetheart', lit. 'little heart')
	mea spēs	('hope')
	meum sōlātium	('comfort')
	meum decus	('glory')

1C

1. The Vulgate

honōrā patrem tuum et mātrem tuam. (Exodus 20.12)

---

honōrō 1 I honour   *māter mātris* 3f. mother

---

uōs estis sal ('salt') *terrae . . . uōs estis lūx* ('light') *mundī.* (Matthew 5.13)

2. Sayings of Cato

These are from a collection of dicta Catōnis *'Sayings of Cato' (= Marcus Cato, 234–149 BC), written in the third or fourth century AD but ascribed to that grand old man who epitomised Roman wisdom and tradition to later generations. They were firm favourites from the middle ages till the seventeenth century in England.*

parentēs (parents) *amā.*

datum (= what you are given) *seruā*

uerēcundiam (= modesty) *seruā*

familiam cūrā

iūsiūrandum = (oath) *seruā*

coniugem (= wife) *amā*

deō (to god) *supplicā* (pray)

3. Beginning of an epitaph

sepulcrum hau pulcrum pulcrāī fēminae . . .

sepulcr-um ī 2n. tomb	*pulcrāī*: note ancient f. s. gen.
hau not (archaic for *haud*)	ending
pulc(h)r- beautiful, fine	*femin-a ae* 1f. woman

1D   *1. Martial*

Martial (*c.* AD 40–104) was a Roman satirical epigrammatist.

> *Thāida Quīntus amat. 'quam Thāida?' Thāida luscam.*
> *ūnum oculum Thāis nōn habet, ille duōs.*

(3.8)

Thāis name of a very famous Roman courtesan (acc. = *Thāida*); *quam* which?; *lusc-us a um* one-eyed; *ūn-us a um* one; *ille* 'but he' i.e. Quintus (sc. *nōn habet*); *duōs* two (eyes). NB The Romans thought of love as blind and lovers as 'blinded'.

> *habet Āfricānus mīliēns, tamen captat.*
> *Fortūna multīs dat nimis, satis nūllī.*

(12.10)

Āfricān-us i 2m Africanus	*captō* 1 I hunt legacies	*nūllī* to no-one
mīliēns 100 million sesterces	*multīs* to many	

2. The Vulgate

Dominus regit mē. (Psalm 23)

rēgo 3 I rule

3. Ordinary of the Mass

in nōmine Patris et Fīliī et Spīritūs Sānctī.

Spīritūs Sānctī of the Holy Spirit

1E   *1. Martial*

> *Tongiliānus habet nāsum: scio, nōn nego, sed iam*
> *nīl praeter nāsum Tongiliānus habet.*

(12.88)

Tongiliān-us ī 2m. Tongiliānus (based on *tongeō* 2 'I know')	*nās-us ī* 2m. discernment (*habeō nāsum* means 'I am critical' – lit. 'I have a nose') *sciō* 4 I know	*negō* 1 I deny *iam* now *nīl* nothing; *praeter* + acc. except.

nōn cēnat sine aprō noster ⌐, *Tite,* ⌐ *Caeciliānus.*
  bellum conuīuam Caeciliānus habet.

(7.59)

(See *Text* p. xix for an explanation of the linking devices used here.)

cēnō 1 I dine	*Caeciliān-us ī* 2m. Caecilianus	a party; Caecilianus ate it
sine + abl. without	*bell-us a um* handsome	when dining alone.
aper apr-ī 2m. wild boar	*conuiu-a ae* 1m. guest,	
noster nostr-a um our	table-companion. NB Boar	
Tite = O Titus	was a dish usually cooked for	

2. The Vulgate

saluum mē fac, domine. (Psalm 59)

pater, sī uīs, trānsfer calicem istum ā mē. (Luke 22.42)

calicem istum this cup	*trānsferō* I let X (acc.) pass

3. Ordinary of the Mass

laudāmus tē, benedīcimus tē, adōrāmus tē, glōrificāmus tē, grātiās agimus tibi propter magnam glōriam tuam: Domine Deus, rēx caelestis, Deus pater omnipotēns.

laudō 1 I praise ('laud')	*grātiās agō* 3 I give thanks	*rēx* king
benedīcō 3 I bless	*tibi* to you	*caelestis* in heaven
adōrō 1 I worship (*ad*+*ōrō*)	*propter* (+ acc.) for the sake of	*omnipotēns* all-powerful.
glōrificō 1 I glorify	*glōri-a ae* 1f. glory	

1F   *1. Sayings of Cato*

(a) *quod* (an amount which) *satis est dormī.*

(b) *āleam* (gambling) *fuge.*

(c) *meretrīcem* (whore) *fuge.*

2. The Vulgate

beātī pauperēs quia uestrum est rēgnum deī. (Luke 6.20)

beātus blessed	*quia* because	*rēgnum* kingdom
beatī pauperēs insert *sunt*	*uestrum* yours	

3. Giovanni Cotta (1480–1510)[1]

amō, quod fateor, meam Lycōrim,
ut pulchrās iuvenēs amant puellās;
amat mē mea, quod reor, Lycōris,
ut bonae iuvenēs amant puellae.

quod fateor 'as I admit'	*iuuenis iuuen-is* 3m. young man
Lycōrim = acc. s. of Lycoris	*quod reor* 'as I think'

1. Latin was the language of scholarship and international communication throughout the Renaissance (fifteenth and sixteenth centuries) and was still felt by and large to be the proper medium for literature also. These are the first four lines of a poem in which the poet's girl gives him some locks of her hair as a love-pledge. The poet burns them, since they have, he claims, 'burned' him – with love!

4. Mottoes[1]

(a) *fac rēctē et nīl timē.* (Hill)

(b) *ā deō et patre.* (Thomas)

(c) *amat uictōria cūram.* (Clark)

rēctē rightly	*ā* on the side of	*uictōria* victory

1. These mottoes originate in medieval times or later. Many families have several.

1G   1. The Vulgate

pānem nostrum quotīdiānum dā nōbis hodiē et dīmittē nōbis peccāta nostra.
(Luke 11.3–4)

pānis pān-is 3m. bread	*dīmittō* 3 I discharge
quotīdiān-us a um daily	*peccāt-um ī* 2n. sin

2. Mottoes (based on the dative)

nōn nōbis, sed omnibus. (Ash, Ashe)

nōn mihi, sed deō et rēgī. (Booth, Warren)

nōn mihi, sed patriae. (Heycock, Jones-Lloyd, Lloyd, Whittingham) *deō, rēgī et patriae.* (Irvine, Duncombe)

deō, patriae, tibi. (Lambard, Sidley)

glōria deō. (Challen, Henn)

rēx rēg-is 3m. king	*patri-a ae* 1f. fatherland	*glōri-a ae* 1f. glory

Additional readings relating to Section 2

2A   *1. Martial*

> *nōn amo tē, Sabidī, nec possum dīcere quārē.*
> *hoc tantum possum dīcere, nōn amo tē.*

(1.32)

Sabidī = O Sabidius	*hoc tantum* this only

Cf. the famous version of Thomas Brown (1663–1704): I do not love thee, Dr Fell. / The reason why I cannot tell. / But this I know and know full well. / I do not love thee, Dr Fell.

> *Veientāna mihī miscēs, ubi Massica pōtās:*
> *olfacere haec mālō pōcula, quam bibere.*

(3.49)

Veientāna (obj.) (name of cheap wine)	*Massica* (obj.) Massic (name of fine wine)	*haec pōcula* (obj.) these drinks (i.e. the Massica)
mihī for me	*pōtō* 1 I drink	*quam* than
misceō 2 I mix	*olfaciō* 3/4 I smell	*bibō* 3 I drink

2. The Vulgate

God speaks to Moses in a cloud: *nōn poteris uidēre faciem meam: nōn enim uidēbit mē homo et uīuet.* (Exodus 33.20)

faciem (acc. s. f.) *face*	*uīuō* 3 live

> *nōn occīdēs . . . nōn fūrtum faciēs . . . nōn concupīscēs domum proximī tuī; nec dēsīderābis uxōrem eius, nōn seruum, nōn ancillam, nōn bouem, nōn asinum.* (Exodus 20.13)

occīdō 3 I kill	*proxim-us ī* 2m. neighbour	*bōs bou-is* 3m. m. ox
fūrt-um ī 2n. theft	*dēsīderō* 1 I long for	*asin-us ī* 2m. ass
concupīscō 3 I desire	*eius* his	
domum (acc.) house	*ancill-a ae* 1f. maidservant	

> *et ego uōbīs dīcō . . . 'quaerite et inueniētis'.* (Luke 11.9)

quaerō 3 I seek	

3. Mottoes

omnia superat uirtūs. (Gardiner)

omnia uincit amor. (Bruce, Rogers)

omnia uincit labor. (Cook)

omnia uincit uēritās. (Eaton, Mann, Naish, Nash)

omnia bona bonīs. (Wenman)

superō 1 I overcome	*labor labōr-is* 3m. work
uincō 3 I conquer	*uēritās uēritāt-is* 3f. truth

2B 1. Martial

cum tua nōn ēdās, carpis mea carmina, Laelī.
 carpere uel nōlī nostra, uel ēde tua.

cum since	*ēdās* you publish	*Laelī* O Laelius
tua = tua carmina	*carpō* 3 I criticise	*uel . . . uel* either . . . or
ēdō 3 I publish	*carmen carmin-is* 3n. poem	*nostra, tua*: i.e. *carmina*

2. Sayings of Cato

cum bonīs ambulā (walk).

rem tuam custōdī (guard).

librōs (books) *lege.*

miserum nōlī irrīdēre.

3. The Vulgate

The Lord to Moses: *ingredere ad Pharaōnem, et loquere ad eum 'haec dīcit dominus deus Hebraeōrum: dīmitte populum meum'.* (Exodus 9.1)

Pharaō Pharaōn-is Pharaoh	*haec* as follows	*dīmittō* 3 I let go
eum him	*Hebrae-ī ōrum* 2m. pl. Hebrews	*popul-us ī* 2m. people

Jesus to the disciples: *'sinite puerōs uenīre ad mē et nōlīte uetāre eōs; tālium enim est rēgnum deī.'* (Luke 18.16)

sinō 3 I allow	*uetō* 1 I forbid	*rēgn-um ī* 2n. kingdom
ueniō 4 I come	*tālium* of such a sort	

4. Mottoes

nōlī irrītāre leōnem. (Cooper, Walsh)

nōlī mentīrī. (Notley)

nōlī mē tangere. (Graeme, Graham, Willett)

dum crēscō, spērō. (Rider)

dum spīrō, spērō. (Anderson, Baker, Brook, Cutler, Davies, Gordon, Greaves, Hunter, Jacobs, Lee, Mason, Moore, Nicholls, Pearson, Roberts, Smith, Symonds, Taylor, Thomason, Walker, Whitehead, Young)

dum uigilō, cūrō. (Cranstoun)

dum uīuō, spērō. (Monteith)

dum in arborem (?) (Hamilton)

fac et spērā. (Armstrong, Arthur, Campbell, Morison, Richardson)

irrītō 1 I annoy	*spīrō* 1 I breathe	*dum* here = 'until', i.e. 'as far
leō leōn-is 3m. lion	*uigilō* 1 I am on guard	as/onto'
crēscō 3 I grow	*uīuō* 3 I live	*arbor arbor-is* 3f. tree (= the
spērō 1 I hope		cross?)

2C   1. Martial

> *laudat amat cantat nostrōs ⌜ mea Rōma ⌝ libellōs,*
> *mēque sinūs omnēs, mē manus omnis, habet.*
> *ecce rubet quĭdam, pallet, stupet, ōscitat, ōdit.*
> *hoc uolo: nunc nōbīs carmina nostra placent.*

(6.60)

laudō 1 I praise	*ecce* but look!	*ōdit* 'he hates'
cantō 1 I sing up	*rubeō* 2 I blush	*hoc, nunc,* are the emphatic words
libell-us ī 2m. book of poems	*quīdam* someone (subject)	here
sinūs (nom. pl.) pockets (a fold in	*palleō* I go pale	*nōbīs* i.e. to me
the toga where books kept)	*stupeō* I look bewildered	*carmen carmin-is* 3n. poem
habet one might expect *habent*	*ōscitō* 1 I yawn	*placeō* 2 I please

2. Mottoes

hoc signum (emblem) *nōn onus sed honor.* (Stoughton)

hoc opus. (Dee)

hoc uirtūtis opus. (Collison)

2D   *1. The Vulgate*

in prīncipiō creāuit Deus coelum et terram. (Genesis 1.1)

fōrmāuit igitur dominus Deus hominem dē līmō terrae et īnspīrāuit in faciem eius spīrāculum uītae. (Genesis 2.7)

septimō autem diē sabbatum dominī Deī tuī est; nōn faciēs omne opus in eō, tū et fīlius tuus et fīlia tua, seruus tuus et ancilla tua, iūmentum tuum . . . sex enim diēbus fēcit dominus coelum et terram et mare. (Exodus 20.10–11)

prīncipi-um beginning	*faciem* (acc.) face	*omne* = any (i.e. all *opus* is
creō 1 I make	*eius* his	excluded)
coel-um heaven, sky	*spīrācul-um* breath	*in eō* in, during it
terr-a earth	*uīt-a* life	*ancill-a* maidservant
fōrmō 1 I form	*septim-us* seventh	*iūment-um* ox
līm-us mud, clay	*sabbat-um* sabbath	*sex* six
īnspīrō 1 I breathe		*mare* sea

2. Mottoes

nīl sine Deō. (Awdry)

nīl sine labōre. (Atkinson, Simpson)

nīl sine causā. (Brown)

nōn sine Deō. (Eliot)

nōn sine causā. (Drury)

nōn sine industriā. (Bevan)

nōn sine iūre. (Charter)

nōn sine perīculō. (Mackenzie, Walker)

labor labōr-is 3m. work	*industri-a ae* 1f. effort
caus-a ae 1f. reason, cause	*iūs iūr-is* 3n. justice, right

2E   *1. Martial*

> praedia sōlus habēs, et sōlus, Candide, nummōs,
>   aurea sōlus habēs, murrina sōlus habēs,
> Massica sōlus habēs et Opīmī Caecuba sōlus,
>   et cor sōlus habēs, sōlus et ingenium.
> omnia sōlus habēs – nec mē puta uelle negāre!
>   uxōrem sed habēs, Candide, cum populō.

(3.26)

praedi-um ī 2n. farm	*Massic-um* ī 2n. fine wine	*ingeni-um* ī 2n. wit
sōl-us a um alone	*Opīmī Caecub-um* ī 2n. Caecuban	*nec mē puta* 'do not reckon that
numm-us ī 2m. coin	wine of Opimius' vintage	I...
Candide O Candidus	(supposedly laid down 121; cf.	*negō* 1 I deny (it)
murrin-um ī 2n. expensive agate	'Napoleon brandy')	*popul-us* ī 2m. people
jar	*cor cord-is* 3n. heart	

2. The Vulgate

> sex diēbus operāberis, et faciēs omnia opera tua... nōn moechāberis... nōn
> loquēris contrā proximum tuum falsum testimōnium. (Exodus 20.9ff.)

sex six	*contrā* + acc. against	*testimōni-um* ī 2n. evidence
operor 1 dep. I am busy	*proxim-us* ī 2m.neighbour	
moechor 1 dep. I commit adultery	*fals-us* untrue	

3. Mottoes

> prō deō et – patriā (Mackenzie) / lībertāte (Wilson) / ecclēsiā. (Bisshopp)

> prō Deō, prō rēge, prō patriā, prō lēge. (Blakemore)

> prō fidē et patriā. (Long)

> prō patriā et – libertāte (Michie) / rēge (Jones, Thomas) / religiōne (Shanley) /
> uirtūte. (Higgins)

> prō patriā uīuere et morī. (Grattan)

> prō rēge et populō. (Bassett)

> prō rēge, lēge, grege. (Shield)

> prō lūsū et praedā. (MacMoran)

patri-a ae 1f. fatherland	*lēx lēg-is* 3f. law	*morior* 3/4 dep. I die
lībertās lībertāt-is 3f. liberty	*fidēs fidē-ī* 5f. faith	*popul-us* ī 2m. people
ecclēsi-a ae 1f. church	*religiō religiōn-is* 3f. religion	*grex greg-is* 3m. crowd, mob
rēx rēg-is 3m. king	*uīuō* 3 I live	*lūs-us ūs* 4m. sport

Additional readings relating to Section 3

3B   *1. Martial*

> *difficilis facilis, iūcundus acerbus es īdem.*
> *nec tēcum possum uīuere, nec sine tē.*

(12.46)

iūcundus sweet } NB Gender *acerbus* bitter }	*īdem* the same (nom.)	*uīuō* 3 I live

2. Motto

agnus in pāce, leō in bellō. (Edmonds)

agn-us ī 2m. lamb	*pāx pāc-is* 3f. peace	*leō leōn-is* 3m. lion

3C   *1. The Vulgate*

Micah 4.2–5 describes the last day:

> *dē Siōn ēgrediētur lēx, et uerbum Dominī dē Hierusalem, et iūdicābit inter*
> *populōs multōs, et corripiet gentēs fortēs usque in longinquum; et concīdent*
> *gladiōs suōs in uōmerēs et hastās suās in ligōnēs; nōn sūmet gēns aduersus*
> *gentem gladium; et nōn discent ultrā belligerāre . . . quia omnēs populī*
> *ambulābunt unusquisque in nōmine Deī suī; nōs autem ambulābimus in nōmine*
> *Dominī Deī nostrī in aeternum et ultrā.*

Siōn (abl.) Sion (the Temple Mount in Jerusalem)	*gēns gent-is* 3f. nation	*aduersus* + acc. against
lēx lēg-is 3f. law	*usque in longinquum* afar off	*discō* 3 I learn
Hierusalem (abl.) Jerusalem	*concīdō* 3 I beat	*ultrā* further, more, beyond
iūdicō 1 I judge (God is the subject)	*gladi-us ī* 2m. sword	*belligerō* 1 I fight
popul-us ī 2n. people	*uōmer uōmer-is* 3m. ploughshare	*unusquisque* each and every one
corripiō 3/4 I control	*hast-a ae* 1f. spear	*in aeternum* for ever
	ligō ligōn-is 3m. pruning hook	
	sūmō 3 I take up	

2. Mottoes

nōn uī, sed mente. (Lincolne)

nōn uī, sed virtūte. (Burrowes, Ramsbotham)

nōn uī sed uoluntāte. (Boucher)

nōn gladiō sed grātiā. (Charteris, Charters)

nōn cantū sed āctū. (Gillman)

ingeniō ac labōre. (Kerr)

ingeniō et uīribus. (Huddleston)

igne et ferrō. (Hickman)

industriā et labōre. (McGallock)

industriā et spē. (Warden)

industriā et uirtūte. (Bolton)

cōnsiliō ac uirtūte. (Rose-Lewin)

cōnsiliō et animīs. (Maitland, Ramadge)

cōnsiliō et armīs. (Stephens)

fidē et amōre. (Conway, Gardner, Hart, Seymour)

fidē et clēmentiā. (Martin)

fidē et armīs. (Fairquhar)

fidē et cōnstantiā (Dixon, James, Lee)

fidē et dīligentiā. (Crawford)

fidē et fidūciā. (Blackman, Gilchrist, Hogg, Wall, Watt)

fidē et labōre. (Allan)

fidē et spē. (Borthwick)

uīs (pl.) *uīr-ēs* s. force; (pl.) strength
mēns ment-is 3f. mind
uoluntās uoluntāt-is 3f. will
gladi-us ī 2m. sword
grāti-a ae 1f. grace

cant-us ūs 4m. song
āct-us ūs 4m. deed, doing
labor labōr-is 3m. effort, work
ferr-um-ī 2n. sword, iron
industri-a ae 1f. industry
spēs spē-ī 5f. hope

arm-a ōrum 2n. pl. arms
fidēs fidē-ī 5f. faith
clēmenti-a ae 1f. mercy
cōnstanti-a ae 1f. constancy
dīligenti-a ae 1f. diligence
fidūci-a ae 1f. trust

3D   *1. Martial*

> *Īliacō ⌐ similem puerum, Faustīne, ¬ ministrō*
> *lusca Lycōris amat. quam bene lusca uidet!*

(3.39)

Īliac-us a um Trojan [hold *Īliacō*: it depends on *similem* and agrees with *ministrō*]	*Faustīne* = O Faustinus *minister ministr-ī* 2m. slave *lusc-us a um* one-eyed	*Lycōris* (nom. f.) Lycoris

NB The 'Trojan slave' is Ganymede, a beautiful young boy with whom Jupiter fell in love. He took him up to heaven to be his cup-bearer.

2. The Vulgate

> *Glōria in altissimīs Deō, et in terrā pāx hominibus bonae uoluntātis.* (Luke 2.14)

glori-a ae 1f. glory *alt-us a um* high	*pāx pāc-is* 3f. peace *uoluntās uoluntāt-is* 3f. will

4A *1. Catullus*

Catullus *floruit c.* 84–54. He was famous for his love poems addressed to his woman, Lesbia. See Section 6A.

> *nūllī sē dīcit mulier mea nūbere mālle*
> *quam mihi, nōn sī sē Iuppiter ipse petat.*
> *dīcit: sed mulier cupidō ⌐ quod dīcit ¬ amantī*
> *in uentō et rapidā scrībere oportet aquā.*

(70)

nūbō 3 (+ dat.) I marry (said of women only) *ipse* himself (nom. s. m.) *petat* 'were to seek'	*quod* what (postponed – in English it would come after *sed*) *cupid-us a um* passionate	*amāns amant-is* 3m. lover *uent-us ī* 2m. wind *rapid-us a um* fast-flowing *oportet* 'one ought'

2. Martial

> *omnia prōmittis, cum tōtā nocte bibistī.*
> *māne nihil praestās. Pōllio, māne bibe.*

(12.12)

cum when *bibō* 3 *bib-ī* I drink	*māne* in the morning *praestō* 1 I provide	*Pōllio* O Pollio

> *numquam sē cēnāsse domī Philo iūrat, et hoc est.*
> *nōn cēnat, quotiēns nēmo uocāuit eum.*

(5.47)

cēnō 1 I dine *Philo Philōn-is* 3m. Philo	*iūrō* 1 I swear *est* 'is the case'	*quotiēns* as often as, whenever

3. Aulus Gellius[1]

cum (*when*) mentior et mē mentīrī dīcō, mentior, an (*or*) uērum dīcō?

1. *c.* 123–165 AD. His *Noctes Atticae* in twenty books is a compendium of scholarly discussions of diverse topics.

4. An epitaph

sum quod eris, fuī quod es.

4B   ### 1. Horace (Quīntus Horātius Flaccus 65–8 BC)

damnōsa quid nōn imminuit diēs?
aetās parentum, pēior auīs, tulit
*   nōs nēquiōrēs, mox datūrōs*
*   prōgeniem uitiōsiōrem.*

(*Odes* 3.6.45ff.)

damnōs-us a um detrimental, causing loss – hold until solved, by *dies* *immineō* 2 I diminish	*aetās aetāt-is* 3f. age *parēns parent-is* parent 3m. or f. *au-us ī* 2m. grandfather *nēquior nēquiōr-is* worse	*prōgeniēs progeniē-ī* 5f. offspring *uitiōs-us a um* corrupt

4C   ### 1. Mottoes

In all of these, the relative comes first, and means 'he who, she who, the thing(s) which' etc. Here are some examples, with translation.

quae habet, manus tenēbit ('What things (or the things which) it has, my hand will hold': Templeman)

quod sors fert, ferimus ('What/that which fate brings, we bear': Clayton)
quī patitur, uincit ('(He) who endures, wins': Kinnaird)

Note the verb 'to be' is often omitted, *e.g. quae rēcta, sequor* ('The things which (are) right, I follow': Campbell)

quae moderāta, firma (Ogilvie)

quae sērāta, sēcūra (Douglas)

quae sursum, uolō (Macqueen, Quin)

quae uult, ualdē uult (Wilmot)

quī inuidet, minor est (Cadogan, Leigh, Pugh)

quī mē tangit, poenitēbit (Gillespie, Macpherson)

quī plānē, sānē uādit (Taylor)

quī stat, caueat (Domville)

quod Deus uult, fīet (Dimsdale)

quod Deus uult, uolō (Mountford)

quod dīxī, dīxī (Dixie, Dixon)

quod faciō, ualdē faciō (Holmes)

quod honestum, ūtile (Lawson)

quod iūstum, nōn quod ūtile (Philips)

quod potuī, perfēcī (Dundas, Turner)

quod tibi uīs fierī, fac alterī (Ram)

quod tuum, tenē (Cheetham)

quod uērum, tūtum (Courtenay, Sim)

quod uolō, erit (Wright)

moderāt-us a um moderate	*inuideō* 2 I am envious	*caueat* 'let him beware'
firm-us a um permanent	*tangō* 3 I touch	*honest-us a um* honourable
sērāt-us a um locked	*poenitet* 2 he regrets (it)	*ūtil-is e* profitable
sēcūr-us a um safe	*plānē* plainly	*iūst-us a um* just
sursum above, in Heaven	*sānē* safely	*tūt-us a um* safe
ualdē strongly	*uādō* 3 I go	

2. Real Latin

(a) *ō fortūnātam nātam mē cōnsule Rōmam.* (Cicero)

fortūnāt-us a um lucky

(b) *nīl dēspērandum Teucrō duce et auspice Teucrō.* (Horace, *Odes* 1.7.27)

dēspērandum 'should be despaired of'	comforting his men as they face another leg of their	*auspex auspic-is* 3m. augur, interpreter of omens
Teucer Teucr-ī 2m. Teucer (brother of Ajax; he is	journey into exile from Salamis)	

(c) *quī uitia ōdit, et hominēs ōdit.* (Pliny)

uiti-um ī 2n. vice	*ōd-ī* (perf.) I hate

(d) *nūllum quod tetigit nōn ōrnāuit* (Dr Johnson's epitaph on Goldsmith)

tangō 3 *tetigī* I touch	*ōrnō* 1 I enhance

3. Unreal Latin

Revise all the cases with the following horrendous 'poem' about the Motor Bus by A. D. Godley. Note that he envisages *Motor* as a 3rd. decl. m. noun, *Bus* as 2m.; and observe what the poem tells you about one school of Latin pronunciation in the early twentieth century. Would *your* pronunciation generate these rhymes?

Motor Bus

What is this that roareth thus?
Can it be a *Mōtor Bus*?
Yes, the smell and hideous hum
Indicat Mōtōrem Bum!
Implet[1] in the Corn and High[2]   5
Terror mē Mōtōris Bī:
Bō Mōtōrī clāmitābō
Nē Mōtōre caedar[3] *ā Bō –*
Dative be or Ablative
So thou only let us live: 10
Whither shall thy victims flee?
Spare us, spare us, *Mōtor Be!*
Thus I sang; and still anigh
Came in hordes *Mōtōrēs Bī,*
Et complēbat[4] *omne forum*   15
Cōpia Mōtōrum Bōrum.
How shall wretches live like us
Cīnctī[5] *Bīs Mōtōribus?*
Domine, dēfende nōs
Contrā[6] *hōs Mōtōrēs Bōs!*   20

1. *implet* 'there fills'.
2. two streets in Oxford (Cornmarket and High Street).
3. 'so that I may not be killed by . . .'
4. *complēbat* 'there filled'.
5. *cīnctī* 'surrounded'.
6. *contrā* (+ acc.) against.

line 4 'points to a Motor Bus'.

lines 5–6 'There fills . . . me a fear of the Motor Bus.'

lines 7–8 'To the Motor Bus I shall shout / so that I may not be killed by the Motor Bus.'

line 12 'O Motor Bus.'

lines 14–16 '. . . Motor Buses, / and there filled the whole market-place / a plethora of Motor Buses'.

lines 18–20 'surrounded by Motor Buses. / Lord, defend us / Against these Motor Buses.'

4D   *The achievements of Augustus*

For sections 4D–4G, we provide passages from the *rēs gestae* (lit. 'things done', i.e. 'achievements') of the first Roman emperor Augustus, written by himself to commemorate himself. He ordered them to be inscribed on bronze tablets and set up in front of his mausoleum.

The period of Roman history in which the Verres story is set was one of increasing turmoil. The Roman republic was passing more and more into the domination of army-backed factions, led by men like Sulla, Pompey, and later Julius Caesar, whose power brought them the leading positions in the state. In 49, civil war broke out between Caesar and Pompey, and Caesar emerged as victor. But on the Ides of March 44, Julius Caesar was murdered by a group of pro-republican activists (led by Brutus) who felt that Rome was becoming a one-man state. In the ensuing civil war, two once allied factions emerged: that of Gaius Octavius, known as Octavian, the adopted son of Julius Caesar, and that of Marcus Antonius (Mark Antony), who looked to the East and the wealth of the Egyptian queen Cleopatra to support his bid for power. At the battle of Actium in 31, Octavian emerged triumphant, but he faced problems as serious as those faced by Julius Caesar, i.e. how to reconcile the Roman aristocracy, with their implacable hatred of any idea of 'monarchy', to the fact that the old-style 'republic' was dead, and that the rule of one man was Rome's only hope of survival. Granted the additional name 'Augustus' by a grateful Roman people and senate in 27, he succeeded by making himself the embodiment of Roman standards, ideals and above all, stability, and by presenting the new order, which was in fact the foundation of an imperial dynasty, to make it look like the old republic restored, though he was in fact in control of it. As we shall see, he restored ancient rituals and customs and temples, and engaged writers (like Virgil and Horace) to play their part in propagating his image and ideals, but the most authentic 'statement' about what he stood for is his own – the *rēs gestae dīuī Augustī* ('the achievements of the divine Augustus'), which he wrote himself.

These extracts are adapted only by the excision of the more difficult passages, so you are reading here Augustus' actual words.

Rēs gestae dīuī Augustī

rēs gestae dīuī Augustī, quibus orbem terrārum imperiō populī Rōmānī subiēcit, et impēnsae quās in rem pūblicam populumque Rōmānum fēcit.

annōs ūndēuīgintī nātus exercitum prīuātō cōnsiliō et prīuātā impēnsā comparāuī, per quem rem pūblicam ⌐ ā dominātiōne factiōnis ⌐ oppressam in lībertātem uindicāuī. senātus in ōrdinem suum mē   5

adlēgit, C. Pānsā et A. Hirtiō cōnsulibus, et imperium mihi dedit.
populus eōdem annō mē cōnsulem et triumuirum creāuit.

cūriam templumque Apollinis, aedem dīuī Iūlī, Lupercal, porticum ad
circum Flāminium, aedēs in Capitōliō Iouis Feretrī et Iouis Tonantis,   10
aedem Quirīnī, aedēs Mineruae et Iūnōnis Rēgīnae et Iouis Lībertātis in
Auentīnō, aedem Larum in summā sacrā uiā, aedem deum Penātium in
Veliā, aedem Iuuentātis, aedem Mātris Magnae in Palātiō fēcī.

Capitōlium et Pompēium theātrum refēcī sine ūllā īnscrīptiōne
nōminis meī. rīuōs aquārum complūribus locīs uetustāte lābentīs refēcī.   15
forum Iūlium et basilicam, quae fuit inter aedem Castoris et aedem
Sāturnī, perfēcī.

ter mūnus gladiātōrium dedī, quibus mūneribus dēpugnāuērunt
hominum circiter decem mīllia.

uēnātiōnēs bēstiārum Āfricānārum in circō aut in forō aut in   20
amphitheātrīs populō dedī sexiēns et uīciens, quibus cōnfecta sunt
bēstiārum circiter tria mīllia et quīngentae.

(*Rēs gestae* 1–4, 19–23)

rēs gestae rērum gestārum 5f.
pl. + 1/2 adj. (lit.) things
done; achievements
dīu-us a um divine
August-us ī 2m. Augustus
quibus [Pl., so what must it pick
up? Dat or abl., but why?
Hold.]
orbis orb-is 3m. circle
(+ *terrārum* = 'circle of the
lands', i.e. world) [Acc., but
why? Hold.]
imperi-um ī 2n. command, rule,
authority. [Dat. or abl., but
why? Hold.]
popul-us ī 2m. people
subiciō 3/4 *subiēcī* I subject X
(acc.) to Y (dat.) [This should
solve *imperiō* and *quibus* (abl.
of means)]
impēns-a ae 1f. money, expense
quās [F. pl., so what must it pick
up? Acc, but why? Hold.]
rēs pūblica rēī pūblicae 5f. +
1/2 adj. republic
fēcit [Explains *quās* in the acc.]
ūndēuīgintī nineteen
nāt-us a um born, aged [Nom.,
m., but who does it refer to?
Hold.]

prīuāt-us a um his own [*prīuātō* is
dat. or abl., but why? Hold.]
5 *comparō* 1 I put together, gather,
raise [Person (tells you who
nātus is)? Explains why
exercitum in acc. Solves
prīuātō . . . impēnsā.]
per quem ['through whom' (i.e.
through me) or 'through
which' (referring to the
army)? Wait.]
dominātiō dominātiōn-is 3f.
tyranny
factiō factiōn-is 3f. political
clique
oppress-us a um crushed, ground
under
in lībertātem uindicō 1 I free (lit.
'I claim into freedom')
[Person? Shows that *quem*
must = army, solves case of
rem pūblicam.]
ōrdō ōrdin-is 3m. order,
membership
adlegō 3 *adlēgī* I enrol
C. Pānsā et A. Hirtiō cōnsulibus
i.e. in 43
triumuir triumuir-ī 2m. triumvir,
member of commission of
three

creō 1 I elect
cūri-a ae 1f. senate house [Acc.,
but why? You will not solve
this sentence till you come to
the very last word! So this is
an important exercise in
holding on.]
templ-um ī 2n. temple [Since it is
linked by *-que* to *cūriam*, one
assumes it also is acc. But
what is the function of the
accusatives? This question
will not be asked again – but
you must ask it.]
Apollō Apollin-is 3m. Apollo
dīu-us a um divine
Iūli-us ī 2m. Julius (Caesar)
Lupercal 3n. the Lupercal
portic-us ūs 4f. portico
10 *circ-us ī* 2m. circus
Flāmini-us a um of Flaminius
Capitōli-um ī 2n. the Capitol (hill)
Feretri-us a um Feretrian
Tonāns Tonant-is thunderer
Quirīn-us ī 2m. Quirinus
(= Romulus deified)

Mineru-a ae 1f. Minerva (Athena)
Iūnō Iūnōn-is 3f. Juno (Hera),
    wife of Jupiter
Rēgīn-a ae 1f. queen
Lībertās Lībertāt-is 3f. freedom
Auentīn-um ī 2n. the Aventine
    (hill)
Larēs Lar-um 3m. pl. the Lares
    (household gods)
deum [Gen. pl., not acc. s.]
Penātēs Penāt-ium 3m. pl. the
    Penates (household gods)
Veli-a ae 1f. the Velian ridge,
    connecting two hills in Rome
Iuuentās Iuuentāt-is 3f. Youth
Māter Magna Mātr-is Magn-ae
    Cybele
Palāti-um ī 2n. the Palatine (hill)
fēcī [At last! Solves all the
    accusatives.]
Capitōli-um ī 2n. the Capitol (hill)
Pompēi-us a um of Pompey
theātr-um ī 2n. theatre [Nom., or
    acc? Hold . . . but not for long.]
reficiō 3/4 *refēcī* I rebuild, restore
īnscrīptiō īnscrīptiōn-is 3f.
    inscription
15 *rīu-us ī* 2m. *aquārum* aqueduct
    [Why acc.? Hold.]
complūr-ēs ium very many,
    several

uetustās uetustāt-is 3f. age [Why
    abl.? Hold.]
lābēns lābent-is collapsing
    (explains *uetustāte*)
Iūli-us a um of Julius (Caesar)
    [Nom. or acc.?]
basilic-a ae 1f. courtyard (used
    for business and law-courts)
    [Its case shows that *forum
    Iūlium* must also be acc.]
inter (+ acc.) in between
Castor Castor-is 3m. Castor (god,
    brother of Pollux)
Sāturn-us ī 2m. Saturn (ancient
    Roman god = Greek Kronos)
ter three times
mūnus mūner-is 3n. public show
    [Neuter, so hold whether nom.
    or acc.]
gladiātōri-us a um involving
    gladiators
dedī [Solves *mūnus*]
quibus mūneribus [Connecting
    relative. But why dat. or abl.?
    Hold.]
dēpugnō 1 I fight [Plural: will
    there follow a subject which
    tells us who fought? *hominum*
    'of men' – it looks like it.]
circiter about
decem ten

mīllia (usually *mīlia*) thousands
    [So we have '*quibus
    mūneribus* about 10,000 men
    fought'. Now translate *quibus
    mūneribus*.]
20 *uēnātiō uēnātiōn-is* 3f. hunt
    [Nom. or acc.? Hold.]
bēsti-a ae 1f. wild animal
Āfricān-us a um from Africa
circ-us ī 2m. circus
amphitheātr-um ī 2n.
    amphitheatre
sexiēns et uīciēns six and twenty
    times
quibus [Pl., so it must pick up –
    uēnātiōnēs? *bēstiārum*?
    amphitheātrīs? Wait.]
cōnficiō 3/4 *cōnfēcī cōnfect-us* I
    destroy [Passive, so something
    'was destroyed'; *sunt* shows
    pl., but why *cōnfect-a* neuter?
    Wait for subject.]
tria mīllia (neuter!) three
    thousands
quīngent-ī ae a 500 [But why *-ae*
    feminine? So we have '*quibus*
    3,500 (of) animals were
    destroyed'. Now tr. *quibus*.]

Other writers

1. Lucretius

C. 95–c. 50. Philosopher poet, author of *Dē rērum natūrā* 'On the nature of matter', 'On the nature of the universe'.

On the nature of the gods
sēmōta ab nostrīs rēbus sēiūnctaque longē;
nam prīuāta dolōre omnī, prīuāta perīclīs,
ipsa suīs pollēns opibus, nīl indiga nostrī,
nec bene prōmeritīs capitur neque tangitur īrā.

(*Dē rērum natūrā* 2.648ff.)

sēmōta removed [It is f., referring
    to *dīuum nātūra* 'the nature of
    the gods' a few lines earlier.]
sēiūncta separated
prīuāt-us a um (+ abl.) relieved of
dolor dolōr-is 3m. pain; grief

perīclīs = *perīculīs*
pollēns pollent-is powerful
suīs . . . opibus 'in (respect of)
    their own resources'
nīl 'in no way'
indig-us a um in need of (+ gen.)

bene prōmerit-a (*ōrum* 2n. pl.)
    good deeds
capiō (here) I win over
tangō 3 I touch, move, affect
īr-a ae 1f. anger

2. Publilius Syrus

First writer of stage 'mimes', full of wit and satire and memorable quotes, *c.* 44.

(a) amāns īrātus multa mentītur sibi.

(b) auārus ipse causa miseriae suae.

(c) amāre iuuenī frūctus est, crīmen senī.

(d) amāre et sapere uix deō concēditur.

(e) amōris uulnus īdem sānat quī facit.

(f) amōrī fīnem tempus, nōn animus, facit.

amāns amant-is 3m. lover	*crīmen crīmin-is* 3n. reproach	*uulnus uulner-is* 3n. wound
auār-us ī 2m. miser	*sapere* 'to be wise'	*sānō* 1 I heal
miseri-a ae 1f. unhappiness	*uix* scarcely	*īdem* (is antecedent of *quī*)
frūct-us ūs 4m. enjoyment	*concēdō* 3 I yield, grant	*fīnis fīn-is* 3m. end

3. Martial

septima iam, Philerōs, tibi conditur uxor in agrō.
    plūs nūllī, Philerōs, quam tibi reddit ager.

(10.43)

septim-us a um seventh	*tibi* 'by you' (dat. of agent)	*reddō* 3 I yield, return
Philerōs (voc.) Phileros ('friend of Eros')	*condō* 3 I bury	

4. Part of the Creed

(Christ) quī propter nōs hominēs et propter nostram salūtem dēscendit dē caelīs.
Et incarnātus est dē spīritū sānctō ex Mariā uirgine; et homo factus est.
Crucifīxus etiam prō nōbīs, sub Pontiō Pīlātō passus et sepultus est.
Et resurrēxit tertiā diē secundum scrīptūrās.

salūs salūt-is 3f. salvation	*spīrit-us -ūs* 4m. spirit	*sepultus est* 'he was buried'
dēscendō 3 *dēscendī* I descend	*crucifīxus* (sc. *est*) 'he was	*resurgō* 3 *resurrēxī* I rise again
dē (+ abl.) from	crucified'	*terti-us a um* third
cael-a ōrum 2n. pl. heaven(s)	*sub* (+ abl.) under	*secundum* (+ acc.) according to
incarnātus est 'he was made flesh'	*passus* (sc. *est*) 'he suffered'	*scrīptūr-a ae* 1f. scripture

4E   *Rēs gestae dīuī Augustī*

mare pācāuī ā praedōnibus. iūrāuit in mea uerba tōta Italia sponte suā, et
mē ⌐ belli quō uīcī ad Actium ¬ ducem dēpoposcit; iūrāuērunt in eadem
uerba prōuinciae Galliae, Hispāniae, Āfrica, Sicilia, Sardinia. omnium
prōuinciārum populī Rōmānī quibus fīnitimae fuērunt gentēs quae nōn
pārērent imperiō nostrō fīnīs auxī. Galliās et Hispāniās prōuinciās, item   5
Germāniam pācāuī. Alpēs ā regiōne eā quae proxima est Hadriānō marī
ad Tuscum pācificāuī. classis mea per Ōceanum ab ostiō Rhēnī ad sōlis
orientis regiōnem usque ad fīnīs Cimbrōrum nāuigāuit. Aegȳptum
imperiō populī Rōmānī adiēcī. plūrimae aliae gentēs expertae sunt p. R.
fidem, mē prīncipe, quibus anteā cum populō Rōmānō nūllum exstiterat   10
lēgātiōnum et amīcitiae commercium.

(Rēs gestae 25–7)

---

pācō 1 I bring peace to X (acc.)
   from (*ā* + abl.) Y
praedō praedōn-is 3m. pirate
iūrō 1 *in uerba* I take the oath of
   allegiance [Await subject, if
   there is one quoted.]
sponte suā of its own accord,
   willingly
mē bellī [Wait to solve both
   these.]
quō ...*Actium* [Relative clause.
   quō picks up *bellī.*]
Acti-um ī 2n. (battle of) Actium,
   31, when Octavian–Augustus
   defeated Mark Antony and
   Cleopatra and became sole
   ruler of Roman world
ducem [Acc. – with *mē.* Yes: *mē
   ducem bellī* solves *bellī.*]
dēposcō 3 *dēpoposcī* I demand
   [Solves case of *mē ducem.*
   Who 'demanded'? Answer:
   tōta Italia from the previous
   clause.]
iūrāuērunt [Pl., so 'they' – but
   who? Await subject(s).]
prōuinci-a ae 1f. province [Ah –
   here come(s) the subject(s).]
Galli-ae ārum 1f. pl. the
   provinces of Gaul
Hispāni-ae ārum 1f. pl. the
   provinces of Spain
omnium ...*populī Rōmānī* [A
   long phrase in the genitive.

Probably 'of all ...', but hold
   till a suitable noun which it
   can qualify emerges.]
quibus ... *nostrō* [Two
   sub-clauses here – first
   quibus ... *gentēs*, then
   quae ... *nostrō.* Hold tight.]
fīnitim-us a um close to (+ dat.)
   [Solves *quibus* – 'to which
   were close ...']
gēns gent-is 3f. tribe, people
quae [By position probably picks
   up 'tribes'. Nom., so 'the
   tribes which ....]
5 *pārērent* '(they) obeyed' (+ dat.)
   fīnēs fīn-ium 3f. pl. boundaries
   [Nom. or acc.?]
augeō 3 *auxī* I increase, enlarge
   [Solves *fīnīs.* But whose *fīnīs*?
   Answer: *omnium* ... ; so we
   only solve *omnium* ... *populī*
   at the end of the sentence.]
item similarly
Germāni-a ae 1f. Germany
Alpēs Alp-ium 3f. pl. the Alps
   [Nom. or acc? Hold.]
regiō regiōn-is 3f. area
proxim-us a um closest (to + dat.)
Hadriān-us a um Adriatic
Tusc-us a um Tuscan (sc. *mare*)
pācificō 1 I pacify, bring peace to
Ōcean-us ī 2m. Ocean, i.e. the
   North Sea
osti-um ī 2n. mouth

Rhēn-us ī 2m. Rhine
sōl oriēns sōl-is orient-is rising
   sun, East
usque ad (+ acc.) right up to
Cimbr-ī ōrum 2m. pl. the Cimbri,
   a German tribe (modern
   Denmark)
Aegȳpt-us ī 2f. Egypt [Case?
   Hold; hold also *imperiō.*]
adiciō 3/4 *adiēcī* I add X (acc.) to
   Y (dat.)
experior 4 dep. *expert-us* I
   experience
p. R. = populī Rōmānī
10 *fidēs fidē-ī* 5f. protection,
   trustworthiness
quibus [Pl., so who must it refer
   to? Case = dat. or abl. Hold.]
anteā previously
nūllum [But no what? Wait.]
exsistō 1 *exstitī* exist [What had
   existed? Since 'exist' cannot
   have a direct object, one
   assumes *nūllum* must be a
   subject, so 'quibus previously
   no something had existed'.]
lēgātiō lēgātiōn-is 3f. embassy,
   i.e. international relations
amīciti-a ae 1f. friendship
commerci-um ī 2n. [Ah! *nūllum*]
   exchange [So 'quibus
   previously no exchange of...'
   Tr. *quibus.*]

Adapted medieval Latin: St Columba subdues the Loch Ness Monster

Adapted by Sidney Morris (*Fōns perennis*) from Adomnan's Life of St Columba, the Irish saint, who was the founder of the monastery of Iona. St Columba lived from about AD 545 to 615. The original of this passage can be read in Keith Sidwell, *Reading Medieval Latin* (Cambridge 1995), pp. 89–90.

ōlim sānctus Columba in prōuinciā Pictōrum per aliquot diēs manēbat et
necesse habuit trānsīre fluuium Nēsam. ubi ad ripām aduēnit, aliquōs ex
incolīs huius regiōnis aspicit humantēs miserum homunculum quem, ut
ipsī incolae dīcēbant, natantem paulō ante in fluuiō aquātilis bēstia
dentibus magnīs momorderat. uir sānctus haec audiēns iussit ūnum ex   5
comitibus suīs natāre ad alteram rīpam et nāuigium, quod ibi stābat, ad sē
redūcere. comes ille, nōmine Lugneus Mocumin, sine morā uestīmenta
exuit et, tunicam sōlam gerēns, immittit sē in aquas.

sed bēstia quae in profundō flūminis latuerat, sentiēns aquam super sē
turbātam, subitō ēmergēns ad hominem in mediō flūmine natantem cum   10
ingentī fremitū, apertō ōre, properāuit. inter Lugneum et bēstiam nōn
amplius erat quam longitūdō ūnīus contī. tum uir beātus haec uidēns,
dum barbarī et frātrēs timōre pauent, sānctam manum ēleuāns, signum
crucis in āēre facit dīcēns bēstiae: 'nōlī ultra prōcēdere; nōlī hominem
tangere sed celeriter abī.' tum uērō bēstia, iussū sānctī uirī, retrō uēlōciter   15
fūgit tremefacta. frātrēs cum ingentī admīrātiōne glōrificāuērunt Deum
in beātō uirō, et barbarī, propter mīraculum quod ipsī uīderant, Deum
magnificāuērunt Christiānōrum.

ōlim one day	*mor-a ae* 1f. delay	*barbar-ī ōrum* 2m. pl. locals
sānct-us a um holy, Saint	*uestīment-um ī* 2n. clothes	*timor timōr-is* 3m. fear
Columb-a ae 1m. Columba	*exuō* 3 I take off	*paueō* 2 I shake, tremble
Pict-ī ōrum 2m. pl. Picts	*tunic-a ae* 1f. tunic	*ēleuō* 1 I raise
aliquot several	*gerō* 3 I wear	*crux cruc-is* 3f. cross
necesse habeō I find it necessary	*immittō* 3 I hurl into	*āēr āër-is* 3m. air
trānseō trānsire I cross	*profund-um ī* 2n. depths	*ultrā* any further
rīp-a ae 1f. bank	*flūmen flūmin-is* 3n. loch	*prōcēdō* 3 I advance
fluui-us ī 2m. loch (lit. river)	(lit. river)	15 *iussū* 'at the command'
incol-a ae 1m. inhabitant	*lateō* 2 I lie hidden	*retrō* back
regiō regiōn-is 3f. region	10 *turbāt-us a um* disturbed	*uēlōciter* speedily
aspiciō 3/4 I spot	*ēmergō* 3 I emerge	*tremefact-us a um* terrified
humō 1 I bury	*medi-us a um* middle of	*admīrātiō admīrātiōn-is* 3f.
natō 1 I swim	*fremit-us ūs* 4m. roar	wonder
aquātil-is bēsti-a ae if. monster,	*apert-us a um* opened	*glōrificō* 1 I glorify
water beast	*ōs ōr-is* 3n. mouth	*mīrācul-um ī* 2n. miracle
5 *dēns dent-is* 3m. tooth	*properō* 1 I hurry	*magnificō* 1 I magnify
mordeō 2 *momordī* I bite	*amplius* more	*Christiān-us ī* 2m. a Christian
nāuigi-um ī 2n. boat	*longitūdō longitūdin-is* 3f. length	
Lugne-us ī 2m. Lugneus	*cont-us ī* 2m. pole	
(*Mocumin* = indecl.)	*beāt-us a um* blessed	

4F   *Rēs gestae dīuī Augustī*

quī parentem meum trucīdāuērunt, eōs in exsilium expulī iūdiciīs
lēgitimīs ultus eōrum facinus, et posteā bellum īnferentīs reī pūblicae uīcī
bis aciē.

bella terrā et marī cīuīlia externaque tōtō in orbe terrārum saepe gessī,
uictorque omnibus ueniam petentibus cīuibus pepercī. externās gentīs,   5
quibus tūtō ignōscī potuit, cōnseruāre quam excīdere māluī. in triumphīs
meīs ductī sunt ante currum meum rēgēs aut rēgum līberī nouem.

cum ex Hispāniā Galliāque, rēbus in iīs prōuinciīs prosperē gestīs,
Rōmam rediī, Ti. Nerōne P. Quīntiliō cōnsulibus, āram Pācis Augustae
senātus prō reditū meō cōnsacrandam cēnsuit ad campum Mārtium, in   10
quā magistrātūs et sacerdōtēs uirginēsque Vestālēs anniuersārium
sacrificium facere iussit.

Iānum Quirīnum, quem claussum esse māiōrēs nostrī uoluērunt cum
per tōtum imperium populī Rōmānī terrā marīque esset parta uictōriīs
pāx, cum, priusquam nāscerer, ā conditā urbe bis omnīnō clausum fuisse   15
prōdātur memoriae, ter mē prīncipe senātus claudendum esse cēnsuit.

lēgibus nouīs mē auctōre lātīs, multa exempla māiōrum exolēscentia
iam ex nostrō saeculō redūxī et ipse multārum rērum exempla imitanda
posterīs trādidī.

(*Rēs gestae* 2–4, 12–13, 18)

---

qui [To be picked up by *eōs.*]
parentem [I.e. Julius Caesar (by adoption).]
trucīdō 1 I slaughter
exsili-um ī 2n. exile
expellō 3 *expulī* I drive out
iūdici-um ī 2n. tribunal [But why dat./abl.? Hold.]
lēgitim-us a um legal
ulcīscor 3 *ultus* I punish [Explains *iūdiciīs* – the means by which he acted.]
posteā afterwards
bellum [Nom. or acc? Wait.]
īnferō 3 I bring, wage X (acc.) against Y (dat.) [Participle, so possibly 'waging war'. Case is acc. pl. (-*īs*). Does it agree with anyone? Yes, with *eōs* 'them', which is not repeated. So it must mean 'them waging war' – in the acc.]

reī pūblicae [Must surely be dat. after *bellum īnferō.*]
uīcī [Subject and verb, explaining why *īnferentīs* is acc.]
bis twice
aciēs aciē-ī 5f. battle-line [Why abl.?]
bella [Nom. or acc. pl.? Wait.]
cīuīl-is e civil
extern-us a um foreign
orbis orb-is 3m. (*terrārum*) the world
5 *uictor uictōr-is* 3m. victor
omnibus [Dat. or abl. pl.? And who are these 'all'?]
ueni-a ae 1f. pardon
petentibus [What are the 'all' doing?]
cīuibus [Ah. Who the 'all' are.]
parcō 3 *pepercī* I spare (+ dat.) [Explains *omnibus… cīuibus.*]

gēns gent-is 3f. nation [*externās* confirms it must be acc., so wait.]
quibus… potuit lit. 'to whom it could safely be pardoned', i.e. 'whom one could pardon safely'
cōnseruō 1 I protect, preserve
quam than [Await verb taking infinitive + *quam.*]
excīdō 3 I exterminate
triumph-us ī 2m. triumph
ductī sunt ['some masculine plurals were led': wait to find out who.]
curr-us ūs 4m. chariot
līber-ī ōrum 2m. pl. children
nouem nine
cum [Followed by ablative? No. So 'when', 'since', 'although'.]
Hispāni-a ae 1f. Spain
Galli-a ae 1f. Gaul

rēbus...gestīs [Looks suspiciously like an abl. abs., and so it is.]

prosperē successfully

Nerō Nerōn-is 3m. Nero (understand *et*)

Quīntili-us ī 2m. Quintilius [I.e. the year 13]

ār-a ae 1f. *Pācis* altar of peace [Why acc.? Wait.]

August-us a um of Augustus

10 *redit-us ūs* 4m. return

cōnsacrandam (*esse*) 'should be consecrated' [Acc. (and inf.) after *cēnsuit*. Since *cōnsacrand-am* is acc. s. f., it must agree with *āram*.]

cēnseō 2 I vote

camp-us Mārti-us camp-ī Mārt-ī 2m. the Campus Martius (of Mars), in Rome [*in quā* (f.), so refers back to what?]

magistrāt-us ūs 4m. magistrate [But nom. or acc. pl.? Do any of the following nouns (to *Vestālēs*) tell you definitely?]

sacerdōs sacerdōt-is 3m. or f. priest(ess)

uirgō Vestālis uirgin-is Vestāl-is 3f. + 3 adj. Vestal Virgin [Still a problem whether these nom. or acc, so continue to hold]

anniuersāri-us a um yearly

sacrifici-um ī 2n. sacrifice [Also nom. or acc, so hold!]

iussit [Singular. So *magistrātūs...uestālēs* cannot be the subject. A 'yearly sacrifice' cannot 'order'. So 'senate' must be the understood subject from the previous clause. Hence 'on which the senate ordered...']

Iān-us ī Quirīn-us ī 2m. the archway (or arched passage) of Janus Quirinus in the forum, with doors at both ends, forming the god's shrine [Why acc.? Hold, till the end of the sentence.]

claudō 3 *clausī claus(s)us* I close

māiōrēs māiōr-um 3m. pl. ancestors

pariō 3/4 *peperī partus* I win, gain [Hold *parta*.]

uictoriīs [Abl. of means after *parta*.]

15 *pāx* [Solves *parta*.]

cum although

priusquam [+ subj.) before

nāscor 3 dep. I am born

condita urbs the founded city, i.e. the foundation of the city

bis twice

omnīnō in all

prōdō 3 I transmit X (acc) to Y (dat.) [The dative is given by *memoriae* 'to history/memory': but what is the subject of *cum prodātur*? No subject is quoted, so try 'it', i.e. 'although it is transmitted to memory/history', when *clausum fuisse* becomes acc. and inf., i.e. 'that (it) had been closed'.]

ter thrice

claudendum esse 'that it should be closed' [What is 'it'? Back to the start of the sentence – *Iānum Quirīnum*.]

nou-us a um new

auctor auctōr-is 3m. initiator

exempl-um ī 2n. example

māiōrēs māiōr-um 3m. pl. ancestors

exolēscō 3 I go out of fashion

saecul-um ī 2n. age

redūcō 3 *redūxī* I bring back

imitanda 'to be copied' [Refers to *exempla*. But still hold case.]

poster-ī ōrum 2m. pl. future generations

trādō 3 *trādidī* I hand down X (acc.) to Y (dat.)

Other writers

1. Martial

ut recitem tibi nostra rogās epigrammata. nōlō.
   nōn audīre, Celer, sed recitāre cupīs.

(1.63)

recitō 1 I read out loud, recite my own poetry

epigramma epigrammat-is 3n. epigram

2. Elio Giulio Crotti c. 1564

Narcissus (who fell in love with himself, looking at his reflection in a pool)

> hicne amor est? hicne est furor? aut īnsānia mentis?
>   nōlo, uolō, atque iterum nōlō, iterumque uolō.
> hicne gelū est? hicne est ignis? nam spīritus aequē
>   mī ignēscit, gelidō ⌐ et torpet in ¬ ōre anima.
> uērum nōn amor aut furor est, ignisue gelūue: 5
>   ipse ego sum, quī mē mī ēripuī ac rapuī.

amor amōr-is 3m. love	*mī = mihi* (dat. of advantage/	**5** *-ue* or
īnsāni-a ae 1f. madness	disadvantage)	*ēripiō* 3/4 *ēripuī* I tear X (acc.)
mēns ment-is 3f. mind	*ignēscō* 3 I catch fire	away from Y (dat.)
gelū n. ice	*gelid-us a um* cold	*rapiō* 3/4 *rapuī* I seize, snatch
spīrit-us ūs 4m. spirit	*torpeō* 2 I am numb	
aequē equally	*anim-a ae* 1f. breath	

Notes

1. Crotti uses much elision (cutting off a final vowel before a following vowel). In line 1 *hicn(e) est;* line 2 *atqu(e) iterum, nōl(ō) iterumque;* line 3 *gel(ū) est, hicn(e) est;* line 4 *m(ī) ignēscit, gelid(ō) et . . . ōr(e) anima;* line 6 *ips(e) ego . . . m(ī) ēripu(ī) ac . . .*
2. He also shortens a long vowel in line 2: *nŏlo* for *nōlō.*
3. See *Grammar and Exercises* p. 273ff. for rules of Latin metre and **186** for the elegiac couplet (the metre Crotti uses here).

4G   *Rēs gestae dīuī Augustī*

in cōnsulātū sextō et septimō, postquam bella cīuīlia exstīnxeram, per cōnsēnsum ūniuersōrum potītus rērum omnium, rem pūblicam ex meā potestāte in senātūs populīque Rōmānī arbitrium trānstulī. quō prō meritō meō, senātūs cōnsultō, Augustus appellātus sum et laureīs postēs aedium meārum uestītī pūblicē corōnaque cīuica super iānuam meam   5
fixa est et clupeus aureus in cūriā Iūliā positus, quem mihi senātum populumque Rōmānum dare uirtūtis clēmentiaeque et iūstitiae et pietātis caussā testātum est per eius clupeī īnscrīptiōnem. post id tempus, auctōritāte omnibus praestitī, potestātis autem nihilō amplius habuī quam cēterī qui mihi quōque in magistrātū conlēgae fuērunt.   10

tertium decimum cōnsulātum cum gerēbam, senātus et equester ōrdō populusque Rōmānus ūniuersus appellāuit mē patrem patriae, idque in uestibulō aedium meārum īnscrībendum et in cūriā Iūliā et in forō Aug. sub quadrīgīs quae mihi ex s.c. positae sunt cēnsuit. cum scrīpsī haec, annum agēbam septuagēnsumum sextum.   15

(*Rēs gestae* 34–5)

cōnsulāt-us ūs
   4m. consulship ⎫
sext-us a um
   sixth ⎬ [i.e. 28 and 27]
septim-us a um
   seventh ⎭
postquam after
cīuīl-is e civil
exstinguō 3 *exstīnxī* I put out
cōnsēns-us ūs 4m. agreement
ūniuers-ī ōrum 2m. pl. everyone
potior 4 dep. (+ gen.) I gain
   control of
potestās potestāt-is 3f. power
arbitri-um ī 2n. judgement,
   arbitration
trānsferō 3 *trānstulī* I transfer
quō [Connecting relative,
   governed by *prō*]
merit-um ī 2n. good deeds
cōnsult-um ī 2n. decree
appellō 1 I call
laure-a ae 1f. laurel-wreath [Dat.
   Or abl.? Hold.]
postis post-is 3m. doorpost
5 *uestiō* 4 I clothe [Solves *laureīs*.]
pūblicē publicly
cīuic-us a um civic

super (+ acc.) above
fīgō 3 4th p.p. *fīx-us* I place, fix
clupe-us ī 2m. shield [See
   frontispiece to *Grammar and*
   Exercises p. ii]
cūri-a ae 1f. senate-house
Iūli-us a um Julian
quem . . . dare lit. 'which (that) the
   senate and the Roman people
   gave to me'
clēmenti-a ae 1f. mercy
iūstiti-a ae 1f. justice
pietās pietāt-is 3f. respect for
   gods, family and homeland
caus(s)ā (+ gen.) for the sake of
   [Follows the noun(s) it
   qualifies.]
testātum est 'it was witnessed'
īnscrīptiō īnscrīptiōn-is 3f.
   inscription
post (+ acc.) after
auctōritās auctōritāt-is 3f.
   authority, prestige
praestō 1 *praestitī* I excel X (dat.)
   in Y (abl.)
nihilō amplius nothing more, no
   more [Governs *potestātis*.]

10 *magistrāt-us ūs* 4m. office
conlēg-a ae 1m. colleague
terti-us decim-us a um thirteenth
cōnsulāt-us ūs 4m. consulship
   [I.e. 2]
equester equestr-is e of knights
ōrdō ōrdin-is 3m. order
patri-a ae 1f. fatherland
ūniuers-us a um whole
uestibul-um ī 2n. forecourt
īnscrībendum to be inscribed
   [Wait to solve *īnscrībendum*
   and *id*, which agree, till end of
   sentence.]
Aug. = *Augustō*, from *August-us a*
   um of Augustus
quadrīg-ae ārum 1f. pl.
   four-horse chariot
s.c. = *senātūs cōnsultō*
   (*cōnsult-um ī* 2n. decree)
cēnseō 2 I vote [Solves
   id . . . īnscrībendum. Subject of
   cēnsuit?]
15 *agō* 3 I pass, live
septuagēnsum-us sext-us a um
   seventy-sixth

Augustus' *rēs gestae*

Octavian realised that he could not rule an empire on his own. He needed the senatorial elite to participate in the task of administration and they had to be persuaded that they still had the opportunity to express their views and use their influence. The satisfactory achievement of these aims came only after a period of experimentation. In January 27 BC Octavian handed over his powers and territory to the decision of the Senate, who duly confirmed his authority as a consul and granted him a huge *prōuincia* in which to exercise his *imperium*. The rest of the provinces were distributed annually by lot to senior senators, as had been the normal practice in the late Republic.

Along with this settlement came the restoration and regularisation of much of the traditional machinery of administration. Octavian could now represent himself as an elected magistrate of the Roman people with a large *prōuincia* granted in regular manner by the Senate. All this worked as long as Octavian continued to hold the consulship each year. But in 23 BC he became dissatisfied and resigned his consulship. But without the consulship the question arose of what was to be the *imperium* he was to use to govern his huge *prōuincia*. So he was invested with the *imperium* of a proconsul, but it was specifically stated to be greater (*māius*) than that of other proconsuls, thus clarifying his relationship with other magistrates of the Roman people.

There was one other power granted in 23 BC which is particularly revealing of Octavian's aims. He was given the power of a tribune (*tribūnicia potestās*). Its significance lay in the way in which it associated the emperor with the tradition of the popular tribunes of the Republic and their role as protectors and promoters of the interests of the ordinary people. (*World of Rome*, **79**)

5A   *Virgil: introduction*

Pūblius Vergilius Marō (Virgil) was born in 70 near Mantua. He early on established powerful connections, notably with the governor of Cisalpine Gaul, C. Asinius Pōlliō, himself a scholar and poet. It was Pōlliō who introduced him to Octavian. In the early 30s Virgil became a member of the circle of Maecēnās, the great literary patron and powerful political ally of Octavian.

Virgil was the author of three major works. The first two were the *Bucolics* (or *Eclogues*), and *Georgics*, whose apparently rural themes have political overtones, e.g. at the end of *Georgics* I, there is an appeal to the native gods of Italy to allow Octavian to come to the aid of the civil-war-stricken land. His final work, begun around 30 and still undergoing final revision at his death in 19, was the *Aeneid*, an epic in twelve books, relating how Aeneas, mythical founder of the Roman race, escaped from the burning city of Troy and finally established a foothold in Italy, after defeating the Rutulian King Turnus in single combat. The ancients saw the purpose of Virgil in this work as twofold: to rival Homer (on whose *Iliad* and *Odyssey* the poem draws heavily) and to glorify Augustus. The latter he achieved in three ways. First he accepted and stressed the family connection between Aeneas and the *gēns Iūlia* (family of Julius Caesar and Augustus), so that the early history of the Roman race was also the family history of Augustus. Secondly, he introduced mentions of Augustus into the poem in prophecies (by Jupiter in Book I and Anchises in Book VI) and on the shield of Aeneas (Book VIII). Thirdly, he reflected the old Roman values which Augustus propagated (and supported even by legislation) in the characters of his epic, especially that of Aeneas, a man distinguished by his *pietās* (respect for gods, family, home and country).

Virgil's Aeneid

Aeneas, storm-tossed from Troy, arrives after many adventures off the North African coast, and is led by his divine mother, Venus, to Carthage. Here he sees the city of Carthage being built.

> corripuēre uiam intereā, quā sēmita mōnstrat,
> iamque ascendēbant collem quī plūrimus urbī
> imminet aduersāsque aspectat dēsuper arcēs.
> mīrātur mōlem Aenēās, māgālia quondam,
> mīrātur portās strepitumque et strāta uiārum.   5
> īnstant ārdentēs Tyriī: pars dūcere mūrōs
> mōlīrīque arcem et manibus subuoluere saxa.
> pars optāre locum tectō et conclūdere sulcō;
> iūra magistrātūsque legunt sānctumque senātum.

hīc portūs aliī effodiunt; hīc alta ⌐ theātrīs   10
⌐ fundāmenta locant aliī, immānīsque columnās
rūpibus excīdunt, scaenis decora apta futūris

quālis apēs aestāte nouā per flōrea rūra	They were like bees at the beginning of
exercet sub sōle labor, cum gentis adultōs	summer,
ēdūcunt fētūs, aut cum līquentia mella 15	busy in the sunshine in the flowery 20
stīpant et dulcī distendunt nectare cellās,	meadows, bringing out the young of the
aut onera accipiunt uenientum, aut agmine	race
factō	just come of age or treading the oozing
ignāuum fūcōs pecus ā praesēpibus arcent;	honey
	and swelling the cells with sweet nectar, or
	taking the loads as they came in or
	mounting
	guard to keep the herds of idle drones out
	of 25
	their farmstead.

feruet opus redolentque thymō fraglantia mella.
'ō fortūnātī, quōrum iam moenia surgunt!'
Aenēās ait et fastīgia suspicit urbis.

(*Aeneid* 1.418–37)

corripiō 3/4 *corripuī* I seize, devour, hasten along
quā where
sēmit-a ae 1f. path
mōnstrō 1 I show
ascendō 3 I climb
collis coll-is 3m. hill
quī plūrimus 'which in its great bulk' [Register nom., so subject.]
urbī [Why dat? Wait.]
immineō 2 (+ dat.) I overlook, loom over [Solves *urbī*.]
aduers-us a um facing [The *-que* suggests another clause or phrase, so 'and the facing . . .', but *aduersās* is acc. pl. f., so we are waiting for a noun which can be described as 'facing', and then (presumably) a verb which explains the acc. case.]
aspectō 1 I look at, observe [So probably 'and looks at the facing . . .']
dēsuper from above

arx arc-is 3f. citadel, stronghold [Solves *aduersās*.]
mīror 1 dep. I marvel at
mīrātur [Subject? Wait.]
mōlēs mōl-is 3f. mass, bulk, size (of the city)
Aenē-ās ae 1m. [Greek declension, see **H6**] Aeneas [Subject]
māgālia māgāl-ium 3n. pl. huts
quondam once upon a time
5 *port-a ae* 1f. gate
strepit-us ūs 4m. hustle and bustle
strāt-um ī 2n. (lit. 'laid flat') paving
īnstō 1 I press on [Subject? Wait.]
ārdēns ārdent-is enthusiastic, eager
Tyri-us ī 2m. Carthaginian [Subject]
pars part-is 3f. some [So we may be waiting for 'others'.]
dūcō 3 (here) build [Infinitive: so why? Wait.]
mūr-us ī 2m. wall
mōlior 4 dep. I work at [Note infinitive.]

manibus [Dat. or abl. pl., but since the men are working, probably abl.]
subuoluō 3 I roll uphill [Note infinitive.]
sax-um ī 2n. stone [Solved infinitive yet?]
pars [Must mean 'others'.]
optō 1 I decide on [Note: still infinitive.]
tect-um ī 2n. building, house
conclūdō 3 I contain, mark out enclose [Infinitive]
sulc-us ī 2m. furrow, trench [But why these infinitives? There appears to be no controlling verb. So they must be – what sort of infinitives?]
iūs iūr-is 3n. law [Subj. or obj? No clue. Wait.]
magistrātūs [Subj. or obj? No clue. Wait.]
legō 3 I select [Do 'laws and magistrates' select?]
sānct-us a um holy, revered [Case? What does this suggest about *iūra* etc?]

10 *port-us ūs* 4m. harbour [Case? So wait.]

aliī [Looks like another string of the *pars* sort above. Await another *aliī*.]

effodiō 3/4 I dig

hīc [So here is another place where they are working: we can surely expect another *aliī* soon.]

alt-us a um deep [Case? Many possibilities. Wait.]

theātr-um ī 2n. theatre [Cannot agree with *alta*, so register dat. or abl. pl. and wait. So far 'here, something about deep things, something about theatres'.]

fundāment-um ī 2n. foundation [Solves *alta*: 'here, something about deep foundations'. So what case is *theātrīs*, with what meaning, probably?]

locō 1 I place [And *aliī* follows, solving the whole thing.]

immān-is e gigantic [Register case, pl.]

column-a ae 1f. column [Immediate agreement, happily.]

rūpes rūp-is 3f. rock [Dat. or abl. pl. Something about 'rocks'.]

excīdō 3 I cut out, quarry [All solved (note force of *ex-*).]

scaenīs [Register cases, wait.]

decus decor-is 3n. ornament, decoration

apt-us a um fit for (+ dat.) [That solves *scaenīs*.]

ferueō 2 I seethe

redoleō 2 I give off a smell of X (abl.) [Plural, so await subject. 'They give off a smell'.]

thym-um ī 2n. thyme (plant noted for its nectar) [Case? Construe with *redolent?* Or wait?]

fraglāns fraglant-is sweet [Make *thymum* depend on *fraglantia?*]

mel mell-is 3n. honey [Pl. for s. A common poetic device.]

20 *fortūnāt-us ī* 2m. lucky man, person

moenia moeni-um 3n. walls

surgō 3 I rise

ait said

fastīgi-um ī 2n. roof, height

suspiciō 3/4 I look up to [Aeneas has by now descended the hill.]

5B *Aeneas, welcomed warmly into Carthage by the queen Dido (who is slowly falling in love with him) is encouraged to tell the story of the destruction of his homeland Troy. Here Aeneas describes how the wooden horse was brought into the city – and laments the blindness of the Trojans.*

> dīuidimus mūrōs et moenia pandimus urbis,
> accingunt omnēs operī pedibusque rotārum
> subiciunt lāpsūs, et stuppea uincula collō
> intendunt; scandit fātālis māchina ⌐ mūrōs
> ⌐ fēta armīs. puerī circum innūptaeque puellae   5
> sacra canunt fūnemque manū contingere gaudent;
> illa subit mediaeque ⌐ mināns inlābitur ⌐ urbī.
> ō patria, ō dīuum domus Īlium et incluta ⌐ bellō
> ⌐ moenia Dardanidum! quater ipsō in līmine portae
> substitit atque uterō sonitum quater arma dedēre;   10
> īnstāmus tamen immemorēs caecīque furōre
> et mōnstrum īnfēlīx sacrātā sistimus arce.

tunc etiam fātīs aperit Cassandra futūrīs ōra deī iussū nōn umquam crēdita Teucrīs. nōs dēlūbra deum miserī, quibus ultimus esset 15 ille diēs, festā uēlāmus fronde per urbem.	Even at this last moment Cassandra opened her lips to prophesy the future, but the gods had ordained that those lips were never believed by Trojans. This was the last day for a doomed people, and we spent it adorning the shrines of the gods throughout the city with festal garlands.

(Aeneid 2.234–49)

dīuidō 3 I open up

mūr-us ī 2m. wall

moenia moeni-um 3n. pl. buildings [Nom. or acc.? Wait.]

pandō 3 I reveal, disclose

urbis [Gen., so must qualify *moenia*.]

accingō 3 I get ready for (+ dat.)

pedibusque [*-que* shows another clause/phrase, so hold 'and something to do with feet in the dat./abl.'.]

rot-a ae 1f. wheel [Can this be 'feet of the wheels'? Seems unlikely.]

subiciō 3/4 I place X (acc.) under Y (dat.) [Are *pedibus* Y?]

lāps-us ūs 4m. slipping [So: 'they place slippings under the feet'. Can *rotārum* construe with 'slippings', i.e. 'they place slippings of wheels under the feet'? But under whose feet? Answer: the feet of whatever is coming into Troy. In other words . . . What might 'slippings of wheels' mean?]

stuppe-us a um made of tow [Hold case possibilities.]

uincul-um ī 2n. halter, rope [Solves *stuppea*: n. pl., nom. or acc. Which? Wait. 'And something about tow halters'.]

coll-um ī 2n. neck [Must be 'on the neck' (dat.).]

intendō 3 I stretch, draw tight X (acc.) on(to) Y (dat.) [Solves it.]

scandō 3 I climb [What climbs? Wait.]

fātāl-is e deadly

māchin-a ae 1f. device, siege-engine [Subject]

5 *fēt-us a um* pregnant with (+ abl.) [Agreeing with what?]

puerī [Probably subject, but hold.]

circum around about

innūpt-us a um unwed

sacra [Cannot agree with 'boys and girls', whatever else it agrees with.]

canō 3 I sing [So 'boys and girls sing . . .' – perhaps *sacra*. What gender and case is *sacra*?]

fūnis fūn-is 3m. rope ['And something to do with a rope in the acc.'.]

contingō 3 I touch [Infinitive. Why?]

gaudeō 2 I rejoice, delight (to) [Solves the infinitive.]

illa [Change of subject, *illa* is f. – so what does it refer to?]

subeō I come up

mediaeque ['and something about the middle'; numerous case possibilities. Wait for agreement.]

mināns [Something in the nom. 'threatening'. Presumably *illa* is threatening, *minor* takes a dat. – is there one about? Not yet . . .]

inlābor 3 dep. I slide in, slip into (+ dat.)

urbī [Ah! Dat., and f., so what agrees with it?]

patri-a ae 1f. fatherland

dīuum = dīuōrum 'of the gods'

Īli-um ī 2n. Troy

inclut-us a um famous [But famous what? Wait.]

bellō [Perhaps shows you in what whatever-it-is is famous, i.e. 'famous in war'.]

moenia moeni-um 3n. pl. walls, town [Solves it.]

Dardanid-ae 1m. pl. (gen. *Dardanidum*) Trojans

quater four times

līmen līmin-is 3n. threshold

port-a ae 1f. gate(way)

10 *subsistō* 3 *substitī* I stop, halt. [What must the subject be?]

uter-us ī 2m. belly, womb [Case? Hold.]

sonit-us ūs 4m. sound [Register case.]

arma [Subject? Object? Probably subject, since *sonitum* must be obj. So the weapons do something to a sound. H'm.]

dedēre = dedērunt [Of course, that's what they do to the sound! This should now solve *uterō*.]

īnstō 1 I press on

immemor immemor-is mindless(ly), forgetful

caec-us a um blind

mōnstr-um ī 2n. monster [Subject or object? Hold.]

īnfēlīx (n.s.) catastrophic, ill-boding

sacrāt-us a um sacred [Register case. Can you solve it yet? No.]

sistō 3 I bring to a halt [Solves *mōnstrum īnfēlīx*.]

arce [Solves *sacrātā*.]

5C   *Aeneas, still telling the story of the fall of Troy, recounts how Achilles' son*
Pyrrhus (also called Neoptolemus) caught up with Troy's aged king Priam and
slaughtered him at the very altar where he and his family had been taking
refuge. His headless corpse now lies on the beach.

sic fātus senior tēlumque imbelle sine ictū	With these words the old man [Priam]
coniēcit, raucō quod prōtinus aere repulsum	hurled his spear, but it did no damage. There
et summō clipeī nequīquam umbōne	was no strength in it. It rattled on the bronze
pependit.	of Pyrrhus' shield without penetrating, and
cūī Pyrrhus: 'referēs ergō haec et nūntius	hung there useless, sticking in the central
ībis	boss on the surface of the shield. Pyrrhus
Pēlīdae genitōrī, illī mea trīstia facta 5	then made his reply. 'In that case you will
dēgeneremque Neoptolemum nārrāre	take this message from me and go with it to
mementō.	my dead father Achilles. Describe my
nunc morere.'	cruelty to him and remember to tell him that
	Neoptolemus [= *Pyrrhus*] is a disgrace to
	his father. Now, die.'

hoc dīcēns altāria ad ipsa trementem ⌐
trāxit et in multō ⌐ lāpsantem sanguine nātī,
implicuitque comam laeuā, dextrāque coruscum   10
extulit ac laterī capulō tenus abdidit ēnsem.
haec fīnis Priamī fatōrum, hic exitus illum ⌐
sorte tulit Trōiam incēnsam et prōlāpsa ⌐ uidentem ⌐
Pergama, tot quondam populīs terrīsque ⌐ superbum ⌐
⌐ rēgnātōrem Asiae. iacet ingēns lītore truncus,   15
āuulsumque umerīs caput et sine nōmine corpus.

(*Aeneid* 2.544–58)

hoc dīcēns [Take together to solve *hoc* (n.) at once.]	*nāt-us ī* 2m. son [Priam's son Polites had just been killed by Neoptolemus.]	*capul-us ī* 2m. hilt [Dat. or abl. Wait.]
altāri-um ī 2n. altar		*tenus* (+ abl.) as far as, right up to [Solves *capulō*.]
tremō 3 I tremble [With *age* not **10** fear, here. Present participle in acc., so something or someone is 'trembling'. If no noun, 'the person trembling'. Await subject and verb.]	*implicō implicuī* 1 I wrap X (acc.) in Y (abl.)	*abdō* 3 *abdidī* I bury
	com-a ae 1f. hair	*ēnsis ēns-is* 3m. sword [So 'he buried the sword right up to the hilt *laterī*: whose *laterī*? Can you now solve *coruscum*?]
	laeu-a ae 1f. left hand	
	dextr-a ae 1f. right hand	
trahō 3 *trāxī* I drag [Solves *trementem*: and who is it who is 'trembling'?]	*corusc-us a um* gleaming [But what? 'something gleaming, nom. or acc.']	*fīnis fīn-is* 3f. end [Sc. *fuit*.]
in multō [But *multō* what? Wait.]	*extulit* [Probably what he does to whatever it is that is gleaming.]	*fāt-a ōrum* 2n. pl. fate, destiny
		exit-us ūs 4m. death
lāpsō 1 I slip [surely the same person as *trementem*]	*efferō* 3 *extulī* I take out	*illum* [Presumably Priam, in acc. Wait.]
sanguine [Solves *multō*.]	*latus later-is* 3n. side [Register dative, wait.]	*sors sort-is* 3f. allocation, lot, fate [Hold.]

tulit [So 'this death took him off *sorte*'. Meaning of *sorte*?]

Trōiam incēnsam [What is this acc. doing? The meaning appeared to be complete, but we now have an unaccountable acc. Be patient. 'Something about "burned Troy" in the acc.']

prōlābor 3 dep. *prōlāpsus* I collapse, fall [Probably acc. pl. n., to complement *Trōiam* in the acc. So 'and something fallen'.]

uidentem [Acc. s. m. At last! Who must this agree with? What does it solve?]

Pergam-a ōrum 2n. pl. the citadel of Troy [Solves *prōlāpsa*.]

tot [Here we go again, when we thought the sense complete.]

quondam once upon a time

populīs terrīsque [Probably with *tot*. Hold dat. or abl.]

superb-us a um proud, arrogant [Could this be acc. s. m. referring to Priam, who has just seen Troy burnt (etc.)? Wait.]

15 *rēgnātor rēgnātōr-is* 3m. ruler [Acc. s. m., so *superbum rēgnātōrem* looks very much as if it does refer to Priam.]

Asiae [Confirms the above.]

iaceō 2 I lie [Who? Probably Priam . . . but wait, *ingēns* 'mighty Priam'? Wait.]

lītus lītor-is 3n. shore

trunc-us ī 2m. torso [Ah. 'He lies, a mighty torso, *lītore*.' How did it get *lītore*? One tradition held Priam was killed at Achilles' tomb on the shore, so Virgil has moved from palace to shore to accommodate it. There may be another reason: Pompey was beheaded on a beach in Egypt (see **6C(v)**). Virgil may be reminding his readers of that.]

āuellō 3 *āuulsī āuuls-us* I rip ['Something ripped.']

umer-us ī 2m. shoulder [Abl., perhaps 'ripped from'.]

Other writers

1. From the 'Life of Aurelian'

A ditty composed by fellow-soldiers of Aurelian (Emperor AD 270) on the basis of his exploits against the Sarmatians (before his principate). He was reported to have slain over 950 in the course of just a few days.

mīlle mīlle dēcollāuimus.
ūnus homo! mīlle dēcollāuimus.
mīlle bibat quī mīlle occīdit.
tantum uīnī habet nēmo, quantum fūdit sanguinis.

mīlle 'a thousand men' (acc.)
dēcollō 1 I behead, decapitate
bibat: mood?

tantum . . . quantum as much . . . as [cf. *satis/nimis* + gen. **31**]
uīn-um ī 2n. wine

fundō 3 *fūdī* I spill, shed (the subject is Aurelian, who is also the *ūnus homo* of line 2)

2. *The Vulgate:* creātiō caelī et terrae

in prīncipiō creāuit Deus caelum et terram. terra autem erat inānis et
uacua, et tenebrae erant super faciem abyssī, et Spīritus Deī ferēbātur
super aquās, dīxitque Deus, 'fīat lūx', et facta est lūx. et uīdit Deus lūcem
quod esset bona: et dīuīsit lūcem ā tenebrīs. appellāuitque lūcem Diem, et
tenebrās Noctem: factumque est uespere et māne, diēs ūnus.   5
dīxit quoque Deus, 'fīat firmāmentum in mediō aquārum: et dīuidat
aquās ab aquīs.' et fēcit Deus firmāmentum, dīuīsitque aquās, quae erant
sub firmāmentō, ab hīs, quae erant super firmāmentum. et factum est ita.
uocāuitque Deus firmāmentum Caelum: et factum est uespere et māne,
diēs secundus.   10
dīxit uērō Deus, 'congregentur aquae, quae sub caelō sunt, in locum
ūnum, et appāreat ārida.' et factum est ita. et uocāuit Deus āridam
Terram, congregātiōnēsque aquārum appellāuit Maria, et uīdit Deus
quod esset bonum. et ait, 'germinet terra herbam uirentem et facientem
sēmen, et lignum pōmiferum faciēns frūctum iuxtā genus suum, cuius   15
sēmen in sēmetipsō sit super terram.' et factum est ita. et prōtulit terra
herbam uirentem, et facientem sēmen iuxtā genus suum, lignumque
faciēns frūctum, et habēns ūnumquodque sēmentem secundum speciem
suam. et uīdit Deus quod esset bonum. et factum est uespere et māne, diēs
tertius.   20
dīxit autem Deus, 'fīant lūmināria in firmāmentō caelī, et dīuidant
diem ac noctem, et sint in signa et tempora, et diēs et annōs; ut lūceant in
firmāmentō caelī, et illūminent terram.' et factum est ita. fēcitque Deus
duo lūmināria magna: lūmināre māius ut praeesset diēī: et lūmināre
minus ut praeesset noctī: et stellās, et posuit eās in firmāmentō caelī, ut   25
lūcērent super terram et praeessent diēī ac noctī, et dīuiderent lūcem ac
tenebrās. et uīdit Deus quod esset bonum. et factum est uespere et māne,
diēs quārtus.
dīxit etiam Deus, 'prōdūcant aquae rēptile animae uīuentis et uolātile
super terram sub firmāmentō caelī.' creāuitque Deus cētē grandia, et   30
omnem animam uīuentem atque mōtābilem, quam prōdūxerant aquae
in speciēs suās, et omne uolātile secundum genus suum. et uīdit Deus
quod esset bonum. benedīxitque eīs, dīcēns, 'crēscite, et multiplicāminī,
et replēte aquās maris: auēsque multiplicentur super terram.' et factum
est uespere et māne, diēs quīntus.   35
dīxit quoque Deus, 'prōdūcat terra animam uīuentem in genere suō,
iūmenta, et rēptilia, et bēstiās terrae secundum speciēs suās.' factumque
est ita. et fecit Deus bēstiās terrae iuxtā speciēs suās, et iūmenta, et omne
rēptile terrae in genere suō. et uīdit Deus quod esset bonum. et ait,
'faciāmus hominem ad imāginem et similitūdinem nostram, et praesit   40
piscibus maris, et uolātilibus caelī, et bēstiīs, ūniuersaeque terrae,
omnīque rēptilī, quod mouētur in terrā.' et creāuit Deus hominem ad

imāginem suam: ad imāginem Deī creāuit illum, masculum et fēminam
creāuit eōs. benedīxitque illīs Deus, et ait, 'crēscite et multiplicāminī, et
replēte terram, et subicite eam, et domināminī piscibus maris, et   45
uolātilibus caelī, et ūniuersīs animantibus, quae mouentur super terram.'
dīxitque Deus, 'ecce dedī uōbīs omnem herbam afferentem sēmen super
terram, et ūniuersa ligna quae habent in sēmetipsīs sēmentem generis suī,
ut sint uōbīs in ēscam: et cūnctīs animantibus terrae, omnīque uolucrī
caelī, et ūniuersīs quae mouentur in terrā, et in quibus est anima uīuēns, ut   50
habeant ad uēscendum.' et factum est ita. uīditque Deus cūncta quae
fēcerat, et erant ualdē bona, et factum est uespere et māne, diēs sextus.
igitur perfectī sunt caelī et terra, et omnis ōrnātus eōrum.
complēuitque Deus diē septimō opus suum quod fēcerat: et requiēuit diē
septimō ab ūniuersō opere quod patrārat. et benedīxit diēī septimō et   55
sānctificāuit illum, quia in ipsō cessāuerat ab omnī opere suō quod creāuit
Deus ut faceret.

(Genesis 1.1–2.3)

creātiō creātiōn-is 3f. creation	15 *sēmen sēmin-is* 3n. seed	*in* (+ acc.) in accordance with
cael-um ī 2n. heaven, sky; pl.	*lign-um ī* 2n. wood, tree	*benedīcō* 3 *benedīxī* I bless
cael-ī ōrum 2m.	*pōmifer pōmifer-a um*	(+ dat.)
prīncipi-um ī 2n. beginning	fruit-bearing	*crēscō* 3 I increase
creō 1 I create	*frūct-us ūs* 4m. fruit	*multiplicor* 1 dep. I multiply
inān-is e empty	*iuxtā* (+ acc.) in accordance with	34 *repleō* 2 I fill
uacu-us a um void	*genus gener-is* 3n. kind, type	*auis au-is* 3f. bird
tenebr-ae ārum 1f. pl. shadows,	*sēmetipsō* 'itself' [Pl. line 48:	*iūment-um ī* 2n. beast
darkness	*sēmetipsīs* 'themselves'.]	*bēsti-a ae* 1f. wild beast
super (+ acc.) over, above	*prōferō prōferre prōtulī* I	*imāgō imāgin-is* 3f. image
faci-ēs faciē-ī 5f. face	produce	40 *similitūdō similitūdin-is* 3f.
abyss-us ī 2f. depths of the sea	*ūnumquodque* each one	likeness
spīrit-us ūs 4m. spirit; breath	*sēmentis sēment-is* 3f. sowing	*piscis pisc-is* 3m. fish
lūx lūc-is 3f. light	*secundum* (+ acc.) in accordance	*ūniuers-us a um* whole, all
quod that (+ subj.) [Also in	with	*mascul-us ī* 2m. male
lines 14, 19, 27, 33, 39.]	*speciēs speciē-ī* 5f. species	*subiciō* 3/4 I subdue
dīuidō 3 *dīuīsī* I divide	20 *lūmināre lūminār-is* 3n. light	45 *dominor* 1 dep. I rule (+ dat.)
appellō 1 I call	*in* (+ acc.) for the purpose of	*animāns animant-is* 3m./f. animal
uespere n. evening	[Also line 49]	*in ēscam* 'for food'
5 *māne* n. morning	*lūceō* 2 I shine	*uolucris uolucr-is* 3f. bird
ūnus = prīmus	*illūminō* 1 I light up	51 *ad uēscendum* 'for eating'
firmāment-um ī 2n. prop; stay;	25 *stell-a ae* 1f. star	*cūnct-us a um* every, all
sky above the earth	*prōdūcō* 3 *prōdūxī* I produce,	*ualdē* very
11 *congregō* 1 I gather	bring forth	*ōrnāt-us ūs* 4m. decoration,
appāreō 2 I appear	*rēptile rēptil-is* 3n. crawling	trimmings
ārid-a ae 1f. dry land	creature	*compleō* 2 *complēuī* I finish
congregātiō congregātiōn-is 3f.	*anim-a ae* 1f. soul, animal	*requiēscō* 3 *requiēuī* I rest
gathering	*uolātile uolātil-is* 3n. flying	*patrō* 1 I effect
ait 'he said'	creature	*sānctificō* 1 I sanctify
germinō 1 I produce	30 *cētē* n. pl. sea-beasts, monsters	*cessō* 1 I stop, cease
herb-a ae 1f. grass	*grand-is e* huge, vast	
uirēns uirent-is green	*mōtābil-is e* moving	

5D   *Dido, for all her prayers and entreaties, has fallen irrevocably in love with*
Aeneas. She lives in his company all day, and when he is absent, clutches
Aeneas' son Ascanius to her bosom. All work on the city stops.

> heu, uātum ignārae mentēs! quid uōta furentem,
> quid dēlūbra iuuant? ēst mollīs flamma medullās
> intereā et tacitum ⌐ uīuit sub pectore ⌐ uulnus.
> ūritur īnfēlīx Dīdō totāque ⌐ uagātur
> ⌐ urbe furēns,

quālis coniectā cerua sagittā, 5	like a wounded deer on the wooded hills of
quam procul incautam nemora inter	Crete. The shepherd who has been hunting
Crēsia fīxit	her has shot his iron-tipped arrow from long
pāstor agēns tēlīs liquitque uolātile ferrum	range and caught her by surprise. As she
nescius: illa fugā siluās saltūsque peragrat	takes to flight and runs over the hills and
Dictaeōs; haeret laterī lētālis harundō.	woods of Crete, the huntsman does not
	know it but the arrow that will bring her to
	her death is sticking in her side.
nunc media Aenēān sēcum per moenia dūcit 10	
Sīdoniāsque ostentat opēs urbemque parātam,	
incipit effārī mediāque in uōce resistit;	
nunc eadem, lābente diē, conuīuia quaerit,	
Iliacōsque ⌐ iterum dēmēns audīre ⌐ labōrēs	
exposcit pendetque iterum narrantis ab ōre. 15	
post ubi dīgressī, lūmenque obscūra	After they had parted, when the fading moon
uicissim	was now beginning to quench its light and
lūna premit suādentque cadentia sīdera	the setting stars seemed to speak of sleep,
somnōs,	she was alone in her empty house, lying in
sōla domō maeret uacuā strātīsque relictīs	despair on the couch where Aeneas had lain
incubat.	to banquet.

> illum absēns absentem auditque uidetque,
> aut gremiō Ascanium genitōris imāgine capta   20
> dētinet, īnfandum sī fallere possit amōrem.
> nōn coeptae adsurgunt turrēs, nōn arma iuuentūs
> exercet portūsue aut prōpugnācula bellō
> tūta parant: pendent opera interrupta minaeque
> mūrōrum ingentēs aequātaque māchina caelō.   25

(Virgil, *Aeneid* 4.65–89)

Dido, yielding to her passion, gets her sister Anna to act as the go-between with
Aeneas. But he will not be moved by their pleas.

tālibus ōrābat, tālīsque miserrima flētūs
fertque refertque soror, sed nūllīs ⌈ ille mouētur
⌉ flētibus aut uōcēs ūllās tractābilis audit;
fāta obstant placidāsque ⌈ uirī deus obstruit ⌉ aurīs.

ac uelut annōsō ualidam cum rōbore quercum 30	As the North winds off the Alps vie with each other to uproot a mighty oak whose
Alpīnī Boreae nunc hinc nunc flātibus illinc	timber has strengthened over long years of
ēruere inter sē certant; it strīdor, et altae	life; they blow upon it from this side and
cōnsternunt terram concussō stīpite frondēs;	from that and whistle through it; the foliage
ipsa haeret scopulīs et quantum uertice ad aurās	from its head covers the ground and the
aetheriās, tantum rādīce in Tartara tendit; 35	trunk of it feels the shock, but it holds on to the rocks with roots plunging as deep into the world below as its crown soars towards the winds of heaven.

haud secus adsiduīs hinc atque hinc uōcibus hērōs
tunditur, et magnō persentit pectore cūrās;
mēns immōta manet, lacrimae uoluuntur inānēs.
tum uērō īnfelīx fātīs exterrita Dīdō
mortem ōrat.   40

(Virgil, *Aeneid* 4.437–51)

---

heu alas!
uātēs uāt-is 3m. seer
ignār-us a um ignorant, blind
mēns ment-is 3f. intellect, mind
quid 'in what respect?'
uōt-um ī 2n. prayer [Subject or object?]
furō 3 I am mad [Since the participle is acc., one assumes *uōta* is subject. So 'in what respect do prayers something the one-who-is-mad?']
dēlūbr-um ī 2n. shrine [Looks like a repeat, i.e. 'in what respect do prayers, in what respect shrines something one-who-is-mad?']
iuuō I help
iuuant [Solves it.]
ēst: 3rd s. pres. of *edō*, I eat, consume [Await subject.]
moll-is e gentle, soft [NB case. So hold.]
flamm-a ae 1f. flame (of love)

medull-a ae 1f. marrow, inmost being
tacitum [New phrase/clause, so hold till solved.]
pectus pector-is 3n. breast
uulnus uulner-is 3n. wound (caused by love)
4 *ūror* 3 I burn
īnfēlīx (nom. s. f) unhappy
Dīdō Dīdōn-is 3f. Dido
uagor 1 (dep.) I range, wander
urbe [Solves *totāque*.]
10 *Aenēān* [Acc. of *Aenēās*.]
Sīdoni-us a um Carthaginian [Case? Hold.]
ostentō 1 I show off, display
opēs op-um 3f. pl. wealth
incipiō 3/4 I begin
effor 1 (dep.) I speak out
resistō 3 I stop
eadem [Nom. s. f. (i.e. Dido)? But why call her 'the same woman'? What other form might it be? Hold.]
lābor 3 (dep.) I slip by

Īliac-us a um Trojan [Acc. pl. m., so hold.]
dēmēns mad [Nom., so whom does it refer to?]
audīre [Why inf.? Hold.]
labōrēs [Solves *Īliacōs*.]
15 *exposcō* I demand to (+ inf.) [Solves *audīre*.]
pendeō 2 I hang on (*ab* + abl.)
nārrantis [Gen. present participle. No noun to agree with it, so 'of the one narrating'.]
20 *illum . . . absentem* [Take together; *absēns* 'she, absent' (i.e. not in Aeneas' presence: subject).]
gremi-um ī 2n. breast, lap [Hold.]
Ascani-us ī 2m. Ascanius, son of Aeneas [Acc. wait for verb.]
genitor genitōr-is 3m. father
imāgō imāgin-is 3f. likeness to (+ gen.)
capta: 'Dido, captivated'
dētineō 2 I hold [So, 'she holds Ascanius *gremiō*' – must be 'in her lap'.]

īnfand-us a um unspeakable, appalling [Neuter nom.? Masc. acc.? Hold.]

sī sc. 'to see'

fallō 3 I elude, beguile, solace

amōrem [Solves *īnfandum*.]

nōn . . . adsurgunt : adsurgō 3 I rise

coept-us a um begun

turris turr-is 3f. tower [Solves *coeptae*.]

arma [Nom. or acc. pl.? Wait.]

iuuent-ūs iuuentūt-is 3f. young men [Subject, so *arma* must be acc. So 'the young men do not — their arms'.]

exerceō 2 I practise with *-ue* or

port-ūs [Case possibilities?]

prōpugnācul-um ī 2n. ramparts (of the city). [Has this solved case problem?]

25 *tūt-us a um* safe [Solves *bellō*: 'in time of war'.]

parant [Who must the subject be, even though that noun is s.? So what case are *portūs*, *prōpugnācula*?]

pendeō 2 I hang idle, stand in idle suspension [Pl., three subjects follow.]

interrupt-us a um broken off

min-ae ārum 2f. pl. (lit.) menaces, threats [But these 'threats' are 'threats' *mūrōrum*, i.e. 'threats (consisting) of walls', i.e. 'threatening walls'.]

aequāt-us a um raised up to, equal to X (dat.)

māchin-a ae if. crane

cael-um ī 2n. sky

26 *tālibus*: abl. 'with such (words, prayers, pleas)'

tālīsque [Await agreeing acc. pl.]

miserrima 'wretched' [Nom. s. f.? Hold.]

flēt-us ūs 4m. tears

referō 3 *rettulī* I bring back

soror [*miserrima*, of course]

tractābil-is e amenable

29 *fāt-um ī* 2n. fate

placid-us a um gracious, kindly, ready to yield [Case? Hold.]

obstruō 3 I block up

auris aur-is 3f. ear [Solves *placidās*.]

36 *secus* differently

adsidu-us a um persistent

hinc atque hinc from this side and that

hērōs (nom.) hero

tundō 3 I pound, assault

persentiō 4 I feel, am aware of

immōt-us a um unmoved

lacrim-a ae 1f. tear

uoluō 3 I roll down

inān-is e useless(ly), (in) vain

39 *īnfēlīx* (nom. s. f.) unhappy

fāt-um ī 2n. fate

exterrit-us a um terrified

Rēs gestae dīuī Augustī

In this passage we read how Augustus was offered oversight of public morals. One wonders how he might have responded to Virgil's picture of Aeneas' entanglement with Dido.

cōnsulibus M. Viniciō et Q. Lucrētiō, et posteā P. Lentulō et Cn. Lentulō, et tertium Paullō Fabiō Maximō et Q. Tuberōne, senātū populōque Rōmānō cōnsentientibus, ut cūrātor lēgum et mōrum summā potestāte sōlus creārer, nūllum magistrātum contrā mōrem māiōrum dēlātum recēpī.

5

(Rēs gestae 6)

posteā afterwards

tertium for a third time [The dates are 19, 18 and 11.]

cōnsentiō 4 I agree (*ut* + subj. 'agree that' X should happen)

cūrātor cūrātōr-is 3m. guardian

creō 1 I make

5 *māiōrēs māiōr-um* 3m. f. pl. ancestors

dēferō 3 *dētulī dēlāt-us* I hand down

recipiō 3/4 *recēpī* I accept, take up

5E   *At the command of the gods, Aeneas abandons Dido (who commits suicide) and continues on his journey. Eventually he arrives in Italy, befriends the local King Latinus, and is offered the hand of his daughter Lavinia in marriage. This*

causes civil war to break out between Aeneas and Turnus, to whom Lavinia had
previously been betrothed. In preparation for this epic contest, Venus has Vulcan
make Aeneas a special shield, on which the whole of Roman history to come is
foreshadowed. Aeneas gazes in wonder at it: the final scene his eyes rest on is
that of Augustus triumphant over his enemies.

at Caesar, triplicī inuectus Rōmāna triumphō
moenia, dīs Italīs uōtum immortāle sacrābat,
maxima ⌐ ter centum tōtam ⌐ dēlūbra per urbem.
laetitiā lūdīsque uiae plausūque fremēbant;
omnibus in templīs mātrum chorus, omnibus ārae;   5
ante ārās terram caesī strāuēre iuuencī.
ipse sedēns niueō ⌐ candentis ⌐ līmine Phoebī
dōna recognōscit populōrum aptatque superbīs
postibus; incēdunt uictae longō ōrdine gentēs,
quam uariae linguīs, habitū tam uestis et armīs.   10

hīc Nomadum genus et discīnctōs Mulciber Āfrōs,	Here Vulcan had moulded the Nomads and the Africans with their streaming robes;
hīc Lelegās Cārāsque sagittiferōsque Gelōnōs	here were the Lelegians and Carians of Asia and the Gelonians from Scythia carrying
fīnxerat; Euphrātēs ībat iam mollior undīs,	their quivers; there was the Euphrates moving now with a chastened current; here
extrēmīque hominum Morinī, Rhēnusque bicornis,	were the Morini from the ends of the earth in Gaul, the two-horned Rhine, the
indomitīque Dahae, et pontem indignātus Araxes. 15	Scythians from beyond the Caspian, never conquered before, and the River Araxes
tālia per clipeum Volcānī, dōna parentis,	chafing at his bridge. Such was the shield that Vulcan made, and Venus gave her son.
mīrātur rērumque ignārus imāgine gaudet	Aeneas marvelled at it, and rejoicing at the
attollēns umerō fāmamque et fāta nepōtum.	things pictured on it without knowing what they were, he lifted onto his shoulder the fame and fates of his descendants.

(Virgil, *Aeneid* 8.714–31)

Caesar: i.e. Augustus	*moenia moen-ium* 3n. pl. city	*ter centum* 300 [*maxima* and
triplex triplic-is threefold [*triplicī*	walls [Solves —?]	*tōtam* both await solution.]
and *Rōmāna* are both	*dīs* from *deus* **16** [Cases? Hold.]	*dēlūbr-um ī* 2n. shrine
adjectives awaiting solution.]	*Ital-us a um* of Italy	*laetiti-a ae* 1f. joy
inuehor 3 dep. *inuectus* I am	*uōt-um ī* 2n. offering	*lūd-us ī* 2m. game, revel
carried into, ride into (+ acc.)	*immortāl-is e* immortal,	*uiae* ['games of/for the road'? Or
triumph-us ī 2m. triumph	everlasting	is this nom. pl.? Answer
[Solves —?]	*sacrō* 1 I consecrate X (acc.) to Y	coming up in verb.]
	(dat.)	

plaus-us ūs 4m. applause, cheers
[Note case and *-que*, linking it
with which previous nouns?]
fremō 3 I resound, echo [With X:
abl. – solves it.]
5 *chor-us ī* 2m. chorus, choir [Sc.
est]
ār-a ae 1f. altar
caedō 3 *cecīdī caesus* I kill,
slaughter
sternō 3 *strāuī* I lie over (+ acc.)
iuuenc-us ī 2m. bullock

ipse [i.e. Augustus]
sedeō 2 I sit
niueō candentis [Both adjectives.
Hold for their solution.]
niue-us a um white
candeō 2 I shine
līmen līmin-is 3n. threshold
Phoeb-us ī 2m. Phoebus (Apollo)
dōn-um ī 2n. gift
recognōscō 3 I review
aptō 1 I fit X (acc.) to Y (dat.)
[What is the (understood) X?]

superb-us a um fine, proud
postis post-is 3m. door-post,
portal
incēdō 3 I march past
10 *quam . . . tam* as . . . as
uari-us a um different
lingu-ae ārum 2f. pl. tongues,
languages [Abl. of respect.]
habit-us ūs 4m. look, fashion
[Abl. of respect.]
uestis uest-is 3f. clothes

**Other
writers**

1. Martial

quem recitās meus est, ō Fīdentīne, libellus.
sed male cum recitās, incipit esse tuus.

(1.38)

recitō 1 I read out, recite
Fīdentīn-us ī 2m. Fidentinus

libell-us ī 2m. book [This is the
antecedent of *quem*.]

incipiō 3/4 I begin

nīl recitās et uīs, Māmerce, poēta uidērī?
quidquid uīs estō, dummodo nīl recitēs.

(2.88)

Māmerc-us ī 2m. Mamercus
poēt-a ae 1m. poet

quidquid whatever

estō be! (= *es*, 2nd. s. imperative
of *sum*)

2. The Vulgate: nātīuitās Christī

factum est autem in diēbus illīs, exiit ēdictum ā Caesare Augustō ut
dēscrīberētur ūniuersus orbis. haec dēscrīptiō prīma facta est ā praeside
Syriae Cyrīnō; et ībant omnēs ut profitērentur singulī in suam cīuitātem.
ascendit autem et Iōsēph ā Galilaeā dē cīuitāte Nazareth in Iūdaeam in
cīuitātem Dauid, quae uocātur Bēthlehem, eō quod esset dē domō et   5
familiā Dauid, ut profitērētur cum Mariā dēspōnsātā sibi uxōre
praegnante. factum est autem, cum essent ibi, implētī sunt diēs ut pareret.
et peperit fīlium suum prīmōgenitum et pannīs eum inuoluit et reclīnāuit
eum in praesēpiō, quia non erat eīs locus in dīuersōriō.

et pāstōrēs erant in regiōne eādem uigilantēs et custōdientēs uigiliās   10
noctis super gregem suum. et ecce angelus Dominī stetit iuxtā illōs, et
clāritās Deī circumfulsit illōs, et timuērunt timōre magnō. et dīxit illīs

angelus: 'nōlīte timēre; ecce enim euangelizō uōbīs gaudium magnum,
quod erit omnī populō; quia nātus est uōbīs hodiē Saluātor quī est
Christus Dominus, in ciuitāte Dauid. et hoc uōbīs signum: inueniētis   15
īnfantem pannīs inuolūtum et positum in praesēpiō.' et subitō facta est
cum angelō multitūdō mīlitiae caelestis laudantium Deum et dīcentium:

Glōria in altissimīs Deō,

et in terrā pāx hominibus bonae uoluntātis.

(Luke 2.1–14)

ēdict-um ī 2n. edict
dēscrībor 3 (pass.) I am subject of
    a census
ūniuers-us a um all, whole
orbis orb-is 3m. world
dēscrīptiō dēscrīptiōn-is 3f.
    census
praeses praesid-is 3m. governor
Syri-a ae 1f. Syria
Cyrīn-us ī 2m. Quirinius
profiteor 2 dep. I make a census
    return
singul-ī ae a (as) individuals
ascendō 3 I go up
Iōsēph nom. Joseph
Galilae-a ae 1f. Galilee
Nazareth [Abl. with *ciuitāte.*]
Iūdae-a ae 1f. Judaea
5 *Dauid* (gen.) of David
Bēthlehem (nom.) Bethlehem

eō quod + subj. 'for this reason,
    that'
Mari-a ae 1f. Mary
dēspōnsāt-us a um betrothed
praegnāns praegnant-is being
    pregnant
impleō 2 *implēuī implētus* I
    complete
pariō 3/4 *peperī* I give birth (to)
prīmōgenit-us a um first-born
pann-ī ōrum 2m. pl. rags, pieces
    of cloth, swaddling clothes
inuoluō 3 *inuoluī inuolūtus* I wrap
reclīnō 1 I lay
praesēpi-um ī 2n. enclosure, pen, 15
    fold; manger
dīuersōri-um ī 2n. hostel, inn
10 *pāstor pāstōr-is* 3m. shepherd
regiō regiōn-is 3f. area
uigilō 1 I am on watch, keep
    awake

custōdiō 4 I guard, keep
uigili-ae ārum 1f. pl. watches
grex greg-is 3m. flock
angel-us ī 2m. messenger
iuxtā (+ acc.) beside
clāritās clāritāt-is 3f. clearness,
    brightness
circumfulgeō 2 *circumfulsī* I shine
    around
timor timōr-is 3m. fear
euangelizō I announce, tell good
    news
gaudi-um ī 2n. joy
saluātor saluātōr-is 3m. saviour
Christ-us ī 2m. Christ
īnfāns īnfant-is 3m. child, infant
mīliti-a ae 1f. soldiers
caelest-is e celestial, heavenly
laudō 1 I praise
alt-us a um high

5F   *Eventually, Aeneas and his rival Turnus come face to face. Aeneas is about to
kill him, but Turnus pleads for his life. In this passage, Aeneas is about to yield
to Turnus' entreaty, when he sees Pallas' sword-belt glittering on him (see note).
Aeneas kills him, and the Aeneid ends.*

                    stetit ācer in armīs
Aenēās uoluēns oculōs dextramque repressit;
et iam iamque magis cūnctantem flectere sermō
coeperat, īnfēlīx umerō cum appāruit altō
balteus et nōtīs fulsērunt cingula bullīs   5
Pallantis puerī, uictum quem uulnere Turnus
strāuerat atque umerīs inimīcum īnsigne gerēbat.
ille, oculīs postquam saeuī monimenta dolōris
exuuiāsque hausit, furiīs accēnsus et īra
terribilis: 'tūne ⌐ hinc spoliīs ¬ indūte meōrum   10

ēripiāre mihī? Pallās tē hōc uulnere, Pallās
immolat et poenam scelerātō ex sanguine sūmit.'
hoc dīcēns, ferrum aduersō sub pectore condit
feruidus; ast illī soluuntur frīgore membra
uītaque cum gemitū fugit indignāta sub umbrās.   15

(Virgil, *Aeneid* 12.938–52)

stetit [Subject? Wait.]
uoluō 3 I roll, shift
reprimō 3 *repressī* I check,
   restrain
iam iamque magis 'now more and
   more'
cūnctantem [Refers to Aeneas.
   Register case and hold.]
flectō 3 I bend, persuade
sermō [I.e. the words (of Turnus).]
īnfēlīx īnfēlīc-is ill-starred,
   disastrous [Wait for noun for
   īnfēlīx and introduction word
   to this new clause.]
umer-us ī 2m. shoulder [Dat. or
   abl.? Hold.]
cum [Introduces the clause.]
appāreō 2 I appear, come into
   view [Where? *umerō*.]
alt-us a um on the top of
5 *balte-us ī* 2m. sword-belt
nōt-us a um well-known
fulgeō 2 *fulsī* I shine, glitter
cingul-a ōrum 2n. pl. baldric
bull-a ae 1f. stud [Solves *nōtīs*.
   But what case?]

Pallās Pallant-is 3m. Pallas, the
   young man entrusted to
   Aeneas' charge by his father
   Evander. Turnus killed Pallas
   in battle (*Aeneid* 10.439ff.)
uictum quem [*quem* introduces the
   clause, object of *strāuerat*.]
uulnus uulner-is 3n. wound
sternō 3 *strāuī* I lay low
inimīc-us a um hostile, of his
   enemy
īnsigne īnsign-is 3n. insignia, a
   sign
gerō 3 I wear [What? Where?
   Solves *umerīs*.]
ille [i.e. Aeneas]
postquam [Introduces clause.]
moniment-um ī 2n. memorial
   (to + gen.)
exuui-ae ārum 2f. pl. spoils
hauriō 4 *hausī* I drink in
furi-ae ārum 1f. pl. the spirits of
   vengeance
accendō 3 *accendi accēnsus* I
   burn up, consume
īr-a ae 1f. anger

10 *spoli-a ōrum* 2n. pl. spoils
indūt-us a um dressed in (+ abl.)
meōrum 'of mine' [I.e. 'of my
   people']
ēripiō 3/4 I snatch away
   [Deliberative subj. 'are you to
   be . . . ?']
immolō 1 I sacrifice
poenam sūmō 3 I take revenge
scelerāt-us a um villainous
aduers-us a um facing
pectus pector-is 3n. chest
condō 3 I hide, bury
feruid-us a um hot, in passion
ast = *at*
illī (dat.) [i.e. Turnus]
frīgus frīgor-is 3n. cold, chill (of
   death)
membr-um ī 2n. limb
15 *gemit-us ūs* 4m. groan
indignāt-us a um complaining
sub (+ acc.) down to
umbr-a ae 1f. shade

Other writers

Martial

quārē nōn habeat, Fabulle, quaeris,
uxōrem Themisōn? habet sorōrem.

(12.20)

Themisōn Themisōn-is 3m.
   Themisron [Subject of *habeat*
   and *habet*.]

aestīuō seruēs ubi piscem tempore, quaeris?
   in thermīs seruā, Caeciliāne, tuīs.

(2.78)

aestīu-us a um hot, summer [Hold
   aestīuō until solved by
   tempore.]
seruēs deliberative subjunctive
   [See **157** note 2.]

piscis pisc-is 3m. fish
therm-ae ārum 1f. pl. baths
   (which were *supposed* to be
   hot)

Caeciliān-us ī 2m. Caecilianus
   (a bath-keeper)

5G   *1. Martial*

cūr nōn mitto meōs ⌐ tibi, Pontiliāne, ⌐ libellōs?
nē mihi tū mittās, Pontiliāne, tuōs.

(7.3)

libell-us ī 2m. book

Pontiliān-us ī 2m. Pontilianus

crās tē uīctūrum, crās dīcis, Postume, semper.
   dīc mihi, crās istud, Postume, quando uenit?
quam longē est crās istud? ubi est? aut unde petendum?
   numquid apud Parthōs Armeniōsque latet?
iam crās istud habet Priamī uel Nestoris annōs.   5
   crās istud quantī, dīc mihi, possit emī?
crās uīuēs: hodiē iam uīuere, Postume, sērum est.
   ille sapit, quisquis, Postume, uīxit heri.

(5.58)

crās tomorrow
numquid 'can it be that it . . . ?'
Parth-ī ōrum 2m. pl. Parthians
Armeni-ī ōrum 2m. pl. Armenians
lateō 2 I lie hidden

5 *Priam-us ī* 2m. Priam (king of
   Troy)
Nestōr Nestor-is 3m. Nestor
   (Greek warrior-king) [Both
   renowned for their longevity!]
quantī (gen.) 'at what price'

emō 3 I buy
sērum too late
sapiō 3/4 I am wise
quisquis who
heri yesterday

īnscrīpsit tumulīs septem ⌐ scelerāta ⌐ uirōrum
'sē fēcisse' Chloē. quid pote simplicius?

(9.15)

īnscrībō 3 *īnscrīpsī* I write upon
   (+ dat.)
tumul-us ī 2m. tomb

scelerāt-us a um infamous
Chloē Chloe (Greek f. nom.)
pote (sc. *est*) 'can be'

simplex simplic-is
   straightforward, frank

2. The Vulgate: sapiēns iūdicium Salamōnis

tunc uēnērunt duae mulierēs meretrīcēs ad rēgem, stetēruntque cōram
eō. quārum ūna ait, 'obsecrō, mī domine; ego et mulier haec
habitābāmus in domō ūnā, et peperī apud eam in cubiculō, tertiā autem
diē postquam ego peperī, peperit et haec; et erāmus simul, nūllusque alius
nōbīscum in domō, exceptīs nōbīs duābus. mortuus est autem fīlius   5
mulieris huius nocte, dormiēns quippe oppressit eum. et cōnsurgēns
intempestae noctis silentiō, tulit fīlium meum dē latere meō ancillae tuae
dormientis, et collocāuit in sinū suō: suum autem fīlium, quī erat
mortuus, posuit in sinū meō. cumque surrēxissem māne ut darem lac filiō
meō, appāruit mortuus; quem dīligentius intuēns clārā lūce, dēprehendī   10
nōn esse meum quod genueram.'
respondítque altera mulier, 'nōn est ita ut dīcis, sed fīlius tuus mortuus
est, meus autem uīuit.' ē contrāriō illa dīcēbat, 'mentīris: fīlius quippe
meus uīuit, et fīlius tuus mortuus est.' atque in hunc modum
contendēbant cōram rēge.   15
tunc rēx ait, 'afferte mihi gladium.' cumque attulissent gladium cōram
rēge, 'dīuidite', inquit, 'īnfantem uīuum in duās partīs, et date dīmidiam
partem ūnī, et dīmidiam partem alterī.'
dīxit autem mulier, cuius fīlius erat uīuus, ad rēgem (commōta sunt
quippe uīscera eius super fīlio suō), 'obsecrō, domine, date illī īnfantem   20
uīuum, et nōlīte interficere eum.' ē contrāriō illa dīcēbat, 'nec mihi, nec
tibi sit: sed dīuidātur.' respondit rēx et ait, 'date huic īnfantem uīuum, et
nōn occīdātur: haec est enim māter eius.' audīuit itaque omnis Israel
iūdicium quod iūdicāsset rēx et timuērunt rēgem, uidentēs sapientiam
Deī esse in eō ad faciendum iūdicium.   25

(I Kings 3.16ff. (Vulgate: III Kings 3.1 6ff.), slightly abridged)

cōram (+ abl.) in the presence of	*silenti-um ī* 2n. silence	*gignō* 3 *genuī* I bear, produce
ait 'said'	*ancillae* 'that is (of me), your	*ē contrāriō* in reply, contradicting
pariō 3/4 *peperī* I give birth	maidservant'	15 *contendō* 3 I squabble
cubicul-um ī 2n. bedroom	*sin-us ūs* 4m. breast, bosom	*īnfāns īnfant-is* 3m. baby
simul = together	*surgō* 3 *surrēxī* I get up	*dīmidi-us a um* half
5 *excipiō* 3/4 *excēpī exceptus* I	*māne* in the morning	*uīscer-a um* 3n. pl. heart, deepest
except	*lac lact-is* 3n. milk	feelings
quippe since [Tends to come late	10 *appāreō* 2 I appear	*super* (+ abl.) for, over
in the clause it controls.]	*dīligēns dīligent-is* close, careful	*Israel* (nom.) Israel
cōnsurgō 3 I rise, get up	*intueor* 2 dep. I examine	*iūdici-um ī* 2n. judgment
intempest-us a um middle of,	*lūx lūc-is* 3f. light	*sapienti-a ae* 1f. wisdom
'dead of'	*dēprehendō* 3 *dēprehendī* I realise	

Total Latin–English Learning Vocabulary

Note

This vocabulary contains all the words in the Learning Vocabularies, together with words learned in the Running Grammar, which are referred to by subsection number, printed in bold. Words which appear in sections of Text in forms significantly different from the basic form are also entered, with a reference to the basic form, e.g. *ablāt-*: see *auferō*; *cuius* gen. s. of *quī/quis*.

A

ā/ab (+ abl.) away from 1D; by (usually a person, after passive verbs) 4D(i)

abeō abīre abiī abitum I go/come away 1C

abiciō 3/4 *abiēcī abiectus* I throw down, throw away 4F(i)

ablāt-: see *auferō*

absēns absent-is absent, away 4C(ii)

abstul-: see *auferō*

absum abesse āfuī āfutūrus I am away from, am absent 4C(i); I am distant 5E(ii)

ac (or *atque*) and 2A
    aliter ac otherwise than
    alius ac different from
    contrā ac contrary to what
    īdem ac the same as
    par ac equivalent to
    pariter ac equally as
    perinde ac in like manner as, just as
    similis ac similar to (see **179.1**)

accēdō 3 *accessī accessum* I approach, reach 4E(iii)

access-: see *accēdō*

accidit 3 *accidit* — (*ut / ut nōn* + subj.) it happens (that / that not) 4F(i)

accipiō 3/4 *accēpī acceptus* I receive, welcome; learn; obtain 2E; sustain, meet with 4E(ii)

accūsō 1 I accuse X (acc.) of Y (gen.) 4A(iii)

ācer ācr-is e keen, sharp, hot 53

acerb-us a um bitter 5D(ii)

aci-ēs ēī 5f. battle-line; sharp edge, point; keenness (of sight) 5G(i)

āct-: see *agō*

ad (+ acc.) towards; at 1A; for the purpose of 4F(i); *usque ad* right up to 6A(iv)

addō 3 *addidī additus* I add; increase 5F(i)

adeō adīre adiī aditum I go/come to, approach 1C

adeō to such an extent 5A(i)

adept-: see *adipīscor*

adferō adferre attulī allātus (or *afferō* etc.) I bring to 5C(iii)

adgredior (*aggredior*) 3/4dep. *adgressus* (*aggressus*) I go up to 2B; attack 4E(i)

adhūc up to now 6B(ii)

adipīscor 3dep. *adeptus* I get, gain, acquire 2B

adiungō 3 *adiūnxī adiūnctus* I join X (acc.) to Y (dat.) 5A(ii)

adloquor (*alloquor*) 3dep. *adlocūtus* (*allocūtus*) I address 2B

adorior 4dep. *adortus* I attack, rise up against 6C(ii)

adsum adesse adfuī adfutūrus I am present, am at hand 2D; (+ dat.) I am present with 3D(iv)

aduers-us a um hostile; opposite; unfavourable 5F(i); in front (i.e. facing the enemy) 5G(iii)

aduertō: see *animaduertō*

adulēscēns adulēscent-is 3m. youth 6B(viii)

aduocō 1 I summon 5F(i)

aedifici-um ī 2n. building 3D(v)

aedificō 1 I build 3B(i)

aedis aed-is 3f. temple; pl. *aed-ēs aed-ium* house 1B

aeger aegr-a um ill 5G(i)

aegrē with difficulty 6D(iv)

Aenē-as ae 1m. (acc. *Aenēan*) Aeneas 3A(ii)

aequor aequor-is 3n. plain; sea 6A(vii)

aequ-us a um fair, balanced, equal 1G; level; calm; impartial 3D(ii)

aes aer-is 3n. bronze 5A(ii)
    aes aliēn-um aer-is aliēn-ī 3n. + 1/2adj. debt (lit. 'someone else's bronze') 5A(ii)

aestimō 1 I value; estimate 6A(iv)

aetās aetāt-is 3f. age; lifetime; generation 5A(ii)

afferō see *adferō*

affirmō 1 I state strongly, assert 4A(iii)

age come! 1G

ager agr-ī 2m. land, field, territory 2B

aggredior: see *adgredior*

agitō 1 I stir up, incite (*agō* + *-it-*) 5A(i)

agmen agmin-is 3n. column 5E(ii)

agō 3 *ēgī āctus* I do, act 2B; drive, lead, direct 4F(ii); spend, pass 5F(ii); (*dē* + abl.) discuss 6C(iii)
    grātiās agō (+ dat.) I thank 2D

Agrigentīn-us ī 2m. person from Agrigentum 4A(i)

aiō irr. I say 6B(iv)

aliās at another time **102**

alibī somewhere else **102**

alicubī somewhere **102**

aliēn-us a um someone else's 5A(ii)

   aes aliēn-um aer-is aliēn-ī debt (lit. 'someone else's bronze') 5A(ii)

aliquandō at some time 6B(viii)

aliquantō to some extent **102**

aliquī aliqua aliquod some (adj.) **102**

aliquis aliqua aliquid someone (pron.) **102**

aliquot several 5A(ii)

aliter ac otherwise than **179.1**

ali-us a ud other 3A(i), 4B(iii) (see **102**) (two different cases in same clause = 'different . . . different': see **102**)

   aliī . . . aliī some . . . others **102**

   alius ac other than **179.1**

alloquor: see *adloquor*

alō 3 *aluī altus* I feed, nourish, rear; support; strengthen 6B(iv)

alter alter-a um one (or other) of two 2A (see **62**)

alt-us a um high; deep 6A(vii)

amb-ō ae ō both 2E (declined as *duo*, see **54**)

amīciti-a ae 1f. friendship 6B(vii)

amīc-us a um friendly 3D(i)

amīc-us ī 2m. friend, ally 3D(i)

āmittō 3 *āmīsī āmissus* I lose 1F

amō 1 I love, like 1B

amor amōr-is 3m. love 3B(ii); pl. girl-friend, sexual intercourse 6A(i)

amplexor 1dep. I embrace 2E

amplius more than 5G(i)

ampl-us a um large, great 5B(i)

an = *-ne* = ? (in direct questions); whether, if (in indirect questions: + subj. = *num*) 6D(iii)

   utrum . . . an = double question, i.e. A or B? (negative *annōn*) 5D(i)

   utrum . . . an (+ subj.) whether . . . or (indirect question: negative *necne*) **172**

anim-a ae 1f. soul, life, breath 5G(iii)

animaduertō (or *animum aduertō*) 3 *animaduertī animaduersus* I observe, take note of 6B(i)

animum aduertō = *animaduertō* 6C(ii)

anim-us ī 2m. mind, spirit, heart 1E

annōn or not? (see *an* or *utrum*) 5D(i)

ann-us ī 2m. year 3A(ii)

ante (+ acc.) before, in front of 2D; (adv.) earlier, before 4E(ii)

anteā before 4G(i)

antequam before **165**

aperiō 4 *aperuī apertus* I open; reveal 5B(ii)

appellō 1 I name, call; address 5G(i)

appropinquō 1 (+ dat.) I approach 6C(ii)

apud (+ acc.) at the house of, in the hands of, in the works of 1F; among 4A(i)

aqu-a ae 1f. water 1C

ār-a ae 1f. altar 5D(iv)

arbiter arbitr-ī 2m. judge 3A(i)

arbitror 1dep. I think, consider; give judgment 2C

arbor arbor-is 3f. tree 6D(iii)

arcessō 3 *arcessīuī arcessītus* I summon 5D(iv)

ārdeō 2 *ārsī ārsum* I burn; am in love 6C(i)

argent-um ī 2n. silver; silver-plate; money 4C(i)

arm-a ōrum 2n. pl. arms; armed men 5A(i)

armāt-us a um armed 5A(iii)

ars art-is 3f. skill, art, accomplishment 6D(ii)

arx arc-is 3f. citadel 5D(iv)

Asi-a ae 1f. Asia Minor 4B(i)

asper asper-a um harsh, cruel, dangerous 3A(ii); rough 5E(ii)

aspici-ō 3/4 *aspexī aspectus* I look upon 4H

at but 2A

atque (or *ac*) and, also 2A (see *ac* for list of comparative expressions learned in **179.1**)

atrōx atrōc-is fierce, unrelenting 6B(vii)

attribuō 3 *attribuī attribūtus* I assign, give 5D(i)

attul-i-: see *adferō*

auctōritās auctōritāt-is 3f. weight, authority 5B(i)

audāci-a ae 1f. boldness, cockiness 1G

audācter boldly (from *audāx*) 3B(i)

audāx audāc-is brave, bold, resolute 1F

audeō 2 semi-dep. *ausus* I dare 2E (see **76**)

audiō 4 I hear, listen to 1D

auferō auferre abstulī ablātus I take away X (acc.) from Y (dat.) 1F

augeō 2 *auxī auctus* I increase (trans.) 5D(iv)

aul-a ae 1f. pot 1A (NB the normal classical Latin form is *olla*, while *aula* generally means 'court' or 'palace')

aure-us a um golden 2D

aur-um ī 2n. gold 1A

aus-: see *audeō*

aut or 1F

   aut . . . aut either . . . or 4D(ii)

autem but, however (2nd word) 1A

autumn-us ī 2m. autumn, fall 6D(ii)

au-us ī 2m. grandfather 3B(i)

auxiliō est (it) is of help to X (dat.), X (nom.) helps Y (dat.) 3D(v)

auxili-um ī 2n. help, aid 3D(v)

B

bell-um ī 2n. war: *bellum gerō* I wage war 3A(ii)

bell-us a um pretty, beautiful 6B(ii)

bene well, thoroughly, rightly 1E; good! fine! 2A (see **79**)

benīgn-us a um kind, favourable 3B(ii)

bibō 3 *bibī* — I drink 4B(iii)

bon-a ōrum 2n. pl. goods 5F(ii)

bon-us a um good, brave, fit, honest 1E

breu-is e short, brief 3A(i)

   breuī (sc. *tempore*) shortly, soon 5C(i)

C

cadō 3 *cecidī cāsum* I fall; die 5G(ii)

caedēs caed-is 3f. slaughter, carnage 5B(iii)

caedō 3 *cecīdī caesus* I cut (down); flog, beat; kill 4B(iv)

caelest-is e in the heavens 6D(iii)

cael-um ī 2n. sky, heaven 6D(i)

caes-: see *caedō*

calamitās calamitāt-is 3f. disaster, calamity 4B(i)

camp-us ī 2m. field, plain 6D(iii)

candid-us a um white; bright, beautiful 6A(vi)

capiō 3/4 *cēpī captus* I take, capture 2A

caput capit-is 3n. head; source 2B

carcer carcer-is 3m. prison; barrier 5E(i)

Carthāgō Carthāgin-is 3f. Carthage 3A(ii)

castīgō 1 I rebuke, chasten 2D

castr-a ōrum 2n. pl. camp 2B

cās-us ūs 4m. outcome; event, occurrence; disaster, death

cāsū by accident; by chance 6B(viii)

caueō 2 *cāuī cautus* I am wary 2B

caus-a ae 1f. case; reason 4F(i); cause 4G(ii)

causā (+ gen. – which precedes it) for the sake of **152.2**

cecid-: see *cadō*

cēdō 3 *cessī cessum* I yield; go 5F(i)

celer celer-is e swift 2A

celeritās celeritāt-is 3f. speed 4B(iv)

celeriter quickly (from *celer*) 3B(ii)

celerrimē very quickly (from *celer*: see **87**) 3C(ii)

cēlō 1 I hide 1A

cēn-a ae 1f. dinner 1F

cēn-ō 1 I dine 3C(i)

centum 100 54

centuriō centuriōn-is 3m. centurion 5G(i)

cēp-: see *capiō*

certē without doubt 1G

certior fīō (fierī factus) I am informed 6B(i)

certiōrem faciō (3/4 *fēcī*) I inform X (acc.) 6B(i)

certō for a fact 1G

certō 1 I struggle, fight; vie 5F(i)

cert-us a um sure, certain 5B(ii)

cess-: see *cēdō*

cēter-ī ae a the rest, the others 4B(i)

cib-us ī 2m. food 4E(i)

circiter (adv.) about 5E(ii)

circum (+ acc.) around 4C(ii)

circumeō circumīre circumiī circumitum I go around 4C(ii)

circumsedeō 2 *circumsēdī circumsessus* I besiege, blockade 6B(ii)

citō quickly 2C

cīuis cīu-is 3m. and f. citizen 1F

cīuitās cīuitāt-is 3f. state 4G(ii)

clam secretly 1B

clāmitō 1 I keep on shouting (*clāmō* + -*it*-) 4G(i)

clāmō 1 I shout 1A

clāmor clāmōr-is 3m. shout; outcry; noise 4A(iv)

clār-us a um famous, well-known 4B(i); clear 6B(vi)

classis class-is 3f. fleet 4D(i)

Cleomenēs Cleomen-is 3m. Cleomenes 4E(i)

coēg-: see *cōgō*

coepī (perfect form: past participle active/passive *coeptus*) I began 4B(ii)

cōgitō 1 I ponder, reflect, consider 1C

cognit-: see *cognōscō*

cognōscō 3 *cognōuī cognitus* I get to know, examine 2B (perf. tense = 'I know', plupf. = 'I knew', fut. perf. = 'I shall know')

cōgō 3 *coēgī coāctus* I force, compel; gather 4H

cohors cohort-is 3f. governor's retinue; cohort 4D(i)

cohortor 1dep. I encourage 5C(ii)

collēg-a ae 1m. colleague 6B(iv)

colligō 3 *collēgī collēctus* I collect, gather; gain, acquire 4C(ii)

collocō 1 I place, station 5A(iii)

coll-um ī 2n. neck 6D(iv)

colō 3 *coluī cultus* I worship; cultivate, till; inhabit 4A(ii)

com-a ae 1f. hair; foliage 6D(iii)

comes comit-is 3m. companion, friend; (pl.) retinue 4B(iv)

committō 3 *commīsī commissus* I commit 4H

commod-us a um satisfactory, convenient 6B(i)

commoror 1dep. I delay, wait 4E(iii)

commoueō 2 *commōuī commōtus* I move; remove; excite, disturb 4C(ii)

commūn-is e shared in, common, universal 5D(ii)

comparō 1 I prepare, provide, get ready, get 4B(iii)

complector 3dep. *complexus* I embrace 6B(iii)

complūr-ēs complūr-ium several 6B(iii)

concidō 3 *concidī* — I fall, collapse; am killed 4F(i)

concordi-a ae 1f. harmony 5D(iii)

concurrō 3 *concurrī concursum* I run together 4B(iv)

condemnō 1 I condemn X (acc.) for Y (gen.) 6B(i)

condiciō condiciōn-is 3f. condition, term 6B(vi)

condiciōnem (condiciōnēs) ferre to make terms 6B(vi)

cond-ō 3 *condid-ī conditus* I found 3A(ii)

cōnfect-: see *cōnficiō*

cōnficiō 3/4 *cōnfēcī cōnfectus* I finish 5C(iii); weaken 6C(iii)

cōnfirmō 1 I state clearly, confirm 4A(iii)

cōnfiteor 2dep. *cōnfessus* I confess, acknowledge 4G(i)

cōnflagrō 1 I burn (intrans.) 4E(ii)

coniciō 3/4 *coniēcī coniectus* I throw 4A(iv)

coniūnx coniug-is 3f. wife; 3m. husband 3B(ii)

coniūrātiō coniūrātiōn-is 3f. conspiracy 5A(i)

coniūrātor coniūrātōr-is 3m. conspirator 5A(i)

cōnor 1dep. I try 2C

cōnscrīptī: *patrēs cōnscrīptī* = senators 5D(ii)

cōnseruō 1 I keep safe, preserve 5D(ii)

cōnsīderō 1 I consider, ponder 5B(ii)

cōnsīdō 3 *cōnsēdī* — I settle down; encamp 5E(ii)

cōnsili-um ī 2n. plan; advice; judgement 1E

cōnsistō 3 *cōnstitī* — I stop, stand my ground 6C(ii)

cōnspicor 1dep. I catch sight of 2E

cōnstit-: see *cōnsistō*

cōnstituō 3 *cōnstituī cōnstitūtus* I decide 4C(i)

cōnsul cōnsul-is 3m. consul 3D(iv)

cōnsulāt-us ūs 4m. consulship 5A(i)

continenti-a ae 1f. self-control, restraint 1G

contiō contiōn-is 3f. meeting, assembly 5F(i)

contrā (+ acc.) against 4H

contrā ac contrary to what 5G 179.1

cōnūbi-um ī 2n. marriage 3B(ii)

conuell-ō 3 *conuellī conuulsus* I tear away 4H

conueniō 4 *conuēnī conuentum* (*ad*) I meet (at) 4B(iii)

conuīui-um ī 2n. party 4B(iii)

conuocō 1 I summon, call together 5A(iii)

cōpi-a ae 1f. multitude, crowd 5E(ii)

cōpi-ae ārum 1f. pl. troops 5E(ii)

coqu-ō 3 *coxī coctus* I cook 1F; 83

coqu-us ī 2m. cook 1A

corn-ū ūs 4n. wing (of army); horn 5G(i)

corōn-a ae 1f. garland 1A

corpus corpor-is 3n. body 3D(iii)

cotīdiē daily 4D(ii)

crēber crēbr-a um frequent; thick, close 6B(ii)

crēdō 3 *crēdidī crēditum/us* I believe in (+ dat.); entrust X (acc.) to Y (dat.) 1G

crūdēl-is e cruel 5D(i)

cui dat. s. of *quī/quis*

cuidam dat. s. of *quīdam*

cuiquam dat. of *quisquam*

cuius gen. s. of *quī/quis*

cuiusdam gen. s. of *quīdam*

culp-a ae 1f. fault; blame (often of sexual misconduct) 6A(vii)

culter cultr-ī 2m. knife 28

cum (+ abl.) with 2A; (+ subj.) when; since; although 4E(iii)

cum semel as soon as 6A(iv)

cum . . . tum both . . . and 5D(ii)

cūnctor 1dep. I delay; hesitate (+ inf.) 5C(i)

cūnct-us a um all, the whole of 6D(iii)

cupiditās cupiditāt-is 3f. lust, greed, desire 4B(ii)

cupiō 3/4 *cupīuī cupītus* I desire, yearn for; want desperately 4B(i)

cūr why? 1A

cūr-a ae 1f. care; worry, concern 1B

cūrō 1 I look after, care for 1B; see to the –ing of X (acc. + gerundive) 4H; am in command 5G(i)

curs-us ūs 4m. running; course; direction; voyage 6C(ii)

custōs custōd-is 3m. and f. guardian 3B(i)

D

dat-: see *dō*

dē (+ abl.) about, concerning 2A; from, down from 4F(i)

de-a ae 1f. goddess 3A(i)

dēbeō 2 I ought (+ inf.); owe 2D

decem ten 54

dēcēp-: see *dēcipiō*

decet 2 it befits X (acc.) to Y (inf.) 5C(iii) and 159

decim-us a um tenth 161

dēcipiō 3/4 *dēcēpī dēceptus* I deceive 2A

decus decor-is 3n. honour; beauty 5F(i)

ded-: see *dō*

dēdecet 2 it is unseemly for X (acc.) to Y (inf.) 161

dēdecorī est it is a disgrace for X (dat.) 5C(iii)

dēdō 3 *dēdidī dēditus* I hand over, surrender 3D(iv)

dēdūcō 3 *dēdūxī dēductus* I lead away, lead down 2B

dēess-: see *dēsum*

dēfendō 3 *dēfendī dēfēnsus* I defend 2C

dēferō dēferre dētulī dēlātus I report, bring news of; accuse, denounce; transfer 4A(iii)

dēfu-: see *dēsum*

dein = *deinde* 6A(iv)

deinde then, next 1A

dēlāt-: see *dēferō*

dēleō 2 *dēlēuī dēlētus* I destroy 2D

dēnique finally; in a word 4E(i)

dēscendō 3 *dēscendī dēscēnsum* I descend 6C(iv)

dēsum dēesse dēfuī dēfutūrus I am missing, am lacking; fail; abandon (+ dat.) 4D(ii)

dētul-: see *dēferō*

de-us ī 2m. god 1B (see 16)

dexter dextr-a um right; favourable 5G(i)

dextr-a ae 1f. right hand 5F(i)

dī nom. pl. of *deus*

dīc imperative s. of *dīcō* 1D

dīcō 3 *dīxī dictus* I speak, say 1D

diēs diē-ī 5m. and f. day 2B

in diēs day by day 3C(i)

difficil-is e difficult 2A

diffīdō 3semi-dep. *diffīsus* (+ dat.) I distrust 6C(iii)

dignitās dignitāt-is 3f. distinction, position; honour; rank, high office 4H

dign-us a um worthy; (+ abl.) worthy of 4H

dīligēns dīligent-is careful, diligent 3C(i)

dīligenti-a ae 1f. care, diligence 5D(iii)

dīmicō 1 I fight 6B(vi)

dīmittō 3 *dīmīsī dīmissus* I send away 5B(i)

discēdō 3 *discessī discessum* I depart; (*in sententiam* + gen.) go over to X's view 5E(i)

discordi-a ae 1f. discord, strife, quarrel (with capital letter, the goddess Discord) 3A(i)

dispōnō 3 *disposuī dispositus* I set, place (in different places) 5E(i)

diū for a long time 3D(v)
   comp. *diūtius* 3D(v)
   superl. *diūtissimē* 3D(v)
dīuers-us a um different 5A(iii)
dīues dīuit-is rich (as noun 3m.
   rich man) 1D, **47**
dīuiti-ae ārum 1f. pl. riches 5F(i)
diūtius any longer 3D(v) (see *diū*)
dīu-us ī 2m. god 6D(i)
dō 1 *dedī datus* I give 1B; *operam*
   dō I pay attention to X (dat.)
   1E
doct-us a um skilled in X (abl.);
   learned 5A(ii)
doleō 2 I suffer pain, grieve
   6A(vi)
dolor dolōr-is 3m. pain, anguish
   5D(i)
dol-us ī 2m. trick, fraud,
   deception 2E
domī at home 1D
domin-us ī 2m. master 1C
domō from home 2A
domum to home, homewards 1D
domum dūcō I take home, marry
   1D
dom-us ūs 4f. (irr.) house, home
   56
dōnō 1 I give 6A(i)
dōn-um ī 2n. gift, offering 4H
dormiō 4 I sleep 1F
dōs dōt-is 3f. dowry 1E
dubitō 1 I doubt; hesitate (+ inf.)
   6B(vi)
dubi-us a um doubtful **174.2**
dūc imperative s. of *dūcō* **37**
ducent-ī ae a 200 **54**
dūcō 3 *dūxī ductus* I lead 1D;
   think, consider 6B(vii)
dulc-is e sweet 5D(iii)
dum (+ indic.) while 2A;
   (+indic./subj.) until; (+
   subj.) provided that (also
   dummodo, modo) **165.4**
duo duae duo two **54**
duodecim twelve 5B(iii)
duodēuīgintī eighteen **161**
dūx-: see *dūcō*
dux duc-is 3m. leader 3A(ii)

E

ē (+ abl.) out of, from (also *ex*)
   1C
ea nom. s. f. or nom./acc. pl. n. of
   is

eā abl. s. f. of *is*
eadem nom. s. f. or nom./acc. pl.
   n. of *īdem*
eādem abl. s. f. of *īdem*
eae nom. pl. f. of *is*
eam acc. s. f. of *is*
eandem acc. s. f. of *īdem*
eārum gen. pl. f. of *īdem*
eās acc. pl. f. of *is*
eāsdem acc. pl. f. of *īdem*
ēbri-us a um drunk 4D(i)
ecce look! see! 2A
ēducō 1 I raise, educate 3C(i)
efficiō 3/4 *effēcī effectus* I bring
   about (*ut* + subj.); cause,
   make; complete 5A(i)
effugiō 3/4 *effūgī —* I escape
   4B(iii)
ēg-: see *agō*
egeō 2 *eguī —* I lack, need, am in
   want of (+ abl. or gen.)
   4E(i)
ego I 1A
ēgredior 3/4dep. *ēgressus* I
   go/come out 2B
ēgregi-us a um outstanding,
   excellent 6B(iii)
ēgress-: see *ēgredior*
eī dat. s. or nom. pl. m. of *is*
eīs dat./abl. pl. of *is*
eius gen. s. of *is*
enim for (2nd word) 1A
eō īre iuī or *iī itum* I go/come 1C
eō to that place 5C(i) *quō* +
   comparative... *eō* +
   comparative 'the more
   X... the more Y' 6B(vi)
eōdem abl. s. m. or n. of *īdem*
eōrum gen. pl. of *is*
eōs acc. pl. m. of *is*
eōsdem acc. pl. m. of *īdem*
epul-ae ārum 1f. pl. meal, feast
   3C(i)
eques equit-is 3m. horseman; pl.
   cavalry 3D(iv); 'knight'
   (member of the Roman
   business class) 4G(ii)
equitāt-us ūs 4m. cavalry 6C(ii)
equus ī 2m. horse 3A(i)
ergō therefore 2D
ēripiō 3/4 *ēripuī ēreptus* I snatch
   away, rescue X (acc.) from Y
   (dat.) 5C(iii)
errō 1 I am wrong; wander
   6B(vii)

et and; also, too; even Intro.;
   et... et both... and 1E
etiam still, even, as well; actually,
   then!, yes indeed 2C
   nōn sōlum (or *nōn modo*)...
   sed *etiam* not only... but
   also 4F(ii)
   etiam atque etiam again and
   again 6B(vii)
etsī although, even though, even if
   6C(iii)
Eucliō Ecliōn-is 3m. Euclio
   Intro.
ex (or *ē*) (+ abl.) out of, from 1C
excēdō 3 *excessī excessum* I
   depart, go out; surpass 6C(ii)
excipiō 3/4 *excēpī exceptus* I
   sustain, receive; welcome;
   catch; make an exception of
   6C(ii)
excōgitō 1 I think up, devise
   4C(ii)
excūsō 1 I excuse 6B(i)
exempl-um ī 2n. copy; example
   5C(i)
exeō exīre exiī exitum I go/come
   out, leave 1C
exercit-us ūs 4m. army 2A
exi-: see *exeō*
exīstimō 1 I think, consider 5B(i)
exiti-um ī 2n. death, destruction
   15
exorior 4dep. *exortus* I arise
   5C(ii)
explicō 1 I tell, explain 1B
expugnō 1 I storm 4A(i)
exsili-um ī 2n. exile 5F(ii)
exspectō 1 I await, wait for 4D(i)
extrēm-us a um furthest 6A(vii)

F

fābul-a ae 1f. story; play 6B(i)
fac imperative s. of *faciō* **37**
facēti-ae ārum 1f. pl. wit 6A(ii)
faciēs faci-ēī 5f. appearance; face
   5E(i)
facil-is e easy 1F
facinus facinor-is 3n. deed; crime;
   endeavour 1E
faciō 3/4 *fēcī factus* I make, do 1E
   certiōrem faciō I inform X
   (acc.) 6B(i)
   faciō ut (+ subj.) I bring it
   about that (cf. *efficiō/*
   perficiō ut) 6C(i)

fact-: see *fīō*

fact-um ī 2n. deed 4H

fām-a ae 1f. rumour, report; reputation 4A(i)

familī-a ae 1f. household Intro.

fān-um ī 2n. shrine 1G

fās n. indecl. right 4H

fāt-um ī 2n. fate 3A(ii)

fēc-: see *faciō*

fēmin-a ae 1f. woman 1D

fer imperative s. of *ferō* **37**

ferē almost 6B(iv)

feriō 4 I strike; beat; kill (perfect active and passive tenses supplied by *percussī percussus* – perf. and perf. part. of *percutiō* 3/4) 4D(ii)

ferō ferre tulī lātus I bear; lead 1E

   mē ferō I betake myself, charge 3B(i)

   condiciōnem (*condiciōnēs*) *ferre* to make terms 6B(vi)

ferōci-a ae 1f. fierceness 5G(iii)

ferōx ferōc-is fierce 3A(ii)

ferr-um ī 2n. sword; iron 3C(iii)

festīnō 1 I hurry 4B(iii)

fidēs fid-eī 5f. loyalty, honour; trust, faith; promise; protection 6B(viii)

fīd-us a um faithful, loyal 6B(viii)

fīli-a ae 1f. daughter Intro.

fīli-us ī 2m. son 1D

fingō 3 *fīnxī fictus* I make up, fabricate 6B(ii)

fīō fierī factus I become; am done, am made (passive of *faciō*) 2D (see **76**)

   certior fīō I am informed 6B(i)

flamm-a ae 1f. flame 6D(i)

fleō 2 *flēuī flētum* I weep 6C(iv)

flūmen flūmin-is 3n. river 3B(i)

fore = *futūrum esse* to be about to be **97**

   fore ut (+ subj.) that it will/ would turn out that . . . **156**

fōrm-a ae 1f. shape, looks; beauty 2C

fōrmōs-us a um handsome, graceful, shapely 3A(i)

fors f. chance (only nom. and abl. *forte* by chance) 3C(i)

fortasse perhaps 6B(viii)

forte by chance, perchance 6B(i)

fort-is e brave, courageous; strong 2A

fortūn-a ae 1f. fortune, luck; pl. wealth 5B(ii)

fortunāt-us a um fortunate, lucky in X (abl.) 5A(ii)

for-um ī 2n. forum, marketplace 2D

frangō 3 *frēgī frāctus* I break 5B(iii)

frāter frātr-is 3m. brother 1D

frīgus frīgor-is 3n. cold; pl. cold spells 6D(ii)

frūment-um ī 2n. corn 5F(i)

fruor 3dep. *frūctus* I enjoy (+ abl.) 4B(i)

frūstrā in vain 5A(iii)

fu-: see *sum*

fug-a ae 1f. flight 5D(i)

fugiō 3/4 *fūgī fugitum* I escape, run off, flee 1F

fugō 1 I put to flight 6D(ii)

fulgeō 2 *fulsī* — I shine 6A(vi)

fundāment-um ī 2n. foundation 3B(i)

fūr fūr-is 3m. thief 1B

furor furōr-is 3m. rage, fury; madness 4F(ii)

futūr-us a um future, to come, destined to be 3A(ii)

G

gaudi-um ī 2n. joy 5G(iii)

gēns gent-is 3f. race; tribe; clan; family; people 3A(ii)

genus gener-is 3n. family; stock; tribe 4C(i); type, kind 5D(ii)

gerō 3 *gessī gestus* I do, conduct 2D

   bellum gerō I wage war 2D

gladi-us ī 2m. sword 3C(ii)

glōri-a ae 1f. glory, renown, fame 4E(iii)

gradior 3/4dep. *gressus* I step, walk, go (cf. compounds in -*gredior*) 6A(vii)

Graec-ī ōrum 2m. pl. the Greeks 3A(ii)

Graec-us a um Greek 4B(i)

grāti-a ae 1f. friendship 3B(ii)

grātiā (+ gen. – placed after the noun it qualifies) for the sake of **152.2**

grāti-ae ārum 1f. pl. thanks, recompense 2D

   grātiās agō (+ dat.) I give thanks 2D

grāt-us a um pleasing (to X dat.) 5A(i)

grauid-us a um pregnant 3B(i)

grau-is e serious, important, weighty; heavy 4E(ii)

grauitās grauitāt-is 3f. seriousness; solemnity; importance, authority 4B(iii)

H

habeō 2 I have 1A; hold, regard 1D

   negōtium habeō I conduct business 1F

   ōrātiōnem habeō I make a speech 5F(i)

habitō 1 I dwell Intro.

hāc this way 2E

Hannibal Hannibal-is 3m. Hannibal (son of Hamilcar, leader of the Carthaginians) 3D(i)

harēn-a ae 1f. sand 6A(v)

haud not 2C

Helen-a ae 1f. Helen 3A(ii)

hic haec hoc this; this person, thing; pl. these; (as pron.) this man/woman/thing; he/she/it 2C (see **63**)

hīc here 2A

hinc from here 2C **63.3**

hodiē today 1E

homo homin-is 3m. human, man, fellow 1E

honest-us a um honourable 3C(i)

honor honōr-is 3m. respect 1B

hōr-a ae 1f. hour 2D

hortor 1dep. I urge, encourage 2B

hospes hospit-is 3m. host; friend; guest; connection 4B(i)

hostis host-is 3m. enemy 2B

hūc (to) here 2E

hūmān-us a um human 4H

hum-us ī 2f. ground 5E(i)

   humī on the ground (locative) 5E(i)

   humum to the ground 5E(i)

I

ī imperative s. of *eō* **37**

i-: see *eō*

iaceō 2 I lie 4D(i)

iactō 1 I discuss; throw; boast; toss about 6B(ii)

iam now, by now, already; presently 2C

iānu-a ae 1f. door 3A(i)

ibi there 2D

idcircō for this/that reason, therefore 5D(i)

īdem eadem idem the same 3C(iii) (see **86**)

   īdem ac the same as **179.1**

idōne-us a um suitable (for), qualified (for) (+ dat.) 5B(i)

igitur therefore 1A

ignāui-a ae 1f. laziness; cowardice 5F(i)

ignāu-us a um lazy; cowardly 5F(i)

ignis ign-is 3m. fire 1C

ignōscō 3 *ignōuī ignōtum* I forgive (+ dat.) 4G(i)

Īli-um ī 2n. Ilium, Troy 3A(ii)

ille ill-a illud that; pl. those; (as pron.) that man/women/thing; he/she/it 2C (see **64**)

illīc there **64**

illinc from there **64**

illūc to there **64**

imāgō imāgin-is 3f. appearance; ghost; idea 3B(ii); image, statue 4H

imitor 1dep. I imitate 6B(viii)

immō more precisely, i.e. no *or* yes (a strong agreement or disagreement with what precedes) 2D

immortāl-is e immortal 4G(i)

impedīment-um ī 2n. hindrance 3D(v)

   impedīmentō (maximō) sum (+ dat.) I am a (very great) hindrance (to) 3D(v) (see **88**)

impediō 4 I prevent, impede, hinder 5A(iii)

imperātor imperātōr-is 3m. general; commander; ruler; leader 3D(ii)

imperi-um ī 2n. command, order; empire 3B(i); power, authority; dominion 5D(ii)

imperō 1 I give orders (to), command (+ dat.: often followed by *ut/ nē* + subj. 'to / not to') 3D(iii)

impetrō 1 I obtain by request 6C(iii)

impet-us ūs 4m. attack 4A(i)

   impetum faciō I make an attack 4A(i)

impiger impigr-a um energetic 3C(iii)

impi-us a um with no respect for gods, parents or fatherland 5D(iv)

impōnō 3 *imposuī impositus* I put X (acc.) on Y (dat.) 6D(ii)

in (+ acc.) into, onto; (+ abl.) in, on 1A; (+ acc.) against 2D

   in diēs day by day, as the days go by 3C(i)

incendi-um ī 2n. fire 4E(ii)

incendō 3 *incendī incēnsus* I set fire to; burn (trans.) 4E(ii)

incert-us a um uncertain 6B(ii)

inde thence, from there; for that reason; from that time 3C(iii)

ineō inīre iniui or *iniī initum* I enter, go in 1F

inerm-is e unarmed 6C(ii)

īnfest-us a um hostile; at the ready; indicating attack 6C(ii)

īnflammāt-us a um inflamed, on fire 4C(i)

ingeni-um ī 2n. talent, ability **15**

ingēns ingent-is huge, large, lavish 1F

ingredior 3/4dep. *ingressus* I enter 2E

inimīc-us a um hostile, enemy 4G(ii)

innocēns innocent-is guiltless 4A(iii)

inquam I say (*inquis, inquit; inquiunt*) 2D

īnsidi-ae ārum 1f. pl. trap, ambush 5A(iii)

īnspiciō 3/4 *īnspexī īnspectus* I look into, inspect, examine 2B

īnstituō 3 *īnstituī īnstitūtus* I begin; construct; resolve 6C(iii)

īnstō 1 *īnstitī* — I press upon; urge, pursue; am at hand, approach; strive after 5G(ii)

īnstruō 3 *īnstrūxī īnstrūctus* I draw up; prepare, equip 4H

īnsum inesse īnfuī īnfutūrus I am in (+ dat.) 5A(iv)

integer integr-a um whole, untouched 5G(ii)

intellegō 3 *intellēxī intellēctus* I perceive, understand, comprehend, grasp 4B(iii)

inter (+ acc.) among; between 4B(iii)

intereā meanwhile 4A(i)

interficiō 3/4 *interfēcī interfectus* I kill, murder 3B(i)

intrō 1 I enter 1A

intrō (adv.) inside 2E

inueniō 4 *inuēnī inuentum* I find 1F

inuideō 2 *inuīdī inuīsum* I envy, begrudge (+ dat.) 5F(ii)

inuitō 1 I invite 4B(iii)

inuīt-us a um unwilling 6A(vi)

inuocō 1 I invoke, call upon 3B(ii)

ioc-us ī 2m. joke, joking, fun 6A(ii)

Iou-: see *Iuppiter*

ipse ipsa ipsum very, actual, self **103**

īrāscor 3dep. *īrātus* I grow angry with X (dat.) 2C

īrāt-us a um angry 2C

irrīdeō 2 *irrīsī irrīsus* I laugh at, mock 1E

is ea id that; he/she/it **70**

iste ista istud that over there/of yours (used especially when referring to opponents at a trial) 4A(iii) (see **91**)

it-: see *eō*

ita so, thus; yes 1D

Ītali-a ae 1f. Italy 3A(ii)

itaque and so, therefore 5A(iii)

item likewise 5C(i)

iter itiner-is 3n. journey, route 5E(ii)

iterum again 2A

iubeō 2 *iussī iussus* I order, command, tell 1D

iūcund-us a um pleasant 5D(iii)

iūdex iūdic-is 3m. judge 4A(ii)

iūdici-um ī 2n. judgement 3A(i)

iūdicō 1 I judge 3A(i)

Iūnō Iūnōn-is 3f. Juno, wife of Jupiter, goddess of marriage 3A(i)

Iuppiter Iou-is 3m. Jupiter, Jove (King of the Gods) 2A

iūs iūr-is 3n. rights, law, privilege, justice 3D(iii)

iūs iūrand-um iūr-is iūrand-ī 3n. oath 3D(iii)

iuss-: see *iubeō*

iussū by the order of X (gen.) 5C(iii)

iuuenis iuuen-is 3m. young man 1G

iuuō 1 *iūuī iūtus* I help; delight, please 6A(iii)

L

labor labōr-is 3m. toil, hard work; trouble 5D(iv)

lābor 3dep. *lāpsus* I slip, glide, fall down; make a mistake 6D(ii)

lacert-us ī 2m. arm, upper arm 6D(iv)

laedō 3 *laesī laesus* I harm 6A(iii)

laetiti-a ae 1f. merriment, festivity, joy 4B(iii)

laet-us a um joyful, happy 3B(i)

Lampsacēn-us ī 2m. person from Lampsacum 4B(i)

lān-a ae 1f. wool 3C(i)

Lar Lar-is 3m. Lar, household god 1A

latebr-ae ārum 1f. pl. hiding-place, lair 6D(iv)

Latīn-us a um Latin 5A(ii)

latrō latrōn-is 3m. robber, bandit 5G(i)

latus later-is 3n. side; flank 5G(ii)

Lāuīni-um ī 2n. Lavinium 3A(ii)

lect-us ī 2m. couch, bed 2B

lēgāt-us ī 2m. ambassador, official 2B; commander 5G(i)

legiō legiōn-is 3f. legion 5E(ii)

legō 3 *lēgī lēctus* I read 3C **83**

lepōs lepōr-is 3m. charm 6A(ii)

lēx lēg-is 3f. law 4A(iv)

līber līber-a um free 4F(i)

līber-ī ōrum 2m. pl. children 3B(ii)

līberō 1 I free, release 4D(i)

lībertās lībertāt-is 3f. freedom, liberty 4G(i)

libet 2 (perf. *libuit* or *libitum est*) it pleases X (dat.) to Y (inf.), X chooses to Y **159**

libīdō libīdin-is 3f. lust, desire 3C(ii)

licet 2 *licuit* it is permitted to X (dat.) to Y (inf.) 3D(v)

līctor līctōr-is 3m, magistrate's attendant, lictor 4F(i)

lingu-a ae 1f. tongue; language 6A(v)

litter-ae ārum 1f. pl. letter 4C(i); literature 5A(ii)

lītus lītor-is 3n. shore 4E(i)

loc-us ī 2m. place; pl. *loc-a ōrum* 2n. region 4A(iii)

locūt-: see *loquor*

longē far 3D(iii) (see **79**)

long-us a um long, lengthy 2A

loquor 3dep. *locūtus* I am speaking, say 2B

lūct-us ūs 4m. grief, mourning 5G(iii)

lūc-us ī 2m. grove, wood 3B(ii)

lūdō 3 *lūsī lūsum* I play 6A(iii)

lūmen lūmin-is 3n. light; pl. eyes 6D(ii)

lūn-a ae 1f. moon 2A

lūx lūc-is 3f. light 5D(i)

M

maest-us a um sad 3C(iii)

magis more 3C(iii) (see **87**)

magistrāt-us ūs 4m. magistrate, state official 4A(iii)

magnopere greatly **79**

magn-us a um great, large 1D

māior māius gen. *māiōr-is* greater, bigger **74**

mālō mālle māluī I prefer (X *quam* Y) 2A

mal-um ī 2n. trouble, evil 2E

māl-um ī 2n. apple 3A(i)

mal-us a um bad, evil, wicked 1C

mandō 1 I entrust X (acc.) to Y (dat.) 5A(i); order X (dat.) (to / not to: *ut/nē* + subj.) 6B(iii)

maneō 2 *mānsī mānsum* I remain, wait 1C

manifest-us a um in the open; obvious, clear; caught in the act 5B(ii)

man-us ūs 4f. hand 2A; band 5B(iii)

mare mar-is 3n. sea (abl. *marī*) 4E(ii)

Mars Mart-is 3m. the god Mars 3B(i)

mātrimōni-um ī 2n. marriage 3A(i)

mātrōn-a ae 1f. wife, mother; lady 5A(ii)

maximē very greatly; most of all (from *magnus*: see **87**) 3C(iii)

maxim-us a um very great, biggest **74**

mē acc. or abl. of *ego* 1A

mēcum with/to me (myself) (= *mē* + *cum*); pl. *nōbīscum* 2C

meditor 1dep. I think 3A(i)

medi-us a um middle (of) 4F(ii)

melior melius gen. *meliōr-is* better **74**

melius (adv.) better **87**

membr-um ī 2n. limb 6A(iii)

meminī (perfect form) I remember 5F(i)

memor memor-is remembering X (gen.); mindful of X (gen.) 5D(iv)

memori-a ae 1f. remembering, memory, recollection; record 6B(i)

mendāx mendāc-is lying, untruthful 2A

mēns ment-is 3f. mind, purpose 3D(i)

mentiō mentiōn-is 3f. mention 4E(iii)

mentior 4dep. I lie, deceive 2B

Mercuri-us ī 2m. Mercury, messenger of Jupiter 3A(i)

mer-us a um unmixed, pure 6A(i)

met-us ūs 4m. fear, terror 4E(iii)

me-us a um my, mine 1B (vocative s. m. *mī*: **17A**)

mī = *mihi* (dat. s. of *ego*) 6A(iv)

mī voc. s. m. of *meus* **17A**

mihi dat. s. of *ego*

mīlēs mīlit-is 3m. soldier 2C

mīlia mīl-ium 3n. pl. thousands (see *mīlle*) **54**

mīlitār-is e military 5C(ii)

mīlle 1,000 (pl. *mīlia*) **54**

min-ae ārum 1f. pl. threats 3C(ii)

Mineru-a ae 1f. Minerva, goddess of crafts and wisdom 3A(i)

minimē very little; no **87**

minim-us a um smallest, fewest, least **74**

minor 1dep. I threaten (+ dat.) 2B

minor minus gen. *minōr-is* smaller, fewer, less **74**

minus (adv.) less **87**

mīr-us a um amazing, wonderful 6B(v)

mīs-: see *mittō*

miser miser-a um miserable, unhappy, wretched 1C

miserand-us a um to be pitied 5D(i)

miseret 2 it moves X (acc.) to pity for Y (gen.) **159**

misericors misericord-is compassionate 5D(i)

miss-: see *mittō*

mittō 3 *mīsī missus* I send 1F; throw 6C(ii)

modest-us a um chaste, modest, discreet 5A(ii)

modo now 2A; only 4F(ii)

   nōn modo . . . sed etiam not only . . . but also (also *nōn sōlum . . . sed etiam*) 4F(ii)

   modo . . . modo at one time . . . at another 5E(ii)

mod-us ī 2m. way, fashion, manner 4C(ii)

moenia moen-ium 3n. pl. walls, ramparts 3A(ii)

moneō 2 I advise, warn 1C

mōns mont-is 3m. mountain 5A(i)

mor-a ae 1f. delay 4G(i)

mōre in the manner of, like (+ gen.) 5F(ii)

morior 3/4dep. *mortuus* I die 3C(ii)

mors mort-is 3f. death 2E

mortāl-is 3m. (or *mortāl-is e* adj.) mortal 3A(ii)

mōs mōr-is 3m. way, habit, custom; pl. character 2C

mōt-: see *moueō*

moueō 2 *mōuī mōtus* I remove X (acc.) from Y (abl.); move **83**; cause, begin 5A(i)

mox soon 2A

mulier mulier-is 3f. woman, wife 2C

multitūdō multitūdin-is 3f. mob, crowd, number 4E(ii)

multō (by) much, far 3A(ii)

multum (adv.) much **79**

mult-us a um much, many 1B

mūnus mūner-is 3n. gift; duty 6A(ii)

mūr-us ī 2m. wall 3B(i)

mūtō 1 I change, alter, exchange 6A(ii)

N

nam for 1A

nārrō 1 I tell, relate X (acc.) to Y (dat.) 5A(i)

nāscor 3dep. *nātus* I am born 3B(i)

nātūr-a ae 1f. nature 5B(i)

nāt-us a um born of/from (abl.) 4C(i)

nāuigō 1 I sail 4E(i)

nāuis nāu-is 3f. ship 4D(i)

naut-a ae 1m. sailor 4D(i)

-ne (added to the first word of a sentence) = ? 1E

nē (+ subj.) not to, that X should not **136**; lest, in order that not, in order not to **150**; that, lest **163**; (+ perf subj.) don't **170**

nē . . . quidem not even (emphasising the word in between) 6B(iii)

nē quis that no one **136**; in order that no one **150**

nec and . . . not; neither; nor (= *neque*) 1D

necesse est it is necessary for X (dat.) to Y (inf.) 3D(iv)

necessitūdō necessitūdin-is 3f. necessity 5F(ii)

necō 1 I kill 2C

nefāri-us a um wicked, vile, criminal 4D(ii)

neglegenti-a ae 1f. carelessness 4G(i)

neglegō 3 *neglēxī neglēctus* I ignore, overlook, neglect 4B(ii)

negō 1 I deny, say that X is not the case (acc. + inf.) 4A(iii)

negōti-um ī 2n. business, work, duty 4A(ii)

   negōtium habeō I do business 1F

   quid negōtī? what (of) business/problem/trouble? 1F

nēmō nēmin-is 3m. no one, nobody 3C(iii) (see **86**)

neque and . . . not; neither; nor (also *nec*) 1C

nēquiti-a ae 1f. wickedness 4E(ii)

nesciō 4 I do not know 2B

nesci-us a um knowing nothing, ignorant (of: gen.) 2C

neu = *nēue* 6C(iv)

nēue (+ subj.) and (that X) should not, and not to 4F(i)

niger nigr-a um black 2A

nihil (indecl. n.) nothing 1E

nihilī of no worth/value 2C

nihilōminus nevertheless 5C(iii)

nīl = *nihil* nothing 1F

nimis too much of X (gen.) 1D

nisi unless, if . . . not; except 2C

nītor 3dep. *nīsus* or *nīxus* I lean on (+ abl.); strive, exert myself 4E(i)

nix niu-is 3f. snow 6D(i)

nōbil-is e renowned, distinguished; well-born, noble 4B(i)

noceō 2 I harm (+ dat.) 5C(iii)

noctū by night 6C(iii)

nōlī (+ inf.) do not **59**

nōlō nōlle nōluī I refuse, am unwilling (+ inf.) 2A (see **52**)

nōmen nōmin-is 3n. name 1D

nōminō 1 I name 5G(i)

nōn no(t) 1A

nōnāgintā 90 5C **161**

nōndum not yet 5B(ii)

nōnne surely not, doesn't/don't? 3C(i) (see **85**)

nōn nūll-ī ae a some 6B(vii)

nōn-us a um ninth **161**

nōs we **43**

nōscō 3 *nōuī nōtus* I get to know (perfect tenses = I know etc.) 5B(i)

noster nostr-a um our 2A

nōt-us a um known, well-known 5B(i)

nōu-: see *nōscō*

nou-us a um new 3B(i)

nox noct-is 3f. night 2A

noxi-us a um guilty; harmful 3C(iii)

nūdō 1 I strip 4F(ii)

nūd-us a um naked 6D(iii)

nūll-us a um no, none 1B (gen. s. *nūllīus*; dat. s. *nūllī*) (see **62**) *nōn nūll-ī ae a* some 6B(vii)

num surely . . . not? **93**; (+ subj.) whether (indirect question) **172**

numer-us ī 2m. number 4D(ii)

numquam never 1C

nunc now 1A

nūntiō 1 I announce 2A

nūnti-us ī 2m. messenger; message; news 3C(iii)

nūpti-ae ārum 1f. pl. marriage-rites 1E

O

ō (+ voc.) O (addressing some one) 2B

ob (+ acc.) on account of, because of 3A(ii)

obdūrō 1 I am firm, hold out, persist 6A(vi)

oblīuīscor 3dep. *oblītus* I forget 2B; (+ gen. of person) 5D(iv)

obscūr-us a um dark; obscure; mean, ignoble 6D(ii)

obsecrō 1 I beg, beseech 4B(iv)

obsess-: see *obsideō*

obsideō 2 *ōbsēdī obsessus* I besiege 5B(iii)

obstō 1 *obstitī obstātum* I stand in the way of, obstruct (+ dat.) 3D(iv)

occāsiō occāsiōn-is 3f. opportunity 5E(ii)

occidī I'm done for! 1E

occidō 3 *occidī occāsum* I fall, die 5G(iii); set 6A(iv)

occīdō 3 *occīdī occīsus* I kill 3A(ii)

occupō 1 I seize 5C(iii)

occurrō 3 *occurrī occursum* I run to meet, meet; attack (+ dat.) 6C(iv)

octāu-us a um eighth **161**

octō eight **54**

octōgintā eighty **161**

ocul-us ī 2m. eye 1C

odiō est (he/it/she) is hateful to X (dat.), X (dat.) hates Y (nom.) 3D(v)

offendō 3 *offendī offēnsus* I meet with; offend 6B(ii)

offici-um ī 2n. duty, job 2A

omittō 3 *omīsī omissus* I give up; let fall; omit, leave aside 5G(ii)

omnīnō altogether, completely 6B(i)

omn-is e all, every; n. pl. *omnia* everything 1F

onerī est it is a burden to X (dat.) 5C(iii)

onus oner-is 3n. load, burden 1E

oper-a ae 1f. attention 1E; service 5A(iii) *operam dō* 1 *dedī datus* (+dat.) I pay attention to 1E

opēs op-um 3f. pl. resources; wealth (s. *ops op-is* 3f. help, aid) 5B(ii)

opīnor 1dep. I think 2B

oportet 2 it is right/fitting for X (acc.) to Y (inf.), X (acc.) ought to Y (inf.) 4B(iii) (see **159**)

oppid-um ī 2n. town 2A

opportūn-us a um strategic, suitable, favourable 5A(iii)

oppress-: see *opprimō*

opprimō 3 *oppressī oppressus* I surprise; catch; crush 2C; press down on 3C(ii)

optimē (adv.) best **87**

optim-us a um best 1D (see **74**)

opus oper-is 3n. job, work, task 2B; fortification 6C(iii)

opus est (+ abl.) there is need of 5F(ii)

ōrāc(u)l-um ī 2n. oracle 6A(v)

ōrātiō ōrātiōn-is 3f. speech 5F(i) *ōrātiōnem habeō* I make a speech 5F(i)

ōrdō ōrdin-is 3m. rank (i.e. section of society or line of soldiers) 5D(ii); order 6D(i)

orior 4dep. *ortus* I arise, begin; spring from, originate 3B(ii)

ōrō 1 I beg, pray 4B(iv)

ōs ōr-is 3n. face; mouth 4F(ii)

ostendō 3 *ostendī ostēnsus* or *ostentus* I show, reveal 1G

ōtiōs-us a um at leisure 6A(iii)

ōti-um ī 2n. cessation of conflict; leisure, inactivity 3D(iii)

P

paene almost 5D(iv)

paenitet 2 X (acc.) regrets Y (gen.) **159**

palam openly 6B(ii)

pandō 3 *pandī passus* I spread out, extend; throw open, disclose 6D(i)

par par-is equal *par ac* equivalent to *pariter ac* equally as (see **179.1**)

parcō 3 *pepercī parsum* I spare (+ dat.) 4B(iv)

parēns parent-is 3m. father, parent; f. mother 5B(iii)

pāreō 2 I obey (+ dat.) 3D(iv)

pariō 3/4 *peperī partus* I bring forth, bear, produce; obtain, acquire 6B(vii)

Paris Parid-is 3m. Paris 3A(i)

parō 1 I prepare, get ready; provide, obtain; I am about (to) 3D(i)

pars part-is 3f. part; faction, party 3D(v); side 6B(vi) *aliī. . . pars* (or *pars . . . pars*) some . . . others **102**

paru-us a um small 3A **74**

pāstor pāstor-is shepherd 3A(i)

patefaciō 3/4 *patefēcī patefactus* I reveal, expose, throw open 5C(iii)

pater patr-is 3m. father 1D; senator *patrēs* = fathers of the city 3B(ii) *patrēs cōnscrīptī* = senators 5D(ii)

patior 3/4 *passus* I endure, suffer; allow 2E

patri-a ae 1f. fatherland 5D(ii)

pauc-ī ae a a few, a small number of 5B(i)

paulātim little by little, gradually 5G(ii)

paulō slightly (cf. *multō*) 4E(i)

paulum a little, slightly **79**

pauper pauper-is 3m. f. poor man/ woman 1D; (adj.) poor **47**

pāx pāc-is 3f. peace 4B(i)

pecūni-a ae 1f. money 1D

pēior pēius gen. *pēiōr-is* worse **74**

peper-: see *pariō*

per (+ acc.) through, by 2C; in the name of 4G(i)

percuss-: see *feriō*

perdō 3 *perdidī perditus* I lose; destroy 6B(ii)

pereō perīre periī peritum I perish, die 6A(vi)

perfēc- :
perfect- : } see *perficiō*

perferō perferre pertulī perlātus I endure (to the end); complete; carry to; announce 6A(vi)

perficiō 3/4 *perfēcī perfectus* I finish, complete, carry out 2B; *perficiō ut/ut nōn* (+ subj.) I bring it about that/that not 4F(ii)

pergō 3 *perrēxī perrēctum* I proceed, continue 2A

perīcul-um ī 2n. danger **15**

peri -: see *pereō*

periī I'm lost 1E

perinde ac in like manner as, just as **179.1**

perit-: see *pereō*

perlegō 3 *perlēgī perlēctus* I read through, peruse 4C(i)

perscrībō 3 *perscrīpsī perscrīptus* I write in detail 6B(i)

persequor 3dep. *persecūtus* I pursue, follow after 5F(i)

persuādeō 2 *persuāsī persuāsum* I persuade X (dat.) ('that/that not', 'to /not to' *ut/nē* + subj.) 4F(i)

peruēniō 4 *peruēnī peruentum* I reach, arrive at, come to (*ad* + acc.) 4A(i)

pēs ped-is 3m. foot 4F(i)

pessimē worst, very badly **87**

pessim-us a um worst **74**

petō 3 *petīuī petītus* I beg **136**; seek 4G(i); proposition, court; attack, make for 5A(ii); stand for (public office) 5A(iii)

Phaedr-a ae 1f. Phaedra Intro.

pietās pietāt-is 3f. respect for the gods (also for family, home and native land) 6D(i)

pīl-um ī 2n. heavy javelin 5G(ii)

pīrāt-a ae 1m. pirate 4D(i)

placet 2 it pleases X (dat.) to Y (inf.); X (dat.) decides to Y (inf.) 3D(i)

plānē clearly 2C

plān-us a um level, flat; plain, distinct 6D(iv)

plēn-us a um full (of) (+ gen. or abl.) 1A

plērīque plēraeque plēraque the majority of 5B(i)

plūrēs plūr-ium more **74**

plūrimum (adv.) most, a lot **87**

plūrim-us a um most, very much **74**

plūs plūr-is 3n. more X (gen.) 3A(i) (see **74**)

pōcul-um ī 2n. cup 4C(i)

poen-a ae 1f. penalty 5C(iii)

polliceor 2dep. I promise 2B

pōnō 3 *posuī positus* I set up, place, position, put 3A(ii); lay aside (= *dēpōnō*) 6D(iv)

pōns pont-is 3m. bridge 5C(ii)

popul-us ī 2m. people 3B(ii)

porrō besides, moreover 5C(iii)

port-a ae 1f. gate 3A(ii)

pōrtō 1 I carry 1A

port-us ūs 4m. harbour 4D(i)

poscō 3 *poposcī* — I demand 1E

posit-: see *pōnō*

possideō 2 *possēdī possessus* I have, hold, possess 1B

possum posse potuī I am able, can 2A; am powerful, have power (+ adv.) 4E(iii)

post (adv.) later, afterwards; (+ acc.) after, behind 2D

posteā afterwards 4A(ii)

postquam (conjunction + indicative) after 5A(iii)

postrēmō finally 4C(ii)

postrēm-us a um last 4E(i)

postulō 1 I demand **136**

posu-: see *pōnō*

pot-: see *possum*

potenti-a ae 1f. power 5F(i)

potior 4dep. I control (+ gen.) 6B(vi); gain control of (+ abl.) 6C(iii)

potius rather 3B(ii)

potu-: see *possum*

praebeō 2 I show, display; *mē praebeō* I show myself to be X (acc. adj./noun) 5C(iii); provide, offer 6D(iv)

praecept-: see *praecipiō*

praecipiō 3/4 *praecēpī praeceptus* I instruct, give orders to X (dat.) (to / not to Y: *ut/nē* + subj.) 5B(ii)

praeclār-us a um very famous, outstanding, brilliant 4D(ii)

praed-a ae 1f. booty 2B

praedō praedōn-is 3m. pirate; robber 4D(i)

praefect-us ī 2m. captain, prefect; (adj.) in charge of (+ dat.) 4D(i)

praeficiō 3/4 *praefēcī praefectus* I put X (acc.) in charge of Y (dat.) 5G(i)

praemi-um ī 2n. prize, reward 5B(ii)

praesēns praesent-is present 6B(iii)

praesidi-um ī 2n. protection, defence, guard 4G(i)

praesum praeesse praefuī praefutūrus I am in charge of (+ dat.) **83**

praetereā besides, moreover 4A(iv)

praetereō praeterīre praeteriī praeteritus I pass by; neglect, omit 6A(vii)

praetor praetōr-is 3m. praetor (Roman state official) 4B(iv)

prec-ēs um 3f. pl. (occasionally *prex prec-is* 3f.) prayer(s) 3C(ii)

precor 1dep. I pray, beg 2B

premō 3 *pressī pressus* I press; oppress 6D(iv)

preti-um ī 2n. price, value, reward 3C(ii)

prīmō at first 4A(iv)

prīmum (adv.) first
ubi prīmum as soon as 5B(i)
quam prīmum as soon as possible 5E(ii)

prīm-us a um first 3D(iv) *in prīmīs* especially 5A(i)

prīnceps prīncip-is 3m. leader, chieftain; (adj.) first 4E(i)

prīstin-us a um former; original 5G(ii)

prius (adv.) before, earlier; first 5A(iii)

priusquam (conjunction) before **165**

prō (+ abl.) for, in return for; on behalf of; in front of 2E; instead of 5B(ii); in accordance with 5G(i)

prōcurrō 3 *prōcucurrī prōcursum* I run forward, advance 6C(i)

proeli-um ī 2n. battle 2B

proficīscor 3dep. *profectus* I set out 2B

profugiō 3/4 *profūgī* — I escape, flee away 4F(ii)

prōgredior 3/4 dep. *prōgressus* I advance 2B

prohibeō 2 I prevent, hinder, keep X (acc.) from Y (abl. / *ā(ab)* + abl.) 5A(iii)

prōiciō 3/4 *prōiēcī prōiectus* I throw down 6C(iv)

prōmittō 3 *prōmīsī prōmissus* I promise 1E

prope (adv.) almost; (+ acc.) near 4B(i)

properō 1 I hurry, make haste 5E(ii)

propius nearer 5C(i)

prōpōnō 3 *prōposuī prōpositus* I set before; imagine; offer 5D(i)

propter (+ acc.) on account of 2E

prōteg-ō 3 *prōtexī prōtectus* I protect 3D(v)

prōuideō 2 *prōuīdī prōuīsus* I take care of (that: often followed by *nē* + subj.) 5D(ii)

prōuinci-a ae 1f. province 4C(ii)

proxim-us a um nearest, next 4F(i)

pudet 2 X (acc.) is ashamed at/for Y (gen.) **159**

pudīciti-a ae 1f. chastity 3C(iii)

pudor pudōr-is 3m. modesty, sense of shame 6D(iv)

puell-a ae 1f. girl 1D

puer puer-ī 2m. boy 3B(i) (see **28**); slave 3D(v)

pugn-a ae 1f. battle, fight 5E(ii)

pugnō 1 I fight 2B

pugn-us ī 2m. fist 4A(i)

pulcher pulchr-a um beautiful 1D; (sup.) *pulcherrim-us a um* **73**; (comp.) *pulchrior pulchriōr-is* **72**

pulchritūdō pulchritūdin-is 3f. beauty 3A(i)

pūniō 4 I punish 5C(iii)

pūtid- us a um rotten 2E

putō 1 I think 4A(iii)

Q

quā where **139**

quadrāgintā forty **161**

quadringent- ī ae a 400 **154**

quaerō 3 *quaesīuī quaesītus* I seek, look for; ask 4G(i)

quāl-is e what sort of 6B(iii)
   tālis . . . quālis of such a kind as **179.2**

quam how! (+ adj. or adv.); (after comp.) than 2C
   tam . . . quam as . . . as **179.2**
   (+ superl. adv.) as ... as possible 5B(ii)
   quam prīmum as soon as possible 5E(ii)

quamquam although 2E

quamuīs (+ subj.) although **146**; (+ adj.) however, ever such a 5A(i)

quandō since, when 2C

quantī: tantī . . . quantī of as much value . . . as **69**

quantum as much as 5D(iii)

quant-us a um how much, how great 5F(i)
   tantus . . . quantus as much . . . as **179.2**

quārē why? 1B; therefore 6A(ii)

quārt-us a um fourth **161**

quasi as if, like 1E

quattuor four **54**

quattuordecim 14 **161**

-que (added to the end of the word) and 1D

quemadmodum how 6B(i)

queror 3dep. *questus* I complain 5B(i)

quī quae quod which? what? **29**; who, which **106**; (+ subj.) since (also with *quippe*) **145**; (+ subj.) in order that/to **150**

quia because 2A

quīcumque quaecumque quodcumque whoever, whatever 6A(vii)

quid what? 1C; why? 4A(ii)
   quid cōnsilī? what (of) plan? 1E
   quid negōtī? what (of) business? what problem? what trouble? 1F

quīdam quaedam quid-/quod-dam a, a certain, some 4A(i)

quidem indeed (places emphasis on the preceding word) 6B(viii)
   nē . . . quidem not even (emphasising the enclosed word) 6B(iii)

quiēs quiēt-is 3f. sleep, rest 6A(iii)

quīn (+ subj.) from —ing; that . . . not; (but) that **174**

quīndecim fifteen **161**

quīngent-ī ae a 500 **54**

quīnquāgintā fifty **161**

quīnt-us a um fifth 4E(i)

quippe quī (*quae quod*) inasmuch as he/she/it **145.2**

quis quid who?, what? **29**

quis qua quid (after *sī, nisi, nē, num*) anyone, anything **136, 144**

quisquam quicquam (after negatives) anyone **176**

quisque quaeque quodque (*quidque*) each **176**

quisquis quidquid (or *quicquid*) whoever, whatever 6B(v)

quō to where? 1E; whither, to where 4E(ii); (see also **139** for *quō* as abl. s. of *quī, quae, quod*)
   quō + comp. + subj. in order that . . . more **155**
   quō + comp . . . *eō* + comp. the more . . . the more 6B(vi)

quōcumque (to) wherever 5F(i)

quod because 1B

quod sī but if 6B(vii)

quōminus (+ subj.) so that . . . not; from —ing **174**

quoque also 1A

quot how many 5F(i) *tot . . . quot* as many as **179.2**

R

rapiō 3/4 *rapuī raptus* I seize, snatch away, carry away, plunder 3B(ii)

ratiō ratiōn-is 3f. plan, method; reason; count, list; calculation 4C(ii)

recēp-: see *recipiō*

recipiō 3/4 *recēpī receptus* I welcome, receive, take in 4B(ii); *mē recipiō* I retreat 6C(iii)

recordor 1dep. I remember 2B

reddō 3 *reddidī redditus* I return, give back 1G

redeō redīre rediī reditum I return (intrans.) 1C

redūcō 3 *redūxī reductus* I lead back 4E(iii)

rēgin-a ae 1f. queen 4H

rēgnō 1 I reign, rule 3A(ii)

rēgn-um ī 2n. kingdom 3B(i)

relict-: see *relinquō*

religiō religiōn-is 3f. sense of reverence, religious scruples 4H

religiōs-us a um sacred, revered, holy, awesome 4A(ii)

relinquō 3 *relīquī relictus* I leave, abandon 3A(ii)

reliqu-us a um remaining, left 4E(ii)

remaneō 2 *remānsī remānsum* I remain 6C(iii)

remittō 3 *remīsī remissus* I send back; remit 6C(iii)

reor 2dep. *ratus* I think, believe, suppose 5G(ii)

repellō 3 *reppulī repulsus* I drive back, drive out 4A(i)

repente suddenly 4A(i)

reperiō 4 *repperī repertus* I find 4A(iii)

reprimō 3 *repressī repressus* I hold back, check 6C(ii)

requīrō 3 *requīsīuī requīsītus* I seek out; ask for 5B(i)

rēs re-ī 5f. thing, matter, business; property; affair 2B

rēs pūblic-a re-ī pūblic-ae 5f. and 1/2adj. state, republic 4H

resistō 3 *restitī* — I resist (+ dat.); stand back; halt, pause 5G(ii)

respiciō 3/4 *respexī respectus* I look round (back) at, turn my gaze upon; reflect upon; care for 6C(i)

respondeō 2 *respondī respōnsum* I reply 2B

retineō 2 *retinuī retentus* I hold back, detain, restrain; maintain 4B(ii)

reuertor 3 dep. *reuersus* I return 6C(iv)

reuocō 1 I call back 4C(ii)

rēx rēg-is 3m. king 2A

rīp-a ae 1f. bank 6D(ii)

rogō 1 I ask 1C

Rōm- a ae 1f. Rome 3A(ii) (*Rōmae*, locative, at Rome 3C(ii))

Rōmān-us a um Roman 3A(ii)

Rōmul-us ī 2m. Romulus 3B(i)

rūmor rūmōr-is 3m. rumour, (piece of) gossip, unfavourable report 6A(iv)

S

sacer sacr-a um holy, sacred 4A(iii)

sacerdōs sacerdōt-is 3m. or f. priest, priestess 4A(iii)

sacr-a ōrum 2n. pl. rites 4A(iii)

saepe often 3D(iv)

saeu-us a um wild; angry 2B

saltem at least 6B(vii)

saluē welcome! 1E

salūs salūt-is 3f. safety 4F(i)

salūtem dīcīt (*S.* or *S.D.* at a letter-head) 'he greets' (+ acc.) 6B(i)

salūtī est (it/he/she) is a source of salvation to X (dat.), X (nom.) saves Y (dat.) 3D(iv)

salūt-ō 1 I greet 2D

salu-us a um safe 1C

sānct-us a um holy 4H

sanguis sanguin-is 3m. blood 4F(i)

sapienti-a ae 1f. wisdom, intelligence 2A

satis enough (of) (+ gen.) 1D

sauci-us a um wounded 5G(ii)

scaen-a ae 1f. stage 1A

scelest-us a um criminal, wicked 2C

scelus sceler-is 3n. crime, villainy; criminal, villain 1E

sciō 4 I know 1F

scrībō scrībere scrīpsī scrīptus I write **83**

sē himself, herself, itself/ themselves **80**

sēcum with/to himself/herself 1E

secund-us a um second **161**

secūris secūr-is 3f. axe 4D(ii)

secūt-: see *sequor*

sed but 1A

sēdecim sixteen **161**

sēd-ēs is 3f. base, foundation 4H

semel once 6A(iv) *cum semel* as soon as 6A(iv)

semper always 1A

senāt-us ūs 4m. senate 3D(v)

senex sen-is 3m. old man 1B

sēns-: see *sentiō*

sententi-a ae 1f. opinion; judgement; sentence; maxim 5C(iii)

sentiō 4 *sēnsī sēnsus* I feel; understand; perceive, realise 4A(ii)

septem seven **54**

septendecim seventeen **161**

septim-us a um seventh **161**

septuāgintā seventy **161**

sepul(h)r-um ī 2n. tomb 6A(v)

sequor 3 dep. *secūtus* I follow 2B

sermō sermōn-is 3m. conversation, discussion 4B(iii)

seru-a ae 1f. slave-woman Intro.

serui-ō 4 I serve (+ dat.) 3D(ii)

seruō 1 I save, keep 1C; keep safe, preserve 4C(i)

seru-us ī 2m. slave 1A

sēsē = sē 5C(ii)

seu (or *sīue*) . . . *seu* (or *sīue*) whether . . . or 6A(vii)

seuēr-us a um strict, stern 3C(i)

sex six **54**

sexāgintā sixty **161**

sext-us a um sixth **161**

sī if 1A

   sī + pres. subj., pres. subj. if X were to happen, Y would happen **144**

   sī + impf. subj., impf subj. if X were happening (now), Y would be happening (sometimes: if X had happened, Y would have happened) **144**

   sī + plupf. subj., plupf. subj. if X had happened, Y would have happened **173**

   quod sī but if 6B(vii)

sīc thus, so 2A

Sicili-a ae 1f. Sicily 4C(ii)

sīcutī (or *sīcut*) (just) as 5C(ii)

sīdus sīder-is 3n. star 6A(v)

sign-um ī 2n. seal, signal, sign 2D; statue 4A(iii); standard; trumpet-call 5G(i)

silu-a ae 1f. wood 6D(ii)

sim pres. subj. of *sum*

simil-is e resembling, like (+ gen. or dat.) 2A

similis ac similar to **179.1**

simul at the same time 4B(iii); together 6A(vii); = *simulatque* as soon as 6B(iv)

simulācr-um ī 2n. image, copy 4A(i)

simulatque (or *simulac* or *simul*) as soon as 6B(iv)

simulō 1 I feign 5B(ii)

sīn but if 6B(viii)

sine (+ abl.) without 2D; *sine dubiō* without doubt, certainly 2D

singul-ī ae a individual, one by one 6D(iv)

sinister sinistr-a um left; unfavourable 5G(i)

sinō 3 *sīuī situs* I allow, permit 2C

sīue (or *seu*) . . . *sīue* (or *seu*) whether . . . or 6A(vii)

soci-us ī 2m. ally, friend 4H

sodāl-is is 3m. friend 6A(ii)

sōl sōl-is 3m. sun 2A

soleō 2semi-dep. *solitus* I am accustomed, am used (+ inf.) 4A(iii)

solit-: see *soleō*

sollicitō 1 I bother, worry 2E; stir up, arouse; incite to revolt 5B(i)

sōlum (adv. of *sōlus*) only 4B(iii)

   nōn sōlum . . . *sed etiam* not only . . . but also 4F(ii)

soluō 3 *soluī solūtus* I release, undo 2D

sōl-us a um (gen. s. *sōlīus*: dat. s. *sōlī*) alone 4B(iii); lonely 6D(ii)

somni-um ī 2n. dream 1B

somn-us ī 2m. sleep 6A(iii)

soror sorōr-is 3f. sister 1D

spati-um ī 2n. space; time 6B(vi)

spectācul-um ī 2n. public entertainment, show 3B(ii)

spērō 1 I hope; expect 5E(ii)

spēs spē-ī 5f. hope(s); expectation 5B(i)

Staphyl-a ae 1f. Staphyla Intro.

statim at once 1C

stet-: see *stō*

stō 1 *stetī statum* I stand 1C

studi-um ī 2n. enthusiasm, zeal 5B(ii)

stultē stupidly 4C(ii)

stult-us a um stupid, foolish 2A

suāu-is e sweet, pleasant, delightful 6B(i)

sub (+ abl.) beneath, under 1A

subitō suddenly 2D

sublāt-: see *tollō*

subsidi-um ī 2n. reserve; help 5G(i)

succurrō 3 *succurrī succursum* I run to help, assist (+ dat.) 5G(ii)

sum esse fuī futūrus I am Intro.

summ-us a um highest, top of 1G

   summum supplicium the death penalty 4G(ii)

sūmō 3 *sūmpsī sūmptus* I take; put on; eat

   supplicium sūmō (*dē* + abl.) I exact the penalty (from) 5D(i)

sūmpt-: see *sūmō*

super (adv.) more than enough; above, over; (prep. + acc./abl.) over, above; (+ abl.) about 6A(v)

superb-us a um proud, haughty, arrogant 6D(ii)

superior superiōr-is higher; earlier 6C(iv)

supplex supplic-is (adj.) suppliant (also as noun) 5D(iv)

supplici-um ī 2n. punishment *summum supplicium* the death penalty 4G(ii)

   supplicium sūmō (*dē* + abl.) I exact the penalty (from) 5D(i)

supplicō 1 I make prayers (to) 1B; (+ dat.) 3D(i)

surgō 3 *surrēxī surrēctum* I rise, arise, get up 6D(ii)

suscipi-ō 3/4 *suscēpī susceptus* I undertake 4H

suspicor 1dep. I suspect 2D

sustineo 2 *sustinuī sustentus* I withstand; support 6C(ii)

sustul-: see *tollō*

su-us a um his, hers/their(s) 3B(i) and **80**

Syrācūsān-us ī 2m. person from Syracuse, Syracusan 4A(iv)

T

taceō 2 I am silent 1C

tacit-us a um silent 2D

tāct-: see *tangō*

tāl-is e of such a kind 4H

   tālis . . . *quālis* of such a kind as **179.2**

tam so 2A

   tam . . . quam as . . . as **179.2**

tamen however, but (second word) 1B

tamquam as though **179.3**

tandem at length 1B

tangō 3 *tetigī tāctus* I touch, lay hands on 1G

tantī . . . *quantī* of as much value . . . as **69**

tant-us a um so great, so much, so important 3D(v)

   tantus . . . *quantus* as much . . . as **179.2**

tard-us a um slow 4E(ii)

tē you (s.) 1A

tēcum with/to you(rself); pl. *uōbīscum* 2C

tegō 3 *tēxī tēctus* I cover 5G(iii)

tēl-um ī 2n. weapon 5A(iii)

templ-um ī 2n. temple 4A(i)

temptō 1 I try, test, attempt; attack 5E(ii)

tempus tempor-is 3n. time 2D

tendō 3 *tetendī tēnsus* or *tentus* I stretch (out); offer; direct; travel 5D(iv); strive, fight 5G(ii)

tenebr-ae ārum 1f. pl. shadows, darkness 6D(ii)

teneō 2 *tenuī tentus* I hold 3C(iii)

terg-um ī 2n. back (6C(ii))

terr-a ae 1f. land 3A(i)

terreō 2 I frighten 6B(viii)

terribil-is e dreadful, frightening 5E(i)

terti-us a um third **161**

testis test-is 3m. witness 4F(i)

tetig-: see *tangō*

thalam-us ī 2m. chamber, bedchamber 6D(iv)

thēsaur-us ī 2m. treasure 1B

timeō 2 I fear, am afraid of 1A; (*nē* + subj.) am afraid that/lest **163**

timid-us a um frightened, fearful 5C(ii)

timor timōr-is 3m. fear 6B(vi)

tollō 3 *sustulī sublātus* I lift, remove, take away 4A(iii)

tor-us ī 2m. couch, bed 6D(iv)

tot so many 4E(iii)

   tot . . . quot as many . . . as **179.2**

tōt-us a um (gen. s. *tōtīus*; dat. s. *tōtī*) whole, complete 4A(i)

trādō 3 *trādidī trāditus* I hand over 5C(ii)

trāns (+ acc.) across 6A(vii)

trānseō trānsīre trānsiī trānsitus I cross 3B(i)

trecent-ī ae a 300 **54**

trēdecim thirteen **161**

trēs tri-a three **54**

trīgintā thirty **161**

trīst-is e sad, gloomy, unhappy 1F

Trōiān-ī ōrum 2m. pl. the Trojans 3A(ii)

Trōiān-us a um Trojan 3A(ii)

trucīdō 1 I butcher 5F(ii)

tū you (s.) 1A

tueor 2dep. *tuitus* or *tūtus* I look after, protect; look at 6B(viii)

tul-: see *ferō*

tum then 1D

   cum . . . tum both . . . and 5D(ii)

tunic-a ae 1f tunic 6D(iv)

turb-a ae 1f. crowd, mob 1F

turp-is e disgusting, filthy, outrageous, ugly 4B(i)

tūt-us a um safe 4G(i)

tu-us a um your(s) (s.) 1C

U

uacu-us a um empty; free (from: + abl. or *ā* (*ab*) + abl.) 6B(vii)

ualdē very much, strongly 6B(v)

ualē goodbye! 1D

ualeō 2 I am strong; am well, am powerful; am able (cf. *ualē* = 'Farewell!' 'Goodbye!') 6A(vii)

uari-us a um diverse, various 3B(ii)

ubi where (at)? 1E; when? 1F

ubi primum as soon as 5B(i)

ubicumque wherever 6B(vii)

-ue (added onto the end of a word: cf. *-ne* and *-que*) or 6A(vii)

uehemēns uehement-is impetuous, violent 5D(i)

uehementer strongly 4F(i)

uel . . . uel either . . . or 5A (ii)

   uel even 5D(iv)

uelim pres. subj. of *uolō*

uellem impf. subj. of *uolō*

uelut as, just as 5C(ii)

ueniō 4 *uēnī uentum* I come 3A(i)

uent-: see *uēniō*

uent-us ī 2m. wind 6D(ii)

Venus Vener-is 3f. Venus, goddess of love 3A(i)

uerber uerber-is 3n. blow; whip 4F(i)

uerberō 1 I flog, beat 1C

uerb-um ī 2n. word 2A

uereor 2 dep. I fear, am afraid 5D(ii) (*nē* + subj. that/lest 163)

uerit-: see *uereor*

uērō indeed 2D

Verrēs Verr-is 3m. Verres 4A(i)

uersor 1dep. I am occupied; stay, dwell; am in a certain condition 5G(ii)

uers-us ūs 4m. verse; pl. poetry 5A(ii)

uertō 3 *uertī uersus* I turn (trans.) 6C(ii)

uērum but 2D

uēr-us a um true 1G

Vestāl-is e Vestal (belonging to the goddess Vesta) 5D(i)

uester uestr-a um your(s) (pl.) 2A

uestis uest-is 3f. clothes, clothing, dress 4D(ii)

uetō 1 *uetuī uetitus* I forbid 4A(iv)

uetus ueter-is (like *dīues* **47**) old; long-established 5A(i)

uexō 1 I annoy, trouble, worry 1C

ui-a ae 1f. way, road 2A

uīc-: see *uincō*

uīcīn-us ī 2m. neighbour 1C

uict-: see *uincō*

uictor uictōr-is 3m. victor 3C(i)

uictōri-a ae 1f. victory 2A

uideō 2 *uīdī uīsus* I see 1B

uideor 2dep. *uīsus* I seem 2C; passive I am seen **121**

uīgintī twenty **161**

uinciō 4 *uīnxī uīnctus* I bind 2A

uincō 3 *uīcī uictus* I conquer 2D

uinc(u)l-um ī 2n. chain, bond 4F(ii)

uīn-um ī 2n. wine 6A(i)

uir uir-ī 2m. man, husband 1D

uīr-ēs ium (pl. of *uīs*) strength, military forces 3D(iv)

uirgō uirgin-is 3f. unmarried woman 3B(ii)

uirtūs uirtūt-is 3f. manliness, courage; goodness 1G; virtue 3D(iii)

uīs-: see *uideō/uideor*

uīs 2nd s. of *uolō*

uīs irr. force, violence (acc. *uim*; abl. *uī*); pl. *uīr-ēs ium* 3f. strength; military forces 3D(iv)

uīt-a ae 1f. life 2E

uīuō 3 *uīxī uictum* I am alive, live 3C(i)

uīu-us a um alive, living 5G(iii)

ūll-us a um (gen. s. *ūllīus*; dat. s. *ūllī*) any (cf. *nūllus* **62**) 4B(i)

ultim-us a um furthest; last; greatest 6A(vii)

umbr-a ae 1f. shadow, darkness; shade, ghost 6D(ii)

umer-us ī 2m. shoulder 6D(ii)

umquam ever 3A(ii)

und-a ae 1f. water, wave 6D(ii)

unde from where, whence 5G(ii)

undecim eleven **161**

undēuīgintī nineteen **161**

unguent-um ī 2n. ointment 1B

ūniuers-us a um all together; whole, entire 6C(ii)

ūn-us a um (gen. s. *ūnīus*; dat. s. *ūnī*) one **54**

uōbīscum with you (pl.) 2C

uocō 1 I call 1A

uolō uelle uoluī I wish, want 1E

uoluntās uoluntāt-is 3f. will, wish 5D(ii)

uoluō 3 *uoluī uolūtus* I roll, turn over (trans.) 5G(iii)

uoluptās uoluptāt-is 3f. agreeable experience, pleasure, desire 2D

uōs you (pl.) **43**

uōt-um ī 2n. vow, prayer 6D(i)

uōx uōc-is 3f. voice; word 2E

urbs urb-is 3f. city 2D

ūs-: see *ūtor*

usque continually, without a break 6A(iv)

usque ad (+ acc.) right up to 6A(iv)

ut (+ indic.) how! 1C; (+ indic.) as, when 1D; (+ subj.) to . . . , that . . . should 4F(i) (**136**); (+ subj.) that (after *accidit*, *perficiō* etc.) **137.**; (+ subj.) that (result) **149**; (+ subj.) in order to/ that (purpose) **150**; (+subj.) that . . . not (after verbs of fearing) **163**

uterque utraque utrumque each of two, both **177**

utī = ut 5B(ii)

utinam I wish that **158.1**

ūtor 3dep. *ūsus* I use, make use of; adopt (+ abl.) 4B(i)

utpote (*quī quae quod*) as is natural (for one who) (+ subj.) **166**

utrimque on both sides 5C(ii)

utrum . . . an (double question) X or Y? (negative *annōn* = or not?) 5D(i); (+ subj.) whether . . . or (indirect question) (negative *necne* = or not) 5D(i)

uulnerō 1 I wound 5G(iii)

uulnus uulner-is 3n. wound 3C(iii)

uult 3rd s. of *uolō*

uultis 2nd pl. of *uolō*

uult-us ūs 4m. face, expression 5G(iii)

uxor uxōr-is 3f. wife 1D